WORLD POPULATION AND DEVELOPMENT

WORLD POPULATION AND DEVELOPMENT

Challenges and Prospects

Edited by

PHILIP M. HAUSER

SYRACUSE UNIVERSITY PRESS 1979

First Edition

Library of Congress Cataloging in Publication Data
Main entry under title:
World population and development.
Includes bibliographies and index.
1. Population—Addresses, essays, lectures.
2. Economic development—Addresses, essays, lectures.
I. Hauser, Philip Morris, 1909–
HB871.W75 301.32 79–15471
ISBN 0–8156–2216-3
ISBN 0–8156–2219–8 pbk.

Manufactured in the United States of America

FOREWORD

THE UNITED NATIONS FUND FOR POPULATION ACTIVITIES (UNFPA) has reached a major milestone in its operation. The year 1979 marks the completion of the first decade of its efforts to implement its United Nations mandate to help resolve world population problems. The decade has been characterized by novel problems because before the 1970s population assistance was a relatively uncharted area. Now, however, some of the population problems of the developing world have been forcefully attacked by the nations themselves and to some extent ameliorated in this first ten years of the Fund's existence.

At this juncture in the life of the agency we should take stock, appraise and evaluate, and chart the course to be followed in the coming years. For this purpose I have invited a number of prominent scholars and experts to review the status of the population and development problems with which the Fund is concerned. In this manner I hoped to obtain a firm foundation of fact and judgment which can serve, on the one hand, as a measure against which to judge the impact of the Fund's activities, and, on the other hand, as a springboard for directing the agency's future policies and programs.

I believe that what has been produced is the best the arts and sciences involved can presently accomplish, and that the product can assist UNFPA in evaluating what it has contributed to date and what is should do to improve its impact in the future.

I am grateful to the contributors to this volume which, I hope, will be found instructive not only to the Fund but, also, to the wider audience of readers interested in population and development.

New York
Spring 1979

Rafael M. Salas
Executive Director
United Nations Fund
for Population Activities

CONTENTS

TABLES

FIGURES

CONTRIBUTORS

B. KWAKU ADADEVOH is Vice Chancellor, University of Lagos, Nigeria.

DILIP AHUJA is Guest Investigator, Laboratory of Brain Evolution and Behavior, National Institute of Mental Health, Bethesda, Maryland.

NANCY BIRDSALL is a doctoral candidate, Department of Economics, Yale University, New Haven, Connecticut.

MARK BLAUG is Head, Research Unit in the Economics of Education, University of London Institute of Education, and Lecturer, London School of Economics, London.

JOHN B. CALHOUN is Head, Unit for Research on Behavioral Systems, Laboratory of Brain Evolution and Behavior, National Institute of Mental Health, Bethesda, Maryland.

KRASAE CHANAWONGSE is Advisor on Health and Rural Development Activities to the Prime Minister, Office of the Prime Minister, Royal Thai Government, Bangkok.

ZHI-YI CHANG is Department Director, Institute of Zoology, Chinese Academy of Science, Peking.

AMITAI ETZIONI is Professor of Sociology, Columbia University, and Director, Center for Policy Research, New York.

JOHN FEI is Professor of Economics, Economic Growth Center, Yale University, New Haven, Connecticut.

RONALD FREEDMAN is Professor of Sociology and Associate Director, Population Studies Center, University of Michigan, Ann Arbor, Michigan.

L. A. PETER GOSLING is Chairman, Department of Geography; Director, Center for South and Southeast Asian Studies; and Associate, Center for Population Planning, University of Michigan, Ann Arbor, Michigan.

ELINA HAAVIO-MANNILA is Acting Professor of Sociology (with tenure as Associate Professor), University of Helsinki, Helsinki.

PHILIP M. HAUSER is Professor Emeritus of Urban Sociology; Director Emeritus, Population Research Center, University of Chicago; Associate, Leo J. Shapiro and Associates, Chicago, Illinois; and Senior Fellow, East-West Population Institute, Honolulu.

KOICHI IIO is Senior Staff Economist, Japan Economic Research Center, Tokyo.

SAGAR C. JAIN is Chairman, Department of Health Administration, School of Public Health, University of North Carolina, Chapel Hill, North Carolina.

FEDERICO JOUBERT is Professor, Instituto de Estudios Superiores de Administration, Caracas, and Consultant to the International Committee on the Management of Population Programmes.

TOSHIO KURODA is Professor of Demography, College of Economics, Nihon University, Tokyo.

SIMON KUZNETS is Professor Emeritus of Economics, Harvard University, Cambridge, Massachusetts, and Senior Consultant, Department of Economics, Economic Growth Center, Yale University, New Haven, Connecticut. He received the Nobel Prize for Economics in 1971.

FERDINAND MÖNCKEBERG is Executive Coordinator, Consejo Nacional para la Alimentacion y Nutricion, Santiago.

GAYL D. NESS is Professor of Sociology; Associate Director, Center for South and Southeast Asian Studies; and Associate, Center for Population Planning, University of Michigan, Ann Arbor, Michigan.

YOICHI OKAZAKI is Chief, Division of Migration Research, Institute of Population Problems, Ministry of Health and Welfare, Tokyo.

SABURO OKITA is Chairman, Japan Economic Research Center, and Special Advisor, International Development Center of Japan, Tokyo.

CHRISTINE OPPONG is Senior Research Fellow, Institute of African Studies, University of Ghana, Legon, Accra, and Visiting Professor, Department of Sociology and Anthropology, University of Rhode Island, Kingston, Rhode Island.

DANIEL G. PARTAN is Professor, School of Law, Boston University, Boston, Massachusetts.

GUSTAV RANIS is Professor of Economics, Economic Growth Center, Yale University, New Haven, Connecticut.

RONALD G. RIDKER is Senior Fellow, Resources for the Future, Washington, D.C.

ALLAN ROSENFIELD is Director, Center for Population and Family Health, and Professor of Obstetrics and Gynecology and Public Health, College of Physicians and Surgeons, Columbia University, New York.

JAY K. SATIA is Professor, Indian Institute of Management, Ahmedabad.

T. PAUL SCHULTZ is Professor of Economics, Economic Growth Center, Yale University, New Haven, Connecticut.

THEODORE W. SCHULTZ is Professor of Economics, University of Chicago, Chicago, Illinois.

SHELDON J. SEGAL is Director, Population Sciences, The Rockefeller Foundation, New York.

MECHAI VIRAVAIDYA is Director, Community-Based Family Planning Services, Bangkok.

WALTER B. WATSON is Senior Research Associate, Center for Population and Family Health, College of Physicians and Surgeons, Columbia University, New York.

MASAAKI YASUKAWA is Professor of Demography, Faculty of Economics, Keio University, Tokyo.

PREFACE

THIS VOLUME was designed to help to commemorate the completion of the first decade of operation of the United Nations Fund for Population Activities (UNFPA). Dr. Rafael M. Salas, Executive Director of UNFPA, invited a distinguished group of scholars to review and to evaluate the status of various aspects of population and of social and economic development, each in the field of his or her own expertise. He also invited me to coordinate and edit this volume—a task made easy by the caliber and product of the individual contributors.

Population has come to be recognized as having a significant impact on a number of world problems. Not all of the interrelationships between the various aspects of population and socioeconomic factors can be expected to be covered in any one volume, but this work, by reason of the subject areas represented and the demonstrated expertise of the authors of the individual chapters, does touch on most of the more important problematic aspects of population. Furthermore, the materials presented have important implications for future international population programs, as will be shown in the Epilogue.

The overview chapter, in part, fills in gaps not covered by the chapters that follow and serves as a framework for them. The brief reference made to the theory of the demographic transition in this preface, for example, is pursued in a broad way by Dr. Ronald Freedman in Chapter 2, "Theories of Fertility Decline: A Reappraisal." With a comprehensive knowledge of the literature and with his own research, Professor Freedman brings both wisdom and empirical evidence to bear on this major theoretical problem in demography. His statement will remain important for some time to come.

In Chapter 3, "Population and Environment: An Evolutionary Perspective to Development," Drs. John B. Calhoun and Dilip Ahuja consider world population retrospectively and prospectively within an evolutionistic time framework. Their conclusions will seem hopeful to some and alarmist to others—but interesting and thought-provoking to all. Especially pertinent in its implications for the UNFPA is the emphasis laid on the importance of the long-term planning and decision-making purposes.

Dr. Ronald G. Ridker explores the relation of both population and economic growth to world resources in Chapter 4, "Resource and Environmental Consequences of Population and Economic Growth," both for the world and for the United States. Especially deserving of attention are the dates presented for "hypothetical exhaustion" of selected minerals and nonrenewable energy sources. His materials may allay the fears of those who believe the world is on the brink of catastrophe in terms of resources, but they may also motivate the appropriate agencies, public and private, to policies and programs to deal realistically with the potential resource crunches that lie ahead.

Dr. Ferdinand Mönckeberg critically examines the relation of population to the world food supply in Chapter 5, "Food and World Population: Future Perspectives." He considers the problem of food shortages and the potential for increasing food production; and he relates the world food problem to the world energy problem. He also raises crucial questions about the interrelations of "have" and "have-not" nations with respect to food production and equitable food distribution.

In Chapter 6, "Health, Population, and Nutrition: Interrelations, Problems, and Possible Solutions," Drs. Walter Watson, Allan Rosenfield, Mechai Viravaidya, and Krasae Chanawongse consider the problem from a medical as well as social and political points of view. The health problems of mothers and children are examined not only in the light of family planning programs, but also parity, age of mothers, birth spacing, and nutrition. The authors see the big problem in this realm as devising ways to get the fruits of scientific advances in health, population, and nutrition to the mass populations in developing countries. Their presentation of possible solutions will be of interest both to policy-makers and to professionals in the field.

Drs. Sheldon J. Segal, B. Kwaku Adadevoh, and Zhi-yi Chang in Chapter 7, "Reproduction, Fertility Regulation, and Infertility," summarize what is known about reproduction and fertility regulation and outline what lies ahead as determined by research already in progress. Although the material is heavily biological in coverage and language, the lay reader will, nevertheless, be able to follow the impressive additions to knowledge about human reproduction mechanisms and processes and fertility control which have been gained through scientific research. The authors clearly demonstrate the magnitude of research that remains to be done before better means of fertility regulation are developed. Progress in solving problems of infertility is also touched upon.

On the vital relationship between population factors and economic development, a sterling team of economists collaborated to produce Chapter 8, "Demography and Development in the 1980s." In this essay, Nancy Birdsall, John Fei, Simon Kuznets, Gustav Ranis, and T. Paul Schultz combined to make a comprehensive analysis of micro and macro models and present a scheme incorporating demographic and economic interrelations using the family as the primary unit of analysis. While more technical considerations may appeal to econometricians, others will find the essay quite illuminating. Also included in this chapter is an interesting sector on "puzzles and prospects" with consideration of priorities for research.

From the theoretical material in Chapter 8 a team of Japanese scholars turn to an analysis of the relation of population and development in Japan, providing an account of the Japanese experience in Chapter 9. Dr. Saburo Okita provides an overview of the Japanese experience; Dr. Masaaki Yasukawa considers the demographic transition in Japan in relation to economic development. Dr. Yoichi Okazaki considers population increase in relation to economic development; Dr. Koichi Iio analyzes the structure of the labor force and development; and Dr. Toshio Kuroda looks into the interrelation of economic growth and migration. The experience of Japan, although unique in a number of ways, points to desirable pathways for less developed countries.

An important aspect of development only recently emphasized in policy and program is taken up by Professor Theodore W. Schultz in Chapter 10, "Investment in Population Quality Throughout Low-Income Countries."Although some demographers and other noneconomist social scientists may dissent on some matters, all would agree on the necessity of investment in human capital being prerequisite to development as discussed by Dr. Schultz. His account of the extent to which such investment has taken place in the LDCs and is still taking place, while moot at some points, is, nevertheless, heartening.

Chapter 11 complements Chapter 10 by elaborating the role of education, formal and informal, in contributing to population quality. This chapter, "The Quality of Population in Developing Countries, with Particular Reference to Education and Training," by Professor Mark Blaug, raises critical policy questions about the allocation of resources among the various levels and types of education and about the experience of an educated labor force in the LDCs. The relatively high incidence of "educated unemployment" is critically examined, and policies and programs to prevent it while improving LDC population quality are explored.

"Population Redistribution: Patterns, Policies, and Prospects" are the subjects of Chapter 12. In this series of short essays, Professor L. A. Peter Gosling, in collaboration with his colleagues John F. Oppenheim, Linda Y. C. Lim, Theodore D. Fuller, Abdul Hamid Abdullah, Donald R. Deskins, Jr., Keith C. Clarke, and Maxine E. Olson, extensively reviews the literature of various aspects of this important field. Among the issues discussed are population redistribution in geographic and economic contexts, rural to urban, rural to rural, and urban to rural migration and migration management, and the relation of population redistribution to economic development.

In Chapter 13, Drs. Christine Oppong and Elina Haavio-Mannila consider "Women, Population, and Development." The authors discuss the increasing international focus on the role of women, problems of equality of men and women, indicators of the position of women in different types of society, and levels of economic development. They also discuss the family and the role of women in production and reproduction and present qualitative and quantitative findings tempered with keen insights and useful perspectives.

In Chapter 14, "Human Rights Aspects of Population Programs," Daniel G. Partan touches on a number of complex and emotional aspects of population policies and programs as they affect human rights. He considers such topics as human rights as legal rights, individual versus collective rights, and individual free will and government coercion. Also discussed are human rights standards in the population field and rights to government benefits and services, including incentives and disincentives. The treatment of human rights embraces a series of individual freedoms—the right to life, abortion in relation to the right to life, marriage and the family, family planning, voluntary sterilization, and various aspects of contraceptive and menstrual regulation. Treatment of the right of freedom of movement delves into problems of population distribution and migration. Partan presents recommendations and points to the implication of human rights for UNFPA policy and program.

The next three chapters have special impact for policy and program agencies concerned with population problems, including a number of implications for UNFPA. In Chapter 15, "Beyond Integration, Toward Guidability," Professor Amitai Etzioni examines the interrelations of population policies and programs and general social and economic policies and programs; and he emphasizes the need for integration of these programs. The need for a holistic approach to deal simultaneously and in an integral manner with population problems in the context of social and economic change is stressed. Recognized also is the fact that population policies should embrace many problematic aspects of population, of which high fertility is but one.

In Chapter 16 Dr. Sagar C. Jain, in collaboration with Drs. Federico Joubert and Jay K. Satia, focuses on the management of national population programs. After presenting conceptual issues and problems relating to the training and functioning of managers, they summarize the evolution of population programs, presenting for a number of developing countries the population policy status, the growth of population programs, the birth control methods used, and the sources of funds. They also describe the population activities of the UN specialized agencies. Finally the majoı managerial concerns of population agencies are considered.

In Chapter 17 Professor Gayl D. Ness critically explores the "Organizational Issues in International Population Assistance," recognizing that "large scale, bureaucratic forms of organization are a dominant factor of life in the modern world." Ness deals with the organizational issues that go beyond problems of structure and function, leadership, resources, and scope of authority—"the common form of much administrative analysis." Drawing on modern theory and research he considers the "environment of action" and the "nature of the technology used." A number of guiding principles for increasing effectiveness in organized population assistance are set forth.

Finally, in the Epilogue the implications of the volume for the future directions of population programs are discussed by the editor of the volume.

All in all, the contents of this volume constitute an inventory, and to some extent an appraisal, of the problems with respect to population and development in the context of a world comprising "have" and "have-not" nations engaged in intense efforts to resolve pressing immediate problems while remaining aware of the even more severe long-run outlook.

Many persons in addition to the authors of the chapters were engaged in this enterprise. A number of seminars and workshops were held in various countries, developed and developing, to consider and discuss the content of individual chapters. The persons involved are too numerous to report here, but their collective and individual contributions were significant. Furthermore, the authors of the individual chapters in a number of instances engaged in research activities in the preparation of their papers which involved other scholars and research assistants, to whom acknowledgment is made in the notes at the beginning of those chapters.

In the coordination and editing work was assigned in many ways which call for acknowledgment. I am indebted to Dr. A. Thavarajah, Chief, Office of Policy Analysis and Statistics (OPAS) of the UNFPA, and to his colleague, Dr. Hirofumi Ando, for wise counsel and implementation of the multitudinous administrative tasks. Thanks are due also to Mrs. Marion O'Connor, Dr. S. L. N. Rao, Mr. A. Kumashiro, and Miss Linda Sherry of OPAS; and Dr. James Collins for their assistance. Valuable secretarial service was rendered by Ms. Florence Banks, Barbara Bazie, Joanne Bernardi, and Wendy Gadd. I am also indebted to my colleagues at the University of Chicago, especially Drs. Evelyn M. Kitagawa and Teresa A. Sullivan of the Population Research Center, for their patience and tolerance in assisting in teaching and research duties when the work on this volume pre-empted time and attention.

Thanks must also be given to the East-West Population Institute where I served as Senior Fellow from December 1978 to April 1979. It was in this capacity that the work on this volume was completed. Acknowledgment is especially due to Dr. Lee-Jay Cho, Director, who arranged for the Senior Fellowship; and to the Institute's support staff, including Minja Choe, Data Analysis Officer, and her statistical assistants; Alice Harris, Resource Materials Specialist, and her associates; and Lynette Tong, Steno Pool Supervisor, and her group of typists. Acknowledgment must also be made of the assistance of Leo J. Shapiro and Associates, whose facilities helped to expedite the early stages of the editorial and administrative tasks.

Thanks must also be given to Barbara W. Sloane for her valued assistance in copyediting. Finally, I am happy to acknowledge my indebtedness to Professor Ronald Freedman for reviewing Chapter 1 and the Epilogue and for providing insightful and helpful counsel. Needless to say, Dr. Freedman cannot be held accountable for the deficiencies that may still be present in these materials.

Honolulu
Spring 1979

Philip M. Hauser

WORLD POPULATION AND DEVELOPMENT

I

Introduction and Overview

PHILIP M. HAUSER

INTRODUCTION

SINCE THE END of World War II, population problems have engaged the attention of humankind on an unprecedented scale. The sharp controversies following the publication in 1798 of Parson Thomas Malthus' *Essay on the Principle of Population* and the bitter public responses generated by such initial advocates of family planning as Charles Bradlaugh and Annie Besant in England and Margaret Sanger in the United States were mere local storms. These pale by comparison with present-day concern with various aspects of population events and trends and the alternative resolutions of their problematic aspects.

Beginning with worries about high fertility and total population growth rates, worldwide attention has broadened to other aspects of population phenomena. These include differential mortality and morbidity rates; problems of population distribution, including global, regional, metropolitan and urban-rural distribution; problems of population quality, including focus on investment in human capital as well as the genetic heritage; problems relating to specific elements of the population—the aged, youth, and women; problems of manpower—the labor force, employment, unemployment, and underemployment; and problems of population heterogeneity—diversity by race, ethnicity, religion, value systems, and life styles—in relation to differential opportunities and socioeconomic status. Much of the growing interest in population matters involves the relation of population to natural resources, food, environmental degradation, and development, social and economic, especially in the less developed countries.

Expanding programs and policies of national and international agencies, in both the private and public sectors, reflect the increasing interest in population. The international attention to population matters was highlighted in the World Population Year, 1974, particularly at the first worldwide population conference of national governments held in Bucharest in August of that year. Over the years the United Nations (UN) and its specialized agencies developed a number of population policies and programs. In 1947, the UN General Assembly, through the Economic and Social Council, established the Population Commission. Before that it had already provided for a Statistical Office and Population Division within the UN administrative organization, including its regional commissions. Specific population programs evolved within the frameworks of the UN technical assistance programs, and the UN Education, Scientific and Cultural Organization (UNESCO), International Labor Organization (ILO), World Health Organization (WHO), Food and Agricultural Organization (FAO), and UN Children's Fund (UNICEF).

The major effort of the UN system to deal with population problems was the creation of the UN Fund for Population Activities (UNFPA). Since 1969, this agency, celebrating the completion of its first decade of activity in 1979, has experienced remarkable growth, expanding from its first budget of $2.5 million in 1969 to a budget of more than $100 million in 1978. The UNFPA has been funded by voluntary national contributions. Rafael Salas, Executive Director of UNFPA, and an Under-Secretary General of the United Nations, observed in 1975:

> Over six operational years, the Fund's donors have steadily increased their contributions, grown in number and tabled no serious complaints on the many formal and informal occasions on which I have met with them. The recipients have also grown in numbers, widened their population programmes and strengthened their political support of the Fund. The agencies and organizations helping to implement the programmes have established close working relationships with both the countries and the Fund and developed new expertise to meet the challenges of untried and innovative programs.[1]

This observation is also applicable to the entire first ten years of the UNFPA's activities.

The first step in examining the emergence of population problems as a national and global concern will be to view the prehistory and history of world population growth.

1. Rafael M. Salas, *People: An International Choice, the Multilateral Approach to Population* (New York: Pergamon, 1976), p. 11.

WORLD POPULATION GROWTH—THE PAST

Although the first complete world census has yet to be taken, it is possible to reconstruct with reasonable accuracy the history of world population growth. During the Neolithic period (7000–6000 B.C.) the population of the world is estimated to have been 5–10 million. By the beginning of the Christian Era, population had reached about 300 million; by the beginning of the Modern Era (1650) about 500 million; and at the present time (1978), total world population is estimated at more than 4 billion.[2] The remarkable acceleration in the rate of world population increase may be understood in summary form as follows. It took most of the time humankind (or close relatives of humankind) has been on the earth, perhaps up to 4 million years, to reach 1 billion people. This is the estimated number of total world population in about 1800. It required another 130 years to add a second billion persons, the estimated world population in about 1930. It took only another thirty years for world population to add a third billion—it was 3 billion in 1960; and it took only an additional fifteen years to add a fourth billion, for world population reached 4 billion in about 1975. If these numbers are translated into growth rates, the data become even more startling. By a process of backward extrapolation, it is estimated that world population grew at rates of about 2 percent per millennium during the 650,000 years of the Paleolithic period. The rate of growth accelerated to a level of 0.4 percent per annum at the beginning of the Christian Era; to 0.8 percent per annum at the beginning of the Modern Era; to about 1 percent per annum between World War I and World War II; and to about 2 percent per annum by the mid-1950s. Thus, world population growth had increased from 2 percent per millennium in the prehistoric past to 2 percent per annum by the mid-1950s—a 1,000-fold increase!

Fortunately, as will be elaborated below, evidence is accumulating that, with the decline in world fertility since about the mid-1960s, the rate of world population growth has also probably declined. But before these recent changes are examined, consideration will be given to the long-run implications of the growth rate of 2 percent per annum reached in the mid-1950s and to the dynamics of population growth—the interplay of birth and death rates and their resultant demographic profiles.

2. *The Determinants and Consequences of Population Trends,* UN Department of Economic and Social Affairs, Population Studies, no. 50, vol. I (New York: UN, 1973), Table II.1.

Long-Run Implications

The rate of world population growth reached in the mid-1950s and persisting to about the mid-1960s would have fantastic implications if projected into the future. At 2 percent per annum, a dozen persons could have produced the 4 billion persons in the world in 1975 in about 991 years. Yet *Homo sapiens* is known to have inhabited parts of the globe in appreciable numbers as early as 25,000 years ago. The 2 percent per annum growth rate could, from a world population of 4 billion, generate one person for every square foot of land surface on the globe (approximately 50 million square miles) in 295 years.

To show that continued population growth in accordance with what has already transpired is impossible, Calhoun, in Chapter 3, points to one of the "absurdities" that playing with numbers can produce. In the past each doubling of world population has taken only half the time required for the preceding doubling. If world population were to continue this pattern for only 50 more years, as it has for nearly 50,000 years over the past, then well before the next fifty years is over all the matter of the universe would have been converted to human bodies.

Space itself may be the ultimate limit to total population growth, although other limits are certain to be in play long before space becomes the limiting factor. Is there any purpose to such demographic calculations? The answer is definitely yes. Such calculations make it possible to reach some indisputable, significant conclusions:

1. Contemporary population growth rates could not possibly have been obtained for any long period in the past.
2. Contemporary population growth rates cannot possibly persist for long into the future.
3. Given the finite limits of the globe, any rate of growth would, in the long run, produce saturation.
4. Zero population growth, over time, is therefore inevitable.

Quite apart from the calculations presented above, a mathematical axiom suffices to support this assertion. Infinite growth is impossible in a finite space, and the world is a finite space.

Dynamics of Growth

For the world as a whole, population growth has only two components: fertility and mortality. For any subdivisions of the world, there is, of course, a third component: net migration. For the world as a whole, then, the interaction of fertility and mortality accounts for changing growth rates, and, as will be seen, generates important differences in population characteristics.

The great acceleration in the rate of population growth in the past has been explained by the "theory of the demographic transition." This theory holds that as a by-product of modernization—social, economic, and political change—mortality declined while fertility levels remained high. As a result, the rise in natural increase, the excess of births over deaths, produced the great rise in the world population growth rate. Painstaking research over the last two decades or so has made it clear that this explanation is simplistic.[3] (See also Chapter 2.) That is, evidence shows that the increase in growth rates has occurred under widely varying conditions before, as well as during, modernization. Although the demographic transition has yet to be fully explained, it is known that by and large, at present, the more developed countries (MDCs) have achieved relatively low growth rates; some are already at, or below, a zero growth level; and others will reach zero growth in the not too distant future. By contrast, the economically less developed countries (LDCs) as a whole are still experiencing rapid growth; and although evidence of declines in birth rates in some LDCs is accumulating, the LDCs as a whole will experience substantial population increases, at least until the end of this century.

Demographic Profiles

The way in which the interaction of fertility and mortality can affect growth rates and also basic population characteristics can be shown by using models of population dynamics.[4] Using model life and stable population tables, Table 1.1 presents varying profiles to illustrate the impact of differing patterns of fertility and mortality.

The impact is shown on broad age structure, dependency, life expectancy, fertility, and survival of offspring. The designations shown in the subheadings of the table—"primitive stationary," "premodern," "transitional," "modern," and "modern stationary"—while arbitrary, do in fact

3. Ansley J. Coale, "The Demographic Transition Reconsidered," International Conference, Liege, 1973 (Liege: IUSSP, 1973), vol. 1; and Michael S. Teitelbaum, "Relevance of Demographic Transition Theory for Developing Countries," *Science* 188 (1975):420–25.

4. Adapted from Philip M. Hauser, "Aging and World Wide Population Change," in *Handbook of Aging and the Social Sciences,* edited by Robert H. Binstock and Ethel Shanas (New York: Van Nostrand Reinhold, 1976), chap. 3.

TABLE 1.1

Model Demographic Profiles under Varying Fertility and Mortality Levels

Population Characteristic	Primitive Stationary*	Premodern†	Tran-sitional‡	Modern§	Modern Stationary‖
Birth rate	50.0	43.7	45.7	20.4	12.9
Death rate	50.0	33.7	15.7	10.4	12.9
Annual growth rate (%)	0.0	1.0	3.0	1.0	0.0
Age structure					
Percent under 15	36.2	37.8	45.4	27.2	19.2
Percent 15–64	60.9	58.8	52.0	62.4	62.3
Percent 65 and over	2.9	3.4	2.6	10.3	18.5
Average age	25.5	25.1	21.8	32.8	40.0
Dependency ratio, total	64	70	92	60	61
Youth (under 15)	59	64	87	44	31
Aged (65 and over)	5	6	5	16	30
Percent surviving to age 15	41.0	55.9	78.8	95.6	98.9
Expectation of life at birth (years)	20.0	30.0	50.0	70.0	77.5
Average number of children born to a woman reaching age 50	6.2	5.5	6.1	2.9	2.7
Average number of children surviving to age 20	2.3	2.9	4.7	2.7	2.0

* Mortality level 1 (for definition of levels, see source).
† Mortality level 5.
‡ Mortality level 13.
§ Mortality level 21.
‖ Mortality level 24.

SOURCE: Ansley J. Coale and Paul Demeny, *Regional Model Life Tables and Stable Populations* (Princeton, N.J.: Princeton University Press, 1966); based on stable populations for "West" female.

have empirical counterparts in the contemporary figures shown in Table 1.2.

Table 1.1 shows that the primitive stationary and modern stationary populations both have zero population growth; but in the primitive stationary population, zero growth is the result of very high fertility and mortality, whereas in the modern stationary population, yet to be achieved in most MDCs, zero growth is the result of both very low birth and death rates. In the premodern population, mortality is assumed to decline much more than fertility to produce a relatively modest growth rate of 1 percent per annum. In the transitional population, mortality is shown to have plummeted to a relatively low level, while fertility has actually increased somewhat, so that population growth rate reaches 3 percent per annum. The increase in fertility in this situation is the result of women living through a

TABLE 1.2
Demographic Profile of the World Classified by Economic Development, *circa* 1965–70

	World	MDCs	LDCs
Birth rate	33.8	18.6	40.6
Death rate	14.0	9.1	16.1
Growth rate	2.0	1.0	2.4
Age structure			
Percent under 15	37.0	26.8	41.4
Percent 15–64	57.8	63.5	55.3
Percent 65 and over	5.2	9.6	3.3
Average age (median)	26	33	23
Dependency ratio, total	74	59	81
Youth (under 15)	65	44	75
Aged (65 and over)	9	15	6
Percent surviving to age 15	85.9	95.0	82.0
Expectation of life at birth (years)	53.1	70.4	49.6
Average number of children born to a woman reaching age 50	4.7	2.7	5.6
Average number surviving to age 20	4.0	2.6	4.6

SOURCE: Adapted from *The World Population Situation in 1970* (New York: UN, 1971) (Department of Economic and Social Affairs), Population Studies, No. 49.

much greater proportion of their childbearing years and their improved health, which must accompany lower death rates. Finally, in the modern population, fertility has declined significantly so that with continued decline in mortality, the relatively modest growth of 1 percent per annum is achieved.

Table 1.2 shows that the transitional and modern models have empirical counterparts in the contemporary LDCs and MDCs, respectively. In Table 1.1 the first two models, the primitive stationary and the premodern, show what may have occurred in the past; modern stationary model shows what probably lies ahead, and, indeed, as will be shown, is being approximated by some MDCs at the present time.

It is informative, especially in examining the relationship between population and development, to observe the variant population characteristics accompanying the differing patterns of fertility and mortality. In the transitional model, descriptive of contemporary LDCs in the aggregate, the population, compared with the modern profile, is relatively young, has a relatively high dependency ratio, lower expectation of life at birth, lower survivorship to age fifteen, a much higher number of children ever born and a much lower number of children surviving to age twenty. More specifically, the average age of the transitional population is only 21.8 years, compared with 32.8 years for the modern population. More than 45 percent of the transitional population is under 15 years of age, compared with the little over 27 percent of the modern population. The youth dependency ratio of the transitional models is 87 (87 persons under age 15 to each 100 persons age 15 to 64), contrasted with 44 for the modern population. Conversely, the aged dependency ratio is only 5 (persons 65 and over per 100 persons 15 to 64), compared with the aged dependency ratio of 16 for the modern population. The total dependency ratio of 92 (92 persons under 15 and over 65 per 100 persons 15 to 64) for the transitional population, is well above that of the modern population, at 60.

The relatively wasteful pattern of survivorship of the transitional population is manifest in the fact that only 78.8 percent of persons born survive to age 15, compared with 95.6 percent in the modern population; and in the expectation of life at birth of only 50 years, compared with 70 years. Demographic waste is also demonstrated in the fact that women in the transitional population have an average of 6.1 births, of whom only 4.7 survive to age 20; whereas women in the modern population average only 2.9 births, but 2.7 of them survive to age 20. The way in which the differences in these population profiles relate to development will be discussed later.

Comparing the transitional and modern models in Table 1.1 either with the primitive stationary and the premodern, or with the modern stationary models yields some even greater contrasts.

In Table 1.2, demographic profiles are presented for the MDCs and LDCs for the period *circa* 1965 to 1970. Similarities can be found between the modern model and the actual profile of the MDCs and between the transitional model and the actual situation for the LDCs. The population growth rate of the MDCs, at 1 percent per annum, is identical with that of the modern model. The growth of the LDCs at 2.4 percent, while lower than that of the transitional model at 3 percent, is nevertheless very high. At this rate, the LDCs would double in about 29 years, whereas the 3 percent growth rate would produce a doubling every 23 years.

The population of the LDCs is significantly younger than that of the MDCs, averaging 23 years, compared with 33. In the LDCs, 41.4 percent of the population is under 15 years old, whereas in the MDCs youngsters constitute only 26.8 percent of the total. In the LDCs only 3.3 percent of the population is 65 and over, whereas in the MDCs the comparable figure is about three times as high, at 9.6 percent. The total dependency ratio of the LDCs is 81, compared with 59 for the MDCs; youth dependency in the former is 75, compared with 44 in the latter. Expectation of life at birth in the LDCs is less than 50 years compared with more than 70 years in the

MDCs. Children ever born per woman age 50 in the LDCs average 5.6, compared with 2.7 in the MDCs. Of the average of 5.6 children ever born per woman in the LDCs, 4.6, or 82 percent, survive to age 20, whereas of the 2.7 children ever born per woman in the MDCs, 2.6, or 96 percent, survive to age 20.

With the estimated decline in fertility since 1965 and the continued decline in mortality, discussed below, the contrasts indicated above have, of course, become somewhat narrowed. But the great differences presented characterize the disparities in demographic profiles between the MDCs and the LDCs during most of the post–World War II period. Updated estimates for both mortality and fertility are presented below.

RECENT MORTALITY, FERTILITY, AND GROWTH

Mortality

The crude death rate in the world as a whole, estimated at 18.5 (deaths per 1,000 persons per year) in 1950–55, dropped to 12.2 in 1970–75 and is projected by the UN to be 11.4 for 1975–80. In the MDCs, the crude death rate of 10.3 in 1950–55 dropped to 9.2 in 1970–75 and is projected by the UN to be 9.4 in 1975–80.[5] In the LDCs, the crude death rate of 22.6 in 1950–55 is placed at 13.4 in 1970–75 and is projected to be 12.2 in 1975–80. Yet despite the continued rapid decline in mortality in the LDCs, there is alarming evidence that some causes of death believed to have been subjected to control have reappeared. For example, deaths attributable to malaria have increased as this disease has again become a health problem in a number of LDCs in Asia and Africa.[6] Moreover, deaths attributable to famine and malnutrition have increased in some local areas because of crop failures.

Fertility

The magnitude of the decline in fertility in the MDCs has been indicated in the model demographic profiles presented in Table 1.1. Crude

5. UN, "Preliminary Report of the Estimates and Projections in Population for the World, Regions and Countries, As Assessed in 1978," mimeographed (New York, October 1978).

6. Rafael M. Salas, "The State of World Population, 1978," Annual Report on UNFPA Activities and Plans to the Governing Council (New York: UN, 1978).

birth rates in excess of 40 (births per 1,000 persons per year) have come down to levels below 20. The average number of children born has declined from more than 6 per woman to little more than 2 and in some countries has fallen below the replacement level. In the United States, for example, the current total fertility rate at about 1.8 is well below the replacement level of 2.1, assuming no immigration.[7]

Declines in the birth rate of the LDCs did not achieve significance until the mid-1960s. Perhaps the most definitive analysis of this decline is that by Mauldin and Berelson of the Population Council, who studied changes in the birth rate in LDCs between 1965 and 1975.[8] The study embraced 94 developing countries with 2.8 billion people, or 98 percent of the population of all developing nations for the period 1965 to 1975. The study reported that the crude birth rate declined during this ten-year period by about 13 percent, or by 5.5 points, dropping from 41 to 35.5. Furthermore, the evidence, while it could be more precise, indicates that the LDC birth rate has continued to decline since 1975.

In assessing the state of population in 1978, the UN assumed a birth rate in the LDCs of 34.3 for the period 1975 to 1980,[9] and the U.S. Bureau of the Census estimated the LDC birth rate in 1976 as ranging from 34 to 39.[10] Needless to say, this decline in the fertility of the developing nations constitutes a major event in the population history of the globe.

Population Growth

For the world as a whole, population growth is, of course, the result of natural increase—the excess of births over deaths. There is considerable error in the figures for both the world birth rate and world death rate. The rate of world population growth, based on subtraction, is a residual of the other two estimates and is, therefore, subject to an even greater percentage of error than either the birth or death rate alone. It should not be surprising that there is no consensus among demographers on whether the rate of *world population growth* has actually declined and, if so, by how much. Moreover, there is no consensus on the precise contributions to changes

7. U.S. Bureau of the Census, *Statistical Abstract of the United States: 1977* (Washington, D.C.: USGPO, 1977), Table 76.

8. W. Parker Mauldin and Bernard Berelson, "Conditions of Fertility Decline in Developing Countries, 1965–75," *Studies in Family Planning* 9 (May 1978).

9. UN, "Preliminary Report," Table 2.

10. U.S. Bureau of the Census, *World Population, 1977, Recent Demographic Estimates for the Countries and Regions of the World,* Advance Summary (Washington, D.C.: USGPO, 1978), p. 14.

in the world population growth rate, of changing fertility, and changing mortality, respectively. That is, although there is consensus on the fact that the *world birth rate* has declined, uncertainties about the extent of the decline and about the world death rate, which in recent years has declined in most countries but probably has increased in some, leave uncertain their impact on the world growth rate.

It is important to note, however, that both the UN and the U.S. Bureau of the Census hold that the world population growth rate has declined during the 1970s. The UN, in making its more recent projection, based on the assessment of world population in 1978, assumes a world population growth rate of 1.8 between 1975 and 1980.[11] The U.S. Bureau of the Census estimates the world growth rate at 1.7 to 2 percent per annum for the year 1976. Moreover, the Census Bureau has expressed the judgment that for the first time in recent human experience, world population growth has not risen and has probably declined to a level of 1.9 percent per annum.

The decline in fertility, of course, tends to decrease the world growth rate. But the determination of whether a decrease has actually occurred, and if so, to what an extent, must await the availability of data more precise than are now at hand. If the world death rate has continued to decline despite the apparent increases in the mortality of some nations, the decline in mortality might well offset the decline in fertility, so that the world population growth rate may not have necessarily decreased with the decreased birth rate.

The United Nations estimates the population growth rates of the less developed nations at 2.2 percent per annum for the period 1975 to 1980. The U.S. Bureau of the Census estimates the growth rates of the population in the less developed nations at 2.1 to 2.4 percent. The UN estimates the growth rates of the more developed nations at 0.74 percent per annum, whereas the U.S. Bureau of the Census estimates it at 0.7 percent per annum.

That most of the more developed nations of the world seem to be approaching zero population growth is noteworthy. A few countries in Europe have already dropped below zero population growth, namely, Austria, East and West Germany, and Luxembourg, which have reported more deaths than births in recent years. The United Kingdom now has about the same number of births and deaths. Furthermore, if present trends in the birth rate continue, a number of other countries will drop below zero population growth in the not too distant future; these countries in-

11. UN, "Preliminary Report," Table 1; and U.S. Bureau of the Census, *Recent Demographic Estimates*.

clude Belgium, Czechoslovakia, Denmark, Hungary, Norway, and Sweden, and, by 1990, Bulgaria, Finland, Greece, Italy, and Switzerland may follow. The continuation of trends will result in the beginning of a decline in the population of Europe as a whole and of the USSR at the end of the century, and of the U.S. in about 2015. These conclusions have been reached on the basis of available data and projections by Charles F. Westoff, of the Office of Population Research, Princeton University.[12]

These trends in the more developed countries, of course, contribute to possible decline in the rate of world population growth, but it must be emphasized that the more developed countries constitute only 28 percent of the world's total population.

PROSPECT TO THE YEAR 2000

What is the prospect for world population by the end of this century? The United Nations has attempted to answer this question.[13] Prospective growth as assessed in 1978, under the "medium variant" projection, would result in a population of 6.2 billion by the year 2000. On the basis of the UN's "high variant" projection, world population would reach 6.5 billion. Under the "low variant" projection, the population of the world would reach 5.9 billion. The range in these projections is produced by variations in the key assumption about the birth rate. The data are given in Table 1.3, in the context of historical growth since 1750.

The effect of declining fertility may be gauged when these projections are compared with those made by the United Nations in 1973.[14] At that time the medium variant projection was set at 6.5 billion, the high variant at 7.1 billion, and the low variant at 6 billion. Because of data limitations, especially for the LDCs, the results of the censuses to be taken in or around 1980 under the aegis of the UN World Census Program are awaited to provide some measure of validity and perhaps greater precision on the estimated decline in fertility in the LDCs and on total world population growth. These data will, of course, also affect the population projections.

Table 1.3 also projects population for the MDCs and the LDCs. The

12. Charles F. Westoff, "Marriage and Fertility in the Developed Countries," *Scientific American* 289 (December 1978): 57 ff.

13. UN, "Preliminary Report," Tables 3, 8, and 10.

14. UN, "World and Regional Population Prospects," ECOSOC, World Population Conference, 1974 (E/Conf. 60/BP/3/ add. 1) (16 May, 1973), pp. 3–16.

TABLE 1.3
Estimates of Past, Present, and Future World Population, 1750–2000

Year	Population (in millions) World	MDCs	LDCs	Percent of Population MDCs	LDCs
1750	791	201	590	25.4	74.6
1800	978	248	730	25.4	74.6
1850	1,262	347	915	27.5	72.5
1900	1,650	573	1,077	34.7	65.3
1950	2,486	858	1,628	34.5	65.5
1970	3,632	1,090	2,542	24.9	75.1
2000					
High variant	6,530	1,402	5,128	21.5	78.5
Medium variant	6,211	1,345	4,866	21.7	78.3
Low variant	5,859	1,295	4,564	22.1	77.9

SOURCES: For 1750 to 1900, J. D. Durand, "The Modern Expansion of World Population," *Proceedings of the American Philosophical Society* 3(3) (June 22, 1967); for 1950, UN, *The World Population Situation in 1970* (New York: UN, 1971); for 1970 to 2000, UN, *Preliminary Report of the Estimates and Projections of Population for the World, Regions and Countries as Assessed in 1978* (October 1978).

table shows that by far the major portion of the projected growth will occur in the LDCs. Of the total anticipated increment of about 2.6 billion persons since 1970, according to the medium variant projections, 2.3 billion, or 90 percent, would be experienced by the developing countries. Thus the LDCs may, in the course of little more than one human generation, between 1970 and 2000, increase by almost as many people as were on the entire globe in 1950.

EXPLANATION OF POPULATION CHANGE

Demographers have shown that although there has been great variation over time and place in the interaction of birth and death rates, it remains true that in general, greatly increased population growth rates have been the product of greatly decreased death rates, which increased the gap between fertility and mortality. The general pattern accounting for explosive population growth is the essence of the theory of the demographic transition, which Freedman discusses in Chapter 2. Factors in the decline in mortality have been well documented and are better understood than the factors in the decline of fertility. Discussion of the factors in mortality decline will, therefore, be succinctly summarized here.

Mortality

The decrease in mortality was in large part the unanticipated and unplanned by-product of social, technological, economic, and political change.[15] Increased productivity in agriculture, improved transportation, and the emergence of national political units, combined, for example, to decrease deaths due to famine and malnutrition because it was possible to effect better distribution of excess agricultural products to areas of deficit within broad regional or national markets. Better environmental sanitation and personal hygiene combined to reduce infectious, parasitic, contagious and communicable diseases greatly, especially the disorders attributable to polluted water and food. Such factors, it has been estimated, may have accounted for about two-thirds of the decrease in mortality before the emergence of modern medicine. Modern medicine in general, climaxed by the relatively recent advent of chemotherapy, can make claim, perhaps, to no more than about one-third of the decline of the death rate in the MDCs.

The decrease in mortality was disproportionately achieved by decreases in infant and child mortality. In consequence, whereas expectation of life at birth has greatly increased, doubling and more than doubling, that at age 60 has gone up relatively little.

For example, expectation of life at birth for females in Sweden in 1755–76 was 35.7 years.[16] By 1973 it had reached 77.7 years,[17] an increase of 42 years, and more than a doubling. Expectation of life for females in Sweden at age 60 in 1755–76 was 13.1 years. By 1973 it had risen to 21.3 years, an increase of 8.2 years. Expectation of life at birth for the MDCs is now above 70 and is about 50 years in the LDCs (Table 1.2).

The dramatic effect of decreased death rates is evident in the fact that in the MDCs in the mid-nineteenth century, one-fourth of the children born were dead by age ten, and half were dead by age 45. A century later, one-fourth of the children born in the MDCs were not dead until age 60, and half were not dead until age 70.[18] The decline in death rates in the MDCs occurred mainly during the latter half of the nineteenth century and first

15. UN, *The Determinants and Consequences of Population Trends* (New York: UN, 1973), Chap. V.

16. Louis Dublin and Alfred Lotka, *Length of Life: A Study of the Life Table* (New York: Ronald, 1936), pp. 48 and 371.

17. UN, *Demographic Year Book, 1976,* Table 21.

18. George J. Stolnitz, "A Century of International Mortality Trends—I and II," *Population Studies* 9 (1955–56):24–55; 10 (1956–57):17–42.

half of the twentieth century. Also noteworthy is the fact that as expectation of life has increased, the gap between the sexes in favor of females has also increased. In Sweden, for example, the difference between male and female expectation of life at birth in 1755–76 was 2.5 years; male expectation was at 33.2, female 35.7. In 1973 the gap in expectation of life by sex had more than doubled: 72.1 years for males and 77.7 for females.

Basic to an understanding of the differential between population growth rates in the MDCs and LDCs is the difference in the timing of mortality declines in the MDCs and LDCs, respectively. Whereas it took the better part of a century to reduce mortality in the MDCs, from premodern levels of 40 or more deaths per 1,000 persons per year to present levels below 10 per 1,000 persons per year, drastic reductions in mortality were experienced in the LDCs over a much shorter period of time. The reason for this lies in the importation of methods of death control from the MDCs to the LDCs. Reduced death rates in the LDCs, unlike those in the MDCs, were not achieved because of basic social, technological, economic, and political change, but were, rather, exogenous, the result of importations from abroad. Thus, whereas it took the United States the first half of this century to cut its death rate in half, it took Sri Lanka less than a decade to do the same after World War II.

Since fertility remained at a relatively high level, rapidly falling mortality in the LDCs produced unprecedent high growth rates. Whereas MDCs rarely achieved population growth rates over 1.5 percent per annum through natural increase (without migration), LDCs at peak achieved growth of 2.5 percent per annum, on the average, and some growth rates as high as, and even higher than, 3 percent.

Fertility

Much more complex and much less understood are the factors that account for declines in fertility.[19] Changes in fertility have frequently been attributed to the process of modernization. The term "modernization" subsumes many economic and social changes, and different researchers have exercised their own biases in emphasizing particular components of the overall modernization process in explaining fertility change. They have considered the relationship of various social and economic indicators to fertility change from both a macro-level and micro-level perspective. At the macro level, both time series and cross-sectional data have been used

19. The section which follows is an adaptation of a summary of fertility literature prepared for this volume by Dr. Ann Way, who received a Ph.D. in sociology with a concentration in demography at the University of Chicago in 1978.

in efforts to identify whether there are "threshold" values for social and economic indicators that must be reached before a country will experience fertility declines. In micro-level studies, by contrast, the nature of the relationship between various social and economic indicators and fertility change within specific populations has been highlighted.

MACRO-LEVEL EXPLANATIONS

To explain differences in fertility rates, analysts have frequently relied on societal, or macro-level, indicators of the social and economic situation. While it could not be expected that a given level of literacy, urbanization, or expectation of life *per se* would influence fertility, these and other similar statistics are generally taken as indicators of changes in the patterns of life in individual households, which collectively result in a given fertility level.

Using time series data, attempts have been made to relate changes in various development indicators to patterns of fertility decline in those countries that have progressed from high to low fertility levels. A UN study in 1973[20] identified seven broad categories of social and economic changes that presumably had some effect on the fertility transition. These were: (1) alterations in family functions and structure; (2) declining mortality levels; (3) rising levels of living and increased costs of raising children; (4) increased education; (5) social mobility; (6) urbanization; and (7) industrialization. But although it may be asserted that these and other developmental indicators had a direct relationship to fertility change in the nineteenth and early twentieth centuries, it is not proven that such factors are necessary, as distinguished from sufficient, conditions for fertility decline. It is not clear, furthermore, which specific elements of general development were most instrumental in bringing about this change, even if the role of development in fertility change is not disputed.

In a detailed study of the process of demographic transition in several different countries and regions, Coale showed that some culturally similar regions moved through the fertility transition at the same pace, although their economic conditions differed substantially, indicating perhaps that cultural factors were more important than economic ones.[21] Evidence has also been presented on the variation in the timing of fertility decline with

20. UN, *The Mysore Population Studies* (ST/SOA/Ser. A/34) (New York, 1961).

21. Ansley J. Coale, "The Demographic Transition," *The Population Debate: Dimensions and Perspectives,* Papers of the World Population Conference, Bucharest, 1 (New York: UN, 1975), pp. 347–55.

respect to several development indicators.[22] Fertility had fallen, it was found, before substantial changes occurred in the mortality levels in several southern and eastern European countries. Similarly, there was considerable variation in whether fertility decline occurred before, during, or after major industrial development. Sweezy found that the Bulgarian birth rate declined despite a lack of significant urbanization or industrialization.[23] These findings do not necessarily suggest, however, that fertility decline bears no relationship to the process of economic and social development and change, but rather that the timing of such fertility decline may be equally dependent on other (e.g., cultural) factors.

Objections have been raised to the use of such historical studies in examining the relationship between development and fertility in a contemporary setting. It has been argued that technological innovations and development in communications media, among other factors, are readily available to developing countries and have so fundamentally altered the process of development as to negate the validity of the use of timetables or relationships derived from historical studies in studies of contemporary development and fertility.[24] A response to such objections has been the use of cross-sectional data on development and fertility under the assumption that current data on the relationship between development and fertility may more accurately portray the future path of development than would the historical path followed by the more developed countries.

Using data from around 1960, the United Nations completed a study of the relationship between a number of development indicators and the gross reproduction rate (GRR—number of daughters born per woman) in a cross-sectional setting. A number of strong correlations were found for these indicators. In general, factors related to communication and health were more strongly related to fertility than were urbanization, industrialization, and income. It was hypothesized, based on these results, that the relationship of these latter variables to fertility may be indirect, operating through other variables which are themselves more strongly linked to fertility.[25]

In a recent, more elaborate study of this type, Srikantan used data

22. Alan Sweezy, "Social and Economic Development and Fertility," in *Population: Perspectives,* edited by H. Brown (San Francisco: Freeman, Cooper, 1973), p. 43 ff.

23. *Ibid.*

24. Dudley Kirk, "A New Demographic Transition," in *Rapid Population Growth: Consequences and Policy Implications,"* edited by R. Ridker (Baltimore: National Academy of Sciences, Johns Hopkins University Press, 1971), pp. 123–47.

25. UN, *Population Bulletin, No. 7* (New York, 1963).

from around 1970 to study the relationship of development with fertility.[26] For the most part, the magnitude and order of the correlations for those indicators shared with the earlier UN study were similar. The computed correlations were averaged into four major areas: communication, health, the status of women, and industrialization. The status of women was found to be the most important factor, followed by industrialization, health, and communication.

In the above investigations, a high degree of association was established between social and economic development and the level of fertility, without claims as to the causal nature or direction of the relationship. Countries with low social and economic development tend to have high fertility. It must be realized, however, that the transition to low fertility and social and economic change are interacting processes. It appears that this relationship may well work in either direction—developmental changes may foster fertility declines, while spontaneous fertility declines may bolster economic and social development. This interaction does not take place in a vacuum; there are other factors that may play an important role in determining the outcome of particular changes. Among such other factors, cultural characteristics, especially value systems, probably deserve emphasis.

THRESHOLD LEVELS

In the light of the relationship, however vaguely defined, between economic and social development and fertility, attention has at times been addressed to the question of whether that relationship is continuous or whether it exhibits certain threshold levels. In a continuous relationship, fertility will be found to vary directly and evenly over the range of the development indicator, while in a relationship characterized by threshold levels, fertility will show little change until such a threshold is reached, at which point change in fertility will occur with change in the development indicator. The concept of a threshold level has a certain intuitive appeal because many aspects of planning are linked to the achievements that are conceptually comparable to threshold levels.[27]

26. K. S. Srikantan, *The Family Programme in the Socio-Economic Context* (New York: Population Council, 1977).

27. United Nations, *Population Bulletin;* and K. S. Srikanta, *The Family Programme;* and F. W. Oeschli and D. Kirk, "Modernization and Demographic Transition in Latin America and the Caribbean," *Economic Development and Cultural Change* 23(3):391–420; and P. Gregory and J. M. Campbell, Jr., "Fertility and Economic Development," in *Population, Public Policy, and Economic Development,* edited by M. D. Keeley (New York: Praeger, 1976), pp. 160–87.

In summary, the experience of researchers is mixed with respect to the identification of threshold values determining the influence of development indicators on fertility. It may not, in fact, be possible to identify threshold levels for a significant number of social and economic factors before which fertility will not decline, and after which fertility will necessarily decline. This is because the causal connection between the development indicator and fertility is extremely complex and is indirect at best. The indicators used reflect, for the most part, only one dimension of an intricate and varied culture. This culture may not be much affected if the level of one of these indicators should change, even substantially.[28] Furthermore, although perhaps appealing from a planning perspective, the application of these threshold levels to the fertility of individual households would be difficult to justify on theoretical grounds.

It should be clear, however, that changes in one of several of the indicators, for example, those reflecting the impact on mortality of the involvement of women in employment outside the home, will have an effect on fertility. But more than any single factor, it is a total environment that determines the pattern of life in a society and thereby affects the fertility level. Efforts to influence fertility levels by manipulating development indicators must recognize the complexity of this relationship.

MICRO-LEVEL ANALYSIS

Macro-level analyses of the relationship between socioeconomic development and fertility have identified a number of social and economic changes that are highly correlated with declines in the fertility rate at the national level. However, such macro-level changes have not been the only focus of attention in efforts to understand and to predict the path of fertility transition. Questions have also been raised concerning the social and economic characteristics that influence an individual couple to break with traditional behavior and practice birth control voluntarily.

In general, socioeconomic status has been found to be inversely related to fertility, using such indexes as educational level, occupation, and income. Studies have also explored the relationship between fertility and economic utility of children, female labor-force participation, family structure, and child mortality. Such studies have in varying degrees shown these factors to be related to fertility, but a coherent model has yet to be devised to show how these factors at the macro and micro levels, in cross section or over time, interact to explain fertility change. An attempt at such a model as perceived by economists is presented in Chapter 8.

28. Kirk, "A New Demographic Transition."

FERTILITY DECLINE IN LDCs, 1965–75

The decline in fertility in the 94 LDCs studied by Mauldin and Berelson of the Population Council, summarized above, was well explained by a combination of factors. Analysis of the data based on several different methodologies resulted in essentially the same conclusions. The highlights of these findings are as follows:[29]

1. The level of modernization, based on seven socioeconomic factors "had a substantial relationship to fertility decline."
2. Better-off countries experienced greater fertility decline than the less well-off.
3. Effective family planning programs had a significant "independent effect over and above the effect of socioeconomic factors." Without question, good family planning programs added considerably to the amount of birth decline.
4. The combination of modernization and family planning program efforts was very effective. These two factors considered jointly explain "about 83 percent of the total variance in fertility decline."
5. To effect a reduction in fertility, a nation should seek economic development—a high level of modernization—and, simultaneously, should adopt a substantial family planning program.
6. Large countries, those with populations of 35 million or more, experienced greater reductions in birth rates than the smaller countries.
7. The longer family planning programs have been in force, the greater their effect on fertility reduction.
8. Countries with population policies designed to reduce fertility have experienced greater declines in the birth rate than countries with family planning programs aiming only to improve the health of mothers and children.
9. Even if China, for which precise data are not available, is left out of the analysis, the conclusions above remain substantially the same.

Although the Population Council report recognizes the limitations of the data available and is aware that demographers disagree about the precise numbers, it expresses the significant well-founded judgment that the general pattern of fertility decline in a number of LDCs cannot be effectively contradicted; nor can there be any doubt about the fact that both

29. Mauldin and Berelson, "Conditions of Fertility," pp. 123–24.

socioeconomic development and family planning programs are associated with the decline.

It must be noted, however, that this study was conducted at the macro level, and so caution is called for in interpreting the way these factors actually operate at the micro level. It is not necessarily true that relationships at the macro level in multicountry analyses will hold true for countries subjected to micro analyses, especially where national policies operate.

Mauldin and Berelson shed further light on the factors in the fertility decline of the LDCs in an additional analysis. Fertility decline is, of course, affected by three factors: changes in age structure, changes in age at marriage, and changes in marital fertility. The study shows that for most of the LDCs, the age structure changes over the past decade or so have been relatively unimportant. After all, ten years is a short period of time for structural change in population. Decreased nuptiality by reason of increased age at marriage has been a significant factor in birth rate decreases; but a more important factor has been the decrease in the birth rate within marriage. In an effort to quantify the respective contributions of these three factors in the decline in the birth rate in the decade 1965 to 1975, Mauldin and Berelson estimated that of the total decline in fertility, 5 to 10 percent was produced by age structure changes, 35 to 45 percent by changes in marital patterns, and 55 to 70 percent by changes in marital fertility.[30]

Fertility vs. Mortality Explanation

Although much remains to be learned about factors that reduce fertility, it is clear that mortality reduction is much easier to achieve than fertility reduction. Death rates go down, to a substantial extent, because of cultural and social changes requiring little or no decision making on the part of individuals. By contrast, apart from the effect of later marriage, birth rates cannot come down until individual couples perceive that birth control is possible, decide to limit the number of their children, have access to means to do this, and are successful in applying such means. In the experience of the MDCs, the later fertility decline began, the greater was the rate of decline.[31] It is yet to be demonstrated that this pattern will also hold among the LDCs. On the other hand, whereas among the MDCs fertility decline occurred often against the wishes of the establishment—the government, church, the medical profession, and conservative social forces

30. *Ibid.*, p. 122.

31. Frank W. Notestein *et al.*, *The Future Population of Europe and the Soviet Union: Population Projections 1940–1970* (Geneva: League of Nations, 1944), p. 29.

in general—the establishment in the LDCs in the main not only supports fertility decline, but actually exercises leadership to bring it about. This is manifest in present family planning programs either for purposes of decreasing population growth rates or improving the health of mothers and infants in about 90 percent of LDC populations. There have been different levels of success among the LDCs in family planning programs. More will be said about this later, including the role of UNFPA in supporting family planning programs. But at this juncture it must be observed, as the Population Council study reports, that strong family planning programs may have a significant impact on fertility with only modest changes in some aspects of modernization.

POPULATION AND WORLD PROBLEMS

In the post–World War II era there has been an increased consciousness of the relation of population factors to a number of major world problems. It has become increasingly apparent that population growth has important effects on the world food supply, the adequacy of world resources—especially the nonrenewable resources—and on world environmental pollution and degradation. Population growth and other aspects of population, as will be seen, also have an important bearing on social change and economic growth, especially in the less developed nations.

POPULATION FACTORS IN DEVELOPMENT

Although much attention has been focused on the relationship of high fertility and high population growth rates to economic development, many other facets of population may also affect both economic and social development. Before exploring these relationships, it is a good idea to clarify what is meant by *development*. The earlier tendency among scholars as well as government officials, including planners, was to use GNP (gross national product), or GDP (gross domestic product), or some measure of income per capita, as an index of economic development. It has been recognized more and more, however, that such an index is simplistic and even misleading. Similarly, it has become increasingly apparent that *development* embraces more than the economic; it includes the social in a broad sense as well. In fact, it is quite erroneous to assume that the division of labor in academia, among economists, sociologists, political scientists, geographers, psychologists, and so on, in any way reflects the real world. Development necessarily involves all aspects of a society and its culture. The need to include the social aspect was recognized by the United Nations in the relatively recent reorganization of its regional commissions: the Economic Commission of Asia and the Far East (ECAFE), for example, was renamed the Economic and Social Commission of Asia and the Pacific (ESCAP).

A number of scholars and agencies have attempted to effect this change in perspective by experimenting with various indicators of development, going beyond GNP per capita for some more meaningful measurements. Among them have been the United Nations Research Institute for Social Development, which has developed a core list of eighteen indicators of development—social, economic and structural—and a synthetic, single index of development based on its core list.[32] This is not the place to review or even to summarize the literature on the measurement of development, but it is important to realize that much more than the economic factor is necessarily involved. In fact, a number of economists concerned with development problems have recognized that the variables with which economists conventionally deal are not adequate either to understand or to prescribe for development. These include such scholars as Simon Kuznets, Henry Bruton, Walt Rostow, Bert Hoselitz, and Michael Todaro.[33]

What are the aspects of population, in addition to high fertility and growth rates, that may accelerate or impede development in the broad sense? A list of such items must include the other component of natural increase, namely, mortality (including differential mortality), and health and morbidity. It must include aspects of population composition, including age structure and degree of homogeneity or heterogeneity of population—ethnic, racial, cultural, and religious. It must also include the distribution of population—regional, urban, rural, metropolitan, and nonmetropolitan. Necessarily involved in considerations of population distribution is migration, international and internal, including the characteristics of in- and out-migrants and the effect of migration on areas of origin and

32. Donald V. McGranahan *et al.*, *Contents and Measurement of Socioeconomic Development* (New York: Praeger, 1972).

33. Simon Kuznets, *Modern Economic Growth: Rate, Structure and Spread* (New Haven: Yale University Press, 1966); Bert F. Hoselitz, *Sociological Aspects of Economic Growth* (New York: Free Press, 1960); Henry Bruton, "Contemporary Theorizing on Economic Growth," in *Theories of Economic Growth*, edited by B. Hoselitz (New York: Free Press, 1960); W. W. Rostow, *The Stages of Economic Growth, A Non-Communist Manifesto* (New York: Cambridge University Press, 1967); Michael Todaro, *Economic Development in the Third World: An Introduction to Problems and Policies and Global Perspectives* (New York: Langwan, 1977).

areas of destination. Also on the list is population quality, as a product of both genetic and social heritages. Especially important is consideration of the process of socialization as it determines population quality, among other things, through education and the acquisition of skills. This focus necessarily embraces the broad topic of investment in human resources—the creation of human capital (see Chapter 10 by Schultz and Chapter 11 by Blaug). Finally, as an essential aspect of population, the labor force requires examination, including labor force participation and differential participation of various elements of the population.

Every one of the above facets of population is related to development, either as an accelerating or impeding factor, and changes in these aspects of population often constitute, at least in part, indications of progress or retrogression in development. Much literature has evolved dealing with the above interrelationships. Only the highlights of the findings of some aspects of this literature will be presented below.

General Considerations

A simplistic indication of the relationships between population and the level of living is given in the equation $L = \frac{O}{P}$, where L is level of living, O is aggregate output, and P is population. The level of living of a people obviously cannot increase unless the output increases more rapidly than population. If output and population increase at the same rate, the level of living remains the same for a larger population; if population grows more rapidly than output, the level of living declines. Thus, all other things being equal, if output can increase while population remains the same, all of the growth in output contributes to higher levels of living per capita. This way of showing the relationship between population increase and level of living is simplistic because it ignores the complex interrelationships between the numerator and denominator in the right-hand side of the equation and the complex character of levels of living, relationships that have elsewhere been explored in depth.[34]

This model illuminates Malthus' "principle" of population, namely, that population inevitably outruns means of subsistence. But Malthus did not anticipate the remarkable increase in productivity flowing from the emergence of science and the application of knowledge in the development of technology. The effect of these developments in the present MDCs, as

34. For example, Harvey Leibenstein, *A Theory of Economic-Demographic Development* (Princeton, N.J.: Princeton University Press, 1954).

documented by Kuznets, was the achievement of high levels of living,[35] not only in spite of high rates of population growth, but also because of them. High rates of population increase under conditions of technological innovation, including employment of sources of nonhuman energy, enabled output to rise more rapidly than even the high rates of population growth. In the experience of the MDCs, rapid population growth along with greatly increased productivity contributed to economies of scale in production and rapidly expanding markets to take up the increased product.

Unfortunately, rapid population growth in the present LDCs is occurring in quite a different context. The population is increasing greatly, without significant increased productivity and product as in the MDCs. Rapid population increase in a traditional agricultural economy with little change in technology and productivity tends to be accompanied by diminishing returns rather than economies of scale. Moreover, the rapid population growth that characterizes the LDCs is occurring at a time when the population is already large in relation to resources, and before critical cultural changes of the type experienced in the Western MDCs, such as the Renaissance, the Reformation, and the emergence of science and advanced technology. Furthermore, population growth in the LDCs, which is much more rapid than was the case in the MDCs, as noted above, is occurring while the great masses of population remain illiterate, unskilled, bogged down in poverty, and, often, in despair.

During the early economic takeoff periods of the present MDCs, a large part of the capital required to finance industrialization and urbanization came from the increased productivity in agriculture, stemming from advances in agricultural technology. In the LDCs today, except for limited areas positively affected by the "Green Revolution," agricultural productivity remains low and, despite various assistance programs, capital remains short.

There is at least one respect in which the LDCs today actually have an advantage over the present MDCs before they achieved relatively high levels of development. Their advantage lies in the worldwide awareness of the great gap in levels of living between the "have" and the "have-not" nations; in the rise of national aspirations to higher levels of living; in the existence of the United Nations and the specialized agencies to provide assistance to the LDCs; and in the various bilateral and multilateral programs of developed nations for providing assistance to the LDCs.

There is nothing unique about the prevalence of "have" and "have-not" nations. As far back as historical records go, it is clear that some areas have been characterized by higher levels of living than others for a

35. Kuznets, *Modern Economic Growth,* Chap. 2.

variety of reasons—differences in the environment, in available resources, in level of technology, and in cultural differences including diverse value systems. The "revolution of rising expectations"[36] which has swept the post–World War II world has, however, made the differences between affluent and poor nations "felt"[37] differences, with resultant significant national and international political implications.

At the beginning of this century, it was estimated that the level of living of the less developed countries was only one-fourth that in the more developed countries.[38] By 1970 this difference had widened so that the level of living of the MDCs was about fourteen times that in the LDCs (see Table 1.4).

More recently, comparative data have been analyzed by the Overseas Development Council. During the period 1960 to 1973, in spite of the

TABLE 1.4
Population and GNP, 1970

Area	Population (in millions)	%	Gross National Product (in billion $ U.S.)	%	GNP per Capita (in $ U.S.)
World	3,600	100	2,640	100	733
More developed regions	1,050	29	2,240	85	2,133
Europe, including the USSR	700	19	1,070	40	1,529
North America	230	7	990	38	4,304
Oceania and Japan	120	3	180	7	1,500
Less developed regions	2,550	71	400	15	157
Asia	1,920	53	240	9	125
Africa	350	10	50	2	143
Latin America	280	8	110	5	393

SOURCE: Willem Brand: "World Resources, Their Use and Distribution," in *International Aspects of Overpopulation,* edited by J. Barratt and M. Louis (London: Macmillan, 1972).

36. Harlan Cleveland used the phrase "the revolution of rising expectations" in a speech at Cornell University in 1949, quoted in *Bartletts' Quotations,* 14th ed., 1968, p. 1077.

37. Warren S. Thompson, *Population and Peace in the Pacific* (Chicago: University of Chicago Press, 1946).

38. Richard J. Barnet and Ronald E. Muller, *Global Reach: The Power of the Multinational Corporations* (New York: Simon and Schuster, 1974), p. 190.

various programs designed to assist the LDCs in raising their living levels, programs of the United Nations and the specialized agencies, and the various multilateral and bilateral technical assistance programs, public and private, the gap between the MDCs and the LDCs has increased in significant ways. From 1960 to 1973 the proportion of the world GNP generated in the LDCs declined from 19 percent to 17 percent; the proportion of world export earnings in the LDCs diminished from 21 percent to 18 percent; the proportion of world public education expenditures in the LDCs declined from 15 percent to 11 percent; and the proportion of world public health expenditures in the LDCs plummeted from 11 percent to 6 percent. Over the same period, the proportion of total world population in the LDCs increased from 71 percent to 74 percent; and, ironically and alarmingly, the proportion of total world military expenditures by the LDCs rose, soaring from nine percent to 13 percent.[39]

In light of the increasing gap in the levels of living between the LDCs and MDCs, despite the LDCs' national aspirations and the MDCs' efforts to date to assist them, it may be readily understood why the LDCs are insisting on a new international economic order (NIEO). Because of their relatively worsening economic position, the LDCs have become more and more aggressive in their efforts to achieve what they perceive to be their fair share of the world's bounty. This became evident during the World Population Conference held in Bucharest during the United Nations Population Year, 1974, the first such conference ever participated in by national governments. Representatives of the MDCs urged the LDCs to increase their efforts to decrease birth rates and population growth rates. Many representatives of the LDCs, however, while cognizant of the relation between population factors and economic development, insisted that before, or simultaneously with, lowered population growth rates, there was a need to achieve an NIEO. Major elements in their demands for an NIEO included the following:

- An end to all forms of foreign occupation and alien domination and exploitation
- A just and equitable relationship between prices that developing countries receive for their raw products and the prices they must pay for imported goods
- Net transfer of real resources from developed to developing countries, including increases in the real price of commodities exported by developing countries

39. Roger D. Hansen, *The U.S. and World Development: Agenda for Action* (New York: Praeger, Overseas Development Council, 1976).

- Improved access to markets in developed countries through a system of preferences for exports of developing countries and through the elimination of tariff and nontariff barriers and restrictive business practices
- Reimbursement to developing countries of customs duties and taxes imposed by importing developed countries
- Arrangements to mitigate the effects of inflation on developing countries and to eliminate the instability of the world monetary system
- Promotion of foreign investment in developing countries in accordance with their needs and requirements
- Formulation of an international code of conduct regulating the activities of transnational corporations
- Measures to promote the processing of raw materials in the producer developing countries
- An increase in essential inputs on favorable terms for food production, including fertilizers, from developed countries
- Urgent measures to alleviate the burden of external debt[40]

In addition, the Conference further declared:

> The response of the developed countries which have by far the greater capacity to assist the affected countries in overcoming their present difficulties must be commensurate with their responsibilities. Their assistance should be in addition to the presently available levels of aid.

Also relevant is the fact that the eighteen-month conference of ministerial representatives of the MDCs and the LDCs that ended in Paris in June, 1977, left many areas of disagreement. The communiqué issued by the LDCs stated that "progress has been accomplished . . . but conclusions of the conference fall short of what is necessary to create a new economic system."[41] The final communiqué listed twenty areas of agreement and twenty-one areas of disagreement.

The conference did foreshadow what lay ahead. It demonstrated that the "have" nations were not yet ready to accept the demands of the poor

40. The Population Council, "A Report on Bucharest," *Studies in Family Planning* 5 (December 1974):364.

41. R. C. Longworth, "Worlds North-South Divisions Still Unresolved," *Chicago Tribune,* June 21, 1977.

nations for the NIEO—even though they recognized that the LDCs were dependent on provision of raw materials for their foreign exchange and required more assistance than they were receiving.

It is important to examine the relationship between total world GNP and population and its implication for correcting the imbalance between the poor and the rich nations. In 1970, world population totaled 3.6 billion, and total world GNP was estimated at $2,640 billion. World per capita GNP was therefore $733. European (including the USSR) per capita GNP was $1,529 (see Table 1.4). The total world product therefore could support 1.7 billion people at the European level of living. GNP per capita in North America was $4,304. The total world product could, therefore, support only 600 million people at the North American level of living. Assuming that these relationships were the same in 1978 as in 1970—a not unreasonable assumption—then the world product in 1978 could support only 1.9 billion persons at the European level of living and 700 million at the North American level of living, compared with the actual world population of over 4 billion. These facts may be interpreted to mean either that the world is already overpopulated or that the world product must be greatly increased. It is clear that an egalitarian distribution of the world product, although it would materially increase GNP per capita in the LDCs, would also significantly decrease GNP per capita in the MDCs.

Since the objective of the NIEO is to decrease the differences in the levels of living between the MDCs and the LDCs, and because it is unlikely that the MDCs are prepared voluntarily and gracefully to diminish their product per capita, the objectives of the LDCs can be attained only through an increase in the total world product. Moreover, it is obvious that if the product per capita of the MDCs continues to rise, the total world product must grow much more rapidly than if the MDCs remained at their present levels of living. These considerations necessarily raise an unprecedented question to which no definitive answer is at present possible, namely, do the earth's resources permit LDCs to reach the European or the North American levels of living? The implications of the answer to this question will be further considered later.

MATCHING EUROPEAN, NORTH AMERICAN, AND MEXICAN GNP PER CAPITA

Consideration is given next to the magnitude of the task that faces the LDCs if, in the aggregate and by continent, they are to match the level of living as measured by GNP per capita of, respectively, the North American or the European, and then the Mexican, GNP per capitas as of 1970.[42] The calculations are made three ways, based on three assumptions with respect to population growth: first, the unrealistic assumption that the LDCs experience no population growth between 1970 and 2000; second, the assumption that the LDCs would experience the UN low variant population projection between 1970 and 2000; and third, the assumption that the LDCs would experience the UN high variant population projection between 1970 and 2000. The UN projections used were assessed in 1978; they are shown in Table 1.5.

To match the 1970 North American GNP per capita by 2000, under the assumption of no further population growth, GNP of the LDCs would have to increase from $400 billion to $10,965 billion, about a 27-fold increase. To achieve such a GNP by the year 2000, the LDCs' GNP would have to grow at a rate (geometric) of 11.7 percent per annum. To match the 1970 European GNP per capita, GNP would have to increase to $3,902 billion by 2000, about a 10-fold increase. To achieve such a GNP by the year 2000, the LDCs' GNP would have to grow at a rate of 7.9 percent per annum. These figures are shown in Table 1.6.

It is, of course, more sensible to assume that the LDCs' population will continue to increase to the end of this century. If the LDCs' population should reach the level of 4,564 million by 2000 (the low variant projection of the United Nations as calculated in 1978), in order to match the 1970

TABLE 1.5
Population in 2000 under Varying Growth Assumptions for LDCs by Continental Region

	Populations (in millions)		
		Projections to A.D. 2000	
Area	Zero	Low	High
Africa	350	759	866
Latin America	280	563	646
Asia	1,920	3,234	3,607
Total LDCs	2,550	4,564*	5,128*

* Will not add exactly because of minor differences in nations included as less developed.

SOURCE: Preliminary Report of the Estimates and Projections of Population for the World, Regions and Countries as Assessed in 1978, October 1978.

42. Following section adapted from Philip M. Hauser, "On Problematic Aspects of the New Economic World Order," in *The Search for Absolute Values in a Changing World,* Proceedings of the Sixth International Conference on the Unity of the Sciences (San Francisco: International Cultural Foundation, Inc., 1978), pp. 371–81.

TABLE 1.6
GNP Necessary for LDCs to Match the GNP per Capita of Europe, North America, and Mexico, under Three Population Growth Assumptions (in $ U.S. billions)

	GNP Necessary to Match 1970 GNP* per Capita in Europe			North America			Mexico		
	Zero	Low	High	Zero	Low	High	Zero	Low	High
Africa	536	1,162	1,325	1,505	3,265	3,725	235	509	580
Multiple†	10.7	23.2	26.5	30.1	65.3	74.5	4.7	10.2	11.6
Rate‡	8.2%	11.1%	11.5%	12.0%	15.0%	15.5%	5.3%	8.0%	8.5%
Latin America	428	862	988	1,204	2,422	2,777	187	359	433
Multiple	3.9	7.8	9.0	10.9	22.0	25.2	1.7	3.3	3.9
Rate	4.6%	7.1%	7.6%	8.3%	10.9%	11.4%	1.8%	4.0%	4.7%
Asia	2,938	4,948	5,519	8,256	13,907	15,511	1,286	2,167	2,417
Multiple	12.2	20.6	23.0	34.4	57.9	64.6	5.4	9.0	10.1
Rate	8.7%	10.6%	11.0%	12.5%	14.5%	15.0%	5.8%	7.6%	8.0%
Total LDCs	3,902	6,972	7,832	10,965	19,593	22,013	1,709	3,053	3,430
Multiple	9.7	17.4	19.6	27.4	49.0	55.0	4.3	7.6	8.6
Rate	7.9%	10.0%	10.4%	11.7%	13.9%	14.3%	5.0%	7.0%	7.4%

* GNP per capita in 1970: Europe $1,530; North America $4,300; Mexico $670.

† Multiple by which 1970 GNP must increase to reach the GNP projected on line 1.

‡ Geometric rate of increase necessary.

North American level of living, the GNP of the LDCs would have to increase to $19,593 billion, a 49-fold increase. Such an increase would necessitate a GNP growth rate of 13.9 percent per annum. To match the European level of living under the same population assumptions, the GNP of the LDCs would have to increase to $6,972 billion, a 17-fold increase. To achieve this, a GNP growth rate of 10 percent per annum would be necessary for a 30-year period.

Under the high variant projections it is assumed that the LDC population will reach the level of 5,128 million by 2000. This assumption provides some basis for gauging the effect of faster population growth. To match the 1970 North American income per capita, the LDCs would have to achieve a GNP of $22,013 billion, a 55-fold increase—a GNP growth rate of 14.3 percent per annum. For the LDCs to match the 1970 European level of living under this assumption, the GNP of the LDCs must increase to $7,837 billion, an almost 20-fold increase, necessitating an annual growth rate of 10.4 percent. Similar calculations have been made for the LDCs by continental region, the results of which are also given in Table 1.6.

A number of significant conclusions can be drawn from these data. Even if the LDCs as a whole experience no further population increase after 1970, they must generate a 10- to 27-fold increase in GNP to match the 1970 European or North American GNP per capita levels, respectively. The annual growth rate required to achieve such GNP increases is clearly beyond their capacity over a 30-year span. Comparable conclusions can be drawn for each of the less developed continental regions shown in Table 1.6, except that Latin American LDCs, if they had experienced no further population growth after 1970, would have had a good probability of matching the 1970 European GNP per capita, but not that of North America. With continued population growth after 1970, the LDCs in each of the three population regions could not, in all likelihood, obtain the 1970 European level of GNP per capita, let alone that of North America.

Using 1970 European and North American per capita GNPs as targets, even if it is assumed that they would have no further population increase from 1970 to 2000, is admittedly setting an extremely high and even unrealistic goal for the objectives of the NIEO. These targets, however, certainly point to what the NIEO cannot possibly achieve.

A lower and more reasonable target is the GNP per capita of Mexico in 1970, namely $670. Using this target, the required increases in GNP and annual growth rates have been calculated under the same three population assumptions: no growth after 1970, low growth, and high growth, respectively, using the same UN projections as assessed in 1978.

The LDCs as a whole, to match the GNP per capita of Mexico for 1970 under the assumptions of no population growth, would have to increase GNP to $1,709 billion, a four-fold increase requiring a GNP growth rate of 5 percent per annum, which was the UN 1960 development decade target rate (see Table 1.6). But, unfortunately, the assumption of no population growth after 1970 is, of course, completely unrealistic. Using the UN low population growth assumption, the LDCs' GNP would have to grow to $3,053 billion, an eight-fold increase, requiring an annual growth rate of 7 percent per annum. Under the high population growth projection, the LDCs would have to achieve a GNP of $3,430 billion, a nine-fold increase, necessitating an annual growth rate for thirty years of 7.4 percent.

Similar calculations made separately for the continental areas shown in Table 1.6 revealed that the achievement of 1970 Mexican GNP per capita is definitely within the possibility for Latin American LDCs in the aggregate, but still not likely to be within the grasp of LDCs in Asia and Africa.

EFFECT OF 5 PERCENT GNP GROWTH RATES IN THE LDCS

Even if the UN target rate of GNP increase set in the first development decade, the 1960s, was achieved from 1970 to the end of the century, the LDCs would still fall far short of matching either the 1970 North American or European GNP per capita. The GNP target rate of 5 percent per annum increase in GNP is well below the GNP growth rates necessary to match 1970 North American or European GNP per capitas, and, for Africa and Asia, well below the GNP growth rates necessary even to match the 1970 Mexican GNP per capita. Only Latin America could match the 1970 Mexican GNP per capita by the end of the century with the 5 percent per annum increase (see Table 1.7).

In 1970, the LDCs' GNP per capita was only about one-tenth that of Europe and less than one twenty-fifth that of North America. Under the unrealistic assumption of no further LDC population growth after 1970, the LDC product per capita would still be below one-fourth that of Europe and about one-sixth that of North America. Under the assumption of either low or high LDC population growth to the end of the century, the LDCs' product per capita would still be less than one-fourth that of the 1970 level for Europe and about one-twelfth that of the 1970 level for North America.

If the more modest GNP per capita of Mexico in 1970 is used as the yardstick, then GNP per capita in the aggregate would reach little more than half of the 1970 Mexican GNP per capita under the low and high

TABLE 1.7

GNP per Capita as Percent of 1970, Europe, North America, and Mexico GNP per Capita under Assumption of 5% Increase in GNP between 1970 and 2000 and under Three Population Growth Assumptions for the Total LDCs and by Continent

Area	Europe			North America			Mexico		
	Zero	Low	High	Zero	Low	High	Zero	Low	High
Asia	35.3	21.0	18.8	12.6	7.5	6.7	80.6	47.9	42.9
Africa	40.4	18.6	16.3	14.4	6.6	5.8	92.1	42.5	37.2
Latin America	111.0	55.2	48.1	39.5	19.6	17.1	253.0	126.0	109.8
Total LDCs	44.3	24.8	22.1	15.8	8.8	7.9	101.2	56.6	50.4

population growth assumptions. Moreover, only the LDCs in Latin America under the low and high population growth assumptions could match the 1970 Mexican GNP per capita by the end of the century.

The importance of population growth in relation to development as measured by GNP per capita has been demonstrated here. But some important caveats are necessary to place the relation of population growth to development in proper perspective. While it is true that lower population growth rates would help to achieve development, population management alone cannot bring about development. But population policies and programs without question must be an integral part of development policies and programs.

BASIC NEEDS APPROACH

In response to the failure of the GNP growth strategy to improve the lot of the poorest people in the LDCs, it has been proposed that the priority target in raising levels of living be that of meeting the basic needs of the poorest population elements.[43] It has come to be recognized that increasing GNP per capita in the developing countries does not necessarily result in the betterment of the most poor. On the contrary, in a number of LDCs, increases in GNP per capita were accompanied by diminished shares of total national income by the poorest elements.[44] To meet basic needs, the objective would be to reach minimum levels of private and social consumption—the former including food, shelter, and clothing, and the latter, potable water, environmental sanitation, public transportation, and health and education facilities. The social consumption levels may also be taken to include opportunity for participation—the achievement of certain nonmaterial things, such as human rights and a voice in public policy and programs. Obviously, meeting basic needs requires, within each LDC, equitable income distribution or, at least, improved income distribution to the lowest income groups.

Adoption of the basic needs approach requires quite a different orientation than that implicit in the analyses made above in calculating GNP per capita requirements. But, as research has shown, GNP per capita cannot be ignored, even when the basic needs strategy is used. Studies have

43. Glen Sheehan and Mike Hopkins, "Meeting Basic Needs: An Examination of the World Situation in 1970," *International Labour Review* 117 (5) (1978):523–40.

44. Cynthia Taft Morris and Irma Adelman, "An Anatomy of Income Distribution Patterns in Developing Countries. A Summary of Findings," International Bank of Reconstruction and Development, Economic Staff Paper No. 116.

shown a high correlation between LDCs meeting basic needs, or making progress toward basic needs objectives, and increases in GNP per capita. Analyses of success in meeting basic needs between the MDCs and LDCs indicate that, although the gap between them is narrowing in such things as life expectancy at birth and literacy, the gap in meeting basic needs widened for most indicators during the 1960s.[45]

Meeting basic needs, then, requires, at least, a dual target for each LDC—an increase in GNP per capita on the one hand, and a redistribution of income in favor of the poor on the other. Population growth, distribution, composition, and quality can have important effects on both of these targets. Much remains to be learned about specific impacts of these facets of population in various social, economic, and political contexts among the LDCs.

UNCERTAINTY OF PROSPECT

Although considerations of the type presented make it appear that the task of reaching 1970 European, North American, or even Mexican levels of living during the remainder of this century is a hopeless one for the LDCs in the aggregate, it must be observed that some absolute gains could be achieved. More specifically, for example, if the UN 1960s growth rate target of 5 percent per annum could be achieved, the LDCs as a whole would increase product per capita, between 1970 and 2000, from $157 to $337 under the high variant population projection, and to $379 under the low variant population projection: a rise of 115 percent and 141 percent respectively.

Although it may be anticipated that LDC populations would enthusiastically welcome such absolute increases in their levels of living, it may, nevertheless, be assumed that, especially under the influence of rising expectations, the LDC peoples will not become unmindful of their relative deprivation. For one thing, except for Latin America, they would not yet have reached the GNP per capita level of Mexico in 1970. The less developed nations may well experience increased frustration and alienation despite the doubling or more than doubling of their present low absolute levels of living. The international and national political implications of increased frustration and alienation will undoubtedly be affected by the extent to which at least basic needs will be met.

At this point, it is well to return to one of the considerations raised

45. Sheehan and Hopkins, "Meeting Basic Needs."

above. Can the earth's resources enable the some 70 percent of the world's population in the LDCs ever to attain either the European or North American levels of living, even if it were to be achieved with different configurations of goods and services? As indicated above, there is at present no definitive answer to this question. One answer, pessimistic in character, is provided by the Club of Rome's *Limits to Growth*.[46] The prospect of limits to consumption of raw materials and energy would, in relatively short periods of time, create a zero sum game situation, in which increases in levels of living of the LDCs could be achieved only at the expense of decreases in MDCs' levels of living. Needless to say, this would be a situation that would tend to exacerbate tensions and increase prospects for international violence.

But at the other extreme is the answer to the question by Herman Kahn of the Hudson Institute in the publication *The Next 200 Years*.[47] This optimistic answer contains the prospect, although certainly not by the end of this century, of substantial increases in the LDCs' GNP per capita, at least to approximate either European or North American levels of living. Under this optimistic framework, it is conceivable that the MDCs' product per capita could continue to rise even while the LDCs' product was increasing faster to narrow the gap between the "have" and "have-not" nations. Should this be possible, then a significant new international economic order could in time be achieved. Under such conditions, the prospect for increased tension, hostility, and violence would certainly be diminished.

Whichever of these extreme answers may turn out to be correct, it is a virtual certainty that the gap in levels of living between the LDCs and MDCs is not likely to narrow much or may increase even further during the remainder of this century. Abraham Lincoln once questioned whether the United States could survive, half slave and half free. The comparable question at this juncture in history is whether, with 70 percent of the population poor and 30 percent affluent, the world can survive.

It is apparent from the above that population growth rates and total achieved population can significantly affect levels of living as measured by GNP per capita. But, as has also been shown, various other aspects of population may have important impacts on development.[48] These other aspects will be summarized in what follows.

46. Donella Meadows *et al.*, *The Limits to Growth, A Report for the Club of Rome's Project on the Predicament of Mankind* (New York: Universe Books, 1972).

47. Herman Kahn *et al.*, *The Next 200 Years: A Scenario for America and the World* (New York: Hudson Institute, 1976).

48. Philip M. Hauser, "The World Population Outlook," *Revista Interamericana Review* 4 (Spring 1974):1–11.

Density

In view of the indisputable fact that in the long run, space itself is a limiting factor for population growth, even though other limits may precede it, potential population density merits attention. High densities could become operative limits to growth in subareas of the globe, of course, long before worldwide density would reach a limit.

The effect of rapid population growth generated by high fertility in increasing density has been well demonstrated in a model developed by Coale, who has illuminated the impact of a number of population factors on economic development.[49] The model assumes an initial population of 1 million persons and rates of fertility and mortality of a typical LDC. If the fertility of population A remains unchanged, and the fertility of population B is reduced 50 percent in 25 years, the following figures result:

Population (in thousands)

	Year			
	0	30	60	150
Population A	1,000	2,757	8,297	245,500
Population B	1,000	2,053	3,420	10,477

It is clear that with unchanged fertility, an initial population of 1 million would have increased more than eightfold in 60 years—in about two and a half generations—whereas, with the reduced fertility assumed, an initial population of 1 million would have increased less than three-and-a-half-fold. Starting with the population of 2.9 billion in the LDCs in the world in 1975, unchanged fertility would produce an LDC population of 24 billion by 2035. By contrast, if fertility declined by 50 percent in 25 years, and even if it remained unchanged thereafter, the LDC world population would be 9.9 billion by 2035, only 41 percent as great. In 150 years, the LDC population of the earth would reach the impossible figure of 712 billion with unchanged fertility and, also improbable, 30 billion, 4 percent as great, with reduced fertility. It should be clear that with unchanged fertility the LDCs alone, within a relatively short period of time, would confront space limits on this globe. But, of course, long before space became the limiting factor, other limits would be reached—water, food, and energy among them.

49. Ansley J. Coale, "Population and Economic Development," in *The Population Dilemma,* edited by Philip M. Hauser (Englewood Cliffs, N.J.: Prentice-Hall, 1963).

Age Structure

All other things being equal, a population with a large proportion of persons below and above working age would have lower production per capita than a population with a smaller proportion of such persons. That is, the former population compared with the latter would have more mouths to feed in relation to hands to do the work. Coale's models also demonstrate the gains in dependency reduction which can be achieved through fertility decline. These can be shown by converting his calculations into dependency ratios—that is, the number of persons below and above working age (below 15 and 65 and over) per hundred persons of working age (15 to 64).[50]

Dependency Ratios

Projection	Year			
	0	30	60	150
Population A	87.3	96.0	97.4	103.2
Population B	87.3	59.5	56.8	58.4

Starting with a total of young and old dependents of 87.3 in Population A, dependents would increase in 30 years to 96.0 with unchanged fertility, whereas they would decrease to 59.5, about a 32 percent reduction, in Population B. In 60 years, dependency in Population A remains at about the same level at 97, but that of Population B declines further to 56.8. Coale indicates the difference in dependency reaches a maximum in about 40 years and remains constant thereafter.

The major proportion of the dependents at the outset in both Populations A and B are the young rather than the old, although the proportion of elders increases with decreased fertility in Population B. At the outset, in both Populations A and B, 43 percent are under 15 years of age. Within 30 years, however, while persons under 15 constitute 45.8 percent of Population A, they make up only 32.8 percent of Population B. In 60 years, when young dependents constitute 46.5 percent of Population A, they diminish to only 29 percent of Population B. The significant decline of young dependents in Population B not only increases product per capita, as has been indicated, but also leads to other potential gains if fertility is reduced. All other things being equal, the decreased proportion of young

50. *Ibid.*, p. 64.

makes it possible to increase investment of relatively scarce savings in LDCs in immediately productive channels, rather than in the social investment required for the rearing of the young—even though such investment may be regarded as investment in human capital. Furthermore, among other things, a decrease in the proportion of young tends to increase the investment possible per child for education and the acquisition of skill investment in human resources essential for improving population quality, which will be discussed later.

Finally, as Coale observed, a high-fertility nation, by reducing its fertility, can make a major gain in increasing potential for product per capita only once. This can come about because in the initial decline in birth rate, while the proportion of young decreases, the proportion of persons of working age is relatively unaffected. That is, if the entrance age for the labor force is taken at 16, it would be 16 years after the drop in the birth rate begins before a decline in the work force begins. Therefore there is a relatively large decrease of young dependents in relation to the work force only during the first generation of fertility decline.

Coale has pursued in greater detail the impact of decreased fertility on development.[51] His models have been subjected to criticism by some economists (see Chapter 8). In a recent article however, Coale, has compared his population projections for Mexico, published in 1958, with what has actually occurred in the last 20 years,[52] and he has also reexamined the relation of population change to development in Mexico. It turned out that population growth in Mexico over the 20 years was almost identical with the Coale-Hoover projection based on the assumption of no fertility decline.[53] Nevertheless, Mexico managed to achieve considerable social and economic development over the period. Thus, considerable progress in development did not necessarily result in decreased fertility, a finding consistent with findings in other areas.[54]

The case of Mexico also illustrates that high fertility and rapid population growth do not necessarily preclude social and economic development. Coale demonstrates, however, that had fertility declined in Mexico over the 20 years surveyed, development would have been even greater. Furthermore, by reason of the continued high fertility, the population of adults, those 15 years of age and older, will double in the next 20 years—raising questions about Mexico's ability to provide adequate em-

51. *Ibid.*, p. 64.

52. Ansley J. Coale, "Population Growth and Economic Development: The Case of Mexico," *Foreign Affairs* (Jan. 1978):415–29.

53. *Ibid.*

54. See sub-section on "Fertility" below.

ployment in the future. In addition, Coale's calculations show that if Mexico's fertility were to be cut in half over the next 20 years and then maintained, her population would increase 11-fold in 150 years to reach 660 million. If there were no fertility decrease after 1975, the population of Mexico would reach the astronomical figure of 15 billion in 150 years—about four times present total world population.

Decreased Mortality

It has been noted that a relatively early demographic consequence of modernization is decreased mortality. Such a decrease may have both beneficial and adverse effects on development. For example, one beneficial effect is to be found in the potential improved productivity of labor, which is possible because decreased mortality must be accompanied by decreased morbidity, and better health is conducive to improvement in work output. Moreover, decreased mortality is reflected in increased person-years of production with increased person-years in the work force (see Chapter 10).

A result adverse to development may lie in the increase in marital fertility brought about by the greater survivorship of women during their reproductive period and improved fecundity as a result of better health. There is some evidence that the decrease in fertility resulting from rising age at marriage because of modernization is to a considerable extent offset by increased marital fertility in some countries. This tendency to keep fertility high could have adverse development consequences of the type already discussed. Furthermore, decrease in mortality, as has been noted, occurs first because of declines in deaths due to parasitic, infectious, contagious, and communicable diseases. These causes of death affect newborn and young the most. Thus, initial gains in mortality operate to increase the proportion of young before fertility decline begins. For the reasons already noted, this tends to maintain an age structure unfavorable to development, at least in the short run. It should also be noted, however, that decreased infant and child mortality resulting in larger family size probably upsets traditional patterns of family life, so that consideration is given by parents to the desirability of reducing the number of total births. Such considerations undoubtedly tend to increase the demand for family planning services.

All in all, then, although decrease in death rates is universally desired as an end in itself, such decrease, at least in some contexts, may tend in the short run to obstruct, rather than accelerate, economic development. Nevertheless, there is doubtless no society that does not strive to achieve lower death rates and increased longevity.

Population Distribution—Urbanization

Throughout the world, in the MDCs as well as in the LDCs, increasing concentrations of people in ever larger urban conglomerations and accompanying migratory streams are generating severe problems—environmental, physical, personal, social, economic, and governmental.[55] The human misery resulting from accelerating rates of urbanization is more intense in the LDCs, because of more severe conditions of life associated with poverty and more rapid rates of urbanization and internal migration.

Although humankind, or close relatives of humankind, have been on the earth for up to 4 million years, urbanization, that is, the emergence of population agglomerations large enough to be called towns, let alone cities, is relatively recent in origin. Archaeological finds have revealed Neolithic villages existing 10,000 years ago which rarely exceeded population clusters of more than 50 to 100 households.[56] Among the prerequisites for agglomerate living are developments in technology, on the one hand, and social organization on the other. Such developments did not make possible agglomerations that in any sense could be called urban until from 5000 to 3500 B.C. Moreover, technological and social organizational developments probably did not make possible a city as large as 100,000 until as recently as ancient Greece and Rome; or a city of 1 million or more until perhaps the nineteenth century.

In 1800, less than 3 percent of the world's population lived in urban places.[57] A century later, world urbanization was still below the 10 percent level. By 1970, the UN had estimated world urbanization at 37 percent, with 66 percent urbanization in the MDCs and 25 percent in the LDCs.[58] By the century's end, the UN has projected that about half the world's population will be living in urban places, more than 80 percent in the MDCs and more than 40 percent in the LDCs. Between 1970 and 2000, world urbanization would proceed, under the UN's projections, at a rate of 2.8 percent per annum. LDC urbanization, however, at 3.8 percent per

55. Philip M. Hauser, "Introduction and Overview," in *The Study of Urbanization*, edited by Philip M. Hauser and Leo F. Schnore (New York: Wiley, 1965).

56. Ralph Turner, *The Great Cultural Traditions. The Foundation of Civilization, The Ancient Cities* 1 (New York: McGraw-Hill, 1941).

57. Kingsley Davis, "The Origin and Growth of Urbanization in the World," *American Journal of Sociology* 60, special issue on "World Urbanism," edited by Philip M. Hauser (March 1955):433.

58. UN, *Trends and Prospects in Urban and Rural Population, 1950–2000: As Assessed in 1973–74* (New York: UN, 1975).

annum, would experience a growth rate about three times as high as that of the MDCs, at 1.4 percent per annum. While urban growth in the world as a whole would absorb 66 percent of total world population growth, that in the LDCs would absorb about 58 percent of the total LDC growth. In the MDCs, the urban increment would exceed the total population increment, that is, migration from rural to urban areas would continue so that the rural population would actually decrease during the thirty-year period to the end of the century.

At present, a large proportion of the urban population in the LDCs does not possess even minimal urban amenities, such as piped water, sewerage, and adequate public transportation and housing. Given these conditions, it is difficult to contemplate the problems with which LDC urban areas would be confronted as their populations triple, as projected, during the course of little more than one human generation. Between 1970 and 2000, the UN projects that urban populations in the LDCs could increase from 632 million to 2 billion. By 2000, although the MDCs would be much more highly urbanized than the LDCs, the number of residents in LDC urban areas would be almost twice as large as those in the MDCs, 2 billion, compared with 1.1 billion.

RURAL GROWTH

The emphasis given here to urbanization cannot be interpreted to mean that rural population growth will be minor or pose relatively few problems. While world urban population from 1970 to 2000 is projected to increase by about 1.8 billion persons, world rural population is projected to increase by 890 million persons, a considerable number. While urban population in the LDCs is projected to increase by about 1.4 billion, rural population will grow simultaneously by more than 1 billion. In the MDCs, while urban population is projected to increase by about 390 million, rural population is projected actually to decline by more than 110 million. Between 1970 and 2000 rural population growth, according to the UN projection, will still constitute more than two-fifths of total LDC population growth.

Rural population growth in the LDCs will, then, also constitute a serious challenge in efforts to increase product per capita and thus to raise levels of living. The emphasis given to urbanization, then, is not to belittle the impact of rural growth but, rather, to focus on the way in which urbanization has special implications for social change and economic development.

URBANIZATION IN MDCS AND LDCS

The relation between urbanization and development, social and economic, has been quite different in the MDCs and the LDCs.[59] In the MDCs, urbanization has been both antecedent to, and consequent of, economic development. Population was pulled from the rural hinterland by higher wages and salaries and higher levels of living permitted by greater productivity.

Urban concentrations in the LDCs, while to some extent the product of similar forces, have predominantly been the result of quite different factors. To begin with, the LDCs are characterized by disproportionately large "primate" cities, which, unlike the large cities in the MDCs, were not so much the product of indigenous economic development as that of imperial economic systems, which they served as entrepôts. The primate cities provided liaison between an imperial mother country and the colony. They achieved great size without corresponding national economic development. In fact, with the collapse of imperialism after World War II and the accompanying disruption of economic relationships, many of the primate cities were left without their major economic bases. Many such cities still await national economic development to justify the size of their present populations. It is in this sense that, without normative connotations, the LDCs may be said to be overurbanized. In brief, the present size of primate cities in the LDCs is in part a product of their colonial heritage, rather than of national economic development, as well as the events discussed below.

A second factor that has fed LDC urban populations has been the troubled countryside, which pushed people into urban places for security, rather than for economic advancement. Insecurity was the consequence of both invasion and liberation during World War II, and of internal disorder after the end of imperial rule as former colonies strove to achieve national consciousness and unity—an objective often obstructed by population heterogeneity and primordial identification. This matter will be discussed below.

Still another factor more important in producing rural-to-urban migration in the LDCs than in the MDCs was the rapid decline in mortality referred to above. The decline of death rates because of exogenous influences produced unprecedentedly high growth rates, with swelling populations that the land could no longer support. Population tended to be pushed off the soil to urban places. Such migration can be more properly characterized as a transfer of poverty from rural to urban areas, rather than

59. Hauser, "Introduction and Overview," pp. 34–40.

as a move to higher levels of living. Even though some increase in marginal productivity and income may occur in such a move, the change from a dispossessed or displaced agricultural worker to a tricycle-taxi operator in a city hardly represents a significant gain in level of living.

Just as the factors associated with urbanization differ in the experience of the MDCs and the LDCs, so do the consequences of urbanization. In the MDCs, urbanization has effected profound changes in the way of life. These changes are evident in social contact and social interaction; in the nature of interpersonal relations; in social control; in attitudes and values; in social institutions, including the family and the church; in the emergence of bureaucracy; in the increasingly interdependent and vulnerable economic and social order; and in the role of government. Urbanism as a way of life has been accompanied by a host of new problems such as those relating to the environment—resource exhaustion and air, water, and noise pollution—the slum and ghetto; the circulation of people and goods, including traffic congestion and the "commuter crisis"; adequate education; educational, health, and recreational facilities; personal and social disorganization evident in delinquency, crime, alcoholism, drug addiction, and family disorganization; the economy—unemployment, underemployment, poverty, consumer exploitation, and abuses of child and female labor; and problems of politics and government, including interrelationships of governments at different levels—national, regional and local—and government corruption, sources of revenue and taxation, and general problems of governance.

Only a few of the aspects of urbanism as a way of life in the MDCs can be considered here, and even then in a limited way.[60] Among the significant changes that urban living has induced in the MDCs arises from the great increase in potential human interaction. The "little community" of a preurban situation has been transformed into the "mass society." In the "little community" contacts may be described as "primary contacts," face-to-face across the whole spectrum of the life space. In contrast, contacts in the urban "mass society" are "secondary contacts" that are highly segmental and arise only as individuals' life spaces intersect. Consequently, relations in the little community are based on intimate knowledge, sentiment, and emotional attachment; while in the urban setting, human interactions are based increasingly on utility. Social control in the little community tends to be informal, the product of common norms and values contained in the social heritage. In the mass society, social control becomes increasingly formal, through legislation, administrative fiat, and the opera-

60. Louis Wirth, "Urbanism as a Way of Life," *American Journal of Sociology* 44 (July 1938):1–24; for criticism see, e.g., Claude S. Fischer, *The Urban Experience* (New York: Harcourt Brace Jovanovich, 1976).

tion of police, courts, penitentiaries, etc. Social institutions in the little community are crescive, that is, the product of group life over long periods of time as populations adapt to their environment and work out means of subsistence and survival. In contrast, social institutions in the mass society are enacted—by legislatures and by administrators both in the public and private sectors—as new problems emerge and new institutional arrangements are required. Even the basic social institution, the family, has experienced great changes in the urban setting. It has tended to become nuclear if previously extended, has achieved independent residence, and has experienced great changes in functions through loss or attenuation. For example, the family in the urban setting in the MDCs is no longer a production unit and often is not even the consumer unit it once was. That is, individual earners within the family often become independent consuming units. Family protection and security functions have become minimal and have been replaced by government functionaries, such as the police, welfare agencies, unemployment compensation provisions, old-age pensions, and the like. The affectional function of the family has certainly changed with greatly increased divorce and remarriage. The family educational functions have been replaced by the schools, libraries, museums, and mass media; recreational functions by the movies, theatres, television, spectator sports, and various outdoor recreational activities.

Perhaps the most important function of the family, that relating to the socialization of the child, has also been greatly transformed. To begin with, the number of children to be socialized has diminished with reduced fertility, and the network of schools has taken over—prenursery, nursery, kindergarten, primary, secondary, and higher schools. Peer groups, various youth groups from scouts to street gangs, increasingly play important roles in the socialization of the child. The mass media also have a significant impact on the child's socialization.

Among the more profound changes accompanying urban life in the MDCs are the changing roles of husbands and wives, parents and children, and siblings to one another. Especially significant is the changing role of women from the relatively restricted functions of wife, mother, and household manager. More and more, women are entering all facets of the life space, from most of which they were previously excluded. In fact, it may be said that the role of women is in the process of changing from female to human being. Especially important is the increased labor force participation of women, including married women with and without children.

Finally, also of great significance, is the evolution of the "urban mentality." This includes a basic change in general orientation, away from dependence on the supernatural to the view that the destiny of humankind lies essentially within human beings themselves through knowledge and its application, rather than in the play of supernatural forces.

These and many other changes that accompany urbanism as a way of life have occurred by and large in the Western world and in the MDCs in general. They are, in the main, not yet manifest to the same extent in urban areas within the LDCs. The chief explanation for the basic changes in urban MDCs lies in the actualization of the great increase in the potential social interaction that increased population size and density afford. In the LDCs, although a similar potential exists, in general, it is not realized. It is not realized because in the urban areas in the LDCs, although population size and density are present, social interaction is generally greatly restricted within various quarters of the city, which are relatively isolated from one another, whether characterized by homogeneity in race, ethnicity, religion, language, or occupational pursuit. Under conditions of relative isolation, that is, limited social contacts and interaction, traditional institutions, customs, beliefs, and behavior patterns may persist, resistant to change, and, therefore, operate actually to retard development.

As economic development is induced in the LDCs, and as technological changes are accepted, the pace of social change tends to increase. It may be anticipated that the acceptance of modern technology and consequent economic organization will inevitably be followed by profound social change. Such change will not necessarily follow the Western pattern, but, nevertheless, will greatly transform the traditional orders that still obtain in the less developed nations. It is necessary to anticipate the great changes which at present have scarcely begun in many areas, and to face up to the transitional problems that will inevitably be involved.

The most critical urban problems in the LDCs are evident among the newcomers to urban areas, the in-migrants. Typically, such newcomers locate in the cheapest and least desirable places to live, often in shantytowns as squatters. The in-migrant tends to experience the extremes of physical and social problems. On the physical side, the squatter family generally lives in a homemade shack of tin or boxwood without piped water, sewerage, or other minimal urban amenities. On the social side, the in-migrants, usually from the rural countryside or small villages, are apt to be completely unprepared for urban life, lacking literacy, occupational skills, and even familiarity with money and a timepiece. The frictions of the transition from little-community to mass-society existence are greatly magnified in the experience of the rural-to-urban in-migrant in the LDCs, especially in the large primate city.

The area of destination of the in-migrant is confronted with many severe problems because it must absorb the in-migrants even while the newcomers are adapting to their new world. In addition, migratory streams have great impact on their areas of origin, as well as their areas of destination. Out-migrants are highly selective in respect to age, sex, education, occupation, and other population characteristics and, therefore, they greatly change the population composition both of their areas of origin and of destination. Transitional problems exist in both types of areas that engage the attention of agencies both in the public and private sectors.

Urbanization and internal migration vitally affect development in a number of ways, and they pose difficult problems for governments. Since the poor countries are characterized by low levels of development in both rural and urban areas, difficult decisions must be made in the allocation of scarce resources to these areas. In the experience of the MDCs, it was increased agricultural productivity that provided the capital as well as the population flows for industrialization, urbanization, and general economic development. In early efforts by LDCs to induce economic development, industrialization tended to get the major attention, but it has become evident that the development of the agricultural sector cannot be overlooked. (See Chapter 5.) Moreover, it has been recognized that the allocation of development funds to rural areas can help to slow the rate of rural-to-urban migration and enable urban areas better to cope with their growth problems. Some countries are actively attempting to decentralize some of the services that have pulled rural inhabitants to urban areas, such as higher education and health services, and they are also trying to provide jobs through decentralized and industrial development.

LDC governments also face difficult problems with respect to the allocation of development funds and programs within the urban sectors. Should funds for industrialization go to the primate cities, with abundantly available labor, or to smaller urban areas to reduce the imbalance in urban population distribution? How much attention should be given to lagging regions through the creation of urban growth poles? Should an effort be made to achieve a pattern of urban population distribution resembling the "rank-size rule" characterizing urban hierarchies in the MDCs?

The answer to the last question should probably be no, since it has been demonstrated that the hierarchy of cities following the "rank-size rule" is a product of stochastic processes in the play of free-market forces.[61] It may be less than wise to attempt to achieve such a distribution pattern in an economy in which central planning, rather than market forces, plays the dominant role.

A fundamental question relates to the rate of urban growth itself. Many LDCs, because of the many difficult problems in urban areas, have attempted to dampen urban growth rates or to stop urban growth completely. Up to this point in history, urban growth in the MDCs has been

61. For example, Brian J. L. Berry and William L. Gamson, "Alternate Explanation of Rank Size Rule," *Annals of the Association of American Geographers* 48 (1958):83–91.

irresistible and irreversible. In the LDCs, efforts to decrease urban growth, short of using force, have, on the whole, not achieved success. It is becoming recognized, however, that efforts to obstruct urban growth are not only futile, but also counterproductive. For despite the many problems urbanization generates, it is a prerequisite, rather than a barrier, to development. There is a need to understand urban growth better and to develop relevant strategies to guide it and to cope with the problems that accompany it. The United Nations Department of Economic and Social Affairs, in discussing the second United Nations development decade, stated:

> The significance of the now universal phenomenon of urbanization has unfortunately only recently been recognized as posing one of the major economic and social problems in developing and developed nations alike. It might have been expected that urbanization would be more of a contributor and less of a problem to contemporary development, as was the case of European and North American cities in the Nineteenth century. However, the powerful cause and effect role of urbanization in development is just beginning to be understood.[62]

The report goes on to state the findings of a United Nations seminar as follows:

> The process of urbanization must be understood as a basic condition for and as a functional consequence of economic, social and technological development. Indiscriminate efforts to avoid urbanization may only serve to delay development.

What then are the strategies to be employed in dealing with the problems of urban growth and urbanization? This question is addressed frontally by the Second United Nations Development Plan in its section on urban strategy for the 1970s. It pointed out that:

> The increase in population and the migration to cities could be made into a major contribution to development if more balanced distribution of population can be obtained, if urban and regional plans can be prepared and put into effect, if building programs could be expanded and productivity raised, if employment can be expanded and savings increased and if the necessary investments are made to underwrite steady increments of effective housing demand.[63]

62. UN Department of Economic and Social Affairs, *Urbanization in the Second UN Development Plan* (New York: UN, 1970), pp. 1–2.

63. *Ibid.*, p. 3.

It is, of course, much more difficult to develop specific strategies, plans, and programs to meet these desired objectives.

Without question, plans and programs will differ in different social and economic situations. But one general caveat is in order, namely, that in efforts to deal with problems of urban growth and urbanization, urban areas must become integral elements in both national and regional plans for development. Urban problems can be solved only within the context of increased employment, increased productivity, and increased effective investment, including investment in human resources.

Goals for the second development decade, which might well be extended to coming decades, might therefore well include the following propositions adapted from the UN recommendations:[64]

1. Urban development itself must be recognized as a major factor in economic and national and regional development plans.
2. Urban development and housing authorities or relevant departments must be endowed with powers to control land use and to improve conditions in slum and squatter settlements so that residents of such areas can contribute to the process of modernization under way.
3. An urban and regional development strategy should be adopted in which urban location and form would be used to stimulate the most productive and diversified use of the nations' resources.
4. Appropriate proportions of national income (the UN recommends the equivalent of 5 percent of national income) should be allocated for direct public programs and publicly stimulated private actions to finance urban development.
5. Savings and credit institutions should be established to mobilize capital and to channel investments into urban development.
6. Urban studies and research centers should be established or expanded and interdisciplinary efforts increased to develop better urban strategies at the national and regional levels.

The achievement of these goals will certainly be facilitated if there is a substantial increase in international resources—financial aid, technical cooperation, and research and training. There is need also for increased worldwide public concern with problems relating to the unprecedented growth and accelerating urbanization in developing regions.

Needless to say, failure in efforts to deal with urban problems would lead to augmented social unrest and political instability. For it is in the

64. *Ibid.*, pp. 36–39.

urban setting much more than in the rural area that the problems of poverty, human misery, frustration, and alienation may serve as the tinderbox for explosive social disorder, including unprecedented threats to world peace.

The failure of the LDCs to use urbanization effectively as a pathway to development is illustrated by the way in which they have in general attempted to deal with squatter settlements. Such shantytowns have often been bulldozed and their populations dispersed, often to peripheral areas of cities far from opportunities to earn a livelihood. A clearance of squatter settlements was often effected for aesthetic reasons, especially if visiting dignitaries, going to and from airports, were likely to see them. Studies conducted by the International Labor Office under their urban employment program have indicated that in-migrants and shantytowns are more appropriately regarded as vanguards to economic development than as urban nuisances.[65] They constitute a bridge between the traditional and modern economic orders and should be viewed as a transitional or informal sector of the economy. Instead of bulldozing shantytowns, consideration should be given to assisting squatters in various ways to continue to perform their very important economic functions and to accelerate economic development. Such assistance could include in-migrant reception centers to assist newcomers to adapting to the urban environment, with at least minimal urban amenities such as piped water, shell houses, sanitation facilities, vocational training programs, placement activities, loans to finance business enterprises, various forms of technical assistance in business activity, and encouragement to participate in social, political, and economic activities at the community and local level.

Also important in coping with the problems of urbanization is the matter of land use. Rational guidance of urban development necessarily entails basic decisions about public and private land use. Zoning practices are required to stimulate and facilitate both business and industrial development and satisfactory residential areas. Physical planning of the urban setting is essential, but consideration must be given to integrating physical planning with social and economic objectives, including the role of the city in the metropolitan, regional, and national economy and society. As an essential element in urban development, a satisfactory arrangement for local governance is necessary not only of the city but also of its hinterland, taking into account its regional and national web of interrelationships.

In general, since the LDCs are necessarily more dependent on central planning than on the play of market forces, the role of government—

65. For example, see International Labour Office, *World Employment Programme: Research in Retrospect and Prospect* (Geneva: ILO, 1976).

central, regional, and local—assumes critical importance. The LDCs are much more dependent on knowledge as a basis for policy and action through planning and its implementation than were the MDCs in their early stages of development. Furthermore, risk in the MDCs' decision making was greatly decentralized to individuals such as entrepreneurs, workers, consumers, and residents. Individual mistakes did not have great import on the community or society as a whole. In economic matters, for example, individual entrepreneurial mistakes were paid for by the individual businessmen in the form of bankruptcy procedures, painful to the individual but with minor impact on the society as a whole. In contrast, mistakes made in central planning, whether national, regional, or local, involve much more risk to the community as a whole and may be much more costly than decentralized mistakes in a market economy. It is ironic that, in consequence, there is much more need for sound data and knowledge to guide decision making in the LDCs than was required in the developmental phases of the MDCs. Unfortunately, knowledge based on the experience of the MDCs may often be unsuited to the needs of the LDCs.

Population Heterogeneity

Technological advances in communication and transportation have tremendously increased social contact and social interaction of peoples of diverse backgrounds—different in culture, language, religion, value systems, ethnicity, race, and life style. Population heterogeneity has been brought about by both international and internal migration that has produced great population mixtures within nations, regions, and localities. Throughout the world, population diversity has been accompanied by social stratification, with minority group status generally being accompanied by inferior social, economic, and political opportunity and status.[66]

Even in antiquity, as in Ancient Rome, population diversity resulted from military conquest as well as migratory population flows. Such diversity in antiquity was accompanied by rigid forms of social stratification which minimized dissension and conflict—forms of superordination and subordination, such as in the caste system, slavery, feudalism, or other forms of class differentiation.

Since the end of World War II, population diversity has increasingly been accompanied by frictions and overt conflict. The world has been swept by the revolution of rising expectations. In consequence, there are

66. Philip Hauser, "The Chaotic Society: Product of the Social Morphological Revolution," *American Sociological Review* 34 (February 1969):1–19.

certainly few populations that do not insist on freedom and independence if they have not yet acquired them; and few minority groups within nations that do not insist on full equality of opportunity for achieving high social, economic, and political status. Communal conflict is evident throughout the world in many forms. Examples are given by the fratricidal conflicts in Northern Ireland and in what was Pakistan. In the former situation, Roman Catholics are struggling against a Protestant majority which has subjugated them for generations; in the latter case, East Pakistan revolted against West Pakistan because of perceived exploitation based in part on tribal differences, the Punjabi versus the Bengali. In Africa, examples are afforded by the conflict in Nigeria involving the Biafrans and in other tribal conflicts; in Asia, the tensions between the Malays and Chinese serve as an example; and in the Middle East, an example is the bitter warfare between the Moslems and Christians in Lebanon. The tensions between whites and blacks, not only in the Union of South Africa and Rhodesia, but also in the United States and the United Kingdom, are further examples. On a milder scale, at least for the time being, are the tensions between the Canadians of French and British origin.

This listing, of course, by no means exhausts the areas of tension and overt conflict within nations arising from ethnic, racial, linguistic, religious, and other bases of differentiation, accompanied by inequalities in opportunity and hence in social and economic status. Humankind has yet to find satisfactory solutions for achieving equal opportunity and raising social, economic, and political status in pluralistic societies.

Tensions and conflicts accompanying population heterogeneity may, of course, also greatly retard development. In the LDCs, especially, population diversity exacerbated by primordial identification, such as with a tribe or region, threatens national unity and purpose in achieving concensus on goals and cooperative programmatic action. In fact, in the short run, at least, rapid urbanization and communal conflict arising from population diversity may obstruct development more than high fertility and rapid population growth. Certainly, problems arising from urbanization and population diversity are relevant in any consideration of population factors in relation to development.

Population Quality

Population quality is still another aspect of population that cannot be ignored in considering the relation of population to development. There is, of course, much literature concerned with population quality as affected both by genetic and social factors. At the extreme, in respect to the genetic, are the unproven assumptions that hereditary differences are the main factors accounting for differences in degrees of development and levels of living. Such assumptions have been racist in character and were embodied in the discredited belief in the racial superiority of Nordic Caucasians, which reached its most repulsive form in Nazi Germany.

Although the genetic heritage is always an element in the quality of the human being, and although it may account for certain types of pathology, and limitations, it has become clear in the study of human genetics that it is not differences in the genetic heritage of large populations varying by race, ethnicity, and culture that account for the great differences in degrees of development and levels of living. In fact, the evidence is irrefutable with respect to two major conclusions. First, there is nothing that the members of one race or other large population grouping can do that the members of other races or large population groupings cannot do. Second, any possible differences in quality based on the genetic heritage of different races (or any other large population grouping) as measured by some central tendency, such as the mean or median, must be significantly smaller than the range of differences in quality within any such group.

Whatever the role of genetic heritage in determining the quality of the human being, it is clear that the role of social heritage is generally not only much more important, but also more mutable. Furthermore, there is ample evidence, especially in the history of the settlement of the Western Hemisphere, that immigrants with limited or no education and with limited occupational skills to offer in the economy, were able to have offspring who, in the course of a single generation, became leaders in business, labor, academia, and, indeed, all spheres of life. That is, illiterate, unskilled immigrants could, under the favorable social and economic conditions that existed in the United States, for example, see their offspring acquire education and skills that enabled them to obtain positions of the highest prestige and remuneration by reason of their favorable social, economic, and political opportunity.

It is only relatively recently that economists have become fully aware of the value of investment in human resources. In neoclassical economics, a unit of labor was judged to be a homogeneous entity in efforts to account for the increase in productivity and product. Consequently, only about half of the increase in gross national product in the United States was explained by the variables of land, natural resources, inputs of reproducible capital, and inputs of labor. With the analysis of differences in the quality of labor based on investment in education, training, skill, and health, about half of the unexplained increase in gross national product was accounted for.[67] In fact, it has become clear that the return on investment in human resources is greater than the return on any other form of investment.

The quality of population as affected by the investment in human capital is, then, a critical element in achieving development. Investment may take a number of forms, such as investment in formal schooling, vocational training, adult education, health, in-service on-the-job training, and migration and adjustment to new community living. Just as investment in human resources has been a major factor in accounting for economic growth in the more developed countries, so also may it be a prerequisite to development in the less developed countries. This subject is further pursued by Schultz in Chapter 10 and Blaug in Chapter 11.

THE LABOR FORCE

The work force of a nation is a major segment of its population crucial in its relation to development. The labor force, in accordance with international usage, is defined as persons above a lower age limit working for pay or profit or seeking work. In the LDCs the lower age limit is generally taken as 10 years of age; in the MDCs the lower age limit is often taken to be the age up to which school attendance is compulsory. Working for pay or profit is taken to include unpaid family work, providing goods or services for the market, but to exclude household work, such as cooking, cleaning, and sewing, not performed for pay.

The size and composition of the work force is a function of three major factors: the size of the population; the age structure of the population; and social, cultural, and economic factors determining labor force participation. Important in the latter are variant cultural definitions of sex and age roles in respect to labor force activity. Such cultural definitions are especially significant in determining the labor force participating rates of women.

More specifically, as Durand pointed out, the crude activity rate (the proportion of a population above the minimum age that is in the work force) is determined by three components: the labor force participation of males by age, that of females by age, and the age-sex composition of the population.[68] Durand's cross-section analysis of international census data

67. Theodore W. Schultz, *Investment in Human Capital: The Role of Education and of Research* (New York: The Free Press, 1971), Chap. 3.

68. John Durand, *The Labor Force in Economic Development* (Princeton, N.J.: Princeton University Press, 1975), p. 80.

for the twenty-year period 1946 to 1966, revealed a U-shaped pattern of crude rates by level of development. Analysis of patterns of intercensal change showed a decrease in crude activity rates; the speed of decline was inversely associated with the level of development; but the rate of decline was controlled by more factors than level of development alone. The impact of these other factors is seen by comparing the contribution of changes in the components to the changes in the crude rates.

Durand's analysis shows that with age controlled, the labor force participation of males decreases as the level of development rises; whereas that of females follows a U-shaped pattern, highest in the less developed countries, falling in the middle range of development, and rising again with higher levels of development. For the fifty-eight countries Durand studied, about half of the decrease in the crude activity rates was attributed to decreased participation of males, and most of the remainder was due to changes in population structure. Durand carries his analysis into greater detail, not to be pursued further here except for the impact of changes in population structure at varying levels of development.[69]

As has been noted above in discussing age structure in relation to development, the factor most important in determining the size of the labor force is the proportion of children to adults. This proportion, as has been shown, is mainly dependent on the birth rate. In the MDCs the proportion of youth is much lower than in the LDCs mainly because of lower fertility. Moreover, as has been noted, as mortality decreases in the LDCs, the relatively great decreases in infant and child mortality tend to increase the proportion of young dependents as more children survive. Decreased fertility, as revealed in the Coale models, greatly lowers the proportion of young in relation to the proportion of adults, persons of working age, especially in the first generation of fertility reduction, because the number of persons of working age is based on earlier higher fertility and will register decline in accordance with lower birth rates only with considerable lag.

The ILO has collated labor force data for the world, the MDCs and LDCs and countries for 1950 to 1970 and model labor force projections to 2000. Table 1.8 shows that in 1970, the crude activity rate of the world for the sexes combined was 41.8, and that of the MDCs, at 45, was higher than that of the LDCs, at 40.4. For the LDCs, the age-specific labor force participation rates for males were higher than those of the MDCs below age 20 and above age 55. For females, labor force participation rates were much higher in the LDCs than in the MDCs for persons under 15 but were

69. *Ibid.*, Chap. 4.

TABLE 1.8
Labor Force Participation Rates by Age and Sex, 1970

Age	Both Sexes			Male			Female		
	World	MDCs	LDCs	World	MDCs	LDCs	World	MDCs	LDCs
All ages	41.8	45.0	40.4	54.2	56.5	53.3	29.3	34.3	27.1
0–9	0.0	0.0	0.0	0.0	0.0	0.0	0.0	0.0	0.0
10–14	14.1	1.8	18.2	16.5	2.2	21.3	11.6	1.4	15.0
15–19	49.1	43.6	51.1	58.6	47.6	62.6	39.3	39.5	39.2
20–24	69.7	75.2	67.4	87.2	85.2	88.0	51.6	65.0	46.0
25–44	74.2	77.9	72.4	96.6	96.9	96.5	51.2	59.1	47.3
45–54	72.5	74.3	71.5	94.8	94.1	95.1	51.0	57.7	46.5
55–64	56.3	50.8	60.7	81.7	76.1	85.7	33.3	30.8	35.6
65+	25.1	14.6	36.8	41.7	24.8	57.1	12.6	8.0	18.5

SOURCE: ILO, *Labor Force, 1950–2000: Estimates 1950–1970, Projections, 1975–2000,* 2nd ed., vol. 5, *World Summary* (Geneva: ILO, 1977).

about the same at age 15 to 19, lower from ages 20 to 44, and then higher above age 45.[70]

In general, what is prominent in the MDC-LDC comparison of age-specific participation rates is the lower activity of both males and females in the MDCs at the younger ages because of schooling, and the lower participation rates in the MDCs of both sexes at the higher ages because of provision for retirement. The high proportion of workers in the LDCs in agriculture, discussed below, is also a factor in the higher labor force activity of both sexes at age 55 and over in the LDCs. At the older ages, it is easier to continue work activity in agriculture than in industry.

Table 1.9 shows that in 1970 the work force of the world as a whole was about half in agriculture (51 percent), over one-fourth in the services, and over one-fifth in industry. The work force in the LDCs was predominantly in agriculture, 66.6 percent, compared with only 18.3 percent in the MDCs. The proportion of workers in industry in the MDCs was 2.4 times that in the LDCs, 37.6 as compared with 15.9 percent; and that in the services in the MDCs was 2.5 times that in the LDCs, 44.1 compared with 17.5 percent. The same general differential pattern characterized each sex; agricultural employment of women was greater than that for men.

The ILO's projections of the labor force for 2000 will be considered next. Between 1970 and 2000, according to the ILO projections, the world's work force will increase 69 percent, from 1,509 million to 2,546 million, or by more than 1 billion workers, as Table 1.10 shows. Of this increase, 887 million would be added to the labor force in the LDCs, 86 percent of the total increment. Such an increase in workers constitutes a major challenge to the LDCs to effect development sufficient to generate jobs for the almost doubling of their work force.

Of the total increase in the world's work force, 688 million, or 66 percent, would be male; and 349 million, or 34 percent, female. Thus, while male workers were increasing by 70 percent in the 30-year period, female workers would increase by 66 percent. In the LDCs, however, male workers would increase by 606 million, or 86 percent, and make up 99 percent of the total world increase in male workers. Female workers in the LDCs would increase by 281 million, or 84 percent, and constitute 81 percent of the total world increase in female workers. In the LDCs male workers would be increasing by 3.4 times the percentage increase of male workers in the MDCs, 86 compared with 25 percent; while female workers in the LDCs would be increasing by about 2.4 times, 84 compared with 35 percent.

70. International Labor Office, *Labor Force: 1950–2000, Estimates 1950–70, Projections 1975–2000,* 2nd ed., vol. 5, *World Summary* (Geneva: ILO, 1977).

TABLE 1.9
Percentage of Work Force in Agriculture, Industry, and Services, by Sex, 1970.

Area	Both Sexes			Male			Female		
	Agr.	Ind.	Ser.	Agr.	Ind.	Ser.	Agr.	Ind.	Ser.
World	51.0	22.9	26.1	49.1	25.7	25.2	54.3	17.9	27.8
MDCs	18.3	37.6	44.1	17.0	44.2	38.7	20.3	27.4	52.3
LDCs	66.6	15.9	17.5	63.0	17.7	19.3	73.8	12.4	13.8

SOURCES: ILO, *Labor Force, 1950–2000: Estimates 1950–1970, Projections, 1975–2000,* 2nd ed., vol. 5, *World Summary* (Geneva: ILO, 1977).

TABLE 1.10
Labor Force by Sex, 1970 and Projected to 2000
(in millions)

	Both Sexes	Male	Female
World			
1970	1,509	980	529
2000	2,546	1,668	878
MDCs			
1970	488	295	192
2000	639	378	260
LDCs			
1970	1,020	684	336
2000	1,907	1,290	617

SOURCE: ILO, *Labor Force, 1950–2000: Estimates 1950–1970; Projections, 1975–2000,* 2nd ed., vol. 5, *World Summary* (Geneva: ILO, 1977).

According to the ILO labor force projections to the year 2000, the patterns of differences between age-specific labor force participation rates in the MDCs and LDCs would persist, but in reduced form at the younger and older ages, as Table 1.11 shows. Whereas in 1970, the activity rate of persons 10 to 14 in the LDCs was ten times that in the MDCs (18.2 percent, compared with 1.8 percent), by the year 2000 this discrepancy would be reduced to 7.5 times. Similarly, whereas the activity rate for persons 15 to 19 in 1970 in the LDCs was 17 percent above that in the MDCs, in 2000 it is anticipated to be but 8 percent higher. Thus the ILO projections assume some increased schooling to compete with labor force participation in the LDCs by the year 2000, but not nearly enough completely to reduce the gap.

Similarly the difference in activity rates of older workers is anticipated to decrease. Whereas in 1970, the activity rate of persons 55 to 64 in the LDCs was 19.5 percent higher than that in the MDCs, in 2000 it would be only about 4 percent greater. Furthermore, whereas in 1970 the activity rate of persons 65 and over in the LDCs was 2.5 times that in the MDCs, in 2000 it would be about twice as great. These patterns, in general, tended to hold for each sex. An important difference, however, is apparent in the crude activity rate. While the female activity rate in the MDCs is anticipated to increase by 10 percent—from 34.3 to 37.7 percent—that for women in the LDCs is anticipated to decrease by 6 percent, from 27.1 to 25.5.

CONCLUDING OBSERVATIONS

The successful management of population and development may well be critical in determining the quality of life and perhaps even the survival

TABLE 1.11
Labor Force Participation Rates, by Sex, Projected to 2000

Age	Both Sexes			Male			Female		
	World	MDCs	LDCs	World	MDCs	LDCs	World	MDCs	LDCs
All Ages	40.7	46.9	39.0	53.0	56.5	52.1	28.2	37.7	25.5
10–14	5.8	.9	6.8	6.9	1.1	8.0	4.7	.7	5.5
15–19	34.4	32.3	34.8	41.0	33.5	42.5	27.6	31.0	26.9
20–24	65.8	74.7	63.9	81.6	79.9	82.0	49.5	69.3	45.3
25–44	73.2	81.1	70.9	95.8	96.3	95.7	49.9	65.5	45.4
45–54	72.1	79.7	68.9	93.1	92.9	93.2	50.9	66.6	44.2
55–64	52.5	51.3	53.2	74.5	69.1	77.1	31.4	34.9	29.6
65+	16.6	10.6	21.1	27.1	16.9	33.6	8.3	6.3	10.0

SOURCE: ILO, *Labor Force, 1950–2000: Estimates 1950–1970, Projections, 1975–2000,* 2nd ed., vol. 5, *World Summary* (Geneva, ILO, 1977).

of humankind in the coming decades. At the interchange between the more developed countries and the least developing countries are the troublesome and fearsome disparities in levels of living and the basic impasse to date in efforts to develop mechanisms and procedures to improve the world situation and to resolve the tensions generated by the demands of the developing countries.

2

Theories of Fertility Decline: A Reappraisal

RONALD FREEDMAN

CLASSICAL DEMOGRAPHIC TRANSITION THEORY

ABOUT FORTY YEARS AGO, sociology and demography were much simpler than they are today. Since relatively few facts were available then, it was possible to state and defend simple, coherent theories to explain population phenomena. Since then, many old theories have been cast into doubt by new data. What follows is a consideration of how new data and ideas have changed thinking about a central problem in the field: the circumstances under which the fertility of a population falls from high to low levels. New observations, both about the history of the West and about recent trends in less developed countries, have shaken the neat theories which once were held.

Two major issues are relevant for understanding fertility decline: (1) what leads to the motivation to have fewer rather than more children; and (2) once the motivation exists, are the concept and the means of fertility control automatically available and inevitably used or do they have independent causal roles in fertility decline?

In the past most demographers had few doubts about what motivates a desire for fewer children. The answer lay in the classical demographic transition model. Briefly, changes in macrodevelopmental variables—urbanization, industrialization, literacy, and the like—resulted in a shift from major dependence on relatively self-contained local institutions to dependence upon larger social, economic, and political units. Such a shift

This chapter is a slightly modified version of the second annual Amos Hawley Lecture, jointly sponsored by the Sociology Departments of The University of Michigan and The University of North Carolina at Chapel Hill, April 11, 1978, and it appears in *Social Forces* (September 1979).

implies a change in the division of labor from one in which the family and local community are central to a larger complex in which the family gives up many functions to larger, specialized institutions. In both areas, new nonfamilial institutions were of growing importance. Greater literacy and the development of effective communication and transportation networks were essential to all these changes.

As units of interdependence expanded and took over familial functions, the benefits and satisfactions derived from numerous children lessened. The costs of children increased, partly because they interfered with new nonfamilial activities and partly because the improving standards of living, the increased education, and the opportunities in the new expanded system of interaction led to rising aspirations. Parents wanted more for themselves and their children. Many satisfactions, such as those derived from the achievements of their children, were more likely to be derived from investing in fewer rather than more children under the new conditions.

In this classical model, primary emphasis was on the changes in the objective structural developmental levels as primary in fertility decline. The new aspirations, the changes in the functions of the family, and new perceptions of the costs and benefits of children were seen as the necessary and almost incidental consequences of the developmental changes which lead to the demand for fewer children.

What is wrong with this formulation? There are, initially, problems in its application to Europe. First, the patterns of developmental conditions actually associated with fertility decline have turned out to be quite varied. Detailed empirical work has been unable to establish combinations of development variables at specific levels which were systematically related to the European fertility declines. Countries which differed widely in industrialization and urbanization began their declines about the same time. Also, examples have been found in which less advanced areas began their declines before more advanced areas.[1]

Secondly, detailed study of the European fertility transition has shown that many areas that were culturally similar, for example in language or ethnicity, also demonstrated similar fertility patterns, without prime reference to socioeconomic developmental indices critical to transition theory. Subregions with a common culture tended to have similar patterns of fertility decline even though they had different developmental

1. Ansley J. Coale, "The Demographic Transition," in International Union for the Scientific Study of Population, *International Population Conference, 1973,* vol. 1. (Liege, Belgium: International Union for the Scientific Study of Population, 1973); and Michael S. Teitelbaum, "Relevance of Demographic Transition Theory for Developing Countries," *Science* 188 (May 1975):420–25.

levels. It is possible that cultural differences in familial institutions involving such matters as inheritance customs and the status of women could be differentiating factors. Coale *et al.* have recently demonstrated that as late as 1970 a number of Asian Soviet republics with modern macro-structural characteristics had high natural marital fertility. The explanations offered are on normative and cultural grounds.[2] In general, the evidence appears to indicate that cultural groupings often are related to fertility in ways that have not yet been explained by the general sociostructural factors central to transition theory.

A third problem with the classical position is that in its empirical tests the macro-structural variables were related directly to fertility. The looseness of this relationship may result from the failure to deal empirically with the changes in the family and in changing aspirations for self and children which are direct links between the macro-variables and fertility in the original formulation.[3]

While this evidence tends to undermine the classical model, it is possible to argue that all of these exceptions in the West are short run and unimportant. All general empirical observations about complex human behavior have exceptions. After all, the whole range of variables did change everywhere in the West across cultural and national lines. The modern Western nuclear family, low fertility, and high aspirations and standards of living are now an integral part of a specialized, highly developed, international social and economic system.

TRANSITION IN LESS DEVELOPED COUNTRIES

Are all of the above factors necessary to motivate fertility decline? Hypotheses which merit consideration are: (1) that subsets of objective development alterations, much smaller than those that characterized the West, can provide motivations for lower fertility today; and (2) that under modern conditions, ideas and aspirations for a different way of life transcending what is actually available are also important in motivating lower fertility.

The fact is that fertility decline already has occurred in a number of countries with only a limited subset of the development changes. For

2. Ansley J. Coale, Barbara Anderson, and Erna Harm, *Human Fertility in Russia Since the 19th Century: The Demographic Transition in a Different Historical Context* (Princeton, N.J.: Princeton University Press, forthcoming.)

3. Rodolfo Bulatao, "On the Nature of the Transition in the Value of Children: Cross Cultural Comparisons," Paper presented at the Conference on Comparative Fertility Transition in Asia, Tokyo, March 1978.

example, fertility has declined in such places as Sri Lanka,[4] Kerala,[5] Thailand,[6] the People's Republic of China, and probably in Indonesia—each with only limited developmental changes and with populations that are overwhelmingly poor and rural.

Just how much change in which subset of conditions is sufficient to motivate fertility declines is not known. Probably more than one combination will turn out to be sufficient. But, consider as examples Sri Lanka, Kerala, and China. They have at least a number of substantive changes in common:

1. Better health and longer life, which means fewer births are needed for the survival of any desired number and which encourages investment in the future.

2. Higher education for both boys and girls, which increases the costs and decreases the benefits while children are in school. Fewer better educated children may provide greater satisfaction than more poorly educated children.

3. Welfare institutions, providing minimum subsistence for the masses, at least in food, which may decrease dependence on children.

4. Communication and transportation facilities capable of providing the information, services, and goods which have produced the other changes.

So, there have been concrete, if limited, changes which may have directly affected the real or perceived costs and benefits of children.

But, there is something more than these objective changes. Increasing numbers of people have become aware of alternatives to their traditional lifestyles and aspire to something different, even though these aspirations often are poorly defined. However, this change process in the realm of ideas and aspirations has a pace and character quite different from earlier changes in the West. One reason for this is that less developed countries (LDCs) today potentially have transportation and communication facilities far more powerful and pervasive than those that were available in the West. These link such areas as those we are discussing to national and interna-

4. D. S. Fernando, "Fertility Trends in Sri Lanka and Future Prospects," *Journal of Bio-Science* 8 (1976):35–43; and Marga Institute, *Welfare and Growth in Sri Lanka,* Marga Research Studies No. 2 (Colombo: Marga Institute, 1974.)

5. J. Ratcliffe, "Social Justice and the Demographic Transition: Lessons from India's Kerala State," *International Journal of Health Services* 8 (1) (1978): 123–44; and United Nations, Department of Economic and Social Affairs, *Poverty and Development Policy, A Case Study of Selected Issues with Reference to Kerala* (New York: United Nations, 1975).

6. Nibhon Debavalya and John Knodel, "Thailand's Reproduction Revolution," *International Family Planning Perspectives and Digest* 4 (2) (Summer 1978):34–49.

tional networks. Furthermore, there is a great difference between the LDCs and the preindustrial West in what is carried by the networks. The LDCs potentially have available as part of their social environment the history, the development, the technology, and the rising standards of living in the West. The influence may be either directly from the network or, more probably, indirectly through local elites. The more literate the LDC and the better the communication system, the greater the potential effect of contact with the cumulative world inventories of models, ideas, and products.

The modern communication system can carry new models of the family and child-parent relations. The Chinese, for example, are loading their communication network with new familial models and have made various changes designed to shift functions and power from the family. However, it is not necessarily such explicit family messages that have the most effect in changing perceptions about the costs and benefits of children. The new ideas and models, covering many aspects of life, may affect the demand for children by changing aspirations for other things wanted both for the children and for the parents. This gets validation through the dissemination into the rural areas of many LDCs of such small items as the bicycle, the motor scooter, the sewing machine, the small pumping motor, the radio, and even the TV. These change the lives both of those who have them and the larger number who want them.

The linkage to the national and world networks affects the self-identity of the individual and incorporates models, ideas, groups, and movements that transcend his family and local community. They may be influenced by whatever image of the new man a government fosters through the communication network. But they are likely to be even more influenced by rock and movie stars, the charismatic political leader, the government bureaucrat, the hero athlete, and a host of other half-real and half-media characters with whom parents and children may identify. Young people who incorporate elements of such images in their self-concepts may be less willing to play some traditional familial roles.

It is not likely that abstract ideas alone can have much effect on fertility. Obviously, there must be at least the changes in communication to provide the means for receiving these ideas. Beyond that, it is doubtful that exposure to the ideas alone could have much meaning without some actual validation in change.

Realistically, the material benefits that can be brought to the LDC masses in the next few decades are limited. But, important added components are rising aspirations and the perception of the possibility of a different life that is considered better by the people and goes beyond what reality offers objectively to all at the moment. Even within a closed society, that perception and aspiration may come from a revolutionary state that effectively links the masses to central institutions and transcends local and familial interactions, as appears to be the case in China. The new perception and aspirations also may come not from revolution but from interdependence with the world-wide communication and trade system. Some combination of minimal changes in life conditions and linkage to the ideas of a larger system seem plausible as a sufficient combination for motivating lower fertility.

Recently, there has been much emphasis on growth from below in the village as the place where developmental and population change must be rooted and motivated. This is often related to the idea that equity in the distribution of goods and services makes for low fertility. It is difficult to know whether it is equity rather than the improvement in the standard of living of the masses which is the relevant variable. However, in either case, such changes at the lowest levels are improbable unless local communities are effectively linked to larger systems of resources and interchange. Without that, rhetoric and grandiose plans in a capital city are irrelevant.

This last observation is especially pertinent to the many negative cases—LDCs with little change in fertility, such as Pakistan or Bangladesh or Zaire. In these countries a common important factor is that the governments have been unable to set up administrative, communication, and transportation systems capable of reaching the village masses, either with the ideas of the outside world or with the minimal services and goods which make the new ideas and aspirations credible.

The causes of fertility decline are very complex. The explanation probably does not lie only in a small subset of sociostructural changes and in new ideas generated by communication systems. It is very likely that there are facilitating and inhibiting factors that depend on the cultural context. For example, in societies in which women have low status, little education, and are highly segregated, they are less likely to get either the limited objective benefits or the new ideas which have been discussed. Women obviously have a special interest in the subject of reproduction. This may help to explain why fertility remains uniformly high in countries in which women are segregated and uneducated. They have neither the access to new ideas nor the stimulus to develop their own. This may be one reason that Moslem countries tend to lag in fertility decline, even when they have family planning programs. On the other hand, in Thailand development is only at moderate levels and contraceptive use is rising rapidly. There, the position of women is unusually good. They are active in the labor force, involved in social and economic affairs, and they are not disadvantaged by any parental preference for sons.

Jack Caldwell, in a recent bold attack on the whole demographic transition concept, goes much farther than this writer on the role of the dissemination of ideas. He argues that the nuclear family as a distinctive emotional unit is beginning to sweep the world—not necessarily as a part of economic modernization, but through westernization—that is, through Western domination of schools and the international network of mass media. He reaches a provocative conclusion: "Fertility decline in the Third World is not dependent on the spread of industrialization or even on the rate of economic development. It will of course be affected by such development in that modernization produces more money for schools, for newspapers, and so on; indeed, the whole question of family nucleation cannot arise in the non-monetized economy. But fertility decline is more likely to precede industrialization and to help bring it about than to follow it."[7]

This writer is in agreement with Caldwell on the possible major role of the dissemination of ideas in motivating a desire for smaller families, and that this may happen through the dissemination of the Western nuclear family pattern is certainly one possible pattern. However, the Western nuclear family is not necessarily a mandatory prior condition.

When it is asserted that people in LDCs are influenced by the ideas of the West, it is not meant that they adopt them whole. For example, while some changes in family life are almost inevitable with lower fertility, adoption of the Western nuclear model and abandonment of traditional familial values is not always a prior condition for large-scale adoption of contraception and a fertility decline. Consider the case of Taiwan.[8] When this writer began to work there seventeen years ago, it was expected that, if the wide-ranging development then underway continued, this would make for fundamental changes in the Chinese extended family structure, resulting in preferences for fewer children, which then would lead to the adoption of contraception. Development and modernization did continue at a spectacular pace. But, the massive adoption of contraception and the rapid fall in fertility occurred while the family retained many traditional forms and attitudes. For example, in 1973 over 80 percent of Taiwanese older parents lived with a married son if they had one. Married sons who do not live with the husband's parents send them money. A large majority of young Taiwanese couples say they expect to live with a married son and to receive financial support from him in their old age. Eighty-eight percent say that having a male heir is important. There is a continuing, very strong prefer-

7. Jack C. Caldwell, "Toward a Restatement of Demographic Transition Theory," *Population and Development Review* 2 (September/December 1976):358.

8. T. H. Sun, H. S. Lin, and Ronald Freedman, "Trends in Fertility, Family Size Preference, and Family Planning: Taiwan, 1965–1976," *Studies in Family Planning* 9 (5) (1978).

ence for sons. There are almost universal aspirations for high education for children and for a high standard of living for both children and parents. There is also a perception of the rising costs of education and higher standards of consumption. *But,* all of this appears to operate along with traditional familial values which are changing slowly but are still very different from ours.

The Taiwanese apparently want to maintain intergenerational extended kinship ties in households equipped with TV and all the latest electronic gadgets. They have rationally decided that this is feasible with fewer children in whom greater investment is made. The costs are similar to those in the West, but the perceived benefits are quite different. Large-scale adoption of birth control and smaller families need not necessarily be preceded by the development of Western nuclear families. It is, of course, possible that there will be a *later* convergence to a Western model.

Careful studies[9] appear to show that children may be net assets to their parents from a fairly early age in some LDC villages. Other studies[10] come to different conclusions. But, the general validity of the studies depends on whether children and parents are willing to play the traditional roles which make children a net asset. The child who acquires a strong taste for blue jeans or even a motorscooter may be less willing to play out the traditional role. In many LDCs as a result of the communication network there is a confusing mixture of values, material goods, and roles. Uncertainty as to how to behave is likely to grow, and uncertainty breeds thinking about alternatives from which social change flows.

It would be naive to think that in Taiwan or anywhere else a changing demand for children, involving new perceptions of their economic and noneconomic benefits and costs, would emerge suddenly in a simultaneous flash of mass insight. It is more likely that it was an emergent phenomenon. As social conditions and aspirations changed, dissatisfactions about such specific problems as housing, school costs, new employment conditions, and the status to be derived from children were only dimly and occasionally seen initially as connected to family size. Such problems provide a latent motive for fewer children, which would be crystallized over time. Within any population there must be a range of motivations for fewer children from latent to explicit, ambivalent to unequivocal.

9. Benjamin White, "The Economic Importance of Children in a Javanese Village," in *Population and Social Organization,* edited by Moni Nag (The Hague: Mouton, 1975).

10. Eva Mueller, "The Economic Value of Children in Peasant Agriculture," in *Population and Development,* edited by Ronald Ridker (Baltimore: The Johns Hopkins University Press, 1977).

DIFFUSION OF THE IDEA OF FAMILY LIMITATION

The preceding discussion has assumed that social change of some kind is necessary to motivate a desire for fewer living children. It is also possible that in some societies significant numbers of couples might have preferred fewer children than they were having but that the concept that it was legitimate to control family size in marriage was not widespread. We do know that infanticide and abortion have been used extensively in pre-modern societies, but it is not clear whether these were used to limit the total number of children to a desired number or as a reaction to emergency conditions.

Assuming that there is a latent or explicit motivation to control family size, what about the second major question—the availability of the concept and the means for family limitation? The classical view, to which this writer once subscribed, is that the concept and the means for birth control have always been potentially available for rapid adoption in all societies, but were not adopted or used much because there was no demand. When social change meant that fewer children were wanted in Western Europe, large numbers of couples apparently adopted coitus interruptus, the condom, and primitive abortion. When the macrodevelopmental changes transformed the family so that parents wanted fewer children, these primitive means were sufficient to produce low fertility. We saw their adoption as incidental and almost inevitable. The fact that such primitive means produced low fertility is often cited as an indication that the idea and means of birth control were not and are not an independent element in the situation.

There is now a case for the thesis that, once motivation is present, both the concept of and the means for family limitation can have independent causal roles in determining both the timing of the onset and the rapidity of the fertility decline. It is important to differentiate the concept from the means of fertility control. That controlling family size in marriage is legitimate is a concept that may be absent or present to varying degrees in a society. Beyond that, there is the question of whether the cost, availability, legitimacy, and other characteristics of methods available and the system for delivering them affect either the acceptance of the concept or the prevalence and effectiveness of practice.

John Knodel recently has written about the possible independent effect of the concept of family limitation.[11] The essence of his argument is

11. John Knodel, "Family Limitation and the Fertility Transition: Evidence from the Age Patterns of Fertility in Europe and Asia," *Population Studies* 31 (July 1977):219–49.

that, before the modern fertility decline, the concept of family limitation in marriage, although sometimes present in small segments of the population, was not a part of mass thinking. The concept that limiting family size in marriage was legitimate and possible was an innovation adopted by significant numbers sooner in some places than in others. While the technology and methods of contraception were and are important, the idea that it is legitimate to use them in marriage can be treated as an additional integral part of an innovative cultural complex. Why it should catch on earlier in some places than in others is an important research question for which no answers are available, but the same uncertainty surrounds the introduction of many technological innovations.

The notion of an independent role for the adoption of the idea of family limitation is consistent with the fact that, once fertility fell in any European country or province by as much as 10 percent or so, it then almost always fell rapidly and continually to low levels. Since the developmental changes which presumably produced the motivation for fewer children occurred much more slowly, one would have expected a more gradual adoption of birth control and a less rapid decline in fertility if contraception were simply an incidental adjustment to growing motivation.

Although Knodel stresses innovation as a neglected element, he indicates that it is not a question of either adjustment or innovation, but of both: "The innovative behavior of family limitation permits fertility to adjust to the prevailing socioeconomic situation. At the same time, socioeconomic change occurred during the period of fertility transition and it seems reasonable to assume that as family limitation diffused fertility continued to adjust to current socioeconomic conditions."[12]

Knodel buttresses his argument by providing evidence that, for a number of countries, the predecline age-specific fertility patterns had a shape that is characteristic of natural fertility. This means that any customs (e.g., breastfeeding) which affect fertility levels are not dependent on how many children a couple has; that is, they are not practiced to achieve a desired family size or to limit the number of children. If Knodel's evidence is valid, then the beginning of the fertility decline was a transition from essentially no family limitation to a rapidly increasing prevalence, with the fertility decline outpacing the rate of development. If the dissemination of the idea of family limitation as legitimate has an independent causal role, this would help to explain the loose fit between macrodevelopmental variables and fertility decline in Western Europe.

That the idea of family limitation had some independent causality also may be relevant to the unexpected clustering in European cultural regions of the onset of European fertility declines. The common language

12. *Ibid.*, p. 248.

and other shared aspects of the cultural regions could produce a culturally bounded communication network for the spread of such an idea.

The argument is that the motivation was necessary but not sufficient without legitimation of this fundamental idea. This also suggests that fertility might have fallen sooner in parts of Western Europe if the idea of family limitation had already been widely available. This was not an idea widely and openly discussed, but a hush-hush matter, adopted despite the opposition of the state, the church, the medical profession, and the information media. Also, the means of contraception were very primitive and not those increasingly chosen today. If modern contraceptives had been available when the concept of family limitation spread, that might have hastened both the adoption of the concept and the practice of birth control.

A second piece of evidence for the possibly independent roles of the concept and means of family limitation is that the rapidity with which contraception has spread and fertility declined in all major population strata in a number of LDCs far exceeds European experience. For example, the rate at which such change has occurred in Taiwan is something which was not anticipated when this writer began research collaboration with the Taiwanese seventeen years ago. This rapid change has affected all strata of the population—rich and poor, urban and rural, illiterates and college graduates. Between 1965 and 1976—in just eleven years—among illiterate Taiwanese wives of childbearing age, the proportion ever using contraception increased from 19 to 78 percent. Overall, fertility fell by 50 percent between 1961 and 1975. Changes of similar magnitude occurred in Korea, Mauritius, and Singapore. In Thailand—far less advanced than Taiwan in many developing indicators—the proportion of rural wives ever using contraception increased from 11 to 35 percent in just six years.[13] In one province of Thailand, Chiang Mai, the total fertility rate declined by 49 percent in fifteen years to just 2.67.[14] Among the 36 LDCs with populations of 10 million or more—with 90 percent of the Third World population—15 had estimated birth rate declines of 10 percent or more between 1965 and 1975.[15] These data indicate that the idea and practice of family limitation can sweep an LDC population far more quickly than was previously imagined possible.

How much fertility decline depends on the concept of fertility control and how much it is affected by the nature of the methods and the delivery

13. Debavalya and Knodel, "Thailand's Reproduction Revolution," p. 40.

14. Tieng, Pardthaisong, "The Recent Fertility Decline in the Chieng Mai Area of Thailand," paper of the East-West Population Institute, East-West Center, No. 47, (1978).

15. Work by Parker W. Mauldin, cited in Bernard Berelson, "Prospects and Programs for Fertility Decline: What, Where?" *Population and Development Review* 4 (December 1978):579–616.

system by which they are provided is an important area for research. It is plausible that methods that are effective, safe, and have other attractive features help both to legitimize the concept and to hasten the dissemination of practice. There is some evidence for this in the work of Westoff and Ryder on the recent rapid spread of modern contraception in the disadvantaged sectors of our own population.

It cannot be argued that the idea and practice of family planning can spread anywhere irrespective of changes in living conditions. For example, with one possible exception, there are no examples of substantial falls in LDC fertility in the postwar world without prior substantial falls in mortality.

Another kind of evidence that acceptance of the concept and availability of means of family limitation may have an independent role is the observation that the effectiveness of organized family planning programs is related to fertility declines above and beyond the effects of development levels. The most recent cross-national multivariate analysis of this issue is a study by Mauldin and Berelson.[16] They find that development levels and family planning program effectiveness have both joint and independent effects on fertility. In addition to a major joint effect, an independent program effect is comparable to an independent development effect. However, where there is very little development, there is no program effect to be observed, presumably because an effective program cannot be mounted without minimal development levels. Good family planning programs are a complex which provide both the idea of fertility control and the means and services under medically optimal, culturally acceptable circumstances. It is probable that the better the services, the more likely that the idea will be accepted and acted upon. However, unless there is at least a latent motivation for fewer children and the concept of family limitation is accepted as the normatively legitimate solution to the problem of too many children, providing the means and services cannot have much effect.

THE CASES OF CHINA AND INDONESIA

Finally, two quite different country cases, China[17] and Indonesia[18] illustrate the possible independent effects of high-pressure, high-priority government

16. Parker W. Mauldin and Bernard Berelson, "Conditions of Fertility Decline in Developing Countries, 1965–1975," *Studies in Family Planning* 9 (May 1978): 90–147.

17. Pi-Chao Chen and Ann Miller, "Lessons from the Chinese Experience: China's Planned Birth Program and Its Transferability," *Studies in Family Planning* 6 (October 1975):354–66.

18. T. H. Hull, V. Hull, and M. Singarimbun, "Indonesia's Family Planning

family-planning programs organized to reach the masses in the village. While the data for both countries is fragmentary and subject to criticism, the cases deserve special attention, both because of the size of their populations and the unusual conditions prevailing. This is not the place for a review of the serious data problems for China, so the following summary descriptive statements represent what can be inferred from scattered and incomplete evidence.

It appears that China's birth rate has fallen from somewhere near 40 to perhaps 25 or so under the present regime. There is a general consensus among most observers that mortality levels have declined substantially, that educational levels have risen, and that the status of women has been improved by more education, more employment, and later marriage, giving them a position less dependent on their fertility. A floor on food and clothing is provided by rationing, and more equitable distribution appears to exist for large parts of the population. There is greater provision for security of older people, particularly in cities. In rural areas the communes appear to be taking over some functions of the family, but it is not clear how far this has really gone. Yet, with all these changes, it is still true that the country is poor, and agriculture, while improved, yields no secure margin of safety for the still burgeoning population. If the birth rate has fallen in China, it has occurred under conditions that are far from those of the modern industrial society. The country is still fundamentally poor and agricultural.

The additional element important for our purpose is the massive Chinese national birth-planning program. This has been organized through the network of political and social organization which mobilizes the masses of the population in primary groups at their places of work and residence and relates these to the party and state hierarchy. That system is used to promote priority objectives—such as birth planning—by persistent and repetitive messages, discussions, and both peer and authority pressure, which is so awesome in its extent that it is hard for us to comprehend. Sociologists have long been respectful of the power of the primary group to mold behavior. The Chinese, in making the mobilization of the masses a centerpiece of their political and economic strategy, are demonstrating applied sociology of a very powerful type.

In China also, then, there is a subset of development conditions which very probably affect the costs and benefits of children, but with something added—a high-pressure, high-priority birth-planning program working through a political-social system capable of reaching the masses of the

---

Story: Success and Challenge," *Population Bulletin* 32 (6) (1977); Jeanne C. Singquefield and Bambang Sungkono, *Fertility and Family Planning in Java and Bali* (Jakarta: Central Bureau of Statistics of Indonesia, forthcoming).

population and influencing their interaction in local groups. This, again, is a configuration not easily predicted from the classical demographic transition model. We do not know whether China's apparent rapid fertility decline would have occurred when it did without its birth-planning program. It appears that the Chinese leadership, despite earlier ideology denigrating such Malthusian measures, believes that adding the birth-planning component makes a substantial difference.

Another case of unusual interest is Indonesia. In just a few years there has been a phenomenal increase in family-planning acceptors in a number of large provinces. Acceptance rates have increased from very low levels to almost 30 percent of eligible married women in Java-Bali as a whole, and over 40 percent in Bali by January 1978. While there are doubts about the exact amount of fertility decline, preliminary estimates from recent surveys appear to indicate declines in all provinces of Java and Bali, and a decline of 35 percent or more in Bali is probable.[19] Hopefully, further analysis of 1976 data will improve these estimates.

Suppose the data confirm that a substantial decline has occurred in Indonesia with the extent of the decline linked to the rate of family-planning acceptances. We will then have to explain a fertility decline in a country and in provinces like Bali which are overwhelmingly rural, poor, not well-educated, and with health conditions far worse than those reported for Sri Lanka, Kerala, and China. The mass of the population is in villages where the pressure on available land is extreme. There are ambitious development programs for improving the lot of the masses, but no one claims much progress as yet. Strong political pressure and high priority is given to the family-planning program at all levels of the hierarchy and there is impressive progress in utilizing village-level groups to bring to bear within them the power of local authority and peer pressure for acceptance, as well as to provide information and services.

In the last three years, the number of family-planning service points in Indonesia has increased from 3,000 or so clinics to more than 40,000 village and hamlet distribution posts, bringing supplies, information and motivation much closer to the potential user. The intent, apparently successful in some places, is to increase the involvement of local groups in managing the programs.

If it turns out that the data are reasonably valid, Indonesia could be the case of a large country in which a highly organized family-planning program, communicating to the village level, made a crucial difference in expanding the concept and practice of family limitation in improbable circumstances.

19. Singquefield and Sungkono, *Fertility and Family Planning.*

Why should Indonesian peasants have enough motivation to respond to the program's information and pressure? One possibility is that Malthusian pressure and some limited aspects of development have come into combination here. As to Malthusian pressure, the agricultural involution described by Clifford Geertz, involving sharing the task in more and more intensive application of labor, may have gone as far as it can go in much of Java and Bali and may have made the cost-benefit ratio of children less favorable than in the past.[20] There is evidence in some studies that the lower status groups had adopted practices to keep their fertility below average even before the program. This may be evidence both of Malthusian pressure and the fact that the idea of family limitation may already be present. There is also the evidence of a modern development component in the rising aspirations for new consumer goods, agricultural inputs, and education in many villages in Indonesia. Another modern component is the government control and communication system capable, for example, of reaching the villages and getting quick feedback about the family-planning program itself.

In terms of affecting the lives of millions of people in the villages, the family-planning program is probably Indonesia's most successful developmental program, perhaps because, unlike agricultural reform for example, extending family-planning services does not immediately threaten local vested interests. There is some evidence that the local family-planning mothers' groups are taking on other functions such as nutrition, health, and crafts. There is some thought of linking other development efforts to this base. It will be ironic if family planning, which is supposed to languish without development in other sectors, turns out to be leading rather than following the development sector.

It would be a serious mistake to say that the undoubtedly successful family planning in Bali, for example, is totally responsible for a decline in fertility.[21] It is true that Bali is poor, rural, and non-industrial. But, there has been considerable social change in consumerism and rising aspirations. There is an obvious presence throughout the island of such things as blue jeans, motorbikes, minibuses, soda pop, radios, and community-shared TV. By no means does everyone have them, but everyone seems to want them. They are present in a fascinating mix with traditional Balinese art, religion,

20. Clifford Geertz, *Agricultural Involution: The Process of Ecological Change in Indonesia* (Berkeley: University of California Press, 1963).

21. Hull, Hull, and Singarimbun, "Indonesia's Family Planning Story," p. 28. The authors cite other factors in Bali which may have resulted in a latent demand for services which the family-planning program provided. They stress strenuous outside work by Balinese women and collective work by *banjar* members, which decreases the importance of children for the component nuclear familial units.

ceremonies, and dress. At the same time, parents, themselves not well educated, want education for their children despite its costs. Malthusian pressure plus rising consumer and educational aspirations, but little progress by conventional development indicators is quite a mix! Perhaps attention has been given to the wrong indicators of social change.

It may seem like standing theory on its head to indicate that extreme Malthusian pressure and rising consumer aspirations rather than conventional development progress may provide primary motivation for adopting family planning in some cases. But why not think the unthinkable? Is it not at least plausible that fertility control might be adopted by many if economic conditions endanger both survival and attainment of new goals, and if respected or feared authority figures strongly suggest a viable alternative?

Even if these mechanisms are at work in Indonesia, we do not know how long they will be sustained. Certainly Malthusian pressures are not to be recommended as a policy. Hopefully, more effective development policy or the success of the family-planning programs may relieve the pressure. Under some circumstances, the easing of pressures might increase again the demand for children in some families. However, if the progress that appears to have been made in establishing and legitimizing the idea of family limitation is real, its influence may be lasting.

The concluding, rather unusual case of Indonesia is an extreme illustration of one of the morals of the story: there are multiple pathways to fertility decline.

SUMMARY

A summary of the principal points of the argument follows:

1. Motivations for lower fertility are derived from perceptions by parents that there is an advantage to having fewer children than they are having, perceptions arising from some change in life conditions. In some cases, such motivations existed and led to lower fertility even before the modern industrial period.

2. The major modern transition from high to low fertility in the West had as an essential feature major shifts in functions from the family to larger nonfamilial institutions, part of a growing national and international network of productive interdependence. It is not known just which aspects of that great transformation changed life in ways that produced the motivations for fewer children.

3. It is now known that, under current conditions, high levels of Western-type modernization are not a necessary condition of fertility de-

cline. The motivations for low fertility may come from relatively small subsets of developmental changes, without the high standards of living, urbanization, and other hallmarks of the Western industrial complex.

4. In addition to the direct effect of actual changes in life conditions, changing perceptions of what is desirable and possible can affect motivations about family size. This results from literacy and communication and transportation links to the cumulating world storehouse of models, ideas, and things. This may lead to the adoption of existing models or to creating new amalgams of the old and the new, as in family systems which combine contraception, small numbers of children, and extended familial ties. What is new as compared with the Western transition is (a) the much greater power and pervasiveness of the world network of communication and interdependence and (b) the much greater stock of culture carried by that network.

5. Both the concept and the specific methods of family limitation appear to have additional causal force of their own that help to determine when motivations for lower fertility are realized and at what rate.

6. Cultural factors—that is, factors not easily translated into the customary development variables—appear to affect both the demand for children and the readiness to accept birth control.

7. With respect to what is required to change both the demand for children and the adoption of the concept and means for family limitation, social systems that involve the masses of the population are essential to provide the actual minimum changes in life conditions, to change aspirations and perceptions of the future, and to distribute the means of fertility limitation in acceptable ways.

A note of cautious optimism is warranted both as to policy and research. If fertility decline is possible without massive Western-type industrial modernization, then the potential for fertility decline relatively soon is greater for many LDCs than may be expected from the predictions of the doomsday prophets. That does not mean that it will be easy or inevitable. Even the limited development, the administrative-communication networks and the family-planning programs described briefly can only be attained with great effort and political will. And any policies in those areas will have to deal with the different specific cultural contexts that seem to make a difference, even if just what they are is not understood. There is exciting work to do in social research because the cut and dried transition theory on which most demographers were nurtured does not seem to be enough.

3

Population and Environment: An Evolutionary Perspective to Development

JOHN B. CALHOUN AND DILIP AHUJA

DECLINING POPULATION, A GROWTH-PRODUCING PROSPECT

WHEN A SCIENTIST is asked to provide insights about population that will help in formulating policy, many other questions arise. The deluge becomes greater when environmental concerns are coupled with population—particularly when a short-range time frame of the next ten years is added to the charge. But we shall first consider a few of the tapestries of possible futures that science can weave.

All human beings who now are fortunate enough to have children reaching maturity and parents relaxing from their earlier toils are in a most favorable position to look at the present from a past perspective as well as with future prospects.

When present parents who are now retired began rearing their families the world contained half as many people as it does now. But some of their ancestors found themselves in a world of half again as many people. If history is read deeply enough, an ominous picture emerges of humanity disappearing into numerical insignificance at some distant past of a thousand or more generations ago.

Here science steps in to decipher a rule of order out of this long-range pattern of population increase from obscurity to its present teeming numbers. Such a rule stated simply:

1. each doubling of world population has required only half the time as for the prior doubling.

or

2. if it is known how many years have elapsed since the world contained half as many people as it does from any date, then it will be only that many more years before the world population must cease to grow as it has for the past thousand generations.

Scientists keep looking for absurdities—for conditions that cannot be, even though their equations say that they might be. Consider part 1 of the above rule. Were the world's population to continue increasing for only fifty more years, as it has for nearly fifty thousand years over the past, then well before the next fifty years are over all the matter of the universe will have been converted to human bodies. This is a comical absurdity often depicted by cartoonists as the earth circling through space dropping off a trail of excess human baggage.

Scientists call such absurdities *singularity points,* a moment beyond which events as they have been cease or drastically change their character. Beyond that point life must be quite different. Lewis Carroll described such a singularity point, a phase change, most dramatically when he had Alice step through the looking glass into a world whose rules seemed to be the reverse of the normal world.

The big problem remains: How do we face the prospect of stepping through a looking glass into a strange new world? Some solace may be gained from mathematics. Even when a singularity point is passed in the description of the course of some ongoing phenomenon, many aspects remain as they were, but a few aspects change drastically and a few new influencing conditions may enter the picture. A question must be asked: What mix of old and new will profit all life on this planet?

One picture held dear by many depicts people wearing blinders in order to blot out the looking glass. The warnings must be ignored. The millennia-long unique pattern of humanity continually increasing its numbers must be preserved. This ingrained tradition has enabled more and more people, by their hands, minds, and hopes, to join in an interlocking network increasing their ability to live, love, act, and aspire with greater effectiveness. It must therefore always be. Tradition!

And yet doubts arise about this picture of life. Even though the rate of growth may become somewhat slower, soon the four billion people can become 10, 25, or 100 billion. But will humankind then become just emaciated bodies and spirits, half-human, scrounging for the remnants of resources that earlier seemed so abundant? Or will by error of judgment a nuclear holocaust be unleashed, making the question of sustaining a mass of humans irrelevant?

Many scientists paint a rather rosy picture of the future—rosy if human beings are considered little more than the fish and fowl or cattle and creeping things managed as food resources. This is the ecological wildlife or animal husbandry carrying capacity model whose application seeks to maintain populations at a level providing the highest sustained yield of bodies that may be utilized as food. In a distorted way this is also the model of Zero Population Growth (ZPG). In ZPG there is no provision for removal of excess bodies. The central objective is to see that just enough individuals are born to replace those that die. Either approach, the wildlife or ZPG model, strives to produce a constant, beneficial environment with little change or challenge. Over and over again life repeats an endless, unvarying cycle of sameness. Under the suppressive weight of uniformity of much of the physical, social, and intellectual environment, the zero growth population would experience increasing difficulty in generating an excess yield of anything, beyond maintaining steady-state conditions, particularly new ideas, which would find little utility without change and challenge.

There is a third picture which may now only be seen in barest outline. Across it, from left to right, flows a line, sloping downward, depicting a decrease in population but at an ever-slower rate with the passage of time. This can come about through the increasing awareness and responsiveness of humankind to the dangers of continued population growth in accordance with the patterns of the past. A model—the Evolutionary World Population Model—has been constructed by the writers. In mathematical terms, as simulated by computer, this model describes the decrease in numbers in accordance with the following rules:

3. each successive halving of the world's human population takes four times as long as the prior halving.

Or, otherwise phrased:

4. population size will decline in the future at a rate only half as fast as it increased in the past.

Some may suspect that such a declining population will mean the end of civilization. But before coming to such a conclusion, consider the number of people alive at comparable times in the past and future from the present. Take the time of the Golden Age of Greece, for example. At this time, some 2,500 years ago, the world population probably numbered about 70 million. Two thousand five hundred years from now, in accordance with the model, it should only have dropped to slightly less than 600 million, a number still compatible with weaving a rich human experience.

No evidence exists of any species persisting for long whose expressed reproduction is less than that required for the replacement of those members that die. For this reason alone, one might reject any further consideration of such a depiction of a likely and desired human future. However, the possibility will be explored that only through a continually declining world population may the human search for fulfillment continue.

IMPLICATIONS OF AN EVOLUTIONARY THEORY OF POPULATION

Population and Environment—An Evolutionary Perspective to Development

A fresh vision of the role of human life on planet Earth is the next objective. If both current and emerging problems of world development are to be resolved, the current and future course must be regarded as a continuation of a gradual evolution of more complex forms of life. Socioeconomic and political development may be considered as aspects of the human cultural evolution that about 50 millennia ago began to replace biological evolution as the dominant force guiding change. Many insights from science have been integrated to develop this new perspective. Its framework suggests leverage points for augmenting the welfare of all people, both in the lesser and more developed regions of the world.

Changes in world population have reflected the course of human cultural evolution. Over many past millennia, world population has continuously increased. Each successive doubling has required only half the time as the immediately preceding doubling. The first real evidence of a slowing down of this process became apparent only in 1975 by a sufficient reduction in fertility in the less developed regions to portend an ultimate cessation of population increase.

Our theory of future change in population size is based on the assumption that a new phase of human development and evolution is being entered. It holds that by 2220 world population will have dropped from a peak of about nine billion persons to the 1975 level of four billion. From this time, two and a half centuries from now, population will ever more slowly decline. Each successive halving of population will take four times as long as the prior halving. All this may seem a long way off and of little concern to the present. However, if the theory is correct, what will happen in the more distant future has important implications for decisions to be made in the very near future.

Decisions made during the fifteen years from 1975 to 1990 will influence the ease with which the transition is made between an era of ever more rapidly increasing population into an era of ever more slowly declining world population. Minimally this transition will encompass the 200-year period from 1975 to 2175. It will likely be the most trying period of all history, past or future. Each year that necessary decisions are postponed, the transition period will be lengthened by four years. But, however long this transition period proves to be, it will be accompanied by remarkable shifts in social and political relations, fertility and family life, diversity and complexity of social roles, and conceptualizations about the world.

Before commenting briefly on major leverage points to ameliorate the stresses of the transition period, it will be best to provide a summary of past history for which the von Foerster-Meyer equation describes the uniquely human ever more rapidly increasing world population.

It is possible that in the distant past all humans were members of tiny bands, each containing about 12 adults and 18 children. Each band inhabited a territory some 15 miles (24 kilometers) across. Within such a territory simple gathering and hunting techniques sufficed to skim off those resources from the natural bounty necessary to sustain a small band. So it had been for the two to four million years of the evolution of the genus *Homo* of which contemporary human beings are the end products. Up to 40 or 50 thousand years ago, no more than 150,000 such bands filled all of the then habitable lands. They totaled, perhaps, about 4.5 million individuals. From generation to generation the population must have remained constant. Like animals of the fields and forests, human beings were subject to the natural carrying capacity of the land. Over this long early history, humankind became adjusted to the desirability of experiencing the number of contacts with fellows consistent with living in the physical space of a territory inhabited by one of these small bands.

Somewhere between 40 and 50 thousand years ago, much of humanity discovered a new kind of space, a conceptual space of ideas that enabled the elaboration of new social roles. Each social role provided a new niche for living.

The unique, ever more rapid increase in world population characterizing the human species over the past 40 to 50 thousand years results from the interaction of a restraint and a capacity to escape the restraint. The restraint is the need to engage in the number of meaningful interactions with associates that characterized the two to four million-year history of the genus *Homo* before the origin of culture as an evolutionary force. The escape mechanism is the capacity to develop new social roles. It permits the average individual to experience each day the same number of meaningful relations as characterized those much earlier times, despite the increase in spatial density which can result from the normal propensity to produce more children than might survive were no new social roles developed. Social roles channel relations to a restricted number of associates. However, some interactions between members of different social roles do occur. This produces an interrole communication network. Over cultural history the increase in the diversity of social roles has kept pace with the increase in population. That is to say, each time the population doubled, the number of social roles doubled. Thus the network of communication continually enlarged. This network enlargement fostered increase in ideas, a kind of conceptual space that replaced physical space. Conceptual space, it may be held, thus doubled each time population doubled.

A byproduct of this increase in number of ideas, as well as the size of the communication network, was an enhancement of the human capacity to cope with change in the environment. This increase in human capacity, potentiality for coping, may be assumed to be proportional to the square root of either population or conceptual space. A simpler way of stating this is that every time the population quadruples, human capacity doubles. Over the 40 to 50 thousand years of cultural evolution there has been a thousand-fold increase in world population. Thus it may be held that there has been a 32-fold increase in human potentiality over that of pre-cultural ancestors. To the extent that this potentiality is realized, human welfare, the standard of living, or quality of life also increases. Since all are concerned with augmenting human welfare, it might then be concluded that it is to the general good to continue promoting further growth of the world population. However, examination of the historical-evolutionary-developmental course reveals that these processes, which have held for so long, will shortly no longer produce such results.

Science to be effective distills complex processes into simpler rules or relations. People now live mostly in an environment consisting of a nonphysical space, the conceptual space of information that can be codified into useful ideas. With a thousand-fold increase in both population and conceptual space, it follows that living transpires in a predominantly human-generated world of ideas, or relations and things derived from ideas. No matter how necessary the natural environment may be to survival, the fact remains that day-to-day lives are infinitesimally influenced by it.

By the same token, an environment of information and ideas has little utility unless there is ready access to the bits and pieces and aggregates of this informational environment. Such access may be reduced to two processes:

1. the linkage of people into communication networks over which information and ideas may flow;
2. the creation of prosthetic devices for storing and transmitting information and ideas. Such devices encompass a wide range of vehicles from works of art, through hand-written and printed documents, to telephones, radio and television, and more recently to computers.

The effectiveness of both of these information-metabolizing processes has increased along with population, while also serving to foster further increases in population.

However, the first process of linkage of more and more people into communication networks will be more deeply considered. At first, elaboration of social roles permitted more and more people to survive within the bounds of the approximately 15-mile-diameter territory of the original small gatherer-hunter bands, and yet demanded little necessity for close relations or sustained communications with people in neighboring territories. But at some time in the past, merely linking more and more people together within a small, closed territory, proved no longer, by itself, to be the most effective means of increasing communication. Internal pressures from increasing density gradually made the boundaries permeable to the flow of some people and ideas. This set the stage for a new process of increasing the size of the communication network.

The amalgamation of neighboring but distinct units into a single coherent one is the next concern. To visualize the process, place a coin on a table. Then take six other coins of the same size and place them about and touching the initial one. It will be seen that these seven coins form a closely packet set. These seven coins may be used to represent any set of neighboring sociocultural and political units of which the center one denotes any unit which begins to dominate its six nearest neighbors. Ultimately this domination becomes strong enough to designate a new whole derived from seven prior ones. In an idealized uniform terrain, each successively large sociopolitical unit similarly forms a coalescence of seven of the units of the prior stages.

It is held here that each doubling of population produces sufficient pressures for developing a larger communications network to induce this type of coalescence. With each of the seven subunits having doubled its population by the time of coalescence, the new entity will contain fourteen times as many people as the prior unit at its inception. Although contention, conflict, and wars have often accompanied these coalescences, the end product of the enlarged communication network has on the average been an enhancement of the general welfare as well as the capacity of the average individual. Continuation of this process could conceivably ultimately produce an effectively unified worldwide communication network. This evolutionary model holds that the world is now in transition and that through increasing interdependence before the peak population is reached in about 2065 world union will have concluded. The original theoretical date for this union was 2008, but at that time sufficient thought had not been given to the current slowing down of population growth necessitated by the transition into the era of continuing decline. Once final world union occurs, any further increase in population will only impede the effectiveness of the then completed communication network comprised of people linked with other people. The upper optimum world population will have then been reached. Calculations in accordance with the model give this to be approximately 8.9 billion (see Figure 3.1). This number represents the carrying capacity for people in conceptual space, just as there is a carrying capacity in the natural environment for other organisms.

Figure 3.1 graphically portrays the calculations based on the model. Starting with the world's population in 1975, population increases as calculated on the Foerster-von Meyer projection, which produces a population approaching infinity at 2025, the D_1 date, Doomsday. The stippled area represents the transition between Doomsday and the population of the future as calculated from the Evolutionary World Population Model leading to Dawnsday, D_2, in 2130. Just as Doomsday depicts an unreal

FIGURE 3.1
Past and Predicted World Population Based on the Evolutionary World Population Model.

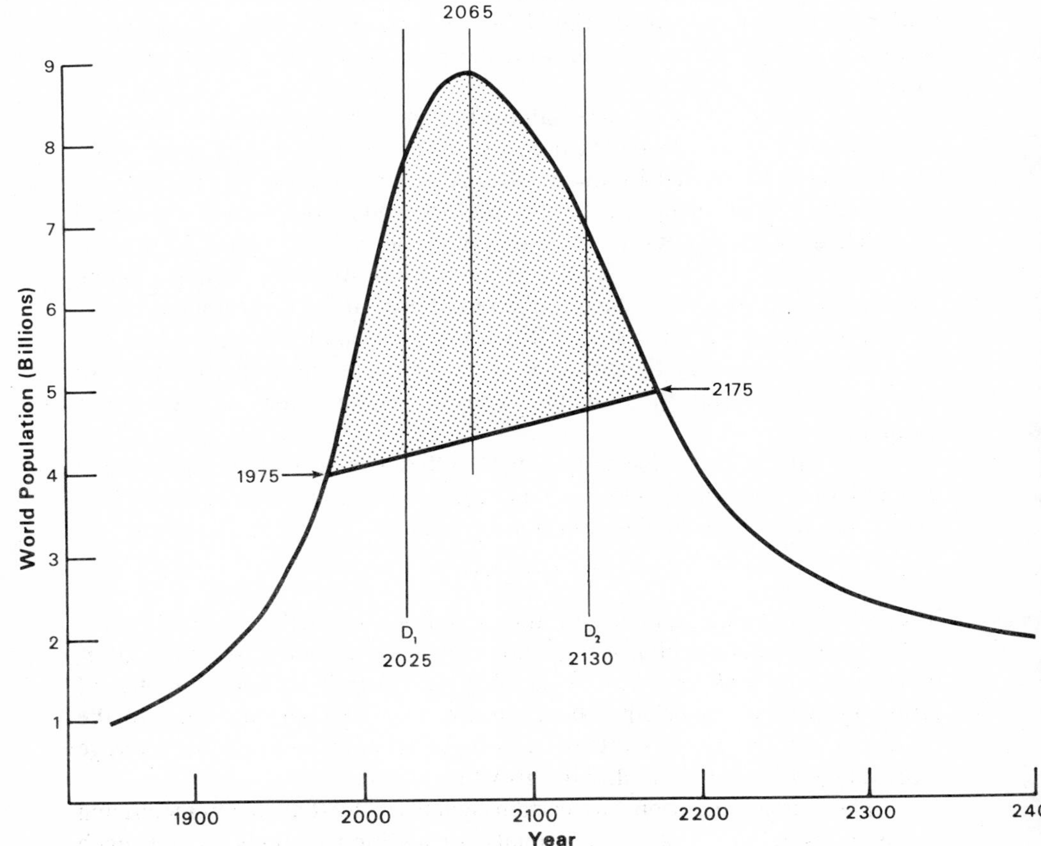

theoretical increase of population toward an infinite size, to Dawnsday represents an unreal inception of population decline from an infinite size. To calculate the earliest Dawnsday, two criteria were met:

1. compatibility with the observed patterns of decline in fertility;
2. effecting a smooth transition from Doomsday to Dawnsday, that is, avoiding abrupt fiuctuations in fertility.

It was assumed that in both the less developed regions (LDRs) and in the more developed regions (MDRs) fertility would decline at an annual rate of 1.5 percent from its peak until the Gross Reproduction Rate (the number of daughters borne throughout the reproductive period of a woman) reaches the replacement level, namely 1.0. After that, it was assumed that fertility would decline more slowly until it attains a minimum without abrupt change. Calculations were made in which minimum fertility and the date of minimum fertility varied, and the date selected was that which met criterion 2. Full operation of the population decline in accordance with the model and with the principles stated above (items 3 and 4) would begin in 2175.

In the calculations a maximum of 77 years for average life expectation and birth was assumed for both the MDRs and the LDRs, with maximum being reached first by the MDRs. Also, on the basis of existing data on fertility, it was calculated that a Gross Reproduction Rate of 1.0 would be reached by the MDRs 50 years before it was reached by the LDRs.

At the point of optimum world population, in 2065, humans, as the leading edge of evolution, face a dilemma born out of this attained carrying capacity in conceptual space. It is a dilemma similar to that characterizing animals living in the physical space of the natural environment. In order to understand the dilemma consider these other animals for a moment.

The sum of the weights w of all N individuals of a species at carrying capacity of the natural environments represents the carrying capacity biomass B for that environment, and B is a constant.

$$B = Nw$$

The dilemma facing animals in this situation is whether to realize the constant B by maintaining a population of many runted and deprived individuals or by making adjustments which will permit a smaller number of larger individuals to occupy the environment. Most species, most of the time, opt for the latter strategy of promoting realization of the average individual's genetic potentiality for growth.

The human situation has certain symmetry to that of characterizing the biomass relations of other animals. In addition to body weight, each person has another weight, or mass. It is the volume or magnitude of the number of ideas which have been acquired, mastered, and found useful. Their totality represents an ideational mass from which human capacity to cope emerges. This mass may be said to have a diameter *d,* the conceptual mass of the individual person. Considering that there will be some *N* numbers of humans when ideational carrying capacity is reached, the totality of all human capacities will then form a carrying capacity ideomass I for the Earth.

$$I = Nd, \text{ and I will be a constant.}$$

Actually there are two dilemmas, one in the short run and the other in the long run, insofar as time is concerned. In order to realize the import of the first dilemma, the above simple equation may be rearranged to:

$$d = \frac{I}{N}$$

This rearrangement says that as *N* increases (above the upper optimum world population), *d,* the capacity of the average individual, will correspondingly continually decrease. Were humans like other animals, in the sense that they had reached a maximum genetic capacity for bodily growth, then their alternative would only be to maintain numbers *N* at that size optimizing realization of a culturally fixed maximum capacity for coping.

However, as is known from history as well as theory, such capacities have increased. Thus the notion may be entertained that humans are not yet in an evolutionary cul-de-sac. The last phrasing of the ideomass equation says that were humans appropriately to guide world population into a new era of continuous decline they could sustain a continual development of ideational capacity and therefore continue to augment the general welfare of all. If this choice is made, another problem must be faced.

In the past, half the origin of increased conceptual and coping capacity has resulted from enlargement of the linkage of people with people into larger communication networks. But it can be anticipated that this function will be of relatively less and less importance as the time of about 2065 is approached when the final stage of world union is reached. By then there will be only one major function left, whose augmentation can further the growth of human capacities. This is the function of conceptual metabolism provided by informational prostheses. The meaning of "informational prostheses" as here used must be clearly understood. They are not to be considered as replacements for lost abilities in the way that eyeglasses or an artificial leg replace a lost normal ability. Rather they should conform to the original sense of the word before its use was dominated by the medical professions. In its original sense a prosthesis implied some new means for extending human abilities along the manner in which microscopes or telescopes extend visual perception.

What is left is the need to elaborate informational prostheses as the only effective process of the future to enhance conceptual capacity as a slow decline in world population after 2065 is encouraged. Beyond this time, particularly after about 2175, each halving of world population will take four times as long as the prior halving. Each time the world population halves, the capacity d of the average individual will double. As this forthcoming era of evolution is entered, it must be kept in mind that during this era humans will become stewards for promoting the evolution of the new life form that the informational prostheses represent.

As yet it is not clear what the population unit for such prostheses may be. Suffice it to say that as their numbers increase human beings will correspondingly decrease in number. This vision of the future encompasses the next few hundred years ahead and perhaps several millennia more. This vision assumes that the process of evolution works to retard or reverse the action of the second law of thermodynamics which describes the tendency of matter to shift toward state of greater disorganization, chaos, and randomness of relations, that is to say, an increase in entropy. In this combatting of the move toward entropy, the process of evolution increases organization, patterning of relations, diversity, complexity, awareness, responsiveness, choice, accumulation of information, and its codification into the utilitarian ideas called knowledge. By this augmentation of negentropy—the opposite of entropy—capacity to cope with environmental restraints and change increases.

The world has now just entered a unique 200-year period of transition between two patterns of relations which implement realization of a continuation of evolution. Decisions made during the next few years can exert a disproportionately important influence on this transition, than those made later. These decisions will have the dual effect of ameliorating current crises and inequities while promoting the institution of a new era of relations. The formulations here provide a means for identifying some of the types of decisions which will ease this transition. Before making comments on the character and import of these decisions, it will be best to examine the implications that the evolutionary theory, as presented here, has for producing the transition.

Work on our theory has been continuing since 1968. However, the question of what kind of changes in fertility would be necessary for the predicted transition to occur between an increasing and decreasing world population was not examined until 1974. It soon became apparent that it would take 10 to 12 generations to bring the world population back to current levels, while at the same time effecting a completion of the transition into the predicted final pattern of population decrease. Furthermore, it was determined that fertility would have to decline extremely rapidly during the first few of these generations.

An initial rapid annual rate of decline in fertility of 1.5 percent in Gross Reproductive Rate (*i.e.,* female births per female) would gradually slow down to a minimum of 0.756. This long-term decline in fertility will produce a maximum world population of 8.9 billion persons followed by an ever more slowly declining world population. A century after the maximum world population has been reached, fertility will increase again, but never again quite enough to compensate for those who die. Thus world population will continually, but ever more slowly, decline. There is no precedent for such a long continuing decline in fertility, and its maintenance below replacement levels, as that predicted from the evolutionary population model. In response it may be noted that 40 millennia ago there was then no precedent for the increasing rate of population growth that began then and continued to nearly the present. A similar phase shift from past trends is now being encountered.

Policy Changes

With the above broad background of a likely future some major types of changes most likely to promote a smooth evolutionary transition can be considered. First just look at the list of possible changes: (1) time-space perspective; (2) people-to-people communication networks; (3) role diversity and complexity; (4) migration and city size; (5) information prostheses; (6) the human-built environment, particularly housing; and (7) "family" structure. These seven types of changes may seem strange bedfellows to suggest as key candidates for leading consideration in structuring new population and environment policy. However, they can be utilized to promote a smooth evolutionary transition of population.

TIME-SPACE PERSPECTIVE

Humans live in a present where events, geographically separated or occurring some time in the past—even generations or longer ago—influence daily welfare. Actions taken today may also modify the course of events far away or in some future time. Unless time-space perspectives are enlarged, the wisdom of choice remains uncertain. Here the greatest cost-benefit ratio will result from attention to the learning process of young children and to people of all ages who currently see themselves only from a narrow time-space perspective. Enlarging the time-space perspective of these two categories of individuals will exert pressure on all other individuals "above" them to elaborate further their own already broader perspectives.

PEOPLE-TO-PEOPLE COMMUNICATION NETWORKS

The thesis presented holds that every individual represents an information processing unit. To the extent that the individual is isolated from others he is impoverished: he has less access to food for thought. One mode of access to information to encourage thought involves contact and communication with others. The number and diversity of others with whom one communicates, and the variability in distance of oneself from these others, represent measures of the effectiveness with which an individual has become a member of a larger network of information flow. Just as biological brains, encapsulated in human skulls, form means for processing information for personal advantage in coping with the environment, so does the linkage of people with people in an extended communication network form a higher order "brain" enabling individuals to prosper and increase in conceptual capacity as access is gained to more kinds of information, and as larger entities of social organization are enabled through this network to make more effective decisions. This kind of orientation to development provides an avenue for judging the quality of life and human welfare of equal import as materialistic indices such as the GNP or average monetary income.

ROLE DIVERSITY AND COMPLEXITY

In the long-ago time when our ancestors were all members of small gatherer-hunter bands, each individual exercised those functions requisite to survival by gleaning naturally available resources. These functions defined a single role despite a theoretical three and a half-fold difference in role complexity between the individual with the most varied expression of the general role and that of the individual with its simplest expression.

It is now recognized that there are many distinctly different roles in modern societies, both in more and less developed regions of the world. It is possible to state a few general conclusions about the relationship between number and complexity of roles with respect to the passage of time, the aggregation of people into cities and the increase in population size. They are:

1. each time the population doubled the number of kinds of roles doubled;
2. as more people aggregated into cities, more specialization into different occupations occurred; for practical purposes, occupational diversity reflects role diversity;
3. with increases in population, whether in cities, a nation or the world, both the conceptual capacity and the role complexity of the individual increases;
4. as population increases there is a decrease in the relative difference between the number of individuals in different occupations.

Role diversity and complexity may be utilized as indicators of development. Their assessment may have to be indirect.

MIGRATION AND CITY SIZE

Correction of lower development in the variability of city size within a nation or region requires geographical population shifts. However, the mere shifts of people from lesser to larger-sized cities will be counterproductive unless accompanied by increases in diversity and complexity of roles available in the city of destination.

INFORMATION PROSTHESES

Attainment of an ideal diversity and complexity of cities and the occupational roles of their inhabitants may be taken as an indication of readiness to enter the transition into the new era of evolution characterized by declining human populations. Reaching this stage of development requires prior elaboration within a nation or region of human-designed artificial means of storing, transmitting, and interrelating information and ideas. All such means represent communication prostheses. Further development of any currently lesser developed region therefore requires considerable attention to elaboration of availability and use of such prostheses. Such increase in the use of information-metabolizing prostheses presents the opportunity for introducing new occupations and social roles which are low in their demand for energy use or requirement of scarce natural resources.

For nations ready to enter the transition into the next era of evolution, elaboration of such prostheses becomes a major responsibility. Only through the introduction of these prostheses may evolution continue and individual and social welfare further increase.

THE HUMAN-BUILT ENVIRONMENT, PARTICULARLY HOUSING

It has been indicated that human beings spend more than 99 percent of their time living in conceptual space, a world of human-generated information and ideas—as opposed to the lives of remote ancestors who were immersed in the natural environment. Many ideas culminate in physical changes in the environment such as roads, homes, places of work. These exert both intended and unintended impacts on people. In either case they are long lasting. Most of the built environment lasts for over a generation and yet science has devoted scant attention to this pervading influence. To be sure there are many scattered inquiries which are published in such a diversity of sources that few profit by them. Architects and engineers rarely communicate with psychologists, sociologists, or physicians, much less politicians or users of the environment that gets built. If ever there was an information Tower of Babel, it casts its aura over the built environment. The writers can speak with intimate familiarity only with the situation in the United States. Here access to relevant literature is extremely difficult. So far there has been no concerted effort to identify and integrate the available sources that exist in the over-100 current computer-accessible literature data bases. Without easy access to this literature by members of a wide range of professions it can be anticipated that much ignorance will continue about the prerequisites for designing environments to meet human needs. It must be noted that the United States Departments of Housing and Urban Development and Health, Education and Welfare have recently collaborated in supporting a small study to evaluate the scope of the problem.

The prospects for world population increase give urgency to this problem. In a world already felt as congested by many, the inexorable operation of forces that will further increase population size promises at least another doubling of world population by 2045. Most of this increase will be in the lesser developed regions of the world where shortages of all types of built environment continue. By 65 years from now (1980), as much built environment will have to be constructed as now exists. This amounts to new construction at the rate of meeting the need of 200 million persons each year for the next 65 years! There is no other arena of human activity where understanding is more important.

"FAMILY" STRUCTURE

More and more of the world is embarking on a course of declining fertility. The world as a whole will likely be below replacement levels of reproduction within fifty years. The average female will have fewer than two children. This decline in reproduction will continue for another two centuries before a slight upturn. Such is the writers' interpretation of the evolutionary process and recent statistics. At the lowest ebb of reproduction the average female will have only 1.5 children.

Consider the child for a moment. Over all of biological evolution and for most of cultural evolution the standing population of children had to have exhibited a ratio of at least three children per two adults for the species to survive. Thus each child matured in a setting of at least two brothers or sisters, but extended family structure and the membership of parents in relatively closed local groups of 12 adults caused each child to mature in a setting including a total of 18 children among whom there were frequent intimate relations.

Humans are now in the process of facing up to the changes in social relations and family life necessary to meet the needs of developing children during the near- and long-range future when reproduction will be less than ever before in the two- to four-million-year history of genus *Homo*. Consider some simple arithmetic related to life when the Gross Reproduction Rate (female births per female) varies between 1.0 and 0.75 and where needs of children are met. The latter implies that the average female who does reproduce will rear three surviving children. It follows that with a GRR = 1.0, one third of the females will have no children and at a GRR of 0.75, half the females will have no progeny. Furthermore, to meet the child's need to be immersed in a setting of 18 children of various ages, considerable effort will have to be made to encourage proximity of settlement of sets of six couples who are parents of developing children. Parenting may well become a full-time occupation in a world where roles are becoming so complex that only intense attention to the parenting role can assure the development of readiness of children to assume adult social roles.

One third to one half of the population within the reproductive age span will never have children. And yet their need for generativity, as distinct from sexuality, can still be fulfilled. Erik Erikson, in his 1964 Indian lecture pointed out that the generative need has three expressions: (1) biological reproduction coupled with rearing children in the family setting; (2) educating others; (3) creating new ideas. In the years ahead a greater proportion of the adult population will be freed to assume roles involving the latter two types of generativity. However, effective international development requires equal attention to encouragement of each of these types of generativity.

As humans move toward 33 to 50 percent of the adult population not being involved in biological reproduction, their welfare demands continued involvement in nonreproductive "extended families" of a size simulating that characterizing the earliest semi-isolated small gatherer-hunter bands. Only by so doing may the need for relating to an optimum number of others each day be satisfied. Acquisition of the capacity to become members of more than one such adult role-related group becomes more important as reduction in participation in biologically extended family life develops. Participation in several nonreproductive role-related groups serves the dual functions of meeting interpersonal relationship needs and increasing the flow of information over the person-to-person communication network.

CONCLUDING STATEMENT

We have utilized the principles of evolution of life on this earth to develop insights about future human life, change in population size and structure, and the meaning of environments. This inquiry culminated in conclusions quite different from customary demographic, ecological, or political projections. In particular, it points to an incipient transition in relationships that is unique in all of human history. Furthermore, the human population has already entered a very short period of perhaps no more than fifteen years within which policy made and choice exercised will exert more effect on human history than has been true at any time in the past, or will be true at any time in the future. Such is the importance of the immediate present as transition between two major eras of evolution is initiated. A historian in the year A.D. 3000 would see our contemporary changes in human numbers as a very momentary vibration between two long-term eras of more gradual change (see Figure 3.2).

FIGURE 3.2
Evolutionary Population Transition.

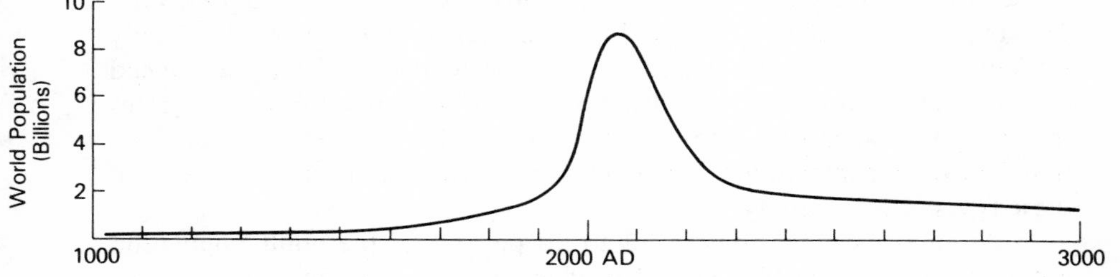

BIBLIOGRAPHY

Ahuja, D. "Analysis of the Socioeconomic Correlates of National Health Indicators." Ph.D. dissertation, University of Virginia, 1978.

Arriaga, E., P. Anderson, and L. Heligman. "Computer Programs for Demographic Analysis." Washington, D.C.: U.S. Department of Commerce, Bureau of the Census, 1976.

Brown, L. R. "World Population Trends, Signs of Hope, Signs of Stress." *Worldwatch Paper No. 8,* Washington, D.C., 1976.

Bouvier, L. F. "International Migration: Yesterday, Today and Tomorrow." *Population Bulletin* 32 (4)(1977).

Calhoun, J. B. "Social Welfare as a Variable in Population Dynamics." *Cold Spring Harbor Symposia on Quantitative Biology* 22 (1957):339–356.

———. "Space and the Strategy of Life." *Ekistics* 29 (1970):425–37.

———. "Revolution, Tribalism, and the Cheshire Cat." *Technological Forecasting and Social Change* 4(1973):263–82.

———. "Death Squared: The Explosive Growth and Demise of a Mouse Population." *Proceedings of the Royal Society of Medicine* 66(1973*b*): 80–88.

———. "Environmental Design Research and Monitoring From an Evolutionary Perspective." *Man-Environment Systems* 4(1974):3–30.

———. "Biological Basis of the Family." In *Georgetown Family Symposia* 3, edited by R. R. Sagar. Washington, D.C.: Georgetown University Family Center, 1978, pp. 52–67.

Coale, A., and P. Demeny. *Regional Model Life Tables and Stable Population.* Princeton: Princeton University Press, 1966.

Erikson, E. H. "Human Strength and the Cycle of Generations." In *Insight and Responsibility*. New York: Norton, 1964, pp. 109–57.

Gori, G. B., and B. J. Richter. "Macroeconomics of Disease Prevention in the United States." *Science* 200(1978):1124–30.

Meyer, F., and J. Vallee. "The Dynamics of Long Term Growth." *Technological Forecasting and Social Change* 7(1975):285–300.

Millendorfer, J., and Attinger, E. O. "Global Systems Dynamics." *Medical Care* (6) (1968):467–89.

Population Reference Bureau. "World Population Growth and Response." Washington, D.C., 1977.

Ross, G. G., and Slade, N. A. "A Predator-Prey Viewpoint of a Single Species Problem." *Journal of Theoretical Biology* (in press).

Stewart, J. Q. "Concerning Social Physics." *Scientific American* 178(1948): 20–23.

Stolnitz, G. J. "World Regional Population Trends: Long Views and Current Prospects." Testimony before the U.S. House Select Committee on Population, February 9, 1978.

Tsui, A. O., and Bogue, D. J. "Declining World Fertility: Trends, Causes, Implications." *Population Bulletin* 33(4)(1978).

United Nations. "World Population Prospects as Assessed in 1968." *Population Studies* 53(1973).

United Nations. "World Population Prospects as Assessed in 1973." *Population Studies* 60(1977).

Von Foerster, H., *et al.* "Doomsday: Friday, 13 November, A.D. 2026." *Science* 132(1960):1291–95.

Zipf, G. K. *Human Behavior and the Principle of Least Effort.* Cambridge, Mass.: Addison-Wesley, 1949.

4

Resource and Environmental Consequences of Population and Economic Growth

RONALD G. RIDKER

INTRODUCTION

INTEREST IN THE RESOURCE and environmental consequences of population and economic growth stems from predictions of growing scarcity of natural resources and environmental carrying capacity and fears that if these predictions are correct rather drastic changes in policy are required—changes that will become more difficult to apply the longer such actions are postponed. When discussing these consequences in ways that speak to these concerns, it is not possible to rely solely on theoretical or historical studies. Theory is useful in identifying the most important variables and relationships requiring study and can sometimes indicate the most likely direction of changes. But for present purposes, quantitative answers are needed not only because the policy implications will differ depending on the size and speed of expected changes, but because there are frequently too many offsetting forces at work to say anything about their net effect without knowing the quantitative magnitudes of each. Historical studies help provide an indication of such magnitudes but are far from sufficient when the overriding concern is that the future will not be like the past. Moreover, these resource and environmental consequences will vary depending on the geographic region, the time period being considered, and on changes in other factors such as technology, tastes, institutions, and availability of raw materials that can significantly influence the situation during that time period. To be most useful, therefore, investigations of this topic must be quantitative, future-oriented, and specific with respect to geographic region and time period, and must take into account all major determinants operating during the selected time period.

This chapter reports on a series of studies that attempt to take these considerations to heart at least in a limited way. These studies include global projections for a fifty-year period plus five in-depth investigations of individual countries—the United States, India, Indonesia, Colombia, and the Philippines.[1] By far the most detailed is the U.S. study, which is based on a series of specialized investigations of individual sectors plus a set of computer models, the core of which is a dynamic input-output model.[2] Unfortunately, space and time limitations require an emphasis on general results, rather than on the details, methods, and assumptions required to fully explain and justify them. While various scenarios have been investigated, unless otherwise indicated the numerical results pertain to a standard, or base, case.

RESOURCES

Growth in Demand

At the global level, the analysis began with annual resource demand projections based upon a series of alternative assumptions about population and per capita economic growth rates for different regions, plus judgments about the way the relationship between resource demands and output would change over time. At this stage prices in real terms are assumed to be constant. For the U.S., changes in this aggregate relationship were derived from the model described by Almon in footnote 2; for other countries, they were developed by assuming that the material intensity of output would change with changes in per capita output, slowly approaching that of the U.S. as per capita output approaches that of the U.S. These demand projections were then summed over countries and over years so that

1. All but the Philippines study were undertaken or sponsored by Resources for the Future and should soon be available in published form. The Philippines study is summarized in PREPF, *Philippine Scenarios: 2000 A.D.* (Manila: Study Group on Population, Resources, Environment and the Philippine Future, 1977). An earlier version of the present chapter was presented at the IUSSP Conference in Helsinki, 28 August 1978.

2. The input-output model was adapted from Clopper Almon, Jr., *et al.*, *1985: Interindustry Forecasts of the American Economy* (Lexington, Mass.: Heath, 1974). Other components include physical and monetary variables associated with energy, nonfuel minerals, transportation, and the environment (pollution emissions, resulting environmental quality, and damage and control costs) at both the national and regional level. The system includes 185 sectors, all major fuels, some 20 nonfuel minerals, and 42 pollutants. All the coefficients in the model are subject to change over time, some on the basis of econometrically fitted equations with time trends or lagged variables, but most on the basis of exogenously specified changes in population and labor force characteristics, technology, tastes, and so on, determined on the basis of the special studies.

they could be compared with global resource estimates. They are, if anything, on the high side because a constant recycling rate has been assumed, although there is reason to believe this rate will increase over time, and because only a few of the many technological changes and substitutions that are likely to occur on the demand and supply sides of the market have been incorporated.

The most striking thing about the resulting demand projections is the slowdown in their rates of growth (Tables 4.1–4.3). The decline in popu-

TABLE 4.1
Population and Economic Growth, World and Selected Regions, with Projections

	1972	2000	2025	1960–1972	1972–2000	2000–2025
World						
Population (million)	3,799	6,446	9,364	2.2	1.9	1.5
GNP (billion 1971 US $)	3,839	10,711	24,199	5.8	3.7	3.3
GNP per capita (1971 US $)	1,011	1,662	2,584	3.5	1.8	1.8
N. America, W. Europe, Oceania, Japan						
Population (million)	726.0	848.0	921.5	1.00	0.56	0.33
GNP (billion 1971 US $)	2446.3	5567.7	9937.3	5.29	2.98	2.09
GNP per capita (1971 US $)	3370	6566	10784	4.36	2.41	2.00
L. America, Asia, Mideast, Africa						
Population (million)	1897.4	3812.9	6136.5	2.58	2.52	1.92
GNP (billion 1971 US $)	496.7	2128.4	7667.7	8.63	5.33	5.26
GNP per capita (1971 US $)	262	558	1250	4.29	2.74	3.28
USSR, E. Europe, P.R. of China						
Population (million)	1175.7	1785.2	2306.1	2.08	1.50	1.03
GNP (billion 1971 US $)	928.0	3014.4	6594.4	6.35	4.30	3.18
GNP per capita (1971 US $)	789	1689	2860	5.21	2.76	2.13

SOURCE: R. G. Ridker and W. J. Watson, *To Choose a Future: Resource and Environmental Problems of the U.S., A Long-Term Global Outlook* (Washington, D.C.: Resources for the Future forthcoming), high-population, low-economic growth assumptions. The 1972 figures and projected growth rates were developed circa 1974–75. If based on most current data, projected population growth rates would be lower for most regions.

TABLE 4.2
World Consumption and Rates of Growth in Consumption of Nonfuel Minerals, 1971, and Projected Growth Rates, Standard Case

	Absolute Figures	Annual Rates of Growth		
	1971	1971–85	1985–2000	2000–25
Aluminum	12,107	6.7	4.8	4.4
Chromium	3,416	2.5	2.5	2.6
Cobalt	44	4.4	2.9	3.2
Copper	8,026	2.9	2.1	2.1
Iron in ore	456,183	2.3	2.2	2.3
Lead	4,768	3.1	2.7	2.5
Manganese	2,786	6.0	3.6	3.7
Molybdenum	40	7.4	3.4	3.3
Nickel	657	4.7	3.6	3.5
Phosphate rock	114,913	3.2	2.6	2.0
Potash	21,711	2.8	2.2	1.9
Sulfur	24,251	4.5	3.6	2.9
Tin	257	3.1	2.6	2.8
Titanium	543	9.2	4.5	3.7
Tungsten	23	4.9	2.9	3.1
Vanadium	22	4.7	3.4	3.0
Zinc	5,525	3.3	2.6	2.7

lation growth rates results from a simple continuation of recent trends assuming no breakthroughs in family planning programs. Indeed, this decline is probably not as rapid as it should be since it was not based on the latest available data—which indicates significant additional declines in

TABLE 4.3
World Consumption and Rates of Growth in Consumption of Commercial Energy, Standard Case

	1950	1960	1972	1975*	2000	2025	2050
Total (10^{15} BTU)	77	124	211	209	548	1,166	2,365
Coal	43	—	—	46	106	175	1,080
Petroleum	22	—	—	100	230	300	27
Natural gas	7	—	—	48	130	255	27
Nuclear	0	—	—	4	58	276	666
Other	5	—	—	11	24	160	565
Annual rate of growth in total energy (% from previous year)		4.9	4.5	—.3	3.9	3.1	2.9

* Values for 1975 are projections from the model.

fertility in many countries—and does not allow for biases that tend to make reported growth rates in recent decades too high.[3] The long-term decline in economic growth rates arises from a variety of factors. For the U.S., these factors involve a continuation of changes in work hours and labor force participation rates, changes in man-hour productivity resulting from shifts in the age, education, and sex composition of the labor force, changes in the composition of output—in particular, the approach of saturation in the purchase of some material-intensive commodities such as automobiles—and a number of transitional factors related to higher energy and environmental cleanup costs. For the rest of the world, the slowdown is postulated to occur because of the elimination of the technological gap between developed countries which has allowed countries like Japan to grow more rapidly than the U.S., emergence of structural problems comparable to those faced by the U.S. as a growing number of countries approach U.S. per capita income levels, and continued problems, especially in less developed countries, in adjusting to high energy prices. The resulting growth rates allow for a substantial improvement in material well-being throughout the world; indeed, they imply the emergence of most Latin American countries from the class considered less developed. But the poorer countries of South Asia remain far from this goal even after fifty years of growth; the average rates of growth for the world are substantially below those of the 1950s and 1960s.

If the use of materials and energy per unit of output were to remain constant, these results would translate directly into declines in rates of growth of resources and waste products. In fact, considerable diversity of experience is likely. For lighter metals such as aluminum, plus cement, plastics, and glass—the beneficiaries of the substitution processes projected for the next several decades—the material intensities of output are likely to rise in most countries. For other minerals and metals, such intensities will probably decline in industrial countries and rise in countries just beginning their period of rapid industrialization. The same is true for total use of energy, though substantial shifts in the composition of fuels are likely as countries attempt to substitute coal, nuclear, and other domestic sources for high-cost petroleum and natural gas imports. For minerals such as sulfur, potash, and phosphates—the major raw materials for fertilizer production—much depends on a country's stage of agricultural development. Growth rates in the U.S. and other major exporting countries are likely to decline, while those for countries attempting to modernize and achieve less dependence on imports are likely to increase. Despite this diversity, the net result is a decline in the rate of growth of demand for

3. See "Puzzles and Prospects" in Chapter 8.

nonfuel minerals taken as a group as well as for total energy measured in British thermal units (BTUs).

This is not to say that the growth in demands that must be met in the future are not going to be substantial. If our projections are correct, annual use of coal will increase 3.8 times, and nuclear power will increase by a factor of 76 from its currently small base. But the result is significantly different from assuming increasing, or even constant, rates of growth, as is done so often, it helps explain the conclusions arrived at when these demands are compared with available resources.

Nonfuel Minerals

The analysis on the supply side has been limited largely to efforts to estimate prospective reserves; that is, quantities likely to be added to current reserves during the next fifty years assuming no changes in prices and only modest improvements in technology, the implicit assumption being that in the long run problems of producing from these reserves will eventually be solved. Our estimates of reserves and prospective reserves are, if anything, on the low side because "speculative" and frequently also "hypothetical" resource estimates[4] are left out, as well as estimates of any kind for some areas (for example, phosphate rock and copper in the People's Republic of China). These estimates were then compared with cumulative demand projections to determine dates when exhaustion would occur in the hypothetical circumstances that there were no changes in prices and no additional efforts to recycle or conserve the resources in question. (In the real world, of course, prices will begin rising well in advance of such dates, including adjustments in both demand and supply so that exhaustion will not, in fact, occur at these dates.)

The results, indicated in Table 4.4, suggest that of the minerals studied, hypothetical exhaustion would occur before 2025 only for cobalt and lead, and before 2050 for cobalt, lead, nickel, copper, aluminum, sulfur, tin, and tungsten. In addition, fluorine and mercury could be in short supply before the end of this period. But in most of these cases, there are special circumstances that make these hypothetical exhaustion dates misleading. Cobalt, copper, and nickel, along with manganese, are the princi-

4. The U.S. Geological Service, from which these estimates were derived, defines speculative resources as those in unknown districts whose existence is postulated on the basis of geological principles and hypothetical resources as deposits postulated to exist in known districts. See U.S. Geological Service, *United States Mineral Resources,* Geological Survey Professional Paper 820 (Washington, D.C.: USGPO, 1973).

TABLE 4.4
Dates of Hypothetical Exhaustion for Selected Minerals, Assuming No Change in Prices,* Standard World Case

	Current Reserves	Current and Prospective Reserves
Aluminum	2025	2038
Chromium	2048	2095
Cobalt	2004	2016
Copper	2010	2041
Iron	2053	2094
Lead	2000	2016
Manganese	2061	2112
Molybdenum	2014	2480
Nickel	2014	2032
Phosphate rock	2034	2120
Potash	2104	2368
Sulfur	2010	2036
Tin	2003	2030
Titan	2043	2151
Tungsten	2009	2037
Vanadium	2060	2180
Zinc	1993	2065

* Also assuming no change in recycling rates, current reserves are used first, and the rate of growth in demand after 2025 is the same as that postulated for the 2020–25 period.

ple minerals likely to be derived from deep-sea nodules; they have not been included in our resource estimates although some experts believe they will be exploited within the next twenty-five years without significant price increases. In the case of aluminum, only bauxite sources have been included in our reserve and prospective reserve estimates despite the fact that 8.3 percent of the earth's crust is composed of aluminum, making it one of the most abundant of the structural metals. While somewhere between a 20 and an 80 percent increase in the price of bauxite would be required to justify switching to nonbauxite sources given today's technology, there is good reason to believe that this switchover price will be reduced substantially in coming decades. Prospective reserve estimates for sulfur are not available for Africa, do not include hypothetical resource estimates for any country, and do not take into account secondary recovery from emission controls associated with the combustion of coal.

This leaves tin, tungsten, lead, fluorine, and mercury for which some price increases may be needed to close the gap between demand and supply. However, it is difficult to believe anything more than a doubling in real prices (compared to the fourfold increase in petroleum prices in 1973–74) would be required, and in most cases this increase would be necessary only after 2025. In addition, there are a few minerals—most notably those associated with deep-sea nodules—that could well fall in price if expectations for that technology prove correct. Thus, we feel reasonably confident that, at least during our time horizon, nonfuel mineral prices in general are unlikely to rise in real terms as a consequence of depletion.

There are, of course, other reasons why the relative price of nonfuel minerals may rise over time. The cost of environmental controls and of energy for mining, beneficiation, reduction, and refining of these minerals tends to be greater per dollar of output than that for other economic activities. There may be added restrictions on land use for mining purposes in the future. Acquisition of sufficient water for mineral processing may prove to be a problem in some areas. And, higher profit rates may be required in the future to induce an adequate flow of investment into these areas in order to offset increased uncertainties and risks. At least these are claims frequently heard.

In the long run, the extent of the price increases necessary to accommodate these factors is unlikely to be very great. Environmental controls, restrictions on land use, and water shortages are likely to affect U.S. production costs more than those in the rest of the world; if U.S. costs are increased for these reasons, imports will rise, holding down domestic prices. The situation with respect to energy is different since these costs will increase universally as ore grades decline or prices increase; but the percentage of energy used in mining and beneficiation as opposed to reduction and refining is small, and according to Goeller and Weinberg, is not likely to increase by more than a factor of two even for the lowest of ore grades ever likely to be used.[5] Uncertainties and risks to investors appear to be growing today because of efforts to impose environmental and land use controls in the U.S. and to gain more local control over company operations and profits abroad. It is not clear, however, that these efforts signal the beginning of a long period of disruptions that will continue to inhibit aggregate investment, that is, investment by public as well as private enterprises. It is just as likely—indeed, perhaps more likely—that we are in a transition period which will not last for more than another five to ten years, and that once the new rules of the game are fully established and accepted, uncertainties and hence reluctance to invest on this count will recede. Of course, the combined effect of all these factors on long-run

5. H. E. Goeller and A. M. Weinberg, "The Age of Substitutability," *Science* 191 (4228) (February 1976):683–88.

prices could be of some significance. But given the fact that the minerals sectors constitute a small and diminishing fraction of total world output, it would take very large increases indeed before any measurable effects on aggregate economic growth were observed.

What an economy cannot absorb with equanimity are sudden disruptions in supply—disruptions which come upon purchasers so rapidly and unexpectedly that there is no time to adjust. Such disruptions for a period long enough to do substantial harm are unlikely, however, because of the diversity of suppliers, the difficulty of forming effective and aggressive cartels in this area—in contrast to petroleum—and the substantial stockpiles held by major consuming countries.

Energy

Whatever the problems in the nonfuel minerals area, they are likely to be minor compared to those of the energy sector. Even here the problems stem less from an insufficiency of resources than from their distribution, environmental consequences, and transitional problems in moving from one energy region to another. Indeed, in terms of *usable* energy resources, vastly larger quantities are available today than were present in 1972, prior to the OPEC price rise; and if real energy prices increase again in the future even larger quantities—including virtually inexhaustible sources such as solar and biomass—will become economically viable.

Projections on the supply side result in a rapid expansion in the use of coal, nuclear power, and synthetic oils and gases from coal, shale, heavy oils, and tars. The early expansion of coal and nuclear power results from the phasing out of oil and gas in the production of electricity plus continued increases in the percentage of energy consumed in the form of electricity. Solar remains an unimportant source of energy until after the turn of the century—in large part because of the absence of significant increases in energy prices before 2010, but also because technological improvements are not expected to lower costs significantly, except in the area of solar electricity and then only late in our period. Geothermal becomes about as important as hydroelectric, which does not expand much at all during the projection period.

Three significant conclusions follow from this analysis. First, even if energy prices do not rise significantly, there is no danger of seriously depleting any of the world's energy resources other than those of petroleum and natural gas within the next half century and probably well beyond (Table 4.5). A possible qualification must be added for uranium because of the uncertainties surrounding estimates of its resource base, but only if

TABLE 4.5
World Cumulative Demand of Nonrenewable Energy Sources and Percent of Resources Used, 2000 and 2025, Standard Case

	1975–2000		1975–2025	
	Cumulative Demand (quads BTU)	Percent of Resources	Cumulative Demand (quads BTU)	Percent of Resources
Coal	2,832	1.6	7,035	4.1
Petroleum	3,907	33.0*	10,567	86.0*
Natural Gas	1,734	17.3	6,062	60.6
Uranium ($U_3 0_8$)	963	2.4–11.7	6,313	15.4–77.0
Oil Shale and Tar Sands	—	—	625	4.0

* Assuming resources of 12,500 quads, that is 10,000 quads of reserves plus prospective reserves, plus 25 percent additional for enhanced recovery and use of heavy oils assumed to become profitable once petroleum prices rise by 30 percent in real terms from the current level.

none of the extensive possibilities for improving efficiency in use of substitution (various forms of plutonium recycling including the breeder, laser enrichment, the thorium fuel cycle, and fusion) come to pass. Even petroleum and natural gas are likely to remain important sources of energy throughout our fifty-year time horizon. In the standard case, 86 percent of the petroleum resources believed to be recoverable today with only modest increases in price or improvements in technology are used up by 2025, and production does not fall to insignificant levels until after 2030.

Second, if there were no constraints imposed on production or sale from any of the world's sources, and if the price were not to fall below its current level in the interim, production of petroleum could keep up with the growth in demand until some time after the turn of the century.[6] At that point, the price would have to rise—unless, of course, alternative sources of liquids became available at competitive prices before that time. In the standard case (in which we assume that the cost of producing synthetics falls slowly over time but never below the current price of petroleum), petroleum prices begin to rise in 2010, reach a peak some 60 percent above the current level, but return to within 15 percent of that level by 2040, when the capacity to produce synthetics has expanded sufficiently. For gas, this transition to a synthetic world begins five to ten years later and does not last as long or involve as great a runup in price.

6. It should be clear that throughout we are talking about changes in price relative to all other prices. In these terms, since 1974, the world price of petroleum has fallen, particularly for countries whose currencies have appreciated against the dollar.

Since these two conclusions differ significantly from those obtained by several others[7] who predict shortages and rising petroleum prices by the latter half of the 1980s, a comment on the reasons for these differences is in order. While the underlying GNP estimates given here are somewhat lower, the principal differences are on the supply side—not with resource, but with production estimates. For example, the CIA report assumes that the Soviet Union will not be able to solve its production problems and will become a net importer, while the WAES study places a ceiling on Saudi production and assumes no trade with the Communist world.[8] Similar conclusions have been generated by constraining global production to 145 quads (145 x 10^{15}Btu or 68.5 million barrels per day) in 1985, 190 quads in 2000, and 200 quads in 2025. In this case, oil prices start rising in 1987, but because petroleum reserves would be stretched out and synthetic liquids would be induced to come on stream more rapidly, the price rise would be limited to a maximum of 40 percent above current levels and would be relatively slow and orderly. Needless to say, a lower ceiling, or a ceiling more abruptly reached, could generate more serious and dramatic results, but there is no economic reason to believe either situation is likely. Petroleum resource estimates for the centrally-planned economics are nearly as large as those for the OPEC countries; surely these countries will solve their production problems—if not by 1980, by 1985 or 1990—and will want to export in order to acquire food, machinery, and raw materials for their own development. So far as Saudi Arabia is concerned, production limits so severe that they hurt the economies of its principal customers will endanger the value of its assets in these countries.

Economic rationality is not the only basis for action in this world. This leads to the third and last conclusion from this analysis. While world production of petroleum and natural gas may become somewhat less concentrated in the next one or two decades as non-OPEC sources become integrated in the system, come "on stream," it is likely thereafter that global production facilities will become concentrated in fewer and fewer

7. In particular, OECD (Organization for Economic Cooperation and Development), 1975, *Energy Prospects to 1985,* vol. II (Paris, OECD); CIA (Central Intelligence Agency), 1977, *The International Energy Situation: Outlook to 1985,* ER 77–1024OU, April, Washington, D.C.; and WAES (Workshop on Alternative Energy Strategies), 1977, *Energy: Global Prospects 1985–2000* (New York: McGraw-Hill).

8. The WAES study also assumes there is minimum reserve-to-production ratio so that, in effect, not all reserves can be used. But this minimum ratio is higher than that currently existing in the U.S.; surely, as the rest of the world approaches U.S. technological capabilities and reserves are diminished, a substantially lower ratio will be achieved. Indeed, as exhaustion approaches, this ratio ought to approach zero. Discussed here is not the petroleum in the ground, but only reserves, that small fraction estimated to be recoverable.

hands. Until such time as synthetic capacity expands, therefore, the world will become more vulnerable to capricious behavior on the part of a few individuals.

There is, of course, a good deal of uncertainty in all this. The recently discovered Yucatan fields of Mexico may prove much larger than believed when the petroleum resource numbers for this chapter were assembled. Solar and synthetics may develop more rapidly than assumed in this scenario. Nuclear power may develop more slowly. The prospects for tapping the vast deposits of heavy oils may have been underestimated. And there is a host of environmental problems associated with energy, which are discussed below. The point here is a limited one: growing shortages of energy resources and rising world energy prices are not the central problems to be faced in the next half century, but rather transitional problems—problems of adjusting to the fourfold increase in prices that has already occurred, problems of bringing new energy sources on stream in an orderly fashion—and problems associated with changes in the distribution of the world's energy resources and resulting shifts in the balance of power.

Food, Forestry, and Fisheries

In the world as a whole, there appear to be adequate quantities of land and water appropriate for food production to meet likely demands during the next half century. But this land and water—plus the know-how, institutions, capital, and proper incentives necessary to achieve decent levels of productivity—are not distributed in the same way as is the world's population, and given differential population and economic growth rates, these disparities could well grow over time. The result could be a continuation of the slow increase in per capita output for the world as a whole at the same time as some regions—most notably South Asia—experience declines. International movements in food will have to grow if per capita consumption in these regions is not to fall.

The U.S., of course, plays a key role in this global picture because of its vast surplus available for export. Although serious doubts have been raised recently about the ability of the U.S. to continue expanding this surplus without substantial increases in prices, our analysis does not support this contention. Largely out of prudence, we have assumed a substantial slowdown in the rate of growth of productivity in this case—from an average of 1.7 percent per year during the last quarter century to 0.9 percent per year during our projection period. But the rate of growth of U.S. consumption, even without increased prices, can be expected to fall even more, fairly quickly approaching the growth rate of population which itself is falling. The result is an increase in exportable surplus compatible with our assumptions about global developments.

On balance, no new land must be converted to cropland in this case, and the rate of growth in use of fertilizers, pesticides, and energy slows down appreciably during this period. Domestic energy prices and environmental control costs do rise somewhat, but not by enough to appreciably affect production costs until close to the end of our time horizon. Also, fertilizer prices could well fall during the next decade or so as recent worldwide efforts to increase capacity come on stream. Beyond 2025, this situation could change as different results are obtained in other scenarios. For example, the most difficult case investigated—involving higher levels of exports and a more rapid increase in U.S. population—requires that 82 million acres of noncropland be converted to agricultural use by 2025. This would virtually exhaust the availability of high quality land that could be converted—there would still be large quantities of lands of more moderate quality that could be used—and would raise production costs by at least 25 per cent. But at least for this base case, and within our time horizon, there seems no reason for significant increases in real prices.

The global situation with respect to forestry and fisheries is quite different. First, the current level of exploitation is probably excessive in the sense that, with current technology, yields cannot be sustained. While there are some unexploitated nontraditional marine species that can be utilized, especially for livestock purposes, most analysts seem agreed that the traditional population is not sustainable without some cutback in the fishing catch. If ocean pollution grows over time, consumption will have to be reduced even further to protect the population, though there are no good numbers to indicate the magnitudes involved. The same holds for fresh water fisheries. So far as forests are concerned, it is indicative of the situation to note that whereas twenty-five years ago forests covered one-quarter of the world's land surface, they now cover one-fifth; if recent trends continue, this fraction will fall to one-sixth in 2000 and one-seventh in 2020. Most of this deforestation will occur in the developing countries where population growth will increase subsistence needs significantly. In richer countries, reforestation projects and a growing range of substitutes for wood may keep price increases within reasonable bounds.

But second, these are two fields in which production technologies could change quite dramatically in the next half century. In contrast to modern agriculture, these industries are still in the hunting and gathering stages. Once they emerge from this stage, when fish and trees are routinely cultivated, sustainable yields could take a substantial jump upwards, just as has happened in the case of agriculture. To accomplish this on a large scale poses many technological, financial, and institutional problems, but there is probably time to forestall major shortages if proper incentives are provided and these tasks are approached with some degree of urgency.

ENVIRONMENT

Present and prospective environmental issues are so many and diverse that some clustering is necessary for this brief summary. It is useful to start with those environmental problems that are currently being controlled or which pose no new control problems: the mass pollutants, solid waste disposal, and routine radiation emissions from power plants. All other problems and issues are discussed in two categories: those that are or may be severe at the local level though they are not severe nationally (for example, siting of power plants and water shortages), and problems that may be serious nationally or globally (for example, erosion, global climate effects, nuclear proliferation, and ocean pollution). With the partial exception of this last category, the emphasis here is on the U.S., first, because we have so little information available on other countries, and second, because it is plausible to assume that despite differences in income, preferences, and economic structures, other countries will not allow environmental problems in the first two categories to become so severe that repercussions are felt beyond their borders.

Relatively Well-Controlled Problems

If the percentage of residuals emitted into the environment were to remain constant in the future, emissions would quickly rise to intolerable levels with the growth of the U.S. economy over time. But emission controls are slated to increase even in the base case which assumes some relaxation from currently legislated standards. While far from optimal, these controls are sufficient to reduce emissions of nine of the eleven mass pollutants that will be studied by 2025—the exceptions being dissolved solids and nutrients. As a consequence, our estimate of damage costs from these pollutants falls from $37 billion to $27 billion between 1975 and 2025, despite the much larger economy and number of units at risk to damage. Control costs, of course, rise from $9.1 billion in 1975 to $68.3 billion, but even when we include costs of controlling other pollutants—solid wastes, nonpoint sources, sulfur sludge, land reclamation, and radiation—they amount to only 1.1 percent of GNP in 1975 and 1.7 percent in 2025. Nevertheless, problems of implementing these controls can be expected because, among other reasons, these costs are not spread smoothly over time and across sectors. The extent of the slippage from legislated standards built into this case represents our estimate of the environmental impact of these problems.

The situation with respect to solid wastes from urban sources and radiation emissions associated with normal operations of power plants is similar—rapidly growing amounts to be controlled and increasing costs of doing so, but not so large as significantly to interfere with aggregate economic growth. In the case of solid wastes, for example, costs per unit of control are likely to rise as distances to acceptable sites increase over time and as more sophisticated procedures are applied in later years to avoid leaching and runoff that could become dangerous because of the buildup of heavy metals and highly toxic chemicals. Controls on radiation emissions associated with normal power plant operations are being built into plant design in increasingly sophisticated ways and (in contrast to other nuclear problems) should not pose serious problems in the future.

Potentially Severe Problems at the Local Level

These problems include conflicts over land use (including siting of power plants, land disturbed by mining, and sulfur sludge disposal), water shortages, reactor accidents, disposal of spent nuclear fuel, and local weather modification. These problems differ from those in the first category in two ways. First, the technologies and institutions for controlling many of them are not as well worked out. Reclamation can keep the land disturbed by mining at any one time within reasonable limits for affordable costs in most areas, but arid regions where much future activity will have to be located pose special problems not yet solved. There is considerable room for improving the efficiency with which water is utilized—and in the process, avoiding shortages and excessive contamination—but the institutional mechanisms for doing so are not adequate in most of the critical regions. The probability of reactor accidents and escape of nuclear materials from waste disposal sites cannot be reduced to zero, any more than can probabilities of accidents in coal mines, but the additional fears associated with nuclear power make the problem of finding acceptable sites far more difficult. Standard procedures for managing solid wastes are inadequate for handling sulfur sludge from coal-fired power plants. All these problems are likely to prove solvable, but until solutions are found, we can expect associated pressures on the environment (along with siting and water allocation problems) to mount as local population and economic growth proceeds. This contrasts rather sharply with what we expect in the case of most mass pollutants.

Second, though these problems may have some social and economic consequences at the national level, their principal impacts—especially their environmental impacts—will be felt at the local level. Compared to most other high-income countries, the U.S. is still a land- and water-rich nation and is likely to remain so during the next half century. This country is not in danger of "paving over" a large fraction of farm land during the next half century, spoiling large tracts of highly valued recreational land, or consuming an excessively large proportion of its available water supplies. Nor is the total number of acres required for nuclear power plants, mines, synthetic energy production, and so on, very large in relation to the number of acres potentially available for such purposes. Thus, if the distributional problems can be solved, the requirements of this scenario can clearly be met.

That may prove to be a rather large "if." A number of regions will have to change character quite dramatically in the next half century. The Delaware River Basin may have to accommodate an inordinately large number of nuclear power plants—32 in the base case in 2025—which means an average of one every nine miles.[9] The Ohio River Valley will be excessively burdened with coal mines, coal-fired power plants, and, eventually, synthetic fuel plants. The Southwest will have to make water available for mining and synthetic fuel production, which will mean less for agriculture. Florida will have to permit the area to be devoted to phosphate mining to expand. In the process, some people and economic activities will have to move to make way for others. The extent of such movements may not be great since there is a good deal of room for other forms of adjustment; for example, getting used to living in more densely populated areas, making a serious effort to conserve water—which, among other things, means raising its price substantially and allowing reallocations among users—and living in and amongst more areas of restricted access. But few regions in the U.S. have the traditions and institutions required to bring about such adjustments quickly and equitably. Judging from past history, conflicts—sometimes bitter and protracted—are likely, particularly in those regions with a confluence of desirable characteristics.

The overall effect of this local turmoil is difficult to judge. If efforts to prohibit the establishment of seemingly dangerous, dirty, or simply distasteful economic activities in one's region become sufficiently widespread, aggregate economic growth could be affected. On the other hand, the need for jobs and desire for profits could win out as they have in the past.

9. Alvin Weinberg has pointed out to me that this way of stating the situation exaggerates the siting problem, for these plants could be clustered into a few large complexes.

Probably, as incomes continue to rise, preferences for environmental amenities will slowly win out over desires for yet more income. This factor adds yet another item to the list of reasons for believing that economic growth in the U.S. will slow down.

Potentially Severe National or Global Problems

Frequently mentioned concerns falling in this category are loss and deterioration of soils, loss of genetic variability, effects on global climate, ozone depletion, release of radon from uranium mill tailings, proliferation and buildup of toxic chemicals in food chains, ocean pollution, and nuclear proliferation. Judging from recent history, this list will change considerably in coming decades.

For a variety of reasons, virtually all the problems in this category are unlikely soon to be controlled effectively. In some cases, control is extremely difficult on technical and institutional grounds. Ultimately, for example, the spread of nuclear weapons depends on the spread of requisite knowledge; the worldwide growth of nuclear power plants—which itself may be impossible to control—may only affect the timing, and then perhaps only marginally. The concentration of carbon dioxide in the atmosphere may be controllable but only by herculean means, involving global agreements to capture it from stack gases, reverse the trend toward deforestation, and, in the end, perhaps reduce combustion itself. And methods of controlling soil loss and deterioration, while well-known, are difficult to apply because of incentives on the part of widely dispersed farmers to maximize short-run production and, if necessary, compensate for such losses by using more fertilizer, adding marginal lands, and reducing fallow periods.

But these difficulties are frequently compounded by absence of knowledge to judge whether controls are needed at all and, if so, how strict they should be. Does CO_2 have to be controlled, or can we wait, hoping that alternatives to combustion—perhaps solar and fusion—will come along before the problem becomes acute? What level of risks are we really subjecting ourselves to when we allow increased nuclear plants to be built, how do they compare with those we accept in other fields and with those we subject ourselves to in the absence of nuclear power? Then, too, it is difficult to mobilize support for such actions. This is particularly the case if effective action requires international agreements; for even with the same facts, countries at different income levels will assess the risks and net benefits of a given action quite differently. But the problem also exists within countries because of differences in preferences and ethics—for example, in how much weight to give to the interests of future generations.

As a consequence, and in contrast to the mass pollutants, these environmental pressures can be expected to increase with population and economic growth. Whether they will become so severe during the next half century as to limit such growth is an open question. They could if the more pessimistic assumptions about CO_2 and risks of nuclear power were justified or if a number of these pressures act in concert to overload ecological or social systems; but little confidence can be placed in these—or any other—assumptions. During this time frame most of these pressures will probably manifest themselves as increased risks of major damages, not actual damages. If so, continued population and economic growth is feasible, but, because of mounting uncertainties and risks, not necessarily desirable.

ROLE OF POPULATION RELATIVE TO OTHER DETERMINANTS

In all this, how important is population growth as opposed to per capita economic growth and other determinants of resource and environmental pressures? This question is most conveniently answered by comparing results for scenarios that differ only with respect to population growth, economic growth, or some other individual determinant, selecting assumptions about these determinants that appear plausible or feasible within the time frame. Three generalizations can be drawn from the materials presented.

First, within the time period being considered, most of the resource and environmental effects of changes in assumptions about population growth are relatively small. Nine of the seventeen minerals studied in depth can be set aside because they have hypothetical exhaustion dates that lie beyond 2050. While simple extrapolation would indicate that a change in population growth assumptions makes a significant difference in these cases, that fact is irrelevant since nothing useful can be said about what might happen to population growth rates, tastes, technology, or any other factor that might influence the situation that far into the future. For the remainder, the impact of a change in population growth assumptions is quite small. Even if scenarios incorporating the highest and lowest *total* GNP projections are compared—a difference of 35 percent from the larger of the figures in 2025—the weighted average of differences in dates to hypothetical exhaustion is only four years for reserves and ten years for prospective reserves. So far as the U.S. is concerned, if current recycling rates and no imports are assumed, six of the seventeen minerals can be set aside either because hypothetical exhaustion dates would occur beyond 2050 or because the U.S. possesses insignificant quantities of the mineral in question. For the remainder, a shift from the highest to the lowest total GNP projection—a difference of 36 percent in 2025—shifts the hypothetical exhaustion dates by two years for reserves and sixteen years for prospective reserves. While the other country studies do not lend themselves to quantitative statements of this kind, the general impression is the same.

The situation with respect to energy resources is similar. The model of the world petroleum market presented in this chapter indicates that the price of petroleum would begin rising in 2012 in the standard case; if the highest (lowest) of the world growth cases prevailed, it would begin rising in 2009 (2014). Comparable dates for natural gas are about a decade later, but the spread between highest and lowest growth rates is somewhat larger. Coal can be ignored because the exhaustion dates lie well beyond 2050. The uranium situation is difficult to judge because its resource numbers are so uncertain. At the country level, population and economic growth rates have even less impact because production in most countries is likely to be determined more by supply constraints—for example, whether petroleum is available or not, how fast nuclear plants can be built or will be permitted—or by international demand considerations in the case of energy exporters rather than by changes in domestic demand.

The situation with respect to most mass pollutants is also similar, though the reasons differ among countries. For mass pollutants in the U.S.—where they are relatively well controlled—alternative population assumptions make very little difference; indeed, as Figure 4.1 demonstrates for sulphates and biological oxygen demand, emissions are likely to fall over time as a consequence of these controls rather than rising as one would expect because of population and economic growth. Similar figures could be drawn using other pollutants or indexes of ambient air and water quality or of per capita damages. Per capita control costs vary somewhat more, but as discussed above, they are such a small portion of per capita GNP that such variations are not significant.

No comparable data are available for other countries. Figure 4.1 does illustrate what might happen to emissions if there were no controls, that is, if emissions were equal to residuals generated. In this case, population and economic growth obviously have significantly more impact. But when applied to less developed countries, this picture probably overstates the effects. Additional population or economic growth in less industrialized and less energy-intensive societies is likely to generate fewer residuals per unit of output than in the U.S., that is, the total height of the bars in Figure

FIGURE 4.1
Gross Residuals and Emissions under Alternative U.S. Scenarios, Strict Abatement Policy

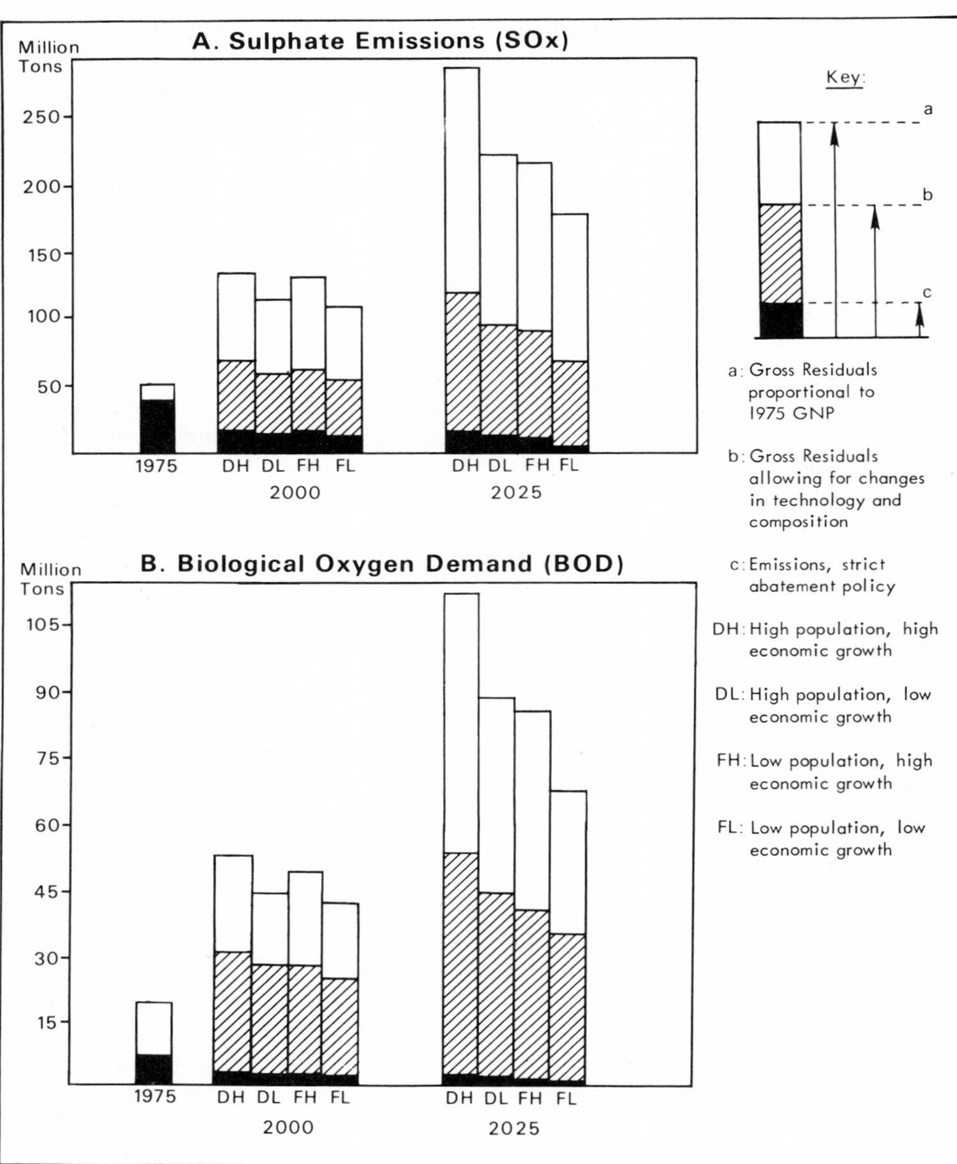

4.1, with or without technological change, is likely to be lower. Environmental concentrations and per capita damages are probably fewer per unit of residuals emitted, given the same levels of controls, because population and economic activities are more disbursed, allowing for more natural dilution and absorption. Whatever the impact of population and economic activities, it represents a small increment to the backlog of problems accumulated from past growth and the absence of adequate pollution control policies.

Second, the resource and environmental impacts of changes in per capita income are significantly larger than those of an equal percentage change in population in early years; but the latter impacts grow over time, so that by 2025 they are roughly equal in magnitude. As a consequence, changes in per capita incomes have larger impacts on cumulative resource requirements over the whole period. This result would be reversed if the projection period were extended. Figure 4.1 indicates a similar result for the mass pollutants. The only exceptions to this general conclusion are minerals associated with fertilizer production and land and water requirements, which—at least so far as the U.S. is concerned—appear more closely tied to population than to per capita income growth in all periods.

Third, other determinants—technological changes, changes in availability of resources, the extent of recycling, and policies aimed directly at reducing the consumption of a specific resource or the emission of a specific pollutant—generally have larger impacts than either population or economic growth rates during our time frame. Figure 4.1 provides a dramatic illustration of the impact of pollution control policies. Other examples pertain to changes in the availability of resources. In early 1978, Venezuela revised upward its estimates of tar sand deposits by a factor of three. Shortly thereafter, Colombia announced the discovery of sufficient natural gas to reduce import requirements in the year 2000 by 15 percent. And a few months later, Mexico released figures on petroleum deposits which are nearly as large as those of Saudi Arabia. Similarly, there can be little doubt that legislated fuel efficiency requirements for new automobiles in the U.S. are having a slow but significant impact on the rate of growth of petroleum consumption. Practically all the sensitivity tests we have conducted on the U.S. model support this general contention.

For the U.S., it is not too surprising to find that population growth plays a relatively small role in generating most resource or environmental pressures. The rate of population growth is low, falling, and unlikely to increase in the near future. This leads to a fairly narrow range within which population projections might realistically be expected to fall. Even if population growth rates were to increase by a significant amount, the U.S. economy is sufficiently rich in resources, income, and technological and managerial capacities that it should be capable of accommodation to most such pressures without significant loss in welfare. Similar findings are likely for other rich countries, though some must rely on imported raw materials and energy to a greater extent. But in poor countries, where the capacity to adjust is less, the resource constraints ought to be more binding. Why then do the four studies of less developed countries reviewed also find small impacts from changes in population growth?

One reason is that the time horizon of these studies is only twenty-five years. During that period a decline in birth rates is not likely to reduce total output significantly; certainly, the labor force will not be appreciably reduced, and if anything, the savings and investment rates will be increased. If output is not reduced, the only effect on resource requirements will be through compositional changes in output, which are generally quite small compared to scale effects. Beyond twenty-five years, the outcome depends on the extent of unemployment that must be absorbed, investment rates, and labor productivity; eventually, however, the size of the economy and hence its aggregate calls on material and environmental resources should be less.

Second, most of these studies began by selecting population and per capita economic growth rates that appeared likely or feasible on non-resource grounds. In particular, the economic growth rates were selected after considering likely changes in savings rates, foreign exchange earnings, and capital and labor productivity—which in turn depend on administrative and managerial capacities, the quality of the labor force, economic incentives, and so on. In general, these factors tend to put a ceiling on economic growth rates that is well within the limits of what is possible on resource and environmental grounds during the time horizon used. The India study, for example, finds that agricultural expansion—the critical element for the next fifteen years in that country—is not limited by insufficiency of land and water but by the rate of development and diffusion of improved agricultural technology, the rate of investment in irrigation facilities, the management of these and other relevant facilities, and economic incentives. The Philippine study finds that, while sustainable timber yields will be inadequate to meet demand (domestic plus a share of foreign demand) by 2000 if there are no policy changes, this situation can be reversed if significant efforts at reforestation, scientific management, and regulation of cutting are introduced reasonably soon. And Indonesia, a major petroleum exporter, has not found that its problems in attempting to achieve higher economic growth rates were greatly alleviated by the four-fold increase in the world price of petroleum in 1973–74. Other studies find that efficiencies in use of energy are very low, no more than 10 to 20 percent of useful energy output being derived from total inputs.[10] Thus, the binding constraints on the development of these countries are not the availability of material and environmental resources per se but the capacity to utilize the resources they have in productive ways. This situation is unlikely to change during the next few decades.

Finally, with the possible exception of petroleum, the resource requirements of these economies are sufficiently small—relative to that of the rest of the world and even in relation to the remainder of their own economies—that whatever shortages develop can be alleviated through imports without an undue foreign exchange burden. The Indian study finds that domestic sources of several metals—notably copper and zinc—may be substantially depleted by 2000, but it goes on to indicate that the total cost of importing the shortfall that might develop is easily manageable. The Colombian study finds that it should not be difficult to increase export earnings to the extent required to meet all their resource and energy shortfalls. The problem in that economy is to decide which export industries to opt for; in particular, whether to promote expansion of agricultural or industrial exports—a risky decision to make, given uncertainties about future world price movements.

Petroleum imports are, of course, an important exception since they can absorb a large percent of foreign exchange earnings in some countries. But the problems here obviously have more to do with the dramatic runup in price and the difficulties of scaling down aspirations for an automobile society than they do with population growth rates per se. As world petroleum resources become depleted and world prices begin rising again, these problems will become more severe. But a decline in population growth rates within the range that is likely to be feasible will not affect the date at which these prices begin rising by more than a few years.

It must be recognized, however, that these findings pertain only to measurable impacts of changes in population growth. Continued population growth also means more local conflicts over land and water use, the need to live with even greater uncertainties and risks of major ecological or nuclear disasters, more dependence on rapid scientific and technological development to reduce these uncertainties and risks, fewer social options, and the continued postponement of the resolution of other problems, including those resulting from past growth. In contrast, a slowdown in population growth purchases time, resources, and additional options; time to overcome our ignorance and redress the mistakes of past growth, resources to implement solutions, and additional freedom of choice in deciding how we want to live in the future. The fact that these effects cannot be quantified does not mean they are unimportant.

10. See Arjun Makhijani, *Energy and Agriculture in the Third World* (Cambridge, Mass.: Ballinger, 1975), and Roger Revelle, "Energy Use in Rural India," *Science* 192 (1976):969.

SOME POLICY IMPLICATIONS

One way to state the principal conclusion presented above is to indicate that the binding constraint on economic and social development in the next several decades is not the availability of material and environmental resources per se, but the capacity to utilize these resources in productive ways. This capacity varies considerably between countries depending on a host of domestic and international factors. In those countries where population growth is pressing against this capacity, economic and social progress can be restricted as severely as if the resources themselves were in short supply; a reduction in population growth would clearly be beneficial. But, given the fact that such capacity can be enhanced—through education, research, the importation of capital and know-how from abroad, and changes in the domestic and international rules governing economic activities—there would seem to be no need nor justification for the application of draconian measures even in the most hard-pressed cases.

A potentially important qualification is global ecological dangers, which if they prove to be real, could require—or force—a severe curtailment of economic and, possibly, also population growth. But for the present, the most urgent need with respect to these dangers is for more information about their nature, imminence, and potential seriousness. The acquisition of such information will not occur easily or quickly, since in many areas basic advances in such sciences as meteorology may be necessary before much headway can be made.

In the meantime, the world is faced with serious regional imbalances in population-resource densities. An important consequence of such imbalances is domestic and international migration. Far too little is known about this topic—about the numbers, occupation, and demographic characteristics of migrants, about the determinants and consequences of migration, and about future prospects. If it is true, as many believe, that the rate of migration is increasing, it will become increasingly important to have such information as a basis for establishing realistic, equitable policies in the future.

Finally, there is a growing need to take demographic variables into account in a more integral way than has been done in the past. To date, most planning exercises have utilized a maximum time horizon of five years—a period sufficiently short that at least fertility and mortality, if not migration rates as well, can be projected independently of economic developments. But, as resource and environmental problems rise on the planner's priority list, this time horizon must be extended. It makes no sense, for example, to make decisions about rates of exploitation of energy and forest resources or lay plans to cope with growing problems of soil erosion and urban environments without taking into account likely developments over several decades. This is a period sufficiently long that economic developments can begin to have an effect on demographic variables. Thus, as resource and environmental issues come to the fore, the demand for more sophisticated demographic analyses, with population treated as an integral part of the development process, will grow.

5

Food and World Population: Future Perspectives

FERDINAND MÖNCKEBERG

PAST AND PRESENT SITUATION

THE HISTORY OF HUNGER in the world is the history of man. The fight of man to obtain his food and his continuous failure to do so since the very beginning of humanity is well known, and it has been documented as persistent undernourishment and periodic famine.[1] However, during recent years, the situation has begun to improve as a consequence of the enormous amount of knowledge now accumulated. The poor harvests of 1972 and 1973, which resulted in almost one million deaths in Asia and Africa, alarmed and worried the world and raised the possibility of an imminent large-scale famine. As a consequence, the United Nations Food and Agriculture Organization (FAO) convened a meeting in Rome to analyze the problem. Although it is true that no definite advances were attained, at least the situation induced intense study of the near future.

As early as 1798, Malthus foresaw a serious feeding problem in the future. In his book *An Essay on the Principle of Population,* he said:

> I think I could formulate two postulates: one, that food is essential for the existence of man and two, that passion between sexes is necessary, and that this state will be thus relatively maintained for the rest of time. Considering then my postulates as being accepted, I say that the growth capacity of the population is infinitely bigger than the land's capacity to produce subsistences to man. When the population is not under control it grows in a geometrical proportion. Instead, subsistence only does it in an arithmetical proportion. A superficial knowledge of mathematics can demonstrate the immensity of the first capacity, in relation to the second

1. P. Parmalee, *Hambre e Historia* (Buenos Aires: Espasa Calpe, 1946).

one. I do not see a way by which man can escape the weight of this law that prevails for every living subject.[2]

One hundred and eighty years have passed since then. What has happened during this time? Has what Malthus predicted come true? At least until today, we must recognize that it has not. On the one hand, the population's growth has exceeded the most pessimistic expectations. From the 800 million inhabitants the world had at that time, population has increased to four billion. On the other hand, however, food production during this period has exceeded the growth of the population. Thus, for example, the rate of the production of cereal, which represents 70 percent of the calories consumed by the world, has remained above the growth of the population, allowing an annual improvement of per capita consumption of about one percent.[3] This has also meant an improvement in nutrition. It could be said that the best levels of nutrition in the whole history of humanity have been reached.[4]

Malthus' prophecy has not yet come to pass, but the recent food crisis of 1972 once again raised the problem. It is true that on the average, the nutritional situation has improved, but never before have there been so many undernourished people in the world. Approximately 500 million individuals are undernourished and two billion are underfed.[5] The situation is uneven and seems to have deteriorated during recent decades. Rich countries have increased their cereal production at a rate of 3 percent per year, and their population by 1 percent per year. This has left a surplus of 2 percent per year available in cereal supplies. In poor countries, the population growth rate has reached 2.5 percent per year, and cereal production has increased by 3 percent per year, leaving only one-half of 1 percent cereal surplus available.[6] As a consequence, the populations of rich countries have improved the quality and quantity of their diets, because their surplus in cereal production has been used to feed animals and thus increase the availability of animal protein. On the other hand, in the poor countries, the increase in cereal production has been used directly for human consumption.

2. T. R. Malthus, *An Essay on the Principle of Population* (London: Macmillan, 1960), p. 6.

3. F. H. Sanderson, "The Great Food Fumble," in *Food: Politics, Economics, Nutrition and Research,* edited by Philip H. Abelson (New York: American Association for the Advancement of Science, 1975), p. 1.

4. Parmalee, *Hambre e Historia.*

5. FAO, "Third World Food Survey," Freedom from Hunger Campaign. Basic Study II (Rome, 1963), p. 51.

6. Sanderson, "The Great Food Fumble," p. 1.

In the past few years, this contrast has sharpened, especially in the countries with a per capita income below $300. In these poorer countries, per capita cereal production increased by only 1.4 percent annually during the decade 1960 to 1970. Moreover, between 1970 and 1976 the situation has further deteriorated in these countries, with cereal production falling to a 0.4 percent per capita annual growth. It is important to consider that these countries represent 56 percent of the population of the developing world (Afghanistan, Bangladesh, Burma, Cameroon, Ethiopia, Ghana, Guatemala, India, Madagascar, Mali, Mozambique, Nepal, Pakistan, Sri Lanka, Sudan, Tanzania, Uganda, Upper Volta). During the same period, in the less developed countries as a whole, per capita cereal production was barely maintained or even decreased slightly.[7] However, the more developed countries have continued to make progress, with per capita cereal production increasing at 2.1 percent annually. In the United States, this growth has reached 3.2 percent per year, taking into account that this country exports two-thirds of its wheat harvest, half of its soy harvest, and 40 percent of its corn. Eighty-eight percent of the cereal that remains in the United States is used for animal consumption. In contrast, only 12 percent of the cereals in developing countries is used for animal consumption, while the rest is directly used for human consumption.

Developed countries, then, have continued to improve the quality of their diet,[8] by increasing the consumption of animal protein. In consequence, the nutritional differences between rich and poor countries have intensified (Figure 5.1).

The future is not promising. It is possible that the nutritional gap between the more developed and less developed countries will increase, because in poor countries rapid population growth has continued, and unless very drastic steps are taken, the possibilities of increasing food production are slight. It has been calculated that during the seventeenth century two million people died of hunger. In the eighteenth century this number increased to ten million and in the nineteenth century to 25 million.[9] What has happened and is happening in this century makes one suspect that the number of people dying of hunger will be still larger.[10]

To analyze the prospect for the near future, one must take into consideration two factors: the growth rate of the population and the world's capacity to produce food. Considering the projections given by the United

7. FAO, *La Cuarta Encuesta Alimentaria Mundial,* Coleccion FAO: Alimentacion y Nutricion (10) (1977).

8. *Ibid.*

9. Ph. Handler, "Los Alimentos y la Poblacion," *Facetas* 9 (1976):14.

10. *Ibid.*

FIGURE 5.1
Animal Proteins and Lipids in Developed and Underdeveloped Countries, 1961–63 and 1972–74

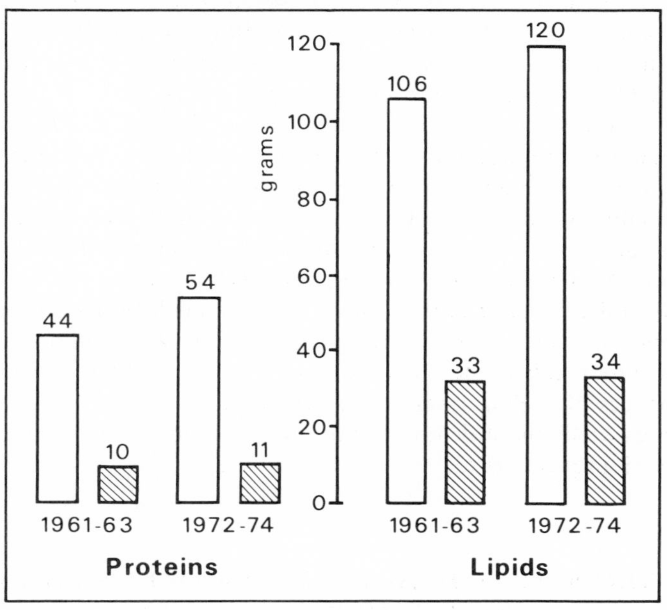

Nations, from now to the year 2000 the average rate of world population growth could be somewhat less than 2 percent per year. Developing countries are expected to grow at 2.2 percent on the average, while the growth of the developed countries is expected to be much lower. Total population could increase from *four billion* people to *6.3 billion* by the year 2000; of this increase, *two billion* would occur in the developing countries and less than 250 million in the developed countries.

According to the Food and Agriculture Organization (FAO) present food availability in the world would be enough, if equitably distributed, to provide a quantitatively adequate amount of food for all of its population. But food is not evenly distributed in the world today. The industrialized countries (Western countries with market economies and socialist countries in Eastern Europe, including the Soviet Union) that represent 30 percent of the world's population produce and consume more than 50 percent of the food. The other 70 percent of the world population consumes less than 50 percent of the food. Similarly, food is unevenly distributed within each of the different social levels.

Reutlinger and Selowsky,[11] in a World Bank report, calculated that the real deficit of cereals in 1965 was only 36 million metric tons, representing only 3.8 percent of world cereal production. The cost, in money, of this amount of cereals is approximately seven billion dollars, equivalent to 2.4 percent of the total Gross National Product (GNP) of all of the developing countries, or expressed in another way, 0.3 percent of the aggregate GNP of every country in the world.

If these estimates are correct, the present food deficit is not very big and it could be manageable. However, projections into the future indicate that even if the relationship of population to food does not worsen, this deficit could increase considerably. Supposing that food production will continue at its present rate, and that population growth will occur as predicted, the cereal deficit for the year 1990 could vary between 120 and 145 million metric tons.[12] This deficit would have its greatest impact in the poorer countries. There, the present deficit is 12 million metric tons, and it could reach up to 70 or 85 million metric tons by 1990.[13] The consequences of such a development would necessarily be very severe, and could mean millions of deaths due to hunger—much greater numbers than those previously observed.

THEORETICAL POSSIBILITIES FOR INCREASING THE RATE OF FOOD PRODUCTION

De Hoogh *et al.*,[14] through analysis of different variables, predicted that it would be possible for food production in the year 2000 to be 2.5 times as high as that of 1975. This would be an important achievement because the increase would be slightly higher than the growth rate of the population. Nevertheless, in spite of this growth, and because of the increasing number of individuals, the number of undernourished people would triple, reaching 1.5 billion.

To prevent this situation, food production must necessarily be increased at a rate higher than at present.Theoretically at least, this seems

11. Sh. Reutlinger and M. Selowsky, *Malnutrition and Poverty* (Baltimore: Johns Hopkins University Press, 1976), p. 25.

12. International Food Policy Research Institute (IFPRI), *Food Need of Developing Countries: Projections of Production and Consumption to 1990* (Washington, D.C., 1977).

13. *Ibid.*

14. J. De Hoogh, et al., *Food for a Growing World Population* (Amsterdam: Economic and Social Institute, Free University, 1976).

possible. Buring *et al.*[15] maintain that even considering the natural restrictions in the possibilities of agriculture, the world could increase its present food production thirty-fold.

But to attain these objectives, some fundamental resources are needed: enough land, adequate water, fertilizers, and fossil energy. It is important to study each of these resources separately to see if Buring's predictions are realistic. This analysis is based on our present knowledge and technologies; however, projections for the future may not be completely valid, since new knowledge acquired in the next 25 years could change the basis of our present calculations.

Availability of Suitable Land

Some countries, such as the United States, have reached extraordinarily high nutritional levels, greatly improving the quality of the diet by consuming enormous amounts of animal protein in excess of man's minimal requirements. It is impractical to consider the average diet of the population of the United States as the ideal for the projected seven billion inhabitants of the world in the year 2000 because, on the basis of present knowledge, available land could not meet such a goal. In 1972, 160 million hectares were cultivated in the United States, for a population of 208 million inhabitants.[16] Discounting the land that produces the food it exports, it may be concluded that the U.S. used 0.6 hectares per inhabitant to feed its population with the present diet. Presently, cultivated land in the world is approximately 1.4 billion hectares, and the population approximately four billion. Thus, the agricultural land per capita is 0.38 hectares. It is also estimated that the present tillable land could be extended to 2.3 billion hectares.[17] On earth there are 13 billion hectares (deducting ice-covered surfaces), but 10.7 billion hectares cannot be considered because they are not suitable, due to adverse climatic factors or physical characteristics. Thus, there could be 0.6 tillable hectares available per inhabitant. If, by the year 2000, the world's population reaches 6 to 7.6 billion inhabitants, maximal availability would be 0.32 to 0.38 hectares per person. That is to say that with the present level of knowledge, it is practically

15. P. Buring, H. D. Van Heemst and G. J. Staring, *Computation of the Absolute Maximum Food Production of the World* (Washington, D.C., 1975).

16. U.S. Department of Agriculture, *Agricultural Statistics 1973* (Washington, D.C.: USGPO, 1973).

17. R. Revelle, "The Resources Available for Agriculture," *Scientific American* 253 (1976):165.

impossible to expect that in the year 2000 all of the world's population could reach the average level of feeding available today in the United States.

However, it is necessary to emphasize that this diet, although it does look attractive, is above minimal requirements, especially as regards animal protein. At present in the United States, more than 90 percent of the cereals, legumes and vegetable proteins are used in animal feeding.[18] This is why in the U.S., the average daily consumption of animal protein is 66 grams per capita, while in Southeast Asia, daily consumption is only five grams per capita. Both situations are extremes.

To cultivate new agricultural lands, high capital investments are required. As these potential new hectares are located in developing areas it will not be easy to bring them into cultivation, because those countries lack the necessary capital.

Efforts must be made not only to incorporate new cultivable lands, but to improve their efficiency as well. Thus, for example, of the 1.3 billion hectares under cultivation, only a small fraction yield more than one crop per year. The potential gross cropped area can be increased by growing more than one crop per year on roughly 1.1 billion hectares, if irrigation is used.[19] On the other hand, a substantial increase in the productivity of each crop can be obtained by using appropriate technology, energy and fertilizers. For example, India has almost the same amount of land under cultivation as the United States, with a comparable soil and water potential. However, its crop yields are only two-fifths as great. Fertilizers, technology, water, pesticides and incentives make the difference. In summary, new soils can still be incorporated so as to increase food production above the present levels, but this would require enormous investment capital that developing countries do not have.

Availability of Water

Water is another resource fundamental to increasing food production. At present, on a global basis, irrigated cropland constitutes about 15 percent of the total cultivated land.[20] Nevertheless, irrigated lands produce over 30 percent of the total food. Water resources are very important if food production is to increase, especially if the new high-yield varieties

18. D. Pimentel, *et al.*, "Energy and Land Constraints in Food Protein Production," *Science* 190 (1975):754.

19. Revelle, "The Resources Available for Agriculture."

20. S. H. Wittwer, "Food Production: Technology and the Resource Base," *Science* 188 (1975):579.

("Green Revolution") are adopted. Irrigation has been intensified in some countries. Thus, for example, China, India, the United States, Pakistan and the Soviet Union have more than 70 percent of the irrigated land in the world. Irrigation of new lands in other countries could markedly increase efficiency per hectare. Less than 4 percent of the fresh water that flows in rivers is now used to irrigate 160 million hectares. The rest of the water is lost in the oceans.[21]

Trickle or drip irrigation has been one of the most impotant advances in water management in the last 15 years. Although it is true that use of this system is still restricted to high yield, high value crops, it could open enormous opportunities in dry or semidesert areas because of its high efficiency. In areas such as California or Hawaii, drip irrigation has been rapidly and successfully adopted.[22] It is evident that the areas under irrigation can be notably increased, and that better water management may influence food production enormously. However, this requires high investment capital that, as has been pointed out, developing countries do not have. Dams, barrages, canals and water courses have to be built to store, divert and distribute river water for irrigation. Elsewhere, large wells with motorized pumps can be built to tap underground reservoirs that are charged by rainfall and runoff. It has been calculated that to improve the use of water and to increase irrigation of new lands, 16 billion dollars would be required.[23]

Availability of Fertilizers

The productivity of land is directly related to the use of fertilizers. Forty percent of the increase in agricultural productivity in the United States in recent years is directly attributable to increased fertilizer use.[24] New high-yielding varieties have brought new demands for fertilizers and pesticides. Forty million tons of synthetically fixed nitrogen were applied worldwide in 1974,[25] but of these, 86 percent was used in developed countries.[26] In the year 2000, 160 million tons of chemically fixed nitrogen will have to be used in world agriculture. The production of nitrogenated

21. Revelle, "The Resources Available for Agriculture."

22. Economic Research Service, U.S. Department of Agriculture, *Foreign Agriculture Economic Report No. 98* (Washington, D.C.: USGPO, 1974).

23. Revelle, "The Resources Available for Agriculture."

24. Wittwer, "Food Production."

25. Revelle, "The Resources Available for Agriculture."

26. Wittwer, "Food Production."

fertilizers needs fossil fuel. One hundred kilograms of fuel are consumed to provide 100 kilograms of nitrogen in the form of chemical fertilizer. In order to produce the amount necessary for year 2000, 250 to 300 million tons of fossil fuel would be needed. This corresponds roughly to 4 percent of present fuel consumption.[27] At the 1975 cost of fertilizers, 30 to 40 billion dollars would have to be spent by the year 2000. It is possible that these sums will be even greater considering the future increases that will necessarily occur in the cost of oil (60 percent of the cost of fertilizers is due to the cost of oil).

During the next 25 years, some 400 nitrogen fertilizer plants, each capable of producing 1,000 tons of ammonia per day (or a corresponding quantity of urea) will be needed. Their total cost will be at least 40 billion dollars.[28] In 1968, 7.6 million tons of phosphorus went into fertilizers. To reach the targets for the year 2000, 30 to 40 million tons should be used.[29] The known reserves of high-grade phosphate rock have been estimated at 18 billion metric tons. At the rates of application expected by the beginning of the twenty-first century, these reserves would be used up in 400 to 600 years. However, additional reserves of lower-grade phosphate are known to exist.

Together with this large volume of fertilizers, larger quantities of insecticides are also needed. These would cost approximately one billion dollars. It is possible to produce adequate amounts of fertilizers, but this will require investments for the fertilizer plants as well as funds for the purchase of their products.

Availability of Energy

The high efficiency level reached by developed countries in their agricultural production is closely related to the use of fossil fuel. When food production was based on human and animal inputs, efficiency was very low. The great advances in scientific and technological knowledge, and their application to production, required the use of available fossil energy. Food production and productivity increased exponentially, completely displacing human and animal work, a change that became very evident between 1940 and 1970. The reason was very simple: during that period, the price of oil was $1.50 per barrel, which was theoretically equivalent to

27. Revelle, "The Resources Available for Agriculture."

28. *Ibid.*

29. *Ibid.*

having a slave work 4,000 hours for $1.[30] Even today, one gallon of gasoline is equivalent to the work produced by one person, working eight hours a day, five days a week, for three weeks.[31] This has made productivity dependent on the use of fossil energy (machinery, fertilizers). In the United States, for example, substitution of human and animal work has been almost complete, so that they contribute less than one percent of the total energy input.

With the displacement of human work, massive migration ensued, resulting in large population agglomerates in the big cities. This led to large changes in the feeding system to adapt it to the new population distribution reality. At the beginning of the nineteenth century, almost 95 percent of the American population was related to agriculture. At present, only 4 percent of the working force is directly occupied in agriculture work.[32]

The adaptive change of the feeding system made it still more dependent upon fossil fuel. The need to supply the urban population adequately meant an increase and improvement in the transport system and in preservation and storage systems, and it became necessary to develop processes for food preparation. All this led to an energy consumption even higher than that required for direct food production. In the United States, approximately 13 to 15 percent of total energy per capita per annum is expended for food.[33] Perhaps this 15 percent does not seem much, but looked at differently, it also means that to feed one person, 1,250 liters of oil are needed per year.

For example, if one takes into consideration the energy spent, 1 kilogram of bread is equivalent to 0.84 kilogram of oil. Eighty percent of this energy is used after wheat has been harvested.[34] Thus, food availability depends on the availability of cheap energy. Pimentel points out that if the world abruptly adopted the agricultural practices of the United States, and if the current world population of four billion inhabitants adopted the American diet, the world's known oil reserves would be used up in just 13 years.[35] This, of course, is a theoretical proposition, but it

30. K. Shoji, "Drip Irrigation," *Scientific American* 237 (1977):62.

31. G. Leach, *Energy and Food Production* (Fashinton, Hampshire, England: Potts and Horsey, 1976), p. 2.

32. D. Pimentel, "Energy Resources and Land Constraints in Food Production. Food and Nutrition and Health and Disease," *Annals New York Academy of Science* 300 (1977):27.

33. Pimentel, "Energy Resources and Land Constraints."

34. Leach, *Energy and Food Production.*

35. Pimentel, "Energy Resources and Land Constraints."

points out that energy will be the main limiting factor in efforts to reach adequate nutrition for world population in the year 2000.

After food has been produced in the countryside, the biggest energy requirements of the feeding system in the developed countries are those needed in food processing and transport. In developing countries this is not the case because most of the population is still rural (Asia and Africa over 80 percent, Latin America 40 percent) and therefore does not need large-scale food processing or transport. On the other hand, the high energy needs of Western European countries and the United States are based on a high consumption of animal proteins that is not really necessary. Pimentel[36] gives the following example: a can of sweet corn contains 270 calories of nutritional energy. To cultivate this corn and have it completely processed at the table, 2,790 calories of energy have been used. But if one wants to obtain 270 calories by consuming beef (100 grams of meat), 22,000 calories are used in its production (one gallon of gasoline contains 38,000 calories).[37]

Thus the availability of fossil energy seems to be a very important limiting factor in efforts to obtain adequate feeding in the year 2000. Fossil energy is rapidly being depleted. Known world reserves of oil and natural gas are expected to be more than half depleted within the next 25 years. One can suppose that new oil reserves will be discovered in the next 25 years so that this source of energy may last for a longer period. Nevertheless, what remains worrisome is the fact that oil reserves are finite while their rate of consumption exceeds that of the rate of growth. Thus, for example, while the population took 300 years to double, energy consumption has doubled in the past ten years.[38] It is expected that new energy sources will be developed, but the speed of this development is unknown. In any case, any other energy source that may come to be used will probably have a much higher cost than oil.

The recent oil crisis has created a very serious problem for the less developed countries. The rise in oil prices has adversely affected them, because they need greater sums of money to import oil and/or fertilizers. In the same way, the rise in the price of oil has also meant a rise in imported food prices. Finally, the world's recent recession lowered the prices of raw materials sold to the developed countries. For example, on account of all these problems, Chile lost more than $1 billion in one year, while in India it is estimated that more than two million people died. This gives some idea of the adverse effects that oil scarcity and higher energy costs could have—effects that most probably could occur in the near future.

36. *Ibid.*
37. *Ibid.*
38. *Ibid.*

From the analysis of the four basic elements—land, water, energy and fertilizer—it may be inferred that these resources are available to increase food production. To maintain the present levels of consumption and nutritional intakes for the projected population in the year 2000, it would be necessary to increase legume production by 66 percent and cereal production by 75 percent, respectively. Even with these increases, however, the number of undernourished people would rise from 500 million to 1.5 billion. With present technologies and resources, it seems possible to increase food production above these levels, but there is still doubt as regards oil energy resources. What really does not seem possible is for all of the world's population in the year 2000 to reach the same levels of food consumption as the developed countries have already reached.

To maintain the nutritional situation after the year 2000 will be very difficult with our present technology. If population growth continues at the rate of 2 percent per year, in the year 2135 there would be 16 billion people. With present land availability, resources and technologies it would be impossible to feed that population.

All the analysis regarding the potential of food production has been made on the basis of scientific and technological knowledge now in use, but it is evident that new technology and knowledge will be produced in the future and could obviously change the outlook. Nevertheless, it seems improbable that new technologies will lead to significant changes in the next 25 years, because the time required between a basic research discovery and its first application is calculated at 13 years.[39] The time necessary for a new technology to reach maximum efficiency is 35 years.[40] Many surprises in the scientific field are likely to be produced in the near future; and some of them can be guessed on the basis of available studies. Nevertheless, at the best, significant increases in food production are not likely to occur in less than 25 years.

In summary, there seem to be basic resources in land and the necessary knowledge to increase present levels of food production. Three main factors are needed to attain this objective: (1) great capital investment; (2) manpower; and (3) knowledge. These three factors are probably the most limiting, because the largest increases must necessarily be made by the less developed countries. They are the ones with biggest food requirements and the highest rates of population growth, and it is in these areas that resources must be found. Estimates made by regions indicate that the

39. M. K. Hubbert, *The Environmental and Ecological Forum 1970–1971* (Oak Ridge, Tenn.: U.S. Atomic Energy Commission Office of Information Services, 1972), pp. 1–5.

40. J. Darmstadler, P. Teitelbaum and J. Polach, *Energy in the World Economy* (Baltimore: Johns Hopkins University Press, 1971).

largest potential growth in cropped areas is in the developing countries of Asia, Africa, and Latin America, which could harvest crops from grossly undercultivated areas outside the humid tropics. These areas are approximately 1,100, 995, and 715 million hectares, respectively.[41] It is, therefore, in the less developed countries that the most fundamental changes must occur. But the developing countries do not have enough capital, they do not have adequately trained manpower and their infrastructure is inefficient. It has been calculated that approximately 700 billion dollars would be needed for the development of irrigation of new lands and modernization of agriculture in Asia, Latin America, and Africa (including the cost of adding lime and other soil supplements).[42] If this cost is distributed over the next 25 years, the annual cost would be about 30 billion dollars—less than one percent of the present GNP of the world. These resources would necessarily have to be provided by the developed countries. Would it be possible to achieve this cooperation? In 1963, the General Assembly of the United Nations recommended that developed countries dedicate at least 1 percent of their GNP to help the less developed. Fifteen years have passed, and these goals are far from being realized. In contrast, the world's military expenditures are increasing every year and are approaching 300 billion dollars a year (Figure 5.2).[43] With only one-tenth of this amount, there would be enough capital in each of the next 25 years to reach the 700 billion dollars target. However, although the proposition seems logical, there is very little probability of obtaining international consensus, so that the rich countries provide the needed help to the poor countries. At least there is no previous historical precedent for humankind meeting such a challenge. Maybe now that the human species is endangered, the more fortunate nations will rise to the occasion. In any case, it will not be easy to establish a supranational mechanism that would resolve the problem. Significant improvement in the lot of the developing nations would necessarily mean a deterioration in living conditions in the affluent nations.

POSSIBILITIES OF DECREASING POPULATION GROWTH RATE

The possibilities of improving feeding in the year 2000 depend basically on food availability and on the number of individuals that must be fed. With the projections of population growth to the year 2000 (at 2 percent per

41. Revelle, "The Resources Available for Agriculture."

42. *Ibid.*

43. J. Tinberger, "Reshaping the International Order," in *A Report of the Club of Rome,* edited by A. Dalman (New York: Dutton, 1976), p. 26.

FIGURE 5.2
World Military Expenditure, 1908–74, in $ U.S. Billions in Constant 1970 Prices

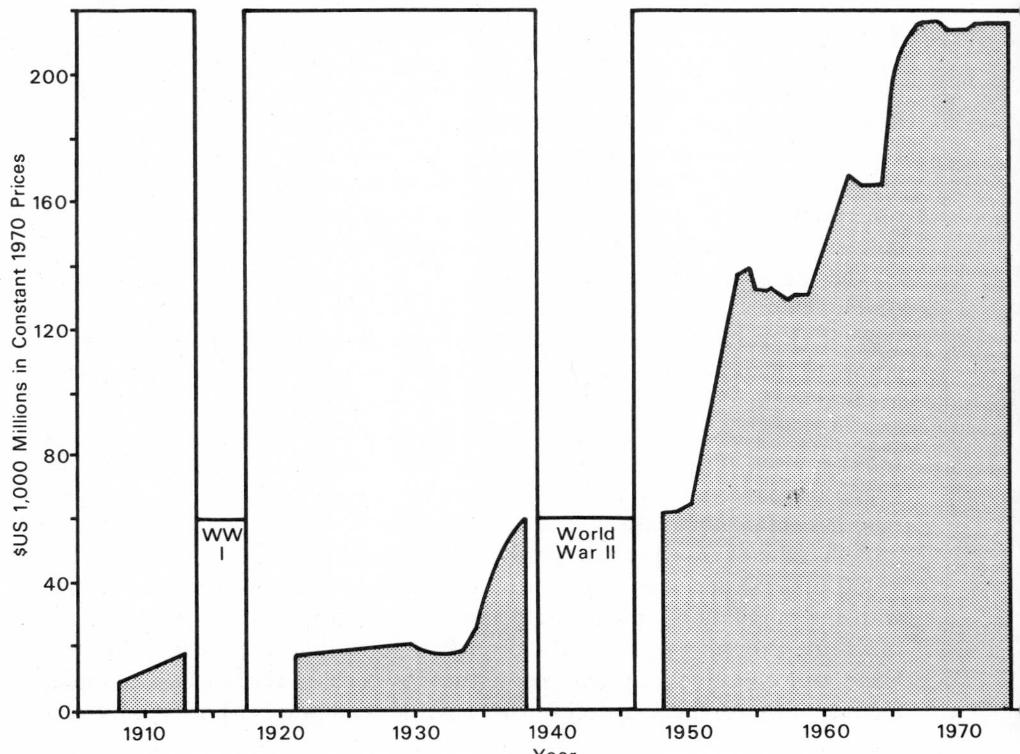

year), it would seem to be difficult to preserve the present nutritional situation and even more difficult to improve it. The problem must be approached by simultaneously considering both the food supply and the many mouths to be fed. This is why it is necessary to study the possibilities of decreasing rates of population growth.

When considering measures to decrease population growth rates, one must realize that they should be applied mainly to developing countries, which exhibit the most explosive growth prospects. According to present projections, by the year 2000, the populations of less developed countries would increase by 2 billion persons, while those of developed countries would increase by only 250 million.

The rate of population growth depends on numerous and complex social, educational and economic factors. In the behavior of populations, two different stages can be distinguished. In the first stage, there would be a decrease in the number of premature deaths as a consequence of the application of health measures and/or environmental sanitation. Thus, for example, the introduction of DDT in Sri Lanka in 1946 eliminated malaria so that general mortality decreased by 35 percent, while a child born in India today has a life expectancy 50 percent higher than the one he would have had in the middle of the century. In the second stage, there would be a decreased number of births that coincides with and probably is the consequence of economic, cultural and social change.

If the rate of population growth is to decrease within a reasonable time frame, it is not possible to depend only on social, economic and cultural development. Moreover, population growth rates and numbers in the developing countries operate to obstruct economic and social development.

It is therefore necessary to design and implement policies and programs to decrease the number of births, especially in those countries that are in their first stage of explosive growth.

In some countries, an important decrease in the population growth rate has been observed in the past few years without a parallel and significant increase in GNP. This may be the case in China, for example. Another interesting case is that of Chile, which in 1970 had a population growth rate of 2.1 percent per year and a birth rate of 30 births per 1,000 persons per year. Since then, a continuous decrease has been noted, with the population growth rate decreasing to 1.5 percent in 1977 and the birth rate dropping to 22 births per 1,000 persons. It is probable that this trend will continue. An analysis of these two cases reveals two common factors: (1) reaching a decision to have a demographic policy; and (2) recognizing the need for a relatively efficient infrastructure to implement it (health infrastructure and educational infrastructure).

These two elements seem absolutely necessary to any country that wants to decrease its rate of population growth. It needs a population policy with clear objectives and consistent programs and, most important, the political decision to implement its policy adequately.

Together with a population policy, efficient infrastructures are required to implement population programs in a coordinated way with other interventions in such areas as health, education and nutrition. This seems possible in countries with intermediate development but it is very difficult in poorly developed countries. Such countries lack adequate structures, qualified personnel and sufficient resources. Unfortunately, it is in these countries that the highest growth rates are to be expected.

As with programs to increase food production, very significant help is needed for population programs from the more developed countries.

Assistance for increasing food production and controlling population growth must be coordinated, because the solution of the food problem necessarily involves a mixture of increases in food production in the developing countries and decreases in the number of mouths to be fed by the year 2000. Isolated aid on food production alone could leave the future quite uncertain. The necessary help of the developed countries should thus have these two components: (1) a policy to increase food production and (2) a policy to decrease rates of population growth.

SOCIOECONOMIC DEVELOPMENT AND UNDERNUTRITION

According to calculations, there will be enough land, water, fertilizers, energy and technology to increase food production over the next two or three decades. Nevertheless, the problem remains of how to obtain an increase in food production in those countries where the deficit is the greatest. Food must not only be produced in greater quantity, but it also must be available to those who most need it. In the less developed countries, individuals are undernourished not only because they do not know what to eat, or because they do not have an adequate variety of food, but also because they lack the necessary economic means to assure an adequate daily diet. In the developing countries, there is a direct relationship between income and amount of calories consumed.[44] With higher incomes, caloric consumption increases and the quality of the diet also improves[45] by greater animal protein intake.[46]

In most of the less developed countries, income distribution is very regressive, with disproportionate concentration of incomes in a very small percentage of the society. Nevertheless, it is also true that in every developing country (except oil producing countries) there is not enough income to distribute.[47] In 1970 in the United States, the annual average per capita expenditure for food was approximately $600. That amount, at that time, was higher than the per capita income of all the developing countries. In the United States, on the average, 16.8 percent of the per capita income is used for food. In Latin America, an average of 64 percent is used and in

44. S. Reutlinger, "Malnutrition: A Poverty or a Food Problem?" Fourth Annual James Memorial Lecture. North Carolina State University, March 24, 1977.

45. F. Mönckeberg, *Jaque al Subdesarrollo* 3rd ed. (Santiago: Gabriela Mistral, 1976).

46. F. Mönckeberg, *Food and Nutrition Policy in Chile* (Santiago: Gabriela Mistra, 1976).

47. Mönckeberg, *Jaque al Subdesarrollo.*

India 84 percent. This can be easily explained because the income per capita in the United States was $6,720, while more than 50 percent of the population in developing countries had a per capita income under $300. The donation of food by developed countries to developing countries might be useful as a transitory measure, but it does not constitute a long-term solution because it only creates new needs and greater dependency, and it inhibits the search for local solutions. It is evident that the nutritional problems of the less developed countries will not be solved until the GNP of these countries increases notably and a better internal distribution of incomes is achieved. It is necessary, of course, to implement palliative measures of nutritional intervention to target groups, but the results will always be limited because the problem of undernutrition cannot be separated from the problem of poverty. As long as the problem of poverty is not solved, undernutrition also will not be solved.

In poor countries, scarce food production is only one manifestation of very complex social and economic problems. The less developed countries do not constitute a homogeneous group. Some are overcrowded while others are sparsely populated. Some have large unexploited food production resources while others do not. In some countries, poverty and undernutrition constitute a desperate situation, while in others, they constitute a less immediate problem. In some, only subsistence is possible, while in others, varying degrees of industrialization and higher levels of living have been reached. Some have an almost exclusively rural population, while others have an important percentage of urban population. Strategies must necessarily be tailored to the situation in each country. In those where almost all the population is rural and agriculture very traditional and primitive, efforts must be made to improve agricultural efficiency. In others, as in most of the Latin American countries in which a high percentage of the population is urban (64 percent), it is not enough to improve subsistence agriculture, because it is necessary to feed the large proportion of the population living in slums in the cities. In the latter countries, it is not only imperative to increase food production, but it is also necessary to achieve economic and social development and to generate new employment with higher incomes that can provide a certain degree of well-being to the growing urban population.

Most of the poorer countries that have severe land limitations and extremely large populations are in Asia. In these countries, food availability is largely a function of rice production, and rice production is, in turn, a major source of income. In these countries the immediate need is to increase the rice harvest (one ton per hectare, compared to five tons per hectare in developed countries). The poor countries lack the capital needed to increase their rice production. For them, sustained assistance in capital, food, fertilizers and appropriate technology is necessary.

The problem is not simple, even when many of the basic techniques to raise yields in developing countries are already known. The transfer of advanced technology is extremely difficult. What happened in those countries that experienced the "Green Revolution" demonstrates the difficulty. The adoption of high yield techniques often was not profitable because there was a limited market, or the prices that farmers received were too low to justify the use of such techniques. A study of rice and fertilizer prices in 1971 demonstrated that in the best rice-producing Southeast Asian countries, the farmer's price for rice relative to the price of fertilizer was far less favorable than in developed countries. Basic economic changes are needed, including greater incentives for increasing rice production in these less developed countries.

THE ROAD TO ECONOMIC AND SOCIAL DEVELOPMENT

The increase of food availability in the less developed countries depends ultimately on their possibilities for economic and social development. If family income and purchasing power increase, a series of events will follow that will make it possible to increase food production efficiently. Food production depends on demand, and demand depends on purchasing power. Purchasing power depends on income and income depends on economic and social development.

During the past decades, the great differences between developed and less developed countries have widened. The "have" nations have increased their riches, while the "have-not" nations have persisted in their poverty. Will it be possible to narrow the gap? Will it be possible for poor countries using technological advances to follow the paths of the developed countries? Or will there be new ways to shorten the road to higher levels of living?

It is evident that the gap between developed and poor countries has increased during this century and especially during the past several decades. The gap started to increase with the industrial revolution and later with the technological revolution. Some countries that now have an intermediate level of development, as in the case of most of Latin America, retained a simple and traditional agrarian economy and participated in the development process only as raw material exporters. Technological progress generates a growing need for complex products, and expanded imports produce a disequilibrium in the balance of payments with increasing trade deficits.

With the close of the Second World War, some countries entered a stage of developing industry to achieve import substitution. They did attain some industrial development but their base was weak because the local market was small. They had limited technological knowledge and they lacked the necessary scientific and technical infrastructure. These new industries could exist only because they were strongly protected. Their products were of inferior quality and their prices were three to five times higher than in the international markets. In consequence they could not successfully compete in the export market. Undoubtedly, this important substitution strategy had a very serious limitation and contributed to very slow economic and social development. This policy also coincided with the neglect of agricultural development. The agricultural sector did not receive adequate incentives for increased production. On the contrary, chronic inflation developed and led to food price controls. In the case of Latin American countries, the rate of population growth exceeded the rate of increase in food production. As a result, as shown in Figure 5.3, wheat imports increased in the period between 1950 and 1975.[48] Not only did productivity decrease, but the number of hectares devoted to wheat also declined.[49] The unemployed in the countryside migrated to the cities, creating belts of poverty around them. Migration was mainly caused by rural misery.

The policy of industrial development based on import substitution did not achieve its objective of improving the balance of payments. The need to develop new, more expensive and more complex products exceeded the industrial capabilities of those countries. The external debt of Latin American countries in the year 1940 was $6 billion; it has now soared to $70 billion (World Bank). It is evident that the import substitution policy has serious limitations and cannot be continued. The world has become an interdependent unit and no country can develop in isolation. Technological progress and economic interdependence make it impossible for any country to achieve economic autarchy. It is not possible to indefinitely continue exporting raw materials, whose prices are fluctuating and are below the price levels of industrial products. It is therefore necessary to find a niche in the international market with products that permit international exchange with a reasonable balance of payments.

The industrial development of the more developed countries has reached a level which makes it difficult for the less developed countries to compete. It is necessary therefore to concentrate development in areas where comparative advantages might be found. This consideration leads to the possibility of finding a solution in agricultural development.

48. M. Valderrama and E. Morcardi, "Current Policies Affecting Food Production: The Care of Wheat in the Andean Region," The World Food Conference of 1976, Iowa State University (1976), p. 219.

49. *Ibid.*

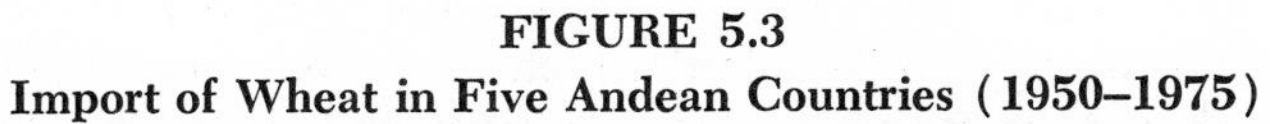

FIGURE 5.3
Import of Wheat in Five Andean Countries (1950–1975)

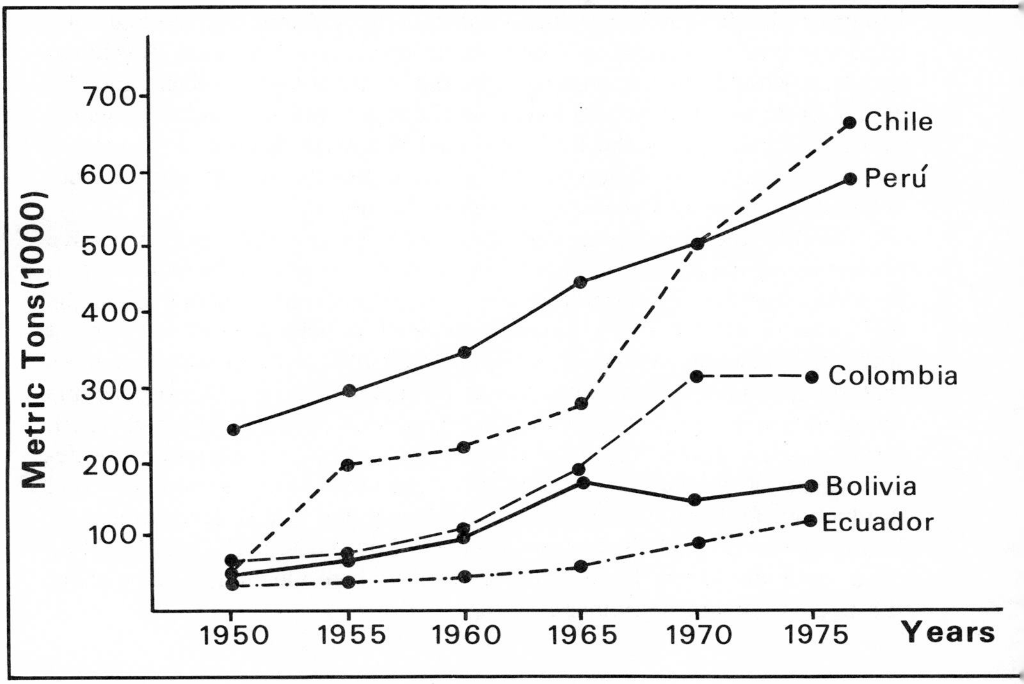

Many less developed countries, as in the case of Latin America and Africa, have enormous potential for increasing agricultural and animal husbandry production by extending their agricultural areas and improving productivity. It is relevant to point out that advanced countries such as the United States have greatly increased their exports of agriculture and animal husbandry products.

Agricultural and animal husbandry development should, therefore, have priority not only to help solve local nutritional problems, but also as a key element in the modernization of the economy. It is also very important to take into account that food self-sufficiency in all countries is neither a desirable nor an efficient use of resources. Agricultural and animal husbandry development should be pursued in accordance with the comparative advantages they offer. If it is not advantageous to produce grains in a given country, these essential foods can be bought in the international market with the earnings of other products sold there, with greater advantage and higher aggregate value. To make this possible, resources and appropriate technology are required which the developing countries lack and which should be provided by the developed countries. Developed countries should not hinder the import of agricultural and animal husbandry products originating from poorer countries. The more developed countries should eliminate direct subsidies to their own products and decrease customs barriers and other mechanisms that discriminate against products coming from the less developed countries. Such actions require the cooperation and understanding of governments in both the less developed countries and the more developed countries.

Within the developing countries, it is necessary to stop excessive protection of inefficient industries by means of customs barriers and to provide incentives to agriculture and animal husbandry as well as to the utilization of available natural resources. Such policies are often in conflict with the immediate wishes of many governments of developing countries that set low prices on food products for the benefit of the poor people living in urban areas. In the long term, permitting these prices to reach normal market levels would be a small price to pay for achieving the development of agriculture and animal husbandry, the increase of food production, and the acceleration of economic and social development. If it is necessary to subsidize prices to benefit poor customers, this should be done without adversely affecting agricultural production, and without subsidizing affluent consumers.

SUMMARY

It is evident that in the coming decades it will be possible to increase efficiency in the use of land resources. But to achieve this, it is imperative that the governments of developing countries, as well as those from developed countries, be aware that the world's food supply is already enmeshed in an international system, and that no one country can obtain benefits at the expense of others. In the near future, world stability will be impossible if a few live in prosperity surrounded by a great mass of people living in misery. Modern communications make it impossible for either poverty or affluence to be hidden. Since the high levels of living in developed countries depends to a great extent on resources that emanate from developing countries, some balance must be achieved. The achievement of the human right, the right to nutrition and growth in healthful conditions, is possible only with cooperative effort and understanding and with a readiness for some sacrifice, especially on the part of the more affluent populations.

6

Health, Population, and Nutrition: Interrelations, Problems, and Possible Solutions

WALTER WATSON, ALLAN ROSENFIELD,
MECHAI VIRAVAIDYA, AND
KRASAE CHANAWONGSE

INCREASINGLY, the fields of health, population, and nutrition are being discussed together because of the many relationships among them. Although the literature in each field is extensive, there is much overlapping in the topics covered. For example, nutrition has an effect on health and fertility, and health and fertility influence nutrition. Similarly, health and population concerns are closely interwoven; and activities in each area affect the other. In this chapter these interrelationships, with emphasis on the effects of maternal age, parity, and child spacing on maternal and infant health, will first be reviewed. Next, problems in delivering essential health care and family planning services to the majority of the world's poor, particularly those living in rural and urban slum areas of developing countries, will be considered. Finally, some of the causes of these problems will be described, and possible solutions, based on apparently successful efforts in a number of different settings, will be suggested.

INTERRELATIONS

The fields of population and health involve many variables and practitioners from many social and natural science disciplines. Mortality, one of the principal variables of demographic analysis, is a key measure of health status. Family planning programs have become one of the most important responses to the problems associated with excessively high population growth rates. They also are seen as a major response to maternal and child health problems. Thus, the numerous links between the fields of population and health have become obvious.[1] Increasingly, students of population have become concerned not only with the quantity, distribution, and characteristics of those living, but also with the relationships of population to the quality of life. Similarly, in the field of health, the definition of health in the narrower sense of the absence of disease has been giving way to a much broader concept involving a positive state of physical, mental, and social well-being—key elements in quality of life.[2]

Recently several writers have extensively reviewed relationships among population, health, and nutrition or family planning and health.[3] In this chapter works by these authors are drawn upon and summarized before issues on international population and health are discussed. Primary sources are cited when necessary to supplement the various reviews.

1. United Nations, World Health Organization, "Health and Family Planning," in *The Population Debate: Dimensions and Perspectives* (New York: Papers of the World Population Conference, Bucharest, vol. 2, 1975), pp. 461–79; "Health Trends and Prospects in Relation to Population and Development," in *ibid.*, vol. 1, pp. 573–97.

2. *Ibid.*, "Health and Family Planning."

3. *Ibid.*, "Health Trends"; W. Henry Mosley, ed., *Nutrition and Human Reproduction* (New York: Plenum, 1978); Robert Buchanan, "Effects of Childbearing On Maternal Health," *Population Reports,* Series J (8) (November 1975); John Cassel, "Health Consequences of Population Density and Crowding," ch. XII in National Academy of Sciences, *Rapid Population Growth: Consequences and Policy Implications* (Baltimore: Johns Hopkins University Press, 1971), pp. 462–78; Erik Eckolm and Kathleen Newland, "Health: The Family Planning Factor," *Worldwatch Paper 10* (Worldwatch Institute) (January 1977); Dorothy Nortman, "Parental Age as a Factor in Pregnancy Outcome and Child Development," *Reports on Population/Family Planning* 16 (Population Council) (August 1974); Dorothy Nortman, "Relations of Fertility and Health," Population Council, unpublished paper, 1978; Abdel R. Omran, *The Health Theme in Family Planning* (Chapel Hill: Carolina Population Center, Monograph no. 16, University of North Carolina, 1971); Abdel R. Omran, "Health Benefits of Family Planning," *Maternity-Centered Family Planning Paper* (Geneva: World Health Organization, October, 1971); Abdel R. Omran, *et al.*, eds., *Family Formation Patterns and Health* (Geneva: World Health Organization, 1976); Joe D. Wray, "Population Pressure on Families: Family Size and Child Spacing," ch. XI in National Academy of Sciences, *Rapid Population Growth: Consequences and Policy Implications* (Baltimore: Johns Hopkins University Press, 1971), pp. 403–61, reprinted in *Reports on Population/Family Planning* 9 (Population Council) (August 1971); Kenneth W. Terhune, *A Review of the Actual and Expected Consequences of Family Size,* Calspan Report No. DP–5333–G–1, Center for Population Research, National Institute of Child Health and Human Development, U.S. Department of Health, Education, and Welfare, publication no. (NIH) 75–779, July 31, 1974; Beverly Winikoff, "Nutrition, Population, and Health: Some Implications for Policy," *Science* 200 (May 26, 1978):895–902.

Health, Nutrition, Population, and Human Rights

Health, nutrition, and population are interrelated, first, in the context of basic human rights. Health, in both its narrower classical and broader modern senses, and nutrition were embodied as universal rights by the United Nations General Assembly in 1948, and maternal and child health were recognized as deserving special attention. Article 25 of the Universal Declaration of Human Rights states:

> Everyone has the right to a standard of living adequate for the health and well-being of himself and of his family, including food, clothing, housing and medical care and necessary social services, and the right to security in the event of unemployment, sickness, disability, widowhood, old age. . . . Motherhood and childhood are entitled to special care and assistance.

From both the health and demographic points of view, access to the means of mortality and morbidity control is implicit in the General Assembly's declaration.

The United Nations also recognized access to knowledge and means of fertility control as well as freedom of mobility and migration in Article 13 of the Universal Declaration of Human Rights. The human rights aspects of population policies and programs are elaborated in Chapter 14.

Health, Nutrition, Population, and Socioeconomic Development

Health, nutrition, and population are also interrelated in the context of socioeconomic development, in which all are significant components.[4] Among the most common indices of socioeconomic development are life expectancy and the infant mortality rate, each of which is also a common index of health, nutrition, and demographic status. Thus, socioeconomic development is taken to mean rising life expectancy, declining infant and maternal mortality, and improved nutritional status, just as it means increases in literacy, education, electrification, industrialization, female labor force participation outside the home, urbanization, and gross national product.

Numbers of doctors and other medical personnel and hospital beds

4. Helen M. Wallace, *et al.*, "World Wide Problems in the Field of Maternal and Child Health and Family Planning Services in the Developing Countries," School of Public Health, University of California, unpublished paper, n. d.

per capita are also frequently used indices of socioeconomic development, as well as of health infrastructure. Indices of fertility might usefully be employed as indices of development as well as of demographic status except that fertility is often regarded as a dependent variable in analyses of the independent and joint effects of socioeconomic development and family planning programs. The independent importance of both factors on declining fertility has been documented.[5]

Health, nutritional, and population variables relate to other developmental variables in independent and dependent ways.[6] For a number of analytic purposes life expectancy, infant mortality, and health infrastructure variables are sometimes also regarded as dependent upon, as well as interdependent with, other development variables. Thus health and nutrition are quality-of-life objectives as well as measures of socioeconomic development.[7] Population control, on the other hand, is usually conceived in the latter sense only. Under certain circumstances this distinction has important implications for the types of programs that will receive the stronger political and budgetary support.[8]

The importance of the interrelationship of population (and, to a lesser extent, health and nutrition) and socioeconomic development was heavily emphasized in the 1974 World Population Conference, the World Population Plan of Action (WPPA)[9] adopted there, and the conference papers.[10] The persistent stress on a new international economic order in a population plan and the call for the establishment of a population unit within the national economic planning apparatus[11] suggest as much. Although to the best knowledge of the authors no serious student of population and family planning or economic development had ever

5. Timothy King, *et al., Population Policies and Economic Development,* A World Bank Staff Report (Baltimore: Johns Hopkins University Press, 1974); W. Parker Mauldin and Bernard Berelson, "Conditions of Fertility Decline in Developing Countries, 1965–75," *Studies in Family Planning* 9 (5) (May 1978):89–147; K. S. Srikantan, *The Family Planning Program in the Socioeconomic Context* (New York: Population Council, 1977); Amy Ong Tsui and Donald J. Bogue, "Declining World Fertility: Trends, Causes, Implications," *Population Bulletin* 33 (4) (October 1978).

6. World Health Organization, "Health Trends."

7. National Research Council, *World Food and Nutrition Study* (Washington: National Academy of Sciences, 1977).

8. Benjamin Barg, "Nutrition and National Development," ch. 6 in *Nutrition, National Development, and Planning,* edited by Alan Berg, *et al.* (Cambridge, Mass.: MIT Press, 1973), pp. 49–69.

9. "World Population Plan of Action," in *The Population Debate,* vol. 1, pp. 155–167, especially preamble and paragraphs 14, 68–70, 78, and 95.

10. *Ibid.,* vol. 1–2.

11. *Ibid.,* "World Population Plan of Action."

advocated to the contrary, the conference and the WPPA stressed that a reduction in population growth could in no way substitute for basic socioeconomic development and that population policies and programs should be viewed explicitly in a more general context as an aspect of development programs and not as a substitute for them. In short, population and development were endorsed, and the hypothetical "straw-man" concept of population programs in lieu of development was rejected.

Health ministries frequently emphasize the contributions of health, nutrition, and population variables and morbidity control to decreased long-term effects of childhood malnutrition and illness, decreased labor absenteeism and school and work days lost, decreased loss from premature death during working life, increased labor productivity, and socioeconomic development generally.[12] Improved health may make possible the opening up of previously uninhabitable areas and the development of their resources. Better health and nutrition and more effective family planning may also have important, but difficult to quantify, indirect effects on stimulating attitudinal change and attacking fatalistic apathy.[13] Despite such arguments, however, in the fierce budgetary competition for scarce funds, health, nutrition, and population programs have frequently encountered difficulties at the hands of economic development planning agencies and personnel vis-à-vis industrialization and military priorities; this is true in rich as well as in poor countries.

Family Planning and Nutrition as Ministry of Health Programs

There are a number of different types of population programs. For example, there are programs to improve the collection of basic demographic data; to conduct social science research on the correlates of changes in fertility, mortality, or migration; to develop and extend population education, family life and sex education, and family planning education; to develop and improve new contraceptives and to conduct related biomedical research; and to develop and extend family planning service delivery,[14] which has commanded considerable attention and resources in many developing countries in recent years.[15]

12. *Ibid.*, "Health Trends."

13. *Ibid.*

14. United Nations Fund for Population Activities, *Inventory of Population Projects in Developing Countries Around the World, 1967–1977* (New York: United Nations Fund for Population Activities, 1976–77).

15. Walter B. Watson, ed., *Family Planning in the Developing World* (New York: Population Council, 1977).

Though the demographic and economic implications of the reduction of fertility, which may be associated with a family planning program, are often recognized, and indeed in many cases have been a principal rationale for the development of a public program, health implications are also almost universally recognized. Consequently, although they have special economic and human rights significance and are related to other social development programs, most family planning programs have been conducted under the aegis of ministries of health or health and population. In some instances they are special-purpose or "vertical" programs; in others, they are linked to the provision of maternal and child health or other health services. Because national or large-scale public family planning programs are conducted by ministries of health, rather than, for example, through the private sector or other government ministries, and because family planning is defined as a sector of health programming, another key health-population relationship has been established. Nutrition programs also appear to be evolving under health ministry auspices.

High-Risk Pregnancy

A number of interrelationships between health and population revolve around the concept of high-risk pregnancy. Prevention of such pregnancies has an impact, in many instances substantial, by lowering rates of fertility and population growth and improving health through the reduction of mortality and morbidity associated, by definition, with such pregnancies.[16]

The concept of high-risk pregnancy, which involves a higher-than-normal medical risk to the mother or infant, is not new. The higher risks associated with pregnancies in the late years of the reproductive period and those to women of quite high parity have long been known. In recent years, however, it has been more explicitly recognized that there are many medical conditions predisposing to high risk. Research on the topic has increased. In addition, considerable interest in the reproductive problems of teenagers has been developing.[17]

The definition of high risk has been substantially expanded, in keeping with more modern notions of what is meant by health, to include a broader spectrum of medical indications, as well as social and economic

16. Bernard Berelson, "18–35 in Place of 15–45," *The Population Council Annual Report 1971* (New York: Population Council, 1972), pp. 19–27.

17. "A Special Issue on Teenage Pregnancy," *Family Planning Perspectives* 10 (4) (July/August 1978):199–235.

factors.[18] The reduction of high-risk pregnancies has become a key rationale for several of the family planning programs in Latin America, where family planning frequently must be justified on health grounds, as opposed to Asia, where the principal rationale has usually been population control. The high risk associated with short pregnancy intervals is well understood in Africa, where child spacing is probably more important culturally as a family planning rationale than in Asia or Latin America. This rationale may well become even more important in Africa in the future as family planning programs develop further and individual interest in family planning deepens. For example, in 1972 President Mobutu Sese Seko of Zaire called for limiting births to "desirable births,"[19] and the government established the National Council for Promotion of Desirable Births.[20]

High Risk to Mothers and Infants in the Early and Late Reproductive Years

As suggested above, many health risks to mothers and to their infants are related to the mother's age at birth. As Omran *et al.* put it:

> Studies have revealed a consistent association between maternal age and mortality and morbidity in mothers and children. These studies uniformly suggest that there is an age-band in the fertility span of a woman during which the reproductive risks are at a minimum; on either side of this relatively safe age-band, the risks progressively increase, describing J-shaped, U-shaped or reversed J-shaped curves. These patterns are particularly typical of late fetal deaths, perinatal mortality, infant mortality, prematurity, and maternal mortality. Congenital malformations, especially Down's Syndrome, increase steadily with age.[21]

The period of minimum risk typically falls in the early twenties, although this may vary slightly between countries and for different risk factors.

Nortman has reviewed the relationships between pregnancy outcome and subsequent child development on the one hand and maternal age on the other in some detail.[22] She noted a J-shaped relationship between

18. Nortman, "Relations of Fertility and Health"; Wallace *et al.*, "World Wide Problems in the Field of Maternal and Child Health."

19. Dorothy Nortman and Ellen Hofstatter, *Population and Family Planning Programs*, 9th ed. (New York: Population Council, 1978).

20. International Planned Parenthood Federation (IPPF), "Family Planning in Five Continents," London, December 1976.

21. Omran, *Family Formation*, p. 34.

22. Nortman, "Parental Age as a Factor."

maternal age and maternal mortality from all causes, and probably also from the specific major causes of sepsis, toxemia, and hemorrhage. By 1969, such a relationship had been found under low general mortality conditions in fourteen countries; under medium mortality conditions in sixteen countries; and under high mortality conditions in twelve countries. Data from the 1974 and 1976 United Nations Demographic Yearbooks suggest that another five countries may be added to these forty-two countries. Similar findings have been reported in Bangladesh[23] and Indonesia.[24] Thus, the curvilinear relationship between maternal mortality and maternal age seems to hold across different world regions and at different stages of socioeconomic development. This provides strong support for the health as well as the demographic rationale in reducing unwanted pregnancies at the very young (below 18, or perhaps below 20) and the older (35 or above) ages of the reproductive span.

Late fetal deaths (stillbirths); neonatal, perinatal, and infant mortality; prematurity; and low birth weight also show a curvilinear relationship to maternal age.[25] Studies in a number of developed and developing countries document a high infant mortality for infants of mothers in their teens, a minimum for mothers in their twenties, and an increasingly steep rise for mothers over age 35.[26] Reducing the births and the deaths associated with these conditions would make a major contribution to public health in areas of the world where infant mortality is high, which includes most of the developing countries, and a not-insignificant contribution in most of the developed countries as well. It would also lower fertility not only directly, but also indirectly through the relationship between family size desires and infant survival (the "child survival hypothesis").[27] For example, Wright estimated for the United States that elimination of all births except first births between ages 20 and 29 and second and third births between ages 25 and 34 would reduce infant and postneonatal mortality markedly.

23. Buchanan, "Effects of Childbearing"; Eckholm and Newland, "Health: The Family Planning Factor."

24. Haryono Suyono and Thomas H. Reese, "Integrating Village Family Planning and Primary Health Services: The Indonesian Perspective," unpublished paper, Jakarta, January 1978.

25. Nortman, "Parental Age as a Factor"; Omran, *Family Formation.*

26. Nortman, "Parental Age as a Factor"; Eckholm and Newland, "Health: The Family Planning Factor"; Peter Kunstadter, "Child Mortality and Maternal Parity: Some Policy Implications," *International Family Planning Perspectives and Digest* 4 (3) (Fall 1978):75–85.

27. Kunstadter, "Child Mortality"; World Health Organization, "Health Trends," pp. 592–95; Omran, *Family Foundation,* pp. 38–43; Omran, *The Health Theme,* pp. 115–32; Samuel H. Preston, "Health Programs and Population Growth," *Population and Development Review* 1 (2) (December 1975):189–99.

"Under optimal assumptions of family size, spacing and timing of first births, infant mortality might be reduced as much as thirty percent."[28] While such estimates involve family size limitation as well as shifts in the timing of births by maternal age, it is likely that the contribution to health would be even greater in developing countries, where infant mortality is much higher.

As Nortman and Berelson have noted, the demographic effects of reducing births by women below age 20 and at age 35 and above, although difficult to estimate precisely, would be quite substantial.[29,30] Estimation is more complicated than it initially appears. In the first place, not all such births are in fact unwanted, so that not all would be eliminated even if the requisite knowledge and access to means were widely diffused and conveniently, inexpensively, and universally available. Age at marriage might increase, leading to delayed fertility in the very early twenties over and above the reduction of fertility below age 20. On the other hand, an opposing influence would be that births which under "normal past" circumstances would have taken place during the later teens might be deferred until ages 20 to 21, rather than eliminated, thereby increasing fertility in the early twenties. With the reduction of births at age 35 and over, the average age at which women bear their children would tend to decline slightly, thereby increasing the crude birth rate.

Frejka shows 29 percent of total fertility (number of live births per woman) outside of ages 20 through 34 for the developing countries and 27 percent foı the developed countries.[31] Bearing in mind the complexities noted above, Nortman suggests, as general orders of magnitude, that elimination of fertility beyond this central age range would decrease world fertility by about one-quarter, would decrease overall mortality (because of decreases in infant, child, and maternal mortality) by about 15 percent(a most impressive contribution to world health), and despite the lowered mortality, would decrease world population growth by about 30 percent.[32] Population growth in the resource-hungry developed world would cease completely, and women in the developing countries would have only slightly more than four births during their lifetimes, as opposed to the 1965–70 level of 5.7.[33]

28. Nicholas H. Wright, "Some Aspects of the Reduction in the U.S. Infant Mortality Rate by Family Planning," *American Journal of Public Health* 62 (8) (August 1972):1130–34.

29. Nortman, "Parental Age as a Factor."

30. Berelson, "18–35 in Place of 15–45."

31. Tomas Frejka, *The Future of Population Growth* (New York: Wiley, 1973).

32. Nortman, "Parental Age as a Factor."

33. Frejka, *The Future.*

High Risk to High-Parity Mothers and Their Infants

Progressively higher parity also entails progressively higher reproductive risks, just as advanced maternal age does. The well-known risks associated with multiparity are not very surprising in view of the close relationship between age and parity. As Wray indicates:

> The effects of increasing numbers of pregnancies on mothers must also be mentioned here. A large number of pregnancies is a necessary precondition for a large number of children, although it is obvious that where infant or childhood mortality rates are high, a mother may belong in the "grand multipara" group and yet have only a few living children. Repeated pregnancies followed by prolonged lactation periods will, among other things, produce sustained needs for high quality protein in the diet. In the many parts of the world where these needs are poorly met, the result is what Jelliffe has termed the "maternal depletion syndrome" (1966). This process may contribute to low birth weight of their infants, to poor performance in lactation and, ultimately ". . . this cumulative process plays a part in the premature ageing and early death often seen among women in developing regions."[34]

Omran *et al.* continue:

> Several studies . . . have found that multiparity, especially grand multiparity, carries increased risks of maternal mortality and obstetric complications such as placenta previa, abruptio placentae, malpresentation of fetus, postpartum haemorrhage, anaemia, toxaemia, and rupture of the uterus. Some evidence also links parity with other maternal health problems, such as prolapse, cancer of the cervix, and diabetes.[35]

Supporting evidence derives from studies in Canada, Finland, the United Kingdom, and the United States in the developed world and Sri Lanka and Thailand in the developing world.[36] Findings of poorer mental health among higher parity women have been reported from Jamaica, Nigeria, South Africa, and the United Kingdom.[37,38]

34. Wray, "Population Pressure on Families," p. 431.

35. Omran, *Family Formation,* p. 29.

36. Wray, "Population Pressure on Families"; Omran, *Family Formation;* World Health Organization, "Health Trends"; Buchanan, "Effects of Childbearing"; Kunstadter, "Child Mortality."

37. Wray, "Population Pressure on Families."

38. Omran, *Family Formation.*

High parity is associated with a higher risk of fetal, perinatal, neonatal, infant, and early childhood mortality and malnutrition as well as maternal mortality. Again there is a parallel to maternal age. Omran *et al.* sum up:

> The general pattern that emerges from various studies [of fetal, perinatal, neonatal, infant, and childhood mortality], mostly undertaken in industrialized countries, indicates that the risk of late fetal death (stillbirth) is relatively high for first births, decreases for second and third births, increases slightly for fourth births, and increases much more sharply for later order births.
>
> The relationship between neonatal mortality rates and birth order shows a similar . . . curve. Both postneonatal and total infant mortality rates increase steadily with increasing birth order, as do the mortality rates for early childhood (1–4 years). If allowance is made for maternal age, infant mortality rates may continue to show a linear increase with parity or they may take the form of a U-shaped curve, especially for older mothers. Some of the more detailed studies indicate that, although a strong inverse relationship exists between mortality and social class, the variations in mortality with birth order are maintained within each social class.[39]

One or more of these risks have been found to be correlated with high parity in studies in Canada, Czechoslovakia, Hungary, Italy, Japan, Portugal, the United Kingdom, and the United States among developed countries and in Bangladesh, Chile, Colombia, Zaire, India, Nigeria, Rwanda, and Taiwan among developing nations.[40]

The exact shape on a graph of the relationships with parity is not as important as with age from a pragmatic public health viewpoint because although the number of births can be reduced among the very young (as well as among older women) by changing their age patterning, no significant reduction in the number of first births is likely to take place. It is feasible programmatically, however, to reduce the incidence of those higher order births (and the associated deaths) which are unwanted through the introduction and expansion of convenient, inexpensive, and high-quality family planning services. As with maternal age, there is a potentially high payoff in public health and demographic terms.

39. *Ibid.*, p. 18.

40. *Ibid.;* Wray, "Population Pressure on Families"; Eckholm and Newland, "Health: The Family Planning Factor"; G. A. O. Alleyne *et al.*, *Protein-Energy Malnutrition* (London: Edward Arnold, 1976).

High Risk from Closely Spaced Births to Mothers, Infants, and Next Youngest Siblings

Birth spacing is obviously not entirely independent of parity or age. To some degree high parity necessarily implies closely spaced births, beginning childbearing early, and continuing it to advanced reproductive age. There are, however, risks associated with closely spaced births even when not of high parity nor at either extreme of the reproductive age span.

Most early family planning accepters in the Taiwanese program were more interested in limiting family size than in child spacing; however, interest in spacing has increased as family planning has spread, and family size has become more effectively controlled.[41] Trends in several other Asian countries are similar. In Africa, on the other hand, child spacing is "cultural" in many areas. Taboos on intercourse for varying lengths of time following a birth or during breastfeeding are common.[42]

Connections between closely spaced births and maternal, infant, and child health appear to have been dramatic enough not to have escaped notice in folk cultures. The "maternal depletion syndrome"[43] associated with a rapid succession of pregnancies, prolonged lactation, inadequate recuperation periods, inadequate protein and caloric intake, and anemia[44] is well known as *shutika* in Bangladesh.[45] Cultural restrictions on intercourse by nursing mothers in Africa were mentioned above, and the name *kwashiorkor,* first used by Cecile Williams, derives from the Ghanian Ga language and means "the disease of the deposed baby (from the mother's breast) when the next one is born."[46]

Excessively frequent childbearing is likely to lead to maternal anemia as documented by studies in India, Nigeria, and Latin America. Anemia in

41. T. H. Sun, "The Impact on Fertility of Taiwan's Family Planning Program," ch. 12 in *Measuring the Effect of Family Planning Programs on Fertility,* edited by C. Chandrasekaran and Albert I. Hermalin (Paris: International Union for the Scientific Study of Population and Development, Centre of the Organization for Economic Cooperation and Development, 1975), pp. 427–504.

42. Thomas E. Dow, Jr., "Breastfeeding and Abstinence among the Yoruba," *Studies in Family Planning* 8 (8) (August 1977):208–14; Carol Valentine and Joanne Revson, "Culture, Tradition, Social Change and Fertility in Sub-Saharan Africa," (Manuscript in preparation, Center for Population and Family Health, Columbia University, 1979).

43. Derrick B. Jelliffe, *The Assessment of the Nutritional Status of the Community* (Geneva: World Health Organization Monograph Series no. 53, 1966).

44. Wray, "Population Pressure on Families."

45. Eckholm and Newland, "Health: The Family Planning Factor."

46. *Ibid.;* Wray, "Population Pressure on Families"; Omran, *Family Formation.*

turn is frequently a contributing factor to maternal and general female mortality.[47] On the basis of studies from Ecuador and India, as well as those from developed countries, Omran *et al.*[48] summarize the state of scientific knowledge concerning the relationship between short birth intervals and infant mortality as follows:

> Many studies from developed countries and some from the less developed countries have shown an association between short birth intervals and higher relative risks to child health. Research concerning the influence of birth interval on family health is scanty and fraught with methodological problems. This is an area for further investigation, especially in developing countries where the factors of lactation and nutrition play an important part in these interactions.

As suggested by the comment on kwashiorkor, the adverse effects of short birth intervals are not limited to mothers and newborn infants, but extend to the next youngest sibling as well. Studies on malnutrition in Colombia and Thailand have documented this relationship,[49] and the Ecuadorian study indicates greater risk of fetal mortality in very short (and also very long) succeeding pregnancy intervals as well as preceding ones.[50]

High Health and Development Risks in Large Families and to Children of High Birth Order

Beyond the risks of maternal, infant, and early childhood mortality associated with early and later maternal age, high parity, and short birth intervals summarized above, there are a variety of infant and child physical and mental health and developmental problems that appear to occur more frequently in larger families than small ones and more to children of higher birth order than low order.[51] The evidence, particularly from developing countries, is neither as extensive nor as clear-cut as one would wish. Nevertheless, Wray was able to summarize as follows:

> The effects associated with family size on the well-being of individuals in a family are varied, but serious: increased illness, including mal-

47. Buchanan, "Effects of Childbearing."
48. Omran, *Family Formation,* p. 36.
49. Wray, "Population Pressure on Families."
50. Omran, *Family Formation.*
51. *Ibid.;* Wray, "Population Pressure on Families"; Terhune, *A Review.*

nutrition, serious enough in younger children to increase mortality rates; less satisfactory growth and intellectual development; increased illness in the parents, as well as clear-cut economic and emotional stresses. Family size is not the only cause of these effects, but it is clearly implicated as an important element in the interacting network of causal factors.[52]

And Omran *et al.* add:

> A number of child health conditions have been linked to family size and birth order (as well as to maternal age). Included are congenital malformation, physical handicaps, malnutrition, dental problems, infectious diseases, emotional problems, and mental illness. Some conditions—like malnutrition—are probably directly related to increased strain on family and maternal resources with each additional child; in the case of common infections, larger family size may simply lead to more frequent exposure to infectious agents through other family members.
>
> Several studies, again mainly from developed countries, describe a detrimental effect of large family (or sibship) size and high birth order on physical and intellectual development. . . .
>
> Birth weight and prematurity provide measures of infant physical development. However, controversy exists about the relationship of birth weight and prematurity to birth order. Mean birth weight seems to increase with birth order (although not consistently), while the rates for prematurity (defined as birth weights below 2501 g) have either a linear or a J-shaped relationship to birth order.
>
> As measured by weight, height, and sexual maturity, the physical growth of children from large families compares unfavorably with that of children from small families. The difference is, however, small and is evident mainly in large studies.[53]

Supporting studies cited by Wray[54] and Omran *et al.*[55] have been carried out in Colombia, Canada, Czechoslovakia, Hungary, Israel, the United Kingdom, and the United States.

Family Size, Intellectual Development, and Educational Achievement

The severe problems of intelligence testing in the developed countries, where much research has been done and literacy is high, are well known. The problems in developing countries, where much less has been done and

52. Wray, "Population Pressure on Families," p. 454.
53. Omran, *Family Formation,* pp. 22, 26.
54. Wray, "Population Pressure on Families."
55. Omran, *Family Formation.*

literacy is low, are presumably at least as great, if not greater. It is clear that tests of "innate ability" independent of sociocultural factors do not exist. Thus, tests that may be valid to some degree for one society or culture or segment of a population, cannot be easily adapted to different sociocultural circumstances. Modesty in stating findings and caution in their interpretation are, therefore, mandatory. Such evidence as does exist from studies in Canada, France, Greece, India, the Netherlands, Sweden, the United Kingdom, the United States, and West Germany tends to support the proposition that large family size is negatively related to the development of infant and childhood intelligence and to educational achievement.[56] Children in large families probably receive less parental attention and encouragement; however, due consideration must be given to such confounding factors as socioeconomic status, nutritional standards, and educational opportunities available. Terhune notes that "parental resources are finite, and the evidence indicates that in general, parental interest and quality of child care diminish with increasing family size."[57] Omran *et al.* summarize the field as follows:

> In regard to intellectual development, increasing evidence shows that children from large families obtain lower intelligence scores than those from small families. Mental retardation is also positively associated with family size. This area, however, will require further research, especially in the developing world.[58]

Nutrition and Fertility

The interrelationships between nutritional factors and reproductive variables are multiple, complex, and in many cases still insufficiently researched. As in other fields, a multitude of interacting social and biological causal factors, some with apparently real but weak relationships to the variable(s) being considered as dependent for the purposes at hand, makes causal analysis difficult. Among the numerous variables involved are maternal, infant, and early childhood nutrition (and health), supplementation, weight gain, breast-feeding (involving mother-child interaction), lactation (a physiological function of the mother), conception, pregnancy, lactational amenorrhea, postpartum sterility, menstruation, fecundity, spontaneous abortion, infanticide (perhaps "disguised" or unrecognized through inade-

56. *Ibid.;* Wray, "Population Pressure on Families"; Terhune, *A Review.*
57. Terhune, *A Review,* p. 189.
58. Omran, *Family Formation,* p. 22.

quate feeding and care),[59] infant and early childhood mortality, menopause, and menarche.[60] Cravioto and DeLicardie list a few of these factors and many others in a model relating biological and social factors to low weight gain in infants and young children.[61] Obviously, this a broad field. The recent volume by Mosley summarizes the present state of knowledge and uncertainty.[62]

The health, nutrition, and population interrelationships summarized above derive primarily from the various reviews and secondary sources noted. However, the summary and the reviews by no means exhaust the topic. Additional relationships are at least implied, if not always explicitly stated, in the programmatic context of practical health, nutrition, and population problems and what to do about them. Before turning to these sets of problems and attempted solutions, the question of integration will be discussed.

Should Health, Nutrition, and Family Planning Programs Be Integrated?

Several arguments have been marshaled to support the proposition that family planning services should be integrated with maternal and child health or other health services.[63] This view has been strongly advocated by the World Health Organization (WHO) and has been gaining ascendancy for several years.[64] It surfaced repeatedly at the World Population Conference in Bucharest in 1974.[65] Family planning has been seen by its advocates as but one of many urgently needed socioeconomic development programs from the perspectives of both population growth control and the

59. Benjamin Viel, *The Demographic Explosion: The Latin American Experience* (New York: Irvington, 1976), especially ch. V, "The Medical Problem," pp. 56–67.

60. Jean-Pierre Habicht, "Field Studies: Introductory Statement," in *Nutrition and Human Reproduction,* edited by H. W. Mosley, pp. 345–52; Henry W. Mosley, "Introduction: Issues, Definitions, and an Analytic Framework," in *ibid.,* pp. 1–7.

61. Joaquin Cravioto and Elsa R. DeLicardie, "The Effect of Malnutrition on the Individual," in *Nutrition, National Development, and Planning,* edited by Alan Berg *et al.* (Cambridge, Mass.: MIT Press, 1973), pp. 3–21.

62. Mosley, *Nutrition and Human Reproduction.*

63. Wallace, "World Wide Problems in the Field of Maternal and Child Health."

64. Jason L. Finkle and Barbara B. Crane, "The World Health Organization and the Population Issue: Organizational Values in the United Nations," *Population and Development Review* 2 (3–4) (September–December 1976) pp. 367–93.

65. World Health Organization, "Health and Family Planning"; and "Health Trends."

improvement of maternal and child health. At Bucharest, however, the view of some delegates, representing a large number of countries, was that many other programs necessary for socioeconomic development and the creation of a new international economic order had been neglected by countries providing aid, relative to the emphasis given family planning. It was felt that family planning services should be provided in a context of maternal and child health and other health services and should be more explicitly and intimately linked to other socioeconomic development programs. Since the Bucharest conference, family planning services have expanded considerably in a number of countries and have been initiated in others, increasingly in a policy context of integration with other health and development programs.

Many countries are now making efforts to extend health and family planning services to broader segments of the population: the rural, the poor, and the otherwise socially or economically disadvantaged. It is clear, however, that this process still has a long way to go in many, if not most, developing countries. It is also an important priority in some developed countries such as the United States, which, despite its great wealth, has a significant population whose access to health and social services is impeded by poverty or ethnic-cultural factors, or both.

Among the arguments for integrating family planning and health services, as summarized by Finkle and Crane, are the following:

> 1. Because of the potentially dangerous but unavoidable complications or side effects of modern contraceptives, it is necessary for "qualified health personnel to provide the techniques as well as to supervise their follow-up" [quoted from WHO 1968].
> 2. Combining health and family planning services results in a more efficient use of resources and personnel, [avoids duplication], and, from the perspective of the potential adopter, makes access to family planning services more "convenient."
> 3. Providing family planning services in a health context is more effective because health services contribute to reducing infant and child mortality, a prerequisite to fertility decline. Health services also reach potential adopters, especially women of reproductive age, more easily and provide a setting for family planning that is more acceptable and attractive to clients as well as to political and medical leaders.[66]

Additional arguments drawn from Wallace *et al.*, Omran, and WHO are as follows:

1. Integration strengthens the health infrastructure and the larger

66. Finkle and Crane, "The World Health Organization," pp. 376–77.

socioeconomic development infrastructure, of which health is one component. Separation of health and family planning, on the other hand, tends to weaken the health infrastructure because of competition for trained personnel, budget, and other resources.

2. The good rapport that health workers develop within the community provides an opportunity to introduce and to discuss family planning and infertility problems. Such discussion may be particularly opportune in a maternal and child health context during premarital counseling and prenatal, postpartum, postabortion, and child health care. Family planning information and services can also be integrated with disease control programs, such as those for tuberculosis or venereal disease, and with nutrition programs. These programs may or may not involve community-based delivery and paramedical or nonmedical workers.[67]

Despite the imposing arguments for integration and their acceptance by WHO and a growing body of international opinion, there remains a substantial body of scientific and "population establishment" opinion to the contrary.[68] Furthermore, it is good to remember that a number of international health program successes have resulted from single-purpose campaigns, which have demonstrated their ability to mobilize sufficient personnel, technology, supplies, funding, expertise, and commitment to do a specialized job. Among these are programs to eradicate, control, or contain smallpox, cholera, malaria, tuberculosis, schistosomiasis, and yaws. Similarly, there have been a number of very successful single-purpose family planning efforts in Asia (South Korea, Taiwan, and Indonesia) and a few in Latin America and the Caribbean, often without the prerequisite of further reduction in infant and child mortality.

Whether the theoretical arguments above are sufficient to overcome the greater practical complexities of planning, retraining, implementing, and managing integrated family planning, maternal and child health, and other health programs, and whether integrated programs can mobilize sufficient personnel, funding, expertise, and commitment with enough speed to generate successes equal to or exceeding those of "undiluted" single-purpose programs, remain to be seen. Programmatically this is a question that each country must answer for itself in light of its own priorities. It is hoped that answers will take into account unique local circumstances and opportunities as well as the international debate on this key issue. The ultimate answers will derive from empirical experience rather than from eloquent arguments or counterarguments.

67. Omran, *The Health Theme;* Wallace, "World Wide Problems in the Field of Maternal and Child Health"; World Health Organization, "Health Trends."

68. Finkel and Crane, "The World Health Organization."

In an important article with policy implications, Kunstadter recently considered the other side of the "child-survival hypothesis" and of the argument that reducing infant and child mortality is a prerequisite to fertility decline.[69] While the correlation seems secure, he has raised serious questions about the direction of causation on the basis of historical evidence in Europe and in modern developing countries and has reemphasized the major contribution to lower mortality and improved health that lower fertility would make in countries where infant and maternal mortality are high. He concludes:

> The available data imply that it is unwise to rely on the reduction of mortality to cause a marked decline in completed family size. On the contrary, if mortality reduction is desired, an effective way to accomplish it is to develop family planning services and education programs aimed at reducing fertility among women at high risk of child loss.
>
> In our survey of the literature and our examination of detailed maternal age, parity and child survival data, we have found little evidence for a strong causal link between health care and a decline in mortality, fertility and completed family size. We have found evidence suggesting the strong effect of parity and of parity relative to age on child mortality and on completed family size. Governments with limited resources seeking to lower mortality and to decrease population growth will be more likely to achieve these objectives by concentrating on family planning programs than by insisting on the primacy of health care services—and they will not be sacrificing humanitarian goals by doing so.[70]

PROBLEMS AND POSSIBLE SOLUTIONS

The Problems

Despite dramatic scientific and technological advances in health, population, and nutrition during the past four or five decades, much of the world's population has been effectively deprived of the fruits of these advances. The most acute problems of access to the benefits of this technology occur in inner-city slums of industrial nations, in the semiurban fringes of the towns and cities that are so rapidly increasing in size in developing countries, and, most importantly, in the vast rural areas of developing countries. Despite the high rates of urban migration in many developing countries,

69. Kunstadter, "Child Mortality."
70. *Ibid.*, pp. 84–85.

from 60 to 90 percent of the population in many such countries still resides in the rural sector.

Among the most fundamental of all human needs are those related to personal health, nutrition, and high or unplanned fertility. Since World War II there has been a decline in mortality in developing societies, in part due to the success of the mass preventive programs aimed at controlling malaria, eradicating smallpox, yaws, and other diseases, and other efforts such as improved sanitation. Also contributing rather significantly to this decline in mortality has been the delivery of antibiotics and other modern medicines through traditional, rather than modern, medical sources.[71]

The picture, however, is mixed. In 1953, the United Nations Children's Fund (UNICEF) and the World Health Organization (WHO) jointly reviewed health policy and health status in the developing world. Their report included the rather devastating statement that "Probably three-fourths of the world's population drinks unsafe water, disposes of human excreta recklessly, prepares milk and food dangerously, are constantly exposed to insect and rodent enemies, and live in unfit dwellings."[72] Thirteen years later a review of health problems in the developing world concluded that infant mortality rates were three to ten times higher than those in the developed world; mortality rates among preschool-age children were thirty to fifty times higher.[73] Forty percent of total mortality occurred in children under the age of five. Unfortunately, these findings remain relatively unchanged in 1978. This situation is particularly distressing, since the technology needed to solve these problems was known and available at the time of these earlier reports, but the necessary steps generally were not taken. The most common causes of death among infants and preschool-age children are the triad of malnutrition, gastrointestinal or diarrheal diseases, and respiratory diseases. These are complicated by various other communicable diseases, such as cholera, diphtheria, whooping cough, neonatal tetanus, malaria, and tuberculosis.

In Indonesia, as one example, a 1972 household survey of morbidity and health demand revealed that 25 percent of all illnesses occurred in preschool children. Gastrointestinal and respiratory infections, coupled with malnutrition, accounted for the majority of these childhood illnesses. Further, deaths among children comprised almost half of all deaths in that

71. Allan Rosenfield, "Modern Medicine and the Delivery of Health Services: Lessons from the Developing World," *Man and Medicine* 2 (4) (1977).

72. UNICEF/WHO, Joint Committee on Health Policy, 6th Session, May 1953.

73. Roy E. Brown, "Medical Problems of the Developing Countries," *Science* 153 (1966):271.

country, the majority in children under the age of five. More specifically, in a country of approximately 125 million people (at that time), each year there were approximately 627,000 deaths among infants less than one year old and another 335,000 deaths among children aged one to five.[74] The infant mortality rate is estimated at about 140 per 1,000 live births, and the 1972 child mortality rate was estimated at approximately 215 per 100,000 children aged one to four.[75] These compare to rates in the United States, for example, of approximately 12 and 70, respectively.

Finally, in Indonesia, UNICEF has estimated that approximately 30 percent of children under the age of six suffer from moderate protein calorie malnutrition; 3 percent have kwashiorkor or marasmus. This is in addition to nutritional problems of iron, iodine and vitamin A deficiencies.[76] Similarly, maternal mortality rates are significantly higher than those found in the West. Rates estimated for Indonesia and other similar developing countries are anywhere from 50 to 800 deaths per 100,000 live births, compared with 5 to 20 in Western nations.

In recent years, schools of "tropical medicine" have been established to study these problems. This term is a misnomer, however, as many of the diseases now seen in the nonindustrialized tropical areas were seen as recently as fifty to sixty years ago in Western countries. These diseases, in large part, are not related so much to the tropics as to a lack of effective preventive measures, inadequate curative services, malnutrition, and conditions of general poverty.[77]

Despite these problems, there has been a decline in mortality since World War II. Until recently, however, birth rates have remained quite high, resulting in the present high rates of population growth. In the past few years, there has been growing evidence to suggest a reversal; growth rates have declined recently in substantial parts of Asia and Latin America, probably due in large part to successful family planning program efforts.[78]

On the individual level, in all societies, there are families who do not wish more children than they already have or who wish to delay a pregnancy to a later time. A major obstacle in many countries for those couples

74. Suyono and Reese, "Integrating Village Family Planning."

75. United Nations Fund for Population Activities, "Draft Report of the 1978 UNFPA Needs Assessment Mission," 1979.

76. *Ibid.*

77. Allan Rosenfield, Walter B. Watson *et al.*, "Health, Nutrition, and Population," ch. 3 in *U.S. Science and Technology for Development: A Contribution to the 1979 UN Conference,* National Research Council (Washington: U.S. Department of State, 1978), pp. 76–112.

78. Tsui and Bogue, "Declining World Fertility"; Maudlin and Berelson, "Conditions of Fertility Decline."

who wish to space or limit pregnancy is the lack of availability of, or access to, effective family planning services. This situation is gradually changing as more than 80 countries, with approximately 90 percent of the developing world's population, have adopted policies aimed at lowering population growth and fertility, or of making family planning services available for health or human rights reasons.[79] Such policies are usually implemented by means of national family planning programs, ordinarily conducted through the public sector, but also frequently supported by the private sector. Despite advances, though, particularly in Asia and Latin America, the delivery of family planning services has been impeded by many of the same obstacles that have faced the health care system in general.

The Causes

A recent report from the National Academy of Sciences in the United States described a number of deficiencies found in programs aimed at delivering simple health and family planning services in developing countries. For example:

—Services simply do not reach or are inaccessible to a large proportion of the population in need (perhaps as many as 80 percent).

—Services are sparse in rural and urban slum areas, largely because of a gross maldistribution of facilities and personnel.

—The health care system is dominated by physicians who usually fail to make optimal use of other health personnel.

—A poor balance exists between curative and preventive care; costly curative, hospital-based, high-technology medicine in urban areas usually dominates.

—The health care system is often strongly centralized, highly bureaucratized, "top-down oriented" and inflexible.[80]

Perhaps the most significant deficiency has been an attempt to adopt, without sufficient cultural modification, the Western medical system. The system as practiced in North America and Europe varies, but in all areas it is heavily physician-oriented, perhaps most extremely so in the United States. Unfortunately, the U.S. system has increasingly become a model for many developing countries. This is particularly ironic in view of the already severe and worsening problem of health and hospital costs in that country, despite its great wealth and high per capita income. Almost all

79. Nortman and Hofstatter, *Population and Family Planning;* Watson, *Family Planning.*

80. Rosenfield, Watson, *et al.*, "Health, Nutrition, and Population."

curative services in the United States are provided by the physician, including routine primary care. Breakthroughs in creating effective roles for other personnel have been slow, although in recent years increased responsibilities have been delegated to personnel such as physician assistants, nurse-midwives, nurse-practitioners, and the so-called MEDEX (graduates of a physician assistant program for former military medical corpsmen).

In the United States there are, on the average, approximately 700 people per physician. In developing countries, on the other hand, the ratios are far higher and usually exacerbated by the fact that more than half of all physicians available are located in the capital and larger cities of the country.[81] In rural areas, where the majority of the people live, the ratio of population to physicians may be as extreme as 50,000 to 100,000 per physician. Despite such grossly adverse ratios, many developing countries, in the process of adopting the health care systems of countries such as Britain, France, or the United States, have generally insisted that curative services be provided only by physicians. This, in effect, denies care to those most in need, while providing medical center–oriented care in urban areas for that small minority of people who can afford to pay for such care. As Dr. Mahler, Director-General of WHO, has stated, the vast majority of the world's population have no access whatsoever to the most essential kinds of health care.[82]

As health services have evolved in most developing countries, an inordinate percentage of the limited funds made available for health care has been allocated inappropriately for urban medical services, often invested in elaborate, costly, modern edifices, which Dr. Mahler has called "disease palaces." Traditional systems of medicine, such as the Ayurvedic system, which is a major factor in service delivery in such countries as Sri Lanka and India, have been neglected. The modern medical centers usually are modeled on major medical centers of the West, with expensive, often exotic, equipment. Because of the significant drain on the national health budget for these centers, very little is left over for urgently needed primary health care, nutrition, and family planning services at the village level. Physicians trained in these hospitals prefer, when their training is complete, to practice in the same type of institution. There is little, if any, attraction to working on the health-related problems in rural villages or urban slums. To give one example, Thailand, a country with a population of more than 40 million people, of whom approximately 80 percent live in the rural areas, has fewer than 250 rural health centers staffed by a physician and

81. Brown, "Medical Problems."

82. H. T. Mahler, Keynote address, International Health Conference, the National Council for International Health, Reston, Virginia, October 1974.

only a few physicians in full-time private practice in these rural areas.[83] More than 60 percent of the physicians in that country live and work in Bangkok.

Possible Solutions

During the past few years, there has been an increasing interest in more appropriate ways to deliver family planning and simple primary health services. Primary health care has been defined in many ways, but, in general, includes the assessment of the initial contact for a complaint and readily accessible services for all individuals and their families. Ideally, there should be full participation of the community in planning such services, at a cost the community and country can afford. Such health care should address the major problems in the community and should include preventive, curative, and, in some cases, rehabilitative services. It might include, for example, basic sanitation, maternal and child health care, treatment of diarrheal diseases and respiratory infections, family planning, immunization programs, promotion of proper nutrition, preventive and curative services for endemic diseases, and health education activities.

Wright has described a moral primary health care system as one that:

> addresses itself to the major needs of the people, places major emphasis on health maintenance, provides available health services to every citizen on the basis of need, regardlesss of all other considerations, is organized to provide a reasonable value for the cost, satisfies the needs of the people, and does no harm.[84]

This should be the goal of an effective program. Unfortunately, as Jelliffe and Jelliffe have written:

> The health services of the Third World countries have tended to be ill-adapted imports from Europe and North America, with emphasis placed on costly curative institutionalized medicine, largely in urban centers and hospitals, manned by highly (and expensively) trained credential-oriented cadres of orthodox health staff, particularly physicians, attempting similar functions and duties of colleagues in developed countries.[85]

83. Allan Rosenfield, "Family Planning: An Expanded Role for Paramedical Personnel," *American Journal of Obstetrics and Gynecology,* 110 (7) (1971):1030–39.

84. Robert D. Wright, "The Immorality of Excellence in Health Care," *Virginia Quarterly Review* 50 (1974):175.

85. Derrick B. Jelliffe and E. F. Patrice Jelliffe, "Nutrition Programs for Preschool Children," *American Journal of Clinical Nutrition* 25 (1972):595.

In areas related to primary health care and family planning, there have been some dramatic examples of approaches that have departed from the more traditional western-oriented, doctor-centered system of service delivery. As Taylor has suggested:

> Auxiliaries, trained specifically to do particular combinations of simple jobs, often produce a better, more consistent quality of work in these jobs than the more broadly prepared doctors—a doctor forced into a position where he is only performing rather simple care tends to become bored, dissatisfied, and ineffectual.[86]

Those functions that are relatively routine and repetitive can be assigned to a variety of health and lay personnel after appropriate training. Taylor suggests that perhaps as much as 90 percent of medical care can be so routinized.

The system of health and family planning care that has generated the most interest in recent years has been that developed in the People's Republic of China.[87] The leading principles of health care in China are patterned after a number of sayings attributed to Chairman Mao, including "Put prevention first," "Serve the people," "Combine Chinese traditional therapy with western scientific knowledge," and "In health and medical care put the stress on rural areas." Dramatic changes have taken place in the provision of health care in China since the revolution in 1949. Between 1949 and 1965, there was an increase from approximately 40,000 modern physicians (most practicing in urban areas) to 100,000 physicians, together with 170,000 assistant physicians, with major changes in patterns of distribution.

Much publicity has been given to the "barefoot doctor," an innovation of tremendous importance. The barefoot doctor is basically a worker, usually a farmer (male or female), selected by the local community, and chosen to receive a short-term (three- to six-month) training course, following which he or she returns to the local community to provide first-line primary care on a part-time basis. Complementing this worker has been a redefinition of the health roles of a variety of nurses, midwives, and auxiliary personnel to include both preventive and curative measures. Procedures previously limited to physicians became part of the

86. Carl E. Taylor, "Health-care Lessons from International Experience," *New England Journal of Medicine* 290 (1974):1376.

87. Victor W. Sidel and Ruth Sidel, "The Delivery of Medical Care in China," *Scientific American* 230 (1974):19; Joe D. Wray, "Child Care in the People's Republic of China: 1973," *Pediatrics* 55 (1975). Anibal Faundes and Tapani Luukkainen, "Health and Family Planning Services in the Chinese People's Republic," *Studies in Family Planning* 3 (7) (Suppl.) (July 1972):165–76.

job descriptions of these various categories of personnel, including suturing wounds, treatment of simple diseases, prescription and distribution of oral contraceptives, insertion of IUDs, and suction curettage for early abortion. A critically important part of the system is an efficient and effective system of referral to increasingly more specialized health centers and hospitals with sophisticated medical centers in the major cities.

The Sidels summarized the achievements in China as an interweaving of three main threads: decentralization, demystification, and continuity with the past.[88] Although policy decisions are made centrally, implementation of these policies has been decentralized to the lowest level in both rural and urban areas. Demystification is an attempt to lessen the mystique in which the medical profession is held. As a result of the innovations introduced in that country, estimates from a variety of visitors suggest that the infant mortality rate is extremely low (in the range of 17 to 20 per 1,000 live births) compared with rates in most of the rest of the developing world of 75 to 125 per 1,000. At the same time, it is estimated that there have been dramatic declines in birth rates in recent years; an extremely active family planning program, which uses all modern contraceptives, sterilization, and abortion, plays a key role.

While some aspects of the Chinese success may be uniquely associated with historical circumstances and the reconstruction of society that has taken place in that country, there are lessons from the Chinese experience that have potentially broad applicability. Similar changes have been described for the health care and family planning systems in North Vietnam[89] and, although through a somewhat different approach, in Cuba,[90] which is alleged to have the most effective and readily accessible health and family planning services for the total population of any country in Latin America. In addition, Cuba is alleged to be the only country in Latin America to have eliminated poliomyelitis and diphtheria and to have eradicated malaria.

On the islands of Java and Bali in Indonesia, the national family planning program has had unique success in moving services from the clinic to the community.[91] In the early 1970s the decision was made that

88. *Ibid.*

89. M. Segall, "Medical Care in North Vietnam," *Lancet* 1 (1970):1224.

90. Zena Stein and Mervyn Susser, "The Cuban Health System: A Trial of a Comprehensive Service in a Poor Country," *International Journal of Health Services* 2 (1972):551; Vicente Navarro, "Health, Health Services, and Health Planning in Cuba," *International Journal of Health Services* 2 (1972):397.

91. Haryono Suyono *et al.*, "Village Family Planning: The Indonesian Model," National Family Planning Coordinating Board Technical Report Series, Monograph No. 13, Jakarta, July 1976.

paramedical personnel, particularly midwives, could effectively be trained to prescribe oral contraceptives and to insert intrauterine devices. As the program spread, it became apparent that while the number of accepters and continuing users was increasing, there were many women at the village level who were not coming to the clinics. Community groups were identified, perhaps most effectively on Bali, and volunteers were chosen by the community to serve in village contraceptive distribution centers. These volunteers were trained to resupply oral contraceptives and condoms to users within their villages. In some of the larger villages, subvillage family planning groups were organized, coordinated by the successful users.

In 1978 there were more than 30,000 contraceptive distribution centers and an estimated 25,000 subvillage family planning groups in villages throughout Java and Bali.[92] This combination of a community-based approach, backed up by health center and mobile service-oriented clinical services, has helped Indonesia to develop one of Asia's most innovative and successful national family planning programs. According to the service statistics, the prevalence of contraceptive practice on Bali by March 31, 1978, was greater than 40 percent, and the figure for all of Java and Bali was 30 percent. This is a dramatic performance in a country in which relatively little socioeconomic development has taken place and is a particularly effective demonstration of the use of nursing, auxiliary, and lay personnel. Plans are now under way in this country to make use of the family planning infrastructure, which now reaches to the subvillage level, to introduce simple primary health care services. If successful, this will be an important example of integrating health care into a family planning program, rather than vice versa.

A private sector program in Thailand, in operation since 1974, is another example of a successful community-oriented activity. The Community-based Family Planning Services, a private, nonprofit agency, has developed a very effective network of grass roots volunteer workers and contraceptive distributors at the village level. By 1978, volunteers had been recruited and were working in approximately one-third of all the villages of the country. A survey was conducted recently, two years after this program was launched, in a sample of villages served by the program. The survey found a contraceptive prevalence rate of 30 percent and a 41 percent decline in the pregnancy rate.[93] This program, which has operated at a cost per accepter significantly lower than that noted in the government

92. UNFPA, "Draft Report."

93. S. Burintratikul and M. C. Samaniego, "CBFPS in Thailand: A Community-Based Approach to Family Planning," ICED, Essex, Conn., Case study no. 6, 1978.

program, has since been expanded. Under the program, in conjunction with the Ministry of Public Health, village volunteers are trained to provide primary health care services, and the Ministry provides clinic-based services and backup. The next step in the program is to build integrated community and economic development activities that aim to reduce fertility further and raise health and economic standards of the village family.[94] This is an example of public and private cooperation and collaboration in providing services at the village level, with significant involvement of the community.

In the delivery of simple health care services at the village level by both health and lay personnel, the following types of services are being considered in a number of countries: oral rehydration for diarrheal diseases; education for mothers about diarrheal diseases, including the need for mothers to continue breast-feeding in the face of diarrhea; the treatment of childhood respiratory infections with antibiotics; nutrition-oriented health education; direct food supplements for children with severe malnutrition; the use of iron and, in some cases, vitamin A to treat childhood deficiencies; treatment of parasitic infestations in young children; the use of iron and vitamins for pregnant women; and general health education.

It is worth noting, at the time of the 1979 United Nations Conference on Science and Technology for Development, that, in general, the discussion has not focused on "hard" scientific and technologic advances, but rather on more appropriate and widespread adaptation, transfer, and application of already available technologies. Admittedly, the scientific and technological community needs to develop a better understanding of both the prevention and treatment of the serious infectious diseases of the tropics, including cholera, schistosomiasis, filariasis, trypanosomiasis, and malaria. Similarly, while such modern contraceptive methods as the IUD and the pill are dramatic advances in family planning, both are fraught with side effects and complications. Priority should be given to the development of improved, safer methods of contraception.

While there are other examples of the need for basic and applied scientific and technologic advances, the fact remains that most of the basic health-related problems affecting the majority of the world's poorest people can be met with technologies already at hand. The delivery of simple primary health care and family planning can be improved dramatically through a number of simple steps including effective and genuine involve-

94. Mechai Viravaidya, "Where Villagers show the way: The Community-Based Family Planning Services in Thailand," paper of the WPS International Population Conference, Manila, 1978.

ment of the community in the decentralized planning and implementation of services at the village level and appropriate delegation of responsibility and activities to varying levels of nursing, auxiliary, and lay personnel. Through changes in medical standards, a genuine revolution is under way in which the health and social well-being of the people can be significantly improved. To date, very few developing countries have succeeded in providing adequate health care or other services for the masses of people in the lower socioeconomic groups. For millions of people living in poverty and deprivation in developing countries, the redistribution of wealth remains a foremost and all-abiding priority. At the same time, the provision of a variety of improved services, including health, nutrition, education, family planning, and social welfare is a high priority. The means are available; the commitment to making the necessary changes is the critical component. The future is promising if this commitment is indeed forthcoming.

7

Reproduction, Fertility Regulation, and Infertility

SHELDON J. SEGAL, B. KWAKU ADADEVOH, AND ZHI-YI CHANG

INTRODUCTION

PREGNANCY AND REPRODUCTION are still largely matters of chance for much of the human race. Less than half of the world's population has access to modern methods of birth control, and folklore methods show little evidence of effectiveness. Throughout the world, couples seldom know when they marry if they will be able to have a baby, and many find that they cannot. Of course, the sex of offspring is also a matter of chance. Yet in some cultures, and for many individual couples, whether a pregnancy yields a girl or a boy makes a difference. All told, people have very little control over their reproductive systems.

That we are so much at the mercy of chance, in this regard, is a challenge to modern science. With today's level of improved mortality throughout most of the world, fertility regulation is important for both individual and national goals. If people could avoid having more children than they want, a number of social and economic problems would be eased—child neglect or abandonment, educational disadvantage, and continued poverty, among others. With improved fertility control, the frequency of certain adverse pregnancy outcomes—including congenital defects, retardation, and maternal mortality—would also decline.

THE BIOLOGY OF REPRODUCTION

The underlying inadequacy in our understanding of the reproductive process constitutes a major obstacle to improving reproductive health and to developing a safer, wider, and more adequate choice of methods of fertility regulation. The following description of the process of human reproduction illustrates some of the major research questions that remain unanswered and problem areas that an enlarged research effort could profitably address.

The human reproductive process may be viewed as an intricate series of events that must proceed in perfect succession. Any interruption in the sequence can stop the process. The role of the male (at least his biological contribution) ends with fertilization. The female, however, continues with the complex process of harboring the newly fertilized egg in a unique nutritive and protective matrix, controlled by a variety of hormones.

The Human Female

Every month, from the time of sexual maturation until menopause, the human female prepares for a possible pregnancy. An egg is produced, the uterine cervix becomes receptive to the passage of spermatozoa, the muscular and secretory capacities of the uterus and the fallopian tubes become conducive to the transport of sperm and egg, and the endometrial lining of the uterus prepares to harbor a fertilized egg. All of this is accomplished by two distinct but cross-linked sequences of events, the ovulatory and the uterine or menstrual cycles.

The key event is the monthly development of an egg. As early as the sixth week of embryonic age of a female, some 2,000 amoeba-like oogonia, or germ cells, migrate into the human ovary from a specialized region of the yolk sac. In the course of embryonic and fetal development their number increases tremendously through cell division. At birth the two ovaries of the female infant contain nearly 500,000 primary follicles: individual oocytes, the precursors of eggs, surrounded by a layer of follicle cells. Most of the follicles, however, are destined for spontaneous degeneration, a process that continues during childhood and adolescence and throughout the reproductive years. It is only the occasional egg that actually ovulates and has an opportunity to participate in fertilization—perhaps fewer than 400 in a woman's reproductive years.[1]

From among the scores of thousands of primary follicles, a few start to develop as the circulating levels of follicle-stimulatory hormone (FSH) from the pituitary gland rise each month a few days before a menstrual period. After about ten days, usually only one follicle continues to flourish and become fully mature, ready to release its egg. At mid-cycle, on approximately the fourteenth day, there is a surge in the pituitary's production of luteinizing hormone (LH), and ovulation occurs with the oocyte

1. E. Witschi, *Development of Vertebrates* (Philadelphia: Saunders, 1956), p. 40.

bursting from the rupture point in a cascade of follicular cells and fluid. The released egg is swept from the surface of the ovary by the undulating open end of the fallopian tube. At this point the egg still has 46 chromosomes, the normal human complement. The process of reduction division, whereby the complement is reduced to 23, to be matched by the 23 chromosomes of the fertilizing spermatozoon, actually begins during a mother's fetal life, but is suspended for many years. How this suspension of development is maintained remains enigmatic. At ovulation, the process is resumed with the expulsion of the first polar body carrying 23 of the chromosomes. The remaining 23 replicate once more, and it is only after a sperm makes contact with the surface of the egg that a second polar body is expelled, again reducing the genetic material by half, so that the union of egg and sperm will produce the normal complement of hereditary material.[2]

Fertilization, once thought to be a simple matter of sperm-egg interaction, is an intricate series of steps that begins when a spermatozoon makes contact with the zona pellucida, a viscous envelope surrounding the egg. By enzymatic action the sperm slices through the zona and makes contact with the surface of the egg. This initiates a series of functional and structural responses. A key event is an immediate blockade against the entry of additional sperm. In fact, without the evolutionary development of a means of preventing polyspermy (the entry of additional sperm), sexual reproduction would not be a successful means of maintaining any species, since polyspermy is almost invariably nonviable. The barriers to polyspermy include changes in the zona pellucida that make it impenetrable and alterations in the egg's surface that preclude the attachment of additional sperm, but the precise nature of the blocks remains unknown.[3] The fertilizing sperm passes through the outer membrane of the egg into the cytoplasm in several stages and, in the process, activates the egg to complete its second reduction division and orients the axis of future development. Even then it is not clear at all that the egg is "fertilized." For about 12 hours the formation within the cytoplasm of distinct egg and sperm pronuclei unfolds. The pronuclei, which are large organelles with a complex structure, move together gradually. Then, following further structural changes, the maternal and paternal hereditary contributions intermingle, and with this event, the first cell division of the zygote begins. After 36 hours the single cell has become two. Two days later the fertilized

2. S. J. Segal, "The Physiology of Human Reproduction," *Scientific American* 231 (3) (1974):51–62.

3. C. B. Metz, "Role of Specific Sperm Antigens in Fertilization," *Federation Proceedings* 32 (1973):2057.

egg may have divided twice more to form a microscopic ball of eight cells. In this condition the egg completes its passage through the fallopian tube and enters the uterus.

Four days after fertilization the egg is a cluster of thirty-two to sixty-four cells, which are beginning to divide more rapidly. This stage corresponds to about day nineteen or twenty of the menstrual cycle. The cluster of cells remains unattached for one or two days and assumes the form of an inner mass of cells encircled by a single row of aligned trophoblastic, or nourishing, cells. This preembryo state is called the blastocyst. Under proper conditions, the outer ring of cells nestles into the endometrium and begins to form the placenta. The inner cell mass, after several more days of cell divisions and internal rearrangments, becomes a human embryo.

In an integrated manner a second sequence takes place concurrently to ensure the egg a protective and supportive nesting place in the uterus. Early in the four-week menstrual cycle, before ovulation, the ovary secretes in ever increasing amounts the estrogenic steroids, principally estradiol. These hormones stimulate the endometrium to proliferate and to become much richer in blood vessels. The final surge of estrogen production heralds (and also induces, by means of the hypothalamic recognition of blood estrogen levels) a mid-cycle peak in the LH level.[4] Ovulation follows within twenty-four hours, and at about this time ovarian steroid production is switched over from a predominance of estrogen to a predominance of progesterone. In response the cells of the endometrium become still more numerous and more corpulent. The endometrial glands grow rapidly in length and thickness and begin to accumulate secretions. The entire endometrial surface, by the twentieth day of the cycle, has become a highly vascular, spongy nest ready to accept, protect, and nurture a fertilized and dividing egg if one should arrive from the fallopion tube. The tube itself has developed cilia and increased its flow of glandular fluids for transporting an egg to the uterus.[5]

The uterine lining is now under the remarkable influence of progesterone produced by the corpus luteum. In a nonfertile month the luteal cells begin to reduce their progesterone production about ten days after ovulation; some four or five days later the level is low enough to result in a sloughing off of the endometrium and menstruation. If an egg is fertilized, the first crisis to be overcome is the avoidance of menstruation. For the pregnancy to survive there must be a source of progesterone to continue the

4. S. J. Segal, "Fertility Regulation Technology: Status and Prospects," *Population Bulletin* 31 (6) (1977):7.

5. R. M. Brenner, "Endocrine Control of Ciliogenesis in the Primate Oviduct," in *Handbook of Physiology* Section 7, "Endocrinology," Vol. 2, pt. 2, edited by R. O. Greep and E. P. Ashwood (Baltimore: Williams and Wilkins, 1973).

support of the endometrium; without it the blastocyst, or, later, the new embryo, would pass out with the sloughed-off endometrium and menstrual blood.

The maintenance of progesterone production—and indeed the synchrony of maturation, release, and fertilization of the egg, on the one hand, and preparation of the uterus as a proper environment for nidation, on the other—is achieved because the hormones involved in each process have such exquisitely integrated and interrelated functions. Consider the implications of the hormonal events of a nonfertile cycle. After ovulation the gonadal steroid hormones feed back at mid-cycle to suppress the pituitary secretion of FSH and LH, and the progressive decline in the concentration of the pituitary gonadotropins in the blood prevents any supplementary ovulations that might interfere with a possible pregnancy. In the absence of a pregnancy, however, a decline in blood steroid concentration in the late luteal phase causes a rise in LH and FSH. In other words, once it is clear that a cycle has been infertile, there is an immediate signal to the brain to initiate the events that prepare an egg for release the next month; menstruation intervenes, but the new cycle has already begun. In response to the increase in secretion of FSH and LH, follicular maturation proceeds, and, with it, egg development and increases in gonadal steroid-hormone production. Late in the follicular phase, approaching the period of the maximal rate of follicular enlargement and maximal steroid production, the patterns of FSH and LH diverge. FSH secretion declines, but LH secretion increases gradually until rising estrogen levels signal the preovulatory surge of both LH and FSH, linking follicular maturation and steroid production to the ovulatory stimulus from the pituitary.[6]

In the case of pregnancy, avoiding the crisis of menstruation requires an uninterrupted supply of progesterone. The initial source is the corpus luteum, which receives a signal to continue making the steroid. The signal comes from the newly formed blastocyst. Even before nidation the outer cells of the early blastocyst copiously produce a gonadotropic molecule, usually called human chorionic gonadotropin (hCG), which is very similar in function and structure to pituitary LH. The blastocyst's gonadotropin stimulates the maternal corpus luteum to keep on producing progesterone beyond the time of the first expected menstrual period. A second critical point lies ahead, however. The corpus luteum, in spite of maximum stimulation, has a limited life span. Before this time limit is reached, at about the fifth week of gestation, the placenta itself begins to produce sufficient quantities of progesterone to maintain the pregnancy. To pass the first

6. G. T. Ross, *et al.*, "Pituitary and Gonadal Hormones in Women During Spontaneous and Induced Ovulatory Cycles," *Recent Progress in Hormone Research* 26 (1970):1.

crisis, in other words, the embryo produces a gonadotropin that stimulates maternal progesterone production; to meet the second crisis, the developing embryo itself assumes the required endocrine function, thus becoming self-sufficient in this respect. By five and a half weeks, the pregnancy can continue even if the maternal ovaries cease to function or are removed.[7]

The noteworthy characteristics of the chain of reproductive events in the female are the restriction of the multiplication phase of oogenesis to the fetal ovary, the dramatic rate of depletion of the oocytes, and the cyclic patterns of pituitary-gonadal interaction. The male reproductive process differs in each of these respects in spite of the similarity of its hormonal system.

The Human Male

Much as in the female, synchronization of successive events characterizes the male reproductive system. The production, maturation, and transport of the sperm and the stimulation of secondary sex functions, including the formation of the seminal fluid, take place in the necessary hormonal milieu. The major difference is that the hormonal production pattern is more or less constant in the male, not cyclic as in the female.

A man produces many billions of spermatozoa in a lifetime, all of which derive from the 1,000 or 2,000 spermatogonia, or germ cells, that migrate into the embryonic testis before the end of the second month of intrauterine life. This process is made possible by the way in which the male germ cells multiply: when the spermatogonia divide, many of the daughter cells are kept in reserve while others undergo further cell divisions and then complete spermatogenesis in the seminiferous tubules. In contrast to the multiplication phase of oogenesis in the ovary, which is confined to a few weeks of fetal life, the multiplication phase of spermatogenesis in the testis begins in the fetal period and continues throughout life. Since there is no significant depletion of the germ-cell stores, there is no gradual loss of gamete-producing function as there is in the ovary; the testis goes on producing millions upon millions of spermatozoa and, in the normal gonad, there always remain additional germ cells to provide the capability of producing millions more. (It is not uncommon, however, for the vascular changes of aging to affect the testis or pituitary and indirectly cause a loss of testicular function.)[8] In the course of spermatogenesis the two important

7. R. L. Van de Wiele *et al.*, "Mechanisms Regulating the Menstrual Cycle in Women," *Recent Progress in Hormone Research* 26 (1970):63.

8. S. J. Segal and W. O. Nelson, "Initiation and Maintenance of Testicular function," in *Endocrinology of Reproduction: Proceedings,* edited by C. Lloyd (New York: Academic Press, 1959), pp. 107–29.

objectives are reduction of the chromosome number from the diploid number (forty-six) of the spermatogonium to the haploid number (twenty-three) of the spermatozoon and the preparation of the spermatozoon for its role in fertilization. A complex series of transformations involving both the cytoplasm and the nucleus changes the large, round spermatogonium into streamlined and motile spermatozoa in approximately seventy-four days.[9]

The testis, like the ovary, must be stimulated by pituitary gonadotropins to produce sex hormones and sperm, but there is still some uncertainty about the relative roles of FSH and LH.[10] It appears that the role of LH is primarily to stimulate Leydig cells, which lie between the seminiferous tubules, to produce their steroid hormones, mainly testosterone; the testosterone in turn has an important effect on the process of sperm production, since the tubules require a high local concentration of the hormone to maintain spermatogenesis. FSH binds specifically to the Sertoli cells of the seminiferous tubules, which implies that its role is in the maintenance of spermatogenesis.[11]

The sperm's voyage can be described, although many of its control mechanisms are poorly understood. A limited number of collecting ducts funnel the spermatozoa coming from the seminiferous tubules to the epididymis, a long tube convoluted into a compact body adjacent to the testis. These immature sperm are not yet able to fertilize an egg or even to move under their own power. As they pass from the head of the epididymis through its slender body to its distended tail, they achieve motility and a degree of maturity, but the final critical changes that enable them to penetrate and fertilize an egg are achieved only in the female reproductive tract, and even there only if the tract is in the proper hormonal balance: precisely the estrogen-dominated status of about the time of ovulation. Thus, remarkably, the interrelations that link the ovary's hormone production and the physiology of the female gamete are extended to the male gamete once it is deposited in the female tract.

From the tail of the epididymis the sperm proceed into the continuation of the epididymal tube known as the vas deferens, which empties into the urethra below the bladder. Some of the sperm die and are disposed of by white blood cells; others enter the urethra in a steady stream and are carried away in the urine. The remainder leave the male tract at ejaculation,

9. Y. Clermont, "Kinetics of Spermatogenesis in Mammals: Seminiferous Epithelium Cycle and Spermatogonial Renewal," *Physiological Review* 52 (1972): 198.

10. E. Steinberger, A. Steinberger, and B. Sanborn, "Endocrine Control of Spermatogenesis," in *Physiology and Genetics of Reproduction,* Part A, edited by E. M. Coutinho and F. Fuchs (New York: Plenum, 1974), p. 163.

11. A. R. Means and J. Vaitukaitis, "Peptide Hormone 'Receptors': Specific Binding of $_3$H-FSH to Testis," *Endocrinology* 90 (1972):39.

when sperm are forced rapidly into the urethra by muscular contractions. These sperm are mixed with the fluid secretions of several accessory glands, including the prostate, whose ducts lead into the terminal portion of the vas deferens or into the urethra. The contributions from these sources and the secretions from the testis, the epididymis, and the vas deferens together constitute the semen, which serves primarily as a vehicle to carry the sperm to the vagina. Most of the spermatozoa go no farther. Of the hundreds of millions that are ejaculated, only tens of thousands enter the cervix, where there is further attrition, so that only a few thousand reach the uterus proper. A few hundred spermatozoa ultimately complete the journey to the upper part of each fallopian tube, where one of them may penetrate and fertilize an egg.

In addition to providing more insight into human biology in general and improved diagnosis and treatment of various diseases and abnormal conditions, increased understanding of the reproductive process has deep significance for the human condition. Recent years have seen important advances in the physician's ability to help people have the children they want to have, notably through the hormonal induction of ovulation[12] and prevention of spontaneous abortion; artificial insemination can also make a pregnancy possible for some subfertile couples. On the other hand, contraceptive technology has improved to the point where it can facilitate efforts to cope with the rapid increase in population that has come with better medical care, public health and nutrition, and the consequent reduction in mortality, first in the developed and now in the less developed countries.

There is, however, a danger of thinking that the regulation of fertility is a simple matter of the development and dissemination of contraceptive technology. The fact is that contraceptive technology is only part of the story along with social and economic conditions and the motivation of individuals. Yet the development of new technology can contribute greatly. It can provide methods that encourage effective family planning at lower levels of motivation, and at any given level of motivation it can provide safer and more effective methods.

CURRENTLY AVAILABLE METHODS OF FERTILITY REGULATION

In this description of methods currently in use, classified by the ways in which they interrupt the reproductive process, emphasis is placed on advantages, disadvantages, and recent efforts to improve the disadvantages.

12. C. Gemzell, "Induction of Ovulation," in *Frontiers of Reproduction and Fertility Control,* edited by R. Greep and M. Koblinsky (Cambridge, Mass.: MIT Press, 1977), pp. 49–54.

Methods That Prevent Entry of Sperm

COITUS INTERRUPTUS

The time-honored way to avoid a pregnancy has been for the male to withdraw prior to ejaculation. The method requires no supplies, expense, preparation, or assistance from physicians. On the other hand, it demands practice, male self-control, and considerable motivation. It may be reliable in highly motivated couples, but failures can result from the escape of semen before ejaculation, from semen deposited externally near the vagina, or from simple delay in withdrawal. Coitus interruptus has been so widely used for so long that it cannot be disregarded. There is hardly a language in which one cannot find a vernacular expression for "pulling out." Some demographers believe it to have been the major, if not the only, method responsible for the decline in birth rates in France in the eighteenth century, in England in the nineteenth century, and in other European countries.

THE CONDOM

A cylindrical sheath that envelops the penis, the condom has the advantage of being cheap and simple to use and available without prescription from a physician. It has the disadvantages, however, of being distracting, of dulling sensation, and, in some cultures, of being associated with prostitution because of its role as a prophylactic in venereal disease. If properly used and carefully manufactured, it is effective, but its actual failure rate can be high since users may sporadically discontinue use. In addition, rubber condoms deteriorate with time, particularly in sunlight and heat, and therefore have a limited shelf life, especially in tropical countries. There are now improved condoms, which are thinner, multicolored, and made of plastic. These have an unlimited shelf life and a more aesthetic appeal and are easy to manufacture.

SPERMICIDES

The introduction of fluid substances of high viscosity containing spermicidal chemicals, also block spermatozoa from entering the cervical canal. They take a variety of forms: gels and creams introduced by means of a syringe-like applicator, suppositories inserted manually, aerosols that produce a dense carbon dioxide foam, and foaming tablets. Their advantage is that they require no prescription, examination, or fitting, are probably harmless, and can be used with little preparation. Disadvantages are the leakage of fluid from the vagina, the need to wait while certain substances have a chance to melt, and poor effectiveness, usually due to poor quality, inadequate quantity, or disregard for the required waiting period. At ejaculation, sperm are deposited right at or into the entrance to the cervix, so a spermicide substance must block the entry to be effective.

THE POSTCOITAL DOUCHE

Retroactive douching with water or a spermicidal solution is the least effective of all methods because sperm have entered the cervix by the time the douche can be administered.

THE DIAPHRAGM

Another means of obstructing the passage of sperm in the female reproductive tract is the diaphragm, a rubber device shaped like a broad, shallow cup, that covers the cervix. The diaphragm must be carefully fitted by an experienced person who can select the proper size, and the woman must be taught how to use it. It is nearly free from side effects or complications (an occasional woman has a reaction to rubber), but the need to insert it carefully before each act of intercourse makes it undesirable for many women. When properly used with a spermicide, its failure rate may be as low as two to three pregnancies per 100 women per year. When used without a spermicide, the results are poor; a very high pregnancy rate can be expected.

STERILIZATION

Although the operation is forbidden (except on strict medical indications) in countries such as France, Italy, and many Latin American nations, in much of the world the absence of definite laws leaves sterilization decisions largely in the hands of the physician and patient. The advantage of this method is that a single procedure gives permanent security against conception, usually without further need for medical supervision, and at a small cost of protection after the expenditure for the initial operation. The disadvantages are that trained surgeons and surgical equipment are needed, there are certain surgical risks, and the procedure is generally irreversible, though that characteristic is precisely what some see as an advantage.

Sterilization of the male (vasectomy) is usually undertaken to protect the wife from pregnancy, either for health reasons or because the desired family size has been achieved. The operation is a simple one, using local anesthesia, and does not require hospitalization. The spermatic duct, or vas deferens, is cut, and the two ends are closed by suture.

Since some men do not want to commit themselves irrevocably to infertility and others eventually change their minds and want their fertility restored, progress toward a reversible technique, termed reanastomosis of the vas deferens, is important. Depending on the skill of both the first and second surgeons, particularly with micro-surgical techniques, the vas can be rejoined, and sperm will reappear. Subsequent pregnancy in the female, however, is less usual. It is possible that, following the original vasectomy, sperm cells are absorbed by white blood cells in large numbers, leading to the production by the body's immune system of antibodies, which enter the semen and cause clumping or agglutination of the sperm cells. As a result, they become nonfunctional. Occasionally, antibodies that have effects on other cells of the body may be triggered, leading to postvasectomy health problems. This is a topic that is still being studied.

A number of techniques are available for female sterilization (cutting the fallopian tubes). They involve either the abdominal or the vaginal route to the surgical field and different ways of tying different parts of the tubes. It is possible to restore normal fallopian tubes, with pregnancy following in about 50 percent of the cases, but it depends, as with the male, on the nature of the earlier operation and the skill of the subsequent operator.[13]

Special procedures involving optical instruments, or endoscopes, which allow the operator to see the field of surgery with a light and a lens, simplify the operation.[14] Laparoscopy involves a small incision in the lower abdomen, coagulating the tube with an electric current, and cutting it with a special instrument. Failure is rare, but uncontrollable bleeding and thermal injury to the intestine are possible risks. Culdoscopy involves access to the fallopian tubes through the back of the vagina, where the tubes are located and brought down for occlusion in the vagina by a standard ligation, by electro-coagulation, or by the application of plastic rings or clips. Another approach, termed mini-laparotomy, although not new, has recently

13. C. R. Garcia, "Oviduct Anastomosis Procedures," in *Human Sterilization*, edited by R. Richart and D. Prager (Springfield, Ill.: Charles C. Thomas, 1972).

14. P. C. Steptoe, "Recent Advances in Surgical Methods of Control of Fertility and Infertility," *British Medical Bulletin* 26 (1970):60.

grown in popularity. It can be performed under local anesthesia through a one-inch abdominal incision. The tubes are reached either by using a clamp or with the surgeon's finger and can be cut or occluded in any of the ways just mentioned. The method is simple and does not require special and expensive instruments, such as the scopes described above.[15] Still another technique, requiring the perfection of instruments and the identification of the ideal chemical agent, would close the tubes at the juncture with the uterus by applications of chemicals or plastic materials that cause obstruction. The particular advantage of this possible method is that it uses a transcervical approach—through the vagina, the cervix, and the uterus.[16]

The complications of tubal ligation or section are those of any gynecological operation requiring the opening of the peritoneum, the sac that lines the abdominal cavity. Estimates of the risk of death are less than for childbirth in most parts of the world, about 1 per 3,000 operations.[17] The risks of the newer, simpler procedures have not been fully measured.

Methods That Avoid or Suppress Ovulation

RHYTHM

The rhythm method, or periodic abstinence timed to avoid coitus near the day of ovulation, was the first method to be based on a scientific understanding of ovulation, the development of the human egg, and the relation of ovulation to the menstrual cycle. In practice, the use of rhythm requires that a woman on a twenty-eight-day menstrual cycle abstain from intercourse from day ten through day seventeen. This period takes into account the variation in the day of ovulation, the fact that the egg is fertilizable for about twenty-four hours, and the fact that sperm are capable of fertilizing for about forty-eight hours. Although there are special problems with cycles of variable length, the time of ovulation can also be determined by taking the basal body temperature.

The rhythm method has the advantage of requiring no special equipment (except a calendar and a thermometer), costing nothing, producing

15. H. Speidel, and M. F. McCann, "Mini-Laparotomy: A Fertility Control Technique of Increasing Importance," *Advances in Planned Parenthood* 13 (2) (1978):42–57.

16. R. M. Richart, A. J. Gutierrez, and R. S. Neuwirth, "Transvaginal Human Sterilization," *American Journal of Obstetrics and Gynecology* 118 (1971):108.

17. L. M. Hellman and J. A. Pritchard, *Williams Obstetrics,* 14th ed. (New York: Appleton-Century-Crofts, 1971), p. 1098.

no side effects, and being sanctioned by the Roman Catholic church. The disadvantages are the need for careful training, the likelihood of miscalculating the safe period, and the high motivation required. The commonest cause of failure is the occasional disregard of the rules.

Research is presently under way to improve the rhythm method, but results are not yet available. The three ways of determining the time of ovulation that are being tested are: use of a small electrical device to measure the electrical charges that occur in the body when the egg is released; the symptothermal method, whereby the woman keeps a daily record of her vaginal temperature and other signs of ovulation such as pain; and the "ovulation" method, whereby the woman evaluates changes in the quantity and quality of her cervical mucus, which becomes abundant and clear at or near the time of ovulation.[18] Overall, although the rhythm method is not the most effective, it is a significant one in that it focuses on ovulation, the key event in the reproductive process. When it is used properly, and if long periods of abstinence are acceptable, it can be very effective indeed.

THE PILL

A greater understanding of endocrinology and physiology dramatically changed contraceptive practice when, in the 1950s, synthetic steroids were developed to serve as oral contraceptive agents.[19] The conventional pill, a combination of estrogen with a progesterone-like chemical, works by suppressing the release of hormones from the hypothalamus that, in turn, release the pituitary hormones FSH and LH. With no FSH and no LH, there is no ovulation. In addition, the synthetic steroids stimulate the endometrium and simulate a menstrual cycle. Usually, the schedule calls for taking pills for twenty-one days and then stopping for seven. The mechanism that makes this work is negative feedback: the brain recognizes the artificially elevated levels of steroids in the blood and therefore cuts down the production of its own hormones. The pill, if taken properly, can be virtually 100 percent effective.[20]

Since the hormones used in the pill have effects on many parts of the

18. N. R. Cohen and H. Haskin, "Detecting Ovulation," *Fertility and Sterility* 11 (1960):497.

19. G. R. Garcia, G. Pincus, and J. Rock, "Effects of Three 19-Nonsteroids on Human Ovulation and Menstruation," *American Journal of Obstetrics and Gynecology* 75 (1958):82–87.

20. G. Pincus, *et al.*, "Fertility Control with Oral Medication," *American Journal of Obstetrics and Gynecology* 75 (1958):1333–46.

body, it is not unexpected that there are side effects associated with its use. Laboratory studies of sugar metabolism and of liver function, for example, have revealed deviations from normal values in many women taking the pill. Although they usually do not produce symptoms, the abnormal laboratory tests are a cause for concern, since their significance for the health of women is not fully understood. There are also minor symptoms similar to those occurring in early pregnancy, such as nausea or a feeling of breast fullness. Other common complaints are intermenstrual bleeding, weight gain, and headache. Most of the symptoms, if they occur at all, are transient.

In addition to the relatively minor changes associated with early use, more serious adverse reactions have been attributed to the pill. The evaluation of these matters is extremely difficult because the conditions under consideration also occur among women who are not using the pill, and it is hard to detect a small change in a rare event in the population at large. The most serious hazard usually associated with the pill is an increased tendency of the blood to clot, resulting in higher risk of heart attack, clots in the lungs (pulmonary embolism), and stroke. These are good examples of the "rare event" problem. The rate of death from these three causes (in Britain, where several studies have been done) among nonpregnant women under age forty is about 1 per 100,000; when the pill is used, the rate may be 3 per 100,000. Among older women who do not use the pill the rate is higher, 12 per 100,000. Among older users of the pill the rate rises to about 36 per 100,000.[21]

These associations are complicated by other factors. Heart disease, for instance, is more frequent among women who smoke, who are obese or diabetic, or who have a history of high blood pressure. The extent to which pill use increases the risk of heart attack depends on these coexisting factors. Smoking is particularly important, since so many women are smokers, at least in the United States and many European countries. It can be concluded that pill taking produces only a slightly greater risk of heart disease than smoking, but there is a considerably greater risk in doing both than in doing either one alone.[22]

Other problems that need further study to establish their association with the pill are an increased risk of urinary tract infections, gall bladder disease, liver disease and tumors, and birth defects if pill use is continued

21. S. J. Segal and L. E. Atkinson, "Biological Effects of Oral Contraceptive Steroids," in *Handbook of Physiology*, edited by R. Greep and E. Ashwood (Baltimore: Williams and Wilkins, 1973), pp. 349–58.

22. A. K. Jain, "Cigarette Smoking, Use of Oral Contraceptives, and Myocardial Infarction," *American Journal of Obstetrics and Gynecology* 126 (1976):301–7.

into pregnancy. Prolonged infertility is also possible after the pill is discontinued, but whether it is caused by the pill itself or masked by the artificial menses during use is unclear. At least ten more years of study are needed before the issue of oral contraceptives and cancer can be closed. Evidence so far shows pill users to have a lower risk of benign breast disease (which may be followed by cancer), fewer ovarian cysts (also a possible precursor to cancer), and unchanged risk of cervical cancer.[23]

Although the advantage of a completely effective method is considerable, the practical aspects of prescription, aside from the safety considerations, require a sophisticated medical apparatus. It is important for a physician or clinic worker to take a preliminary medical history and do a physical examination before starting a woman on the pill. Directions for use, information on side effects, and systematic follow-up visits are essential. At present there is no good way of screening women to identify those for whom pills are especially risky, beyond avoiding prescribing the pill for women who are heavy smokers or obese and therefore already at risk of heart disease.

Since the original pill was approved and marketed in 1960, major improvements have been made, primarily by using lower steroid doses. Some pills in use in 1977 contain less than 5 percent of the original amount of synthetic steroids. Low-dose progestins, in the so-called minipill, have the advantage of eliminating the estrogens and their associated side effects, while allowing ovulation to continue. The actual effectiveness of this method is somewhat uncertain. The major side effect is considerable menstrual cycle irregularity. These pills offer hypothetical advantages regarding safety at the expense of effectiveness in preventing pregnancy.

Methods That Prevent Implantation

THE IUD

Intrauterine contraception did not begin with fundamental chemical and biological discoveries. It began with the empirical observation that the presence of a foreign body in the uterus prevents pregnancy. Intrauterine devices (IUDs) do not disrupt an established pregnancy; they prevent fertilization or implantation by rendering the uterus hostile to either the sperm or the fertilized egg, if there is one. Since in general the causes of implantation are not well understood, no more precise explanation can be given.

23. S. Ramcharan, *The Walnut Creek Contraceptive Drug Study,* vol. I, DHEW Publication No. (NIH) 74–562 (Washington: USGPO, 1974).

Although various intrauterine devices were used as early as the nineteenth century, they were not regarded favorably until the early 1960s, when new materials—such as plastics and stainless steel, which can remain in the uterus indefinitely—could be used. Antibiotics have reduced concern about pelvic inflammatory disease, considered to be a possible side effect of devices at an earlier time.

IUDs are highly reliable, but not completely so; pregnancy rates of one or two per hundred women per year can be expected with the best devices. The essential requirements for the intrauterine device, aside from effectiveness, are dependable retention, ease of insertion and removal, minimal side effects, and availability of a location aid such as a "tail" that passes through the cervical canal into the vagina and can be felt by the wearer herself. These needs have led to the development of about forty different devices, varying in size, shape, and material, and often satisfying one need at the expense of another. Small size, for example, tends to reduce bleeding and pain, but increases expulsions; rigidity tends to decrease expulsions, but increases bleeding and pain. Common shapes are coils and loops (the Lippes loop), rings and closed devices (the Ota ring, the Birnberg bow), a shield (the Dalkon shield),[24] and a T shape.

When a pregnancy proceeds to term with an IUD in place, there is no change in the frequency of fetal abnormalities.[25] Serious complications are rare but possible, the major one being perforation of the uterine wall, if the device is inserted by an unskilled operator. There are reports of an increased incidence of pelvic infection among IUD users. This may be a problem, particularly for segments of the population that experience a high incidence of pelvic inflammatory disease (PID) anyway. The IUD does not create permanent sterility after removal,[26] but a woman who has had PID while using an IUD may end up with closed tubes as a result of the infection.

24. H. J. Tatum, *et al.*, "The Dalkon Shield Controversy: Structural and Bacteriological Studies on IUD Tails," *Journal of the American Medical Association* 231 (1975):711. The Dalkon shield is an example of a device whose disadvantages outweighed its advantages. Although it has good retention, if pregnancy does occur with the device in place, there appears to be a particular risk of severe infection. Perhaps this is caused by the shield's unique tail serving as a wick that permits bacteria to ascend from the vaginal canal. The original device had to be withdrawn from the market in 1975.

25. H. S. Tatum, F. S. Schmidt, and A. K. Jain, "Management and Outcome of Accidental Pregnancies Associated with Copper T Intrauterine Devices," *American Journal of Obstetrics and Gynecology* 126 (1976):863.

26. C. Tietze, "Fertility after Discontinuation of Intrauterine and Oral Contraception," *Proceedings of the Sixth World Congress on Fertility and Sterilization* (Tel Aviv, Israel, 1968) p. 237.

There is no evidence of any relationship between the IUD and increased cancer. (Indeed, it is possible that IUD use has a beneficial effect through early cancer detection as a result of IUD checkup examinations.) In short, the individual advantages of the device are considerable: prolonged protection without the need for a regular regimen of pill taking, the precoital preparation of traditional contraceptives, privacy, or high motivation. The advantages for a family planning program are that it is simple to manufacture, inexpensive, can be inserted by trained paraprofessionals, and, particularly for the newer devices described below, can be inserted in women who have had no children (nulliparous women) and in women immediately following delivery (postpartum women).

Methods That Prevent Birth in Established Pregnancy

ABORTION

Abortion as a means of birth control elicits a wide range of opinions. The recent liberalization of opinion on this subject around the world has been based primarily on respect for the rights of women and concern over morbidity and mortality stemming from illegal abortion under adverse circumstances. In many countries, traditional medicines are reported as being able to cause abortion, and are used widely. Whether they are, indeed, effective has never been established; these claims should be explored carefully.

Different techniques of abortion are available, depending on the stage of the pregnancy. For pregnancies of less than twelve weeks, the traditional method is dilation and curettage (D & C), consisting of two steps: dilation of the cervical canal in order to reach the uterus, and careful scraping, with an instrument called a curette, of the uterus in order to remove the fetus and the early placenta (along with most of the uterine lining). General or local anesthesia is used, and strictly sterile conditions are required. If some of the placental tissue is accidentally not removed, hemorrhage or infection may result. Because the uterine wall becomes softer with pregnancy, perforation is a risk.

Before the thirteenth week, curettage is possible also through suction or vacuum aspiration. Some dilation of the cervix is needed after the sixth week. Negative pressure serves to collect the embryo, fragments of the placenta blood, and fluid. The pressure can be generated with an electrical pump, a foot pedal, or hydraulic suction. Bleeding and early complications are rarer with vacuum aspiration than with D & C,[27] though the same care to avoid infection and injury must be taken.

When menstruation has been delayed for up to two weeks and pregnancy is suspected but not diagnosed, an office procedure that is a modification of suction curettage can be performed using a source of negative pressure and a special plastic tube, not requiring dilation of the cervical canal. This procedure has a number of names: "mini-curettage," "endometrial extraction," and "menstrual regulation."

After the twelfth week of gestation, the technical difficulties of abortion increase because of the size of the embryo relative to the diameter of the cervical canal. One technique used after this time is a miniature cesarean section, termed abdominal hysterotomy, whereby an incision is made in the abdomen and the uterus, and the fetus and placenta are thereby removed. When sterilization is indicated, an advantage of this method is that the fallopian tubes are accessible during the operation and can be tied in a few minutes.

A method that is steadily replacing the hysterotomy, and that does not require an operation, is the injection of a hypertonic saline solution into the uterine cavity through the abdominal wall in order to bring about uterine contractions, labor, and subsequent expulsion of the fetus and placenta. It is not clear how the saline solution induces labor, but it is thought that it suppresses progesterone production by the placenta, which is responsible for relaxing the uterine muscles. Without such a relaxing agent, muscular contractions, or labor, begin. The complications of such a mid-trimester abortion relate to the injection as well as to labor and delivery. (Some of these complications are thought to be avoidable by careful injection.) The main risk is injection of the salt solution into the bloodstream, which could cause death. Even with a good intra-amniotic injection, there is a high level of serum sodium causing headache, numbed fingers, and, possibly, coma. Retention of the placenta and long waits for expulsion of the fetus occur in a very small percentage of cases.

Complications of abortion that develop later are possible but rare: infertility, if an inflammation closes the fallopian tubes or the endometrium is damaged by excessive curettage; a predisposition to premature labor or spontaneous abortion; higher risk of ectopic pregnancy; and the development of Rh antibodies in Rh-negative women from an abortion after the early weeks (a condition that can be corrected by Rh immunization).

27. C. Tietze and S. Lewit, "A National Medical Experience: The Joint Program for the Study of Abortion (JPSA)," *Studies in Family Planning* 3 (1972):97–122.

Disadvantages include not only these possible complications when the procedures are inexpertly performed in unsterile conditions, but the fact that no permanent protection is provided against pregnancy. Advantages for the woman who does not want the pregnancy for health or other reasons are considerable.

Newer chemical abortifacients, discussed in detail below, are now in use. The methods outlined in this section are those that have been used for centuries or have been developed and used over the last decade and a half.

HEALTH EFFECTS OF REDUCED FERTILITY

Each year there are approximately 335 million conceptions throughout the world; of these, perhaps 160 million terminate as blighted ova, spontaneous miscarriages and stillbirths; about 50 million terminate by induced abortion; and the remainder (about 125 million) result in live births.[28] The evidence suggests that 30 million to 55 million of these births are neither planned nor wanted by parents at the time of conception. One-fifth of all births are to women below age twenty or above age thirty-five. Of the 125 million babies born, 20 million are born prematurely, and many of them are unlikely to survive or grow normally; about 14 million die before the end of their first year; an additional 18 million would be expected to die before age fifteen; at least 6 million have chromosomal abnormalities, hereditary biochemical disorders, or major congenital defects at birth, with handicaps that are either untreatable or require intensive care involving sophisticated health resources; perhaps 3 million to 4 million are seriously retarded, and most will remain so as long as they live; an unknown but large number are malnourished, prenatally or postnatally, with the resultant risk of susceptibility to chronic debilitating illness.[29]

Of women who carried these pregnancies, at least 200,000 die before the gestational period is completed or during parturition; an unknown but large number suffer from maternal malnutrition, anemia, infection, or chronic illness, often with lifelong effects; and about 25 million experience serious illness or complications of pregnancy and delivery.

28. B. Berelson, "The Population Problem, Conceptions and Misconceptions," *Anesthesia and Analgesia* 50 (4) (1971):481–89.

29. B. Berelson, "18–35 in Place of 15–45?" *Population Council Annual Report* (1971), pp. 19–27.

There is, of course, some overlap among these adverse pregnancy outcomes. But the malformed, retarded, and sick babies who survive face limited opportunities to participate meaningfully in the lives of their families and societies. Their ability to obtain an education will be more restricted than that of other children in their societies, as will their ability to learn a trade and engage in productive employment.

These estimates are only rough orders of magnitude, but they illustrate the importance of the human reproductive process for the health, well-being, and future functioning of individual women and children. If more adequate epidemiological data were collected, it is highly likely that the accounts would show even greater problems in human reproductive effort. Biological imperatives make some reproductive problems unavoidable, but additional knowledge and its application would reduce these risks to levels closer to the irreducible biological minimum and thereby enable more of the world's children to be born healthy and to lead productive lives.

These health and social consequences are not confined to the individual women and their babies; they also affect the functioning of families, communities, and nations. The problems facing individuals aggregate to a series of intractable social problems in industrialized nations: illegitimacy, early marriage, educational disadvantage, the perpetuation of poverty, family disruption, the need to divert considerable resources from the maintenance of health to the intensive care of the seriously ill and disabled. Each of these problems necessarily commands societal attention and requires societal resources that in some industrialized countries account for a significant share of governmental expenditures. In developing nations that are not yet able to sustain extensive health and welfare programs, the consequences are expressed differently and are less visible at the national level, but they are nonetheless similar in principle.

Thus, human reproduction, which is essential to the survival of the species, can also exact high costs from both individuals and societies. These adverse consequences have multiple causes, ranging from our ignorance of many aspects of the basic biological processes of reproduction to the poverty and malnutrition that afflict much of the world and the inadequacies of our educational and health systems. In the complex web of interacting factors adversely affecting reproductive outcome, the inability of millions of individuals to regulate pregnancy adequately—to determine whether and when they will bear children—is critically important.

Bearing children at too young or too old an age or too close together and having too many children are major factors contributing to infant and maternal mortality and morbidity, malformations, and congenital defects. Unplanned and unwanted pregnancies, particularly among younger and older women, respectively, are estimated to comprise between 24 and 45 percent of pregnancies worldwide. The younger and older ages of childbearing are precisely those at which the risks of adverse health outcomes are greatest and the socioeconomic consequences most acute.

These interrelationships have been documented in detail in numerous studies,[30] and improvements in the health of mothers and children resulting from more effective regulation of pregnancy can be demonstrated in many ways. To take but one example, the risk of mortality for the woman and of mortality or malformation for the fetus is generally related to the age of the mother. Because unwanted and mistimed births are concentrated at young and old maternal ages, the reduction of unintended fertility would tend to reduce the incidence of such age-related problems. For example, one estimate is that if all unwanted births in the United States in the period 1965 to 1970 had been avoided, the incidence of serious sex chromosome defects such as Down's Syndrome would have been about 12 percent lower. If all births to women over age thirty-five had been avoided, a reduction in incidence of about 25 percent would have been expected.[31]

The effort to solve these varied problems proceeds on several fronts. Some lines of biomedical research attempt to find direct solutions for adverse health outcomes (such as the important work in perinatology aimed at developing better means of managing threatened pregnancies). Other researchers seek to unravel the mysteries of genetic development and to determine the causes of and remedies for retardation.

In the past fifteen years, another branch of biomedical research, the reproductive sciences and contraceptive development, has emerged. This branch seeks indirectly to affect all of these health, social, and economic consequences of the reproductive process. This is the worldwide effort to develop safer, simpler, and more effective techniques for regulating fertility. The reproductive sciences branch complements (and to some extent overlaps) ongoing research in perinatal development, genetics, and endocrinology. Unlike these other branches, however, it adds to fundamental biomedical knowledge findings particularly applicable to the task of discovering improved ways for human beings safely to control the reproductive process.

30. D. Norman, "Parental Age as a Factor in Pregnancy Outcome and Child Development," *Reports on Population/Family Planning* 16 (1974): 1–51.

31. M. S. Teitlebaum, "Some Genetic Implications of Population Policies," *Demographic and Social Aspects of Population Growth* (U.S. Commission of Population Growth and the American Future), vol. 1 (Washington: Government Printing Office, 1972), pp. 491–501.

SAFETY AND HEALTH EFFECTS OF FERTILITY REGULATION METHODS

When drugs or medical devices of any type, including contraceptives, are first introduced for wide-scale use, information can be provided regarding effectiveness and most short-range safety matters. It is virtually impossible, however, to anticipate all safety issues that can develop. Side effects that occur after a long period of latency, for example, can be detected only after many years of use. Some health issues may be race- or culture-specific and need attention on a geographic basis. For these reasons, it is difficult to say that contraceptives now in use are "safe" without qualification. As with all drugs or devices, they require constant surveillance on issues of safety and health effects.

The record for maintaining a safety surveillance for methods of fertility regulation is not good. One of the problems has been in cross-cultural transfer of technology. Chemical contraceptives that could affect lactation, for example, are usually tested in countries where breast-feeding is rare, and then distributed in locations where breast-feeding is not only usual but essential for the survival of infants. Another problem is geographic specificity of potential problems based on local health or dietary conditions. IUD-associated bleeding is usually studied when new devices are developed, but the significance of the blood loss can be masked if the device is tested in a population with uniformly high hemoglobin levels and iron reserves and then used in a society with the opposite characteristics.

Nearly fifty specific topics can be identified that need to be studied to resolve safety or reversibility issues relating to oral contraceptives, injectable contraceptives, postcoital pills, intrauterine devices, surgical sterilization, surgical abortion, or spermicidal chemicals.[32] The issues requiring investigation can be studied by long-term prospective cohort studies, case-control studies, or Phase IV pharmacology studies. Case-control studies have been the most frequently used safety evaluation conducted thus far for fertility control methods. Prospective studies are far more costly, but yield information on incidence rates not obtainable directly through case-control studies. The study of pharmacological issues, which can be resolved by laboratory investigations, has usually been determined by the scientific interest of individual investigators.

Long-term prospective studies with oral contraceptives are being carried out in the United Kingdom and in the United States. It may be

32. S. J. Segal, "A Challenge to Research," in *Reproduction and Human Welfare,* edited by R. Greep, M. Koblinsky, and F. Jaffe (Cambridge: MIT Press, 1976), pp. 562–65.

unrealistic to believe that such studies could be done in countries without sophisticated medical record systems.

Short-term epidemiological studies and pharmacological studies on health issues particularly significant to developing countries need to be undertaken. The epidemiological work should concentrate on retrospective case-control studies and similar designs that can be done relatively quickly. Pharmacological studies should also be done, using random assignment, double-blind design, drug crossover studies, or other designs that could be expected to give definitive answers in a short time. International, multi-center studies should also be organized so that geographic specificity can be examined. The most important issues in developing countries should be determined by how generally the results may be taken geographically. A partial list of important topics, excluding long-term prospective studies, follows:

Hormonal Contraceptives

effect on milk volume and quality
passage of steroid into milk
suppression of immune response
hematological effects
metabolic effects
restoration of fertility
incidence of thromboembolic disease, stroke, and renal disease on geographic and age-related bases

Intrauterine Devices

effect on tubal patency
effect on endometrial histology
incidence of pelvic inflammatory disease
restoration of fertility
pregnancy outcome
age-specific side effects
ectopic pregnancy rates

Surgical Abortion

incidence of short-term morbidity
rate of subsequent ectopic pregnancy, prematurity, infertility
age-specific side effects

Surgical Sterilization

failure rates
immune effects in men
effects on hormone levels in men
poststerilization menstrual irregularities
comparative morbidity of different methods

ADVANCES IN FERTILITY REGULATION

New Methods

Recent research has led to the testing and use of several new fertility control methods. Some are refinements of present methods; others, based on applications of fundamental research, are new.

MEDICATED IUDS

So-called pharmacologically active, or medicated, devices have been developed to achieve maximum protection from pregnancy with minimal side effects. The T-shaped device had been shown to cause fewer complaints of pain, bleeding, and expulsion compared with the Lippes loop, but these substantial advantages were canceled out by a higher pregnancy rate. To correct this, two antifertility agents that act locally on the uterus have been added to the plastic T: copper and progesterone. Several versions of copper-bearing devices have been tested, and two (the Copper T and Copper 7) have been approved for use in a number of countries. Although at present the copper-carrying devices have a life span of about three years (a potential disadvantage in developing countries where it is difficult for women to return to a clinic regularly), a newer model of the Copper T has a much longer life span.[33] The progesterone-releasing device must be replaced every year.[34] Both the progesterone-releasing and the copper-bearing devices can be worn by women who have never been pregnant.

POSTCOITAL ESTROGENS

A synthetic estrogen, diethylstilbestrol (DES), if given for five days within 72 hours of unprotected coitus, will prevent pregnancy.[35] The action of the drug is thought to be on the corpus luteum and its role in providing progesterone in the very early stages of pregnancy. Because of its side effects (intense nausea and vomiting), a risk of disrupting subsequent

33. H. J. Tatum, "Copper-Bearing Intrauterine Devices," *Clinical Obstetrics and Gynecology* 17 (1) (1974):93.

34. J. Martinez-Manautou, R. Aznar, and A. Rosado, "Clinical Experience with Intrauterine Progesterone-Releasing Systems," in *Analysis of Intrauterine Contraception,* edited by F. Hefnawi and S. Segal (Amsterdam: North Holland, 1975).

35. L. K. Kuchera, "Postcoital Contraception with Diethylstilbestrol," *Journal of the American Medical Association* 218 (1971): 562–63.

ovarian cycles, and a long-term carcinogenic potential, the method cannot be used routinely. Despite the practical disadvantages, the principle is important. It is possible that other types of estrogens might accomplish the same purpose with fewer side effects, and a "morning-after" or "minutes-after" pill might be developed.

CHEMICAL ABORTIFACIENT: PROSTAGLANDINS

A new compound is being used in aborting mid-trimester pregnancies, or pregnancies of twelve to sixteen weeks' duration that are too far along for vacuum aspiration and not far enough along for saline abortions. It is based on a scientific breakthrough in 1960, namely, the purification of naturally occurring substances called prostaglandins.[36] They are now used, in place of saline, for intra-amniotic administration to induce late abortions. This method works by initiating uterine contractions and causing evacuation of the uterus. Prostaglandins, however, have their disadvantages. According to a comparative study, they are not as safe as saline injection or hysterotomy, and they have troublesome side effects (nausea, vomiting, headache, and sometimes diarrhea).[37] Various prostaglandin compounds are being tested in other forms: intrauterine injection, vaginal or rectal suppositories, and oral medication.

These new methods are in use now because of the fundamental studies, the testing in animals, and the product development work over the last several years, which have prepared them for use by people.

Methods under Investigation

Any new method that is going to be ready for use in the next three to five years has to be at a very advanced stage of testing now, including clinical trials with human subjects. Any project not yet in the clinical stage will take much longer to develop.

VACCINATION AGAINST THE PREGNANCY HORMONE

Researchers in several countries are working to develop a long-term, safe, and effective contraceptive vaccine. The focus of the work is human chorionic gonadotropin (hCG). As we have seen, this is the hormone

36. S. Bergstrom, and J. Sjovall, "The Isolation of Prostaglandin from Sheep Prostate Glands," *Acta Chemica Scandinavica* 14 (1960):1693–1700.

37. W. Cates, *et al.*, "World Health Organization Studies of Prostaglandins versus Saline Abortifacients," *Obstetrics and Gynecology* 54 (4) (1973):493–98.

secreted by the fertilized egg that signals the corpus luteum to continue producing the progesterone necessary for the continuation of the early pregnancy. The objective is to develop a vaccine that would influence the body's immune system to form antibodies to hCG, the pregnancy hormone. Such antibodies would then intercept the crucial message, should the egg indeed have been fertilized, and the corpus luteum would regress, progesterone levels would decline, and menstruation, accompanied by the disappearance of the fertilized egg, would occur. Each cycle therefore would end with menstruation, whether or not fertilization had occurred.

A number of issues need to be studied before the vaccine can move beyond the preliminary testing stage. The pregnancy hormone, hCG, is similar in structure to a pituitary hormone (LH). The formation of antibodies that would cross-react with LH could be risky and could interfere with normal ovarian and menstrual cycles. An important resolution of this problem has been to use only one part of the hCG molecule, a part that it not fully shared by the LH molecule. This, however, contributes to a second problem: the part of the hCG used, the beta-subunit, is quite small and is not a good antibody stimulant. To overcome this, the hCG-beta molecule has been linked with the familiar tetanus toxoid, widely used by humans. Results to date in tests with volunteer subjects show that the vaccine causes the production of antibodies that neutralize the activity of hCG without interfering with ovarian and menstrual cycles.[38] Clinical chemistry studies have not revealed any toxicity or abnormalities in liver and kidney function, but more work needs to be done on both the safety and reliability issues before the substantial promise of the method is realized. Similar work in the United States, the United Kingdom, and Australia, using a fragment of the beta-subunit of hCG, is still at the animal level.

PHARMACOLOGICAL SUPPRESSION OF THE CORPUS LUTEUM

Also at the animal level are studies to identify a compound that would directly suppress the progesterone function of the corpus luteum—a process referred to as luteolysis. The principle is to eliminate the only source of progesterone that can prevent the expected menses in a fertile month. The action would probably be based on inhibiting a specific enzyme in progesterone production, but there are other possible mechanisms. If a proper compound could be identified, the high degree of specificity, af-

38. G. P. Talwar, *et al.*, "Isoimmunization against Human Chorionic Gonadotropin with Conjugates of Processed Beta-Subunit of the Hormone and Tetanus Toxoid," *Proceedings of the National Academy of Science* 73 (1) (1976):218–22.

fecting only the corpus luteum, would reduce the chances of side effects or complications beyond its intended effect: prevention of pregnancy. The only thing required of the woman would be to know that she was expecting a menses on a given day. On the three or four occasions a year when she is one or two days late, she could take a pill that would bring about menstruation. Others might prefer to use the pill on a regular monthly basis, to induce menstruation without knowing if there were any question of being "late." So far, the search for a purely luteolytic agent has turned up a few substances: an extract called Zoapatle from the Mexican plant *Montanoa tuberosa;* a synthetic nonsteroidal drug made in India named Centchroman; a few steroid inhibitors of progesterone synthesis; and a synthetic prostaglandin.[39] Other approaches to luteolysis, described below, are at even earlier stages of fundamental investigation and must await more information about the control of progesterone synthesis and the role of cell receptors in the action of hormones.

Closely related to this field of research is work with a chemical substance extracted from an herb used in China to induce abortion. The root tubes of *Trichosanthis Kirilowii Maxim* is the source of the substance. The protein extracted is called trichosanthin. It is believed to be effective as an abortifacient through its cytotoxic effect on cells that produce chorionic gonadotropin.[40]

LONG-ACTING FORMS OF CONTRACEPTIVE STEROIDS

To overcome some of the disadvantages of the pill, such as the need to remember to take it daily and the sudden absorption into the blood stream (and directly to the liver) of the synthetic sex hormones, better forms of steroidal contraception are sought. Ease of administration, the medical preference for constant dosage levels in the system, and the acceptability of injections by women who are accustomed to them for disease control are factors influencing this research. The attempts to find an effective and long-acting steroid take the forms listed below. Most are based on the same principle as the pill.

Injections

Injections of progestins, given at lengthy intervals, are being tested clinically. The injection of Depo Provera every three months is widely

39. S. J. Segal, "Fertility Regulation Technology."

40. Shanghai Institute of Experimental Biology, "Studies on the Mechanism of Abortion Induction by Trichosanthin," *Scientia Sinica* 19 (6) (1976):801–28.

used for contraception throughout the world, but this use is not approved by the United States Food and Drug Administration, The synthetic progestin that is the active ingredient of Depo Provera has not performed well in long-term toxicity studies in beagle dogs. This fact, plus clinical experience suggesting a post-treatment loss of fertility, contributed to a cautious interpretation by the U.S. regulatory agency of the compound's risk/benefit ratio. The concern over safety has been reinforced by recent findings in rhesus monkeys. On the other hand, in South America, the Caribbean Islands, and many Asian and African countries, Depo Provera is used regularly as an injectable contraceptive in spite of the safety issues and its serious disruption of menstrual bleeding patterns. Scientists are studying another injectable progestin, called norethisterone enanthate.[41] It is a close chemical relative of the progestin in one of the most popular contraceptive pills.

Implants

To avoid the need for return visits to a clinic and to assure the constant and gradual release of steroids, various implants have been tested. These are tubes or rods made of a rubber-like compound containing the synthetic steroids that are implanted, with a small incision, under the skin—usually in the arm or the buttocks. One implant regimen that would last for one or two years uses a new progestin, norgestrienone; another uses levonorgestrel, a popular drug when used in pill form, and could last for as long as six years. Also being tested, but at a much earlier stage of research, are biodegradable implants or steroids coated with biodegradable substances like those used in absorbable surgical sutures. The advantage of this development is that the implants would not need to be removed, but would simply disintegrate under the skin as they progress through their effective lifetime. The six-year implant of levonorgestrel is highly effective in terms of pregnancy prevention. Its main problem is bleeding irregularity, a side effect that makes the method unacceptable for about 18 percent of those who use it.[42] This particular form of the implant method is ready for field study, and will probably be introduced for general use in 1980 or 1981. This timetable assumes the absence of unforeseen safety issues in chronic animal studies or as the method is used more extensively.

41. World Health Organization, "Multinational Comparative Clinical Evaluation of Two Long-Acting Injectable Contraceptive Steroids: Norethisterone Enanthate and Medroxy-Progesterone Acetate," *Contraception* 17 (1978):395–407.

42. E. Coutinho, *et al.*, "Contraception with Long-Acting Sub-Dermal Implants: An Effective and Acceptable Modality," *Contraception* 18 (4):315–334.

Vaginal Ring

Steroids can be absorbed through the vaginal mucosa. Taking advantage of this property, researchers have incorporated progestins into a plastic ring, similar to but smaller than the rim of a diaphragm, which is introduced into the vagina behind the cervix. The woman can insert the ring herself and leave it in place for three weeks before removing the ring, thus precipitating a menstrual flow. The schedule of three weeks in and one week out is similar to the contraceptive pill regimen. The advantage is that the user does not have to remember to take a pill every day. The steroids are released at a more constant level, a feature which may avoid significant side effects of the pill. The ring needs to be replaced with a new one about once every six months when the steroids are exhausted. This method shows clinical promise and could be in general use by 1980.[43]

Intracervical Devices

Unlike IUDs, which are placed in the uterus, or vaginal rings, which are placed in the vagina, other devices can be placed in the cervix (the opening of the uterus at the end of the vaginal canal). The purpose is to accomplish local contraception without affecting the rest of the body. The intracervical device would release sufficient progestin to cause thickening of the cervical mucus.[44]

PHARMACOLOGIC CONTRACEPTION FOR MALES

Although for centuries contraception was left up to males, who used coitus interruptus and the condom, attention to chemical methods for men began in earnest with clinical trials only in 1971. A difficulty encountered in the field of contraceptive research in the male is the small number of links in the reproductive chain of events, compared to the number of vulnerable points identified in the female system. The focus has been on suppressing the production of sperm through the action of synthetic male hormones in a manner analogous to the suppression of egg production and

43. D. R. Mishell, Jr., *et al.*, "Clinical Performance and Endocrine Profits with Contraceptive Vaginal Rings Containing a Combination of Estradiol and D-Norgestrel," *American Journal of Obstetrics and Gynecology* 130 (1978):55–62.

44. R. Nakamura, Clinical Experience with Intracervical Devices. Personal communication, 1978.

ovulation in the female with the pill. The problem, as with the female pill, is to achieve a balance between dosages of steroids that would stop sperm production on the one hand and not cause unacceptable side effects, on the other.

Combinations of the male sex hormone, testosterone, and a progestin have been used to stop sperm production. Their effect is reversible, and they do not introduce unacceptable hazards.[45] The main problem with the compounds at dosages tested is inability to maintain low sperm counts for a protracted period. In too many cases, sperm production breaks through after a few weeks or months. The problem appears to be proper compound identification and establishment of proper dose. A male contraceptive, like the female contraceptives still under investigation, could take the form of a pill, an implant, or an injection. A report from China describes successful clinical trials in men with a compound extracted from cottonseed oil. The studies were undertaken on the basis of reports of a high incidence of male infertility in regions where raw cottonseed oil is used widely in the diet. A known toxic substance, gossypol, was extracted from the cottonseed oil and tested in animals. It was found to suppress sperm production and was subsequently introduced into clinical trials. The cumulative toxicity of gossypol in certain animal species is a cause for concern with this drug, even though the Chinese studies are being carried out with low doses of the substance. The nearly complete effectiveness described in the published report is an encouraging finding.[46] However, the toxicological potential of gossypol makes the establishment of an acceptable pharmacological ratio (toxic dose:effective dose) a critical issue.[47]

In addition to these new methods, investigation is continuing on refinements of other methods discussed earlier: improved IUDs, better techniques of female sterilization, and reversible vasectomies.

New Areas of Research

In the long process of development of practical methods of fertility control, a number of new areas of possibility are still "at the bench" in the laboratory.

45. S. B. Schearer, "The use of Progestins and Androgens as a Male Contraceptive," *International Journal of Andrology,* Supplement 2 (1978).

46. National Coordinating Group for Male Contraceptives, Shanghai, "Gossypol—A New Male Contraceptive," *Chinese Medical Journal* 58 (8) (1978):455–58.

47. L. C. Bernardi and L. A. Goldblatt, "Gossypol, Food Science and Technology," *Toxic Constituents of Plant Food Stuffs,* edited by I. Liener (New York: Academic Press, 1969).

Many of these have come about through major breakthroughs in methodology, such as the development in the last ten years of very sensitive assays, or tests, to measure tiny quantities of hormones in the blood and other body tissues. It is now possible, using just a finger prick sample of blood, to test for the presence of hormones that could not be tested with any degree of accuracy before. Another significant methodological advance is amino acid sequencing, the ability to determine the amino acid or chemical structure of any protein. The application of this technique by protein chemists preceded the isolation and use of the beta-subunit of the pregnancy hormone, hCG, in the antipregnancy vaccine described above. The prospect of such a vaccine was postulated 30 years ago, but the development had to await the methodology to isolate and identify the pure hCG molecule.[48] Polypeptide synthesis, another major methodological discovery that has contributed to human reproductive research in the last five years, is the process of making a synthetic protein, once its structure is known. It is now possible through this technique to make artificial molecules that are identical to the ones in the body and that can be used as substitutes. Another advance, the electron microscope, has permitted study of the egg and sperm at the subcell level.

These fundamental methodological advances and other discoveries in protein chemistry, neuroendocrinology, and molecular biology have great potential for a future generation of contraceptives. In some cases, we know enough to have reached certain levels of application already touched on in this paper. In other cases, knowledge is still at such an early stage that we do not even know how the basic processes work in detail. Nevertheless, we now know much more about what we don't know—the gaps in our information base. Where, then, are these fundamental areas of laboratory research that may have future payoff for fertility control?

INFLUENCING THE BRAIN

The protein produced in the brain that triggers the production and release by the pituitary of the hormones that stimulate the ovary and the testis is the luteinizing hormone releasing factor, LRF. It is now possible to isolate and synthesize LRF, a decapeptide, or a chain of ten amino acids, and make similar or antagonistic compounds.[49] One possible application would be an antagonist to suppress ovulation. A second applica-

48. R. E. Canfield, *et al.*, "Studies of Human Chorionic Gonadotropin," *Recent Progress in Hormone Research* 27 (1971):51–62.

49. J. E. River and W. W. Vale, "A Potent Luteinizing Hormone Releasing Factor Antagonist *in vitro* and Inhibitor of Ovulation in the Rat," *Life Sciences* 23 (1978):869–76.

tion would be to stimulate ovulation on a predictable basis, administering the synthetic protein as a pill, a tablet absorbed under the tongue, a nasal spray, or a vaginal tampon. The message would reach the brain; LRF would cause the production of LH, and ovulation would occur at a precise time, allowing a woman to use the rhythm method with greater certainty. Since such a method would affect only the cells in the pituitary that produce LH, it would avoid the more general side effects of less specific compounds, such as the steroid pill. In the male, analogues of LRF could be used to prevent sperm production.[50]

Another point of action between the brain and the reproductive system that may be useful for intervention is the pineal gland, which produces a biologically active chemical called melatonin. In lower mammals, melatonin inhibits ovulation. We do not know what it does in the human, but it may be related to pineal control of the function of the ovary. From work in this area, a pill or some other method may be developed to inhibit the ovary, again without having an effect on the rest of the system and therefore without producing the risks of the steroid pill.

OCCUPYING THE BINDING SITES

The gonadotropins that bind to special cells on the surface of the ovary and stimulate the ovary to function are large strings of amino acids or chemicals with sugar molecules called glycoproteins attached to them. Without these special carbohydrates, the proteins bind onto their special target cells, but move off so quickly that they will not do what they are supposed to. This suggests that counterfeit molecules could be synthesized. These altered molecules could occupy the binding cells in place of the real ones and therefore block their action.[51] With hCG competitors, this "first-come-first-bind" process might lead to a chemical abortifacient. If a woman has missed a period, she could take the antagonist. A fake message would arrive at the ovary and, in effect, fail to tell the corpus luteum to continue to deliver progesterone. By keeping real hCG off the binding sites, the new drug would induce menses.

IDENTIFYING THE RECEPTORS

Work is going on to learn more about the chemistry of the receptors, or binding sites on the surface of cells of the ovary or testis for the gonad-

50. F. Labrie, *et al.*, "Inhibitory Effect of LHRH and Its Agonists on Testicular Gonadotropin Receptors and Spermatogenesis in the Rat," *International Journal of Andrology*, Supplement 2 (1978).

51. O. P. Ball, L. Marz, and W. P. Moyle, "The Role of the Carbohydrate in

stimulating hormones in both the male (testis) and the female (ovary). Altering the binding capacity of these cells might also inhibit gonad function.[52]

UNDERSTANDING THE INTRACELLULAR ACTION OF STEROIDS

A very important field is the biology of steroid hormones at the level of single cells. In the last ten years we have learned that many cells in the reproductive system tell their own internal factories what to produce according to a complex chain of messages starting with the entry into the cell of the steroid hormones. The hormone attaches to receptors in the cytoplasm of the cell, which carry it into the nucleus.[53] There interaction with the chromosomes determines the pattern of which genes are active and which genes are not active. The message is given to add amino acids in the right sequence to make the right protein. Implications of this new knowledge for contraception are that we might be able to allow the ovarian cycle to continue normally, but then interfere with the action of the steroids on the cells of the endometrium so that the uterus does not have the right secretions to prepare properly for pregnancy. Different impact points in the normal steroid-receptor interaction are possible: the formation of the receptors in the cytoplasm; the rate of degeneration of the receptors; the binding process of the steroid to the receptor; and the binding of the steroid-receptor complex to the chromosomes. Chemical substances have been synthesized to block some of these actions, at least in laboratory experiments.[54] It is a giant step to clinical application, but not an improbable development.

AFFECTING THE MEMBRANES OF EGG OR SPERM

When the first sperm touches the egg in the fallopian tube, changes in the membrane of the egg block the entry of more sperm. This block

---

the Biological Function of Human Chorionic Gonadotropin," in *Hormone Binding and Target Cell Activation in the Testis,* edited by M. Dufau and A. Means (New York: Plenum, 1974), pp. 32–46.

52. N. L. Dufau, O. Ryan, K. J. Cott, "Disulfide Groups of Gonadotropin Receptor Are Essential for Specific Binding of Human Chorionic Gonadotropin," *Biochemica et Biophysica Acta* 343 (1974):417.

53. G. P. Talwar, *et al.,* "The Binding of Estradiol in the Uterus: A Mechanism for the Depression of RNA Synthesis," *Proceedings of the National Academy of Science, USA* 52 (1964):1058–66.

54. B. W. O'Malley, *et al.,* "Steroid Hormone Induction of a Specific Translatable Messenger RNA," *Nature New Biology* 240 (1973):2031.

to polyspermy is what keeps the egg alive; if it is penetrated by more than one sperm, it would never develop or survive and would be sloughed off in menstruation. Research on marine invertebrates, such as the sea urchin, suggests that the first sperm chemically alters the egg membrane so that the remaining sperm receptors on its surface are inactivated. Therefore one approach would be to develop a surrogate sperm that would beat the real sperm to the egg, induce this change in the egg membrane, and block the penetration of the real sperm. Another possibility would be to change chemically, with a pill or an implant, the egg membrane from its pre-fertilization delicacy to a tough skin. An additional route would be to encourage polyspermy and the subsequent passing of the nonviable egg with menses. At present, we need to know a great deal more about fundamental membrane biology before we can pursue this.

INTERFERING WITH SPERM AND EGG DEVELOPMENT

In a process that is not very well understood, sperm mature between leaving the testis and entering the fallopian tube of the female. Important changes occur during the journey through the male epididymis, including alterations in structure, metabolism, pattern of motility, and fertilizing capacity.[55] Once more is learned about the biochemical nature of this process, the epididymis may serve as a site for interrupting capacitation so that the male ejaculate contains "blanks."

In the human female, the egg is in a state of arrest for a number of years, a condition apparently caused by a maturation inhibitor produced by the follicles. It has been shown with marine organisms like the starfish that when certain follicular maturation factors are applied to the ovary,[56] the eggs in the ovary will start to develop. Work is under way to determine whether a natural or chemical agent can be used to inhibit or stimulate egg maturation in the follicles of mammalian ovaries,[57] a development that would have the greatest usefulness in fertility control application, because of its specificity to the reproductive process.

55. M. R. M. Prasad, G. G. Gupta, and T. Karkum, "Control of Epididymal Function," *Journal of Reproduction and Fertility,* Supplement 18 (1973):215.

56. H. Kanatani, "Maturation-Inducing Substances in Starfishes," *International Review of Cytology* (New York: Academic Press, Inc.) 35:253–98.

57. C. P. Channing, *et al.,* "Studies on an Oocyte Maturation Inhibitor Present in Porcine Follicular Fluid," *Novel Aspects of Reproductive Physiology,* edited by C. H. Spelman and J. W. Wills (New York: Spectrum, 1978), pp. 37–60.

ADVANCES IN INFERTILITY TREATMENT

Significant improvements have been achieved over the past decade in the diagnosis and treatment of sterility. For diagnostic purposes, the development of very sensitive assays, described above, has been invaluable. It is now possible to test levels of steroid or protein hormones that previously could not be tested with any degree of accuracy. From bioengineers have come instruments to evaluate the reproductive organs visually, using fiber optics as a component of endoscopes; devices that use ultrasound to scan and project on a cathode tube every millimeter of the surface of the uterus and oviducts; and instruments to evaluate the flow characteristics of cervical mucus. Immunology has also contributed to the diagnostic procedures to evaluate infertility in either the female or male.

The first effective treatment of ovarian failure was the direct stimulation of the ovaries with extracts from human pituitary glands, or from postmenopausal urine.[58] Subsequently, two other chemical approaches to ovulation induction have appeared, and literally thousands of previously untreatable couples have been assisted to parenthood. This success in hormonal therapy has been matched by surgical advances for the treatment of blocked tubes, a major cause of female infertility. Less sensational perhaps, than the highly publicized work with *in vitro* fertilization and egg transfer from petri dish to uterus,[59] sound surgical management of tubal closure, along with the new hormonal treatments for ovulation induction, are the chief reasons for new hope for the infertile couple.[60] Infertility due to male factors, estimated to be the cause in about 50 percent of infertile couples, has not yielded to attempts at therapy so far and represents a major challenge for scientific inquiry in the coming years.

PREDETERMINATION OF SEX

Predetermination of sex is a scientific goal of considerable interest. Research in this field is stimulated by the commercial advantage to be gained in the breeding of farm animals. When that goal is achieved, the choice of sex of offspring may also be available to parents everywhere.

58. C. Gemzell, and E. D. B. Johansson, "Human Gonadotropin: Control of Human Fertility," *Nobel Symposium 15* (Stockholm: Almquist and Wiksell, 1971), pp. 241–54.

59. P. C. Steptoe and R. G. Edwards, "Birth after the Reimplantation of a Human Embryo," *Lancet* 2 (1978) 8085:366.

60. C. R. Garcia and J. Allen, "Surgical Approach to Tubal Disease," *Clinical Obstetrics and Gynecology* 17 (1974):102–14.

Biologists have successfully altered the sex ratio of nonmammalian vertebrates. By ingenious experiments, amphibian offspring can be made either 100 percent male or 100 percent female.[61] With a view toward human application and the advantages for the rearing of farm animals, physiologists have attempted to influence the sex ratio of mammals. One approach has been physically to separate the X-bearing spermatozoa (which produce females) and the Y-bearing spermatozoa (which produce males).[62] From time to time, claims of success appear, but prove to be unduly optimistic when put to the test of statistical significance and adequate experimental design.[63] A second approach to sex predetermination is based on selective elimination of the X or Y spermatozoon, either chemically or immunologically.[64] Although not yet successful, this approach has a reasonable theoretical basis. The development of a technique to stain selectively and identify the Y chromosomes in human cells has been of major importance to research in sex predetermination. Now, with the application of this special fluorescence procedure, the ratio of X-bearing and Y-bearing sperm in semen samples can be established visually so that experimental interventions can be evaluated rapidly.[65] This advance in basic science brings much closer ultimate success in sperm separation as a basis for sex predetermination.

CONCLUSION

The future of contraceptive technology, the management of infertility, and other aspects of reproductive medicine depend to a great extent on how much is invested in fundamental research in reproductive and developmental biology. It is vital to recognize that the work and study going on in the laboratories is doing more to advance the state of the science than much of the applied work that attracts public attention.

61. C. Y. Chang and E. Witschi, "Breeding of Sex-Reverse Males of Xenopus Laevis," *Proceedings of the Society of Experimental Biology and Medicine* 89 (1955): 150–52.

62. P. E. Lindahl, "Separation of Bull Spermatozoa Carrying X- and Y-Chromosomes by Counter-Streaming Centrifugation," *Nature* 181 (1958):784.

63. M. J. Gordan, "Electrophoretic Separation of Rabbit Sperm," *Scientific American* 199 (1958):87–94.

64. T. Caspersson, "Identification of the Philadelphia Chromosome as a Number 22 by Quinacrine Mustard Flourescence Analysis," *Experimental Cell Research* 63 (1970):238–40.

65. *Ibid.*

The process is basic to science. Improvements applicable to the regulation of human fertility begin with fundamental studies of the reproductive system and extend to applied product development. It is a task that engages chemists, biologists, physicians, and a host of other professionals. Seldom has there been such an opportunity to use science for the benefit of all humanity as there is in this area now.

8

Demography and Development in the 1980s

NANCY BIRDSALL, JOHN FEI, SIMON KUZNETS, GUSTAV RANIS, AND T. PAUL SCHULTZ

INTRODUCTION

MALTHUS GAVE TO ECONOMICS a relatively simple model linking family behavior, individual welfare, and economic growth. In his model, reproductive behavior was attuned to economic conditions. New families formed more rapidly and had more children in good times; thus more income per capita led inexorably to larger populations. Larger populations, however, put pressure on limited land; the law of diminishing returns then dictated lower labor productivity, forcing per capita consumption below subsistence levels. Deprivation then assured both higher mortality and a drop in the rate of family formation and reproduction. Thus, in the classical system, economic growth in the sense of increased total output could occur, but for most families the standard of living would not improve.

The family and its response mechanisms represented a necessary ingredient in this classical framework of Malthus and Ricardo; but the analysis was essentially aggregative, with little attention to the precise nature of the underlying family decision-making process. Yet the family is the locus of many decisions that affect both production and population; the family is also society's principal redistributive unit, especially in the poorer countries, and thus the logical focus of income distribution analysis. It must be a central building block in any future theory- and policy-reformulation effort.

This chapter represents a collaborative effort in the sense that all the authors have benefitted from a substantial interchange of comments and suggestions. It should be noted, however, that T. Paul Schultz had primary responsibility for the third section and Simon Kuznets for the sixth section. They are not necessarily to be held responsible for other material in this chapter.

In the second edition of his *Essay on Population,* Malthus introduced the notion of preventive checks to rampant human reproduction, and his axiomatic "fixity of passion" gave way to the sociological assertion of a tendency of the "lower" classes to reproduce too much—a tendency curable, however, by policy measures and education. Though popularly known today for his doomsday views, in this later edition, a more sophisticated version, Malthus became a social reformer; and it is within the latter tradition that the interest in public policy and individual birth control programs has developed.

As it turned out, Malthus and Ricardo were wrong, both in their assumptions regarding family reproductive behavior and those regarding the potential for increasing agricultural production, for the Industrial Revolution ultimately ushered in a new type of society. Even as Malthus wrote, the transition to what has been called "modern economic growth" had begun. The persistent search for new scientific principles and their routine application to production processes were beginning to yield productivity gains that outstripped population growth and guaranteed increases in per capita incomes. Moreover, by the end of the nineteenth century, the eighteenth century economic transition had been complemented by a demographic transition to lower fertility, making per capita income increases even greater for given increases in economic output. The economic and demographic characteristics of typical industrial economies were set: sustained productivity increases, steady but slow population growth, and improving consumption standards for the working majority.

Malthus and the classicists are remembered not because they were right (indeed they were not), but because they helped suggest the notion of a "system," and one in which aggregate economic and demographic change were tied together by behavior at the family level. Between the classicists and the present, subsequent "systems" of population and development have been based on two contrary views: first-edition Malthus, represented today by the limits-to-growth advocates, with energy sources and pollution a constraint even for the developed countries; and reformist, second-edition Malthus, emphasizing the power of accumulating useful knowledge in creating technology for sustaining a larger population and in designing social policy to encourage lower fertility. In the second view, moreover, the determinism of the early popularized Malthus is rejected; it provides the basis for governments administering policy measures to enhance economic growth, improve distribution, and speed the demographic transition.

But the precise causes of fertility decline and its relationship to economic change and income distribution patterns are still far from completely understood. Policy design and government intervention require such a fuller understanding of a system which in operation involves demographic, economic, and social phenomena vastly more complicated than Malthus implied. Modern demographic theory provides much of what is needed on the relations among rates of fertility, nuptiality, mortality, the age and sex distribution of the population, and rates of population growth. Modern economic theory relates population and economic growth to capital accumulation, technology change, and, to some extent, patterns of income distribution. The new home economics of the family analyzes family decisions, particularly fertility and marriage, and female labor force activity which affect demographic change. Social history and modern anthropology inform us about changes over time in the definition and role of the family which are relevant to understanding the interrelations between economic growth, population change, and the distribution of income. Thus, progress is being made.

But specialization, while expanding the available information, has also narrowed perspective. How can new knowledge be organized to provide the broader perspective necessary for intelligent policy interventions? The device proposed is a modest descendant of Malthus' second-edition system. First, we offer a description in some detail of this "general" economic-demographic system, emphasizing especially those aspects of it which are novel and which help to incorporate family decisions into the conventional economic and demographic frameworks. An effort is made to indicate the data or information which would (and in some work does already) help analysts and policy-makers to infer what drives the system. The discussion is, moreover, focused on the three principal social purposes which seem to prevail in today's developing countries: the *efficiency* of resource allocation, the *equity* with which income is distributed, and the rapidity of *growth* and structural change.[1] Recent research and analysis in these areas which addresses (sometimes only implicitly) policy issues is discussed relating work in each of these areas to the general system presented here.

In the next section, "Microeconomic Aspects of Family Behavior," it is shown how a model which treats the family as an efficient and rational—indeed, profit-maximizing and cost-minimizing—unit, can be useful in policy design. Family economic and demographic decisions, including fertility and labor supply, are shown to be influenced by structural change and growth in the economy within which families operate.

"Development and Demography: Macro Models" considers the extent to which various aggregative growth models effectively incorporate demographic variables and indicates how the less aggregated family-level

1. A fourth purpose, commonly the concern of economists, is the *stability* of the economy. This is omitted here; it is primarily relevant to the industrialized mature economies.

data framework developed in "The General Economic-Demographic System" can be exploited in the construction of macro models.

"Population Growth and the Size Distribution of Income Among Families" focuses attention on that body of income distribution work at an intermediate level of aggregation which incorporates family and demographic variables. It shows how work on family income distribution may provide a heretofore missing portion of the analytical chain which links economic growth, distribution, and population change.

"Puzzles and Prospects" considers the extent to which currently available data, particularly demographic data, permits or inhibits fuller analysis of some of the policy issues raised in the preceding sections. Some puzzles presented by current data on demographic trends in developing countries are discussed, with emphasis on how future data collection and analysis focusing on demographic trends among socioeconomic subgroups within less developed countries (LDCs) might help resolve such puzzles. In the course of this discussion currently emerging trends in both mortality and fertility in developing countries are considered within a longer-run perspective.

Finally, in "Conclusions for Research and Policy," the policy issues which emerge from this consideration of the general economic-demographic system are given more explicit emphasis. Evidence on fertility change now indicates the beginning of the end of the so-called demographic transition for large portions of the developing world; a clear trend of falling fertility has emerged in Latin America and in portions of Southeast and East Asia. As some countries shed transitional characteristics, new growth, distributional and demographic issues are arising; and so will the need for a shift in our policy emphasis. Ultimately new directions in future research and policy design must be sought—directions attuned to a world in which the diversity among types of developing countries and, within countries, among socioeconomic subgroups, is becoming an increasingly important economic and political reality.

THE GENERAL ECONOMIC-DEMOGRAPHIC SYSTEM

The phenomena normally defined as demographic, particularly marriage and fertility, are the product of individual personal decisions long viewed as outside the realm of economics. To understand and relate apparently personal decisions to the larger changes wrought by economic growth requires a broadening of the conventional economic framework to accommodate the family and the household. In this section a type of general economic-demographic system is outlined which does this, and which suggests the types of data necessary to analyze how the system operates.

In conventional economics, the population is treated in terms of both its production and consumption dimensions. In a flow system (portion A of Figure 8.1) the population enters production as manpower or labor, along with the stock of physical capital and natural resources. The output resulting from that production is then consumed or saved and invested by members of the same population. The system describes an economy which is closed with respect to labor mobility; net emigration or immigration is not allowed. (This is not unrealistic for most of today's developing countries.)

The major difference between this simple version of the conventional system and a more general economic-demographic system is the addition of the household production sector to the market production sector (portion B of Figure 8.1). The limited labor time of all members of the population must be allocated between the traditional or market sector and the household sector. The latter produces maintenance services (e.g., cooking, cleaning, fuel gathering) and the care of the nonactive population: the children and the elderly. Household services are critical to every economy and, as will be seen below, absorb a large portion of one of the few resources available to the poor in developing countries: their own time.

The general system, like the conventional economic system, can be pictured as a flow of capital and labor owned by members of the population either to market or to household production; and of goods and services produced in those sectors back to the population, which then allocates its receipts of those goods and services to consumption or further production, i.e., investment.

Investment in physical capital in the market production sector is a concern in the conventional economic system. In the general system, equally important is the investment in human resources, especially in health and education; this investment takes place both in the market sector and in the household sector. Some of the market production sector investment in human resources is supported by the government.

In this demographically oriented system—neutral with respect to institutional choices—the focus is on the family and government as organizational units, complementing the analysis of firms in conventional mixed-economy settings. The family, perhaps the most permanent and durable of human institutions, is the natural managerial and decision-making unit for household production, though it has no monopoly on household services, as public schools, centrally coordinated nursery systems and state nursing homes demonstrate. It is, however, usually within the family unit that a household budget is administered and the consumption of family members

FIGURE 8.1
General Economic-Demographic System

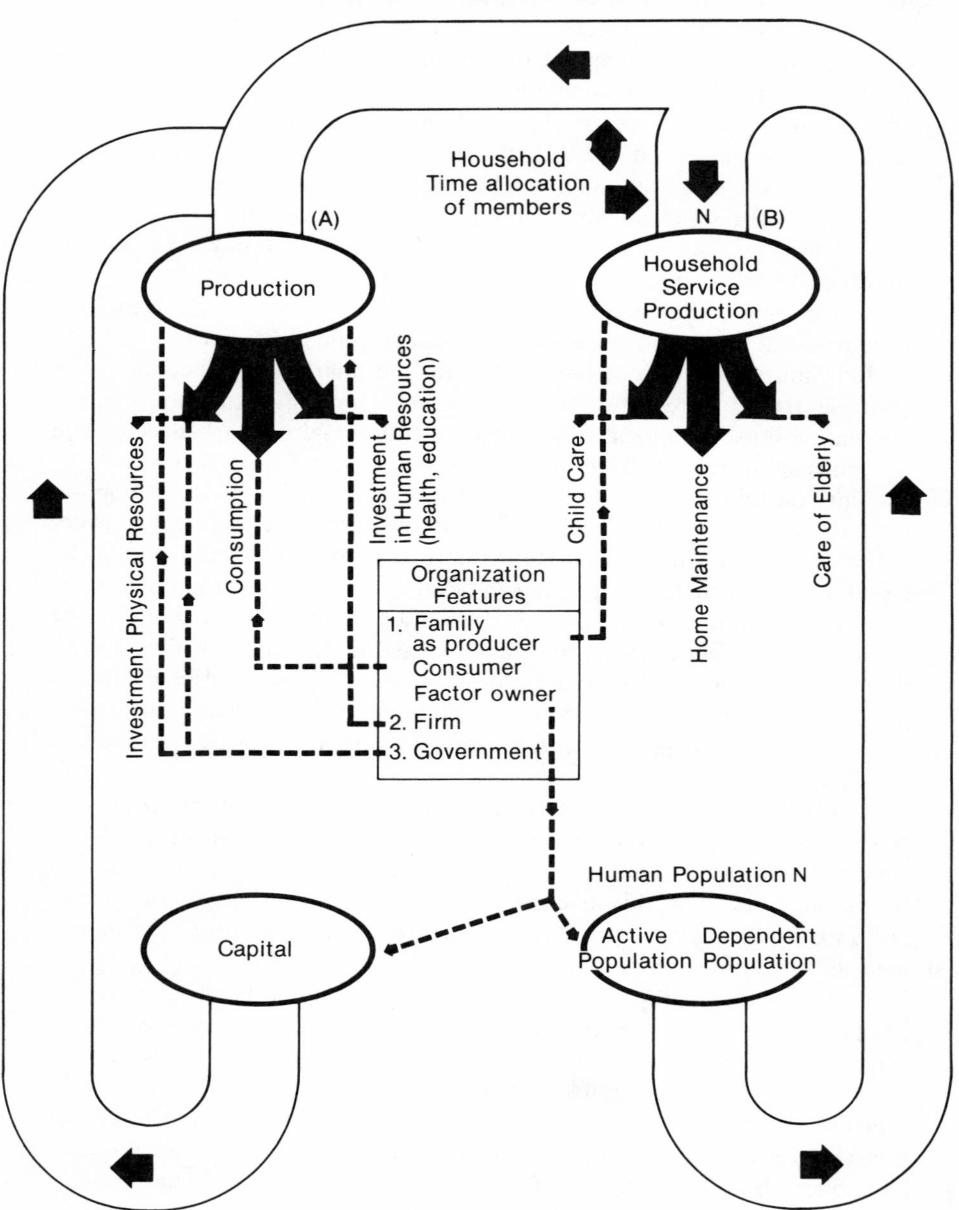

organized. It is the family which "owns" labor, one of the inputs to production in both the market and household sectors. In some, but not all, societies, families also own capital and land. It is the family which manages much of society's total investment in human resources, particularly that which occurs during the crucial years of infancy and early childhood. "Families" are organized differently in different societies; in fact in some cultures, production, consumption, and reproduction decisions are not made within coincident "families." Still, the nuclear family, with modest and variable extensions and adaptations, remains the predominant type.

In most societies governments organize the production of certain goods, either because of the requirements of large-scale production or because of the indivisibility of public goods. Governments deliver services which complement household investments in human resources in the form of expenditures on education, health, and family planning. While all societies, regardless of their institutional preferences, choose some mixture of family and government decision making in these areas, most of the contemporary developing countries are "mixed," that is to say, the economic and demographic decisions of individual families are coordinated through some combination of government planning plus reliance on the market system in which relative prices, including wages, are the main signals to which individual families respond.

Distinguishing Themes

Before indicating the kinds of data which will be needed to analyze the general economic-demographic system, attention is called to several major themes which will recur throughout the remainder of this section. First is the use of the family as the unit of analysis. The family, rather than the individual of conventional economics, is the primary consumption unit. Moreover, a major component of total societal production, that is, the household sector, is organized and carried out by the family—and it is within the family context that the decision about allocation of labor to the market production sector is made. Families also, as mentioned above, manage much of society's investment.

A second theme is the importance of time and the time constraint faced by individuals and families in the system. In the textbook economic system, there is some recognition of the limits of time: individuals must allocate their time between "labor" and "leisure," whereby labor is actually meant to be work in the market sector, and leisure is "all other time." In the general economic-demographic system, much non-market-labor time of individuals is seen to be not leisure at all, but work in the household production sector: caring for children and the health of family members, via cooking, cleaning, fetching water and fuel, and other home chores.

Traditional labor-surplus models of developing economies often seem to imply that time is an abundant resource for the poor. Indeed, time is one of the poor's few resources; the poorest families have little schooling, few tools, virtually no capital, and often no land. But where labor may be "surplus," it is likely to be so defined in relation to the scarcity of other production factors—capital and land—rather than in terms of the availability of leisure to individuals. In fact, women work an average of eleven hours per day in Bangladesh and Java; ten hours in the Philippines, eight hours in Israel and seven in the U.S.[2] Because the poor have little but their time, they work many hours. Their decisions regarding use of time between household and market work, and among consumption, production and investment within the household, are keys to the understanding of underdevelopment, and the escape from it. In fact, an important characteristic of economic growth is the increase in lifetime leisure available to members of wealthier societies. With development, not only do hours per day or week of those in the labor force decline, but the proportion of a lifetime during which persons are in the labor force declines, as participation rates among the very old and the very young drop off.

This leads to a third theme: full income. In the general economic-demographic system, "full income" is the counterpart to the "full" production described, i.e., production including not only the market, but the household sector, just as money income is the counterpart in the traditional system to market production alone (GNP). By a household's or family's full income is meant the total resources available to the household, including not only income from capital and income from labor allocated to the market sector, but also the time available for home production or leisure. If household members choose leisure (as may many of those who retire at early ages in wealthy societies) rather than the higher money income associated with more hours of work, their full income does not decline, though money income does. In developing societies, if teenage children attend school rather than work on a family farm, full income of the family does not decline, though money income may (most obviously if hired help substitutes for child labor).

While the measurement problems are severe and can only be solved over time, the full income concept has significant policy implications. Cross-section comparisons of income per capita may in one sense minimize

2. See Robert E. Evenson and Elizabeth K. Quizon, "Time Allocation and Home Production in Philippine Rural Households," paper presented at International Center for Research on Women, Elkridge, Md., April 1978.

differences among countries or among households within countries, if the wealthier enjoy not only more money but more leisure. On the other hand, if, with development, there is a tendency to specialize through the market the level of measured market income will tend to increase more rapidly than full income. Data on increases in market and nonmarket income over time in any one society will understate improvements in welfare if members cash in on increases in full income partially by working less (earlier retirement), or investing more (extended schooling). Societies concerned with investment in human resources, and thus the health and education of children, must attend to the full income of particular households rather than money income alone. For example, two households may have the same money income and the same number of adults and children, but if in the first, all adult members are working in the market full time and, in the second, one or more adults are available at home for child care, the second is clearly better off—as a full income comparison would confirm.

Finally we have a fourth theme: the need to avoid confusion of cause and effect within the general system, and to propose what may be the direction of causality between variables only when theory and empirical findings clearly permit. A defining characteristic of any "system" which is "general" is that all parts are affected by and affect other parts, indirectly if not directly. Where human behavior in areas such as reproduction and care of children interacts with society-wide economic forces, opinion will vary considerably as to the "effect" of either on the other; careful attention to available facts and extraordinary methodological care is necessary before conclusions regarding cause-effect relationships are warranted. Causal relations are often hypothesized and tested in partial equilibrium models, i.e., when some conditions of a general system are taken as given, and the effect of those conditions or variables on other parts of the system is examined. This is the case, for example, when the effect of extant wage and price conditions on a couple's fertility is measured; or, for the contrasting example, when the effect of current fertility rates on (future) wages is examined. Various degrees of partial equilibrium analysis are, of course, a necessary input to an understanding of the general system. But one purpose of organizing current economic and demographic work under a general system rubric is to underscore the artificiality, in the larger sense, of the partial approach, and the care required in using partial equilibrium frameworks if the pitfalls of policy design based only on their conclusions are to be avoided. In the general system presented, the traditional distinction between causes and effect is temporarily set aside; for example, the distinction between the impact of fertility on economic development, or the impact of development on fertility, becomes no more than an expository convenience. In this general framework, fertility cannot sensibly be discussed or analyzed in isolation; it becomes only one of several interlocking phenomena, all to be explored simultaneously as an effort is made to unscramble the total development puzzle. This last theme is treated several times below, as in the presentation of the distinction between static and dynamic information models, and when policy-conscious means of data collection and analysis are suggested. Reference to it is also implicit throughout the discussion of work in macroeconomic modelling, family economics, and income distribution.

Information Requirements of the General System

As rich and complex as the information described below is, it by no means exhausts what should and could be utilized in the study of the workings of the full system. Only essential and quantifiable information currently used or potentially useful for analytical and policy approaches to economic-demographic issues in the future is incorporated here.

The data described may be thought of as approaching an ideal. Some of it is already regularly collected within most countries—but not all. In some cases, the required raw data exists but is not organized in the proposed manner. In others, its full definition and collection is still a long way off. Where we refer to household and family-level data, we have in mind the results of carefully drawn samples of households. Recognizing the incompleteness of the data set suggested for inclusion here, decisions on this will have to be continuously and flexibly guided by considerations of both feasibility of collection and theoretical need. Whenever possible, age, education, and other categories which already are in standard use by the UN and other international organizations are included.

The information system presented below should thus be viewed as illustrative, on the one hand, and as wedded, as much as possible, to the national income accounting and assets accounting system used in conventional economic analysis, on the other. It highlights the demographic and family dimensions of the more general system, and indicates some of the essential linkages between these and the more conventional forms of information. In contrast to the national accounts this flexible and still amorphous system may be conceived as a multipurpose microfile in which information on individuals and families may be preserved in a disaggregated fashion but can be aggregated along different dimensions of the population to answer particular questions. As in a complex household survey file with individual and household records, this data base should lend itself to presenting information by conventional demographic breakdowns such as by age, sex, and educational attainment for the study of, say, labor force participation, or by women's current marital status, age, and number of children born, to study the frequency of births. Family aggregation may weight members by the productive potential of their time to attempt to calculate "full income" or by time worked at the current wage to arrive at the total market income of the family. To explore how the industrial composition and sales of firms are related to income distribution it might be important to collect some information about the employment setting which has heretofore only been available in censuses of manufacturing, or agriculture, for example, but which needs to be combined in future studies with household economic and demographic data.

To illustrate these points, in the F(a) curve of Figure 8.2 are shown the age and sex distribution of a population; along with education, this comprises the basic static information on demography. Any population can be roughly divided into productive and dependent categories. The actual ages at which members of a population begin and end their working lives vary considerably across populations and probably cover a wider range in poor than in rich countries. In a closed system without external migration, the ratio of males to females is likely to be close to 50 percent at most ages; but within certain countries and regions it can vary considerably by age due to differential rates of migration by sex.

Because definitions of at what ages members of a population are productive as opposed to dependent should be country-specific and may also change within countries over time, dotted lines are used to delineate the two groups in the figure. Typically, macroeconomic and demographic planning models impose such age categories, taking as given a phenomenon which is probably a function of development and changing economic constraints—in fact, a phenomenon which should be examined in its own right. At the country level, planning officials may wish to impose such age delineations, as a deliberate aid to understanding, for example, the effect of demographic structure on the future size of the labor force.

The family demographic matrix (Figure 8.2) transforms the above-described aggregate demographic data into information at the family level. There are n-families F_1, F_2 . . . F_n indicated in the rows. The columns of the matrix correspond to the age classification of the top portion of the figure, so that the total frequency in each column of the family matrix is exactly F(a) for each age. The population is thus organized exclusively and exhaustively into families (and unrelated individuals).

For each individual, within each family, the matrix indicates his or her sex (a circle for a female and a triangle for a male), age group (by column), education (subscripts N, P, S, H for none, some primary, some secondary, and higher), and enrollment in school status (enrolled, not enrolled). Other family-level demographic information, e.g., family size,

FIGURE 8.2

Family Demographic and Economic Information (Static)

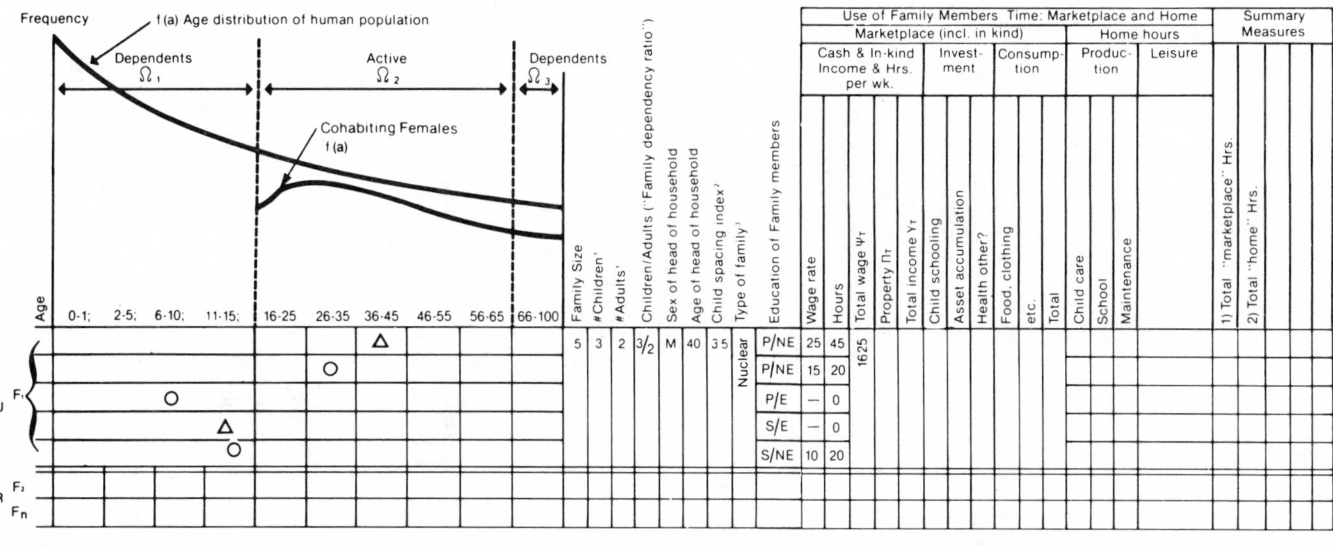

E=Enrolled in school
NE=Not enrolled
1. Ages for "children" & "adults" defined on a country basis by local planning officials
2. Equals (age of oldest-youngest)/(#children-1)
3. e.g. nuclear, stem, etc.
U=urban
R=rural
○ females
△ males

the family dependency ratio (number of dependents, age-defined, to number of productive-age members), the age and sex of the head of the household, and a child spacing index are shown for each family at the end of each row.[3] On the basis of such a microfile, summary data for particular questions can be organized. For example, the family dependency ratio and the household head's age may be critical inputs to an analysis of the family distribution of income, as will be discussed more fully below.

The data on which member is the head of the household, and the relationship of others to him or her, implicitly indicates family formation rules in the society, i.e., what proportion of families are nuclear, consanguineous, stem, joint etc. Types of families are denoted in the figure $t_1, t_2 \ldots t_n$. The number of various family types in a given society or country is an important, if somewhat overlooked, input to understanding the nexus of family decisions and economic change. Much economic analysis of demographic and family variables assumes that the types of families which prevail in a society are predetermined, i.e., conditions within the economic system, such as wages, relative prices, and the pattern of income distribution are not assumed to influence what types of families are formed, or the rules by which families are formed. The assumption is at best only justified at a given point in time; over the long run, as work by anthropologists, sociologists, and social historians attests, family formation rules and family types are hardly inalterable, and changes can probably be systematically related to economic as well as social forces.[4] Household composition may be a consequence of inheritance rules, the nature of the agricultural system, degree of wealth, commercialization of the economy, and so on. These are translated into household decisions to marry, migrate, take in cousins or uncles, encourage elder kin to remain, take on a hired hand, send children to relatives, and, most familiar in the population policy literature, the household decision to have another child.

Historian Peter Laslett has noted the statistical predominance in western countries of households consisting of no more than one nuclear family and no non-family members.[5] Though others contest his historical

3. The child spacing index can be defined in terms of actual fertility or surviving children—most simply as the age of the eldest minus the age of the youngest child divided by the number of children minus one. The index is useful in analyzing relationships between fertility and mortality at the household level, and in relating fertility to other household decisions, such as market labor force participation of women and schooling of children.

4. Examples are: William Goode, *World Revolution and Family Patterns* (New York: Free Press, 1970); Peter Laslett, *The World We Have Lost* (London: Methuen, 1971); and Edward Shorter, *The Making of the Modern Family* (New York: Basic Books, 1975).

5. Peter Laslett, *The World We Have Lost* (London: Methuen, 1971).

evidence,[6] the nuclear family is indisputably a prevalent type today and is probably even more isolated than Laslett's historical nuclear family, which could include unmarried adult relatives. Yet, even given the prevalence of nuclear households, the "family" is no simple matter. What, after all, is the relevant defining characteristic for a "family"? Clearly not the household itself, i.e., joint residence. A family, for the purposes of decisions regarding marriage, fertility, investment in children, and a host of other economic-demographic decisions, may well include a cluster of households, e.g., the parents of a married couple and the households of adult siblings.

Whether the nuclear family in Europe contributed to low fertility rates throughout several centuries and to the nineteenth century fertility decline, or whether the nuclear family type and low fertility were jointly determined by larger economic, cultural, and social forces is not clear from extant demographic and historical analyses.[7] The rules which determine the formation of different family types are complicated and still unclear, particularly as they relate to economic growth and changes in population size and structure. Family formation rules represent a missing link in the full specification of the general economic-demographic system, an issue which is put aside here but returned to below.

Turning now to economic data, each family can also be described in terms of conventional "economic" characteristics.[8] The economic portion of the family matrix, on the right hand side of Figure 8.2, includes "marketplace" and "home" production and income variables. It indicates the family's consumption (including its "investment" in education and health) and its total market (cash and in-kind) income for the period. Market income is further divided into wage and property income. Total wage income is the sum of income of individual family members who work in the market sector of the economy. For each such member the matrix also shows the wage rate and the proportions of market work time and household work time to total time; this work time information is especially relevant for women and children, whose household work time is often overlooked.

6. Lutz K. Berkner and Franklin F. Mendels, "Inheritance Systems, Family Structure and Demographic Patterns in Western Europe, 1700–1900," in *Historical Studies of Changing Fertility,* edited by Charles Tilly (Princeton: Princeton University Press, 1978).

7. Tilly, *Changing Fertility,* pp. 46–49. Low fertility is also linked to what Hajnal has characterized as the European marriage pattern (late age at marriage and low rates of nuptiality).

8. The distinction between data termed demographic and economic is not in itself important; the education of family members is as much an economic as a demographic variable.

The conventional economic portion of the family matrix (i.e., marketplace income) can be compiled as the basis for more aggregated economic data. For each family, a wage and prices structure is given; the distinction shown in the matrix between urban and rural families underlines the possibility that families face different wage and price structures, depending on residence. (Care must be taken, however, to allow for family-level adjustment to differentials through migration.) The prices apply to all commodities consumed and are required for the calculation of the family's pattern of consumption expenditure. The wages are specified for specific types of labor; the heterogeneity of the labor force follows from different combinations of age, sex, education, and rural vs. urban residence. There are in total 160 wage rates for each of the possible combinations of two sexes, four education groups, and ten age groups (as specified in the matrix), in rural and urban areas. In any one period, these prices and wages are given for the families. It should be noted, however, that in a dynamic model, the education of individuals is itself determined by prior family decisions regarding schooling of members.

For simplicity, the market labor force "experience" of family members is not specified as an economic variable, though experience is clearly an important determinant of any individual's marketplace wage. For men, age tends to be an adequate proxy for experience; for women, who move in and out of the marketplace labor force and do not always work full time in the market, age will often but not always overestimate experience. The marketplace wage commanded today is clearly a function of earlier decisions regarding marketplace work, in a manner analogous to earlier family decisions governing a child's schooling and thus affecting the child's wage today. On the other hand, in terms of full income and full production, the age of women should not overestimate *total* experience, including that in household work.

Such family data, once aggregated, yields portions of the conventional economic data on national income, the shares of income going to labor and to property. But these aggregates—summarized at the bottom of the family matrix—tell us only half the story since cash income alone does not fully reflect either the extent and nature of a household's production or its consumption and thus welfare. Aggregation of child-care hours over families and hours spent in school over families, if compared to nationwide dependency ratios, would provide planners with a summary indicator of society's investment in children. Across countries at different development levels, surprisingly little is known about differences, if any, in total hours and per child hours spent in child care—nor how such differences shift with age of children. Similarly, summary measures of leisure, as mentioned above, could provide a measure of welfare level which would complement the money income measure, just as expectation of life at birth or nationwide literacy rates are often used to complement money income. As with all such measures, problems arise; in the case of leisure, a careful correction for involuntary leisure due to unemployment or discouragement of workers would be required (though time spent searching for a job should be entered as marketplace work hours). In fact, the entire area of household production and time allocation represents a challenge to measurement as well as to the economic analysis of family decisions and their role in development. Time budget surveys, i.e., the collection of data on the use of time of household members, are one mechanism for investigating household production, full household income, and their relevance to general development strategy. In the conclusion, the utility of future time use studies to policy and program planners is discussed.

Next, dynamic information is considered; on the demographic side it includes birth, death, and cohabiting rates, and such component parts as infant and child mortality rates. (The term "cohabiting" rather than "married" is used in recognition of the fact that in some societies, e.g. parts of the Caribbean and Latin America, reproduction occurs within unions which, though they may be more or less stable, are not as formal as marriage. In the interests of semantic simplicity below, we sometimes revert to the term "marriage.") These rates determine the change in F(a) from one period to the next, which in turn is of interest because it influences the division of the population into its more productive and more dependent portions in the next period. Schedule b in Figure 8.3 shows age-specific mortality; schedule c shows age-specific marital fertility. Schedules b, c, and d are vertically lined up under the F(a) age distribution of the population, which, as seen in the figure, changes from one period to the next as a function of the rates pictured.

The death schedule is U-shaped, with the first year of life representing a critically high risk period. The proportion of married females is represented by an inverted U, beginning at about age 15. With fecundity falling off after age 35, the birth rate is the weighted average of age-specific marital fertility rates. The difference between death and birth rates is the natural rate of increase of the population, the single piece of demographic information most widely used in conventional economic growth models.

With fixed birth and death rate schedules, the relative age structure of a population eventually will not change from one period to the next, and a "system" is said to attain a stable population structure at some given rate of growth. Though stable population theory permits certain types of demographic analysis in the absence of complete information on vital rates in a population, no populations actually exhibit such stable characteristics at this time. In fact, for developing economies, it is changes in F(a)

FIGURE 8.3
Dynamic Demographic Information

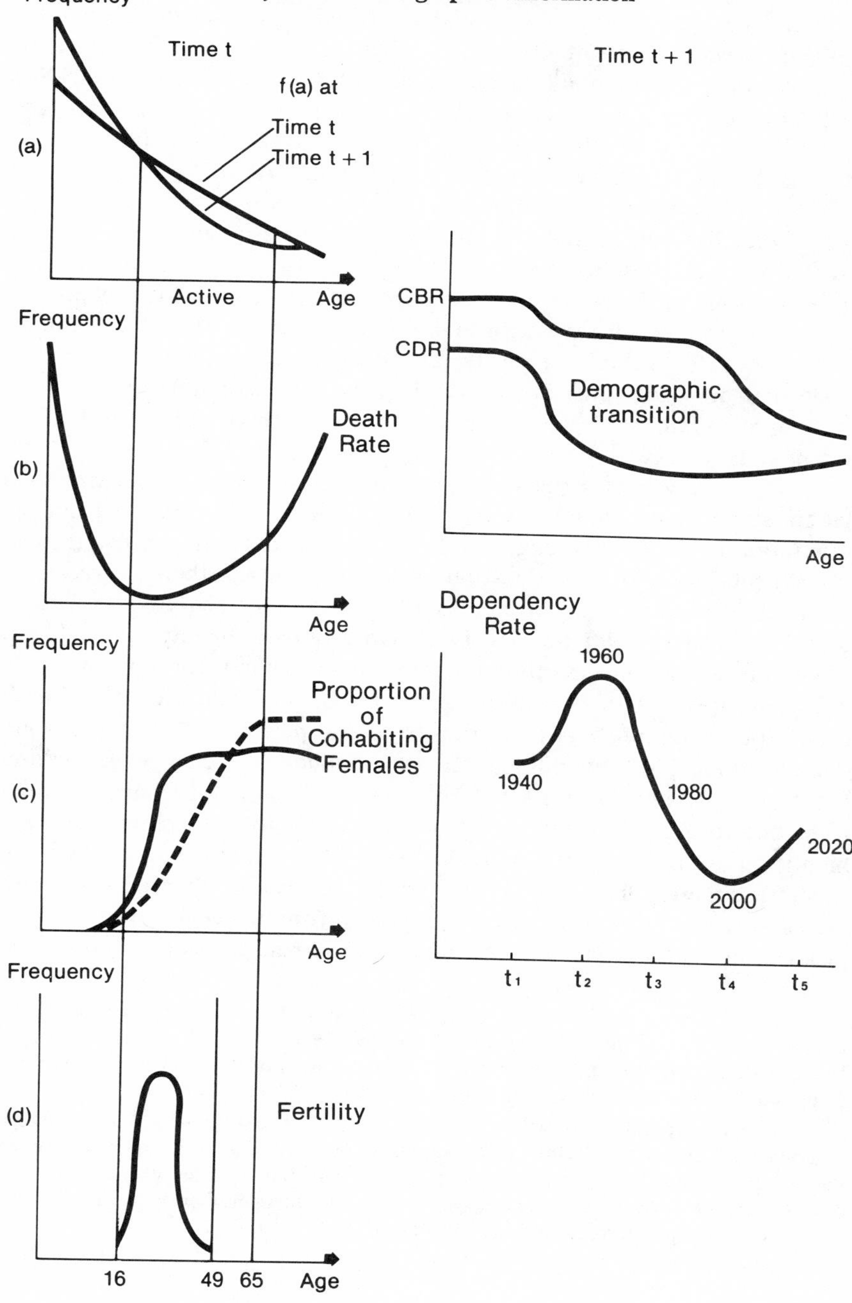

through time which are likely to be particularly important. During the demographic transition, as mortality rates decline, the population typically becomes younger in terms of its age composition, so that the dependency ratio increases; the resultant drain on physical resources is built explicitly into economic-demographic macro models of developing economies.[9] Subsequently, as the new, larger cohorts become old enough to seek entry into the labor force, unemployment may be related to this short-run phenomenon of the entry of large cohorts of demographic transition babies into the labor force of developing countries.

What lies behind shifts in the fertility and marriage schedules is the sum of various decisions made within families—to marry, to have children, to leave home in the case of older children. These decisions are reflected in changes in the family matrix through time.[10] What lies behind shifts in the death schedule can only be partly related to conscious family choice; also important are exogenous factors which vary with economic development, such as government expenditures on public health or the control of environmental disease through public sanitation systems.

The family is also the focal point for certain information which can be classified as dynamic economic. The family transfers wealth from one generation to the next through bequests of physical assets but also through investments in children's education and investments in their migration, as when children are given or loaned the "grubstake" required to make a move, or assisted with housing by urban relatives. Family ownership of labor will change through time for three reasons. First, for a given family, individual members may acquire experience in the labor market and additional formal or informal education from one period to the next. Second, the partitioning of the population into families will change as children exit from one family group and form another (including perhaps migration from one to another labor market where their skills are on average more highly valued), as older family members die, and as couples join and separate. Finally, there may be changes in the way family groups organize themselves—for example, as rural extended families which form a single production unit become less common and urban nuclear families more

9. See Ansley J. Coale and Edgar M. Hoover, *Population Growth and Economic Development in Low-Income Countries* (Princeton: Princeton University Press, 1958); and also the discussion of descendant models in "Development and Demography: Macro Models," which appears below.

10. For example, a delay in the average age at marriage (the dotted curve in schedule c) can cause a decline in the aggregate population growth rate both because the actual fertility of younger women is higher than that of older women (schedule d) and because with higher average age at marriage, the time between generations is increased—barring interrelationships between the two.

common. This last reflects a change in family formation rules—a field of interest for sociologists and social historians, not yet, as pointed out earlier, well integrated into the general economic-demographic system.

Dynamic economic information in the general system also includes the conventional measures: saving, the accumulation of capital (both physical and human), technology change (usually considered solely in the context of market production, but it can apply to household production as well). Installation of a well can reduce time spent fetching water for cooking and washing, as well as alter agricultural production methods, to cite but one example.

Thus, from a dynamic point of view, the general system will reflect demographic changes in the population as a whole, in the form of birth and death rates, changes in the number, composition and characteristics of families, and changes in the traditionally defined economic system. The interaction of these changes through time, and the nature of the causal relations among parts of the system are portrayed in Figure 8.4, in which two time periods are shown (a period in this case being sufficiently long to allow certain forces within the system to be played out, say five to ten years). At time t, the basic information is the age and education distribution of the population and the capital stock of the economy, circles A and B in Figure 8.4. The population is partitioned into family groups, and the family ownership of labor is described by the family matrix (C in Figure 8.4). The firms make decisions regarding the use of the capital stock (D) while the families make decisions regarding the allocation of labor time to the market sector, one of the decisions in the E circle (family economics). As a result of these two sets of decisions, resource allocation and prices are determined simultaneously in the market. The prices thus determined in turn represent part of the information basis for the family decisions, the economic portion of the family matrix, shown as E in Figure 8.4.

In addition to its decision regarding the provision of labor supply to the market sector, the family makes a host of other decisions regarding production and consumption in the household sector, all central to the workings of the general economic-demographic system. Fertility and marriage decisions, along with the death rate (in part determined by factors outside family control) determine the age distribution of the population in the following period, and the change in the number and types of families. For example, family savings decisions contribute to the capital stock in the following period; family "investment" decisions regarding schooling and child care at home determine the educational quality of the population in the next period; family labor supply determines the experience qualifications of market labor force participants in the next period: migration deter-

FIGURE 8.4
Economic-Demographic System: Dynamics

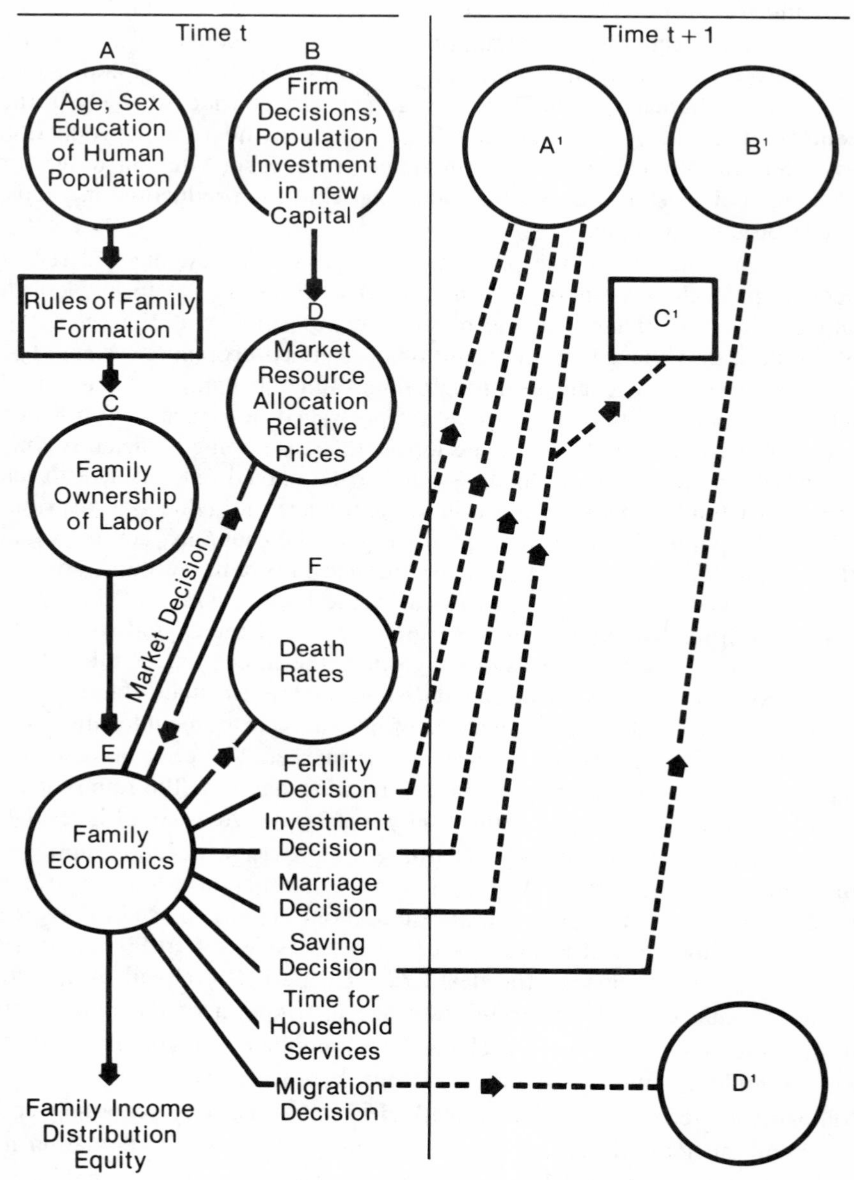

mines the rural-urban allocation of workers and hence their relative supplies.

Figure 8.4 emphasizes certain intertemporal causal relations. For example, the effect of individual families' decisions regarding fertility, time for household services vs. market labor (including that of children), and investment in children's education are seen to clearly affect the A circle in the following period, in which are shown the age, sex, and education of the population at time t + 1. Less well understood relations, for example the effect of the family distribution of market and full income on family fertility in the current period, are not causally specified here. The division of the population into urban and rural, components which could be based on a further division of the production sector encompassed by the D circle, is sometimes invoked as relevant to the level of aggregate fertility. The literature abounds with possible correlations, but not well-formulated theories. Consequently, for purposes of preliminary analysis of the general system, the focus here is exclusively on structural relationships interpreted as causal and capable of description by the information outlined above.

Figure 8.4 is intended to underscore a central point made above, namely that cause and effect relationships are difficult to isolate in the general system, but are best understood in a dynamic framework, i.e., when the passage from one period to the next permits the sorting out of meaningful causal relations from the much larger number of observed correlations.

MICROECONOMIC ASPECTS OF FAMILY BEHAVIOR

Economic development generally involves the transfer of production from household to factory—from small, diversified, family units to more specialized production units. Before development, families are relatively self-sufficient. Development entails increasing dependence of both family and new firms on the market for purchase of inputs and sale of outputs. In the course of development, the market signals transmitted to the family change, and families adjust their own production and exchange accordingly; thus the productive organization of society is transformed. These changing demands on the family mediated through the expanding market typically involve notable changes in the balance of activities performed by women and children. In most societies women and children are partly employed in the production of goods and services that are not traded in the market but consumed within the household, such as child care, housekeeping, and food preparation. Modern economic growth erodes the comparative advantage of the household in some of these activities for a variety of reasons:

economies of scale in new technology result in large scale firms and market specialization; urban concentrations of production increase wages in certain regions and encourage migration; and rapid change in labor and goods markets makes the allocative and adaptive skills learned in school more valuable than time-honored home skills. Women's work at home rarely conflicts with high fertility; as other factors motivate couples to restrict their fertility, household work becomes more costly in terms of alternative opportunities women forego. Since these final consumption services and reproduction are, by convention, largely neglected in national income accounts, these services are often overlooked by economists. Yet household production and reproduction bulk large in the resources and welfare of poor people; so the concerted study of the full array of production, consumption, and reproduction decisions made by families promises to identify ways in which economic growth could be fostered and its inequities tempered. Moreover, insofar as production and reproduction decisions made within the family affect the welfare of those outside the family, for good or ill, development strategy ought to try to close identified gaps between family motivations and social objectives, and capture or offset the gains and losses that accrue to bystanders.

The issues, theoretical models, and empirical evidence of family organization and behavior are far too vast to survey at one time, and so only a few aspects of the subject receive comment here in order to suggest how an economic framework has been applied to the analysis of interrelated areas of household economic demographic behavior. Many disciplines are involved in the accretion of observation, conceptualization, and statistical interpretation, though the economic theory of demand has provided the starting point. Market labor force behavior, as traditionally studied by economists in industrially advanced countries, has been successfully reformulated around the ultimate constraint of time to deal with nonmarket household production. The extension of this approach to the study of such personal decisions as fertility and marriage represents the current controversial frontier of the field.

Interdisciplinary Research Strategy and Policy Rationale

The task of linking the demographic attributes of the family to the development process requires a description of the manner and timing of the adjustment of family members to the transformation of production with the advent of modern growth. What is the accommodation by which husband, wife, or children switch from traditional home production and processing of various food, clothing, fuel, and staple commodities to work in a modern, specialized labor market with the increasing purchase of such commodities in the market? A careful description in each cultural-technological setting of this accommodation in production and consumption should clarify how this generally inevitable process of market penetration of the household sector impinges upon the production and consumption of each household member and thereby on the status and welfare of men, women, and children.

Given that private household demographic and economic behavior has social ramifications, reasons are frequently advanced for a society to encourage or discourage certain forms of private behavior to further social objectives of efficiency and equity. But by their very nature as private choices on the fringes of regular markets it is extraordinarily hard to regulate by legal statute such activities as school attendance, child labor force participation, internal migration, fertility, distribution of nutrition among family members, and the use of health services, to name only a few. For example, a school lunch program in Brazil may provide children from poor families with one good meal a day, but their families may in response reallocate the child's portion of food at home to other uses that the family now views as more important. Society cannot influence household demographic and economic behavior, no matter how ingenious the legal statute or how hortatory the message. The ways of people have a logic of their own. They grow out of a subtle and informal calculus that is designed to advance their own interests. Though individuals and families may not always appear to be well informed, their "traditional" practices have survived the test of time. To change behavior by public intervention, this private logic must be appreciated and behavioral outcomes must be traced back to the conditions that made them privately desirable. For one thing, such understanding will point the way to the least-cost approach to intervention; it will indicate those settings where policies which foster socially sought forms of behavior in the private interest are best initiated and pursued, and those settings where such policies would be too costly in the immediate future.

Clearly, the most attractive policy options are those which promote a change that is desirable in its own right, such as reducing child mortality, and also have the secondary effect of reducing the private demand for further births. Most policies, however, do require the evaluation of trade-offs; the introduction of new improved crops that require distinctly less labor input from children may improve the schooling, health, and future incomes of children, but reduce the current income of poor large families. Intergenerational or interpersonal trade-offs of this nature raise difficult welfare issues for any society; such programs call for explicit study and political caution to determine if the social consensus exists to mandate such transfers among persons.

It is essential that analysis focus on both the *outputs* of the household sector that may embody social externalities, such as health, schooling, fertility, and migration, and on the *inputs* that can be most readily altered by development strategy, such as education, extension, infrastructure, and the relative prices that are often affected by food policies, marketing boards, and foreign exchange and trade policies. For example, small changes in the relative price structure or composition of local public expenditures may elicit considerable changes in the mix and level of domestic activity, increasing (or decreasing) the health, schooling, and productivity of children while reducing (or increasing) the average number of births women will want. How various market-oriented production activities complement or conflict with traditional domestic functions, such as childrearing, is only partially understood and tends to be variable from one cultural-technological environment to the next.

To proceed in identifying how social policy impinges on family behavior, one needs a model. First, descriptions of family production and social organization between generations and sexes are required; this topic has been the bailiwick of anthropologists. Their distillation of observations advances us toward verifiable hypotheses as to what represent cause and effect relationships. The economist has a comparative advantage in abstracting from the culturally specific; the objective is to obtain empirically refutable predictions, develop a structure of consistent concepts to guide measurement and link hypotheses, and formalize these hypotheses to admit to statistical testing.

Refinement of hypotheses concerning how the members of the household adapt to economic development and the mortality transition will require, therefore, the joint efforts of economists and anthropologists, among others. Much of this work can be done now with available survey and aggregate census data. At the same time new and better data must be developed. For example, a major difficulty in inferring how the allocation of time in households has changed in response to the recent reduction in mortality and the increase in economic growth is the lack of satisfactory *time series* for countries or communities where such documented change has occurred. Typically in such cases of slow, unobserved, social evolution, a good deal can be learned by studying the correlates of *cross-sectional* differences across countries or areas within a relatively homogenous portion of the world's population, e.g., a country, and by statistical interpretation of differences among individuals in their behavioral propensities. Aggregate and individual analyses based on multipurpose survey and census samples of the sort discussed elsewhere in this chapter promise to improve markedly understanding of these processes. In the next decade, moreover, the availability of repeated panel surveys and individual retrospective histories from representative samples should provide the basis for much new methodological and substantive social science research. In the field of family behavior and economic-demographic interrelations these new sources of time series and cohort information will permit researchers to confirm and extend the insights currently being accumulated from cross-sectional investigations. The economic framework of individual choice must be elaborated to describe the multiperson family, and extended to deal with interrelated life cycle economic and demographic decisions, subject to time and resource constraints, relative market prices, and technological possibilities.

Described below is an overview of various aspects of microeconomic analyses of family behavior including consideration of a useful model for observing how family members adjust to the transformation of production with modern growth. The demand theory of household time allocation is applied to changing labor force patterns in LDCs and to changing fertility; also considered are the determinants of mortality and reproductive response to mortality change, and the relationship between age composition, and the personal distribution of incomes.

Demand Theory of Household Time Allocation

Household demand theory implies that the desire to engage in nonmarket activities is a function of the schedule of wages offered in the market, market prices, physical assets, or the flow of unearned income. It is common to extend this framework to a two-person household, in particular the husband and wife, even though this implies a strong symmetry between the conjugal pair in their respective valuations of the time each spends in nonmarket activities. In some cultural settings the production and consumption unit may include additional relatives, and the pooling of resources may be more evident among siblings than it is within the reproductive unit. But this classical demand approach to labor supply behavior has proven a powerful abstraction to guide the study of labor force behavior in industrially advanced countries and has been fruitfully applied to urban and rural labor markets in low-income countries.[11] Women generally tend to work more in the market if their own wage opportunities are greater, and those of their husbands are lower. Among husbands, their supply of time available for the market is less

11. D. A. Oliveira, "Labour Supply and Employment in Belo Horizonte, Brazil," (Ph.D. dissertation, the London School of Economics and Political Science 1978); M. R. Rosenzweig, "Neoclassical Theory and the Optimizing Peasant: An Econometric Analysis of Market Family, Market Supply," Yale University Economic Growth Center Discussion Paper No. 271 (1977).

elastic, in part because they customarily work full time in the market labor force, and hence the income effect embodied in their own response to wage variation outweighs any substitution effect at the margin.

If both husband and wife work for a given market wage, demand for other lifetime activities may be interpreted as a function of the same set of initial constraints on the household: the skills and time of husband and wife, and the nonhuman capital resources they bring to marriage. Because children can absorb a substantial share of a couple's available time and market income in certain periods, and augment family resources in other periods of the life cycle, market prices, levels of husband, wife, and child wage rates, interest rates, and nonhuman wealth are considered by economists as potential determinants of the number of children parents want. This demand framework has been used to interpret individual differences in labor force, marriage, migration, and schooling behavior as first conceptualized by Mincer, Becker, and T. W. Schultz, and empirically applied in a growing number of countries to the study of reproductive behavior.[12]

Labor Force Behavior

Several tendencies are evident in the labor market in virtually all countries, both in cross sections and over time.[13] Age-specific labor force participation rates among the very young and very old tend to decline with development. Much of this decline in participation rates among the young is due to the gradual increase in school enrollment rates, but how much is not known. If the view is accepted that schooling is often under-

12. J. Mincer, "Market Prices, Opportunity Costs, and Income Effects," in *Measurement in Economics: Studies in Mathematical Economics and Econometrics in Memory of Yehuda Grunfeld,* edited by C. Christ *et al.* (Stanford: Stanford University Press, 1963); G. S. Becker, "A Theory of the Allocation of Time," *Economic Journal* 75 (September 1965):493–517; T. W. Schultz, ed., *Economics of the Family* (Chicago: University of Chicago Press, 1974). See also T. P. Schultz, "Interrelationships between Mortality and Fertility," in *Population and Development: The Search for Selective Interventions,* edited by R. G. Ridker (Baltimore: Johns Hopkins University Press, 1976).

13. Although labor force activity statistics are infamously incomparable among societies, particularly in the rural sector, John Durand, *The Labor Force* in *Economic Development: A Comparison of International Census Statistics: 1946–1966* (Princeton: Princeton University Press, 1975), has performed the yeoman task of assembling much of this data from some 80 censuses available from about 1945 to 1965. The story his data tells is full of puzzles and tantalizing irregularities in need of explanation. Such a comprehensive examination of census data complements nicely the thought-provoking collection of hypotheses and case studies of Ester Boserup, *Women's Role in Economic Development* (New York: St. Martin's Press, 1970).

taken with the anticipation that the earnings foregone by reduced current labor force participation will be recouped by later improved earning opportunities associated with higher productivity and nonpecuniary rewards, it can be misleading to interpret this decline in participation as a decline in labor inputs applied to market production. Rather, schooling should be directly incorporated into analyses of labor force behavior as an investment process.

The extent and intensity of child schooling is beginning to be analyzed in conjunction with the parents' fertility, for it is often noted that voluntary control of family size reflects the predominance of maximizing the education of one's children over maximizing their number.[14] Whatever factors convince parents to invest more in the schooling of their children are also very likely to lower their fertility, whether it is achieved by delay of marriage, spacing, or termination of births by lactation, abstinence, or other methods of birth control.

The decline in labor force participation that is generally observed beyond the age of 55 may be due to either increased wealth, permitting people to demand more time out of the market for themselves or, more worrisome, it may be due to declines in the productive opportunities of the aged, whose skills may have lost their relevance to modern market production. An important aspect of one's wealth is the number of surviving children one has for support in old age, and in this respect the wealth of old people has certainly increased. The sudden reduction in infant and child mortality following the Second World War placed an unanticipated burden of support on young parents in the 1950s and 1960s, requiring of them greater productive efforts and labor force participation. Today these parents are moving into a period in their life cycle when the resources for child support will diminish and a reverse flow of transfers to parents may increase, with consequences on their labor force behavior and regional mobility. Few data have as yet been collected on these intergenerational flows of funds and the degree to which they substitute for or complement other patterns of savings and expenditure. Similarly, the relative importance of wealth and market wage effects in explaining the pattern of diminished labor market activity of the old has received little empirical attention, despite the distinctly different policy and welfare implications that follow from these alternative interpretations of recent events.

Among men between the ages of 25 and 54, the vast majority participate in the labor force, and economic development, if it has any effect,

14. J. C. Caldwell, "Fertility Differentials as Evidence of Incipient Fertility Decline in a Developing Country, The Case of Ghana," *Population Studies* 21 (July 1967).

may increase participation slightly by improving the health and schooling of workers and thereby increasing the opportunity cost of nonmarket time. Women, however, fall into no single pattern either across countries by income level or over time during periods of economic development. Here it is most difficult to generalize from the empirical record. One thing is clear: it is rarely possible to interpret labor force participation patterns of women without also analyzing as jointly determined (1) family structure, (2) marriage patterns, and (3) reproductive behavior.

The association between fertility and female participation in the market labor force is inverse in high-income countries, but becomes more subtle and ambiguous in low-income countries, notably in West Africa and in portions of Southeast Asia where women hold a prominent position in many economic activities including trading and agriculture, and yet these responsibilities do not appear to interfere with high levels of fertility. Study must clarify (1) the degree of compatibility of jobs and childbearing, (2) the cost and adequacy of child-care substitutes for the mother's time, and lastly, (3) the effect of increased market wealth on the couple's demand for more children. Numerous combinations of these underlying conditions and the behavioral parameters associated with income and price-of-time effects could explain occasions in which market labor force commitments of women increase without depressing fertility. But despite such instances, the most common relationship is an inverse one between completed fertility and women's participation in modern nonagricultural activities. Even among African and Malay populations this may become the predominant pattern in the 1980s.

Fertility, Mortality, and Household Demands

Given the plausible assumptions that women contribute more time to childrearing than men, and that women's time so allocated has a lower opportunity value than that of men, the simplest version of the demand framework predicts that advancement in women's market productivity in activities that are *not* readily combined with childbearing will diminish reproductive goals. Increases in the labor productivity of men and children, on the contrary, are likely to enhance the attractions of a larger family. The returns to schooling and migration may complicate, however, the net effects of child wages on desired fertility. The demand framework emphasizes the relative economic status and power of women to men as a crucial variable for understanding the decline in surviving family size that is associated with economic growth.

Increases in the household's nonhuman wealth increases the couple's demand for all ordinary goods, including children. But more wealthy parents are also likely to want to endow their offspring with more human and nonhuman resources, which may deter them from indulging in a larger family. Land and assets used in home production tend to raise the productivity of child labor, in general, and thereby encourage greater fertility, though technical change may work in the other direction by encouraging investment in the schooling of children. Beyond these central economic variables, a host of more specific technological, ethnic, and community factors are found to be relevant to reproductive decision making in particular household settings.

The last major factor affecting fertility is *child mortality,* even though its effect on reproductive demands is too complex to summarize here. The "demographic transition," during which mortality *and* fertility decline, remains an imprecisely characterized process in demography. One finds in the literature little agreement on what is the causal relationship, if any, transmitting the decline in mortality into a compensating decline in fertility. Conflicting empirical evidence adds to the ambiguity: cross-sectional data suggest that fertility and child mortality are closely related in low-income countries,[15] whereas aggregate time series show crude death rates falling for three decades before crude birth rates widely decline.[16] But this conflict may be resolved in part if our base of data admits to analysis at various levels of aggregation. First, a decade may elapse in the process of family formation before the decline in child mortality substantially affects marginal fertility decisions, and at this time only the fertility of older women who have reached their family size goals would decline, but they are a small proportion of the population of childbearing age in most low-income countries. This lag in the emergence of the replacement effect is further extended or initially concealed by the shift in age composition that follows a couple of decades after the onset of mortality declines. These trends in age composition favor a rise in crude birth rates and a decline in crude death rates even when age-standardized fertility and mortality measures are unchanged. Thus, the separation through time of the downturn of crude death rates and distinct downturn of crude birth rates may be largely a reflection of age composition changes that are generated by the age pattern of mortality reductions.

At the individual and cohort level, the magnitude of the direct association found between child mortality and fertility is generally several

15. Schultz, "Interrelationships."

16. Simon Kuznets, "Recent Population Trends in Less Developed Countries and Implications for International Income Inequality," Yale University Discussion Paper No. 261 (1977).

times that which can be attributed to an involuntary *biological* feedback.[17] Although the association between fertility and child mortality is strong, the majority of studies has not found fertility variation in the cross section to compensate completely for variation in child mortality. Consequently, the size of the surviving family tends to be somewhat larger for couples who have recently sustained lower levels of child mortality, and it is this burden of dependency that is associated with the early phases of the population explosion. Still the reduction of child mortality is likely to elicit within a generation a substantial reduction in cohort fertility, but, at least in the short run, increases in the rate of population growth are virtually inevitable. Additional social and economic conditions must change if parents are to be motivated to reduce their "surviving" family-size goals.

One important implication of this demand framework applied to the study of fertility is that development and increased income levels need not contribute to decreasing fertility. On the contrary, the effect on fertility depends on the source of the increment to income, and hence the "price effect" embodied in that source. Increasing the supply of cultivable land or raising its productive value is often associated with *increased* fertility and possibly diminished child schooling, other things equal.[18] The twentieth century decrease in the factor income share of land and physical capital in the more industrial countries may be related to the concurrent durable downtrend in fertility, even though historical linkages remain a subject of controversy.[19]

Increases in labor productivity may also not necessarily translate into decreased reproductive goals. The existing empirical evidence from cross-sectional studies suggests that the education of husbands, a proxy used to measure men's market wage offer, is often positively associated with fertility, holding constant for their wife's educational attainment. On the other hand, the wage rate of women or their education is generally

17. This biological mechanism is thought to operate through the effect of cessation of lactation on the length of the mother's postpartum nonsusceptible period, and may be increased somewhat in a malnourished population.

18. W. Stys, "The Influence of Economic Conditions on the Fertility of Peasant Women," *Population Studies* (November 1957); M. R. Rosenzweig, "The Demand for Children in Farm Households," *Journal of Political Economy* 84 (December 1976); M. R. Rosenzweig and R. Evenson, "Fertility, Schooling and the Economic Contribution of Children in Rural India," *Econometrica* 45 (July 1977):1065–79; M. T. R. Sarma, "Economic Value of Children in Rural India," Yale University Economic Growth Center Discussion Paper No. 272 (1977).

19. Simon Kuznets, "Quantitative Aspects of Modern Economic Growth: The Distribution of Income by Factors," *Economic Development and Cultural Change* (January 1959); P. Lindert, *Fertility and Scarcity in America* (Princeton: Princeton University Press, 1978).

inversely associated with accumulated fertility, even when adjusted for child mortality losses. These studies would seem to imply that for effective reproduction or surviving family size to decrease substantially, the gains from economic growth must accrue increasingly to women; the educational achievements of women relative to men and their economic status must rise, and thus the rising opportunity costs of women's time in childbearing is likely to be the critical force gradually restricting reproductive goals as development proceeds.

The education of children also represents a key variable for understanding the fertility differentials found in low-income countries and perhaps one that has a more immediate effect on the fertility of today's parents. Where children are withdrawn from market and nonmarket labor force activities in the home and their current and often considerable output is sacrificed in order to have them attend school, fertility is lower. This allocation of the child's time is dominantly determined by parents, who are responding to perceptions of the returns that accrue to the educated youth, the extent to which better jobs are allocated according to individual training rather than family and class origins. Much remains to be understood in terms of how the character of derived demands for labor generated by modern economic growth, technical change, the development of competitive labor markets, and the effect of class and caste restrictions on occupational mobility interact to shape the returns to schooling. But it seems likely that where these returns are increasing at the primary and secondary school levels, and the educational infrastructure is minimally adequate to meet the demand, parents will both increase their investments in the education of each of their children and have fewer. Needless to say, these suggestions of relationships drawn from repeated cross-sectional studies remain to be confirmed by analyses of slowly accruing time series.

In societies in which marriage is a well-defined and readily measured event and most births occur within wedlock, analysis of marriage patterns and their timing, extent, and dissolution, promises to provide insights into the time path and age structure of fertility declines. In diverse premodern and preindustrial societies the age at marriage is observed to be an important regulator of lifetime reproductive performance and population increase. To perpetuate society and maintain family lines in the face of heavy child mortality and limited schooling opportunities, parents encourage their children to marry young and not delay childbearing. When livelihoods are limited by the scarcity of land and occupational niches, intergenerational support for early marriage is withheld, and population growth is checked.[20]

20. D. Dumond, "The Limitation of Human Population: A Natural History," *Science* 187 (1975):713–21.

Little is as yet known about the determinants of today's rapidly changing marriage patterns, and whether the delay of marriage represents a response to mortality change, the educational advance of women, urbanization, or declining segregation of opportunities for women in the market labor force. Unanticipated and substantial shifts upward in the age at marriage are linked to declines in fertility in such countries as Sri Lanka, South Korea and Colombia.[21] In contrast, in Taiwan, where the age at marriage had already obtained a relatively high level before child mortality declined, the early declines in fertility occurred largely within marriage. Even polygyny has been studied with some insight as responsive to demand conditions within a particular cultural setting.[22]

It would be premature to say that the demand approach to fertility and family behavior has yet restructured the design or influenced widely the evolution of population or development policy. But the framework, and its growing body of supporting evidence and extensions, has ratified if not initiated a shift in attention from technological solutions involving only birth control and their dissemination, to broader consideration of the setting in which poor people live that motivates them, with reason, to want and to have a large family.[23] This changing perspective on the issues of population and development was also perceptible at the Accra African Population Conference in 1971, where Samir Amin cogently summarized one aspect of this argument: "The demographic variable is however neither a variable 'of no importance' nor a variable to which 'nothing can be done.' It may well be that, under given specific conditions, an authentic development strategy will incorporate a population policy, either to slow it down, or to accelerate it, according to circumstances. But this policy has no chance of yielding results unless the micro motivations of families are consistent with the macro objectives of the nation."[24]

Understanding the micro motivations and economic logic of family behavior is the necessary starting point for population policy research and may also provide fundamental insights into the design of better development policy.

21. G. A. Hernandez, *Hacia un Analysis de la Nupcialidad en Colombia* (Bogota: Corp. Centro Regionale de Poblacion, 1978).

22. Amyra Grossbard, "Towards a Marriage between Economics and Anthropology and a General Theory of Marriage," *The American Economic Review, Papers and Proceedings* 68 (May 1978).

23. R. S. McNamara, "Possible Interventions to Reduce Fertility," address at Massachusetts Institute of Technology, 28 April 1977. Reprinted in part in *Population and Development Review* 3 (1–2) (1977):163–76.

24. Samir Amin, "Under Populated Africa," paper prepared for the African Population Conference, Accra (9–18 December 1971), pp. 11–12.

The Determinants of Mortality and Reproductive Response

Much has been written about why mortality declined. For simplicity, these explanations are grouped here under two headings: (1) developments associated with increased levels of private material well-being and (2) developments that either depend on public investments or derive from new medical knowledge and technology that reduce the cost of effective health measures. In economic terms, the first class of factors is linked to individual *wealth effects* and the second to social-policy interventions and changes in *relative prices*.

In low-income countries innovations in public health and sanitation and not increases in overall income levels are often considered to be the cause of declining mortality. Mortality trends are "remarkably neutral with respect to economic events. . . . Economic misery as such is no longer an effective barrier to the vast upsurge in survival opportunities in the underdeveloped areas."[25] Other scholars stress the catalytic role of international agencies and outside assistance in reducing death rates without increasing material levels of living correspondingly. It is frequently asserted, therefore, that levels of private wealth and resulting opportunities for consumption are much less relevant to the secular trends and differentials in mortality in low-income countries today than they were in high-income countries at a similar stage in their demographic or economic development.

Although this widely accepted view may be plausible, it has not been rigorously inferred from quantitative analysis of mortality trends and differentials. The possible exception may be programs for the eradication of malaria in a few countries. But even in the most dramatic instance of Sri Lanka, only a quarter of the postwar decline in mortality is attributable to control of malaria, and the remainder is *not* associated at the district level with various public health services or their utilization.[26] Socioeconomic development and redistribution of income would appear to be responsible for a large part of the "unexplained" decline in Sri Lanka's death rate.

There is also clinic-level evidence in low-income countries that further declines in mortality will depend increasingly upon improved economic conditions for the mass of the population. Field research shows that high levels of childhood mortality found in low-income countries are primarily due to gastroenteritis and diarrheal disease, which are on the whole immune to Western modern medical technology, and which are

25. G. J. Stolnitz, "Recent Mortality Trends in Latin America, Asia and Africa," *Population Studies* 19 (November 1965):117.

26. R. H. Gray, "The Decline of Mortality in Ceylon and the Demographic Effects of Malaria Control," *Population Studies* 28 (July 1974):205–29.

likely to be the cause of death only in an already malnourished population. In many low-income societies this remaining major cause of childhood mortality is intimately related to the private, physical wealth of families and the educational attainment of mothers.

There are strong indications that a large part of the decline in mortality in this century, in both high- and low-income countries, is due to control of infectious and parasitic diseases and respiratory tuberculosis. The persisting high levels of diarrheal disease and resulting mortality among children in low-income countries are not readily linked to the provision of modern medical services, but to the provision of better nutrition and living conditions that depend, for the most part, on increases in levels of private income and their more nearly equal distribution among persons. In these low-income countries, the further decline in childhood mortality increasingly depends on improved levels of living, particularly among the poor, and perhaps also the increased educational attainment of women. These nontraditional interventions of policy to reduce mortality warrant increased quantitative study. Only when they are analyzed together with the relationship between fertility and mortality will we obtain a clear picture of the way in which economic development has contributed to, and been influenced by, recent demographic changes.

Parents seem to respond to the decline in child mortality by having fewer births, perhaps to some extent because of the biological effect of an infant's death, which often interrupts lactation and shortens the mother's sterile period following a birth. But this association also appears to reflect strong behavioral preferences of parents to replace an infant who dies. As indicated above, this replacement motivation cannot be derived from a simple economic model: many related economic effects of a child's death on family wealth, prices, risks, and returns on human capital might contribute to the observed positive behavioral relationship between fertility and child mortality. Declines in mortality increase the real value of income streams, and in particular they raise the relative value of human versus physical capital goods in their investment decision during their lifetime. Since these human assets are less unequally distributed among persons than are physical assets, such as land and reproducible physical capital, the general decline in mortality may also have an equalizing effect on the personal distribution of income, at least in the short run.

Existing empirical evidence does not permit a precise attribution of the response of fertility to mortality or between biological and behavioral factors, yet the noticeable pattern of reproductive response coefficients obtained for women of different ages and according to the sex of the deceased child indicate that behavioral aspects of this relationship should not be underrated. Future investigations of pregnancy histories should permit separation of the biological from the behavioral effects.[27]

Fortunately, the *sum* of the biological and behavioral effects is of principal interest for policy or the *total* reproductive response to child mortality. With all their deficiencies, almost half the studies contain evidence that the reproductive response of mothers is about sufficient to maintain a nearly constant surviving family size while adjusting to lower child mortality. In the other half of the cases, the response was sufficient to compensate only partially for the observed differences in child mortality. Empirical evidence from many different sources has, therefore, not yet added up to much general quantitative knowledge of the magnitude of these relationships.

Extending human life is viewed as an indisputable good, requiring no justification. But it is suspected that a consequence of this attitude has been a certain demotion in the claims to public resources of public health programs in low-income countries. Without serious efforts to measure the effects of development policies on mortality across social and economic groups, and an equally diligent effort to quantify the consequences of mortality on fertility, child schooling, labor productivity, and personal welfare, policy interventions to reduce mortality are likely to continue to be unfocused and gradually lose out in the competition for development funds.

Age Composition and the Personal Distribution of Incomes

The distribution of personal income in a society is directly and indirectly linked to the demographic structure of that population and its change. The demographic transition and modern economic growth affect the demographic structure in many ways, and in all probability the distribution of personal income influences in turn the pace and character of demographic change. The problem is how to simplify the many possible causal connections to a few that are tractable to analysis and which can be explored with existing data across many populations and within some populations over time. The need exists to develop and apply conceptual and statistical methodologies that will clarify socially meaningful dimensions of income inequality that are a consequence or cause of the pace and pattern of demographic change in a society. Several issues warrant study.

27. T. P. Schultz, "Interrelationships"; S. H. Preston, "Introduction," at CICRED Seminar on Infant Mortality in Relation to the Level of Fertility, Paris (1975).

THE COMPOSITION OF FAMILIES

First, there is the family or household that functions as a means of coordinating production and consumption. How do individuals choose to arrange themselves into household units, how do they divide their time among the labor market, home production, and leisure activities, how do they privately arrive at fertility goals, and under what circumstances do they absorb parents, unmarried adult offspring and other relatives of the household heads? These individual decisions are undoubtedly strongly shaped by cultural constraints and evolving social norms, yet they have nonetheless changed rapidly as economic conditions favored a restructuring of the family unit. The meaning of standard measures of inequality among families is called into question by such structural change in the size and composition of families, and yet this appears often to be a development that parallels demographic transition, urbanization, and industrialization.

The classic hypothesis of Goode is that of convergence across non-Western societies toward the nuclear family, a development that he traces to economic and social pressures of modernization. Goode also suggests that the predominance of the mobile nuclear family favored industrialization in the West and vice versa.[28] Laslett and Wrigley have empirically documented the predominance of the nuclear family unit well before the modern era of industrialization in Britain and northwestern Europe, but they have not answered why it existed there.[29]

Although the nuclear family may have been the predominant unit of social and economic organization in Europe back to the Middle Ages, there is substantial change in its size and structure over time within a region and across regions. It has been proposed to divide these differences into that portion which is attributable to differences in surviving fertility (or natural increase) and that portion which is due to the propensity for adults to live together.[30] The former source of change in family composition is dealt with directly by investigations into the determinants of fertility and mortality discussed above. But the latter propensity toward common living arrangements among kin is rarely studied, and may also have significant implications for the incentives surrounding fertility and mobility.

To understand the causes and consequences of family size and composition, one objective should be to clarify the conditions under which change in family income inequality involves real changes in the distribution

28. Goode, *World Revolution and Family Patterns.*

29. Laslett, *World We Have Lost;* E. A. Wrigley, *Population and History* (New York: McGraw Hill, 1969).

30. Kuznets, "Recent Population Trends."

of economic welfare and when it reflects only shifts in the composition of families. Two such periods of family composition change are notable in the U.S., immediately after the Second World War and today. These questions will undoubtedly be more difficult to answer in some cultural settings, such as sub-Saharan Africa, where the family's role may differ more notably from that known in the West.

INEQUALITY AND AGE STRUCTURE

A second area in which simplifying methodological tools are needed is in the decomposition of overall aggregate measures of personal income inequality into elements that are directly associated with (1) the age composition, (2) the age-income profile, and (3) the inequality within age groups. The preferred time frame for comparisons of income inequality is the lifetime. Equity is often defined in terms of the distribution of lifetime (or even intergenerational) opportunities, and individual investment decisions are stressed in the human capital literature as one increasingly important source of differences in individual age-income profiles. Income differences by age (2), may not, therefore, represent inequitable variations in income to the extent that individuals are likely to experience in part the full sequence of the age-income profile over their lifetimes. Similarly, although differences in the age composition (1) of a population may affect importantly aggregate measures of income inequality, it is unclear that these differences reflect inequities in individual lifetime opportunities. It is not known how much of the variation in conventional measures of income inequality, such as the Gini coefficients publicized by World Bank studies, can be attributed to differences across countries in age composition, with the young LDC population structures contributing to more "inequality" and the older age structure of industrialized countries contributing to less measured "inequality." Needless to say, the differences in age structure reflect largely recent vital rates, and hence high-fertility populations will have more *measured* "inequality" without necessarily having more individual lifetime inequality. Using an age-standardized measure of inequality would be an improvement over the current literature, but even this straightforward step is not readily undertaken for many countries because the underlying survey and census data are rarely tabulated by age and sex.

The third component of income inequality is that within age groups, which most nearly coincides with the individual equity concept of inequality. However, a procedure is needed to "average" or summarize these measures across ages and to do this correctly one must also know the covariation of income for individuals as they age. Clearly, if one's position in the within-age income distribution were randomly determined in each successive time period, income would be more equally or equitably distributed than if one's relative position (rank) in the within-age income distribution were fixed over time.

For example, the logarithmic variance of personal individual incomes, a common measure of income inequality, can be decomposed into three elements based on stratification of the population by age. One component of inequality is directly associated with the age composition of the population; a second component is associated with the difference between the age group's (geometric) mean income and the (geometric) average of the entire population; and the third component is the within-age group logarithmic variance in income.[31] It would be instructive to perform this form of inequality decomposition for several countries experiencing quite different demographic transitions.

There is also reason to anticipate that the age composition would affect *indirectly* the age-income profile (2) observed in cross-sectional data and within-age group inequality. The former case is precisely the demographic-economic mechanism that Easterlin and Ronald Lee argue has caused long-term swings in the relative income status of a sequence of U.S. birth cohorts.[32] Relatively large (small) cohorts are expected to relatively depress (inflate) their lifetime earnings and thus distort the steady state age-income profile as observed in a single cross section. The high unemployment among youth in many LDCs today is a reflection of the lower income opportunities available to the unusually large postwar birth cohorts surviving to labor force age.

No one has presented convincing evidence that periods of high (surviving) fertility or those *yielding* relatively large birth cohorts are also marked by greater *within-age group* income inequality, though this hypothesis is plausible and also worthy of testing. For the reasons stated above, it should be clear that intercountry comparisons of aggregate Gini coefficients do not directly test these conjectures as discussed below. Of course there may also be an effect of within-cohort inequality or even aggregative inequality on fertility. Much of the existing research has simply correlated crude birth rates and aggregative Gini coefficients of family market income inequality. The positive correlation across countries has been presented as evidence that fertility is reduced by a more equal distribution of income. As noted above, the reverse causal relationship from

31. T. Paul Schultz, "The Distribution of Personal Income: A Case Study of the Netherlands," Ph.D. dissertation, MIT, 1965.

32. R. A. Easterlin, *Population, Labor Force, and Long Swings in Economic Growth: The American Experience* (New York: National Bureau of Economic Research, 1968); Ronald Lee, "Marital Fertility in the U.S.: 1949–1974."

fertility to measured inequality is undoubtedly responsible for much of the correlations between them reported across countries.

Changes over time in age composition during the early phases of the demographic transition may also largely explain the scattered evidence that aggregative inequality has tended to increase in many LDCs in recent decades. However, one does not have to rely on the example of low-income countries to observe the sizeable impact of age composition changes on income inequality comparisons over time. Data for the U.S. and the Netherlands also document this fact.[33] Calculations for low-income populations are now needed, both over time and across countries, to identify the purely demographic and socioeconomic sources of differences and changes in measured income inequality.

INTERGENERATIONAL TRANSMISSION OF WEALTH: DEMOGRAPHIC FACTORS

A third line of new research would seek to illuminate at the individual and family level how intergenerational inequality is affected by the recent changes in mortality and fertility in low-income countries. Numerous difficult problems of statistical inference arise. Data requirements will be particularly severe as one seeks detailed information regarding the economic conditions and reproductive performance of two successive generations. It will take much time to formulate in this case an adequate research methodology, but the general approach can be crudely outlined. The starting point would be to estimate for both generations of parents a model of fertility determination, including compensation (biological and behavioral) to child mortality. Generational differences in reproductive performance could then be traced through to differences in underlying conditions facing the two generations and differences in response parameters that might reflect improved family-planning techniques. In addition to such a straightforward decomposition of intergenerational change it would also be useful to observe the level and variance in actual reproductive performance among specified quartiles of the full-income distribution. Particular care is required to specify the fertility equation to admit to nonlinear effects of various sources of income arising from the husband's wage, the wife's wage, and nonhuman wealth. Of central interest in such an exercise would

33. Considering aggregate data on the size distribution of personal incomes in age groups in the Netherlands in 1950, one would have concluded that in the subsequent decade the log variance of personal income declined eight percent. If the overall log variance of incomes had been simply standardized for the 1950 age and sex composition of the population (16 groups), the remaining within-age group log variance in personal income would have declined by 28 percent (Schultz, "The Distribution of Personal Income").

be the level and variability of natural increase (fertility less mortality before reaching the mean age of childbearing) by full-income class and the average level of schooling and physical wealth bequests parents transfer to offspring according to their sex and birth order. The question to be answered is whether today's structure of natural increase and transfers of endowments by income class is more likely to widen the disparity in personal incomes in the future than was the structure existing a generation ago. One might hope that active family-planning programs could mitigate such a tendency if it indeed exists.

DEVELOPMENT AND DEMOGRAPHY: MACRO MODELS

As pointed out in the introduction to this chapter, much of the macromodeling work in this field has its antecedents in the classical tradition. It might, in addition, be fair to say that the models focusing on the consequences of population growth take their inspiration from the crude version of the Malthusian/Ricardian model, while those dealing with the determinants, of somewhat later vintage, are descendants, if somewhat removed, of the more sophisticated version of the Malthusian/Marshallian view of the world.

The reader will be aware of the fact that there was a long hiatus, in terms of the concern of the economics profession with economic growth itself, between the classical school—to some extent Marx—and the revival of this interest in the post-Keynesian, post-World War II era. It is also evident that the population growth dimension, when it was reintegrated at all in the course of this revival of interest in development, was initially largely dealt with in terms of the impact of exogenous changes in numbers on the prospects for development, i.e., the consequences side of the equation. The effort at reintegrating the determinants side, i.e., rendering population growth endogenous, less pronounced even in the context of the classical "magnificient dynamics," has occurred only in relatively recent years. As a consequence, there is today a good deal of aggregative modeling, incorporating the consequences side of the demographic equation, but still relatively little spillover from recent advances in analyzing the determinants of fertility and mortality at the micro level for macro models. Partial exceptions are the relatively large general equilibrium simulation models of the ILO/Bachue type[34] which try to accommodate all the interactions between demographic and economic variables in a projections context.

34. G. B. Rodgers, M. J. D. Hopkins, and R. Wery, *Population, Employment, and Inequality: Bachue-Philippines* (London: Saxon House, 1978).

Consequences Modeling

The essential ingredients of the macro-consequences modelling consist of the tracing of population growth impact on the labor supply, on the one hand, and on savings, on the other. With respect to the labor supply, simple models will translate fertility changes into lagged (by fifteen years or less) labor force changes; more complicated ones will examine the age-specific impact of mortality changes; and still more complicated ones may look into the impact of morbidity on labor force productivity. At the same time the impact of population growth on the volume of available cooperating factors of production, specifically physical capital and, in more sophisticated versions, human capital formation, can be traced. The assumption under which part of the early models operated is that household saving, total investment, and expenditures on education are diminished as there are more dependents for the household to maintain and as the composition of total investment shifts from more to less productive areas.

The focus then was largely on how the exogenous expansion of population and labor force exerts pressure on the resulting even scarcer complementary factors of production, especially land in the preponderant agricultural sectors of the LDCs, and capital in the smaller nonagricultural sectors, thus impacting on both total and per capita income. The potentially positive contribution of population growth—after a lag—via increases in the labor force was given increasingly less weight, especially in an initially underemployment or labor abundance context, while increases in population were seen as leading to a decline in total savings rates for the economy and thus a decrease in the relative amounts of cooperating capital.

Just how serious these twin impacts are depends in large part, of course, on the type of aggregative production relation that is assumed. For example, if a Leontief or Harrod-Domar fixed-proportions type is accepted, the positive impact of labor force growth on income is bound to be zero; thus the impact on per capita income must be negative—without even taking into account any effects on the saving rate, hence the growth of the capital stock. If a neoclassical or substitutable kind of production function is accepted, the contribution of the extra labor to income per capita can continue to be substantially positive—under normal elasticity of substitution assumptions—as long as the overall growth of the labor force does not exceed that of the capital stock. To the extent there is technology change, and an innovation inducement mechanism is at work responding to relative factor supply pressures at the margin, the contribution of labor can be substantially positive even then.

It might be added that in the context of such modeling much less attention was paid to the family distribution of income than to the functional distribution which is closely related to aggregative production function analysis. Thus, for example, the elasticity of substitution, and the strength and bias of technology change, are essential ingredients in models which trace the more rapid growth of the labor force relative to cooperating land or capital and predict alternative outcomes for the functional distribution of income. If labor does grow over time faster than capital this should normally favor the share of the capital, i.e., in the absence of an unusually favorable type of technology change.

The classical economists, it should be remembered, were writing at a time when population growth suddenly accelerated, as has already been noted, and it is easy to understand why those who accepted the relatively crude version of Malthus were especially seized with the problem in the aftermath of World War II, when a new accelerated burst of population growth was in evidence as a consequence of the rapid decline in LDC mortality. Models in the Coale-Hoover tradition were clearly seized with this Ricardian view of the world, with the focus on diminishing returns, i.e., the domination of the agricultural sector which is implied thereby and the down-playing of increasing returns in industry and/or the potential for technology change on the production side in both the agricultural and nonagricultural sectors. The classical fear that urban-centered activities may only be temporary and that a successful transition to modern growth is likely to be impeded by cheaply obtained bursts of mortality decline unaccompanied by fertility decline dominated such models. Whether the modern descendants of this framework handle two or three factors of production; whether they employ a simple Harrod/Domar fixed proportions production function or a more sophisticated substitutable neoclassical alternative; and whether or not the models are small and simple or multisectored and more complicated, they clearly are in this same mold, i.e., they deploy an aggregative framework; they focus mainly on population as an exogenous variable; they analyze its quantitative relationships with other more scarce factors of production; and they are geared to a projection of the future on the basis of assumed alternative increases in population growth. From the scientific point of view, they emphasize the production rather than the demographic aspect of the problem.

Determinants Modeling

More recently an effort is discernible to strengthen the determinants side of such models in the context of general equilibrium projection models of the ILO/Bachue type. The demographic dimension of such macro models has been substantially strengthened and, in the process, more attention has been paid to the full range of interactions between income growth and population growth. On the other hand such models (the Bachue model in particular) while complicated in their overall structure and the number of equations, are often quite naive in terms of the individual behavioral relations posited. Constant coefficients are used; output growth in the basic reference model is predetermined; in application to particular countries cross-country parameter estimates are deployed—to cite just a few examples. The use of macroeconomic models of this kind for planning and simulation thus suffers from a lack of realism and richness in some of the behavioristic foundations as well as from an overemphasis on capital accumulation and a neglect of such dynamic considerations as technology change. Thus while there is no law of nature which forces detailed interactive macro models to give up the strength of the individual behavioral building blocks, a relevant observation would be that, in fact, this is what does happen, i.e., energies are either placed on relatively simple models with some effort at capturing behavioral realities, or on fairly complicated models which sacrifice the strength of individual causal relations for the sake of a general equilibrium approach capable of capturing complicated interactions and feedbacks.

With the exception of these Bachue-type models most of the past effort in macro modeling has, as has been seen, focused on the consequences rather than the determinants side of population growth. In recent years, moreover, it has become clearer that the facile assumptions about the definitive negative influence of population growth on income growth are not necessarily warranted—either in terms of the impact of labor force growth or in terms of the impact of family size and composition on savings and investments. For one, if economies of scale are important in the economy, faster population growth may in fact, be helpful, both statically and in terms of the inducement of innovations. In this category of argument must also be placed Esther Boserup's view that the shortage of complementary factors, such as land in particular, may induce workers in agricultural households to work harder and longer hours, thus obviating a decline in the marginal product of labor even though one will find a decline in the marginal product of labor hours. For another, evidence is inconclusive partly because these models focus only on personal rather than on total savings, partly because the savings estimates themselves are usually residuals, and partly because often it is found that the reaction of father and mother to additional children may be to work harder, thus increasing total income and total household savings, and partly because, in general, child care in developing countries seems to be less competitive with market activity than in the advanced countries. What meager evidence there is seems to indicate that consumption may go up with increases in family size but less than proportionately to income and that people may change their desire for assets and savings in terms of the bequest motive. At a minimum there is doubt as to the strong conclusions which once were believed to hold. While macroeconomists used to have much more confidence in their ability to determine the consequences of population growth, they have now become more circumspect. On the other hand, they have become more bullish in their expectations with respect to work on the determinants side in recent years. But this is only a relative statement, since, as will be noted, much work remains to be done on the determinants side as well.

It should be emphasized here that the data framework presented above constitutes what appears to be a reasonable compromise to guide future effort in macro modeling. It is a general equilibrium framework which, however, does not rush to judgment on particular behavioral relationships until they are empirically tested and proven within a particular country context. Neither is the other extreme adopted of insisting on only partial equilibrium verification in disregard of relationships among a complicated set of economic and demographic variables. The proposed economic-demographic data framework, in fact, provides a setting within which a gradually improving set of behavioral relations can be accommodated and a mapping of the future research effort intelligently focused.

Since countries represent customary units of observation there can be little doubt that the ultimate purpose of this search for a better understanding is the construction of an aggregative framework or model applicable to the whole system and within which its performance in relation to output, equity or, for that matter, any other dimension, can be assessed. The really interesting question, then, is how to get there, i.e., how is the growing partial equilibrium storehouse of knowledge to be organized, on both the consequences and determinants side, most effectively in terms of a strategy for future research and policy formulation?

The answer here would be not to force the pace of theorizing ahead of empirical verifiability and, for the decade ahead, to concentrate on gradually filling in the pieces of a general equilibrium framework rather than building general equilibrium simulation models. The kinds of frameworks that might be useful would at a minimum differentiate between the agricultural and nonagricultural sectors of a developing economy—reflecting the reality that the economic-demographic transition of concern is part and parcel of a gradual shift from agrarianism to modern growth. Secondly, the framework should undoubtedly be sensitive to important typological differences among developing countries which may affect the nature of the behavioral relations linking parts of an economic-demographic matrix. Such typological differences are likely to be significant both on the economic and demographic side of the ledger, i.e., differences in family structure as well as differences in country size and in the initial endowment conditions are likely to matter.

Given the substantial heterogeneity among contemporary LDCs, it would be foolhardy to set out for a general theory of development recognizing all the economic-demographic interactions alluded to.[35] The role of population growth in the context of a large labor abundant economy is found to be very different from that in a small, natural resources-rich country situation; the same holds for the impact of nuclear vs. extended family configurations in the context of analyzing rural/urban migration processes. Both a typological view of development and a sensitivity to the dynamics of the transition process, including the identification of meaningful subphases across which the mode of operation of the system may differ substantially, represent important ingredients of meaningful macro models. Only when reasonable confidence is felt that such models do a good job of tracing the past, including the existence of meaningful turning points with respect to output, population growth, and income distribution, should confidence be achieved enough to engage in simulations and projections for use by policy makers.

POPULATION GROWTH AND THE SIZE DISTRIBUTION OF INCOME AMONG FAMILIES

The issue of the equality or inequality with which incomes are distributed to families in a society has always been of concern to mankind. Economists, however, have traditionally focused their attention on the functional distribution of income related to the determination of factor prices and factor shares. While the size or family distribution of income (FID) has by no means been totally neglected—witness the use of the Lorenz curve for almost seventy years—it is fair to say that the topic has been treated mainly descriptively in the past, i.e., aiming at the measurement of the degree of inequality.

During the early postwar period (1950–60), the main social problem in the newly independent LDCs was a concern with growth, based on the notion that, in a poor country, policies must first be geared to increasing income levels before "redistribution" can really be meaningful. In more recent years, there has been an increased unwillingness, by all parties, to accept the "grow now and redistribute later" prescription, possibly due to an increasing skepticism as to whether "later" would, in fact, ever come.

35. For example, the difference between Chad and Brazil is undoubtedly greater than that between Brazil and Japan.

Since the distribution of income is related, on the one hand, to the ownership of assets by families, and, on the other, to the composition of the membership of these families, the equity or inequity of income over all families must be related to the accumulation of capital and human assets over time. It is thus a growth-related issue, dependent on family decisions with respect to the accumulation of physical and human assets over time.

The focus here is on the relations between income growth, the distribution of income, and population growth. In recent years, the notion has been accepted that there exists a two-way relationship between mortality and fertility, on the one hand, and income and its distribution, on the other. While the causal nexus is not yet fully understood, it is currently being asserted that "there appears to be no explicit dissent from the view that lower fertility contributes to greater income equality." Likewise, for the determinants side, the current assertion is that "poverty itself is likely to encourage high fertility."[36] While these still represent sweeping generalizations based on inadequate evidence and reasoning, at this point in time they are representative of current awareness of the importance of these two types of issues which will be discussed in this section.

An extension of the economic-demographic system presented above will provide a holistic framework for such reasoning. On the one hand, in Figure 8.5 identification is made of the roles of the families (indicated in the circle in the middle for n-families).[37] On the other hand, the stock of heterogeneous workers, differentiated by age, sex, and education (and indicated as $T_1, T_2, \ldots T_m$) are included in the "labor force circle." Families as owners of this labor force and capital stock, receive wages (W_i) as well as property incomes (π_i) leading to the total family income pattern ($Y_1, Y_2, \ldots Y_n$) the "equity" of which is the focus of attention of income-distribution theory.

Such a figure provides a general perspective to identify and to classify ideas related to family distribution of income (FDI) developed in recent years by economists. The boxes in this diagram (labeled A, B, C, D, E, F, G) contain names that describe a particular approach—the arrows leading from a box point to the relevant phenomenon (or concept) essential to that approach. For example, Box A refers to the traditional functional distribution approach involving the wage share and the property share determined by the aggregate production function plus bargaining. These boxes should help readers both find and maintain their bearing in the discussion that follows.

36. World Bank, *Population Policies and Economic Development* (Baltimore: Johns Hopkins University Press, 1974), pp. 35, 37.

37. Figure 8.5 neglects the household services production sector of Figure 8.1. At the present state of knowledge, the full income concept in relation to income distribution analysis is thus neglected, but only as a first approximation.

FIGURE 8.5
Economic Approaches to Family Income Distribution as viewed within Holistic Economic System

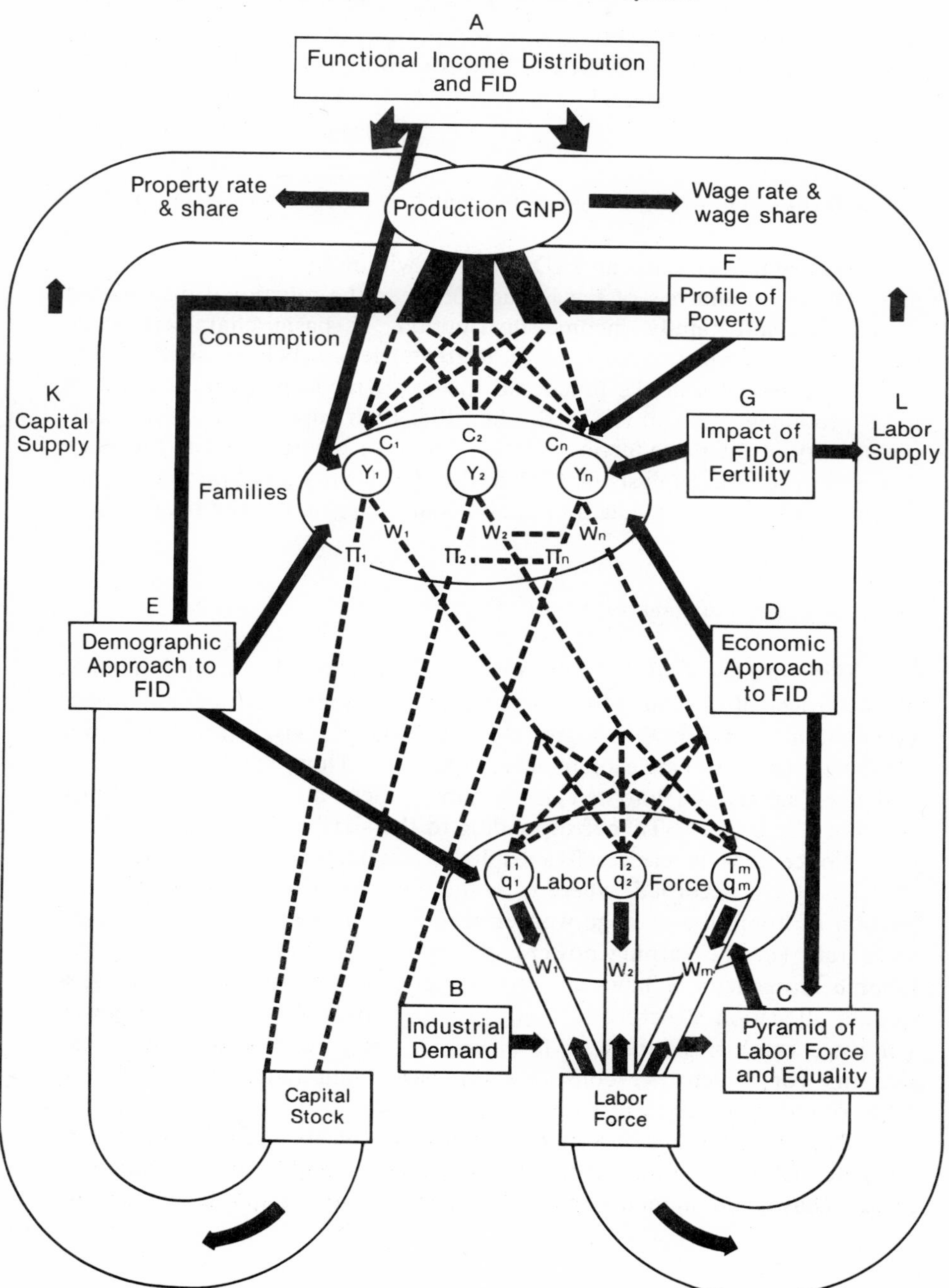

Factors Affecting FID Equity

If $Y = (Y_1, Y_2, \ldots Y_n)$ is the pattern of family income distribution, the degree of inequality of Y is measurable by an index of inequality such as the Gini coefficient G(Y). In this section, certain ideas developed by economists are discussed with respect to the factors affecting G(Y).

THE AGGREGATE FUNCTIONAL INCOME DISTRIBUTION APPROACH (BOX A)

This approach imbeds FID analysis within the neoclassical model and aims at an analysis of the linkage between the functional distribution of income and family income distribution. A basic characteristic of this approach—which is considered at greater length below—is its affinity with the classical school's functional theory of income distribution which gives prominent recognition to the fact that both capital and labor, complementary in their production relation, must be incorporated in the same framework for the analysis of FID equity. In all the other approaches, the capital stock and the production relations are relegated to the background.

THE LABOR-ORIENTED APPROACH (BOXES B, C, D)

With respect to these three related approaches, the starting point is the heterogeneity of the labor force, itself an essential demographic phenomenon as emphasized in Figure 8.2. For example, given just three labor attributes, i.e., *sex* (male or female), *education* (low, medium, or high), and *age* (subdivided into ten age groups), there already are sixty types of labor $T_1, T_2 \ldots T_{60}$ corresponding to the sixty cells of Figure 8.6.

Notice that in each cell a triplet of numbers (h_i, w_i, q_i) $(i = 1, 2, \ldots 60)$ is recorded, where q_i is the quantity of workers, h_i the proportion of hours the average worker spends in market activity and w_i the wage rate (or the earning power) of labor of the i-th type. Thus, given labor heterogeneity, a labor quantity structure $q = (q_1, q_2, \ldots q_{60})$, a market allocation structure $h = (h_1, h_2, \ldots h_{60})$ and an earning power (or wage rate) structure $w = (w_1, w_2, \ldots w_{60})$ can be defined. These patterns (or structures) constitute the basic data requirements for the labor-oriented approach to FID.

The labor market of a modern industrial society evaluates the heterogeneous labor force differently. There are both equilibrium or "rational" forces (based on human capital differences) and disequilibrium or "ir-

FIGURE 8.6
Labor-Oriented Approach to FID Equity

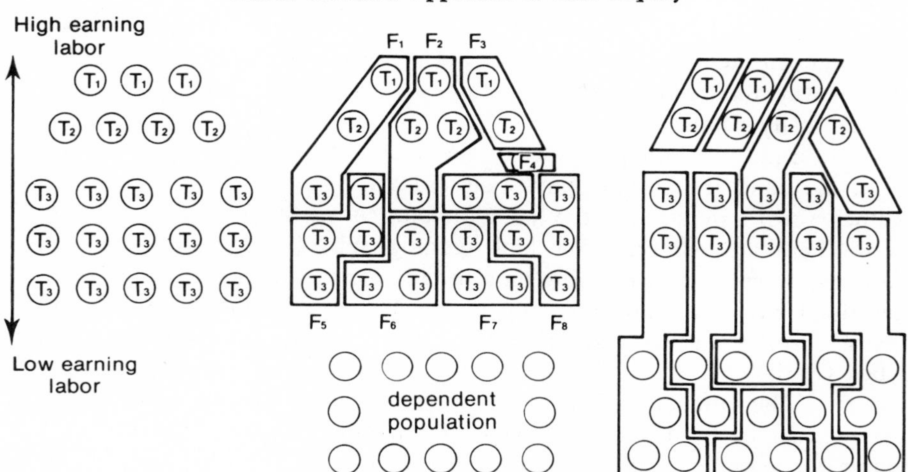

b) Family irrelevant Pyramiding of Industrial Labor Force

c) Family grouping of Active Population — family "income" orientation

d) Family grouping of active & dependent Population — family "welfare" orientation

(a) Classification of Labor Force

sex	edu \ Age	15-20	21-25	26-30	31-35	36-40	41-45	46-50	51-55	56-60	61-over
Male	Low	T_1 (h_1, w_1, q_1)	T_2 (h_2, w_2, q_2)	T_3 (h_3, w_3, q_3)	– –	– –	– –	– –	– –	– –	T_{10} (h_{10}, w_{10}, q_{10})
	Med.	T_{11} (h_{11}, w_{11}, q_{11})	T_{12} (h_{12}, w_{12}, q_{12})	T_{13} (h_{13}, w_{13}, q_{13})	– –	– –	– –	– –	– –	– –	– –
	High	¦	¦	¦							
Female	Low	¦	¦	¦							
	Med.	¦	¦	¦							
	High	¦	¦	¦							T_{60} (h_{60}, w_{60}, q_{60})

Heterogeneous labor types: $(T_1, T_2, \ldots T_{60})$

Quantities: $q = (q_1, q_2, \ldots q_{60})$

Market Allocation rate: $h = (h_1, h_2, \ldots h_{60})$

Earning Power: $w = (w_1, w_2, \ldots w_{60})$

rational" factors (based on factor market distortions) that enter this evaluation process. The industrial labor demand analysis (Box B) makes use of an "earnings function approach," based on regression techniques, in order to weight the relative importance of the various individual characteristics. In this way, the earning power structure $w = (w_1, w_2, \ldots w_{60})$ is at least conceptually determined.

In a modern industrial society, the quantitative structure $q = (q_1, q_2, \ldots q_{60})$ and the earning power structure $w = (w_1, w_2, \ldots w_{60})$, together, form a pyramid of the labor force as shown symbolically in Figure 8.6. There are relatively few high earning units (e.g., medical doctors, lawyers, entrepreneurs) resting on a broad base of low earning units (e.g., unskilled workers). The resulting pyramid appears to be natural—comparable to the rank structure of an army. Given such a labor force pyramid (box C) the extent of its inequality can be measured (through the computation of the Gini coefficient for $G(w,q)$). It should be immediately apparent that to the extent that such "pyramiding" of the labor force is a natural consequence of the modernization process, $G(w,q)$ can be expected to change over time. The analysis of the change of $G(w,q)$ through time as a consequence of the increased division of labor and industrialization process has not been attempted to date, as far as is known, and constitutes a researchable issue for the future.

Since families, not individuals, are being dealt with, however, the labor force pyramid of Figure 8.6b may be partitioned into family groupings $F_1, F_2, \ldots F_8$ (see Figure 8.6c). The total family wage income pattern is $W = (W_1, W_2, \ldots W_8)$ where W_i is the total wage income of all the wage earners in the i-th family ($i = 1, 2, \ldots 8$). The economic approach to family wage income equity (Box D) aims at an analysis of causation of family wage income inequality as measured by $G(W)$, the Gini coefficient of $W = (W_1, W_2, \ldots W_8)$.

In case the "structure" of the labor force owned by each family is the same (e.g., every family has one Ph.D. and two unskilled labor members), it is conceivable that $G(W) = 0$—showing the complete equality of wage income. The fact is, however, that this is extremely unlikely. Unequal distribution of the earning power associated with unequal distribution of educational opportunities and the right of inheritance under the existing family system are likely to cause total family income inequality in general and family wage income inequality in particular.

THE DEMOGRAPHIC APPROACH

In the context of this approach (Box E), the active as well as the dependent population are taken into consideration in the family grouping (see Figure 8.6d). Given this broadened notion, the focus of attention falls not only on family income ($Y_1, Y_2, \ldots Y_n$) but also on family size and on the family consumption, or welfare pattern ($C_1, C_2, \ldots C_n$).

One analytical dimension of this demographic approach stresses the age of the head of the household as a variable that is related to both family size and family income. *Ceteris paribus* a family headed by an "older parent" tends to have a larger family size as well as higher income (because of a skill and/or experience premium as well as the greater opportunity to accumulate more family assets through savings and inheritance). A systematic investigation along this line leads invariably to the idea of "life-long earnings" of an individual, on the one hand, and the development of the "family cycle" (e.g., marriage, the growing up of children, and the formation of new families) on the other. Here is an additional fruitful area for interdisciplinary research involving both economists, sociologists, and, to the extent the family concepts differ across societies, anthropologists.

THE PROFILE OF POVERTY APPROACH

The profile of poverty approach (Box F) concentrates directly on the income distribution pattern, with special attention given to the poor families below a certain poverty line. This descriptive approach is usually combined with a study of the consumption pattern ($C_1, C_2, \ldots C_3$) with some stress on the meeting of the basic needs of these families. It places emphasis on the specification of the specific bundle of consumption items including nutrition, shelter, education, and health, as related to family size.

The Impact of Fertility on Family Income Distribution

The most obvious way that high fertility may worsen FID is through increasing the supply of labor relative to the other factors of production, thus restraining the growth of real wages, perhaps even reducing them. Higher fertility and population growth rates can thus worsen family distribution of income through a worsening of the functional distribution of income. It is by no means obvious, of course, that there must always be a one-to-one relationship between the functional and the size distribution of income. First of all, therefore, the elements of functional distribution are examined to be followed by an analysis of the way in which the functional distribution operates on family income distribution equity.

The aim of the neoclassical functional distribution theory (see box A in Figure 8.5) is to explain the economic forces that determine the wage rate (w) and the rate of return to capital (π) in the context of a market economy in which labor and capital are jointly involved in (an aggregate) production process. In a competitive market economy context, each factor of production receives its marginal product; furthermore, under the assumption of the "law of diminishing returns" (that stresses the necessity of "complementarity" in the production process) when the quantity of one factor (e.g., population) increases (i.e., becomes more abundant relative to the other factor) its price (i.e., the wage rate) declines. Thus the functional distribution theory is a theory on factor prices, and, as such, is in and of itself not relevant to family income distribution. Indeed, the family ownership pattern of labor and capital, which is central to family income distribution equity, is quite irrelevant to the functional distribution of income.

When population increases, given the decline of the real wage, the wage share (i.e., the wage share as a fraction of total national income) is likely to decline whether labor and capital are "normally" substitutable in the production process (i.e., when the elasticity of substitution is less than one) and when technology change of a labor-using type cannot be counted on. The family ownership pattern of labor and/or capital is, again, not directly relevant to the direction of change in the wage share.

There is no automatic relationship between a worsening of labor's relative share and a worsening of the distribution of total income. In order to link the functional with the size distribution, it should be apparent that the family wage income distribution pattern $W = (W_1, W_2, \dots W_n)$ and the property income distribution pattern $\pi = (\pi_1, \pi_2, \dots \pi_n)$, as determined by the family ownership patterns of labor and capital assets, are the two additive factor components of the total income pattern $Y = (Y_1, Y_2, \dots Y_n)$. If $G(Y)$, $G(W)$, and $G(\pi)$ are the Gini coefficients of Y, W, and π, respectively it can be shown that[38]:

$$G(Y) = \phi_W G(W) + \phi_\pi G(\pi) \tag{8.1}$$

which states that $G(Y)$ is (approximately) the weighted average of the factor Ginis (i.e., the wage Gini $G(W)$ and the property Gini $G(\pi)$), where the two distributive shares (i.e., the wages share ϕ_W and the property share ϕ_π) constitute the weights (i.e., $\phi_W + \phi_\pi = 1$).

It can readily be seen that an improvement of a functional distribution in favor of labor (i.e., an increase of ϕ_W) can improve the equity of the total family income distribution [(i.e., lower the value of $G(Y)$] if, and only if, the following condition is fulfilled:

$$G(W) < G(\pi) \tag{8.2}$$

38. Under certain simplifying assumptions which are normally met; see: J. Fei, G. Ranis and S. Kuo, "Growth and the Family Distribution of Income by Factor Components," *Quarterly Journal of Economics* (February 1978).

which states that wage income must be distributed more equally than property income. There is ample evidence to support the customary empirical validity of (8.2) so that the improvement of the wage share (brought about, for example, by an increase of the relative wage and/or the reduction of unemployment) will almost always improve the equity of the family distribution of income.[39]

To reflect important typological, e.g., dualistic, characteristics of a developing economy it may be important to distinguish between agricultural and nonagricultural households and generalize the above relationships to include undifferentiated agricultural income. An additional important determinant of the overall equity of income distribution then becomes the relative importance of agricultural income in total income which is a proxy for the combined effect of rural/urban migration and of the rural location of industries. The extent to which income changes in rural households, arising, for instance, from additional agricultural incomes, additional cottage industry activities, or additional organized rural industry activities, is likely to have a differential effect on fertility. The labor requirements of the particular growth activity—total and as between male and female—whether additional agricultural output or by type of industrial expansion, can be assumed to affect the demand conditions for additional children. The protoindustrialization literature relating to the demographic transition in Western Europe has not yet been plumbed for its possible relevance to the contemporary developing countries.[40]

The Impact of Distribution on Fertility

The notion that a redistribution of income, in favor of the poorer families, may contribute to a decrease in fertility has received considerable attention in recent years and some quantitative analysis.[41] To analyze this notion, certain vital demographic and economic information can be extracted from the economic-demographic matrix developed above. By way of illustration of the type of analysis needed for the fuller investigation of this issue families may be ordered (or classified) by family income as relatively poor, middle income, and wealthy (see Table 8.1). With

39. *Ibid.*

40. J. D. Chambers, "Enclosure and Labour Supply in the Industrial Revolution," *Economic History Review* 5 (1953).

41. For example, Robert Repetto, "The Relation of Size Distribution of Income on Fertility and the Implication for Development Policy," in *Population Policies and Economic Development,* World Bank; J. E. Kocher, *et al., Rural Development, Income Distribution and Fertility Decline,* World Population Council Occasional Paper (New York: World Population Council, 1973).

respect to the demographic information, the same families may be classified according to the age of the head of the household ($_{16}\Omega_{23}$, $_{24}\Omega_{35}$, $_{36}\Omega_{49}$). Thus, in the example, there are nine cells (i.e. nine types of families). In each cell the vital information on cell frequency (n_{ij}, or number of families), family income (y_{ij}), and fertility rate (b_{ij}) are recorded. These vital rates are indicated in the matrix form below the table and make up all the information needed for our analysis.

There are many ways, some of which will be illustrated here, in which such demographic information can be used to investigate the impact of family income distribution on fertility. First of all, a type of approach, typical of "crude empiricism," may be differentiated from a type which calls for more careful "economic modeling" in which deductive reasoning plays a more prominent and formal role. As will be apparent later on, careful economic modeling will ultimately be essential if the analytical significance of income distribution inequality is to be fully explored.

Formal economic models, of course, also differ in complexity. In this respect, a type of "demographically insensitive approach" can be identified by temporarily suppressing many "demographic" dimensions of the problem as a first approximation. These "demographic" dimensions include such concepts as family size, the age structure of the population, and a careful distinction between the fertility rate and the net reproduction rate (as the difference between the age standardized fertility rate and the mortality rate), as well as the significance attached to the full income in contrast to the market income. These demographic dimensions are traditionally neglected by economists.

Work with the demographically insensitive approach is discussed first in order to highlight the analytical issues involved with respect to the distribution of income. In this approach, certain simplifying assumptions are made with respect to the demographic dimensions. For example, for the model in Table 8.1, for analytical convenience it is assumed that all families have the same size. When this "constant" family size is normalized to be "one" (i.e., one person per family), a family in our model amounts to an individual income recipient. The age dimension of the problem can also be suppressed via an aggregation procedure (see below). The fertility rate can be thought of as the net reproduction rate if the mortality rate is assumed to be constant. Finally, the full income can be identified with the market-related income if the output of the "household service" sector is neglected. After the demographically insensitive model is logically worked out, the question as to the significance of the various neglected demographic dimensions can then be raised by relaxing these restrictive assumptions one by one.

One relatively crude way to examine the impact of "income distribu-

TABLE 8.1
Impact of Family Income Distribution on Fertility

Demographic variables		Age-specific specification			FID and Fertility (age suppressed)	
Family income	Vital information	${}_{16}\Omega_{23}$	${}_{24}\Omega_{35}$	${}_{36}\Omega_{49}$	Sum	Indicator
Poor	Frequency	n_{11}	n_{12}	n_{13}	$n_1 = \Sigma n_{1j}$	$N_1 = n_1/N$
	Income	y_{11}	y_{12}	y_{13}	$y_1 = \Sigma n_{ij} y_{1j}$	$S_1 = y_1/Y; Y_1{}^* = y_1/n_1$
	Fertility Rate	b_{11}	b_{12}	b_{13}	$b_1 = \Sigma b_{1j} n_{1j}$	$B_1 = b_1/n_1$
Middle Income	Frequency	n_{21}	n_{22}	n_{23}	$n_2 = \Sigma n_{2j}$	$N_2 = n_2/N$
	Income	y_{21}	y_{22}	y_{23}	$y_2 = \Sigma n_{ij} y_{2j}$	$S_2 = y_2/Y; Y_2{}^* = y_2/n_2$
	Fertility Rate	b_{21}	b_{22}	b_{23}	$b_2 = \Sigma b_{2j} n_{2j}$	$B_2 = b_2/n_2$
Wealthy	Frequency	n_{31}	n_{32}	n_{33}	$n_3 = \Sigma n_{3j}$	$N_3 = n_3/N$
	Income	y_{31}	y_{32}	y_{33}	$y_3 = \Sigma n_{ij} y_{3j}$	$S_3 = y_3/Y; Y_3{}^* = y_3/n_3$
	Fertility Rate	b_{31}	b_{32}	b_{33}	$b_3 = \Sigma b_{3j} n_{3j}$	$B_3 = b_3/n_3$

$$(n) = \begin{pmatrix} n_{11} & n_{12} & n_{13} \\ n_{21} & n_{22} & n_{23} \\ n_{31} & n_{32} & n_{33} \end{pmatrix} \downarrow \quad N = \Sigma n_{ij}$$

(no. of families)

$$(y) = \begin{pmatrix} y_{11} & y_{12} & y_{13} \\ y_{21} & y_{22} & y_{23} \\ y_{31} & y_{32} & y_{33} \end{pmatrix} \downarrow \quad Y = \Sigma y_{ij} n_{ij}$$

(total income)

$$Y^* = Y/N$$

(per family income)

$$(b) = \begin{pmatrix} b_{11} & b_{12} & b_{13} \\ b_{21} & b_{22} & b_{23} \\ b_{31} & b_{32} & b_{33} \end{pmatrix} \downarrow \quad b = \Sigma b_{ij} n_{ij}/N$$

(fertility rate)

$(N_1, N_2, N_3): N_1 + N_2 + N_3 = 1$ (Family shares)

$(S_1, S_2, S_3): S_1 + S_2 + S_3 = 1$ (Income shares)

$(Y_1{}^*, Y_2{}^*, Y_3{}^*): Y_1{}^* < Y_2{}^* < Y_3{}^*$ (Income level)

$(B_1, B_2, B_3): B_1 > B_2 > B_3$ (Birth rate)

$b = N_1B_1 + N_2B_2 + N_3B_3$ (Aggregate birth rate)

$B_1 = B_1(Y_1{}^*), B_1 = B_2(Y_2{}^*), B_3 = B_3(Y_3{}^*)$ (Behavioristic)

$b = N_1B_1(S_1Y^*/N_1) + N_2B_2(S_2Y^*/N_2) + N_3B_3(S_3Y^*/N_3)$ (Basic equation)

tion" on fertility is via an investigation of the correlation between per capita income and the fertility rate (identified with the net reproduction rate for the time being) for the whole economy. With the aid of the primary data in Table 8.1, the following can be defined:

(8.1a) $N = \sum_{ij} n_{ij}$ (total number of families)

(8.1b) $Y = \sum_{ij} n_{ij} Y_{ij}$ (total income of all families)

(8.1c) $b = \sum_{ij} n_{ij} b_{ij/N}$ (aggregate fertility rate)

(8.1d) $Y^* = Y/N$ (per family income[42])

If per capita income and the aggregate fertility rate are computed for m countries (using cross-country data), a crude empirical approach might aim at determining whether or not an inverse relationship exists between Y^* and b for the m countries. Such a straight empirical approach, however, entails a number of difficulties. First of all, if cross-country data are used to calculate this correlation coefficient, the relationship may be found to be positive, negative, or nonexistent. This is due primarily to the fact that there really exists no a priori reason to expect a significant positive correlation to exist in the first place.[43] Moreover, even when a perfectly linear relation is observed, it tells little about the causal relation between the fertility rate and income inequality. Such a straightforward empiricist approach should be viewed only as a first step.[44]

Dissatisfaction with such straightforward empiricism leads to the search for an approach in which income distribution equity is formally recognized as a factor affecting aggregate fertility. The essence of this approach begins with the following definitions in the model:

42. At the present level of abstraction, Y^* is identified with per person income because every family is assumed to contain one person.

43. Suppose, for a given country with n-families, with per family income $Y = (Y_1, Y_2, \ldots Y_n)$ and fertility rates $b = (b_1, b_2, \ldots b_n)$, $b = f(Y)$ satisfies a perfectly curvilinear relationship. Suppose we arbitrarily classify these families into p-groups $G_1, G_2, \ldots G_p$ such that G_i contains n_i families $(n_1 + n_2 + \ldots + n_p = n)$. We can then calculate the per capita income $Y^* = (Y^*_1, Y^*_2, \ldots Y^*_p)$ and the net reproduction rates $b^* = (b^*_1, b^*_2, \ldots b^*_p)$ for the p groups. We do not expect a significant positive correlation between Y^* and b^* because the aggregation itself suppresses much of the information in $b = f(Y)$.

44. Repetto, "The Relation of Size Distribution of Income on Fertility and the Implication for Development Policy."

(8.2a) $n_i = \sum_j n_{ij}$ $(i = 1,2,3)$ (total number of poor, middle income, and wealthy families)

(8.2b) $y_i = \sum_j n_{ij}y_{ij}$ $(i = 1,2,3)$ (total income of poor, middle income, and wealthy families)

(8.2c) $b_i = \sum_j n_{ij}b_{ij}$ $(i = 1,2,3)$ (fertility rate of poor, middle income, and wealthy families)

In Table 8.1, these numbers are indicated in the "sum column" in order to show that, when these triplets (n_i,y_i,b_i) $(i = 1,2,3)$ are worked with, the age dimension of the problem in terms of our demographically insensitive approach has, in fact, been suppressed. From these triplets further definitions follow:

(8.3a) $N_i = n_i/N$ $(i = 1,2,3)$ (proportion of poor, middle income, and wealthy families)

(8.3b) $S_i = y_i/Y$ $(i = 1,2,3)$ (family income shares of poor, middle income, and wealthy families)

(8.3c) $B_i = b_i/n_i$ $(i = 1,2,3)$ ("aggregate" fertility rates of poor, middle income, and wealthy families)

(8.3d) $Y^*_i = y_i/n_i$ $(i = 1,2,3)$ (family income levels of poor, middle income, and wealthy families)

These numbers are indicated in the "indicator columns" of Table 8.1 and constitute the basic information base for the FID analysis. It is apparent that the overall family income inequality can now be defined by the Gini coefficient (or some other inequality index).

(8.4) $G = G(N_1,N_2,N_3,S_1,S_2,S_3)$ [the Gini coefficient defined from (8.3ab)]

A precise formulation of the problem of the impact of income distribution equity on fertility (or the net reproduction rate) requires an investigation of the relationship between G [defined in (8.4)] and b [defined in (8.1c)] In particular, in order to show that a "worsening of income distribution leads to a higher fertility rate" it is necessary to prove, deductively, that a high value of G always leads to a high value of b through the postulation of some behavioristic assumption. For example, it is possible to postulate the following "impact function":

(8.5) $$B = f(Y^*) \text{ with } f' < 0$$

which states that the fertility rate is a function of the family income level.[45]

45. In other words, $(B_i Y^*_i)$ $(i = 1,2,3)$ satisfies (8.5).

One step further is then possible by postulating the underlined condition that the fertility rate is lower when the family income level is higher.

Whether or not this proposition can be defended is a matter of demographic speculation at the microscopic level, as noted in "Development and Demography" above. The assumption is more likely to be false when B is interpreted as the "net reproduction rate" (rather than the fertility rate) since the mortality rate (less subject to rational choice) is likely to be lower (and hence the net reproduction rate higher) for the wealthier families. Whether or not the fertility rate is lower for the wealthy family depends, among other things, on the full-income versus the price effects in the "demand for children." While these are matters for demographic theoretical speculation at the micro level, it is possible to proceed to analyze the theoretical consequence on the assumption that (8.5) is in fact satisfied. If it is not satisfied, the theoretical reasoning can be carried out in a different but analogous fashion. Of course, if the relationship between B and Y* in (8.5) turns out to be random, the analytical effort would be stymied. But the investigation of this matter in this careful fashion is a matter of high priority.

If it is assumed that (8.5) is, in fact, satisfied, then the following can be defined:

(8.6a) $$Y^*_i = S_i Y^*/N_i \quad (i = 1,2,3) \text{ by (8.3) or}$$

(8.6b) $$Y^*_i/Y^* = S_i/N_i \quad (i = 1,2,3)$$

where Y^*_i/Y^* is the "income parity" of each group (in relation to overall per capita income). Furthermore

(8.7) $$b = N_1B_1 + N_2B_2 + N_3B_3$$

which shows that the overall fertility (or net reproduction) rate is the weighted average of the rates pertaining to each income group.

Finally, then the basic equation is

(8.8) $$b = N_1f(S_1Y^*/N_1) + N_2f(S_2Y^*/N_2) + N_3f(S_3Y^*/N_3)$$

which may constitute one possible analytical framework for the study of the relation between FID inequality and the rate of population increase within a given LDC.

Notice that income distribution equity (e.g., as measured by the Gini coefficient) is determined completely by (N_1,N_2,N_3) and (S_1,S_2,S_3) (the family proportions and family income shares) which appear as the explanatory variables in the basic equation. For example, the FID becomes more equal when S_1 gains at the expense of S_3 (poor families gain a larger income share) and/or N_2 gains at the expense of N_1 or N_3 (the middle class becomes more numerous at the expense of the very poor or the very wealthy families). It would then be a simple matter to predict the impact of the variation of FID on long-run rates of population growth. For example, if S_1 gains at the expense of S_3 (holding N_1 constant), i.e., income distribution becomes unambiguously more equitable, then

$$db/dS_1 = Y^* \, [f'(Y^*_1) - f'(Y^*_3)]$$

The obvious economic explanation is that the overall fertility rate will decline if and only if $|f'(Y^*_1)| > |f'(Y^*_3)|$, i.e., when the poor family's fertility is more income-sensitive than the wealthy family's. When this condition is fulfilled, an increase in equity exercises a direct influence on fertility decline.

The above analysis is only meant to suggest that additional deductive reasoning is needed to establish a logical link between the Gini coefficient and the aggregate fertility rate (b). At the present time, it is not known whether it is generally true theoretically, that there is a positive relation between G and b (i.e., that a decline in G always leads to a decline in b). The simple empirical correlation efforts to date must be viewed as strictly heuristic in character.[46]

It should be noted that all that has been attempted here is to outline one possible approach to the question of the impact of equity on fertility. The key behavioristic assumption underlying this approach (that a family's fertility rate is related to its income) must be examined more closely in the light of demographic research at the micro level. This approach may thus provide a link between the micro demand analysis of fertility and the macro issue of income distribution inequity.

Other micro links between distribution and fertility are discussed above in "Microeconomic Aspects of Family Behavior." The productivity of both these approaches emphasizing the mutuality of interactions might well be enhanced by focusing more attention on the differential characteristics of the population of a given LDC as reflected in our general economic/demographic data framework. The age of the head of the household, or the age of the mother, or the location of the household, or the specific source of family income may be key explanatory variables through which the comparative fertility behavior of different socioeconomic groups can be explained and, in this way, a richer two-way relationship between the Gini (G) and the time path of fertility and mortality can be established.

46. For example, those of Repetto, "The Relation of Size Distribution of Income."

PUZZLES AND PROSPECTS

Priorities for relevant research in the 1980s and beyond are best perceived and evaluated against a background of recent major trends in the underlying demographic processes. Experience indicates that such trends are never fully expected and foreseen before they occur, i.e., there is usually some delay in the perception of their emergence, and an even longer delay in the analysis of their causes and of their economic and social consequences. When analytical probing does begin, it is often followed by the discovery, not really so surprising, that the conventional data sources, while possibly providing valuable evidence on the trends and their magnitude, do not contain the more telling data on their timing, and particularly on their spread. Major, somewhat unexpected, demographic trends generate the explanatory or interpretive puzzles which must be the natural starting point for research and action in the years ahead. These puzzles identify the topics for further data collection and research; analytical and policy-related gaps in knowledge are revealed by the juxtaposition of recent major trends with the inadequate explanatory or even inferential analytical framework heretofore in use.

In dealing below with the major trends over the last three to five decades and the analytical questions they raise, one has to be satisfied with an impressionistic review rather than a complete census of observed reality and, even less, of the resulting analytical concerns. The latter would demand an impossibly large input of research effort; and in the absence of testable criteria of selection and evaluation, large elements of arbitrary judgment would be bound to remain even then.

A second limitation is to focus attention on the trends and research problems of the developing countries.[47] It needs hardly be emphasized that

47. The reason for omitting the experience and problems of the developed countries is *not* the absence of striking demographic trends or of analytical problems involved in interpreting both the causative antecedents and the major economic and social implications of these trends. The resumption of a striking decline in fertility in the developed countries within the recent decade or two, combined with the marked aging of the population, accelerated entry of women into the labor force, and the declining size of family households have given rise to a variety of important economic and social questions that could fill the research program of a large number of demographers, economists, and sociologists in the developed countries for decades to come. Indeed, one reason for even mentioning such trends and their implications for the developed countries in this footnote is that only a limited fraction of the relevant intellectual talents are likely to be available for work on the specific problems of the developing countries—not an unusual situation in the international distribution of resources, but one that should be of obvious relevance to the planning efforts of such international agencies as the UNFPA.

the major demographic trends over the last three to four decades in these countries had a profound impact on their much needed economic and social growth—raising analytical and policy problems of severe acuteness in their wake.

Decline in Mortality

The most conspicuous and pervasive of these demographic trends over the recent three to four decades in the less developed regions of the world has, of course, been the decline in death rates. Whether one takes the four decades back to the late 1930s or the period covered by the far more abundant data, i.e., since the 1950s, death rates declined at rates far greater than was true of the downtrends in mortality in the currently developed countries which began in the late eighteenth and early nineteenth centuries. Even more significant, this recent decline in mortality was observed not only in those less developed countries that enjoyed fairly rapid economic growth but also in countries in which per capita product is still low and in which current growth rates in output are moderate.

A few striking comparisons will illustrate the unusual character of these recent downtrends in mortality. According to the United Nations,[48] the crude death rate in India was 25.2 per thousand in 1950–55 and declined to 15.7 in 1970–75. This drop by close to 10 points in about twenty years could be found in a number of other less developed countries in Asia and some in Africa (e.g., Indonesia from 26.4 to 16.9; Morocco, from 25.7 to 15.7). But when the long-term records for currently developed countries are examined, it is found that crude death rates as high as 25 per thousand obtained as early as the beginning of the nineteenth century and that these rates were above 16 or 17 per thousand as late as the end of the nineteenth and the beginning of the twentieth century.[49] The crude death rate for England and Wales in 1890–1900 was 18 per thousand, for the United States 19 per thousand, and for Germany 22 per thousand. Even if one allows for the differences in underlying age structure, the fact remains that by the mid-1970s the developing countries, with per capita income and the overall degree of development far below that prevailing in the leading developed countries at the close of the nineteenth century, have attained mortality levels equal or lower. This comparison reveals the im-

48. United Nations, Population Division, *World Population Prospects Assessed in 1973* (New York: United Nations, 1977).

49. Simon Kuznets, *Modern Economic Growth* (New Haven: Yale University Press, 1966), table 2.3, pp. 42–45.

pact of new technological, income, and related price changes affecting mortality. One of the analytical puzzles is the extent to which declines in age-specific mortality resulted from accelerated socioeconomic change and the extent to which it could occur as a result of the availability of technology and without the underlying economic and social transformation that appear to have been required in the earlier history of the currently developed countries. Would comparisons of the levels and rates of decrease in different developing countries and among different socioeconomic groups within countries over the last 25 years provide clues to the correct answer? For example, has the decline in death rates stalled in parts of Africa, where socioeconomic change has been less pronounced, as compared with, say, urban Latin America? And what differences are perceived by income groups within the same country?

Second, given countries with different cultural and political systems, can the effect on mortality of increases in private household income and consequent complementary expenditures, be distinguished from the effect of publicly provided health and other services? Is the public provision of such services always associated with a more equitable distribution of the increase in the real income such services provide to the populations served? What is to be learned by comparison of Sri Lanka, with low rates of economic growth, large declines in death rates, and well-distributed health services, with Brazil, with high rates of economic growth, poorly distributed health services, and average rates of mortality decline? Similar questions might be addressed in the study of the relatively early demographic transitions in one of the lower income but more equitable states of India, i.e., Kerala.

Because of the distinctive features of the recent decline in mortality in LDCs, novel in terms of their sustained magnitude even in poor countries with slow growth rates, and partly because of the scarcity of data for the less developed and populous countries of Asia and Africa, the recognition of the new trends and their application to population projections and hence to policy formation were delayed. This delay can be seen in observing the successive projections of world population by the UN in the 1950s, with particular stress on the Asian and African LDCs. In the first projection of the three distinct groups within the world population (1951), only Group III, comprising Asia (excluding Japan and Asiatic USSR) and Africa, lies wholly in the less developed category (Latin America is included in Group II).[50] For Group III, the UN assumed a "high" projec-

50. United Nations, Population Division, "The Past and Future Growth of World Population—A Long-Range View," *Population Bulletin of the United Nations* 1 (December 1951):3–12.

tion of a natural rate of increase of at least 13 per thousand.[51] The projected rise in this rate over the next thirty years was seen as 3 points; for this increase in population, death rates would have had to decline from just above 30 to just below 30. The actual decline in the twenty years following 1950–55 was much greater—close to 10 points.

There was still a lag in the perception of the mortality trends in the next UN projection of 1954.[52] It was only by the time of the 1957 projection that we finally find recognition of the mortality trends as they have, in fact, emerged and are perceived today, although room for further revision, of course, remained.[53]

The delay in recognizing the magnitude and the likely persistence of the recent declines in mortality in LDCs was only to be expected in view of the novel features of the trend and absence of data on vital rates for a sufficiently long period covering the decline. The purpose of dwelling on this delay lies in the value of recognizing that, when new trends emerge, their full perception and the data base needed to gain such a perception are still to follow; and this unavoidable time-consuming learning process in turn delays the analysis of causal antecedents and consequences. Such analysis, once initiated and expanded, can be counted on to reveal the need for additional data and further probing.

51. *Ibid.*, table 3, p. 3.

52. See "Framework for Future Population Estimates, 1950–1980, by World Regions," *Proceedings of the World Population Conference 1954*, Vol. 3 (New York: UN, 1955).

53. See United Nations, *The Future Growth of World Population* (New York: UN, 1958). The following comparison of the projections of population for 1980, high variant, for Group III (East Asia, except Japan and the Asiatic USSR; South Asia; and Africa) may be of interest.

UN ESTIMATES, Selected Years

	Total Group III				Group ex. East Asia		
	1951 (1)	1954 (2)	1957–58 (3)	1973–77 (4)	1954 (5)	1957–77 (6)	1973–77 (7)
1. Pop. 1950 mill	1,387	1,435	1,495	1,503	895	900	912
2. Proj. 1980 mill	2,043	2,415	2,731	2,882	1,529	1,651	1,900
3. % Growth, 2/1	47.3	68.3	82.7	98.4	70.8	83.4	108.3

The totals were derived from the four United Nations studies already cited (including the 1977 publication on *World Population Prospects as Assessed in 1973*). It should be noted that even with the exclusion of East Asia (largely Mainland China), the 1957–58 projection was still substantially short of the 1973 assessment (compare cols. 6 and 7, line 3).

A large and sustained decline in mortality, of the magnitude that occurred in the less-developed regions, particularly in Asia and Africa since 1960, has enormous implications for economic growth and social advance. Given the U-shaped age-specific death rate schedule, a large proportion of the total decline was in the extreme left-hand horn of the U, i.e., in infant and children's (under 5) mortality, while the contribution to the total increased longevity at the well-advanced ages (the right horn of the U) was relatively moderate. Such reduction in infant and children's mortality meant not only the removal of a heavy economic and personal burden involved in the failure of infants and children to attain the potential of productive maturity. It was also a necessary (although not sufficient) condition for the modern pattern of demographic growth to assert itself, i.e., for family choices of a smaller number of children with greater investment in their nurture, education, and training. These aspects of the recent decline in mortality in the LDCs are major and obvious; but they have tended to be overshadowed in the natural concern about the explosive rise in the rates of natural increase of population which resulted from the combination of a sharp downtrend in mortality with the persistence of high crude birth rates.

With the steady expansion of data on crude death rates and life expectancy in a variety of less developed countries and regions, and an emerging consensus on the complex of factors lying behind it, i.e., a combination of technological innovations in the medical and health fields with greater ease of communication and organization, and the rising economic capacity to sustain and feed the larger populations, one major topic clearly appears to deserve increased attention. It is the process by which lower LDC mortality rates spread among different economic and social groups within the total population. It is known that, at any given time, there tends to exist a negative correlation between mortality rates and socioeconomic status. This means that in a given less developed country, *before* the significant decline in death rates even begins, mortality is appreciably lower among the upper economic and social groups than among the lower (for the same demographic, i.e., age, sex, etc.) classes. But what happens when death rates begin to decline? Will they decline more in absolute terms for the lower economic and social groups for whom the initial mortality levels are higher and the effect of contributions of mortality-reducing factors have been longer delayed? Or are there distinct phases in the spread of lower mortality? Is there an initial phase in which larger absolute reductions occur among the upper or upper-middle economic and social groups? Is there a second phase in which mortality decline, reaching the lower income groups belatedly, is then found to show larger and faster reductions than the concurrent downtrend in mortality among the higher status economic and social groups?

Underlying such an analysis of the diffusion of mortality rate declines must be a better understanding of the underlying causes in terms of the differential access to the new technology, the differential private income capacity to make complementary expenditures, and possibly differential innovational responses to a superior new available technology. One interesting and potentially very important conclusion would be whether or not—and to what extent—mortality differentials first widen and only begin to close at a later stage in the development process.

These questions are of obvious importance for understanding the growth implications of the downtrends of mortality, even though a fuller answer would have to include the connection between declines in mortality and the reduction of fertility that will come as the eventual response. Yet the general summary sources do not provide an answer, and, indeed, fail to discuss the questions explicitly.[54] Stolnitz's comment that a "pervasive aspect of twentieth-century mortality changes is that countries which were late to embark upon sustained transitions have tended consistently to outperform the countries with earlier transitions" suggests that, within a country, an initial delay in the spread of lower mortality to the lower economic groups will mean a much faster reduction once the transition begins.[55] But whether such delays in fact occur is not indicated, except perhaps in the case of rural populations as compared with urban, the latter enjoying easier access to the services of modern medicine and health. Yet if there is an unequal spread of declines in mortality, with the earlier declines occurring among the upper economic groups, the initial result will be to widen the economic and social differentials in mortality, thus exacerbating economic and social inequality problems—and this exacerbation will take place even though the persisting high mortality among the lower economic groups will keep down the size of the completed family. The continued heavy burden of infant and child mortality will reduce the economic returns to the low-income family in the longer run far more than would be the case for the reduced lower mortality among the higher status economic and social groups. To deal with these questions new data are required on mortality differences and on trends by economic, social, and educational classes.

54. For example, United Nations, "Mortality," in *The Determinants and Consequences of Population Trends,* Vol. 1 (New York: UN, 1973), pp. 107–158; and George J. Stolnitz, "International Mortality Trends: Some Main Facts and Implications," in *The Population Debate: Dimensions and Perspectives,* Vol. 1 (New York: UN, 1965), pp. 220–36.

55. *Ibid.,* p. 224.

Trends in Fertility

The recent trends in fertility in the less-developed regions have appeared to be, at least until very recently, far less conspicuous than in mortality. The main 1977 United Nations source (summarizing prospects as assessed in 1973) shows crude birth rates for Africa moving from 48 per thousand in 1950–55 to 46 per thousand in 1970–75 (medium projection, here and below); for South Asia from 44 to 42 per thousand, for Latin America from 41 to 37, and for China from 37 to 27. Only for the exceptional case of China was the decline in birth rates of a magnitude approaching that in death rates—and this case is still to be examined on the basis of more abundant and testable data than have been provided so far. For the other less-developed regions, with the few exceptions of countries that had an impressively high record of economic growth, crude and even refined fertility levels moved down slowly and at rates far lower than the drop in mortality. It was this delay that produced the substantial rise in the postwar rates of natural increase and in the concern as to its implications for economic growth and social advance. This concern in turn led to widespread analysis as to the reasons for this delay in the response of fertility to the large and sustained declines in death rates. Since fertility decisions appear to be more subject to personal and institutional influences than, at least on the surface, changes in mortality, a substantial volume of work has focused on trying to present explanatory factors—ranging from governmental failure to adequately encourage family planning to the rational calculus of economic advantages accruing from larger numbers of surviving children relative to a smaller number of children with greater investment in their nurture and training.

As with the downtrends in mortality in the LDCs, the differentials in fertility rates within the less-developed countries among groups at different economic and social levels and, particularly, the diffusion of declines in fertility among such socioeconomic groups, are still incompletely reflected in data of sufficient coverage. During the last two decades the amount and quality of demographic data has undoubtedly improved enormously. It is easier today, for example, to identify and isolate factors which have tended to mask and delay the emergence of an observed decline in fertility. For most countries, reasonably reliable information on the size and age structure of the population has now been collected in censuses and representative national surveys at several points in time, permitting one to begin to transform crude birth and death rate indicators into intrinsic measures of age-specific and normalized rates of fertility and mortality. Sophisticated tests of internal consistency applied to these data, constructed in accordance with "stable population models," have improved the assessment of trends as well as the current estimates of birth, death, and population growth rates. As the range of uncertainty on the level and age structure of national death rates has narrowed appreciably, new and generally unanticipated evidence has been found of fertility changes occurring in a large number of countries in Latin America, Asia, North Africa, and portions of the Middle East. Changes in the age composition of the population induced by the disproportionate reduction in infant and child mortality have exaggerated the decline in crude death rates far below the level that would be maintained in the long run as the age structure of the population stabilizes. At the same time, the shift in age composition in LDCs, due to the structure and unprecedented rate of mortality decline, has contributed to a more modest increase in crude birth rates beginning in the 1960s, as a growing fraction of these populations enters into the more fertile childbearing ages. In addition, birth registration figures used to construct crude birth rates have been improved, as the degree of underenumeration declines with urbanization and improved rural communications. Trends in registered birth rates that are often officially cited have thereby been subjected to a spurious upward bias over time.

It is therefore quite plausible that a period of rapid, though probably very uneven, decline in fertility in a substantial number of LDCs has been reached. As in the case of assessing the changing trends in mortality, it seems likely, however, that the figures on birth rates and resulting population growth projection rates as prepared from official UN statistics will mirror these new and diverse trends only with a considerable lag. For example, according to the UN population projections published in 1975, the rate of growth of the world's entire population was expected to continue to increase from 1.90 percent per year in the period 1970–75 to 1.96 percent per year in 1975–85.[56] But more recent evidence suggests that by 1977 world population growth had already levelled off, and probably begun to decline, to the vicinity of 1.7 to 1.8 percent per year, or to about the rate of growth recorded during the 1950s.

In recent years several organizations have begun to prepare worldwide demographic estimates including the US/AID and the U.S. Bureau of the Census. Increasing controversy attaches to projected trends in fertility in regions where population statistics are relatively poor and collected infrequently. In particular, there is growing disagreement on population growth rates in such countries as China, Indonesia, India, Bangladesh, Pakistan, the Philippines, Thailand, Colombia, Mexico, and Brazil. And

56. UN, Population Division, *Selected Demographic Indicators by Countries, 1950–2000,* ESA/P/WP/55 (New York: UN, 1975).

today these ten countries contain two billion people or half of the world's population.[57] Little, moreover, is known about China, whereas Indonesia, India, the Philippines and Thailand in Asia, and Brazil and Colombia in Latin America appear to be in the midst of fertility declines of as yet indeterminate magnitude. Pakistan and Bangladesh could well be experiencing a decline but the data are as yet sufficiently inaccurate, to be sure. As indicated earlier, the issues for research in this crucial period when fertility trends give evidence of beginning to change reside not only in gaining a better understanding of the determinants of national trends but also in studying the nature, extent, and spread of fertility differentials among social and economic groups within countries. These differentials, which probably increased during the early phases of a general fertility decline, can be somewhat narrowed by population programs that seek to reach specific target groups, i.e., the poorer, rural, traditionally employed segments of LDC populations, by providing them with information about and subsidized access to modern means of birth control. The early collection of relevant data plus research and action at the policy level are needed to shorten the lags in perception, policy evaluation, and program commitment.

In the absence of adequate data and of an adequate inventory of specific analytical findings, it is easy to envisage, but not to choose among, scenarios of different combinations of socioeconomic group differentials on both the mortality and fertility fronts that would yield the observed aggregate trends in mortality and fertility, but with different implications as to the phasing and changes in intergroup differentials. The task is to determine which combination is the proper one, i.e., best founded in behavioral terms. Thus one may assume an initial slight decline in mortality but also a decline in morbidity and involuntary sterility. Both the limited reduction in mortality and the delay in the fertility response of the parental generation might mean a slight rise rather than a decline in the crude birth rates among the lower-income groups. This would be concurrent with a sharp decline in both mortality and fertility among the economic groups above the average. The result might be a slow downtrend in fertility, and a widened disparity in rates of natural increase (surviving children) between the two economic groups. All of this may change in the next phase. Alternatives to such a sequence of phases and combinations of economic group differentials in levels and changes in mortality and fertility can, presumably, be derived. Indeed, a systematic elaboration of the several plausible se-

57. For a comparison of various organizational estimates of crude birth, crude death, and population growth rates, see R. Kramer and S. Baum, "Comparison of Recent Estimates of World Population Growth," U.S. Bureau of the Census, Population Division (April 1978).

quences of phases and changes in economic group differentials in both mortality and fertility would be extremely useful as an underpinning for future policy actions. But there exists as yet no fully adequate data base of the kind outlined here for testing the alternatives; and the implicit effects on group economic inequalities are still to be considered in terms of actually observed alternative patterns of demographic differentials and their trends in the transition to the modern type of demographic behavior.

The Broader Thesis

These comments clearly suggest a broader thesis: a major requirement for the observation and analysis of the growth and distributional implications of demographic trends is to have the latter available, in whatever full demographic detail needed, for the major socioeconomic groups within the population. It is only when the demographic processes are observed in connection with economic and social groupings that their implications for economic growth and distribution can be fully studied. Information on the behavior of such groups should be available *within* countries, permitting us to move away from the almost total past reliance on cross sections of countries at different levels of development to infer socioeconomic differences. The essence of a country's economic growth resides not only in the rise of its aggregate product (total or per capita) but also in structural change, which means changes among different socioeconomic groups within the population, both as producers and consumers. To study these differentials in a dynamic context involves much less extreme *ceteris paribus* assumptions than those which need to be made in the use of aggregate intercountry cross sections.

The requirement of a close tie between demographic processes and parameters and the distinction of significant socioeconomic groups is valid whether mortality, fertility, natural increase, or internal and external migration are considered; whether, within mortality, age- and sex-specific death rates or the changing composition of the population by age and sex are examined; whether, in dealing with fertility, distinctions are made among such intermediate variables as nuptiality and intramarital fertility; and whether the impact of a changing or different age-sex structure of population relevant to each particular process is studied. Indeed, one could legitimately argue that if the objective is to learn about the implications of demographic processes for economic growth and social advance, and if the unit of observation for policy purposes—as most everyone would agree—is the politically sovereign and independent state, the main topic on the agenda should be these differentials in demographic processes, at whatever level of demographic detail needed, differentials that are also of analytical significance in observing and analyzing economic growth and equity.

The socioeconomic groups that should be distinguished in observing the intracountry incidence of major demographic trends are those relevant to the study and analysis of economic growth and equity—because of their specific and changing roles within the economic structure in its transition to higher levels of aggregate, and particularly per capita, product. These groups are usually identified by their role within the structure of production, i.e., the participation of its active members in various production sectors (agricultural, industrial) and at different levels of performance within the latter. Such participation also determines the type or place of residence, conditions of preparation for the functions, and conditions of life of both the participants and the related members of their family or family household. In the course of any such suggested attempt to define socioeconomic groups for studying the impact of demographic trends on them, advantage must be taken of accumulated definitions and knowledge of these groups in current classifications, geared though they are at this time largely to developed countries. Such reference to already established categories should, however, be with a wary eye to the distinct possibility that they may distinguish groups of little importance in LDCs, and, more important, that they may prematurely merge smaller subgroups into broad groups and thus blur a distinction which may be of crucial importance for analyzing related growth and distributional aspects in the less developed countries.

Since demographic trends are being dealt with here, and differentiation of their impact among socioeconomic groups is the objective, the underlying basic units which will be grouped are families, persons related by blood, marriage, and adoption ties who, given such ties, form units whose members cooperate in their economic and demographic functions. These involve, among others, making a living to be shared with the dependent members of the family, producing and nurturing to maturity the next generation, and, in many societies, sheltering and sustaining the older generation that has passed beyond the productive age. The concept of a family is complex, not surprising in view of the long span and the variety of societies in which this institution has flourished; and in recent times, there have arisen statistical problems in defining the extended family as distinct from the family household, the latter identified by joint production and consumption involving the family members. Co-residential or dwelling units may, in some African societies, have little bearing on the family as the basic unit of production, consumption, and reproduction. Alternatively, in temperate climates the dwelling unit may be most important.

But all such conceptual and statistical difficulties are common to analyses of the interrelations of complex processes—particularly in the early attempts to bring together aspects of social processes that for too long were studied separately; or were brought together by the simple joining of aggregates that failed to distinguish among the basic human decision units. For it is not persons as individuals who make decisions about life, death, and succession, or about training and lifetime work; and it is not the country's total population that is the direct decision-making unit concerning growth and structure of either people or product. The working assumption here is that it is instead the family units that make these decisions within an institutional framework suggested in the general models noted elsewhere in this chapter. But knowledge of the impact of demographic trends on socioeconomic units grouped by families (often households as a first approximation) is still meager, even for the developed countries, let alone the LDCs.

Families and family households differ in size through the long life cycle from the wedding through the child-bearing years and to the older ages, when the children mature and leave to form their own households; and they may differ in size even for comparable phases of the life cycle. The usual statistical data on the economic position of family households record their income and components—usually for a single year, usually incompletely, and relatively rarely with adjustment, for every family household, for differences in size and characteristics, of both active and dependent members.[58] Hence, the conventional data on the size distribution of income among households by income per household are deficient as a measure of disparities in long-term levels of income (or related measures of economic status), adjusted for the size and other short-term characteristics of the household.[59] While these deficiencies can be reduced in the long run by gradual improvements in the definitions of recipient units and income, corresponding changes in the tabulation of the primary data, and the increasing availability of raw survey/census files, classifications based on the criterion of the size of annual income per household must be used with circumspection. Increased attention might be paid to alternative criteria of the kind captured by the age and education of the head of the family household and spouse. Corrections for differences in the average size of households or similar changing demographic characteristics such as rural/urban residence and industrial attachment will also become feasible as micro data files become more flexible.

58. There are practically no data, for adequate comparative purposes, on the structure and economic levels of families at large, i.e., associated by ties of blood, marriage, or adoption but living in different places.

59. For more detailed discussion, see Simon Kuznets, "Demographic Aspects of the Size Distribution of Income: An Exploratory Essay," *Economic Development and Cultural Change* 25 (October 1976):1–94.

This suggested area of research is wide in scope and demanding in the combination of demographic and economic data that it requires. Reducing it to feasible dimensions might mean selecting a smaller number of less developed countries, representing different regions and different phases in the transition to the modern pattern of population growth; and attempting, for these countries, to secure data on the demographic differentials and trends for a comparable range of socioeconomic groups within each. There is no substitute for fresh theorizing concerning the precise nature of the subtle interrelationships among demographic change, income growth, and changes in the distribution of income. But the theorizing must be able to be checked against an adequate, if always improving, data base. Once the general direction of priority research and policy concerns has been set in this fashion, such data sets, used at whatever level of disaggregation appropriate to the particular problem, should provide the basis for the construction of firmer building blocks of causality underlying the plausibility of relevant theories.

CONCLUSIONS FOR RESEARCH AND POLICY

Casting a backward look over the past quarter century of thought and policy in the field of economic demography one might, at first blush, be tempted to conclude that the great surge of concern over the so-called LDC population problem is currently abating. The accent on development emerging from the Bucharest Conference of 1974, plus some evidence that fertility has begun to decline in several developing countries, has strengthened sentiment that the dangers of the new (LDC) demographic transition were exaggerated or, in any event, lie safely behind, or represent problems which are not understood and about which much cannot be done anyway. There are still dire warnings from those who fear the disastrous effects of past fertility on employment and the environment throughout the globe during the next quarter century. And prescient observers are aware that even though total population numbers may diminish over the long run, in the short run the momentum of population growth built into the large numbers of young people, only now entering their reproductive years, will present severe problems. But in general, the level of concern with the demographic dimension of development during the past decade has undoubtedly diminished; and there is the danger that population will simply be added to the large catalog of "relevant factors in economic development."

What does the future hold in terms of this view of the past and the present? Acknowledgment must be made that there was overzealousness in both the realms of science and of affairs in depicting the scope of the neo-Malthusian dangers during the 60s, and in selling oversimple solutions to complicated problems. Subsequent disavowals seem equally overzealous. Has demography really been "dethroned" as a central area for research and action in economic development? On the basis of the present tour d'horizon, the conclusion is clearly not. The reduction in decibel count may reflect the growing realization that the web of relationships binding demography and development is complex indeed. Clearly an era is being entered in which the recognition of the more subtle and complicated nature of the relevant relationships must increasingly be accepted by researchers and policy makers. Moreover, this realization may really be the first step in the construction of a sturdier throne—reconfirming the central place of population in the development context.

Directions of Future Policy-Oriented Research

Two major ingredients are essential to the construction of this sturdier throne for the population dimension of development: the increased recognition of the importance of the family and family behavior; and the increased realization that the behavior of families when distinguished by socioeconomic groups may permit the forging of the needed links between demography, development, and the distribution of income. It may, in fact, be a happy coincidence that both the current research frontier in economic demography and the growing concern with the size distribution of income point in the same direction, i.e., toward the study of behavior at the family level as it affects the more aggregative performance indicators for the society as a whole.

It is families, not individuals, who make decisions about consumption and savings as well as about the number and quality of children. It is families, not individuals, who own capital and within which members of a differentiated labor force are organized for productive activity. The heterogeneity of any population, differentiated by location, age, sex, education, and other relevant socioeconomic attributes, follows from the differentiated quantity and quality of the membership of various families. Members' characteristics determine labor earnings, and, together with asset holdings, determine family income and the distribution of income across families. It is, moreover, income from family labor which weighs most heavily in the determination of the overall distribution of income, in terms of the weight of labor income in total income by source.[60] Property income is usually

60. J. Fei *et al.*, "Growth and the Family Distribution of Income."

distributed less equitably than overall income and labor income; thus the distribution of characteristics of family members which determine family earning power is important in determining the overall distribution of income.

The foundations for general equilibrium analysis linking population, income, and the distribution of income, are best constructed at an intermediate level of aggregation, between the holistic and the individual. At the level of the family, heterogeneities suppressed at the aggregative level can be taken into account, at the same time as individuals are summed up to the level at which decisions are made which affect aggregate demographic and economic outcomes. International organizations concerned with family welfare, like the UNFPA, can encourage analysis at this level in as many countries as possible. Moreover, attention is called below to ways data now available can be exploited in a manner consistent with the general economic-demographic data system of the type described above, and to ways new data can be collected to improve our ability to apply and refine such a framework—with help from national and international institutions.

The practical implications of this emphasis on family behavior and on equity raises the issue of research strategy. As noted earlier in this chapter, the field of relevant scientific inquiry has moved a considerable distance from the pioneering but crude macro models of the Coale-Hoover type in the classical tradition. Early models focused only on the consequences of population growth for development, in terms of the size of the labor force and the amount and allocation of savings. Today a few models, such as the ILO/Bachue type, include as well effects from per capita income and other socioeconomic changes on population variables—fertility, mortality, and migration. Bachue-type models emphasizing the web of interactions between economic and demographic variables, a web woven most densely about the family, illustrate how intuition regarding the plausible outcomes of policies can often be wrong, due to the cumulative and unexpected impact of indirect effects. Such models have, by and large, tended to overemphasize the number of equations, subroutines, and feedbacks, and the carrying out of various simulation experiments, at a cost of not enough work on careful specification of the underlying behavioral model. The requirement now is to organize existing data and to assure new data collection of a sort which will permit the kind of intermediate level behavioral analysis essential for really viable future general equilibrium models. In any event, the existing models appear all too often to be relatively "sexless" multipurpose machines which cannot sufficiently guide the direction of future research and policy; in fact, their construction and intelligent application may require further articulation of the central problem areas and of a research and policy agenda guided by this assessment. Based on earlier discussions in this chapter, some thoughts on what these priorities might be are considered, as are also the data requirements which underly pursuit of this strategy.

Basic preference clearly goes to the improvement of individual behavioral building blocks and their fortification on the research side before utilizing them at aggregative levels either in focusing on the consequences or determinants, or within a neutral general equilibrium context. Moreover, the search for causal rather than simple gratuitous relationships should be carried on not only as between fertility and mortality, on the one hand, and output as a whole, on the other, but between the demographic outcomes and the distribution of income as well. Such analyses of demographic and distributional relationships may, in fact, better illuminate the relationships of both with output growth.

For the immediate future, emphasis on smaller models focusing on the interrelations among population, output, and income distribution will provide better building blocks. Such models should have greater sensitivity to typological differences among developing countries and be able to accommodate varying historical subphases within particular types of countries. Moreover, the important laboratory for furthering understanding of these relationships lies less with aggregate cross-country studies as a proxy for socioeconomic differences within populations, and more with disaggregation of a particular society's population according to its socioeconomic characteristics. For particular types of developing countries—large or small, labor-abundant or land-abundant, natural-resource rich or natural-resource poor—more emphasis should be placed on within-country analytical/historical studies than has been true in the past. History remains our most reliable laboratory. Not only is the record of the so-called demographic transition available in Western Europe and, perhaps more relevant, in Japan, but also a quarter century of increasingly well-documented development experience in the contemporary developing countries can be drawn upon.

Acceptance of a focus on the family as the relevant unit of observation and action entails acceptance of the full income or product concept, a central ingredient of the proposed general economic-demographic system, both conceptually and empirically. This means more focus on activities within the household, both in their static and dynamic dimensions. Technology change in household non-market activities has hardly been considered in the literature or in program planning. Studies of the shift of household members, male and female, from nonmarket to market activities and the effects of labor shifts on household full income, market income, fertility, and the distribution of household income have great potential for improving our understanding of the overall development process. It is known that children affect the full income of households differently depending, for example, on the returns to child labor and schooling; such calculations, implicit or explicit, clearly affect the extent of the joint production system inside, and the composition of output outside the household.

Finally, it seems clear that virtually all the important linkages between population and income, running through income distribution directly or indirectly, can be clarified through analysis of the "differential demographic transition" being experienced by various socioeconomic groups within a country. Take, for example, the effect of fertility change on income and income distribution. If a lowering of fertility is initially confined to urban, higher income groups, the distribution of income will worsen, at least temporarily; when rural or lower-income families experience a subsequent and more substantial (percentage-wise) decline in fertility, income distribution will improve later on. Regarding the causal impact of income distribution on fertility it is known that as income increases fertility does fall but probably at a diminishing rate. Therefore, as income increases and is redistributed across the deciles in the population more fertility decline per unit of per capita increase may be registered in the lower deciles. But it is not known exactly why that happens or whether this result depends, as the demand framework suggests, upon the source of the income, i.e., whether it arises from land or labor or whether it is reflected in male or female labor productivity. A fuller analysis points to the need for not just looking at the income level and its distribution but at just how income is earned by the families. It is likely to make a substantial difference for nuptiality and fertility whether or not the additional income of rural families is generated in a secondary food crop, in cottage crafts, or in rural, organized industry. The literature on proto-industrialization within the Western European demographic transition may be relevant to this question, but it has not as yet been fully explored in terms of its relevance for contemporary developing economies.[61] Labor-intensive rural activities have clearly been a key part of the explanation for success in the small subset of LDCs where rapid growth has been consistent with the absence of the generally expected deterioration in the distribution of income.[62]

61. Franklin F. Mendels, "Proto-Industrialization: The First Phase of the Industrialization Process," *Journal of Economic History* 32 (1972); P. Deprez, "The Demographic Development of Flanders in the Eighth Century," in *Population in History*, edited by D. V. Glass and D. E. C. Eversley (London, 1965).

62. Based on a decomposition analysis of the Gini index across households, rural and urban, but without explicitly taking into account life cycle problems. However, the same study indicates that the age of head of household is not an important explanatory variable in determining the distribution of wage income, e.g., the wage Gini; thus it is not felt that the usual inability to handle the life cycle problem completely discredits these results. See J. Fei, G. Ranis, S. Kuo, *Growth with Equity: The Taiwan Case* (Oxford: At the University Press, 1979).

Interrelationships between mortality and income/income distribution have been even more neglected and should come in for more attention in the future. Regarding the consequences of mortality change for income/income distribution, the results on labor force and savings, of course, will depend again on the differential changes in mortality by socioeconomic group. Differential mortality across socioeconomic groups can increase inequality at first as the better-off capture more of the benefits of improved environmental health conditions. Later inequality may decline as mortality is reduced among the poor and rural families. For many parts of the world current tabulations of country data do not allow analysis of this question, and it is not really known at what stage the differential mortality transition is at present. Related sets of problems, also obstructing fuller understanding, include the interrelations between morbidity declines and labor productivity, and between mortality and fertility.[63]

But perhaps the most under-investigated area of all is the determinants of mortality, i.e., the effects of income/income distribution on the death rate and life expectancy. It is insufficiently understood, for example, the extent to which infant mortality decline is due to differential access to public investment such as information and technology, the extent to which it is due to private income differences which permit the household to make differential complementary investment and consumption decisions, and the extent to which the rate of diffusion and acceptance of innovations is itself related to education and other socioeconomic characteristics of families. If different income groups react differently with respect to these three possible explanations, different patterns of a relationship between income/income distribution and mortality rates will emerge. Such differences provide clues not only as to which of the above explanations dominates at the aggregative level but also as to the time path and location of the mortality decline that can be expected as an economy undergoes socioeconomic change.

The general conclusion here is that the forces bearing on both fertility and mortality in a given society differ both by income and other socioeconomic characteristics, such as location, and that the recognition of such differences is likely to be a necessary prelude for both analysis and policy. Such recognition may be one of the only ways to separate endogenous from exogenous variables, a serious problem in this field. There is an opportunity here not only to obtain illumination from differences by socioeconomic groups at one point in time but, also, from an investigation of the dynamics for given income and equity levels. Once the demographic transition is under way the establishment of phases by socioeconomic subgroups

63. The effects of child mortality on fertility are by now well established as a fruitful area for further within-country analysis to complement previous cross-sectional analysis. See Schultz, "Interrelationships."

with respect to both the consequences and determinants dimensions of the problem constitutes an invaluable input into the effort to enrich analysis. A combination of disaggregation and phasing analysis may be the best way to separate the "more" exogenous from the "more" endogenous in the fuller general equilibrium system of the future.

The role of the family as the critical analytical and decision-making unit both in terms of the determinants and the consequences side of the general equilibrium framework under discussion has been consistently emphasized. But the family concept itself as is well known is not the same in all societies and certainly is not a static concept in any given society. While change may be slow in any given cultural context, the evolution of the family structure itself in response to changing socioeconomic conditions can be observed. Thus, while in the short run the family may be treated as institutionally given or exogenous and the reactions of that family analyzed in a given societal environment with respect to the variables of interest, in the longer run it is endogenous and adapts itself to changing circumstances. Here the typological dimension of research emphasis on the comparisons between groups of developing countries is once again relevant, and here cross-country behavior differences are likely to be more instructive than in-country historical analysis. Nevertheless, in phasing of within-country economic-demographic behavior patterns over time, endogenous changes in the family structure may well be possible to identify by means of socio-economic decomposition analysis. Such changes in the family, from extended to nuclear, for example, are likely to constitute a relatively slow process. In this area, in particular, analysis would be substantially enriched by contributions from anthropologists and sociologists.

The importance of the meaning of "family" is illustrated most aptly in connection with the issue of migration and the possibility of a distinction between "family" and "household," depending on the socioeconomic milieu in which a society finds itself. Thus, partial migration may mean a return each night of family members to the family household or the part-time migration of males to the city, as in Africa, or females, as in Latin America, all of which have their special impact on the meaning of income, the nature of the intrafamily contract, the direction and size of remittance flows, and the impact on fertility and mortality as well as on income and income distribution.

The focus of attention on the family as opposed to the strict definition of the household places it at the crossroads between population, income, and equity which are the major objectives of contemporary development policy. The direct action or policy implications of constructing sturdier partial equilibrium building blocks within this general equilibrium economic-demographic framework will, of course, depend on the enhanced incremental understanding to be achieved in the course of time. For practical reasons, however, second-best policies must continue to be used as this accumulation of knowledge takes place; a policy moratorium can hardly be declared.

In recent years, for example, the emergence of a closer link between family planning and various dimensions of a broader family welfare goal has been witnessed. Nutrition or working opportunities for women have been included in population programs—while elsewhere the general call has gone out to examine the demographic dimension of all developmental activities. Some of this represents a shotgun approach; much of it is not really implementable in the absence of more detailed guidelines, but all of it would benefit from a more specific focus on socioeconomic groups. Future family-planning activities can be redefined and substantially strengthened in their effectiveness by being focused on particular socioeconomic target groups, particularly as research on differentials in fertility and mortality by group clarifies our understanding.

Another example of a possible arena for future government and international agency action is in the area of providing information and education on the nature of the relationships described at an easily comprehensible level for central and local government, as well as professional personnel. Because household production lays a claim on large portions of poor people's time, education and extension programs which fail to take into account the household sector may well be needlessly inefficient. Agricultural extension programs directed only at males will have less impact if women and children who are responsible for food storage and preparation are ignored. If crop changes require weeding or watering, chores often assigned to children, an increase in market income could simultaneously discourage child schooling, an unexpected result which should not be ignored. Many such mistakes arising from both the political oversell of past years and a lack of appreciation of the subtleties of the interactions matrix described can be avoided. A gradual shift, of say 10 percent a year, of human and budgetary allocations from traditional family-planning programs towards these kinds of activities might yield very substantial beneficial results. In some countries, moreover, it may be appropriate to support networks which provide traditional contraceptive information and technology within broader family welfare types of packages and focus on the socioeconomic setting within which, for example, family decisions on fertility and mortality, on savings and consumption are constantly being made. Using different types of family-planning packages or the same family-planning package over different socioeconomic groups may yield controlled experiments as a by-product, and constitute an important raw material for additional research to guide national and international policy interventions in the future, as discussed further below.

An incidental and not unimportant additional by-product of such research at the socioeconomic group level—for example, by urban vs. rural location of the families—is that it enhances the receptivity by decentralized public or private decision makers and thus encourages overall implementation via the imbedding of the results in their own activities in the field. An LDC central government can often obtain critical local decision-making cooperation only in this fashion. It is clear that the forces which bear on fertility and mortality in a given society differ markedly by income and by other socioeconomic indicators within the population. A better understanding of these is just as clearly a necessary prelude for the successful formulation of central government policy in the future.

Directions of Future Data-Related Efforts

It is not unusual to conclude that data lacunae inhibit the full development of our theoretical understanding and the subsequent improvement of our decision-making capacities. However, the opportunities to better use the experience of what has already been done, in the policy sense, and of what is already being collected in the statistical sense, are rather unique in this area of economic-demographic inquiry. The key here is relating already existing data to each other in a meaningful fashion, as well as the collection of new series. Both will be required before substantial headway can be made; but it is essential that it is first recognized that substantial information resources are already available, or at least potentially available, at the same time as an effort is made efficiently to fill in some of the gaps in the general economic-demographic matrix.

First of all, as has been suggested throughout this chapter, there is a growing need to understand the sources of variation across families and of change over time in family demographic and economic behavior. To proceed with the necessary analysis of these household behavioral patterns and resulting outcomes, data must be widely available in a form that admits to many forms of cross tabulation and ultimately the application of multivariate statistical techniques at the level of the individual family or household.

This requires that information from a large number of households drawn representatively from the population be converted to machine readable form and made available on magnetic tape that is readily used with modern electronic data-processing equipment. While collecting more detailed and refocused household economic-demographic surveys that can advance our knowledge of many specific and important processes in the household, existing data bases should be exploited without delay.

A population census enumeration may represent a very powerful resource for research and policy on these questions if it is converted to a machine readable sample in which only one in twenty or one in a hundred of the enumerated households is coded. It is understandably difficult to convince responsible officials that in spite of the great effort to collect a census of all persons in a country, a sample of only a few percent of this total can represent a more powerful resource for policymaking than the publication of several dozen two- and three-way tabulations by administrative units of the country. Yet the cost of sampling and coding a small percent of a census for multipurpose household studies can be a small fraction of the total census budget and is likely to be even cheaper than expanding the standard published tabulations marginally.

For the purposes of planning the regional allocation of public infrastructure such as roads and sanitation facilities, or the extension of public services such as schools and hospitals, a relatively large census sample can be far more useful to policy makers than a new large survey that inherently must be small by comparison with the census and therefore less accurate for questions regarding the small regions served by many public-sector projects and programs. Program evaluation, discussed in the next section, will also be greatly strengthened.

A relatively small survey can provide some evidence on the level and structure of national fertility because about one in four persons in a low-income country tends to be a woman of childbearing age, and as many as one-fifth of these women will have a birth each year. Thus the incidence of fertility may be as high as one in twenty. Migration may occur even more frequently among rural residents. But much larger samples are required to study mortality or fertility differentials across many socioeconomic groups. Only in the first year of life is mortality on the order of one in ten in very low-income populations; thereafter it is much less frequent. To obtain statistically meaningful estimates of the differences in mortality across socioeconomic groups of adult males or even preschool children, very large samples are imperative. Mortality estimates from simple retrospective information contained in censuses are being refined rapidly by Samuel Preston of the UN Population Division, and if large samples become widely available from national population censuses, knowledge of mortality determinants and consequences in low-income countries could progress markedly in the 1980s, with undoubtedly important repercussions on health and population policies.

As a reflection of the substantial value of the one-tenth of one percent public-use samples drawn from the 1960 U.S. census, this innovation was replicated on a much expanded one percent basis for many subsamples of the U.S. 1970 census. Indeed, the U.S. National Science Foundation has recently sponsored a multimillion dollar project to create similar multipurpose household samples from the 1940 and 1950 U.S. census manuscripts. With the opening of the U.S. census archives to the public after the lapse of a century, historians have begun individually to sample questionnaires collected in 1840 and 1860, years in which the census collected unusually detailed materials on fertility, income, and wealth. Several countries of Latin America have also begun sampling their censuses and creating public use files, and Costa Rica and Colombia now have two census samples in widespread use. Technical and financial support from UNFPA could be a catalytic agent in encouraging countries to prepare public use samples from their censuses of population before the original manuscripts are forever destroyed. Indeed, many countries would probably benefit from undertaking a similar task as being performed by the United States, namely, reconstructing a working sample from recent past censuses to facilitate a better understanding of how the demographic transition has progressed across various social and economic groups in the population. Unfortunately, many countries in the 1960 round of censuses did not collect valuable information on children ever born, recent fertility, child mortality, labor force attachment, and income. But where some of this information was collected in combination with the standard age, sex, education, and occupational detail, the census sample would be a valuable resource for social science research and, more important, for improved policy making in the future.

Secondly, research needs can more effectively be coordinated with current programs and policies. Population and development policy measures invariably alter not just one aspect of family behavior but exert their effect on a host of interrelated choices which diffuse over time to slowly change longer term, life-cycle allocational choices. Ideally, to understand the effects of policy interventions it would be desirable to have data based on an experiment in which randomly selected households were exposed to the policy. In principle, nothing more than a contingency table analysis would then be required to infer how behavior of experimental and control families differs, and thus what the effects of the policy intervention have been during a specified period. In other words, with such a classical controlled experiment, no theory identifying other exogenous conditioning factors in the family's environment or distinguishing jointly determined endogenous behavioral outcomes is required.

But, in fact, controlled experiments are rare, time consuming, costly, and often on reconsideration have defects of design that limit their generality. Some "natural experiments" are provided by nature, when climate, pests, disease, or luck affect different persons or groups or regions randomly. Political developments may scatter program interventions across regions in a seemingly random manner, but in this case caution is advised, for the allocation of public goods is undoubtedly responsive to political and economic pressures that are probably themselves dependent on the socioeconomic conditions and behavior of families.

In general, however, program interventions are not often experimentally allocated across families or communities. Hence, there is great value in the household-demand framework, since it enables the singling out of exogenous determinants of behavior, so that these determinants may be held constant with standard statistical techniques. The view of the family as an allocational unit coordinating demographic as well as economic decisions also clarifies which forms of household behavior are jointly determined and should not be directly held constant in evaluating the effect of policy interventions. The more complete is the understanding of the demand determinants of family behavior, such as fertility, the more precise an evaluation can be made of the effects of policy on fertility. This would be particularly so in the instances where the intensity of program activity or policy effort is associated with other exogenous socioeconomic circumstances that are thought to affect reproduction goals and the timing of fertility declines. For example, the use of family-planning clinics may be greater and the decline in birth rates initially more rapid in urban areas of a low-income country not because the clinics are responsible for the decline in fertility but because other "urban factors"—low child mortality, more educational opportunities, and better jobs for women—favor lower reproductive goals among urban residents. Both improvements in the household behavioral models and in the public availability of multipurpose family data files can strengthen social welfare policy evaluation in a number of important fields.

Still, even as theory is utilized and further developed as a substitute to controlled experiments, it would also be extremely valuable for evaluation purposes if new programs and variations in program strategies were extended first to a randomly selected set of administrative units. Systematic allocation of particular public services across regions could be coordinated to assure roughly similar expenditure levels in each administrative area for the *sum* of all program interventions, while still retaining the regional variation in program mix that is required for confident program evaluation. At the same time, it would be highly beneficial if UNFPA would encourage social welfare programs in family planning, maternal and child health, public sanitation, home economics and health extension, and child and adult schooling and training to maintain activity records by common administrative geographic units in which all activity was conventionally costed out in terms of identical current and capital accounting procedures. By such standardization in regional accounting and pilot program design in health, education, and family welfare programs, UNFPA would thereby set the stage for vast improvements in program evaluation in the social sector of developing countries in the 1980s.

Finally, some of the information specified in our proposed matrix, needed to understand the complex of family decisions and the manner in which these decisions are affected by economic change, does not exist in conventional demographic data collections—certainly not in censuses, and even not in many "fertility" surveys, such as KAP (knowledge, attitude, and practice of contraception) surveys or even the central module of the World Fertility Survey. Bits and pieces can be gleaned from, e.g., household expenditure surveys, farm management surveys in rural areas of developing countries, labor force surveys. But often information on the use of time within the household, especially by women and children, is missing; thus "full income" information is incomplete.

Time use studies are one approach to close this data gap. Though widely discussed and written about, only in a few isolated cases have such studies been successfully completed in developing countries, including one in the Philippines (Laguna), sponsored by the Agricultural Development Council and one in Malaysia, conducted under the auspices of the Rand Corporation and sponsored by U.S. AID.

Much of the knowledge gained from doing such pioneering work can be put to use in subsequent surveys in key countries. Given some overall technical guidance and financial support such studies could be arranged and conducted in selected countries by local research organizations. Their multiple value would be significant. It is one way to familiarize policy and program people in the developing countries with some of the problems and issues raised in this chapter. Individual researchers will use these data at different levels of aggregation for different purposes. But there can be little doubt that if the understanding of these subtle and complicated relationships is to be improved, continuing comparable data sets of this sort will be needed, permitting analysis to focus on relationships at different socioeconomic levels. Only in this way can a more than incrementally better understanding of the aggregative performance of the total system be ultimately achieved.

It should be re-emphasized that such a data system would have both static and dynamic dimensions. It would be general equilibrium in character as has been depicted above, but agnostic as to the nature of the causal relationships and certainly not premature in assigning causality. It would thus be possible to accommodate new parameter estimates as well as new theoretical linkages as and when better behavioral relationships are established through research in the various priority areas.

The way to get there is likely to be via smaller models, less ambitious in character, the results of which can be accommodated within the context of this general equilibrium framework without immediately aiming at a detailed, full-blown general equilibrium model. Since individual researchers at various institutions around the world are not in a position to initiate, much less maintain, such a broad economic-demographic data system, it is largely up to international institutions to support its creation and maintenance. Both the direction and quality of future work may largely depend on the initiation of such a strategy—starting perhaps in a few countries and moving on to a comprehensive international system over time. Such a framework would in time become a companion to the UN system of national accounts which now focuses mainly at the level of aggregative and market production sectors.

It should, in summary, be recognized that the objective here has essentially been limited: through emphasis on the general equilibrium character of behavior patterns suggesting ways in which the family as a decision-making unit can be related to aggregate growth and distributional equity, and exploring some of the conclusions for policy that flow from this better understanding. Neither all the facts nor the full conceptual apparatus are available to do so without considerable modesty; and, undoubtedly, as many questions have been raised as have been answered. But it is hoped and expected that greater awareness of these questions and their relation to each other, in the ways outlined in this chapter, will assist the search for better analytical and policy designs, both in international organizations and within countries at national and local levels.

9

Population and Development: The Japanese Experience

SABURO OKITA, TOSHIO KURODA,
MASAAKI YASUKAWA, YOICHI OKAZAKI,
AND KOICHI IIO

THE JAPANESE EXPERIENCE—AN OVERVIEW

Introduction

IT IS HOPED that this chapter, on the process of change in Japan's population and labor force under which economic growth occurred and the impact of this economic development on the population and labor force, will shed some light on the interrelationship between population and development.

The section entitled "Demographic Transition and Economic Development" examines how postwar Japan was able to complete in only ten-odd years the demographic transition which took Western Europe a half century. Demographic transition and economic growth in Japan are shown to have proceeded in parallel fashion but, as opposed to the Western European experience, to have arisen from separate sets of factors. The next section traces the relationship between population increases and economic development in Japan from the late nineteenth century and touches upon the effect of the rapid postwar aging of Japan's population on future economic development. "Structure of Labor Force and Economic Development" examines the progress of Japan's economic development in relation to the employment structure—primary, secondary, and tertiary industries. The final section discusses the socioeconomic factors behind Japan's massive internal migration during the post–World War II period of economic recovery and the subsequent years of rapid economic growth.

In-depth coverage of the relationship between economic development and population change cannot, of course, be provided by just the topics mentioned above. A comprehensive treatment of the subject would entail discussion of education, health and nutrition, government population policies, and the status of women. The present authors have directed their efforts more at a preliminary statement than at an all-embracing one, intending it to serve as a first step toward a more comprehensive approach in the future.

Population and Food

In the Japanese experience, the process of industrialization and development of agriculture from the late nineteenth century had a significant effect on the increase of the urban population and the industry-wide labor force composition. For example, the number of persons employed in the primary industries remained almost constant at 14 million from the late 1860s to the 1930s, while during that same period the population had doubled. This population, therefore, streamed to the secondary and tertiary industries. In the postwar period, the secondary and tertiary industries developed to the point where they began rapidly to absorb labor from the primary industries. The case is, however, different in today's developing countries. In the Japanese experience, the rate of population increase remained low in the early period of development. In today's developing countries, not only is the rate of population growth high but it is, also, not synchronized with industrialization. Population increase in the developing nations must, therefore, be absorbed by the agricultural sector, and consequently, economic development will be more difficult.

The age composition of Japan's population proved to be extremely advantageous during its period of rapid growth. The Japanese labor force was characterized by a young age structure with a relatively small proportion of aged—an age structure favorable to development. It may be said from the Japanese experience that if a developing country reaches a certain stage of development in the future, it may have a labor force structure similar to that of Japan.

Looked at from another angle, one of the most striking population changes in Japan was the postwar rise in the average life expectancy. In 1935, it was 46.92 years for males and 49.63 years for females. By 1977, this had risen to 72.69 and 77.95 years, respectively, giving the people of Japan one of the longest life expectancies in the world. On the other hand, the infant mortality rate, which stood at a high 138 per thousand in 1926, has recently fallen to 9.3. Advances in medicine and hygiene were the major contributors to this decline, but the general improvement in Japanese nutrition cannot be ignored. Before World War II, the average Japanese diet consisted primarily of rice, with protein being obtained from soybeans and fish. Postwar economic development and increased exports of industrial goods, however, created a substantial reserve of foreign currency with which it was possible to import large quantities of animal feed. This then increased the availability of meat and poultry.

This point should not be overlooked. Industrial development, therefore, both encourages the increase in urban population and leads to an improved diet through acquisition of foreign currency. The former often contributes to lowering fertility; the latter, to lowering mortality. A trial calculation shows that the per capita caloric intake, including calories in animal feed (original calories), is 10,000 per day in the United States and 4,000 per day in Japan. Japan can therefore feed a population 2.5 times greater than the United States with the same grain supply.

As several Food and Agriculture Organization studies[1] have previously shown, if the world population continues increasing at its present rate, most of the developing countries will lose almost all hope of improving the nutritional level of food intake of their people. The time factor is extremely important. Should effective measures fail to be taken within the next ten years to restrain the increase in population, the chance to solve the food and population problem may be lost altogether.

Solving these problems on a global scale is no easy matter. Japan, however, succeeded on a national scale: the food situation in the postwar period was extremely serious, but the government managed to improve radically the health and nutritional conditions of the people by disseminating information on good nutrition and conducting vigorous local campaigns. It enacted legislation promoting the study of dietetics and encouraging improved nutrition, helped train dietitians, and initiated a program of school lunches. Annual surveys on national nutrition were conducted and recommended nutritional standards established. Local campaigns featuring "kitchen-cars" and other measures were also launched. These campaigns were used simultaneously to spread information on family planning and birth control, effectively reducing the psychological inhibitions of housewives toward participation in family planning practice and promotional activities. Excellent results were also obtained from an integrated project for family planning and parasite control, started for similar reasons.

Education

A study of the interrelationship of economic development and population must necessarily include the role of education. Japan had already achieved a widespread grade-school education among its people in the late 1860s, and thus has traditionally had a high literacy rate. Freer access for

1. For instance, FAO *Agricultural Commodities; Projection for 1975 and 1985* (Rome: FAO, 1967).

mothers to information on contraceptive techniques proved to be a great plus in population control and was probably significant in the spontaneous spread of birth control practices.

Japan's early educational pyramid was extremely broad based. The government expended considerable time and effort in grade-school education but less so at the high school level. The general trend in developing countries, especially former colonies, is for a narrow educational base. The propagation of grade school-level education, however, may be considered one of the keys to successful population control and effective family planning.

Higher education in Japan became even more widespread after World War II. The percentage of students reaching high school rose from 52 percent in 1955, to today's high figure of 93 percent. This has been one of the factors behind the change in the life style of the average Japanese. For example, the considerable expense involved in putting one's children through high school increased the desirability of small families. Higher education among the female population has also encouraged more women to enter the labor pool, which is directly related to low fertility.

Higher education has even reached the rural areas in Japan. The effect this has had on closing the various gaps between the cities and rural areas should not be overlooked. Education undeniably plays a significant role in changing life styles and encouraging lower fertility and mortality.

Urbanization

The increase in the urban population which accompanies industrialization stops after a certain stage is reached, and the nature of the urbanization changes, i.e., when the growth rate of large cities reaches a plateau, local urban centers start to expand, and the gap between the standards of living in urban and rural areas narrows. As will be indicated below, Japan has already entered the stage of transition from concentration in large cities to rural dispersion. Developing countries will not have to face this for some time to come. The Japanese experience, however, demonstrates the possibility of this process.

Attention should be drawn to the role played by social overhead capital, especially the advancement of communication and transportation, in closing the gap between the large cities and rural areas. This has been one of the major factors promoting regional migration. Improved communication and transportation facilities encourage the concentration of population at one stage, but conversely, enable dispersion at the next. In the past, life in the big cities held a strong fascination for people in rural areas, especially for the young. Today, however, pollution, the deterioration in living conditions, the rise in housing costs, the increasing distance from natural surroundings, and other factors have reduced the allure of urban life. Japan has reached the stage where the people are re-evaluating large, medium, and small cities. Therefore, a certain stage in economic development, particularly development of the infrastructure, may be thought of as having a significant effect on the regional distribution of population.

Income and Population Dynamics

Japanese data may be used to clarify the relationship between income and birth and death rates. When the per capita income in Japan reached US $200–300, there was a sudden drop in both rates. Of course, conditions differ in other countries, but by plotting data from several Asian countries on a graph, as has been done in Figures 9.1 and 9.2, it can be shown that the above trend is fairly widespread.

There are exceptions. For example, the birth rate has refused to drop in Latin American countries even though the per capita income has reached a fairly high level. Several complex factors are involved here, primarily religious beliefs and income distribution.

It is widely believed in some advanced nations that an increase in the income of developing countries would only lead to larger populations. This is not necessarily true; indeed, the higher the income the lower the birth rate seems. Others hold that achievement of economic development and higher income must be given priority over everything else. True, the two are important factors leading to population stability, but because of the rapidity of today's world population increase, it would take too much time for the birth rate to drop naturally through just an increase in income. Two measures must be taken in tandem: indirect stabilization of population through higher income and direct reduction of the birth rate. The population dynamics of today's developing countries are somewhat different from those of yesterday's Japan. The drop in death rates is faster, and the birth rates are still high. Because of this, populations in these countries have been increasing extremely rapidly. This hard fact makes the use of direct measures advisable.

This all implies that the combination of the following five factors is important in effectively reducing the birth rate: a broad-based grade school education, an increase in the income level, improved nutrition, a rise in the social position of women, and decisive government action in population policies.

FIGURE 9.1
Birth Rate and Per Capita National Income

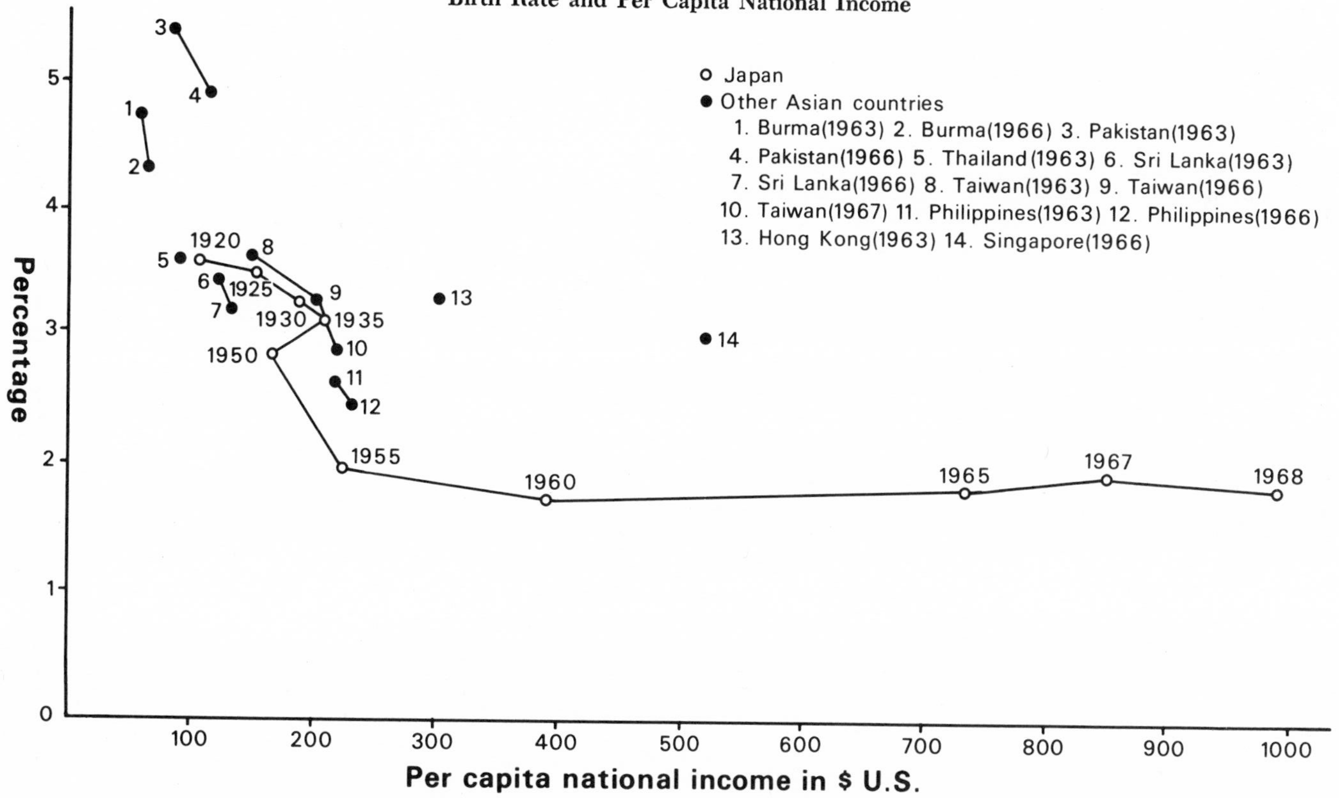

FIGURE 9.2

Death Rate and Per Capita National Income

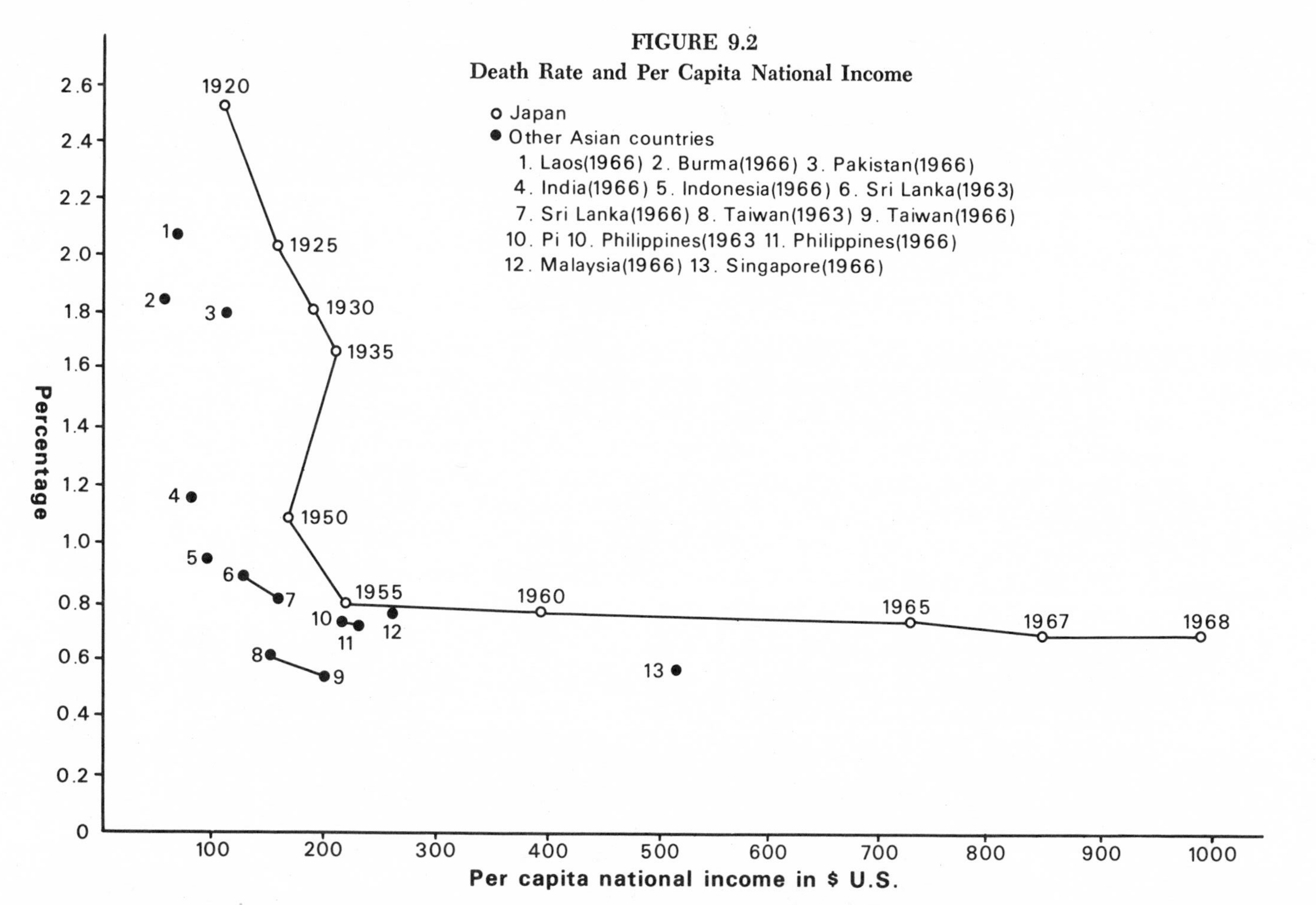

The demographic process which led to Japan's modernization was condensed in a relatively short period. It is possible to trace back the roles of employment, education, nutrition, and other factors in the process of Japan's transition from an undeveloped to a developed society. And since Japan began collecting statistical data at a relatively early date, it is also possible to obtain relatively long-term time series. The fact that Japan has historically not experienced major changes in its national boundaries nor massive external migrations means that its economic development was achieved in a kind of pure culture medium. Japan's experience in economic development and population change should, therefore, provide many useful examples on the best path for modern developing countries.

DEMOGRAPHIC TRANSITION AND ECONOMIC DEVELOPMENT

Modernization and Population in Japan

Both economic development and the population trends acting upon it are topics of great significance in the 100-year history of Japan's modernization. Japan's modernization began with the first attempts at copying and imitating Western European civilization. Although the process of development was not always direct, it was for the most part steady. In the meantime, Japan was blessed with both a large population and a plentiful labor force. The size of the labor force meant workers could be hired for low wages—it was cheaper to employ manual labor than to purchase machinery. Economic development from the late 1860s was assisted by both the cheap and ample labor supply and the greater amount of work the people had to perform because of their low wages and remuneration. Japan's characteristic thirst for knowledge and other factors also contributed significantly to rapid development.

The hard life of the people created a "poverty mentality" which exists today. This has had the effect of suppressing overpopulation. In other words, it was commonly believed that the smaller the population, the better life would be. In 1868, Japan had a population of 35 million. Today, it holds more than three times as many people, 110 million, and its economy has developed to the point where its GNP ranks third in the world. A threefold rise in population over 100 years might seem rapid at first glance, but it actually amounts only to an annual one percent increase. Looking back, Japan's population increase has been fairly low since the start of its modernization. The economic growth rate from 1868 to 1912 is estimated to have been approximately 4 percent per year. Consequently, an average 3 percent improvement per year can be inferred for the standard of living during that same period.

Postwar Population Trends

Japan's population passed 100 million in 1967, and reached 114.15 million in 1977. This means that there was an increase of thirty-eight million, from the seventy-two million in 1945, in only a thirty-year period. From a contemporary viewpoint, the population at the end of the war might seem to have been small; however, these seventy-two million were living in a war-devastated, defeated country and were hovering around the starvation line. The people became conscious of the dangers of overpopulation because of food shortages.

At the same time there was a vast influx of soldiers and civilians returning to the islands. Even with the large-scale repatriations of Koreans, Taiwanese, and other nationals from Japan, these soldiers and civilians swelled the population by another five million. Peace also brought with it a temporary explosion in the birth rate, resulting in eight million more children in the three years from 1947 to 1949. By 1950, the population had thus risen to eighty-three million.

The effect of newly introduced medicines and hygienic practices on the death rate soon became felt. The death rate dropped from the postwar 16–17 per 1,000, finally settling at the slightly over 6 per 1,000 of today.

Though the birth rate had shot up to 34 per 1,000 from 1947 to 1949, it was subsequently brought under control. The people were too busy providing for their existing families to want to produce more children, and the rate of births began to follow the downward path taken by the death rate. In less than ten years it had already halved and by 1957 had dropped to slightly over 17 per 1,000. Bottoming out at 17.0 in 1961, it hovered for a while and then showed a slight upturn. (The 13.8 recorded in 1966 was a special case due to the traditional folk belief that girls born in this year, Hinoe-uma, "Firehorse," would make poor wives.) This rise resulted from the young people born during the 1947–49 baby boom reaching the marrying age. The birth rate rose slightly from 19.2 to 19.4 in 1971 to 1973, but dropped again to 18.6 in 1974, and continued falling, reaching 17.1 in 1975, 16.3 in 1976, and 15.5 in 1977. This signified the end of the second baby boom.

The economy of Japan during the postwar period was fraught with confusion and inflation, but the outbreak of the Korean War in 1950 set Japan on the path toward steady economic reconstruction. As for population, the number of births declined, the burden of child raising lightened, and a potential for high purchasing power built up, a factor of value in economic development. The government formulated a program to double income in 1960 and was subsequently able to achieve rapid growth.

The government had a difficult time providing people with food and employment in the first ten years after World War II. The economic programs of the late fifties, however, eliminated the danger that the pressure of the increasing labor force would make modernization of the low productivity sectors difficult.

After 1960, technical revolutions stimulated the growth of the heavy and chemical industries. The changes in the industrial structure caused by Japan's rapid growth resulted in different conditions in the labor market and brought about a need for a larger labor force. Up until then, migration in Japan had been due to pressures from overpopulated rural areas. This condition changed with Japan's increasing industrialization and urbanization, and migration became due to the attraction of urban areas; it is the cause of today's crowded cities and underpopulated rural areas. What needs to be discussed are the effects of the migration, rather than the migration itself, and the changes they work on the community.

The period up until the late sixties or early seventies is known as Japan's high growth era or "golden age." All effort was directed to achieving the economic goal of boosting the GNP. Japan managed to develop its economy to a level comparable with the advanced nations and to implant the concept among the people that Japan was an economic giant. It was here that Japan's population problem became detached from the food problem. The traditional population problem disappeared.

Demographically, Japan changed quickly to a nation characterized by low fertility and mortality, as exemplified by the change in the average life expectancy. In 1971, it finally broke through the Western European level of 70 years for males and 75 years for females and by 1977 had reached a record 72.69 years and 77.95 years, respectively. It might appear from this that Japan had solved its population problem, but in reality this was not the case.

Although Japan managed to join the ranks of economically advanced nations, it simultaneously became burdened with new population problems. The giant industrial productivity of the advanced nations serves to increase the consumption of its beneficiaries. Consequently, consumption of natural resources rises, and the problems of ecological damage and pollution as well as energy shortages then become added to the list of national considerations. As noted above, even the slow population increases in advanced nations have now become problematical. Considering this along with the population explosion now occurring in the developing nations, it becomes clear that the world will soon be pressured by population on one side and limited resources on the other. The only path remaining for survival of the human race is controlling births to match the declining death rate. Of course, conditions differ in each country. In applying such controls, a more sophisticated approach must be used, taking into consideration various internal factors.

Japan has recently entered a stage of low economic growth, and labor surpluses are troubling the industrial world. Surveys show that during the high-growth era of the sixties, city residents, who formed the majority of the total population, felt for a while that living conditions were too crowded, and there was a shortage of people in productive sectors. Today, Japanese society has become more diversified, and there are regional variations in population and a distorted age distribution.

The regional variations in population were caused by the population concentration in the cities. The problem is excessive concentration and overdispersion. The distortion in age distribution manifests itself as an extremely large population in the age groups caused by the postwar baby boom. The large numbers of children born between 1947 and 1949 have now reached 29–31 years of age. This boom was followed by a decline in births, and there is consequently a smaller younger population.

The increase in the average life expectancy of the Japanese has also produced larger numbers of senior citizens. Social security and medical insurance for the elderly have now become important issues. Vigorous efforts to adjust the population imbalances and the distorted age distribution for the future welfare of society have become essential.

Demographic Transition

Studies of recent structural changes in Japan's population reveal the great significance of postwar population movements. Especially important were the drop in the death rate and the subsequent fall in the birth rate. Figure 9.3 shows the trends in Japan's population changes since 1900. The postwar period is particularly noticeable. But first, the population trends caused by the changes in the economy and society will be considered.

There is a basic relationship between population and economic development. Countries with high birth and death rates rank low in economic development. Conversely, countries with highly developed economies have low rates. Every highly developed nation had high birth and death rates in the past when it was still economically immature but achieved low rates upon reaching its present position.

The demographic transition in postwar Japan is of particular interest. Western Europe took more than half a century to complete the transition to low fertility and mortality. This same transition was accomplished in Japan in just ten years. The Western European experience, however, is understood as a manifestation of the rapid economic growth of the late

FIGURE 9.3
Birth Rate and Death Rate

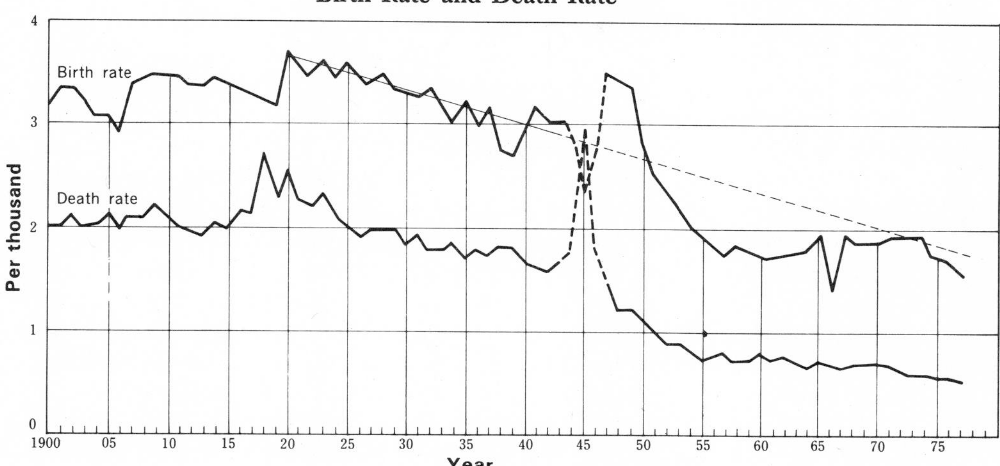

nineteenth century. In Japan's case, the demographic transition was a separate phenomenon, caused by factors unrelated to economic growth, yet proceeding in parallel with it.

Bearing this in mind, the period directly after World War II as shown on Figure 9.3 is especially noteworthy. The Japanese economy and society were in a state of confusion and saw no real development. However, the death rate began to fall, and a rapid decline was also seen in the birth rate after the 1947–49 baby boom. Both rates declined more than half in the ten years after the war, an unprecedented world record.

The drop in the death rate resulted from the introduction of new medicines and dissemination of new hygienic practices. This proves once more that economic development is not necessary for such a drop, as developing countries today are experiencing.

The drop in the postwar birth rate, too, was not a result of economic development but was, rather, a product of the confusion which followed the war and the hard life during that period.

There was a temporary spurt in the birth rate causing the baby boom, but this occurs in all countries after a war due to the repatriation of overseas personnel after the termination of hostilities and their return to married life, plus an increase in marriages. After this temporary period passes, the birth rate generally begins to decline.

To determine the actual period when Japan's demographic transition began, the trend from 1920 to 1945 was found and the line extended to the postwar period. This line intersects the postwar birth rate between 1951 and 1952. Of course, the line cannot be extended indefinitely, but the fact that the birth rate after 1955 remained below it indicates that the birth rate was consciously suppressed. Japan's postwar demographic transition can, therefore, be considered to have started around 1950. The rate later bottomed out at 17.0 in 1961 and then showed a gradual recovery (the 13.8 recorded in 1966 was a special case). The line then intersects the birth rate again in 1972. It may be assumed that if World War II and the subsequent period of confusion had not occurred, the slow decline of the birth rate which began in 1920 would have continued. Thus the rapid postwar demographic transition began in 1950 and ended roughly twenty years later in 1972. Japan has now returned to the slow prewar demographic transition which began in 1920. However, since the children produced in the postwar baby boom have now come of marrying age and a second baby boom has been experienced, a new situation must be projected for the future. That is to say, the rapid postwar demographic transition ended in 1972. The prewar demographic transition also saw its completion here. This is of particular interest in studying future birth trends.

It is interesting to compare the Japanese experience in its demographic transition with that of Western Europe, where the transition accompanied a continuous process of economic development. Postwar Japan's experience was different in that it resulted from conscious efforts on the part of the people, who at that time faced serious hardships in their daily lives. Thus such a demographic transition need not be coupled with economic growth. This is one of the lessons to be gained from Japan's experience by nations on the road to development.

In brief, Western Europe's demographic transition from the nineteenth to the twentieth century resulted from a prior process of continuous economic development. Japan's demographic transition in the twenty years after World War II, however, was a conscious one proceeding in parallel with the full-scale economic reconstruction starting in 1950. The case of developing countries today is the opposite of that of the Western European nations. If the demographic transition does not precede development, it will be impossible to improve the standards of living of the nation.

Migration

Migration is one of the strongest of the structural changes of population that influence population trends. Migration will be discussed in more depth later; here its main features are discussed only in terms of changes in the employment structure.

Migration in a stable economy and society is of the outflow type and is caused by population pressure; people are pushed out from rural areas and stream to the cities. This migration is, therefore, only the search for employment opportunities; even though when these people reach the cities, they are forced to work for low wages.

With a technical revolution, however, as was the case in Japan in the sixties with its heavy and chemical industries, labor productivity rises and there is a simultaneous stimulation of related industries. The opening up of new employment opportunities resulted in the start of inflow migration. Society itself is modernized through this industrialization, and rapid urbanization is encouraged. The concentration of people from rural areas in the cities intensifies the migration. At the same time, the people are awakened and the old way of life is destroyed. Education becomes more widespread and the age of marriage rises. Even reproductivity is influenced.

Industrialization also leads to the development of new medicines and public hygiene, which brings down the death rate. With migration, however, the decline is generally due to the move from high mortality poor areas favoring early marriages and large families to low mortality areas with greater economic opportunities and higher standards of living which favor late marriages and small families. It must be remembered that this promotes the drop in the death and birth rates. Now, the city not only stirs up the dreams of young people living in backward areas, but it also attracts a young labor force because of its industrialization. Therefore, migration also affects age distribution and plays a large role in changing the nature of a population.

POPULATION INCREASE AND ECONOMIC DEVELOPMENT

Japan's Population Increase

Japan's modern growth period began in 1868, the year of the Meiji Restoration. Approximately 260 years before that, the period starting with the establishment of the Edo shogunate government and commonly known as the Edo Period, was also an important phase for Japan. During the Edo Period, Japanese society was basically agricultural in nature and was built along feudalistic lines. Society was controlled by a strong centralized government. Yet, in those years various socioeconomic conditions changed.

Two contrasting trends in population in the Edo Period are apparent: strong growth in the first half and weak growth in the second. Studies by contemporary historical demographers indicate that the population at the beginning of the seventeenth century was from ten to twelve million people.[2] By the middle of the eighteenth century, this had risen to about thirty million. This means there was an increase of from 18 to 20 million in about 120 years, or an annual rise of 0.8 percent to 0.9 percent. This was almost the same as that experienced in the late nineteenth century, but the reason for this comparatively high rate must be examined.

The population increase in the seventeenth and early eighteenth centuries was caused by a rapid rise in both the marriage and birth rates. More than 200 castle towns, including the giant cities of Edo (modern Tokyo) and Osaka, were formed throughout the nation. In the rural areas, the small family unit, based around the husband and wife and including the lineal relatives, made its appearance.

On the other hand, the improved standard of living brought the death rate down sharply, especially for infants and children, which proved to be another major factor behind the population increase.[3] It is possible to observe here an example of the interrelationship between population increase and economic growth in a premodernization period.

In contrast to this, the population increased only slightly during the mid-eighteenth to nineteenth centuries. The population in 1868 has been estimated at approximately thirty-five million people. Consequently, there was an increase of only 5 million in slightly under 150 years, or an annual rate of only 0.1 percent. In the prewar period, it was theorized that this was due to the loss of vigor of the feudalistic society.[4] Recently, however, historical demography has provided information suggesting that the demographic characteristics of the cities of the premodern society, e.g., the high death rate and the low birth rate, were the main causes.[5] This new theory will have to be checked as further studies on the historical demography of Edo Period cities are made. It is highly significant, however, in that it provides a new explanation for the premodern population-economy relationship.[6]

Now, what about the population increase from 1868 to the present? Much more reliable statistical materials on population are available for

2. Hiroshi Shinbo, Akira Hayami, Shunsaku Nishikawa, *Introduction to Quantitative Economic History* (Tokyo: Nihon Hyoron-sha, 1975), pp. 42–49.

3. *Ibid.*, p. 47.

4. Ryozaburo Minami *et al.*, eds., *Encyclopedia of Population* (Tokyo: Heibonsha, 1967), p. 329.

5. Hiroshi Shinbo, Akira Hayami, Shunsaku Nishikawa, *Introduction to Quantitative Economic History*, p. 58.

6. The following is a representative work on this subject: Society of Socioeconomic History, ed., *In Search of New Concepts of Edo Period History* (Tokyo: Toyo Keizai Shimpo-sha, 1977).

this period. However, modern population surveys, that is, censuses, only began to be made from 1920. And estimates of demographers have to be used for the years before 1920. There has been considerable research in this area, however, and fairly definitive estimates have been established only since World War II. Table 9.1 gives figures for Japan's population from 1865 to the present. Figures from 1865 to 1920 are based on estimates of Masaaki Yasukawa of Keio University,[7] while those from 1920 on are from government population censuses and population estimates.

Table 9.1 reveals the following: First, the slow population increase which had lasted from the mid-eighteenth to nineteenth centuries accel-

TABLE 9.1
Population Increase in Japan

Year	Total population (thousands)	Increase (%)
1865	34,505	0.51
1868	35,033	0.50
1870	35,384	0.64
1875	36,528	0.88
1880	38,174	0.75
1885	39,634	0.69
1890	41,020	0.70
1895	42,472	0.88
1900	44,393	1.07
1905	46,825	1.17
1910	49,637	1.29
1915	52,949	1.11
1920	55,963	1.31
1925	59,737	1.52
1930	64,450	1.44
1935	69,254	1.08
1940	73,114	−0.25
1945	72,200	2.84
1950	83,200	1.41
1955	89,276	0.91
1960	93,419	1.01
1965	98,275	1.08
1970	103,720	—

SOURCE: 1865 to 1920: Estimates of Masaaki Yasukawa, Keio University; 1920 to 1970: Population Census.

Note: Rate of increase is the average annual rate compared with the next year.

7. Masaaki Yasukawa, *Economics of Population,* 3rd rev. ed. (Tokyo: Shujusha, 1977), pp. 182–83.

erated once again with Japan's modernization drive. Second, the population increase rate was comparatively low during the period when the government was devising measures to modernize the country and striving for economic and social development. The rate was strikingly different from those of countries now in their early stages of development. Third, the rate of population increase began to rise as the industrial and social base for modernization grew stronger and the economy was set on the road to steady development. It reached its highest levels during 1925–35. Fourth, the rate of population increase gradually declined after 1935. Severe fluctuations in the increase rate were seen during the Sino-Japanese War, World War II, and the postwar period due to such disruptive factors as the dispatch overseas and subsequent return of military personnel and civilian employees and the postwar baby boom. The leap in the rate of increase after 1970, as shown in Table 9.2, reflects the arrival at the connubial and childbearing age of the group born in the postwar baby boom and the subsequent second baby boom.

Economic Development and Population Increase

The relation between economic development and population increase from 1968 to the present has changed with each development stage. This suggests that although it is possible to discuss the relationship between population and development in theory, such a discussion would yield few results of any practical value.

TABLE 9.2
Recent Population Increase in Japan

Year	Total population (thousands)	Increase (%)
1970	104,665	1.37
1971	106,100	1.41
1972	107,595	1.40
1973	109,104	1.35
1974	110,573	1.24
1975	111,940	1.03
1976	113,089	0.94
1977	114,154	—

SOURCE: Government of Japan, Prime Minister's Office, Bureau of Statistics, *Estimated Population.*

Note: Figures after 1970 included Okinawa, though actual reversion was in 1972.

THE PREWAR PERIOD

The population increase in the late nineteenth century was rather a slow one and consequently, as already pointed out, did not obstruct economic or social development. In addition, as explained in the section on demographic transition and economic development, the population increase during this period was induced and caused by the development of the economy. In other words, the increase of the economy kept pace with the expanding population-supporting capacity on the economic side. While the population was increasing passively in this way, it also served as the source of supply for the labor force required by the growing industries. In this sense, it contributed positively to Japan's early economic growth.

Of note here was the dual structure of the economy. Two sectors existed side by side: a growth sector based around the modern industrial plants, originally managed by the government and later transferred to private ownership; and a traditional sector consisting primarily of small farms continuing from before 1868. The former demanded more people for its labor force, and the latter supplied them. Fertility was high in the traditional farm sector. After the labor force needed for its own reproduction was secured, the excess was sent to the growth sector. Because of this, for example in the roughly thirty-year period from 1878 to 1911, although the population had increased by 12.79 million and the number of employed by 7.42 million, there was an increase of only 610,000 employed in the primary industries. During this same period, the number of persons employed in the secondary industries had risen by 3.06 million and in the tertiary industries by 3.75 million.[8]

As the economy developed in this way, Japan's population increased at an ever faster rate. The economic structure shifted from light industries to heavy and chemical industries and was transformed from a labor-intensive model to a capital- and technology-intensive model. Japan became more and more overpopulated from the turn of the century on.

When the post–World War I economic boom ended, the world was thrown into an economic recession. Japan did not, of course, escape its effects. It was then that the seriousness of Japan's overpopulation was realized—directly and indirectly. Scholars began to discuss the problem, and the government deliberated on measures to cope with it, establishing a special committee to study population and food problems in 1927. Two years later, the American demographer Warren S. Thompson pointed out

8. Kazushi Ohkawa, ed., *The Growth Rate of the Japanese Economy Since 1878* (Tokyo: Kinokuniya, 1956), pp. 130–31.

the potential threat to world peace of Japan's overpopulation in his book, *Danger Spots in World Population.*[9]

Japan's population increase thus gradually began to obstruct rather than aid its economic and social development. A rational solution to the population problem was not found, and Thompson's prophesy finally came true when Japan resorted to war.

THE POSTWAR PERIOD

In the end, Japan was not able to solve its population problems through force. In fact, the war struck a stinging blow to its economy and swelled the population on the islands by another five million people. The military personnel and civilians returning from overseas areas more than offset the Koreans, Taiwanese, and other foreign nationals repatriated from Japan. Added to this was the natural increase of five million caused by the postwar baby boom. Thus from 1945 to 1950, Japan's population grew at the abnormally high rate of 2.8 percent per year for a total increase of 11 million, and Japan was confronted with a population problem even more serious than that of the prewar years.

The only method of birth control open to the people at this time was illegal abortion. Information on contraception and contraceptive implements were still not readily available. The situation changed in 1948 when the Eugenic Protection Law was enacted, legalizing abortions in certain cases. This law was amended several times, and the conditions under which abortions were permitted gradually relaxed. Then, in 1952, the family planning program and related activities of the Ministry of Health and Welfare began to start on a full-scale basis.

Because there was a strong conscious desire among the people to keep the number of births down, and because of the measures taken, Japan managed to realize a sharp drop in its birth rate. For example, there were 2.68 million births in 1947 for a crude birth rate of 34.3 per thousand. Ten years later, in 1957, this had fallen to 1.57 million and 17.2 per thousand, respectively. Since there was a sharp parallel decline in the death rate, however, no pronounced decline in the actual rate of population increase was shown. The settling of Japan's population in the postwar period into a low-fertility and low-mortality model was extremely significant from the point of view of economic development.

Postwar Japan was blessed with unexpectedly favorable economic conditions, which encouraged its rapid growth. This growth both created

9. Warren S. Thompson, *Danger Spots in World Population* (New York: Knopf, 1929).

the conditions under which low fertility and mortality became possible and set off a massive, rarely seen migration altering the distribution of the population and labor force. While demographic factors had little directly to do with this rapid growth itself, they played an important role in determining what its effects were.

At the end of its economic reconstruction period, Japan entered a new growth phase. Table 9.3 shows the economic growth rate after 1955 (real gross national expenditure) and the rate of population increase. The table makes it immediately apparent that the economic growth rate was generally extremely high. While the prewar economic growth rate was an average 4 percent per year, considered high compared with other nations,[10] it more than doubled after the war. Compared to this, the increase in the

TABLE 9.3
Postwar Economic Growth and Population Increase

Year	Economic Growth (%)	Population Increase (%)	Difference (%)
1955	6.1	1.0	5.1
1956	7.8	0.8	7.0
1957	6.0	0.9	5.1
1958	11.2	1.0	10.2
1959	12.5	0.8	11.7
1960	13.5	0.9	12.6
1961	6.4	0.9	5.5
1962	12.5	1.0	11.5
1963	10.6	1.1	9.5
1964	5.7	1.1	4.6
1965	11.1	0.8	10.3
1966	13.1	1.2	11.9
1967	12.7	1.1	11.6
1968	11.0	1.2	9.8
1969	10.4	1.2	9.2
1970	7.3	1.4	5.9
1971	9.8	1.4	8.4
1972	6.4	1.4	5.0
1973	—0.3	1.4	—1.7
1974	3.4	1.2	2.2
1975	5.7	1.0	4.7

SOURCE: Economic growth percentages are based on *Annual Report on National Income Statistics* published by the Economic Planning Agency, Government of Japan, annually for the period of 1955–75; population increase percentages are based on, *Estimated Population in Japan* published annually by the Bureau of Statistics, Prime Minister's Office, Government of Japan.

10. Kazushi Ohkawa, Nobukiyo Takamatsu, Yuzo Yamamoto, *National Income* (Tokyo: Toyo Keizai Shimpo-sha, 1974).

postwar population was low, but not so low as a rate, per se. The average annual increase was about 1 percent, while in the early seventies it was a fairly high 1.4 percent.

This high economic growth was supported by an uncommonly fast rise in productivity. Despite this, the demand for labor became stronger. The traditional agricultural sector was not able to fill this demand with its excess labor force alone, unlike in prewar days, and consequently, was seriously drained of its own manpower. This drain is visible in the absolute and comparative decline in both the number of persons employed in the primary industries and the rural population. In 1955, there were 16 million persons employed in the primary industries, 41 percent of the total number of employed. By 1970, this had fallen to 10 million, or 19 percent. The rural population dropped in the same period from 40 million people, or 44 percent, to 29 million, or 28 percent. In addition, during the high growth period, approximately eight million production units, composed of the group born during the postwar baby boom, reached productive age. All this meant that the growth industries were favored with a plentiful new labor force. The rapid economic growth of the postwar period brought a temporary solution to the overpopulation problem—one which the government had previously attempted to solve by force of arms. In addition, it dissolved the old dual structure of the economy which had characterized prewar Japan and spread the practice of birth control from the prewar urban white-collar class to the blue-collar and farmer classes. An epochal change was realized in population reproduction, with low fertility becoming the pattern nationwide. Together with the simultaneous drop in mortality, it set the population trends of the future and is of great significance in economic development in the years to come.

Aging of Population and Economic Development

Assuming that the birth and death rates remain stable at their current low levels,[11] it is possible to project fairly accurately the future trends of Japan's population. Table 9.4 shows the estimated size of the population in the future as well as the proportion of the over-65 group. The following may be pointed out in relation to the table.

1. The population increase will continue for the time being. By the end of the century, there will be over 130 million people on the islands. The increase will continue further until a stationary population is achieved in the middle of the twenty-first century.

11. Although the birth rate dropped after 1974, breaking the previous stability, this point is not considered here.

TABLE 9.4
Future Population Projections

Year	Total Population (thousands)	Increase (%)	Over-65 Group	Proportion of over-65 Group (%)
1975	111,940	1.0	8,865	7.9
1980	117,563	0.8	10,436	8.9
1985	122,333	0.6	11,909	9.7
1990	126,280	0.6	13,909	11.0
1995	130,065	0.6	16,503	12.7
2000	133,676	—	19,061	14.3

SOURCE: Government of Japan, Ministry of Health and Welfare, Institute of Population Problems, *Estimated Future Population of Japan,* 1976.

2. The rate of population increase, however, will gradually decline, falling below 1 percent a year. At the start of the twenty-first century, the rate of increase will be even more sharply curbed, finally dropping to zero.

3. Both the size of the over-65 group and its proportion in the total population will rapidly rise.

4. The proportion of children (fourteen years and under) will gradually decline.

5. The proportion of dependents (children and the over-65 group) to the productive age group (15–64), or what is known as the dependency ratio, will rise.

6. Although there will be almost no increase in the strata of the productive-age group (15–39), the middle-age strata (40–64) will increase greatly. In other words, the productive-age group will become more middle-aged.

The above changes are almost postulates of what will take place in Japan's population in the future. The question now is what impact these will have on economic development and what new measures will be required to deal with them.

Of course many factors besides demographic ones have an influence on economic trends. It would be extremely difficult to predict exactly how the economy will move in the future, and a monumental amount of work to do that is involved. Here, only the direct and indirect effects of future population changes on economic development will be examined:

1. The increase in the number of dependents, primarily the over-65 group and their proportion in the total population will bring a corresponding increase in consumption expenditure in the Gross National Expenditure (GNE). The proportion of investment expenditure, including demographic investment for children, will drop.

2. Since there will be an increase in the demand for health, medical,

and welfare services for the elderly, a considerable proportion of the manpower in the productive age group will have to be directed toward those sectors.

3. The comparative decline in the young, new labor force in the working population will reduce the flexibility of the industrial structure to make changes.

4. The comparative increase in the middle- and upper-age labor force will cause the amount of wage payments of companies operating under Japan's traditional seniority-based wage system to swell.

5. The burden of support for dependents shouldered by the middle and upper groups will become much heavier, both directly and indirectly, with less child support more than offset by the higher costs of support of the elderly.

Judging from this, the economic burden caused by the aging of the population will more than offset the benefits of the gradually reduced rate of population increase. In the same way as people gradually lose their energy after reaching an advanced age, the population also loses its energy as it ages. Japan will have to be satisfied with a correspondingly low economic growth. The experience of the advanced Western European nations is a precedent, and Japan's population is fated to follow the same course.

STRUCTURE OF LABOR FORCE AND ECONOMIC DEVELOPMENT

Long-Term Trends of Employment Structure

The trends in Japan's working population over the last century are given in Table 9.5 for the primary, secondary and tertiary industries. The following may be pointed out:

1. Roughly 100 years ago, agriculture and other primary industries accounted for 82.3 percent of persons employed. After the end of World War I, their proportion had fallen to approximately 50 percent, and the decline continued. Although a temporary rise was shown in the period of confusion following the end of World War II, the speed of decline in general accelerated rapidly, and by 1975, their proportion had shrunk to 13.9 percent.

2. The secondary industries, principally manufacturing, illustrate the progress of Japan's economic industrialization. In direct opposition to the primary industries, they showed a tendency to increase proportionately. The secondary industries absorbed a particularly large labor force during the rapid industrialization that followed World War II.

TABLE 9.5
Composition of Working Population by Industry

Year	Primary	Secondary	Tertiary
1878–1882	82.3	5.6	12.1
1898–1902	69.9	11.8	18.3
1913–1917	59.2	16.4	24.4
1920	53.6	20.7	23.8
1930	49.4	20.4	30.0
1940	44.0	26.1	29.2
1950	48.3	21.9	29.7
1955	41.0	23.5	35.5
1960	32.6	29.2	38.2
1965	24.6	32.3	43.0
1970	19.3	34.1	46.5
1975	13.9	35.1	50.7

SOURCE: For 1878 to 1917, Kazushi Ohkawa, ed., *The Growth Rate of the Japanese Economy since 1878* (Tokyo: Kinokuniya, 1956); and for 1920 to 1975, Government of Japan, Prime Minister's Office, Bureau of Statistics, *Population Census* for each year.

3. The proportion of population engaged in the sectors of primary and secondary material production has steadily declined, while those employed in the tertiary industries has, conversely, expanded. Recently, the number of persons employed in the material production sector and service industry sector have been roughly the same.

Therefore, Petty's Law has proven consistently valid in Japan. As W. Petty and C. Clark emphasized, the income elasticity of demand for farm produce is less than 1 while that for other produce is greater than 1. As a result, the proportion held by the primary industries in the production value sharply dropped while those of the secondary and tertiary industries rose.[12]

Internationally, Japan belongs to that group of nations with a fairly high proportion of tertiary industries. To reach this point it underwent the process outlined above. Many developing countries already have had a very large proportion of tertiary industries from an early stage. It must be noted that even though the proportions of persons employed in the tertiary industries are large, the process by which Japan reached that point differed from other developing countries. Discussed below is the process of economic change Japan's employment structure underwent to reach its present form, by industrial grouping.

12. William Petty's experimental law that the labor force or capital tend to shift from the primary industry to the secondary and then to the tertiary in the course of industrial development. See C. Clark, *The Conditions of Economic Progress* (New York: Macmillan, 1960), pp. 490–520.

Vicissitudes of the Primary Industries

Agriculture has played an extremely important role in the process of development of the Japanese economy since 1868. It provided a supply of food sufficient for a growing population and higher levels of income, and through exports of raw silk and other commodities was a major source of foreign currency. In the late nineteenth century, over 80 percent of the labor force was engaged in the primary industries. These industries have continued to supply the workers needed by the nonagricultural sectors up until the present, when they account for slightly over 10 percent of the work force. Further, the capital needed for development of the nonagricultural sectors was supplied from agriculture to the nonagricultural industries through, e.g., land rents.

Japan's agricultural development from 1880 to 1965 is often classified into six major periods, as shown in Table 9.6. Production of rice, Japan's main crop, has increased about 2.5 times in the approximately 90-year period, while other cultivated crops increased 3.5 times. Cultivated crops as a whole increased approximately three times. On the other hand, sericulture reached a peak around 1930, when it increased to ten times that of the late nineteenth century. During World War II, however, it sharply declined and currently stands at less than one-third the prewar level. Livestock showed the most development by far, growing more than 100 times in size during the 90 years.

TABLE 9.6
Sector-Wise Growth of Agricultural Production (%)

	Period	Cultivated crops			Sericulture	Livestock
		Rice	Others	Total		
I	1880–1900	0.9	2.1	1.3	3.9	6.8
II	1900–1920	1.7	1.4	1.6	4.7	3.8
III	1920–1935	0.4	0.7	0.5	1.7	5.7
IV	1935–1945	−0.4	−1.6	−0.8	−10.3	−7.6
V	1945–1955	1.4	4.5	2.5	−0.5	16.3
VI	1955–1965	2.2	1.9	2.1	−0.3	11.0
Prewar period	1880–1935	1.1	1.5	1.2	3.6	5.4
Postwar period	1945–1965	1.8	3.2	2.4	−0.4	13.6
Total period	1880–1965	1.1	1.5	1.2	0.9	5.6

SOURCE: M. Umemura *et al.*, *Estimates of Long-Term Economic Statistics of Japan since 1868, Series No. 9, Agriculture and Forestry* (Tokyo: Toyo Keizai Shimpo-sha, 1966).

This sector-wise difference in growth rates, in terms of 1934–36 prices, resulted in the proportion of rice, the largest agricultural crop, dropping from slightly under 70 percent to 45 percent in the 90-year period. The percent composition of other cultivated crops remained in the 30-percent range throughout the period. Sericulture peaked at over 10 percent in 1923–37, but later declined to the two percent range. In contrast to this, livestock expanded widely after World War II and has now passed the 20-percent mark.

The level of agricultural production is determined by the input and quality of production factors and the state of technology combining the two. A glance at the general way in which input factors changed in the ninety-year period reveals that the labor force shrank from 15.5 million to 11 million, or to two-thirds.[13] Labor was the only agricultural input to have shrunk. The area of cultivated land increased close to 30 percent, from 4.7 million hectares to 6 million hectares. Fixed capital, consisting of livestock, machinery, buildings, etc., in terms of 1934–36 prices, increased close to four times. Current assets from purchases of fertilizers, feed, etc., increased twenty-five times. In other words, while the labor force declined, agricultural production became supported by a gradual increase in land and a wide increase in capital assets, especially current assets.

The trends of agricultural input differed considerably at times. Labor input, however, declined continuously except for the postwar period when the economy was in confusion and large numbers of people were repatriated from overseas. This is tied into the fact that agriculture has supplied the labor force for the nonagricultural industry sector during Japan's process of economic development. The decline in period VI (1955–65), which at times reached 3 percent a year, resulted from the strong influence of the high growth of the postwar economy. Compared to the prewar average, there was approximately two-thirds reduction in the postwar period. Of note is the fact that the male worker rate of decline was at times twice that of the female.

It is instructive to trace the factors causing the change in persons employed in the primary industries. Columns 1 and 2 of Table 9.7 give the annual increase in persons employed in the primary, secondary, and tertiary industries. Column 3 shows the natural increase in the persons employed in the primary industries. Column 4 is the net outflow (outflow-inflow) derived by subtracting the figures in column 1 from column 3.

13. The decline started after 1920. Before that the labor force remained fairly constant.

TABLE 9.7
Factors of Change in Number of Persons Employed in Primary Industries (Annual Average)

	Increase in Number of employed		Persons employed in primary			
Year	Primary (1)*	Secondary and tertiary (2)*	Natural increase (3)*	Net outflow (4)*	Net outflow rate (%) (5)	Contribution rate (%) (6)
1906–10	–164	268	64	228	1.47	85.0
1910–20	–73	237	93	166	1.12	70.0
1920–30	5	233	132	127	0.88	54.5
1930–40	–30	319	135	165	1.15	51.7
1950–55	–219	955	321	540	3.24	56.5
1955–60	–353	1,153	290	643	4.22	55.7
1960–65	–523	1,371	120	643	4.92	46.9
1965–70	–333	1,231	194	527	4.84	42.8

SOURCE: R. Minami, *The Turning Point in Economic Development: Japan's Experience* (Tokyo: Sobunsha, 1973).
* Thousands.

As shown in Table 9.7, the net outflow was higher than the natural increase in all except the 1920–30 period. This resulted in a decline in the number of persons employed in the primary industries. Also, the natural increase for the postwar period was higher than for the prewar period. Since the net outflow increased widely after the war, an unprecedented drop was consequently seen in the numbers of employed. That is, the net outflow remained at from 127,000–228,000 a year in the prewar period, but more than trebled in the postwar period, reaching 527,000–643,000. Column 5 shows the rate of outflow, derived by dividing the net outflow by the increase in the number of persons employed in the primary industries. This jumped from 0.9 percent to 1.5 percent in the prewar period, to 3.2 percent to 4.9 percent in the postwar period. Column 6 shows the outflow from the primary industries divided by the increase in the number of persons employed in the secondary and tertiary industries. It also attempts to show how many of the persons employed in the secondary and tertiary industries can be accounted for by the outflow from the primary ones. The contribution rate was as much as 85 percent up until 1906–1910, but in those days, the weight of the primary industries was great, and the other industries were still immature. This gradually fell later, despite the sharp increase in the net outflow after the war, and reached 43 percent by 1965–70.

Attention must be drawn to the fact that the outflow from the primary industries shown in the table includes farmers' children who become employed in nonagricultural industries immediately after graduating from school. Because of this, the occupational trend in terms of new graduates also becomes an important factor in determining the employment structure. Data on the prewar period is scarce, but from 1929–38 there were about 900 thousand new grade school graduates of whom 400 thousand became employed in the primary industries annually—40 percent to 50 percent. Data for 1971–75 indicate this fell to no more than 6.3 percent for even male middle school graduates and dropped to slightly under 3 percent for new graduates as a whole. Incidentally, 41 percent of the graduates found employment in the secondary and 55 percent in the tertiary industries.

Now, the long-term forecast of the Japan Economic Research Center indicates that the proportion of the tertiary industries in the employment structure will expand still more. By 1990, primary industries will account for 6.8 percent, secondary industries for 35.7 percent, and tertiary industries 57.2 percent. Japan will be faced with the serious problem in the future of how to ensure a certain degree of self-supply in key agricultural products with a continually shrinking and rapidly aging pool of farm workers. More than 50 percent of all farm workers today are over 50 years old, and the situation is expected to worsen rapidly in the future.

Changes in the Secondary and Tertiary Industries

In the section above a look was taken at the primary industries, especially agriculture. In the process of Japan's economic development, these functioned primarily as a labor supply source. Below, an analysis will be made of the development of the secondary and tertiary industries which absorbed this labor force, focusing on changes in the employment structure.

The dynamic force behind the economic growth of Japan from the late nineteenth century was the expansion of manufacturing. In the 1880s, the manufacturing industries accounted for only slightly over 10 percent of the net national income. By 1926, however, they had climbed to 26 percent. (The peak was 30.5 percent in 1969; it has subsequently declined.) During this same period, agriculture had dropped from 40 percent to 6 percent, industry in the broad sense (manufacturing, mining, construction, transportation and communications, public utilities) rose from 20 percent to 43 percent, and service industries increased from 40 percent to 51 percent.

Recent studies have provided estimates of Japan's industrial production back to 1874. According to these estimates, production increased 29.5 times from 1874 to 1940. During most of World War II—1941 to

1945—industrial production remained almost the same, but it was sharply reduced by the destruction wrought in the last months of the war and the confusion of the postwar period. The peak was in 1944, when a level of 30.7 times that of 1874 was attained. If the 1944 level is assigned a value of 100, then industrial production fell to 42.4 in the final year of the war, 1945, and to 16.0 in 1946. The 1946 level was equivalent to that reached in 1912. The war, consequently, set Japan's production back 34 years.

Damage to the capital stock and labor force, however, was not as serious as the drop in production, and Japan had not lost its technological and educational reserves, the building blocks of industrialization. Japan's experience showed that, so long as there is no major damage to the fundamentals, production will start to recover rapidly from any temporary slump as soon as exterior restraints are removed. Table 9.8 shows the growth rate of industrial production after World War II. A growth of over 30 percent a year was shown from 1946–51, the period directly after cessation of hostilities, and in 1955 the prewar peak was reached. With the exception of the striking growth years of 1946–51, the average annual growth rate for the twenty years from 1951–71 was 14.1 percent.

The growth rate of industrial production in the last century was 3.8 percent in the thirty-one years from 1874 to 1905, 6.0 percent in the thirty-nine years from 1905 to 1944, and 8.4 percent in the twenty-seven years from 1944 to 1971, or an increase of slightly over 2 percent in each period.

Three growth phases in industrial production can be discerned from the late nineteenth century to World War II: 1885–95, 1905–15, and 1925–35. Of note here was the change in industries leading the growth. A study of the degree of contribution to growth, considering the nature and scale of the industries, shows that during the first phase, food and textiles were by far the most important, while the heavy and chemical industries were still relatively insignificant. During the second phase, the food and textile industries and the heavy and chemical industries (chemicals, metals,

TABLE 9.8
Growth Rate of Industrial Production After World War II

Year	Percentage
1946–51	31.2
1951–56	14.4
1956–61	16.3
1961–66	10.7
1966–71	15.2
(1951–71)	14.1

SOURCE: *Indexes of Manufacturing Industries' Production,* published annually by the Ministry of International Trade and Industry, Government of Japan.

and machinery) became almost equal. During the third phase, the heavy and chemical industries became the strongest.[14]

During the recovery period directly following the end of the war, the degree of slump in each industry differed. Each industry, however, subsequently achieved a high growth rate of 20–30 percent. Later, during the high growth period from 1955–71, a marked gap appeared between the growth rates of each sector. This was due to the trend of heavy and chemical industrialization. New technology was incorporated, further strengthening this trend which had already begun before the war.

It was mentioned before that there were three phases in the rise of industrial production from the late nineteenth century to World War II. The annual increase rate in persons employed in the secondary industries was an average 4.7 percent for 1885–95, 2.5 percent for 1905–15, and 2.5 percent for 1925–35. The growth rates in the total number of employed during the same phases were much lower—1.2 percent, 0.4 percent, and 1.0 percent. Because of this, the proportion of persons employed in the secondary industries expanded from 7.3 percent in 1885, to 19.8 percent in 1935. In absolute numerical terms, this amounted to a fourfold rise over a fifty-year period, from 1.55 million to 6.22 million.

In 1955–71, the period of high growth after the war, industrial production expanded by an annual average of 14 percent. Consequently, a strong demand for labor from the primary industries was generated. From 1955–65, there was an outflow of as many as 640 thousand workers a year from the primary industries, while from 1965–70 there was a similar outflow of 530 thousand (see Table 9.7). Not all of this outflow was absorbed by the secondary industries, of course, but the number of persons employed in them did almost double in the fifteen-year period from 1955, when it stood at 9.25 million, to 1970, when it stood at 17.78 million. Therefore, the rate of increase during this period reached an average annual 4.5 percent. The proportion of persons employed in the secondary industries to the total number of employed climbed to 34 percent by 1970. Japan can thus legitimately be said to have been transformed into an industrialized nation in both name and reality in those fifteen years.

The proportion of persons employed in the tertiary industries expanded extremely steadily, as shown in Table 9.5, from 12 percent around 1880, to 51 percent in 1975. In contrast, income produced expanded from 26 percent in 1880, to 58 percent in 1975. This implies that the productivity of the tertiary industries was higher in the past compared with the other material production sectors. Productivity gradually declined as the

14. M. Shinohara, *Estimates of Long-Term Economic Statistics of Japan since 1868, Series No. 10, Mining and Manufacturing* (Tokyo: Toyo Keizai Shimpo-sha, 1972).

proportion of the relatively low productivity primary industries dropped and that of the secondary industries rose.

Statistical restrictions do not permit any meaningful study of persons employed in the tertiary industries earlier than 1920, when the first population census was conducted. Table 9.9 shows just how tertiary employment changed from 1920, when it was 23.8 percent of the total employed, to 1975, when it reached 50.7 percent. Of note is the drop in the proportion of the service industries, which had accounted for the largest share in 1920. The major factor behind this drop was the almost total disappearance of live-in household help, which had accounted for more than half of the service industries at the time. Recently, the number of persons employed in the medical, educational, automative servicing, and other industries has rapidly expanded, but this has not been enough to offset the drop in household help. Further, the share of finance, insurance, real estate, transportation, and public utilities has grown, since they are strongly tied to the development of the secondary industries. Japan's wholesale and retail trade were previously characterized by small-scale operations and were said to harbor excess labor. The percent composition of 1975 shows them accounting for the largest share. This may still be true at the present time. Government jobs expanded 120 times from 1920 to 1975. Heated debates over the number of public officials are often conducted. In general, Japan can be said to have been different in its early development stage from contemporary developing nations.

As previously mentioned, the proportion of Japan's tertiary industries, primarily education, research services, and medicine-related industries, is expected to continue to expand in the future. By 1990, it is projected to reach 57 percent. The proportion of the service economy in the employment structure will also probably become stronger.

TABLE 9.9
Changes in Tertiary Employment (thousands)

Year	Wholesale and retail trade	Finance, insurance, and real estate	Transportation and public utilities	Services	Government	Total
1920	828	13	65	1,074	16	1,995
	(41.5)*	(0.6)*	(3.3)*	(53.8)*	(0.8)*	(100.0)*
1975	11,293	1,790	3,690	8,730	1,954	27,456
	(41.1)*	(6.5)*	(13.4)*	(31.8)*	(7.1)*	(100.0)*

SOURCE: Government of Japan, Prime Minister's Office, Bureau of the Census, *Population Census*, 1920 and 1975.

* Figures in parentheses are percent of total employment.

MIGRATION AND ECONOMIC DEVELOPMENT

Migration and Economic Growth

Modernization is a combination of two main factors: industrialization and urbanization. Industrialization and urbanization are made possible by the demographic factor known as migration. Consequently, without migration there can be no successful modernization. The history of the two are closely intertwined, as exemplified by the long-term rural-to-urban regional migratory pattern.

One of the fundamental features of Japan's modernization during the last century was the migration of population from the rural areas to the cities, even though the numbers of migrants fluctuated at times. Demographically, it was a movement of people from the high-fertility rural areas to low-fertility urban areas and may be understood as the pressure value of the overpopulated rural areas which led to the regional redistribution of population throughout the country. Economically, it supplied the labor force required in the urbanized and industrialized regions and contributed to both a higher GNP and national standard of living.

Migration continued to increase at a great speed in Japan's economic recovery period after World War II and even more so in the subsequent period of high economic growth. It is commonly spoken of as "the great Japanese migration."

Japan's manufacturing industries and heavy and chemical industries, which provided the main thrust behind its accelerated economic growth, flourished primarily in two centers of long historical significance, the Tokyo and Osaka metropolitan areas. As a result, there was a massive flow of the labor force from rural villages and small cities all over Japan and a massive concentration and crowding of population in the small region known as the Pacific Industrial Belt.

The tremendous labor force required for the high economic growth commencing in the late fifties was provided by the more than six million overseas repatriates living in rural areas (including military personnel and civilians) and the large numbers of soldiers demobilized in Japan after the war. The number of people supported by the primary industries, 14 million in prewar days, reached over 17 million in 1950. In 1965, however, fifteen years later, this had fallen sharply to 11.7 million, illustrating indirectly the influence of the available labor supply. Incidentally, it should be remembered that the baby boom of 1947–49 became the source of supply of the large young labor force in the sixties.

This large-scale migration also had its detrimental aspects. Major cities became overcrowded and local rural areas underpopulated, so much so that serious concern was stirred up in the government and among experts.

Migration theory has been concerned with the causes of migration. Theories emphasizing economic factors, such as regional disparities in standards of living and income, have been dominant.[15] From the micro-economic viewpoint, people move to cities in search of job opportunities through which they can raise their standard of living. Cities offer a wide selection of diverse employment opportunities as well as many social and public facilities. The lure of the big city with its ample entertainment facilities is particularly strong for the young people in local rural areas.

Not all the people in rural areas, in particular the young, leave their villages for the cities. There is more or less a fixed number of young people who never migrate in the first place and some young people who return after having once left. Aside from purely economic reasons, one can imagine the strength of Japan's family, inheritance, or land system as being factors in migration behavior. No general theory exists to explain the complicated factors determining whether or not a person will move. Migration differs in form with each country, each region, each time period, and each social, economic, and cultural level.

The Japanese government began to show concern over the intensified concentration of population in the cities at a fairly early stage and moved to suppress overconcentration in the major urban areas.[16] In 1962, for example, it enacted the New Industrial Cities Promotion Law. Designed to contribute to development of local areas and the national economy, this law acted on industrial land conditions and municipal facilities in an attempt to prevent overconcentration of industry and population in the major cities, correct regional disparities, and stabilize employment. The Comprehensive National Development Plan, submitted and passed the same year, also emphasized as one of its goals the correction of urban overcrowding.

In 1969, the government adopted the New Comprehensive National Development Plan, which was directed at dispersion of industrial development to local areas and at large-scale developmental projects. Its basic policy

15. M. Tachi's works may be cited as representative studies in this field: "Regional Income Disparity and Internal Migration of Population in Japan," *Economic Development and Cultural Change* 12 (2) (Jan. 1964); M. Tachi, ed., "Major Cities and the Economic Role of Migration, Issues," *Urban Populations—Internal Migration of Population in Japan* (Tokyo: Kokon Shoin, 1962), pp. 1–22; and M. Tachi, ed., "The Role of Internal Migrations of Population," *Internal Migration of Population in Japan* (Tokyo: Kokon Shoin, 1967), pp. 146–77. Also R. Minami and A. Ono, "Economic Theory of Migration," *Theory and Analysis of Population Urbanization* (Tokyo: Keiso Shobo, 1965), especially Chapter 3, Section 2.

16. Bernard Berelson, ed., M. Muramatsu and T. Kuroda, Chapter 23, "Japan," *Population Policy in Developed Countries* (New York: McGraw-Hill, 1974), pp. 704–30, especially pp. 728–30.

called for balanced coordinated development throughout Japan. The Third Comprehensive National Development Plan was proposed and passed in December 1977. It may be described as a typical policy of population dispersion through migration, designed to establish "human habitation zones."

A statistical analysis of the changes in migration in postwar Japan reveals the stages of intensification of the classical pattern of migration from the agricultural village to the city and, also, the occurrence of subsequent new migratory patterns, called "mobility transition." Migratory behavior is viewed as the response to new stages of development which lead people to new decisions in selecting places of residence.

Changes in Amount of Migration and Features of Regional Migration

The numbers of migrants, rates of increase compared with the previous year, and total migration expressed as a percentage of Japan's total population in the approximate quarter century from 1954–77 are given in Table 9.10.

Japan is considered to have entered its era of high economic growth in about 1957. The same year saw a general long-term increase in the numbers of migrants, although considerable fluctuations were seen in the actual year-by-year increase rates. The average number of migrants in the late fifties was 5.2 million a year, in the early sixties 6.5 million, in the late sixties 7.6 million, and in the seventies over 8 million, reaching 8.5 million in 1973. The year 1973 was also the one in which the Arabs instituted their oil embargo. The numbers of migrants peaked and later declined sharply, falling to 7.5 million in 1975, and 7.4 million in 1976.

The large migration of people in the Japanese islands also seems to have reached a peak in the early seventies and then entered a new stage of change. The changes in the total number of migrants is examined from the standpoint of movement among different regions. Japan's forty-six prefectures (excluding Okinawa) were classified into fifteen regions and the net migration (in-migration minus out-migration) calculated for each five-year period from 1955 (three-year period from 1975 to 1977). The results are given in Table 9.11.

Table 9.11 indicates the following (see also Figure 9.4): First, regions E and J, what are today known as the Tokyo and Osaka metropolitan areas, absorbed a vast amount of people from almost all of the other regions. Second, this migratory trend began to change from around 1965: net in-migration in the Tokyo and Osaka metropolitan areas sharply declined. An excess of out-migrants over in-migrants is already being shown in the Osaka metropolitan area. This change in migration to the

Figure 9.4
Region, Prefectures, and Major Cities of Japan, 1975

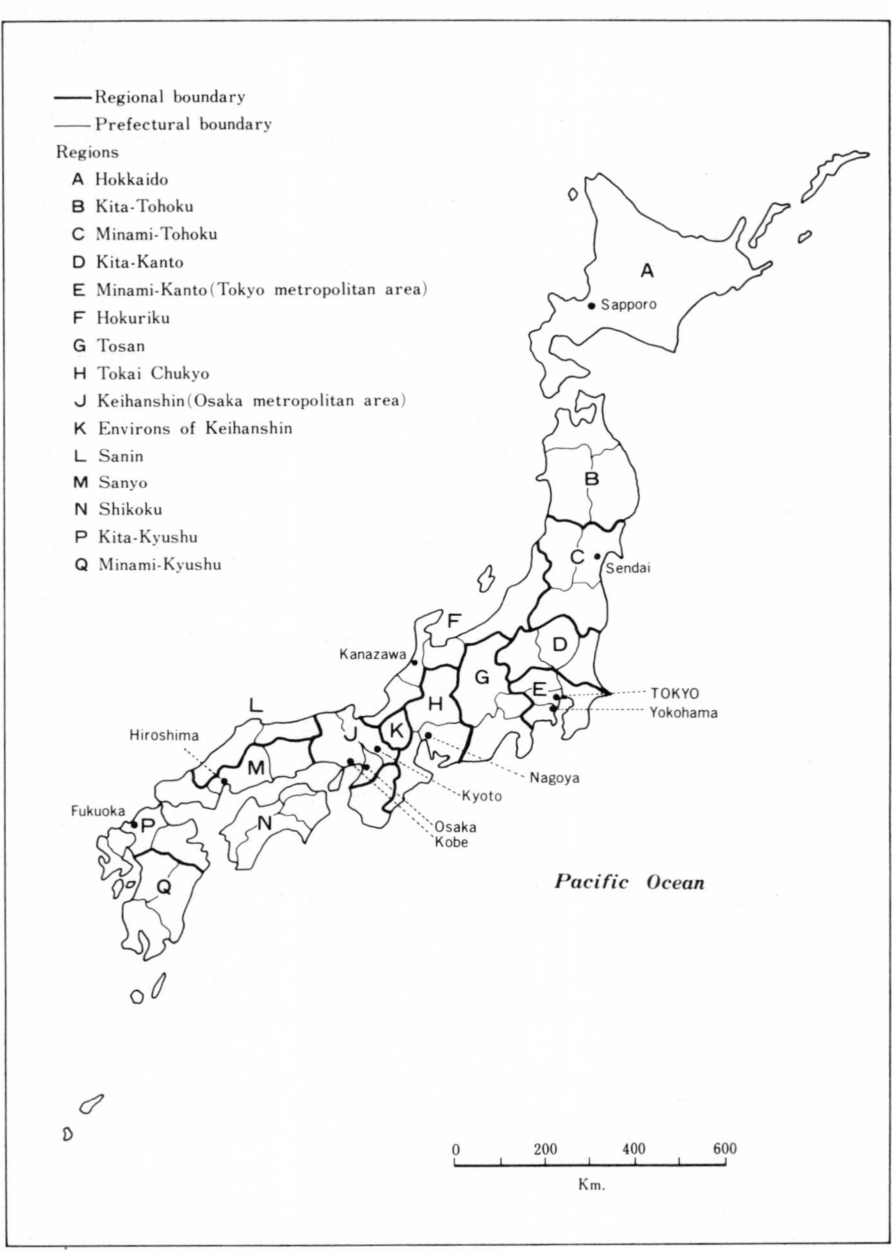

TABLE 9.10
Trends in Numbers of Migrants* in Japan

Year	Numbers (thousands)	Increase (%)	Total Migration (%)	Year	Numbers thousands	Increase (%)	Total Migration (%)
1954	5,498		6.27	1966	7,432	0.7	7.55
1955	5,141	−6.5	5.80	1967	7,479	0.6	7.51
1956	4,860	−5.5	5.43	1968	7,775	4.0	7.72
1957	5,268	8.4	5.83	1969	8,126	4.5	7.97
1058	5,294	0.5	5.81	1970	8,273	1.8	8.02
1959	5,358	1.2	5.82	1971	8,360	1.1	8.01
1960	5,653	5.5	6.09	1972	8,225	−1.6	7.78
1961	6,012	6.4	6.42	1973	8,539		7.90
1962	6,580	9.4	6.95	1974	8,027	−6.0	7.34
1963	6,937	5.4	7.26	1975	7,544	−6.0	6.78
1964	7,257	4.6	7.51	1976	7,392	−2.0	6.58
1965	7,381	1.7	7.56	1977	7,395	0.0	6.52

SOURCE: Government of Japan, Prime Minister's Office, Bureau of Statistics, *Annual Report on the Internal Migration in Japan Derived from the Basic Resident Registers*, 1977.

* Numbers of migrants refers to numbers of people moving between cities, wards, towns, or villages. Migrants to and from Okinawa included only after 1973.

TABLE 9.11
Changes in Net Regional Migration in Postwar Japan

Region	1955–59	1960–64	1965–69	1970–74	1975–77
A. Hokkaido	+23	−151	−199	−217	−10
B. Kita-Tohoku	−160	−298	−250	−204	−30
C. Minami-Tohoku	−280	−361	−219	−79	−8
D. Kita-Kanto	−285	−201	−90	+95	+53
E. Minami-Kanto (Tokyo metropolitan area)	+1,422	+1,854	+1,452	+876	+169
F. Hokuriku	−245	−254	−212	−121	−30
G. Tosan	−222	−137	−87	−20	−22
H. Chukyo	−70	+311	+157	+111	−24
J. Keihanshin (Osaka metropolitan area)	+633	+929	+526	+62	−164
K. Environs of Keihanshin	−57	−37	+22	+107	+62
L. Sanin	−88	−115	−93	−46	−4
M. Sanyo	−127	−185	−53	+25	−19
N. Shikoku	−212	−289	−199	−79	−3
P. Kita-Kyushu	−177	−606	−407	−241	+25
Q. Minami-Kyushu	−293	−461	−349	−228	+9

SOURCE: Computation based on *Annual Report on the Internal Migration in Japan Derived from the Basic Resident Registers,* Bureau of Statistics, Prime Minister's Office. Data up to November 9, 1967, are based on the Resident Registration Law, superseded by the Basic Resident Register Law enacted in November 1967.

NOTE: The fifteen regions and boundaries of the forty-six prefectures contained in each region are as follows: A. Hokkaido; B. Aomori, Iwate, Akita; C. Miyagi, Yamagata, Fukushima; D. Ibaraki, Tochigi, Gunma; E. Saitama, Chiba, Tokyo, Kanagawa; F. Niigata, Toyama, Ishikawa, Fukui; G. Yamanashi, Nagano, Shizuoka; H. Gifu, Aichi, Mie; J. Kyoto, Osaka, Hyogo; K. Shiga, Nara, Wakayama; L. Tottori, Shimane; M. Okayama, Hiroshima, Yamaguchi; N. Tokushima, Kagawa, Ehime, Kochi; P. Fukuoka, Saga, Nagasaki, Oita; and Q. Kumamoto, Miyazaki, Kagoshima.

(+) Indicates an excess of in-migrants over out-migrants.

(—) Indicates an excess of out-migrants over in-migrants.

metropolitan areas is examined below from the viewpoint of the other local areas. Some local areas have been shifting in the long term from out-migration regions to in-migration regions (Kita-Kanto, Kita-Kyushu, Minami-Kyushu). Others have continued to show an excess of out-migrants over in-migrants, but on a sharply reduced scale, (e.g., Kita-Tohoku, Minami-Tohoku, Tosan, Sanin, Shikoku).

These changes in migration in Japan indicate that the concentrated migration to the giant urban areas has also reached a peak and new changes have begun. Migratory patterns have started to diversify—to a decline in the inflow of metropolitan areas, an increase in the outflow from metropolitan areas to local areas (U-turn), a transition from migration to the larger cities to migration to medium and small cities, and an increase in migration between local neighboring areas (for example migration between Kita-Tohoku and Minami-Tohoku, or Kita-Kyushu and Minami-Kyushu). These may be thought of as the first stirrings in the movement toward population redistribution in the Japanese archipelago.

Migration in Three Metropolitan Areas

Examined here are the changes in the net number of migrants in the three metropolitan areas where migratory changes appear the most pronounced (see Table 9.12). Overall in-migration in the three areas was

TABLE 9.12
Changes in Net Migration of Three Metropolitan Areas (thousands)

Year	Tokyo area‡	Osaka area§	Chukyo area‖	Total*
1955	235	95	23	353
1956	247	612	42	401
1957	295	169	44	507
1958	273	123	26	422
1959	300	145	45	490
1960	333	189	72	594
1961	359	221	75	655
1962	364	211	72	647
1963	354	185	80	619
1964	327	174	76	578
1965	298	131	52	481
1966	266	103	37	406
1967	255	107	42	404
1968	259	112	48	418
1969	250	121	55	426
1970	248	91	54	393
1971	206	47	37	289
1972	159	24	24	207
1973	97	−5†	22	114
1974	53	−21	7	39
1975	45	−30	−4	11
1976	26	−41	−7	−23
1977	35	−45	3	−6

SOURCE: Computation based on *Annual Report on the Internal Migration in Japan Derived from the Basic Resident Registers*, published annually for the period of 1955–77 by the Bureau of Statistics, Prime Minister's Office, Government of Japan.

* Figures for each area are rounded off, and the total of the three may not necessarily correspond to the figures in the Total column.

†— Indicates an excess of out-migrants over in-migrants.

‡ Included in the Tokyo metropolitan area are Saitama, Chiba, Tokyo, and Kanagawa.

§ Included in the Osaka metropolitan area are Kyoto, Osaka, and Hyogo.

‖ Included in the Chukyo metropolitan area are regions in Aichi, Gifu, and Mie Prefectures.

over 600 thousand a year in 1961, 1962, and 1963. In-migration declined after that, totaling only 110 thousand in 1973, the year of the oil embargo, and in 1976 an excess of out-migrants over in-migrants was recorded for the first time. This suggests the migration in Japan had entered a crucial stage of transition.

Attention should also be drawn to the marked change in the position held by migration in the population increases of metropolitan areas. Changes in regional population are obviously not due to migration alone but also to natural increases. The change in the relative weight of migration and natural increases in the growth of the Tokyo and Osaka metropolitan populations are given in Table 9.13. Up until 1965, more than 50 percent of the population increase in both areas was attributable to the excess of in-migrants over out-migrants. The relative weight of migration started to decline after that year, however, and in the five-year period 1970–75 had fallen to no more than 3 percent in the Osaka area. Natural increase accounted for 97 percent of the population rise. Even in the Tokyo area, the relative weight of migration had fallen to 30 percent in the 1970–75 period. In the Third Comprehensive National Development Plan, the government envisioned a population increase in the metropolitan areas no greater than the amount from natural increase. The level of a so-called "closed population" was able to be maintained because of this recent reversal in the relative weights of migration and natural increase.

It may also be discerned from Table 9.13 that 1965 was the transition point of migration in Japan.

Study of Mobility Transition

The statistics given in each previous section clearly point to a new transition of migration in Japan, i.e., changes in the behavior of people in selecting places of residence. These statistics are analyzed below to allow this transition to be touched upon further.[17]

First, the trend of population redistribution manifests itself as a rapid increase of medium and small city populations, an increase in the proportion of Japan's total population held by those populations, a pronounced drop in the rate of increase of large city populations (over one million), and a declining trend in the rate of population increases in areas centered

17. T. Kuroda, "The Role of Migration in Population Distribution" in *Japan's Demographic Transition,* Papers of the East-West Population Institute, no. 46 (July 1977).

TABLE 9.13
Changes in Migration and Natural Increase in Population Growth of Tokyo and Osaka Metropolitan Areas (thousands)

Time period	Tokyo Area				Osaka Area			
	Population increase A	Natural increase B	Migration C	C/A (%)	Population increase A	Natural increase B	Migration C	C/A (%)
1950–55	2,346	889	1,457	62.1	1,142	533	609	53.3
1955–60	2,440	877	1,563	64.1	1,230	510	721	58.6
1960–65	3,153	1,294	1,859	59.0	1,665	758	907	54.5
1965–70	3,096	1,740	1,356	43.8	1,469	973	495	33.7
1970–75	2,926	2,039	887	30.3	1,157	1,122	35	3.0

SOURCE: Census results published by the Bureau of Statistics, Prime Minister's Office, Government of Japan, and vital statistics on population movement, published by the Ministry of Health and Welfare, Government of Japan.

Increase caused by migration (excess of in-migrants over out-migrants) computed by subtracting five years' natural increase from five years' population increase of each metropolis or prefecture comprising the metropolitan area. Prefectures (Tokyo) comprising the metropolitan areas correspond to those in other statistical tables.

around giant cities. A Hoover Index analysis[18] was made to ascertain the degree of concentration of urban populations by data from 644 cities in Japan. This analysis showed a rapid rise in the index to 1965 signifying increased concentration. The speed of the rise in concentration slowed down somewhat after that between 1970 and 1975. It then dropped in 1976 and in 1977, suggesting that dispersion of urban population had actually begun.

Second, this mobility transition implied a trend toward redispersion, as discussed previously, and manifested itself as a change in the regions selected by migrants for residence. This change in the regions migrated to is clearly suggested in Tables 9.6 and 9.7. It is impossible, however, to determine the concrete nature of this change, therefore a preference index is used. An analysis of the 1955–77 period using this index reveals the following.[19] There has been a pronounced outflow from the metropolitan areas to several local areas. For example, there was an increase in selective outflow from the Tokyo metropolitan area to Kita-Kanto, Minami-Tohoku, Tosan, Kita-Tohoku, and Hokuriku (almost all migrants returning to home-town regions), and an increase in selective outflow from the Osaka metropolitan area to its environs (suburbs), Sanin, Shikoku, and Minami-Kyushu. There has also been a striking outflow increase to neighboring

18. N. Sakashita, "Concentration and Dispersion of Urban Populations—Easy Economics," *Nihon Keizai Shimbun (The Japan Economic Journal)*, July 24–30, 1978.

$$\text{Hoover Index} = \frac{1}{2}\sum_{i=1}^{n}\left| X_i - S_i \right|$$

X_i = the proportion of the population in unit i of the total national population.
S_i = the proportion of the space of unit i over the total land area.
n = the total number of the units in the country.

19. S. Uchino, "Two Major Migration Streams in Japan," *The Journal of Population Problems*, 139 (July 1976). Data for 1977 from unreleased provisional calculations of Ms. Uchino. The following method was used to compute the preference index:

$$PI = \left(\frac{Mod}{mPo \dfrac{Po}{\Sigma Pi - Po}} \right) 100$$

Mod: Actual out-migration
m: Ratio of regional migrants to total population
Po: Population of outflow area
Pi: Population of intake area
ΣPi: Total population

regions. Up until 1965, for instance, the Tokyo metropolitan area was the region of strongest selective outflow for Kita-Tohoku. After 1965, however, Minami-Tohoku laid claim to this position. The Osaka metropolitan area had the highest selective index for both Sanin and Sanyo until 1960, but after 1965 this had changed to Sanyo for Sanin and vice-versa. The same held true for Kita-Kyushu and Minami-Kyushu.

Third, there was a change in the age group of the migrants. The majority of migrants is known to be generally young. Existing statistics do not contain information on the age composition of migrants in Japan, consequently, a census survival ratio was used to compute the change in prefectural populations by sex and age caused by migration. Examined was the increase or decrease in age groups by prefecture or metropolis. The changes in males 20–24 years old (in 1965) were especially noteworthy. In 1970, an excess of out-migrants over in-migrants of this group was shown in Tokyo, Osaka, Kyoto, and Fukuoka, with the net outflow exceeding 20 percent in the first two. Almost all the other prefectures showed a net intake of this group. This suggests a flow of young people from the metropolitan prefectures to the local areas.[20] Also examined was the change during the 1970–75 period.[21] Males 20–24 years old (in 1970) had declined in the Tokyo, Osaka, and Chukyo metropolitan areas by 1975 (9.3 percent, 7.1 percent, and 0.2 percent declines, respectively). The same group increased in all other regions. The rate of increase was especially high in Sanin and Shikoku, 19.1 percent and 17.8 percent, respectively. Even more noticeable was the decline in the three metropolitan areas by 1975 of males 25–29 in 1970, (30–34 in 1975). The other regions in Japan, except Hokkaido, each showed an increase. This indicates an expansion of the age group of migrants to rural areas from 20–24 years to 25–29 years.

Conclusion

A study was made of the notable transitional stages in the numbers, regional selection, and age of Japan's population migration. Two basic trends were assessed: a change from concentration in metropolitan areas to dispersion in local areas, and a predominance of the young productive age group in the 20s among migrants. This "U-turn" in the young labor

20. S. Nishikawa, "The Reversal of Population Migration," *Nihon Keizai Shimbun (The Japan Economic Journal),* April 27, 1973; Shunsaku Nishikawa, "Economic Analysis and Policy," *Regional Migration of Labor—1970 to 1975* (Tokyo: Nihon Keizai Shimbun Ltd., 1975), pp. 109–128.

21. Based upon unreleased provisional calculations by S. Uchino.

force was made possible by the Comprehensive National Development Plan of 1962, the New Comprehensive National Development Plan of 1969, the many measures taken to encourage local development, and the comprehensive development plans of each individual prefecture. These created more developed regional economies and greater employment opportunities. Additional factors encouraging this "U-turn" were the simultaneous deterioration of living conditions in the large cities and changes in attitudes toward life in general.

The basic concept behind the Third Comprehensive National Development Plan of 1977 was a human habitation scheme.[22] Behind it may be seen the aforementioned mobility transition. The government hopes to keep future population increases in the Tokyo and Osaka metropolitan areas below that of a closed population, in other words, below a natural increase. It is planning to establish 200–300 human habitation zones throughout Japan which will act as basic areas for regional development. Just how the government will coordinate and equip the habitation space and spaces for economic activities in these zones is a topic for the future.

The massive internal migration in postwar Japan proved to be a significant contribution to the rapid economic growth and development of Japan's metropolitan areas. However, at the same time it not only obstructed development of those regions supplying the large young labor force, but also created overcrowded conditions in the high-density industrial and population regions. A new method of development aimed at upgrading the quality of life must be studied when redirecting migration for redistribution of the population.

22. Government of Japan, Land Agency, *Third Comprehensive National Development Plan,* Nov. 1977.

10

Investment in Population Quality throughout Low-Income Countries

THEODORE W. SCHULTZ

INTRODUCTION

As a graduate student, the writer's analytical interest in population growth came close to being aborted. It happened that Professor Edward A. Ross was late in meeting his seminar the day that his book *Standing Room Only* appeared. A Japanese student and the writer had taken to the blackboard to calculate how much of the earth's surface would be required to provide standing room for the then world's population. The figures showed that a small part of Dane County in which the University of Wisconsin is located would suffice. Professor Ross caught us in the act and he called on us to explain our figures. Noting his great displeasure, the economics of agriculture and food was obviously a safer topic than population growth.

It has come to pass that economics is less dismal about population growth than Malthus, and is also less dismal than the main stream of demography. The reasons for these differences in pessimism are basically conceptual. Malthus' original (first edition) concept deals with the arithmetic of population growth in response to economic "progress." His population arithmetic, which is constrained by Ricardo's diminishing returns to land, caused economics to be labelled the "dismal science." Modern demography is both sophisticated and rigorous in producing and handling population data. Its projections of population growth, however, are long on statistics and short on theory from the viewpoint of economics. Clearly, its projections for low-income countries have in general been exceedingly pessimistic. There has been an obsession with statistics which computers extrapolate with ease, and what they have been telling us is horrendous. These extrapolations support the appeals to spaceship Earth and indicate

I am indebted to Gary S. Becker, Donald McCloskey, and T. Paul Schultz for their helpful comments.

that before long the world will arrive at Ross's standing room only. These statistical projections imply that poor people breed without regard to their own well-being. But this implication, so it seems, is patently false. It is false with regard to our own rich countries, as a look at their social and economic history when they were poor testifies. It is contended here that it is also false in the case of the population growth in today's poor countries.

Our cultural roots are mainly European, where birth and death rates were very high for many generations, where the fertility transition occurred slowly, where the "extended" family was one of the ways of living with severe poverty, and where various population explosions occurred in response to improvements in economic opportunities. Some non-European populations have, during the recent past, progressed toward a population equilibrium at a more rapid rate than the European populations did during the more distant past. Ross did not anticipate, nor did anyone else at that time, the rapid decline in fertility in Japan. Viewed historically, the recent declines in death rates and, to a lesser degree, in birth rates of various low-income countries must be judged as a remarkable social change. These declines in death and birth rates are certainly not slow by historical standards. If they are accompanied by increases in the life span of people, as they are in many of these countries, then the economic implications are favorable. A longer life span implies a real gain in welfare. The extension of the period during which people are effectively in the labor force adds to their full life productivity. Moreover, a part of the population growth is undoubtedly a response to economic improvements, a response that should have been expected in view of past population increases in Europe and North America.

But is there any point in looking for increases in population quality in low-income countries? Surely it is not an idle venture on a par with searching for the Holy Grail, because in fact the quality of the population in many low-income countries is rising and it has been doing so over recent decades. It is one of the major achievements of these countries. Why, then, has this achievement pertaining to population quality not been reckoned by population experts? One reason could be that it is very difficult to identify and measure quality. The writer is not inclined, however, to give any appreciable weight to this reason, inasmuch as the increase in population quality has in general been overlooked. It could be argued that the underlying reason is that population research is dependent on a quantity theory of population. But, if there were an awareness of this limitation, there should have been endeavors to develop a quantity-quality theory. Yet except for a small group of economists, there has been a lack of such endeavors. The basic reason is the widely held belief that rapid population growth in low-income countries forecloses the possibility of improving their population quality. This belief rests on the assumption that the resource constraints in these countries are such that they are hard pressed to increase national income and savings sufficiently to maintain the level of well-being of the rapidly growing population and, therefore, savings do not suffice to invest in population quality. Instead of an analysis of the social and economic processes that are contributing to population quality in low-income countries, the issues related to population that have been on the research agenda feature a wide array of adverse developments. The list of such issues is indeed long. There are studies that support the belief that these countries are increasingly vulnerable to famine, to malnutrition, and to poverty. Following the food grain production success of the Green Revolution many "analysts" in India and abroad turned to making unwarranted predictions about the unfavorable side effects of such economic dynamics instead of searching for ways of duplicating the Punjab success in other agricultural spheres. With respect to declining death rates, what is featured on the agenda is their effect on population growth while their important favorable implications for human welfare are omitted.

There is also the belief that the lot of city dwellers declines as cities become more massive and crowded. Simple population arithmetic readily supports the belief that the creation of additional jobs to keep pace with growth in the labor force becomes increasingly less possible, so that ever more unemployment follows. Still another adverse development attributed to population growth is that it "causes" a decline in savings for investment as a proportion of national income. The argument is that rapid population growth implies more private consumption and more public expenditure on welfare programs, which leaves less of the national income available for savings. One of the errors in this argument is that the costs of the increases in schooling are treated as if schooling was pure consumption, whereas it is in large part an investment in an important form of human capital.

Counting the number of people measures the quantity of human beings in a population. This is what demographers do with increasing precision. Malthus developed a particular *quantity theory of population,* the dynamics of which (as already noted) are constrained by diminishing returns to the supporting resources. Malthus' concept of quality is a crude minimum level of quality, i.e., the subsistence level of living of the rank and file of the population. In going beyond subsistence, the concept and measurement of population quality still consist mainly of *ad hoc* applications, except for recent extensions in economic theory. Economic theory is now capable of dealing with population quality. It does so at the micro level (family) and at the macro level (country), treating it as human capital.

ECONOMIC CONCEPT OF QUALITY

Although it is difficult to reckon and maintain a reliable count of people, it is much more difficult to specify and measure the quality of a population. The concept of quality, however, is not new in economics. Differences in the quality of the original properties of land are an essential part of Ricardian Rent. Then, too, the quality of cropland, specifically its productivity, can as a rule be improved by means of investment. In general, factors of production and the goods and services that are produced differ importantly in quality. For the purpose of this chapter, attributes of acquired population quality are valuable and they can be augmented by appropriate investment which will be treated as human capital.

At this point, quality attributes and human abilities will be equated in order to distinguish between two basic classes of human abilities. Consider all human abilities to be either innate or acquired. Every person is born with a particular set of genes that determines his innate ability. Although there is a wide range of innate abilities, it is convenient to assume that in large populations by countries the distributions of these innate abilities tend to be similar. Proceeding on this assumption, it follows that the differences in population quality between such countries are a consequence of the differences in acquired abilities. It is this class of population quality to which this essay is devoted.

Any element of quality that a human being acquires from birth on through his life cycle entails a measure of costs. Whenever it is worthwhile to incur these costs, there is an incentive to invest in the quality component. Child care by parents, primarily by mothers, is a variable source of quality. So is home and work experience, schooling, and health. Experience that children derive from their part in family activities and from on-the-job work throughout later life is a major source of useful skills. Economic modernization has an appreciable positive effect in producing new opportunities and incentives to acquire additional human capital. Learning and experimenting are important. For example, farm people in the Punjab, in adopting the Mexican variety of wheat, experimented with a view to obtaining needed information as they participated in the Green Revolution. Modernization is a source of many new experiences that entail learning valuable new skills and acquiring information of value. The positive effects of schooling are pervasive, and schooling will be considered in some detail, with special reference to India, later in this essay. Ranked high in importance are the improvements in health. The evidence that is presented on improvements in health and their economic implications also pertains to India. The opportunities and incentives to invest in each of these forms of human capital are interdependent. To understand the actual investment in acquired human capital, it is necessary to be ever mindful of the interactions among the various processes that contribute to population quality.

The relevance of this economic approach is widely resisted by most population experts. It is opposed because in their view economic theory is suspect when it comes to analyzing the behavior of poor people. In the population domain, the unsettled question here is, who actually wants quality and who is prepared to pay the price of acquiring it? Experts often bemoan the lack of quality; they see governments as hard pressed for resources to get on with economic development and they believe that poor people in low-income countries can ill afford it even if they want it. Much of the population literature implies that the rank and file of poor people in these countries are not motivated to acquire human capital because they are too strongly bound by tradition to do so. Thus if the quality of the population is to be improved, experts must persuade the government to devise public programs that mandate the acquisition of quality. But this assessment of the behavior of poor people rests on untenable assumptions. People in low-income countries are not indifferent to opportunities that reveal to them worthwhile incentives to undertake investments in their own human capital. The belief that they are dull, listless, unperceptive of new opportunities and passive creatures of habit is not consistent with their behavior. They are in fact calculating human agents. Although they are poor, they tend to be efficient in allocating their meager resources with a fine regard to marginal costs and returns.

ACTIVITIES AND AN AGENDA

As already noted, the principal activities that contribute to the acquisition of human capital are child care, home and work experience, schooling, and health. The value of this human capital depends on the additional well-being that people derive from their additional human capital. Their well-being is enhanced by gains in labor productivity, and by increases in entrepreneurial efficiency in acquiring information, and in adjusting to the disequilibria inherent in the process of modernization as it affects farm and nonfarm production, household production, the time and other resources that students allocate to their education, migration to better job opportunities and to better locations in which to live, and, importantly, the gains in satisfaction that are an integral part of future consumption.

The stock of acquired human capital in this context consists of abilities and information that have an economic value. In ascertaining the stock of this capital at any given date, sex and age are important considerations. Both in theory and in empirical work, child quality is receiving increasing attention. We then have the quality of youth and that of adults, both as parents and as productive agents at work, including activities pertaining to their consumption.

This approach to increases in population quality leads to an economic agenda. It being an economic approach, quality is treated as a scarce human resource. The concept of a scarce resource implies that it has an economic value and that its acquisition entails a price. In analyzing human behavior that determines the type and amount of quality acquired over time, the key to the analysis is the incentive. When the incentive is sufficient and the necessary conditions exist, the stock of population quality will be enhanced. This means that increases in the supply of any quality component is a response to the demand for it. Moreover, it is a supply-demand approach to investment behavior because all quality components are here treated as durable scarce resources that are useful over some period of time.

It is beyond the scope of this chapter to set forth the economic theory to deal with the quality-quantity interactions and the appropriate empirical models for testing the implications of the theory. The implied theory to which appeal is made is that the returns to various quality components have been increasing over time in many low-income countries; for example, the rents that entrepreneurs derive from their allocative ability have risen (see footnote 5), along with the returns to child care, schooling, and improvements in health. Furthermore, the rates of return have been enhanced by the reductions in the costs of acquiring most of these quality components. Over time the increases in the demand for quality, e.g., in children and on the part of adults in enhancing their own quality, depresses the demand for quantity, i.e., for more children.

Special consideration is given to the improvements in the ability of farm entrepreneurs in low-income countries. This is clear because much of the writer's professional work has been on agricultural production.

When child quality is considered, the improvements that appear to account for the decline in infant mortality and the increases in the quality of young children will be examined briefly.

Investment in schooling is quite manageable. Available data make it possible to gauge the increases in this quality component. As an investment it is large, given the resources that low-income people allocate to investment. Moreover, when the investment in schooling is reckoned it increases very much the total implied savings of these countries.

On-the-job training and other forms of useful experiences are very difficult to get. What can be said on the increases in such training and experience is at best based on plausible assumptions which will be mentioned briefly when consideration is given to the implications of the improvements in health and increases in lifespan.

The achievement pertaining to health on the part of many low-income countries must be viewed as remarkable. As yet all too little is known with respect to the precise contributions of the various public and private activities that account for the observed improvements in health. The economic implications of these achievements, however, are highly instructive and empirically testable.

HUMAN CAPITAL: FARM ENTREPRENEURS

There has been a large, measurable increase in the ability of farmers in low-income countries to modernize agricultural production. Millions of them have learned how to use land, labor, and capital efficiently in response to the production opportunities associated with agricultural modernization. They are no longer bound to the long-established "routine" farming of traditional agriculture.[1] They are a new breed of farmers, capable of doing what needs to be done. Their performance has become robust; to wit: in the production of more food grains despite the distortions in agricultural incentives caused by ill-advised government interventions.[2] In view of the contributions of agricultural research oriented to the requirements of low-income countries and the large amounts of additional capital being committed to agricultural development in these countries, the acquired capacity of this new breed of farmers to transform these research contributions and the additional capital into increases in food production bodes well for the future, especially so if the distortions in agricultural incentives are reduced.[3]

Population experts who take a dim view of the future supply of food err seriously when they overlook the fact that farmers the world over, in dealing with costs, returns, and risks, are calculating economic agents. Within their small, individual, allocative domain they are fine-tuning entre-

1. The economic conditions that characterize traditional agriculture are set forth in the writer's *Transforming Traditional Agriculture* (New Haven: Yale University Press, 1964). Events and studies since this book support the analysis that was presented.

2. See the writer's *Distortions of Agricultural Incentives* (Bloomington: Indiana University Press, 1978).

3. D. Gale Johnson, "Food Production Potentials in Developing Countries," Occasional Paper No. 1, Bureau of Economic Studies (St. Paul, Minn.: Macalester College, 1977), and "The World Food Situation: Recent Developments and Prospects," University of Chicago, Graduate School of Business, 1978.

preneurs, tuning so subtly that many experts fail to see how efficient they are. On most farms there is also a second enterprise, namely the household. Housewives are also entrepreneurs in allocating their own time and in using farm products and purchased goods in household production. This entrepreneurial talent is supplied by millions of men and women on small-scale producing units, and on this score agriculture is a highly decentralized sector of the economy. Where governments have taken over the entrepreneurial function in farming, they have been far from efficient in modernizing agriculture. Where governments have not nationalized agriculture, the entrepreneurial roles of farmers and of farm housewives are important and the economic opportunities open to them really matter.

One measure of the entrepreneurial ability of farmers is the high rate at which the high-yielding varieties of wheat and rice have been adopted. New high-yielding varieties, deemed to be suitable to the requirements of low-income countries, became available to farmers only a little more than a decade ago, except for a few countries where they were introduced a few years earlier. The suitability of these varieties differed by countries; new complementary inputs had to be purchased, notably fertilizer, and the appropriate changes in farm practices had to be learned. There were new risks and uncertainties. The data in Table 10.1 summarize what had been achieved by 1976–77.[4]

TABLE 10.1
Crop Land Devoted to High-Yielding Varieties of Wheat and Rice, 1976–77

Area allocated to high-yielding varieties*			High-yielding varieties as a portion of the total particular crop area allocated to wheat and rice		
	Wheat (in millions of hectares)	Rice		Wheat (in percent)	Rice
Asia (South & East	19.7	24.2	Asia (South & East)	74.2	30.4
Near East (West Asia & N. Africa)	4.4	.04	Near East (West Asia & N. Africa)	17.0	3.4
Africa (excl. N. Africa)	.2	.12	Africa (excl. N. Africa)	22.5	1.7
Latin America†	5.1	.92	Latin America†	41.0	13.0
Total	29.4	25.28	Total	44.2	27.5

* Either planted or harvested area.
† A rough estimate.

4. Dana G. Dalrymple, *Development and Spread of High Yielding Varieties of Wheat and Rice in the Less Developed Nations,* USDA, Foreign Agricultural Economic Report, No. 95, 1978, adapted from data on pages x and xi.

In the crop year 1965–66, India planted or harvested 3,000 hectares of high yielding wheat. In twelve years, by 1977–78, it had risen to 15 million hectares. The increases in the area allocated to high yielding rice in India reveal a pattern similar to that of wheat.

The ability of farmers in low-income countries to perceive, interpret, and respond to new events in a context of risk and uncertainty is an important part of the human capital of these countries. In economics, this particular ability is treated as the *allocative ability* of farmers. The observed increase in this allocative ability is one of the components contributing to the quality of the population. Moreover, there are many more farmers relative to the size of the population in low-income than in high-income countries.

Although farmers have been featured, increases in the ability to reallocate resources in response to new events is not restricted to farm entrepreneurs. It should be stressed that people who supply labor services for hire or who are self-employed are also reallocating their services in response to changes in the value of the work they do. So are housewives in using purchased goods and services in household production. Students, likewise, are reallocating their own time along with the educational services they purchase as they respond to changes in expected earnings and in the personal satisfactions they expect to derive from their education. Consumption opportunities are also changing and, inasmuch as pure consumption entails time, here, too, people are reallocating their own time in response to changing opportunities. Clearly, in an economy that is undergoing modernization, the value of the ability to reallocate resources in response to new events is pervasive. Although it is, as a rule, more difficult to identify and measure the increases in the allocative ability of nonfarm people than of farmers, judging from the studies that have been made, it is plausible that this entrepreneurial capacity, which encompasses consideration of risks and uncertainty, as an integral part of the allocative ability, has been increasing throughout the population of many low-income countries. *The supply curve of entrepreneurial capacity has been shifting to the right.* [5]

5. See the writer's "The Value of the Ability to Deal with Disequilibria," *Journal of Economic Literature* 13 (September 1975):827–46. To show this supply curve graphically, scale the economic value of entrepreneurs' capacity vertically and scale their capacity horizontally. The economic value is the *rent* they derive from their allocative ability. The rent for any given capacity is a function of the disequilibria that the entrepreneurs face. Entrepreneurial capacity is a function of the original capacity of human agents, their experience in dealing with disequilibria, their schooling and health. The positions of this supply curve under two different economic conditions are as follows: For traditional agriculture, which has long been in a state of equilibrium, production activities tend to be routine. There is little or no rent to allocative ability. This supply curve is far to the left in this graph, indicating a small

No reference has been made to the role of schooling and health as these contribute to the increases in the capacity of farmers to deal efficiently with new events. What has been stressed by implication is their having learned from participating in the modernization process. The favorable interaction between learning from their experience and their schooling and their health status will be considered later in this essay.

INVESTMENT IN CHILD QUALITY

The arithmetic of the increasing numbers of children in low-income countries seems fairly simple compared to the task of determining whether or not the quality per child has risen over time. Mothers' parental care and the care of infants and of the child that is provided by the parents and by public programs on health and early schooling will be treated as an investment in child quality. Have these components of child quality improved in the low-income countries? Are infants and children of tender ages receiving a better start in life than they did two or three decades ago? Although infant mortality has declined markedly, there is no reliable direct evidence that such acquired abilities as the health of surviving infants has improved or that the vitality and early training of young children have been enhanced. The measurement of these attributes of child quality throughout the population in any low-income country is at best exceedingly difficult. Some insights pertaining to child care, however, can be inferred from the implications of theory, along with some indirect evidence in support of these implications.

The response of households to new opportunities in providing child care to be had from new products and facilities that are more efficient relative to their costs than the traditional ones is in principle similar to the response of farmers to new high-yielding wheat and rice varieties and to public irrigation facilities that become available to farmers. Households in many parts of low-income countries have been purchasing new antibiotics (drugs) and acquiring advice and information from new health centers; moreover, the members of these households have been benefitting from various public school and health programs. Although there are many

amount of revealed entrepreneurial capacity because it has little value under such equilibrium conditions. Once agricultural modernization has been under way for an extended period, the rent derived from allocative ability becomes important, and the entrepreneurial capacity of farmers is increased by learning from experience, by the acquisition of more schooling, and by improvements in health. The supply curve therefore appears definitely to the right of that indicated for traditional agriculture.

studies that feature malnutrition, these studies are not designed to measure the changes in the nutrition of populations by countries over time. Food consumption per capita has in general been increasing, albeit slowly. The implication is that nutrition has been improving.

In analyzing the behavior of households, there is a private demand for useful drugs, for schooling, for health services, and for more and higher quality food. It is argued here that the supply curve (schedule) of these products and services has been shifting to the right, which implies that these products and services have become available to households at a lower price than in the past. In this context, housewives are in general the entrepreneurs who perceive, interpret, and (when they find the new opportunities worthwhile) respond to the implied incentives to improve the welfare of the family, including the well-being of their children. There is also a public demand for programs that improve the supply of drinking water and that reduce the incidence of various widespread diseases.

The indirect evidence that supports the hypothesis that child quality has been increasing in low-income countries is of three parts. Per capita food consumption has increased somewhat. Pre-primary and primary school enrollment has been rising substantially relative to the number of children. The increase in the survival rate of children is the most telling indirect evidence pertaining to this hypothesis. Since developments with respect to schooling and health in India will be considered, for which there is good evidence in the two sections that follow, some evidence is introduced at this point on the increases in the survival rates of children. These data imply that child quality has been increasing.

The survival rates of children shown in Table 10.2 are obtained by dividing the number of living children by the number ever born to women of specific ages. In Table 10.2, the survival rates of women ages 30–34 are compared with those of ages 50 to 54. Thus, the age-specific differences between these sets of women is 20 years or more. For each of the eleven countries, the survival rates of children of the younger women is clearly higher than those which the older women experienced. The survival rates of the younger women in eight of these countries is in the neighborhood of 20 percent higher than that shown for the older women. It is noteworthy that the rural survival rates are somewhat lower than those for urban residence in all but one of these countries for which estimates by residence are shown. Tentatively and with qualifications, the increases in the survival rates, shown for the younger women in column 4, are here viewed as a proxy for the improvement in child quality.

There are a considerable number of economic studies that pertain to child quality, but in using the relevant theory, most of the empirical work deals with the family behavior in high-income countries. Leibowitz's analysis of investment in children shows that home investments increase the measured stock of childhood human capital.[6] Even within a sample of very able children, the home investment variables were positively and signifi-

TABLE 10.2
Survival Rate* of Children by Age of Women and by Residence, Where Available

(1)	Survival rates young mothers age 30–34 (2)	Old mothers (3)	Relative increase in survival rates for young mothers in percent (4)
Taiwan, 1967			
Five Cities	.963	.772 age 60+	20
Other Area	.930	.753 age 60+	19
Malaysia, 1970—Sarawak			
Urban	.961	.933 age 50+	3
Rural	.894	.807 age 50+	10
Korea (South), 1970			
Cities	.945	.709 age 60+	25
Countryside	.925	.702 age 60+	24
Liberia, 1970			
Urban	.88	.77 age 50+	12
Rural	.84	.72 age 50+	14
Brazil			
1940	.782	.683 age 50+	13
1970	.870	.780 age 50+	10
Syria, 1970			
Urban	.859	.642 age 50+	25
Rural	.805	.595 age 50+	26
Tanzania, 1967			
Urban	.84	.67 age 50+	20
Rural	.74	.58 age 50+	22
El Salvador, 1971			
Urban	.837	.664 age 50+	21
Rural	.816	.666 age 50+	18
Indonesia, 1965	.779	.634 age 50+	19
Jordan, 1961			
Urban	.777	.576 ages 55–59	26
Rural	.731	.570 ages 55–59	22
Central African Republic (year not indicated)	.67	.51 age 50+	24

* The survival rate is the average number of living children divided by the average number of children ever born.

SOURCE: T. Paul Schultz, "Interrelationship Between Mortality and Fertility," in *Population and Development,* edited by Ronald G. Ridker (Baltimore: Johns Hopkins University Press, 1976).

6. Arleen Leibowitz, "Home Investment in Children," in *Economics of the Family: Marriage, Children and Human Capital,* edited by Theodore W. Schultz (Chicago: University of Chicago Press, 1974).

cantly related to her measure of the children's human capital. The positive effect of the allocation of time by parents to their preschool children on their education is also reported by Hill and Stafford.[7]

The approach of Butz and Habicht to the effects of nutrition and health rests on the assumption that family response behavior to new and better opportunities is in principle similar to that of farmers in low-income countries to better opportunities.[8] In a recent Rand study, De Tray, with the advantage of the contributions of various earlier studies, analyzes child schooling.[9]

The interaction in family behavior between child quantity and quality of children is high on the research agenda of human capital-oriented economists. De Tray's Ph.D. research deals directly with substitution between quantity and quality of children in the household.[10] His analysis was then extended, concentrating on child quality and the demand for children. His tentative findings, using the U.S. data, are that female (mothers) education increases the relative efficiency with which child quality is produced.[11] In a seminal-theoretical paper Becker and Lewis then extended the analytical framework of the interaction between quantity and quality of children.[12] They concluded "that the observed price elasticity of quantity exceeds that of quality, just the opposite of our conclusion for observed income elasticities. This reversal of quantity-quality ordering for price and income elasticities . . . gives a consistent interpretation of the findings of De Tray and others." In extending the Becker-Lewis model, some additional determinants of the demand for the quality of children are presented by Becker.[13] Further progress in analyzing this set of interactions is re-

7. Russell C. Hill and Frank P. Stafford, "The Allocation of Time to Preschool Children and Educational Opportunity," *Journal of Human Resources* 9 (1974).

8. William P. Butz and Jean-Pierre Habicht, "The Effects of Nutrition and Health on Fertility," in *Population and Development,* edited by Ronald G. Ridker, (Baltimore: Johns Hopkins University Press, 1976).

9. Dennis N. De Tray, *Child Schooling and Family Size* (Santa Monica, Calif.: Rand, April, 1978).

10. Dennis N. De Tray, "The Substitution Between Quantity and Quality of Children in the Household," Ph.D. dissertation, University of Chicago, 1972.

11. Dennis N. De Tray, "Child Quality and the Demand for Children," in *Economics of the Family: Marriage, Children and Human Capital,* edited by Theodore W. Schultz (Chicago: University of Chicago Press, 1974).

12. Gary S. Becker and H. Gregg Lewis, "Interaction Between Quantity and Quality of Children," in *Economics of the Family: Marriage, Children and Human Capital,* edited by Theodore W. Schultz (Chicago: University of Chicago Press, 1974).

13. Gary S. Becker, "A Theory of Social Interactions," *Journal of Political Economy* 82 (1974).

ported by Becker and Tomes.[14] A unique test of the quantity-quality model by Rosenzweig and Wolpin, using the twins experiment in a national sample of 2939 farm households in India, shows the theoretically expected negative effects of twins on schooling.[15]

SCHOOLING: AN INVESTMENT IN QUALITY

Progress in schooling accounts for a considerable part of the observable improvements in population quality. The costs of schooling and the distribution of schooling by age within the population have distinctive attributes. In reckoning the costs of schooling in these countries, the value of the work that young children do for their parents must be included. Thus, even for very young children during their first years of school, the rank and file of parents forego (sacrifice) the value of the work that these children perform. This cost component consists of earnings foregone. Another distinctive attribute of the progress in schooling is the vintage effect by age over time. Starting from a state of widespread illiteracy, as more schooling per child is achieved, the adults continue to proceed through life with little or no schooling, whereas the children on entering into adulthood are the beneficiaries of the additional schooling. Accordingly, a comparison of the schooling of the population who are presently ages 45 to 65 is approximately what it was for that age class two decades ago. For young adults ages 20 to 40, however, the level of schooling is presently considerably higher than it was for the same age class two decades ago.

Schooling is more than a consumption activity in the sense that it is not undertaken solely to obtain satisfactions (utility) while attending school. On the contrary, the public and private costs of schooling are incurred deliberately to acquire a productive stock, embodied in human beings, that provides future services. These services consist of future earnings and future capacity in self employment, in household activity and in future consumer satisfactions. Accordingly, the acquisition of schooling is here viewed as an investment in human capital. As an investment, schooling adds appreciably to the savings of these countries, but is omitted in the conventional national economic accounts because the reported savings are confined to the formation of physical capital.

14. Gary S. Becker and Nigel Tomes, "Child Endowments and the Quantity and Quality of Children," *Journal of Political Economy* 84 (1976).

15. Mark R. Rosenzweig and Kenneth I. Wolpin, "Testing the Quantity-Quality Fertility Model: The Use of Twins as a Natural Experiment," unpublished paper. Yale University, Economic Growth Center, October 1978.

There are a considerable number of studies that show that the supply of entrepreneurial capacity is definitely increased by additional schooling. The writer's survey of these studies clearly shows the pervasiveness of the favorable effects of schooling in both high- and low-income countries on the ability to deal with disequilibria associated with economic modernization.[16] The studies pertaining to agriculture provide the best evidence on this issue, mainly because the data are better than they are for other types of economic activity. Welch's recent essay is a further contribution, extending the analysis of the role of human capital in agriculture.[17]

The value of the contribution of the work that very young children do at home and on the family farms in India, and the effects that this cost component has upon school attendance, is a major part of the Ph.D. research by Makhija.[18] She also surveyed the literature bearing on this issue, including the recent studies by Shortlidge and by Rosenzweig and Evenson.[19]

The increase in schooling relative to population growth in India is indicated by Ram and Schultz. Table 10.3 shows that over the period from 1950/51 to 1970/71, the population increased by 52 percent. Pre-primary and primary enrollment, however, rose by 217 percent and that of middle and secondary schooling by 329 percent.

The remarkable increase in public school expenditures and in private opportunity cost of students relative to the increase in national income in India is evident in Table 10.4.

Since schooling is primarily an investment in future earnings and future satisfactions, it is a serious error to treat schooling outlays as current consumption. This error arises from the inference that schooling is like food, which is a consumer good, and from the treatment of increases in public expenditures on schooling that are associated with population growth as "welfare" expenditures, as a burden on the state, and as a use of resources that has the effect of reducing "savings" that would otherwise

16. See the writer's "The Value of the Ability to Deal with Disequilibria."

17. Finis Welch, "The Role of Investments in Human Capital and Agriculture," in *Distortions of Agricultural Incentives,* edited by Theodore W. Schultz (Bloomington: Indiana University Press, 1978).

18. Indra Makhija, "The Economic Contribution of Children and Its Effects on Fertility and Schooling: Rural India," Ph.D. dissertation, University of Chicago, December 1977.

19. Robert L. Shortlidge, Jr., "A Social-Economic Model of School Attendance in Rural India," Occasional Paper No. 86, Department of Agricultural Economics (Ithaca, New York: Cornell University, January 1976); Mark R. Rosenzweig and Robert E. Evenson, "Fertility, Schooling and the Economic Contribution of Children in Rural India," *Econometrica* 45 (July 1977).

TABLE 10.3
Population and Enrollment Increases, India 1950–51 to 1970–71

	1950–51	1970–71	1973–74	Percent from 1950/51 to 1970/71
Population (millions)				
Total	361	548	580	52
Age 6–10	44.5	75.2	NA	69
Age 11–14	32.0	51.0	NA	59
Enrollment (millions)				
Primary	18.7	59.3	63.2	217
Middle	3.3 } 4.8	13.4 } 20.6	14.7	306 } 329
Secondary	1.5	7.2	7.5	980
Post-secondary	2.0	5.2	NA	160
University	.17	1.95	2.23	1047

SOURCE: Population estimates for 1950–51 and 1970–71 are from the 1951 and 1971 census of India and for 1973–74 from Reports on Population and Family Planning, Population Council, New York. Enrollment estimates are from Government of India Planning Commission, *Draft Five Year Plan 1978–83*, 1978, p. 226, except for post-secondary which is from Rati Ram and Theodore W. Schultz, "Life Span, Health, Savings, and Productivity," *Economic Development and Cultural Change* (April 1979).

be available for investment purposes. Thus a serious conceptual error is committed in treating schooling as consumption whereas it is primarily an investment.

Clearly the expenditures on schooling, including higher education, are a substantial fraction of national income in most countries. What is less

TABLE 10.4
Investment in Schooling Relative to National Income, India, 1950–51 to 1970–71

		1950–51	1970–71
1	National income in billion rupees, current prices	95.1	344
2	Public schooling expenditures in billion rupees, current prices	1.1	10.8
3	Private opportunity cost of students' time in billion rupees, current prices	3.9	27.9
4	2 + 3 as a percentage of 1	5	11

SOURCE: Rati Ram and Theodore W. Schultz, "Life Span, Health, Savings and Productivity," *Economic Development and Cultural Change* (April 1979).

well known is that these expenditures are *large* relative to the conventional national accounting measures (concepts) of savings and investment which exclude expenditure on schooling. Taking India as an example, as Table 10.4 shows, the proportion that schooling expenditures bear to national income, savings and investment is not only large but it has tended to increase substantially over time.

HUMAN CAPITAL: THE STOCK OF HEALTH[20]

A house built to last 50 years adds a good deal more to the stock of housing than does a house that lasts only 30 years. Quality of construction makes the difference and the better house is the more valuable property. Human capital has comparable dimensions. The economic value of human capital, be it entrepreneurship, skills, or schooling, is enhanced when its useful life is extended. The life span of a population is an important factor both in determining the incentives to invest in various forms of human capital and the value of the stock of such capital. Human capital theory treats everyone's state of health as a stock, i.e., as health capital and its contribution as health services. A part of the quality of the initial stock is inherited and a part is acquired by investment in health capital, which depreciates over time and at an increasing rate in later life. There are acquisition and maintenance costs which make up the gross investment in health capital. These investments include child care, nutrition, housing, medical services, exercise and use of own time. The flow of services that health capital renders consists of "healthy time" or "sickness-free time" which are inputs into work, consumption and leisure activities.[21]

The notable improvement in health that is revealed by the longer life span of people in low-income countries is undoubtedly the most important advance in population quality. Moreover, this quality attribute has improved at a remarkable pace over the last three decades. Despite the stress that has been put on the adverse effects it has in causing population growth, there is no other quality attribute that is as important and pervasive in its contributions to the welfare of people in these countries. What, then, are the specific implications of better health and the longer life span?

20. This section draws primarily on the study of Rati Ram and Theodore W. Schultz, "Life Span, Health, Savings, and Productivity," *Economic Development and Cultural Change* (April 1979).

21. See Alan Williams, "Health Service Planning," in *Studies in Modern Economic Analysis,* edited by M. J. Artis and A. R. Nobay (Edinburgh: Blackwell, 1977); and M. Grossman, *The Demand for Health,* Occasional Paper 119, National Bureau of Economic Research (New York: Columbia University Press, 1972).

One implication that has received much attention relates to population growth. It is obvious that the large decline in the death rates and persistent high traditional birth rates, which, however, are now beginning to decline substantially, account for the prevailing rapid population growth. But what has been overlooked is that population growth is not necessarily incompatible with advances in human welfare. On the contrary, there are important favorable implications that are consequences of the increases in life span. First and foremost is the additional satisfaction (utility) that people derive from longer life. Hard to measure, of course, but there is little room for doubt that value of life is enhanced by its extension. Nor is the measurement of the value of this achievement wholly out of the cards. Usher has developed an ingenious approach to determine the additional utility that people derive from increases in life expectancy.[22] His application of this extension of theory to particular low-income countries suggests that the real rate of economic growth is appreciably higher than that shown by the national statistics of these countries.

There is also a set of implications that pertain to the incentives to acquire more human capital, namely the incentive to acquire more schooling and on-the-job experience as investments in future earnings which are to be had over the longer period and the incentive on the part of parents to invest more in the human capital of their children. Gains in the state of health and the longer life span also imply increases in the productivity of workers as a consequence of longer participation in the labor force, greater physical ability to do work, and less loss of working time because of illness.

It is well known that since about 1950 the life expectancy at birth has increased 40 percent or more in many low-income countries. This remarkable achievement, however, has received all too little attention. The people of Western Europe and North America never attained so large an increase in life expectancy in so short a period. Since there are no comparable developments in Western economic history, to account for this unprecedented achievement on the part of many low-income countries and to analyze its effects calls for a direct appeal to the human condition and circumstances that have characterized these countries.

The decline in the mortality of infants and of very young children is only a part of this story. The mortality of older children, youth, and adults has also declined very substantially. The term "life span" is used here to refer to life expectancy at ages 10, 20, and at older ages. The longer life

22. Dan Usher, "An Imputation to the Measure of Economic Growth for Changes in Life Expectancy," *The Measurement of Economic and Social Performance,* edited by Milton Moss (New York: National Bureau of Economic Research, 1973).

span of children who have reached the age when they are in school and of young adults is central to the approach here.

The Ram-Schultz study deals mainly with the economics of these demographic developments in India. The gains in life span achieved by low-income countries are well illustrated by developments in India. Over the period from 1951 to 1971, life expectancy at birth of males rose from 32.4 to 46.4 years, which is an increase of 43 percent, and that of females rose from 31.7 to 44.7 years, an increase of 41 percent. The notable increases in life span that occurred over these two decades are shown for selected ages from 10 to 60 in Table 10.5. The increases in the life span of males ranges from 25 to 35 percent and of females from 20 to 22 percent. However, the expected life span in years for males and females at ages 40, 50 and 60 are virtually the same for 1971. The full range from birth to age 60 of these increases in life spans is depicted in Figure 10.1; the difference in years in favor of 1971 is shown on the vertical scale.

The story on schooling, including the increases in savings that the additional schooling has called forth, is covered in the preceding section. That substantial increases in on-the-job training and experience have occurred is highly plausible in view of the additional incentives to gain such training and experience. But data on this activity do not permit estimates of the extent of the response to these incentives and the magnitude of the increases. The Ram-Schultz paper, however, provides some evidence on the gains in the productivity of agricultural labor in India that has been realized as a consequence of improvements in health.

Using a simple production function approach to account for the increases in agricultural production during each of two recent decades, the

TABLE 10.5
Increase in Expected Life Span of Males and Females in India between 1951 and 1971 at Selected Ages

	Expected Life Span				Increase 1951–1971			
	Males		Females		Males		Females	
Age	1951	1971	1951	1971	Years	%	Years	%
10	39.0	48.8	39.5	47.7	9.8	25	8.2	21
20	33.0	41.1	32.9	39.9	8.1	25	7.0	21
30	26.6	33.3	26.2	32.0	6.7	25	5.8	22
40	20.5	25.9	21.1	25.4	5.4	26	4.3	20
50	14.9	19.2	16.2	19.7	4.3	29	3.5	22
60	10.1	13.6	11.3	13.8	3.5	35	2.5	22

SOURCES: 1951—*Census of India 1951*, Paper No. 2 of 1956, pp. 35–38; 1971—*Census of India 1971*, Paper No. 1 of 1977, pp. 16—19. Rati Ram and Theodore W. Schultz, "Life Span, Health, Savings, and Productivity," *Economic Development and Cultural Change* (April 1979).

FIGURE 10.1
Age-Specific Life Expectancy, India, 1951 and 1971 Censuses

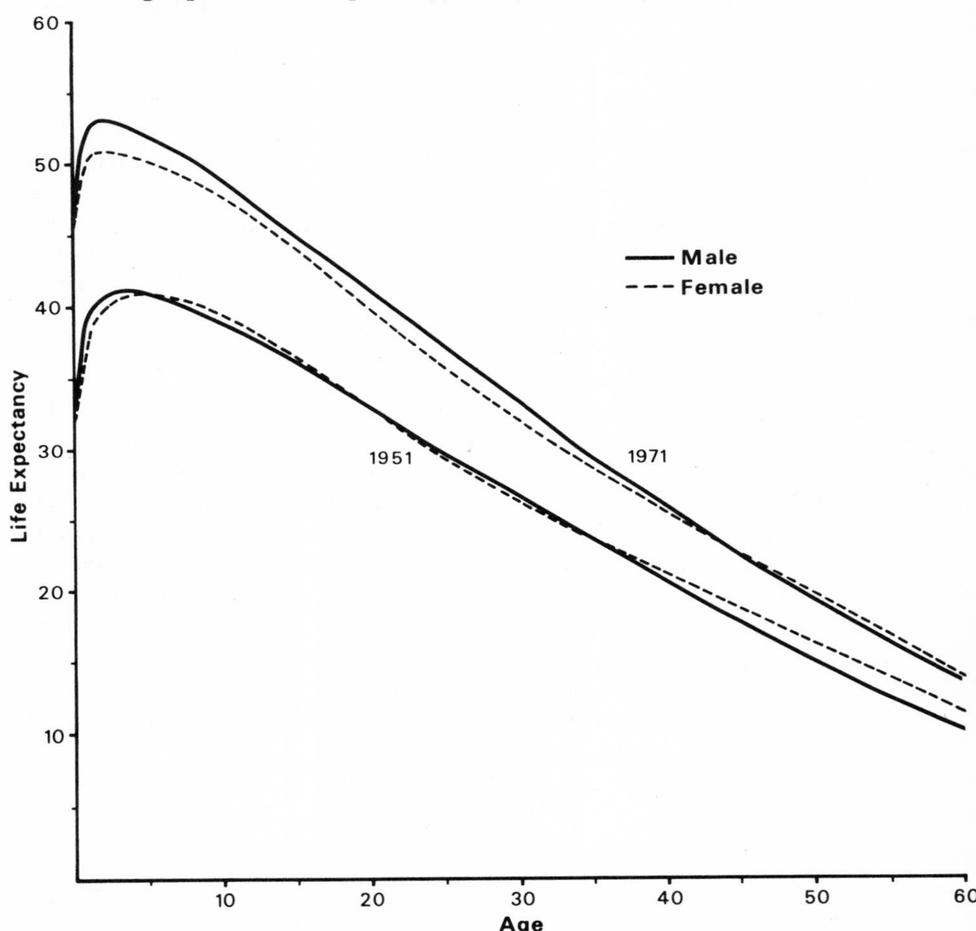

SOURCE: Rati Ram and Theodore W. Schultz, "Life Span, Health, Savings, and Productivity," *Economic and Cultural Change* (April 1979).

unexplained part of the increases in output is approximately 36 percent over the period from 1951 to 1961 and only 19 percent during the period from 1961 to 1971. These unexplained residuals in this growth accounting approach are attributed to "technical progress" and to the consequence of the improvement in the health of workers. The difference between the magnitudes of these two residuals (36 and 19 percent respectively) presents a puzzle. The Green Revolution, the hallmark of technical progress, was actively underway during the later decade. It was not so during the 1951–1961 period. Yet this residual was much the larger during the decade before the Green Revolution occurred. In searching for a solution to this puzzle, we found that the differences in the production effects of the improvements in health of the labor force appear to be the explanation. Public health programs initiated during the First Five Year Plan (1951–56) and carried through the Second Plan (1956–61) had a much larger favorable effect on health than did the programs undertaken later. The program to suppress malaria tells the story. Official data indicate that the incidence of malaria dropped from 75 million in 1952–53 to about 1.1 million in 1959–60. But the malaria program suffered a setback after 1965, although the incidence of malaria did not revert to the old level. It should also be noted that a massive drive against tuberculosis was launched in the 1950s, and, by the end of 1959, 138 million people had been tested and about 48 million vaccinated.

The observable difference in the decline in mortality alone explains about 28 percent of the interstate variation in agricultural productivity. An additional test, based on effects of the suppression of malaria by districts in India, shows that the increases in crop output in the "high incidence" districts rose 45 percent while in the "low incidence" districts the increase was less, as expected, namely 38.6 percent. The evidence seems reasonably good in support of the proposition that the near-eradication of malaria during the early part of the decades under consideration contributed significantly to increases in agricultural production. What applies to the favorable production effects of malaria programs also applies to the other public and private activities that lead to improvements in health and increases in life span.[23]

23. Other studies on the favorable productive effects of malaria control lend support to this analysis: Robin Barlow, "The Economic Effects of Malaria Eradication," *American Economic Review* 57 (2) (May 1967). Jere Behrman, *Supply Response in Underdeveloped Agriculture: A Case Study of Four Major Annual Crops in Thailand, 1937–63* (Amsterdam: North Holland, 1967). G. Borkar, *Health in Independent India* (New Delhi: Ministry of Health, Government of India, 1957). Wilfred Malenbaum, "Health and Productivity in Poor Areas," in *Empirical Studies in Health Economics,* edited by H. E. Klarman (Baltimore: The Johns Hopkins University Press, 1970). Rati Ram, "India's Agriculture During 1950–70: An Exercise in Growth Source Analysis," The University of Chicago Agricultural Economics Paper 74 (14) (1974) unpublished. N. V. Sovani, *Population Trends and Agriculture Development: Case Studies of Sri Lanka and India,* United Nations Economic and Social Council Paper E/Conf. 60/SYM. 1/11 (April 1973). C. E. A. Winslow, *The Cost of Sickness and the Price of Health* (Geneva: World Health Organization, 1951). World Bank, *Health: Sector Working Paper,* Washington, D.C., 1975.

SUMMING UP

Human capital theory is sufficiently robust to gauge particular improvements in population quality. Many low-income countries have during the past two or three decades made large investments in various stocks of capital that are embodied in people. The growth in the stock of health capital is more impressive. The improvement in health that accounts for the 40 percent and more increase in life span is an unprecedented achievement. People of all ages throughout the population have participated in this achievement. Child quality has risen. When account is taken of large increases in schooling per pupil along with the gains in health, the quality of school-age children and young adults is clearly much better than it was for the same age class some decades ago. The effects of the additional schooling and of the improvements in health on labor productivity have been favorable. The supply of entrepreneurship throughout the economy has increased considerably; people are taking more effective advantage of the new economic opportunities associated with modernization. Annual savings have also been enhanced substantially by the investment in human capital.

As noted elsewhere, in a society where life is short, labor earns a pittance; work is hard and life is harsh.[24] Vitality is low, illiteracy abounds, and people languish. A turn to a better future comes when the span of life increases. Incentives become worthwhile; to invest in more schooling and the time spent at work becomes more productive. Investment in human capital and the resulting improvements in population quality matter. "Standing room only" becomes a myth.

24. Ram and Schultz, "Life Span, Health, Savings, and Productivity."

II

The Quality of Population in Developing Countries, with Particular Reference to Education and Training

MARK BLAUG

INTRODUCTION

THE "QUALITY" OF POPULATION in a country is usually taken to mean its state of health, its nutritional standards, and the level of its skills and competencies. The problem of health and nutrition in developing countries is a vast subject in its own right. The subjects of concern in this essay are those population qualities that can be improved by formal and non-formal education and training programs. Much has been achieved in this regard in Asia, Africa and Latin America over the last two or three decades, and yet educational and training issues in the three continents of the Third World continue to be matters of profound controversy. The aim here is a twofold one: to sum up the accomplishments to date and to convey the flavor of current debates. There is in fact a widespread sense throughout the Third World that something has gone wrong of late with development policies in general, and with educational and training policies in particular. Indeed, to any economist who, like the writer, has long been concerned with questions of educational planning in developing countries, the intellectual landscape has recently undergone an amazing sea change.

In the 1950s and 1960s, economists were thick on the ground in every ministry of education in every capital city of the less developed countries (LDCs). Those were the days when all indications pointed toward the rapid expansion of educational systems at all levels and when economists were welcomed for producing new arguments to support an educational inflation that was desired anyway on political grounds. What did it matter that manpower forecasting was crude and that cost-benefit analysis was based on rather implausible assumptions, when in fact they led to answers that called for still more education? No one likes to look a gift horse in the mouth, and politicians are always thankful for all the help they can get. Economists who still remember those days have reason to look back at them with nostalgia.

To be an economist interested in education in the 1970s is not quite so easy. The streets of Calcutta, Karachi, Cairo, Accra, Bogota and Buenos Aires are filled with unemployed university graduates, even as the civil services in these countries are overstocked with graduates. In Africa, the so-called school leaver problem, which only ten years ago referred exclusively to unemployed leavers from *primary* schools, now designates the unemployed products of secondary as well as primary schools. In the famous Addis Ababa Conference of 1961, African ministers of education looked forward confidently to universal primary education by 1980. Nineteen hundred and eighty is only one year away and yet in more than half of the 46 countries in tropical Africa, it is now perfectly obvious that universal primary education will not be achieved even by the year 2000. Everywhere there is deep dissatisfaction with the quality of education—the curriculum, the examination system, the standards of teacher training, and so on. There must be something wrong with an educational system, it is argued, that encourages students to gear all their efforts to the passing of examinations, leading to the next cycle of education and still more examinations, for the sole purpose of gaining entry into wage employment in the modern sector of the economy when so many of them clearly never will achieve this goal. Ivan Illich's books appear to be addressed to audiences in advanced countries, and yet his thoroughly subversive idea of deschooling has not fallen entirely on deaf ears even in developing countries. The new American theories of screening, namely, that educational certificates serve no other function than to discriminate between individuals in terms of achievement drive, adds strength to the impact of Illich's writings. The "diploma disease" may be a worldwide phenomenon,[1] but, surely, it is Third World countries that are really obsessed by "credentialism."

The new circumstances of the 1970s have produced new priorities in educational planning. No longer are ministries of education solely preoccupied with the building of more schools to accommodate ever larger enrollments, and with the expansion of teacher training facilities to equip the new schools with more teachers. Nowadays, educational plans in the Third World consist largely of ambitious schemes to (1) introduce work experience into the primary school curriculum, (2) to integrate adults with children in a more flexible system of first-stage education, (3) to vocationalize the curriculum of secondary schools, (4) to introduce a mandatory period of labor market experience between secondary and higher

1. R. Dore, *The Diploma Disease. Education, Qualifications and Development* (London: Allen and Unwin, 1976).

education, and (5) to recruit the dropouts of the educational system into a national youth employment service. Everywhere there is an interest in reforming the examination system so as to minimize the testing of academic achievement and to maximize the testing of natural aptitudes that cannot be acquired by rote learning. Some countries have begun to introduce geographical quotas as a basis for educational selection, and there is even talk of imitating the Chinese by using social quotas in terms of family background. If the slogans of the 1960s were "universal primary education," "manpower planning," and "investment in human capital," the slogans of the 1970s are "basic education," "earning while learning," "lifelong education," and "aptitude testing instead of examinations."

In such an atmosphere, the arguments of economists appear to be both unnecessary and irrelevent. Nevertheless, economists still have valuable lessons to impart to educational planners in developing countries. No doubt many of these lessons will be harder to teach than the old ones, more easily resisted than the lessons of yesterday, and more politically dangerous to implement than the recommendations of ten years ago. Still, economists have insights they can bring to bear on the outstanding issues in the field of education and training that are easily missed by noneconomists. In that sense, economists still have a contribution to make to educational planning in poor countries.

EDUCATION AND ECONOMIC DEVELOPMENT

It is useful to think of educational planning as consisting of a definite hierarchy of decisions:

1. How much of the total resources of an economy should be devoted to education and training?
2. How much should be spent by government, relying on private finance to fill out the rest?
3. How should public expenditures on education and training be divided between formal education provided by educational institutions and nonformal training provided by industry and various government agencies (subsidies for on-the-job training, off-the-job training, adult education, literacy campaigns, agricultural extension, and so on)?
4. How should public expenditures on formal education be divided among the different levels of the educational system?
5. How should these in turn be divided among the institutions comprising a level of education?

Consider now the first two of the items in the list. Clearly, if these two decisions are made irrationally, all subsequent decisions in the list must be suboptimal. Now what can the economist say about these two grand overall planning decisions? Very little, if the truth be told. No doubt there is a positive relationship between the volume of education and training provided, on the one hand, and the level and rate of growth of national income, on the other. But such general knowledge is of little use to a particular government interested in accelerating the pace of economic development. After two decades of intensive research on the association between education and national income around the world, little more can be said than that a 10 percent rate of enrollment in primary schools and a 40 percent literacy rate is a necessary but, alas, not a sufficient condition for rapid economic advance.[2] It is, in fact, easier to show that nations are better educated because they are rich than that they are rich because they are better educated. Even at the level of a given occupational category within a given industry, no universal relationship can be laid down between the education of workers and the output of the productive processes in which they participate. Countries progress along a variety of manpower growth paths, and the range of alternatives is almost as wide as the range of their living standards. Differences in social attitudes and in political systems, not to mention the costs and finance of educational systems, widen the range even further. In short, what is learned from international comparisons is that nothing is learned from international comparisons.

Even if the first item on the list of decisions is taken for granted, the second item would itself raise insuperable problems. If the general principle is accepted that there can be no *economic* justification for devoting more resources to any particular use—and thus less to all others—unless this results in greater measurable economic benefits per unit of costs, cost-benefit analysis of each and every area of government activity clearly cannot be carried out so as to equalize cost-benefit ratios in all lines of public expenditure. The notion that educational planning cannot be done until the problems of the economics of, for example, health, housing and social insurance are solved is a counsel of despair. Besides, experts in the other social services are likewise waiting for educational planners to solve their problems so they can in turn determine the optimum level of expenditure in such areas as health and housing.

Like it or not, therefore, scholars seem doomed to analyzing allocative efficiency in the field of education and training at a suboptimal level. The constraint within which operations are possible—total public expenditures

2. M. Blaug, *An Introduction to the Economics of Education* (London: Penguin, 1970), chap. 3.

on education—is determined by a political process that is only vaguely connected with any objectives that might be described as economic. Thus, effective educational planning begins not with item 1 or 2, but with item 3 in the preceding list.

THE OPTIMUM SHAPE OF THE EDUCATIONAL PYRAMID

A broad historical look at some of the most prominent advanced countries that fifty or sixty years ago were underdeveloped—say, Japan and the Soviet Union—will reveal the following pattern. The typical picture of the expansion of schooling—in the case of Japan since about 1890, and in the case of the Soviet Union since the October 1917 Revolution—illustrates a policy of first attaining universal primary education while holding back secondary and higher education. Then, having almost reached universal primary education—in Japan around 1912, and in Russia around 1930—a more generous attitude was taken toward secondary education, while higher education was still kept tightly under control. Only when secondary education had become almost universal in these countries—in the case of Japan about 1930, and in the case of the Soviet Union about 1950—was higher education allowed to expand.[3] This classic pattern of allowing the educational pyramid to grow at the base and only thereafter allowing it to grow in the middle and at the apex has been completely reversed in the recent experiences of the Third World. Ever since 1950, in practically all of the hundred or so developing countries in the world, secondary education and higher education have grown faster than primary education both in terms of enrollments and in terms of educational expenditures. Or, to express the same thought in other words: secondary and particularly higher educated manpower has been overproduced in most of Africa, Asia and Latin America beyond all possible hopes of absorption into gainful employment, whatever the feasible rates of future economic growth in these countries. Therefore, the first priority in educational planning in the Third World is to reduce somehow the rates of growth of secondary and higher education, shifting resources from the upper to the lower levels of the educational system.

3. For Japan, see R. P. Dore, "Education in Japan's Growth," *Pacific Affairs* 14 (Spring 1964); and W. E. Lockwood, "Employment, Technology and Education in Asia," *Malayan Economic Review* 16 (2) (October 1971):21. For the USSR, see N. De Witt, *Education and Professional Employment in the USSR* (Washington, D.C.: USGPO, 1961), pp. 37, 130–39, 439–41, 449; and K. Nozhko *et al.*, *Education Planning in the USSR* (Paris: UNESCO-IIEP, 1968), pp. 21, 26.

What is the evidence for such a bold assertion? It is evidence of three kinds. Firstly, there is the evidence of growing open unemployment of secondary and higher educated individuals throughout Asia, Africa, and Latin America, which is further considered below. Secondly, there is the fact that forecasts of manpower requirements in Third World countries increasingly predict middle-level and higher-level manpower surpluses rather than shortages in the decade to come.[4] Thirdly, there is evidence that the social rate of return on investment in education is almost always lower in secondary and higher education than in primary education.[5]

One may quarrel about the reliability of unemployment statistics in developing countries. One may dismiss the technique of manpower forecasting as little more than guesswork dressed up in numbers. One may likewise throw doubt on rate-of-return analysis for relying too much on monetary earnings as a measure of the economic contribution of education. And one may also point to certain countries, such as Burma, Mali, Botswana, Bolivia, and Ecuador, that continue to face serious shortages of middle-level and particularly higher-level manpower. But by and large in the three continents with most of the less developed nations, it is true to say that all indications point toward the past overexpansion of the upper levels of the educational system and a concomitant underinvestment in the lower levels. Even if only the planning targets of these countries themselves are considered, the point would still remain valid. For example, primary enrollments in Africa were in 1977 well below the Addis Ababa targets set in 1962, whereas enrollments in secondary and tertiary education were well above the original planned targets. Most of the overexpansion in higher education in Africa has so far been disguised by overemployment of university graduates in the public sector,[6] in consequence of which, overexpansion of education in Africa has only shown up dramatically to date in the form of open unemployment among secondary school leavers. But now that many African governments are beginning to be unwilling to absorb university graduates in the civil service, owing to increasing fiscal pressures,

4. See D. Turnham, *The Employment Problems in Less Developed Countries. A Review of the Evidence* (Paris: OECD, Development Centre Studies, Employment Series 1, 1971), pp. 119–20; ILO, *Growth, Employment and Equity. A Development Plan for Sudan* (Geneva: ILO, 1976), pp. 403–406 (referred to hereafter as the ILO Sudan Report).

5. See G. Psacharopoulos, *Returns to Education. An International Comparison* (Amsterdam: Elsevier, 1973), ch. 4; H. H. Thias and M. Carnoy, *Cost-Benefit Analysis in Education. A Case Study of Kenya* (Baltimore: John Hopkins University Press, 1972), pp. 93–94, 128–32; and ILO Sudan Development Plan, pp. 406–408.

6. Egypt's policy of guaranteed employment for university graduates has for long been the most striking example of this tendency in Africa. But the Sudan is another example: see ILO Sudan Development Plan, pp. 115–16.

we can expect to see Africa following Asia in massive open unemployment of university graduates.

NATURE AND MAGNITUDE OF EDUCATED UNEMPLOYMENT

Educated unemployment, and particularly graduate unemployment, has slowly emerged as the major educational problem of LDCs in the 1970s. To convey the magnitude of the problem, the facts for a few Asian and African countries will be briefly surveyed. The term "educated unemployment" refers in each case to open unemployment among those who at least completed a given level of education, but the particular level will vary from country to country: for example, in India it refers to "matriculates" and college graduates; in Bangladesh it refers to all those with a secondary school certificate or above; in Sri Lanka it refers to those with 0-levels and above; and throughout Africa it generally refers to those who have at least completed primary education.

The best data on educated unemployment in the Asian continent are found in India. The Expert Committee on Unemployment Estimates, better known as the Dantwala Committee, devoted several pages to a review of the Indian evidence on educated unemployment; 1969 saw the publication of an entire book on the subject, and more recent figures are given in a special enumeration of the 1971 Census of Population.[7] Recent data on educated unemployment in Sri Lanka are found in the country mission report of the International Labour Organization (ILO) World Employment Programme,[8] and there is some partial evidence for Bangladesh in recent years.[9]

7. *Report of the Committee of Experts on Unemployment Estimates* (Delhi: Planning Commission, Government of India, 1970), pp. 149–51 (referred to hereafter as the Dantwala Committee Report); M. Blaug, R. Layard, and M. Woodhall, *The Causes of Graduate Unemployment in India* (London: Allen Lane, Penguin, 1969); Ministry of Labour and Rehabilitation, Department of Labour and Employment, *Report of the Committee on Unemployment* (Delhi: Government of India, 1973), app. 15, 16 (referred to hereafter as the Bhagvati Committee Report); and K. V. E. Prasad, "Education and Unemployment of Professional Manpower in India," Zakir Husain Centre for Educational Studies, Jawaharlal Nehru University, New Delhi, 1977.

8. ILO, *Matching Employment Opportunities and Expectations. A Programme of Action for Ceylon* (Geneva: ILO, 1971) (referred to hereafter as the ILO Sri Lanka Report). See also P. J. Richards, *Employment and Unemployment in Ceylon* (Paris: OECD, Employment Series, 3, 1971).

9. See A. Josefowicz, *Unemployment Among the Educated Youth* (Karachi: Planning Commission, Government of Pakistan, 1970). See also M. Obaidullah, *A Study of Employment Survey of Graduates* (Dacca: Institute of Statistical Re-

In all developing countries, it appears to be true that unemployment is higher among educated groups than among illiterates and higher at the middle levels of the educational system than at the lower or upper ends. These characteristics also obtain in India.[10] Likewise, the incidence of educated unemployment the world over is heaviest among the younger age groups, and again this characteristic is found in India.[11] A much more controversial but nevertheless general feature of educated unemployment in developing countries is its concentration among first job seekers. The rate of open unemployment among the educated is high because so many of them take from 6 to 12 to 24 months to find their first job; the rate of unemployment among those who have worked before is in fact trivial. Blaug, Layard and Woodhall estimated the "waiting period" after graduation of an average matriculate in 1967 at 18 months, and that of an average university graduate at 6 months, a finding which has been endorsed by the Dantwala Committee.[12] This may be contrasted with an average waiting period of 3–4 weeks for university graduates in countries like the U.S. and U.K.

Since then, a special enumeration of the 1971 Census shows that the average "waiting period" of first degree holders in 1971 had crept up to 12.7 months for males and 14.2 months for females; among male master's degree holders, it was even higher than that, namely, 13.1 months, and even among Ph.D.s it was as high as 12 months.[13] Since some graduates, particularly those with first class degrees, get a job immediately after leaving college, an *average* waiting period of 12 months implies that 10–20 percent of all graduates actually search for work over a period as long as 4–5 years. Lest it be thought that such long waiting periods are mostly due to the large proportion of graduates with "general" degrees in liberal studies, it should be noted that the average waiting period for graduate civil engineers in 1971 was 11.4 months; likewise, for master's and doctoral degree holders in physics it was as high as 13 and 11.6 months

---

search and Training, University of Dacca, 1971); and J. M. Ritzen, J. B. Balderston, *Methodology for Planning Technical Education. With a Case Study of Polytechnics in Bangladesh* (New York: Praeger, 1975). For data on other Asian countries, see UN-ECAFE, *Economic Survey of Asia and the Far East, 1973, Part One, Education and Employment* (Colombo, Sri Lanka: ECAFE, 1974), pp. 47–50.

10. See Turnham, *Employment Problems in Less Developed Countries,* pp. 51–52.

11. *Ibid.*, pp. 47–51.

12. Blaug, Layard, and Woodhall, *Causes of Graduate Unemployment in India,* pp. 74–81, 89–90; and Dantwala Committee Report, p. 150.

13. Bhagvati Committee Report, App. 15.

respectively.[14] The total number of educated unemployed in India in 1978 may be crudely estimated at about 3 million.

The rate of unemployment among university and polytechnic graduates in Bangladesh has in recent years been as high as 25 percent and the average "waiting period" for polytechnic graduates has been calculated to be 5 months.[15] Still higher rates of educated unemployment have been reported for Sri Lanka, at least for primary and secondary school leavers.[16]

Turning to Africa, it is likewise found that rates of unemployment among primary school leavers are sometimes lower than among persons of the same age who have never been to school.[17] This should not be surprising because education in Africa has for a long time been a major criterion for selecting those that are eligible for formal sector employment in both government and private firms. At the same time, it is also true that African school leavers have been finding it increasingly difficult to obtain wage-earning employment, or at least to obtain it on the same favorable terms as five or ten years earlier. A number of tracer studies in Africa have documented the employment experience of school leavers over the first few years after leaving school.

Table 11.1 summarizes the results for school leavers in Ghana, Kenya, Swaziland and Zambia. Most of the rates of unemployment for recent years are high, although not necessarily higher than the rates of other persons in the same age bracket; rates of job-seeking in Africa among all young people aged 15 to 24, especially if they are unmarried and without dependents, are invariably extremely high. Note also that for each cohort, the rates of unemployment decline over time, suggesting that after a period of search, most of the school leavers do find work.[18] In these respects, the school leaver problem, like the general employment problem, is somewhat different from what is often imagined. But there is no reason to be complacent: given the expected rates of growth of school leavers in Africa, as against the expected rates of growth of formal sector employment, there is

14. Prasad, "Education and Employment of Professional Manpower in India."

15. See Ritzen and Balderston, *Technical Education*, pp. 70–72.

16. ILO Sri Lanka Report, Table 8 and Diagrams 1, 2, pp. 28–29.

17. Kenya is one such example: see ILO, *Employment, Incomes and Equality. A Strategy for Increasing Productive Employment in Kenya* (Geneva: ILO), Table 19, p. 59 (referred to hereafter as the ILO Kenya Report).

18. The decline in educated unemployment as time passes after graduation also comes out clearly in Manpower Services, Ministry of Economic Planning, *Survey of the Pattern of Employment and Employment Prospects of Polytechnic Graduates in Ghana* (Accra: Ministry of Economic Planning, 1975), Table 13; and ILO Sudan Report, Table 97, p. 374.

every reason to think that the so-called school leaver problem in Africa will get worse over the next ten years.[19]

THE CAUSES OF EDUCATED UNEMPLOYMENT

When a developing country suffers from general, open unemployment and underemployment—as all LDCs do—it is not surprising to find that some of the unemployed are by no means without some schooling and even that they include a certain proportion of secondary school leavers and university graduates. However, the magnitude of educated unemployment in Asia and sub-Saharan Africa, and perhaps even more the persistence of the phenomenon in certain Asian countries over decades, if not generations, is in fact somewhat surprising. For obvious reasons, unemployment of educated people is a more serious problem than unemployment in general:

TABLE 11.1
Percentage of Junior Secondary School Leavers Unemployed One or Two Years Later in Selected African Countries, 1963–73

Countries	Year of leaving	One year after leaving	Two years after leaving
Kenya	1965	2	—
	1966	1	—
	1967	1	1*
	1968	15	9
	1969	16	4
Zambia	1971	38† 20	10
	1973	22‡ 7§	—
Swaziland	1963	11 ‖	
Ghana	1963	—	15
	1964	—	40
	1965	44†	

SOURCE: UN-ECA, *Survey of Economic and Social Conditions in Africa 1976–1977 (Part 1)*. Addis Ababa: UN, 1978, p. 66.

* 3 years after leaving.
† 6 months after leaving.
‡ 8 months after leaving (includes 4 percent unknown).
§ 14 months after leaving.
‖ Including persons working in South Africa.
18 months after leaving.

19. See R. P. Dore, J. Humphrey, and P. West, *The Basic Arithmetic of Employment* (Geneva: ILO, 1976).

in most cases, social as well as private resources have been invested in educated individuals in the hope, among other things, that education would render them more employable; moreover, educated individuals are likely to regard gainful employment as a human right, and their discontent upon finding themselves unemployed can become a potent threat to national security. For all these reasons, governments are likely to attach high priority to the elimination of educated unemployment or, at any rate, are likely to entertain the belief that it can be eliminated long before full employment of all labor is achieved.

It is perfectly conceivable that general unemployment and educated unemployment stem from different causes and that, in this sense, the latter can be eliminated without necessarily curing the former. Educated unemployment, some will argue, is due to the effects of education on the career aspirations of students, creating what is in effect a gap between expectations and opportunities; this kind of structural imbalance can be removed by appropriate educational reform, even though an overall imbalance between the demand and supply of labor might continue indefinitely.[20] But despite the plausibility of this argument, it is far from obvious that the causes of structural and overall imbalance can be distinguished in this way.

Overall imbalance of labor means that there is an excess supply of labor over the volume of employment that is generated by the structure of production, the existing technology, the current rate of wages, and the range of product prices ruling in the market. Structural imbalance, as exemplified by educated unemployment, may mean that the labor force is too highly educated for that volume of employment; in other words, there are just too many educated people for the prevailing job opportunities, whatever their aspirations and expectations. It cannot be denied that if educated people were willing to accept any job that was offered to them, including manual work at substandard wages, educated unemployment would virtually disappear overnight. But this can also be said of general unemployment. It is always unrealistic to discuss the problem of unemployment without taking some account of the given job aspirations of people. It remains an open question, therefore, as to whether the educational system in the Third World is *artificially* raising the expectations of graduates, so that they end up demanding more well-paid, white collar jobs than are in fact available.

To put it more sharply, is it really true that the type of education they have received robs them of the capacity to adjust their expectations to the prevailing realities of the labor market? Unless the question is put this

20. L. Emmerij, "Research Priorities of the World Employment Programme," *International Labour Review* (May 1972), p. 415.

sharply, it is pointless to debate educational remedies for the situation. It is hardly practical to argue, for example, that the graduates of urban schools and colleges are unemployed because they refuse to "get their hands dirty" by migrating to farms in the countryside, and that the educational system should be thoroughly reformed so as to instill a "love for farming" among town-bred youngsters. If feasible educational reforms that might make an impact on the employment problem are to be discussed, it must be taken for granted that educated youngsters will always aspire to the better-paid jobs in society, whatever the content of education and whatever the level of economic development.

Enough has now been said to suggest that there are difficulties in accounting for educated unemployment in the absence of general unemployment and underemployment, and there is always the possibility that the former is simply a by-product of the latter. Be that as it may, the attempts to date to single out educated unemployment as a special problem in developing countries come in essentially two versions, with innumerable variations thereon.[21] The first stresses the unprecedented rates at which the total population, the economically active population, and the urban educated population have been growing in Africa since about 1950. Rates of growth of 3.5 percent for total population, 3 percent for the labor force, 6–7 percent for the urban labor force and 8–10 percent for the stock of educated people with primary education and above are now common in many developing countries, and these rates are unprecedented in a double sense: they exceed what the developing countries experienced before 1950, and they exceed what the advanced countries experienced at early stages of their industrialization. Given these rates of growth, it would take an equally unprecedented pace of economic expansion, as well as an unusually flexible labor market, to prevent the emergence of heavy unemployment. In addition, most of Africa has recently been pursuing an economic policy of promoting import-competing, capital-intensive manufacturing industry, and this type of economic growth has generated surprisingly little extra employment, thus exacerbating the employment problem. These pressures do not necessarily show up in mass unemployment because in largely agrarian countries, the rural sector will tend to soak up redundant labor in the form of underemployment on family farms. Open unemployment will only surface in cities and, of course, the educated tend to concentrate in urban areas. To arrive at a more or less self-contained theory of educated unemployment needs only the additional citation of (1) the presence of an extremely wide salary differential owing to past scarcities of highly qualified

21. For a different typology of explanation, see S. G. Fields, "The Private Demand for Education in Relation to Labour Market Conditions in Less-Developed Countries," *Economic Journal* (December 1974).

manpower and the historical influence of colonial administration in Asia and Africa, if not Latin America; (2) the tendency of a rapidly growing public sector in LDCs to define entry pay scales strictly in terms of educational attainments; and (3) the traditional prejudices of urban middle-class families against manual blue collar employment. This theory is set forth, with rich variations on the theme, in Volume II of Gunnar Mydral's influential book, *Asian Drama* (1968).

The second type of explanation of educated unemployment in African-type economies takes for granted the sort of facts cited above, but stresses the economic rationality in the prevailing circumstances of both the private demand for education and the length of job search after leaving school: despite long periods of unemployment, schooling is profitable to students and their families. It argues that labor markets in the countries of the region do adjust to the presence of unemployment, but, for various cultural and political reasons, the adjustment is too slow to eliminate unemployment in any finite period of time. Low job mobility and the tradition of the extended family create long lags in the demand for and supply of educated people; low job mobility, or the certain knowledge that the first job will be the last job, lengthens the search period for the first job and the extended family guarantees that the long search period will somehow be financed. In addition, heavy government subsidies to education, particularly at the tertiary levels of the educational system, tend continually to underwrite the explosion in the demand for education.[22]

What differences exist in these two types of explanations lie less in the facts which they both invoke as in the policy perspectives which they offer. The first explanation points directly to the content of education as forming, or at any rate encouraging, traditional antipathies to manual work and, consequently, emphasizes the need for curriculum reform. This approach also directs attention to the imperfections of labor markets and usually culminates in the recommendation of a wages and incomes policy, designed to reduce sharply the existing inequalities between wages and salaries. The second explanation, on the other hand, places major emphasis on the financing of education and, in general, on questions of quantity rather than quality of education. According to this view, educated unemployment in Asia, Africa and Latin America is essentially a problem of excess supply rather than deficient demand, and its recommendations for policy are chiefly directed at the problem of shifting resources from the upper to the lower levels of the educational system, while at the same time attempting to improve the flexibility of the labor market.

22. See Blaug, Layard, and Woodhall. *Causes of Graduate Unemployment in India.*

These distinctions in types of explanations and in associated policy proposals are not clear-cut, and some writers, such as Phillip Coombs in his popular book, *The World Educational Crisis: A Systems Analysis* (1968), neatly combine elements of both points of view. Nevertheless, it is useful to keep in mind the different standpoints which different authors bring to bear on the problem of educated unemployment in developing countries, which largely account for the wide array of practical recommendations that are encountered in the literature.[23]

Elsewhere, the writer has drawn a sharp contrast between the "quantitators" and the "qualitators" in the educational planning literature; that is, between those who trace all educational ills to a quantitative discrepancy between the supply of educated people and the demand for them, and those who instead trace them to qualitative failures of the educational system.[24] And although this contrast is too extreme, it is nevertheless true that different writers on the subject tend to emphasize either quantitative or qualitative dimensions of the employment problem of educated people in LDCs and, in many cases, it is illuminating to keep them distinct. Thus, we take up first with those who hold out purely quantitative remedies to the problem of educated unemployment and underemployment in LDCs.

QUANTITATIVE REMEDIES

Many countries are now agreed that current rates of growth of secondary and higher education cannot be allowed to continue, although very few have gone so far as the Philippines in asserting that these rates of growth

23. There is a rich literature on the employment problem of educated youths in Africa and Asia. For Africa, the Kericho and Niamey conferences outlined the essentials of the problem ten years ago: *Education, Employment and Rural Development,* edited by J. R. Sheffield (Nairobi: East African Publishing House, 1967), and *Youth Employment and National Development in Africa* (Addis Ababa: UN-ECA, 1968). Two UNESCO-IIEP African Research Monographs deal directly with the same question: G. Hunter, *Manpower, Employment and Education in the Rural Economy of Tanzania* (Paris: UNESCO-IIEP, 1966) and A. Callaway, *Educational Planning and Unemployed Youth* (Paris: UNESCO-IIEP, 1971). For additional African references, see *The School Leaver in Developing Countries,* edited by P. Williams (London: NFER, 1976), App. 3. For Asia, see the wide-ranging UN-ECAFE, *Economic Survey of Asia.*

24. M. Blaug, *Education and the Employment Problem in Developing Countries* (Geneva: ILO, 1973), ch. 6. For another statement of these different approaches, see R. Jolly, *et al., Third World Employment. Problems and Strategy* (London: Penguin Education, 1973), pp. 171–73.

will not be allowed to continue.[25] Some countries, such as Tanzania, Zambia, and Egypt, even agree that primary education should be expanded *at the expense* of the growth of secondary and higher education; that is, they agree that resources are to be reallocated from the top to the bottom of the educational system. But all this is easier said than done. Public opinion throughout the Third World is firmly opposed to enrollment ceilings and, in these circumstances, it would be suicidal for a politician to demand quantitative restrictions on secondary and higher education. Moreover, most Third World governments are deeply committed to the principle of higher education as a right and not a privilege for all those who are properly qualified, and this commitment militates against the attempt to clamp down on the growth of higher education. Moreover, there is an equally firm commitment to *free* higher education, including the commitment to finance cost of residence and out-of-pocket expenses of attendance. These commitments in fact deny to a government the lever of increased tuition fees as a device for discouraging demand for higher education.

Although governments may seek to curtail the growth of enrollments simply by setting ceilings on admissions or expenditure limits on new buildings, experience has shown how easily such government plans may be abandoned in the face of strong public demand for more places. To achieve success, therefore, it is necessary to supplement direct with indirect measures. One such indirect measure is higher tuition fees combined with a limited number of scholarships for poor students from the backward regions and a student loans scheme for all students, to be financed by a special graduate tax on future incomes. Some African countries, such as Tanzania, and some Asian countries, such as Sri Lanka, have begun to draw the attention of the public to the fact that university students are in fact a privileged élite. Indeed, a survey of the social composition of students in higher education in Third World countries would reveal that the average university student is, to put it mildly, much better off than the average taxpayer, not to mention the average peasant or urban worker.[26] So long as this is true, *free* higher education is a form of regressive taxation

25. Presidential Commission to Survey Philippine Education, *Education for National Development, New Patterns, New Directions* (Makati, Rizal: Presidential Commission, 1970), p. 27.

26. It must be admitted, however, that the evidence on this point is scarce and far from unambiguous: for India, see Blaug, Layard and Woodhall, *Causes of Graduate Unemployment in India,* pp. 130–33; for the Philippines, see ILO, *Sharing in Development. A Programme of Employment, Equity and Growth for the Philippines* (Geneva: ILO, 1974), pp. 327–30 (referred to hereafter as the ILO Philippines Report).

which makes a mockery of the policy of egalitarianism to which most Third World governments are dedicated.[27]

It is sometimes argued that a student loans scheme or graduate tax would be impractical in developing countries where income tax exasion is widespread and where individuals frequently pool their incomes with distant relatives. But the ILO Philippines Report suggests that a student loans program could be rigorously confined to able, poor students by asking them to make a sworn declaration that parental income did not exceed a stated level; in case of dispute, parental income could be assessed on the basis of the father's occupation and an arbitrary scale of income per age per occupation applied to the father's occupation. Students themselves would, in addition, have to satisfy a minimum standard of educational achievement, but this would be set deliberately below the average standard achieved by their peers on the grounds that an insistence on equal merit as the criterion for eligibility would immediately discriminate against students from poor families.[28] In short, student loans schemes could be made to work in LDCs and, of course, a number of African and Asian governments operate such schemes on a limited basis.[29]

The idea of stemming the growth of higher education by either direct or indirect means sometimes meets with the objection that the effect of cutting down on higher education is simply to multiply the number of unemployed secondary school leavers; and unemployment among secondary school leavers is no easier to deal with than unemployment among university graduates. But this argument ignores the object of the exercise, which is to release current resources invested in higher education, so that these can be applied either to the lower levels of the educational system, or to income-earning opportunities generated elsewhere in the economy. Nothing that we do to educated unemployment solves the problem of general unemployment. It merely ensures that public funds are not invested unproductively. President Nyerere of Tanzania expressed the argument succinctly:

> It is essential that we face the facts of our present economic situation. Every penny spent on education is money taken away from some other needed activity—whether it is an investment in the future, better medical services, or just more food, clothing and comfort for our citizens

27. See G. Psacharopoulos, "The Perverse Effects of Public Subsidization of Education or How Equitable is Free Education?," *Comparative Education Review* (February 1977), for a development of this theme.

28. ILO Philippines Report, pp. 339ff.

29. See, for example, P. Williams, "Lending for Learning: An Experiment in Ghana," *Minerva* 12 (3) (July 1974).

> at present. And the truth is that there is no possibility of Tanzania being able to increase the proportion of the national income which is spent on education; it ought to be decreased. Therefore, we cannot solve our present problems by any solution which costs more than is at present spent, in particular, we cannot solve the "problem of primary school leavers" by increasing the number of secondary school places.[30]

We can control secondary and higher education directly by admission ceilings, or indirectly by higher private costs. But there are still subtler indirect means of making upper secondary and higher education less attractive to students. For example, the ILO Kenya Report recommended postponement of entry into university courses by two or three years, with eventual admission being conditioned on evidence of work experience and community service. Universities in Kenya would make the final selection of students as in the past, but they would now do so on the basis of examination results and employers' reports, and full credit would be given for part-time courses attended while working.[31] Since then, the idea of postponed entry into higher education has been taken up elsewhere, as in Tanzania, Zambia, and Ethiopia. There is hardly any doubt that postponed entry, particularly for a period as long as two or three years, would serve to discourage some students from taking up higher education who otherwise would have done so, not to mention its effect in strengthening the motivation of students who did reenter the educational system.

The case for expanding primary education at the maximum possible rate is as strong on economic grounds as it is on social and political grounds. There is some scope for cost-saving measures in primary education itself, but these could finance only a small part of the expansion required to achieve universal primary education. The bulk of the resources will have to come from the contraction of secondary and higher education. And as long as a year of higher education costs 100 times as much as a year of primary education—a median figure for Africa and Asia—even a marginal shift of resources from tertiary to primary education could work wonders in increasing enrollments in first-level education. It has been calculated that in six African countries, primary enrollment ratios could be raised to 100 percent overnight merely by shifting 20 percent of current educational expenditure on secondary or higher education to primary education.[32] To achieve such a shifting of resources throughout the Third World remains a primary objective of educational planning.

30. J. K. Nyerere, *Education for Self-Reliance* (Dar es Salaam: Ministry of Information and Tourism, 1967), p. 14.

31. ILO Kenya Report, p. 242; and Republic of Kenya, *Sessional Paper on Employment* (Nairobi: Government Printer, 1973), p. 49.

32. UN-ECA, *Survey of Conditions in Africa,* pp. 96–97.

QUALITATIVE REMEDIES

We turn now to a wide class of policy reforms, all of which travel under the general label of "vocationalization of education." The general theme which runs through all these reform proposals is the failure of the formal educational system in the Third World to be oriented to "the world of work": in primary and secondary education, teaching is almost exclusively geared to the next stage of education, ignoring the large proportion of children who will enter the labor market after completing the cycle in question; education is academic, bookish and obsessed with examination questions; it enforces traditional social values that accord low prestige to manual work and self-employment; and in consequence, it renders students unemployable except in white collar occupations in the modern, organized sector, and sometimes not even in those. The root cause of educated unemployment in this view, therefore, is the content of formal education. The theory that lies behind the vocationalization movement has been widely endorsed throughout the Third World, and there is hardly a country in Asia and Africa which has not made earnest efforts to "vocationalize" education. Many, but not all, of these efforts are concentrated at the secondary stage, and they have run all the way from the creation of special secondary vocational schools, to the introduction of vocational tracks in comprehensive high schools, to the addition of "work experience" or "practical arts" in all years of secondary and even primary education, to the planned allocation of students in higher education between science and liberal arts degrees. In rural schools, these proposals have taken the form of calling for a revision of the curriculum, either to include the teaching of agricultural science, or at any rate to instill an agricultural bias into the teaching of all subjects; sometimes it is recommended that a garden-farm be added to each school or, alternatively, that all children should engage in some practical farming as part of the schedule.

A brief review of Asian experience in this field will serve as a background for a critical discussion of these proposals. The Indian Education Commission of 1964–66, the last influential review on a major scale of the problems of Indian education, recommended that by 1986 some 20 percent of all enrollments at the lower secondary level and some 50 percent in the upper secondary level should be in part-time or full-time vocational and professional courses, but they failed to indicate precisely how this was to be accomplished. Even more to the point, they recommended the introduction of "work experience" as an integral part of education at all stages. They defined work experience as "participation in productive work in school, in the home, in a workshop, on a farm, in a factory, or in any other productive situation," and explained that it would involve "earning while learning";[33] a pilot project to adopt "work experience" in schools has been in operation in the State of Maharashtra since 1971, but no results have yet been published.[34] Pakistan announced a plan in 1972 to introduce workshops in all middle schools so that "pupils may engage in activities such as weaving, book-binding, wood-work, blacksmithy, leather-work, food preservation, home management, etc., related to the local agricultural/industrial environment"; these changes in middle schools are designed to complement work-oriented curriculum changes in elementary education.[35] In Singapore, it was recently proposed that one-third of all students in the third and fourth years of secondary education should enter technical secondary schools, which combine academic education with technical training in broad basic skills.[36] The Presidential Commission to Survey Philippine Education recommended "that high priority be given to the provision of technical and vocational education and training programs in order to meet current and projected needs for trained manpower in developing society."[37] It proposed not only to increase the number of specialized vocational secondary schools but also to lengthen the vocational track in general high schools from two to three years. The last proposal has been rejected, but the Philippine government has just made vocational education compulsory in all years of the four-year high school program, leaving students the option in the last two years of further increasing the amount of vocational shop courses in the schedule. Similarly, Sri Lanka has replaced 0-level subject examinations at the end of the secondary cycle with a National Certificate of Education, and the new certificate includes the testing of competence in a number of manual skills.

These brief descriptions are perhaps sufficient to convey a flavor of the activities in Asia in the area of vocational education. It is apparent that the phrase "vocational education" may cover shop courses, work experience, prevocational training, and proper vocational education as such. The line of demarcation among these is hard to draw, but it must be drawn if the

33. Education Commission, *Education and National Development, Report of the Education Commission 1964–66* (Delhi: National Council of Educational Research and Training, 1971), pp. 350 ff.

34. But see E. Staley, "Work-Oriented General Education," *International Development Review* 16 (1) (1974).

35. Government of Pakistan, *The Education Policy 1972–1980* (Islamabad: Government of Pakistan, 1972), p. 7.

36. D. H. Clark, "Manpower Planning in Singapore," *Malayan Economic Review* 16 (2) (October 1971):195.

37. Presidential Commission to Survey Philippine Education, *Education for National Development*, p. 88.

desirability of expanding vocational education is to be assessed. The Pakistan concept of shop courses in secondary education is perhaps the simplest to grasp, and such courses exist to a greater or lesser extent in schools all over the world. It is, of course, a striking fact that they are more common in secondary schools in advanced countries than in developing countries, but, in the advanced countries, their purpose is a relatively modest one: it is not imagined that they will serve as any kind of introduction to an occupational environment, but, rather, they are designed to relieve the tedium of cognitive learning and to afford those with little aptitude for academic education some scope for an expression of their abilities. In Pakistan, on the other hand, it is hoped that "the knowledge and skills imparted, attitudes implanted, and the learning methods employed will ensure that those not proceeding to secondary [or tertiary] education can be usefully absorbed into the economy of the local community."

It is indeed doubtful whether an hour or two a day of shop courses can accomplish all these aims. The most that can be said is that they will facilitate post-school vocational training. Even greater doubts are raised by the Indian idea of "work experience" in schools, although they are doubts not so much about its effectiveness as about the feasibility of organizing a scheme of "earning while learning" in thousands of schools for tens of thousands of pupils. A program of work experience embodied in formal schooling is heavily dependent on the enthusiasm of teachers and administrators who would have to be specially trained to monitor children's work activities inside and outside of the classroom. No country, not even the most advanced, has ever succeeded in mounting such a program, and it is even questionable whether a sufficient number of earning activities could be found in any country to keep all 7 to 14-year-olds busy for a few hours a week. There is perhaps scope for this idea in some schools in some areas for certain age ranges, but surely not as a general solution for the academic orientation of schooling in developing societies.

Prevocational education, or "occupational education" as it is sometimes called,[38] seems to be a more relevant idea. The stress in prevocational education is on turning out a *trainable* person, rather than a person whose acquired skills make him immediately employable. The idea is that general education should be augmented with curriculum offerings that focus on attitudes, skills, and knowledge relevant to a selected range of occupations, fairly broadly defined. In principle, this is similar to the proposal to add shop courses to an academic curriculum but, in practice, it goes beyond this by treating shop courses seriously as a learning activity and by grouping them meaningfully for each student. Furthermore, pre-

38. See E. Staley, *Planning Occupational Education and Training for Development* (Delhi: Orient Longmans, 1970).

vocational education aims to supplement an occupational orientation by career guidance and counselling, so that each student has some opportunity to discover his own aptitudes in the light of labor market information. It is precisely the latter component which creates difficulties: few countries in Asia can provide each primary and secondary school with a career guidance officer; in addition, the paucity of labor market data would give career guidance officers little to work with.[39] Lastly, there is the still open question as to how much prevocational education is required to render a student trainable after leaving school, not to mention giving him the opportunity to explore his aptitudes. In some Asian countries, shop courses, or whatever they are called, constitute barely 5 percent of class time; in most countries they constitute at best 10–15 percent of class time at certain grades. The inadequacy of the time allotted to such courses, therefore, makes it impossible to actually realize the aims of prevocational education, even if all the objections mentioned previously fell to the ground.

These depressing facts do not, however, invalidate the concept of prevocational education. The question which must be asked is: is prevocational education a viable idea, and would it be worth expanding the provision of prevocational education as a way of solving the problem of educated unemployment? It will serve to sharpen the argument if this discussion closes by looking at vocational schools as such, about which little has yet been said. It may then be asked whether the criticisms that have been levelled at vocational education strictly defined are or are not applicable to prevocational education.

Most critics of vocational education in developing countries emphasize its costliness, the difficulty of finding suitable teachers to run vocational courses, or the tendency of students to regard vocational schooling as a second-best chance of receiving further education. A more fundamental criticism, however, runs in terms of the poor record of manpower forecasting around the world: it would appear that the demand for precisely specified skills cannot be accurately predicted more than a year or two ahead.[40] Since a cycle of vocational schooling is bound to be as long as three or more years, the preparation of students to take up specific occupations runs the constant danger of being out of touch with the pattern of demand in the labor market. Therefore, a policy of imparting general, academic education may be conceived as a rational device for hedging against the uncertainty of a continually changing economic environment.

39. Only 4,000 of India's 50,000 secondary schools now have a "career's master," and India has devoted more effort to building up a system of vocational guidance than other countries in Asia.

40. For the evidence, see *The Practice of Manpower Forecasting. A Collection of Case Studies,* edited by B. Ahamad and M. Blaug (Amsterdam: Elsevier, 1973).

To these considerations the notion may be added that education renders students employable primarily by inculcating definite behavioral traits and only secondarily by imparting cognitive knowledge; in most cases, it might be argued, the social and communicative skills that employers value are much more efficiently fostered by academic than by vocational education. This does not deny the case for accelerated training courses provided on a part-time basis after working hours, or even on a full-time basis for several months in the year in a rural out-of-school context. Nor does it deny the case for "vocationalizing" secondary school curricula, if what is meant thereby is the provision of some work-oriented shop courses, combined with take-home projects of a practical kind. But to ask schools to prepare students to take up clearly defined occupations is to ask them to do what is literally impossible. The most that schools can do is to provide a broad technical foundation for on-the-job acquisition of specific skills.

There is very little hard evidence to back up this case against formal vocational schooling. It is true that the available tracer studies of the graduates of vocational and academic secondary schools generally reveal little difference in the unemployment rate between the two groups. Nevertheless, what evidence there is is so thin that little is gained by examining it. What is clear is that vocational schools are much more expensive to operate than academic schools; thus in that sense, the case against them is made if they are only as effective as academic schools from the standpoint of the labor market. They must be *more* effective if they are to be judged desirable, and this much has never been convincingly demonstrated.

So, on balance, the case for vocational schooling appears to be weak. However, the same reasons that throw doubt on vocational schooling only serve to strengthen the case for prevocational education. However, while endorsing prevocational education as "good education," a warning is necessary against the belief that it is capable by itself of fundamentally changing pupils' attitudes to manual and clerical work. Schools make only a marginal contribution to the prevailing ethos of a society, and, while this is no reason for not trying to make an impact, the history of educational experiments around the world cautions against optimism about such efforts. In particular, there is no evidence whatsoever that schooling can foster the desire to take up self-employment, thereby creating jobs in the literal sense of the term. There is a vast literature on entrepreneurship, but little of it implies that schools have much to do with the making of entrepreneurs.[41]

The issue of "vocationalization" of education takes on special force when considered in the light of the needs of the rural sector. There is broad

41. This question is explored at greater length in Blaug, *Education and the Employment Problem*, pp. 53–55.

agreement among Asian countries that there is little merit in actually teaching agricultural science in primary and secondary schools; instead, an agricultural bias ought to permeate the general curriculum. The Indian Education Commission of 1964–66 summed up the prevailing view:

> The introduction of agricultural education at the primary level is not, in our opinion, likely to achieve, by itself, the objective of inculcating a liking for agriculture as a way of life or of halting migration of rural people from the land. . . . The same broad conclusion will be valid at the lower secondary stage also. It has been the opinion of most people contacted by us that the training given in institutions of formal education does not lead to vocational competence. Farming implies hard work and mature judgement and the age group concerned (13+ to 16+) is neither physically nor mentally prepared for this. We also think that over-specialization at an early age is not at all desirable. . . . This does not mean, however, that the school system till the end of the lower secondary stage has no contribution to make to the development of agriculture. On the contrary, we believe that some orientation to agriculture should form an integral part of all general education. . . . We therefore recommend . . . all primary schools . . . should give an agricultural orientation to their programmes . . . orienting existing courses in general science, biology, social studies, mathematics, etc., towards the rural environment.[42]

The difficulty with this policy is that of extending it to urban schools, because in towns, an agriculturally biased curriculum is regarded as alien by both students and teachers. On the other hand, to provide an agricultural orientation to the curriculum of rural schools but an industrial orientation to the curriculum of urban schools creates a sense of second-class citizenship in rural areas, which is likely to encourage still further an exodus to the towns. This remains an unresolved dilemma in most developing countries. Although these are all basically agricultural economies, they are also countries where much of the growth that is taking place is concentrated in cities. In other words, urban growth is the dominant feature of social and economic development in all these countries; in these circumstances, it is virtually impossible to reform education in the direction of "ruralizing" the curriculum. What would be required to give bite to such a policy is a wholesale program of rural mobilization as the centerpiece of a development strategy. If all the planning efforts of a country were focused on the rural sector as the priority sector, the idea of "ruralizing" the curriculum of both rural and urban schools would call for very little extra effort and would indeed be a natural by-product of such a develop-

42. Education Commission, *Education and National Development*, pp. 658–60.

ment strategy. But so long as the economic advantages of urban life are in fact much greater than rural life, mere changes in the educational content of rural schools will neither stem the exodus of school leavers from rural areas, nor bring about an improvement in agricultural productivity. That is not to say that all efforts to ruralize curricula should now cease. Such efforts are part and parcel of a larger design to place increasing emphasis on the rural sector in development planning. It is merely to warn that curriculum reform in the direction of "ruralization" cannot be expected to work wonders in the near future.

The current debate about curriculum "relevance" is not a new one to the African continent; in Africa it goes back to the first half of the nineteenth century. In 1842, for example, a Select Committee of the British Parliament noted that in Ghana no efforts had been made to offer agricultural instruction, or to establish school farms, and recommended that these deficiencies be made good. Similarly, a report from the Educational Committee of the Privy Council, circulated to the British colonies in Africa in 1847, recommended the establishment of "industrial schools" with the objectives of teaching the rudiments of health care, sanitation, handicrafts, and agricultural techniques suitable to the local environment. The first Education Ordinances for Sierra Leone (1881) and Ghana (1882) included provision for the establishment of such schools, and during the last decade of the nineteenth century, many of the mission schools in those countries established agricultural plots where students spent considerable time each week doing manual work. Similar innovations occurred in East Africa in the early part of the twentieth century, as in Tanzania, where "native authority schools" from 1928 onward introduced agriculture, carpentry and tailoring into the timetable. Such initiatives were applauded by the Phelps-Stokes Report of 1922—the first comprehensive report on education in Africa—which strongly emphasized the need for vocational rural education in primary schools. However, all these early experiments failed in the sense that they were eventually abandoned. In most cases the climate of popular opinion was against them. The examinations were set and administered by bodies in the metropolitan countries, and all modifications of the syllabus in the direction of practical studies were seen as a digression, a threat to standards elsewhere in the curriculum, and a deliberate attempt to give second-class education to Africans. Over the hundred years or so up to 1960, the same pattern has been repeated in many African countries. Local or even national initiatives in practical education were generally shortlived and always ended in a return to the teaching of the standard academic subjects as determined principally by the nature of public examinations.

This is not to say that there has been no progress in curriculum development in Africa. On the contrary, and particularly since independence, there has been a significant shift away from the content and subject structure of curricula that were imported from Western countries. Increasingly, the official medium of instruction is the *lingua franca,* and in some cases even the *lingua mater,* at least during the primary stage of education. This necessitates the production of textbooks and materials in many different languages—eleven in the case of Ethiopia and twenty in the case of Zambia, to take two examples. Similarly, the topics treated in subjects like history, geography, and social science are becoming increasingly localized in most countries. Examinations, now under local rather than metropolitan control, have been redesigned to reflect these changes in the subject content of the curriculum.

Despite this innovative attitude to traditional curricula, however, the introduction of practical subjects has never met with great success in Africa, at least when limited to particular schools. The new view, however, is that the effort to integrate education and production may prove successful if approached at the national scale for the entire educational system. Such thinking is echoed in the World Bank's new proposals for "basic education."[43]

In brief, the World Bank argues that universal primary education in developing countries can only be achieved by providing a new, flexible, low-cost education called "basic education" as a supplement to standard primary schooling, so that those children and adults who have failed to gain access to the existing system will nevertheless be provided with the 3 Rs, plus some minimum functional skills. Some, if not all, of the elements of "basic education" are already taught in many developing countries in a wide variety of nonformal education programs. Education that is provided in farmers' training centers, community education centers, rural education centers, literacy programs, and even settlement schemes, includes important elements of "basic education" as described above.

The growing disillusionment with the quality of primary and secondary schooling, together with the impossibility in many countries of ever absorbing all their products in the modern sector, have increased the appeal of basic education programs. Basic education has the advantage of being designable to fit the specific needs of rural communities. It can be shorter, more functional, and, it is argued, cheaper than the education that is provided within the orthodox school system. Since basic education courses generally do not involve certification of students, it is widely believed that they represent a means whereby useful attitudes and skills can be developed without at the same time encouraging aspirations for gainful employment in the modern sector.

43. IBRD, *Education. Sector Working Paper* (Washington, D.C.: World Bank, 1974), pp. 29–30.

But there are real dangers in the basic education approach. The establishment of a dual education system, comprising standard schools and colleges for a minority of the population and basic education programs for the rest, would run directly counter to the aim of equality of educational opportunity. Governments following such a strategy are open to the charge that their policies are institutionalizing existing inequalities among social groups in the community. This is, indeed, the major reason why, historically, approaches very similar to basic education have generally failed in Africa and elsewhere. Though the basic education program may be popular in its early stages, students and parents quickly come to regard such schemes as a temporary expedient that should be replaced by primary schooling at a later date. If this does not happen, basic education soon becomes a symbol of discrimination against rural people and the program begins to collapse.

Besides, it is very doubtful that basic education would, in fact, be cheaper than the rock-bottom costs of an ordinary primary school. A teacher facing a mixed class of children and adults would have to be more experienced or better trained than the average primary school teacher and would, therefore, be more expensive. Most primary schools in Africa do not, in fact, succeed in teaching children more than reading, writing, and arithmetic, yet basic schools are supposed to achieve that, in addition to knowledge required for running a household and bringing up a family, not to mention functional rural skills. Even if this were possible, it strains credulity to believe that it would be an equally effective education.[44]

44. In the words of one commentator: "Though in the literature on the subject basic education is often advocated as a means of reducing the costs of education, there is very little analysis of the ways in which this might be achieved. It is well known that the recurrent costs of primary schooling are mainly determined by the level of teachers' salaries and by the teacher-pupil ratio. Thus, the costs of basic education schools would only be lower if classes were larger (or if teachers taught more classes) or if salaries were reduced. For the latter to be achieved—unless the salary structure as a whole were changed—the calibre of the teachers would almost inevitably be lower than in orthodox schools. In any event, . . . if the costs of basic education were less than orthodox primary schools, it seems likely that the quality (and therefore equality) would be similarly reduced"—(C. Colclough, "Basic Education—Samson or Delilah?" *Convergence* 9 (2):46. In a similar vein, another critic of "basic education" has observed: "Although a *non-competitive* substitute for the primary school might be feasible in areas of low demand for schools, in areas of high demand and inadequate supply it would probably be workable only either at a greater cost or at a greatly lesser effectiveness than the primary school itself. Even though such an institution might present itself as a custodial holding centre, willing to care for a child constructively until a primary school place becomes available, the problems of acquiring trained staff, an adequate staffing ratio, attractive equipment to stimulate learning, would more than likely rule it out of court"—

Despite all these arguments against basic education, many governments in Asia and Africa are undoubtedly attracted by the general thinking that lies behind the drive for basic education. Algeria, Tanzania, Zambia, and India are all reforming their educational systems to include large elements of the basic education philosophy. On a less comprehensive scale, Upper Volta, Senegal, Ethiopia, and Sri Lanka have instituted experimental basic education programs for out-of-school youths which emphasize vocational subjects. Community schools, that is, self-sufficient rural schools that are closely linked to their local communities, are being developed in a range of countries, including Ghana, Zaire, and Tanzania. A theme that recurs again and again in all these reforms is the view that education and production ought to be closely linked and, indeed, that the school should become a productive unit. This is generally seen as having two advantages. On the one hand, the integration of education and production, and particularly the possibility that schools can begin to market products for sale, means that some of the costs of running the schools can be subsidized by this production and hence that the total costs of expanding the school system can be greatly reduced. On the other hand, the integration of education and production is expected to discourage the attitude of students which leads them away from rural areas in search of wage employment in the cities. In short, it is hoped that this new type of school will minimize the alienation of students from their home community and will encourage aspirations for self-help and community work.

The country that has had most experience in these moves to incorporate "earning while learning" into the school curriculum is Tanzania. Although the Tanzanian experience is relatively recent, a number of lessons are already beginning to emerge.[45] For present purposes, the main lesson is that neither students nor their parents will treat even compulsory practical school work seriously unless doing so improves the chances of progression within the school system. In Tanzanian primary schools, the criterion of a subject taught in the curriculum is a perceived connection of the subject with the daily activities of people in the neighboring area. Though the amount of time devoted to practical work varies from school to school, the majority of schools in rural areas are involved in agricultural work, while poultry-keeping and other activities are practiced in urban schools. But systematic evaluations of these curriculum innovations in Tanzania have shown that the vocational aspects of school life are not

J. Oxenham, "Reflections on the 1974 Education Sector Working Papers," *Prescription for Progress? A Commentary on the Education Policy of the World Bank,* edited by P. Williams (London: University of London Institute of Education, 1976), p. 43.

45. See UN-ECA, *Survey of Conditions in Africa,* pp. 124–28.

taken as seriously as the academic side for the simple reason that the former are not at present assessed in final examinations.[46] This deficiency is recognized by the authorities in Tanzania, and they intend in future to test the abilities of students in vocational subjects as part of the Primary School Leaving Examination; they also plan to reduce the power of the examinations by introducing greater dependence upon continuous assessment methods.

Tanzania's experience demonstrates the naivety of believing that the problem of educated unemployment can be solved merely by curriculum reform. The question thus becomes whether or not changes in curriculum, together with changes in selection systems embodied in new types of examinations, are capable of having an impact on the school leaver problem. The evidence here is not conclusive, if only because no African country has yet had experience with this type of comprehensive reform. It is clear, however, that a change to alternative selection methods will introduce new problems. Continuous assessment methods tend, on balance, to be less "objective" than formal written examinations because they give scope to teachers' social biases in rewarding compliant and obedient students. In other words, there are reasons to believe that the abolition of terminal examinations and their replacement by continuous assessment would aggravate the tendency of academically inclined students to forge ahead of those who are more practically oriented.

Having such considerations in mind, the ILO Employment Mission Report on Sri Lanka came up with a radically new proposal for examination reform, namely, to replace the old achievement tests in secondary schools by aptitude testing. For example, the Ministry of Education might offer a one-week radio and correspondence course on an announced subject towards the close of the academic year; all students in secondary schools would devote that week to studying the subject, and they would then be examined at the end to see how much of it they had mastered; their mark on this test would then be entered on their record cards as a supplement to their standard examination score, and selection for higher education would depend on both marks; similarly, private and public employers would have access to both marks.[47]

46. The ways in which student pressures prevent subjects that are not to be examined from being taught or studied effectively are described more fully for Kenya by K. King, *Primary Schools in Kenya: Some Critical Constraints on their Effectiveness* (Nairobi: Institute of Development Studies, Discussion Paper No. 130, 1973). For a general analysis of the "backwash" effects of examinations on the content of schooling in the Third World, see R. P. Dore, *Deschool? Try Using Schools for Education First* (Brighton: Institute of Development Studies, University of Sussex, Discussion Paper No. 6, 1972).

47. ILO Sri Lanka Report, pp. 139–40; also ILO Kenya Report, p. 243.

The principal advantage of this scheme is that it would create a measure of educational achievement which could not distort the curriculum that led up to it; not knowing the subject that would be announced, teachers could not drill students beforehand in basic information about the subject; it is true that they could still drill them in the techniques of summarizing information about any subject, but that would be all to the good. Secondly, this scheme would yield a score which comes much closer to measuring a student's basic aptitude and intelligence than the results of a standard examination. Thirdly, as countries gained experience with this new testing device, its weight in a student's overall score could be gradually increased; as the weight of traditional examinations declined, the whole of the curriculum during the secondary stage would then be liberated for creative learning divorced from the necessity of passing examinations. Lastly, the idea could be adopted without any additional investments other than those involved in providing a one-week radio and correspondence course plus the processing of an additional set of test scores.

The possible objections to this attractive proposal are recognized and discussed in the Sri Lanka Report. Examinations perform three functions in the school system: (1) certifying the possession of certain competencies and attributes for purposes of being hired in the labor market; (2) predicting successful performances in the next cycle of education; and (3) ensuring attendance and enforcing discipline in the preceding cycle of education. It is precisely the latter which gives rise to doubt. The Sri Lanka Report considers the problem of "the carrot and the stick" and concludes that this particular function of examinations must be repudiated as much for the sake of teachers as for the sake of students.

Assuming that teachers would accept increasing reliance on aptitude rather than achievement tests, there is hardly any doubt that the growing tendency to demote the traditional examination would have a liberating effect on the process of education. What is much more questionable is whether it would succeed in rendering secondary education terminal. The trouble is that the correlation between the marks on the two types of tests, while far from perfect, would probably be very high. The type of student who scores well on a traditional achievement test would also score well on a written aptitude test. Unless the aptitude test involved making things with one's hands, as well as relatively culture-free questions testing reasoning ability and spatial relationships, it would largely measure the same competencies as an achievement test. Since achievement testing has never discouraged students from wanting to stay on to acquire higher education, aptitude testing with results highly correlated with those of achievement testing would fail to make secondary education terminal.

Besides, aptitude testing would pose a serious threat to teachers for whom the existing curriculum and examination system has the merit of solving the problem of what to teach and when to teach. In fact, the trouble with all these qualitative reforms that we have been discussing is that every one of them increases the demand made upon teachers in Third World countries. The strength of the orthodox system, at least as far as the teachers were concerned, was that it laid down very strictly the specific information that had to be mastered by students if they were to be successful, both in terms of promotion within the education system and more generally in society at large. The vocationalization of the curricula, the decentralization of syllabi, the integration of production and education, the move away from examinations, all require teachers who are enthusiastic, innovative and highly trained. When we consider the typical rural teacher in an African primary school who has himself had no more than primary education, it is difficult to believe that he will prove equal to the task that will be imposed upon him by the new educational reforms. Even the inservice teacher training courses that are currently planned by Third World governments about to engage on major educational reforms may fail to equip the teaching cadre with the skills and confidence it needs to implement the reforms in question. It is this which may prove to be the Achilles' heel of this new wave of educational reform in Asia and Africa.

A further critical variable concerns the earnings that regularly accrue to persons with advanced levels of schooling in developing countries. The appeal of standard examinations, for example, stems not merely from the wish of students to achieve entrance to higher education. Rather, it derives from the very high earnings and status associated with jobs to which higher levels of education give access. While changes in examination and in systems of selection may be expected to bring educational benefits, it is unrealistic to suppose that such changes will make people content to accept work at very low incomes in rural areas if they believe themselves to be eligible for highly paid urban jobs. In short, as long as employers continue to use the level of education attained as the main criterion for hiring recruits into first jobs, and as long as the existing income differentials between the highest and worst-paid jobs in the occupational hierarchy remain what they are, the phenomenon of educated unemployment and underemployment in Asia, Africa, and Latin America is unlikely to be more than marginally affected by even major changes in the qualitative aspects of education.

RECURRENT EDUCATION

The proposal to replace orthodox examinations by aptitude tests is only one of a number of proposals that have been produced by ILO Employment Missions to promote the "terminalization" of secondary education in developing countries. In both the Sri Lanka and Kenya Reports, achievement testing is linked up with educational selection by quotas and with the concept of postponed or recurrrent education. Selection by quotas involves selecting students into upper secondary education by school quotas within each school district; selection within each school quota is then by a mixture of achievement tests. The purpose of selection by quotas is that of equalizing educational opportunities between poor and rich families and between rural and urban districts; in effect, therefore, the quotas will be as much geographical as social quotas, and they are designed to strengthen the selection of students for further education by factors other than examination results. Similarly, both the Sri Lanka and Kenya Reports recommend postponement of entry into university courses by two or three years, with eventual admission being conditional on evidence of work experience or community service. The universities themselves would make the selection as in the past, but they would now do so on the basis of examination results, aptitude tests, employers' reports and teachers' reports, and full credit would be given for part-time courses attended while working.[48] Postponed entry, the reports suggest, would help to cut down on college enrollments and would, in addition, strengthen students' motivation and improve their career choices.

It is apparent that this proposal to postpone entry into higher education by a few years is one version of the general concept of recurrent education, which is now under heated discussion in most European countries.[49] In other versions, higher education is taken on a part-time basis concurrently with employment; it is never completed in one sequence but recurs at intervals throughout a person's working life. The ILO proposal is a relatively modest interpretation of the concept of recurrent education; all that would be called for is greater flexibility on the part of employers in offering part-time work to youngsters and some increased sophistication in the admission procedures of universities.

There is little doubt that to interpose two or three years between completion of secondary education and entry into higher education would reduce the demand for higher education; that is to say, some proportion of secondary school leavers would in all probability lose their incentives to take up higher education. In addition, there is also little doubt that it would alter their aspirations and strengthen their motivation to study if they should decide to return to the educational system. Thus, whether it is believed that educated unemployment is due to excessive education, or to

48. ILO Sri Lanka Report, p. 141; ILO Kenya Report, p. 242.

49. See E. Faure et al., *Learning To Be* (Paris: UNESCO, 1972); International Commission on the Development of Education (Edgar Faure Commission).

a structural imbalance represented by a mismatch between aspirations and opportunities, the impact of postponed entry into higher education is entirely in the right direction. What is much less certain is that the magnitude of the impact will be very large. Here, as elsewhere, experiments are needed to point the way. Sri Lanka has now adopted the concept of a six-month interval between the completion of secondary education and entry into higher education, and the latter is in fact governed by a set of geographical quotas. In that sense, an experiment is now under way, and whatever its results, the ice has now at least been broken.

The ILO mission reports saw the period of postponed higher education as being devoted to either gainful employment or community service. Reference to community service provides an opportunity to say something about the question of out-of-school involvement of youngsters in voluntary social services, or in a compulsory national service, as devices for altering their attitudes to the world of work. A significant example, but only one example, of a voluntary service of this kind is the *Shramadana* (Gift of Labour Movement of Sri Lanka), in which young people work with villagers on such projects as constructing roads, digging wells, improving sanitary facilities, developing water resources and irrigation canals, and providing educational and recreational facilities. In other Asian countries, such organized youth activities as scouting, Junior Red Cross, and National Cadet Corps, which are generally confined to school children, have been extended to cover out-of-school youth. The results have been generally encouraging but the coverage of such programs to date is still very minimal. What it shows, however, is that there is a wide variety of devices available for attempting to alter the values and aspirations of youngsters. It is not true that this can be done only in schools. It may not even be best done in schools. Indeed, in all Asian countries there are vast complexes of activity (which may be bundled together under the label "nonformal education"), which are currently engaged in teaching new skills to out-of-school youths and adults.

NONFORMAL AND INFORMAL EDUCATION

The more critical attitude to formal education in recent years has led to new appreciation of the importance and potential contribution of nonformal and informal education. By their very nature, data on these varied, decentralized and often overlooked forms of education and training are partial and inadequate. But it is important to have at least some grasp of the range of activities in these areas, if only to avoid the impression that all or even most education takes place in the formal school system.

"Nonformal education" is defined by the International Council for Educational Development as "any organised educational activity outside the established formal system—whether operating separately or as an important feature of some broader activity—that is intended to serve identifiable learning clienteles and learning objectives."[50] Such programs include youth services, agricultural extension programs, settlement schemes, cooperative training, vocational agricultural training, adult literacy campaigns, and national awareness programs using the mass media. At the risk of some oversimplification, three categories of nonformal educational programs can be distinguished: (1) programs which are designed to upgrade the skills of persons in employment; (2) programs which are organized as a bridge between formal schooling and employment, which usually include some specific vocational training; and (3) programs which are organized as an alternative to formal schooling for those persons who are presently excluded from the school system. Although only fragmentary data on nonformal education are available,[51] it may be useful to indicate something of the range of educational activity within each of the above three categories.

Programs in the first category—those that are designed to upgrade the skills of persons in employment—include on-the-job training and in-service courses of various kinds for workers in the formal sector. Many governments in Asia and Africa have adopted a positive policy towards increasing and improving on-the-job training schemes; in addition to training on the job, a large number of nonformal in-service courses are also provided. These are sometimes run by private employers, but most of such courses are available only in the public sector. Furthermore, many governments in Africa make available a number of places in their technical training institutes specifically for the purpose of upgrading workers during a period of release from employment. In Kenya, for example, under the provisions of the Apprenticeship Training Scheme, workers spend part of their time in training courses at the National Industrial Vocational Training Centres. And most of the training at the polytechnics in Kenya comprises in-service courses for people who are sponsored by their employers either in the public or the private sector. Many other governments (including those of Ghana, Zambia, Botswana, and Swaziland) have similar

50. P. H. Coombs, R. Pressner, M. Ahmed, *New Paths to Learning for Rural Children and Youth* (New York: International Council for Educational Development, 1973). See also P. H. Coombs, M. Ahmed, *Attacking Rural Poverty. How Non-Formal Education Can Help* (Baltimore: John Hopkins University Press, 1974).

51. But see J. Sheffield and V. Diejomaoh, *Non-Formal Education in African Development* (New York: African-American Institute, 1972), for a useful survey of African nonformal programs.

schemes. Most of these government training courses are "nonformal" in our terms; that is, they are organized in response to specific occupational needs, they lie outside the purview of the ministry of education, and they rarely lead to the acquisition of certificates. In this sense, they contrast with many of the preservice training courses that fall more squarely within the formal training system.

Finally, one of the most important and widespread forms of nonformal education in the first category is the agricultural extension service. In most countries, this service is responsible for encouraging farmers to apply new methods of cultivation and animal husbandry; it aims to increase the use of fertilizers, insecticides, manure, draft animals, and equipment, and to promote the introduction of new crops. In the mid-1960s, expenditure on agricultural extension in Tanzania accounted for up to one-third of the recurrent budget of the Ministry of Agriculture, and up to three percent of total government recurrent expenditure.[52] This experience has also been fairly typical of other countries. Extension services are thus an extremely important item of nonformal education in terms of the financial resources allocated to them.

The second category of nonformal education covers pre-employment training programs. In Africa, many of these would be included in the category of formal rather than nonformal education. Apart from the more usual examples of vocational training—those for teachers, nurses, artisans, technicians, and so on—there is a wide range of other preemployment, nonformal programs. These programs are offered by both government and private sector agencies, particularly the latter. Many recently established programs have their origins in the attempt to provide some kind of vocational opportunity for primary school leavers unable to find modern sector jobs. A Kenyan example is the training given by the Christian Industrial Training Centre in Nairobi. The majority of such schemes, however, have been conceived from the very beginning as training programs which promote a transition to self-employment rather than wage employment in the modern sector. Training programs for weaving, cottage industries, carving, carpentry, building, electrical trades, mechanics, and almost every other conceivable, marketable low-level skill have appeared in Africa over the past twenty years. As in the case of the Kenyan Village Polytechnics, many of these programs are explicitly organized on a self-help basis, using student labor and local materials. Though often highly structured, such programs are characterized by low recurrent costs, by pupil-teacher ratios higher than in the formal training system, by the absence of formal require-

52. J. King, *Planning Non-Formal Education in Tanzania* (Paris: UNESCO-IIEP, 1967), pp. 25–26.

ments for admission, and by the absence of certificates at the end of the program.

In spite of these features, the success of many of these programs still tends to be judged by the number of their graduates who succeed in finding wage employment. This is so because, regardless of the focus of the course on self-employment, the students themselves have their eyes on the training as a means, however remote, of gaining access to a wage-earning job. Furthermore, the emphasis on skill training in these programs ignores all the other, deeper problems that an inexperienced youngster faces in entering the labor market on his own account. Seldom is the major constraint simply the lack of a vocational skill; more frequently, it is a lack of capital, a lack of knowledge concerning marketing possibilities, a lack of business acumen, a lack even of the knowledge of basic bookkeeping practices. In short, these preemployment training courses are addressed to what is, in fact, only one of the shortcomings of a would-be entrepreneur. As the glut of potential and qualified workers seeking entrance to the modern sector increases in Africa, more and more of these schemes are recognizing the inadequacy of the preparation they provide.

The third major category of nonformal education includes programs that are deliberately established as an alternative to formal schooling. African and Asian interest in these second-chance facilities has grown considerably over the last five years. Most of such programs are still on an experimental basis, but their initiation in an increasing number of countries is a portent of the future. These programs have come to be referred to as "basic education," which we have already discussed. The growing disillusionment with the quality of formal education has increased the appeal of basic education programs. Basic education has the advantage of being able to be designed to fit the specific needs of rural communities. Since basic education courses generally do not lead to any certification of students, it is widely believed that they represent a means whereby useful attitudes and skills can be developed without at the same time encouraging aspirations for gaining employment in the modern sector. Their chief role, in Africa at any rate, has been less to provide alternatives to formal schooling for youngsters than as supplements to the school system for adults. Such adult programs are aimed at a wide range of social and economic objectives. They include community development programs, literacy programs, cooperative education and development schemes, and mass campaigns using radio. Radio learning has been most notably used in Tanzania in order to contact groups of largely illiterate people living in rural areas. Other governments, including Botswana and Zambia, have also begun using this approach to the promotion of a limited range of learning objectives in health, nutrition, agriculture, rural development, and civics.

The last comment perfectly illustrates the range and complexity of nonformal education in Africa. While it would be desirable to generalize about its development, and its prospects for the future, it is hard to do so because of the diversity of aims and methods involved. However, it is clear that the main provider of nonformal education in Africa is at present the public sector. Though private initiatives have been of key importance in some countries, resulting (as in the case of the Botswana Brigades and the Kenya Village Polytechnics) in a large student population created without government help or subsidy, these are the exceptions rather than the rule. In general, bearing in mind the importance of agricultural extension, literacy programs, and inservice and upgrading training, the scope of private training schemes is tiny compared with the resources and the people involved in government programs. The initiative for the future development of nonformal education thus lies firmly in governments' hands.

So far comments here have been related to *organized* systems of learning that take place outside the orthodox or formal school system. It is being increasingly recognized, however, that the vast majority of the labor force throughout the Third World learn the skills they need for their livelihood not in the systems of formal or nonformal education, but informally, on the job or in the home. To return to the Kenyan examples mentioned earlier, technical skill training within the formal system is available to only about 5,000 students each year. Thus, only a tiny proportion of the 225,000 primary school leavers in Kenya can gain entry to these programs. It is incorrect to imagine that the remainder are condemned to unskilled manual jobs. On the contrary, a high proportion eventually enter some kind of indigenous apprenticeship arrangement in the informal sector, or acquire skills on the job that eventually promote their transition to self-employment.

In parallel with the attention given to the informal sectors of the economy from the perspective of helping the poorest groups in the economy, there has also been a growth of interest in the role played by informal or indigenous learning systems. The fact that the latter systems provide the gateway to the former is important from an analytic and a policy perspective. Work on informal education is as yet in its infancy.[53] Nevertheless, recent studies for Africa do support the following generalizations: (1) informal education/training is the main vehicle for skill acquisition in a wide variety of skilled and semiskilled jobs, particularly those in the informal and rural sectors; (2) informal artisan training is often closely

53. But see the substantial amount of historical and sociological analysis presented in K. King, *The African Artisan* (Edinburgh: University of Edinburgh Centre for African Studies, 1975), and C. Wallace and S. Weeks, *Success or Failure in Rural Uganda: A Study of Young People* (Kampala: Makerere University, 1974).

similar to the apprenticeship schemes promulgated by governments—fees may be paid by the trainee, and the training period may last over a period of years; (3) informal training schemes tend to promote skill acquisition relevant to local resources and products—*prima facie* they tend to be more usable in a rural environment, or in cases where capital is a key constraint; and (4) informal wage structures are more determined by productivity than by certification—this means that informal learning systems may be more effective as instruments to promote relevant knowledge and skills than the formal system, geared as the latter is to the needs of a formal sector labor market.

These characteristics are now confirmed by studies in a number of countries, and it is clear that the *de facto* importance of informal education has been overlooked in the past. Nevertheless, the importance of informal education from the point of view of government policy relates more to the lessons that can be learned for educational developments in the formal system than to the desirability of governments becoming more involved in these informal learning processes. At present, the best thing that could happen to informal education is that it be left alone, not least because it appears to achieve a wide range of educational objectives more successfully than the formal system. Meanwhile, there is a need to conduct more descriptive research in a variety of rural and urban settings, both to increase our knowledge of the range of skills that are effectively taught informally, and to gain insights concerning the actual and potential linkages to organized systems of learning.

AN ACTIVE MANPOWER POLICY

Left to the last is the question of tackling educated unemployment by direct intervention in labor markets. When an economist examines the comprehensive educational reforms that are now under way in a large number of Asian and African countries, the overwhelming impression gained is that the direct links between the educational system and the labor market are still not adequately appreciated in developing countries. Again and again, he will witness countries overhauling their entire educational system without taking steps to alter the prevailing salary differentials by levels of schooling. Even when such countries pursue an incomes policy designed to restrain the upward movement of wages and salaries, no effort is made to monitor and publicize the squeezing of differentials that such a policy frequently entails, as if levels were everything and differentials nothing. There may be circumstances in which governments are powerless to affect the general pattern of rewards in the labor market, at least in the short run, but any government in Asia or Africa can in fact make significant inroads on the rewards of educated people merely by altering its own hiring and promotion practices, for the simple reason that they are generally a major employer, as in the case of Asia, or a principal employer, as in the case of Africa, of the products of secondary and tertiary educational institutions.

The ILO mission Reports on Sri Lanka and Kenya both place emphasis on policies designed to reduce earnings differentials in labor markets.[54] They take the view that the differentials between unskilled and skilled workers and between less and more educated workers are "excessive," in the sense that they exceed the differentials required to give people an incentive to acquire both skills and education. These excessive differentials produce a high private rate of return to investment in education and thus feed the demand for upper secondary and higher education. Moreover, they distort the motives of youngsters and thus contribute to educated unemployment. For example, a survey of university students in Sri Lanka carried out by the ILO Employment Mission showed that most unemployed arts graduates were willing to consider a job at Rs. 300 per month, which is about half the going rate for university graduates; furthermore, a graduate training scheme which offered 5,000 jobs at Rs. 200, rising in two years to Rs. 400, led to applications from half of the new arts graduates in the country.[55] Clearly, these graduates are willing to work at less than the current salary for university graduates. It is worth noting that the public sector in Sri Lanka pays educated people more than the private sector at every age and, in addition, offers fringe benefits which are more generous than those offered by private industry. No wonder that Sri Lanka university students prefer public sector employment, citing superior fringe benefits, greater job security and more personal freedom as the justification for their preference.[56]

The ILO Kenya Mission Report attacks the problem directly by proposing that the entry points on public pay scales should be reduced by 25 percent for a five-year period, after which entry points should no longer be defined in terms of formal education; however, this suggestion was not accepted by the Kenyan government.[57] Nevertheless, the Kenyan government did accept the principle of working toward a narrowing of skill differentials in the years ahead. Incomes policies, to use a widely accepted shorthand, are now a regular feature of economic policy in a number of

54. ILO Sri Lanka Report, pp. 118–20; ILO Kenya Report, pp. 268–69.

55. ILO Sri Lanka Report, p. 175.

56. *Ibid.*, p. 135.

57. ILO Kenya Report, pp. 268–69, and Republic of Kenya, *Sessional Paper on Employment*, p. 50.

Third World countries, and although they are rarely designed to deal expressly with the problem of depressing the relative earnings of university graduates, they all have the effect of doing so.[58] Nevertheless, even a general incomes policy that narrows earnings differentials in labor markets, and thus effectively saps the private incentive to acquire higher education, is not enough, unless accompanied by specific changes in public sector hiring practices. As the principal employer of the bulk of educated people, Asian and African governments share a heavy responsibility for the excessive growth of the upper levels of the educational system. In most countries, they tie salary scales rigidly to educational qualifications; they promote almost automatically by age, with little resort to performance rating; they fail to provide job specifications and fail to practice scientific job evaluations; and they invariably provide absolute tenure and generous fringe benefits. Even if they paid graduates no more than secondary school leavers, this would be enough to create a large demand for university education. In short, the recruitment and promotion policies of the public sector in Asia and Africa have done much to foster "the diploma disease." Large salary differentials and free or almost free university education have done the rest.

A COMPREHENSIVE STRATEGY

By now, a formidable list of policy proposals has been collected for an attack on the problem of educated unemployment in developing countries: they range from quantitative restrictions on entry at various levels; to a rise in the private costs of secondary and higher education joined to income-related scholarships and loans to equalize educational opportunities; to structural reforms allowing flexibility for a number of different routes through both formal and informal education; to "vocationalization" of curricula and the reform of the examination system; to a strengthening of out-of-school provision; and, lastly, to an incomes policy or at least a change in public sector employment practices. All of these may be expected to have an impact on the employment problem, but, in the present state of knowledge, it is not possible to know which of these would be more or less effective. It may be concluded, therefore, that the hope of gearing education to employment opportunities demands a multi-pronged attack. Apart from the fact that changes affecting the labor market should precede, or at

58. For some African evidence, showing that Egypt, Ghana, Tanzania, Zambia, and Kenya have all succeeded in recent years in squeezing earnings differentials by the device of freezing top salaries and raising statutory minimum wages, see UN-ECA, *Economic Conditions in Africa*, pp. 113–15.

least go hand-in-hand with, educational reforms, it is evident that educational remedies to the problem of educated unemployment have to be considered as a whole. The need is for a comprehensive educational strategy, embodying all the reforms which have been noted.

The precise weight assigned to each component of the comprehensive attack on the problem of educated unemployment will vary from country to country. As between the formal system of schooling and informal educational activities, between universal primary education and selective secondary education, between comprehensive schools and specialized technical institutes, between regular university degree courses and short career courses, between a uniform, urban-oriented curriculum and a "ruralized" curriculum, between an uninterrupted learning stage and recurrent education with "sandwiched" periods of work and learning, not to mention the choice among fees, scholarships and loans, the alternatives are so numerous that the choice must ultimately depend on each country's national objectives. In these circumstances, a few, but only a few, generalizations by way of a conclusion are ventured.

The greatest educational need for the Third World, and particularly for countries in Asia and Africa, is still universal primary education. The large numbers of children who are not in school, either because they never entered one or because they have dropped out of school too early, have to be given the benefit of a minimum quantum of education. This first stage of education should be both free and compulsory. The period of such compulsory primary education should in practice be as long as a country can afford, although the tenets of educational psychology would demand that it last a minimum of 7 to 8 years. Universal primary education, followed by selective education to satisfy identified manpower needs in modern sector employment, is not a new policy in Asia or Africa. But where it has been operative hitherto, the tendency has been to select students only in respect of certain high-level professions, allowing the rest either to drop out of the system or to be relegated to less expensive and unfocused courses of study. The current situation in the Third World demands a system of postprimary education which is accessible to all those who want to pursue full-time, part-time, or "own-time" education, not as a right but as a privilege. In general, everyone should pay for postprimary education unless they can show that they are too poor to do so. Alternatively, students may be lent their fees to be repaid out of future earnings, if they have earnings and not otherwise. Some countries may want to combine low fees and minimum loans with some scholarships for particularly disadvantaged groups. But, in general, countries must be prepared to shift an increasing burden of the costs of postprimary education to parents. Universal primary education in the Third World cannot be achieved unless the locomotive of higher education can somehow be slowed down, and there is little chance of that unless it can be made more expensive to students and their families.

The content of education must move gradually towards the ideal of comprehensive schooling for everyone that includes "shop courses," "practical arts," "prevocational education," or whatever it is called, whose purpose it is to introduce children to manual work without pretending to prepare them for a specific job, or even a range of specific jobs. Examinations ought to contain an increasing number of objective questions, unrelated to the previous syllabus, and aptitude tests may be gradually introduced alongside standard examinations of the old type. A period of work experience as an essential prerequisite to admission in higher education ought to become universal in developing countries (not to mention developed ones). And the role of relating education to the so-called manpower requirements of a growing economy should fall increasingly on informal education and on training schemes offered on a part-time or short-term basis. In general, new attention ought to be given to the location of educational activities as between town and country. Future economic planning will, in any case, be focused on the rural sector, and it is rural education, and particularly out-of-school education for rural youths and adults, that must now become the linchpin of educational policy in Asia and Africa.

The policy proposals outlined above are designed to affect the quality of population. They may also contribute to the solution of the quantitative population problem in the Third World, but that cannot be their principal motive. The effect of formal schooling, whatever its magnitude and character, has only indirect, long-term influence on the birth rate, and hence the rate of population growth, in particular countries.[59] In consequence, no specific education and training policies can be derived from a country's official programs aimed at reducing the population growth rate. It is true that UNFPA, FAO, WHO, and UNESCO have long been concerned with both school and out-of-school programs of what is called "population education," namely, the insertion in school curricula and in formal youth training programs of the study of population dynamics and policies.[60] But, as yet, the number of nationwide population education programs is small: although there have been different programs in more than fifty countries, less than twenty have so far committed themselves to

59. See R. M. Bjork, "Population, Education and Modernization," *Education in National Development,* edited by D. Adams (London: Routledge and Kegan Paul, 1971), pp. 118–45.

60. See UNESCO, *Population Education: A Contemporary Concern* (Paris: UNESCO, 1978).

official national programs.[61] That is no reason for not encouraging the expansion of such programs in future years, but the fact remains that even a massive expansion of population education programs could not be expected to affect fertility rates for many years to come and would in any case absorb only a small proportion of educational budgets around the world. Meanwhile, the vast educational and training problems of Third World countries would still remain unsolved. The argument for better educational planning in the Third World has to be that effective planning would contribute to a wider process of modernization, in which policies aimed primarily at the quality of population complement associated policies designed to affect the quantity of population, which would not necessarily have impact today, or tomorrow, but would, surely, the day after tomorrow.

61. *Ibid.*, p. 28.

12

Population Redistribution: Patterns, Policies, and Prospects

L. A. PETER GOSLING

INTRODUCTION

THE CONCERN with population problems in developing countries has, until recently, focused almost exclusively on overall population numbers and growth and on policies to control fertility in these countries. Now, however, increasing recognition is also being given to the location or distribution of population within nations. Developing countries have become increasingly concerned with the spatial maldistribution of population manifest in such phenomena as overurbanization, rural overpopulation, and the associated problems of rural and urban poverty, unemployment, and urban blight. A wide range of population redistribution policies has evolved to deal with these problems. They include policies to control, restrict, or reverse rural-urban migration; to move "surplus population" out of cities; to control spontaneous, or even planned, population redistribution within rural areas; to develop land settlement projects and such urban projects as squatter eviction, slum clearance, urban renewal, and public housing.

Most of these population redistribution policies evolve in response to specific problems such as poor and landless rural population and urban overcrowding and unemployment. They do not deal with the underlying causes of these problems, which lie in social and economic structures and

This chapter is a summary of a monograph of the same title which incorporates nine individual papers, written by L. A. Peter Gosling, Linda Lim, John Oppenheim, Donald Deskins, Keith Clarke, Theodore Fuller, Abdul Hamid Abdullah, and Maxine Olson, and edited by L. A. Peter Gosling and Linda Lim. The reader is referred to this monograph, to be published in its entirety by UNFPA, for more detailed discussions and extensive footnotes and references. An abbreviated list of references is appended to this chapter.

relationships which cannot be altered by simply shifting people from place to place. Fragmented policies may conflict with one another, or are contravened and frustrated by other government policies which have direct and indirect impacts on population movements. Sometimes the various redistribution policies which deal with specific problems can be joined into a comprehensive national population redistribution plan, but even this may be frustrated if it does not fit in with the direction and goals of national economic planning. Population redistribution usually takes place for reasons which may be untouched by specific redistribution policies.

Because population redistribution involves changing the prevailing patterns of residence and movement, it often involves government *intervention* in the freedom to move or not to move. Governments are accustomed to high levels of intervention in implementing redistribution undertaken for political reasons, but in general, low level intervention policies are preferred for non-political population redistribution.

It is possible to identify several levels of intervention. *Spontaneous* redistribution refers to situations in which *no direct* government intervention or planning is involved which affects either the area sending migrants, or the area receiving them. *Managed* redistribution refers to situations in which there is intervention in either the sending or receiving area, such as job training or employment counselling among potential migrants in the sending area, or the provision of employment opportunities or migrant housing in the receiving area. However, these components may not be linked. *Sponsored* redistribution involves linked government intervention, in which a specific population is induced to move from one location to a specific new location, such as the case of settlers recruited for a new land settlement. *Compulsory* redistribution involves maximum intervention in which people are forced to move from one location to another, such as the resettlement in new communities of population flooded out by reservoirs. Politically motivated population movement, such as resettlement for security purposes, is an extreme form of compulsory redistribution. The increasing level of intervention in the above typology does not necessarily involve increasing coercion, as there may be direct or indirect coercion or compulsion at any of these levels.

This range of intervention levels is sometimes seen in terms of a "free market" in population redistribution at one pole, and a "planned economy" control of population movement at the other. The "free market" view assumes that population migration is a natural phenomenon of economic life, involving movement within national boundaries and—when permitted—across national boundaries. The natural economic self-interest of the individual causes him to move to the place where he is most needed and can therefore obtain the highest returns for his labor. That is, free migration or labor mobility efficiently distributes population to meet the requirements of the economy without government intervention. The ideal "planned economy" counterview considers that population is a resource which, like any other resource, should be managed for the collective national benefit. Because population is more mobile than fixed resources such as agricultural land or optimal industrial locations, government-sponsored movement of population to meet national goals is both acceptable and efficient. While both "free market" and "planned economy" elements are included in most population redistribution programs, the trend is toward increased central planning and government intervention.

The following sections of this paper attempt brief reviews of the state of the art in population redistribution studies and policies in these areas: determinants of population distribution, rural-to-urban migration and migration management, rural population redistribution including land settlement and resettlement, urban population redistribution, urban-to-rural population redistribution, refugee resettlement, human rights issues in planned population redistribution, and population redistribution in the context of economic development. They include selective surveys of the relevant literature, assessments of the state of theory, some original case material, and identifications of important areas of needed research in each area.

Over the coming decade, problems arising from the maldistribution of population, especially in developing countries, will intensify and be perceived with a greater sense of urgency than is now the case. Deliberate population redistribution will increasingly be viewed as necessary, with governments increasingly accepting responsibility for intervening in and planning population movements. The need for information on population redistribution patterns, policies, and their outcomes will grow. Ultimately, since, as we will argue, population redistribution is primarily determined by national economic development patterns and the spatial distribution of economic opportunities that they condition, population redistribution analysis and planning must be integrated into broader social and economic development efforts in a comprehensive national planning context.

DETERMINANTS OF POPULATION DISTRIBUTION

The Geographic Context

A majority of the world's population is distributed on only a small part of the earth's surface. Only about 30 percent of the world's land area is permanently inhabited, with another 35 to 40 percent being physically uninhabitable. Population densities vary greatly by region, with about 65 percent of the world's land area being sparsely inhabited, and most population settlement occurring in increasingly concentrated areas. Over time, populations tend to cluster, especially in urban areas: by the year 2000, world population may reach 6.5 billion, with up to 50 percent of the population residing in urban areas. In the last two decades, urban population has grown more rapidly than rural population, more so in developing than in developed nations. But despite major rural-to-urban population movements, pressure on land and resources in rural areas continues to increase significantly, especially in developing countries.

In general, people are settled in particular areas for historical reasons, based on the relative importance of physical factors in combination with different resource uses conditioned by economic development, especially through market forces. Physical factors determine the outer limits of inhabitable land, although these limits themselves are constantly shifting through the application of technology, which affects population distribution through its impact on the carrying capacity of the land. Population density varies with types of economic activities, such as nomadic activities, agriculture, and industrial production—all of which are associated with cultural preferences which also shape distribution patterns. Political factors influence distribution largely through boundary control and their impact on resource exploitation and economic activities.

Analyses of the relationship between population and resources have resulted in measures such as population density, man-land ratios, and cropland production. These measures are used to define the support capacity of mainly natural resources but are inadequate for assessing general patterns of population-resource relationships. Attempts have been made to include environmental and ecological factors in carrying capacity estimates, but it is still difficult to assess the crucial human and capital resources in relation to population. Until recently policymakers concerned with population-resource ratios have concentrated on the expansion of resources, but now it has become fashionable to view population growth limitation as the deciding factor in establishing balance and stability in this relationship.

Geographers have developed various theoretical models in attempts to provide abstract generalizations about population-environment relationships. These include central place theory, analyses of the rank-size relationships between cities, and growth center theory, all of which have proved to be deficient. They fail to integrate micro-level human decision-making activities with macro-level distribution patterns. Taking the city as the starting point of analysis generates an urban bias in the theory which is of limited relevance to developing countries. All the theories contain, at least implicitly, the concept of some optimum pattern of population distribution, but this remains barely defined. No sound theoretical criteria for evaluating distributions have been developed.

The Economic Context

The spatial distribution of population is very much a product of a dynamic historical process of economic development. Development has occurred unevenly in different places and times and is inadequately captured by the typically static and ahistorical theoretical models found in the geographic literature. For most of human history, most populations were directly dependent on nature for survival—distribution was mostly determined by the physical characteristics of the environment. As technology developed, and as economic activities diversified, human settlement patterns shifted. The size, density, and distribution of population was determined by the type of production (nomadism, hunting and gathering, shifting cultivation, settled agriculture) and the population's social organization (in settled agriculture, for example) according to whether peasant, feudal, or commercial farming systems predominated.

Over the past few centuries economic development has become a worldwide process with the colonial expansion of market forces greatly altering land carrying capacities and population distribution patterns throughout much of the developing world. Vast tracts of previously inhabited and uninhabited land have been turned into commerical farms and plantations producing for a world market. Different forms of organization of production and increased inputs of capital and human resources may increase the productivity of given tracts of land, but the gains of such increases may be experienced more at the point of consumption, e.g., in developed Western nations, than at the point of production in the developing countries. This suggests that assessments of population distribution, and especially *maldistribution,* should be made, not on a national, but on a worldwide basis. For example, much of what is seen as overpopulation in terms of excessive numbers of people and their maldistribution in relation to resources in the Third World might be better characterized as a worldwide maldistribution, with excessively high per capita consumption of Third World products in developed countries adding to the population pressure on resources in developing countries.

The historical growth of towns usually reflects a higher development of technology and human social organization. Urban areas are able to support much higher population densities than rural areas and are much less dependent on the physical characteristics of the material environment. Even in urban areas, however, the population carrying capacity is determined by the particular system of production and distribution. If urban activity involves largely capital-intensive industrial enterprises paying high wages, it can support fewer fully employed people, though at relatively higher standards of living (characteristic of many Third World countries). Labor-intensive industries and services can employ larger numbers of people, but at lower income levels.

This discussion suggests that the need for some theoretical criteria to assess population distribution and maldistribution can only be met by a dynamic concept of optimal population distribution based on a dynamic population-resources relationship. The optimum—defined, for example, by full employment of the labor force—will change over time, but it should be possible to specify a range within which it will lie in any developmental context. Then the difference between this moving optimum target and the actual or projected level and distribution of population shown by demographic data will indicate the degree of maldistribution and the targets for distribution.

In most countries, market forces remain the main determinant of population distribution. Thus a government interested in planning population redistribution (e.g., because market forces alone lead to maldistribution) will be more successful the more it is able to affect those market forces. This may imply only marginal changes and indirect policies or major attempts to supplant market forces through a radical restructuring of the organization of production and distribution. (Discussions below indicate, however, that even major attempts to supplant market forces have been of only limited success in changing patterns of population distribution.) Economic development, especially higher standards of living for the population, is both the objective and the determinant of population distribution. There is no optimum distribution pattern outside of the economic context, hence no population redistribution policy is relevant or effective unless it is conducted within the framework of general economic development in a comprehensive national planning effort.

RURAL-TO-URBAN MIGRATION AND MIGRATION MANAGEMENT

Rural-to-urban migration constitutes one of the major migration streams in the developing world today. Until recently this process of urbanization was thought to provide a stimulus for economic development. There is now, however, gathering consensus that the transfer of labor from rural to urban areas is outstripping the ability of many developing countries to generate urban employment. Rural-to-urban migration may simply add to the difficulties to be overcome in the process of development. Already a majority of the world's urban population lives in the cities of the developing world, which are growing much faster than cities in the developed world did a century ago. It is estimated that during 1970–75 there was a net transfer of approximately 100 million people from rural to urban areas—a movement of considerable magnitude in developing countries.

In 1885 Ravenstein posited six major propositions on migration: (1) the rate of migration is inversely related to distance; (2) stage migration is common, with a series of moves culminating in a move to the fastest growing cities; (3) for each migration stream there is a counter stream; (4) net migratory streams will usually be from rural to urban areas; (5) increases in technology and communications will increase migration rates; and, (6) economic factors will be most important in influencing migration.

Since then, few additional generalizations have been advanced. Most writers on migration have employed some form of differential benefit perspective in their analysis of rural-to-urban migration. Migrants are drawn to urban areas when they perceive greater benefits there than they enjoy in rural areas. Higher urban wages and employment, a greater variety and higher level of services, and a perception of greater opportunities in urban areas lead people to move in that direction. Most theories also recognize that consideration must be given to conditions at the place of origin as well as at the destination of migration, to the intervening conditions between the two, and to such things as feedback channels and patterns of information flow.

Almost universally, young adult males are overrepresented in rural-to-urban migration streams. This can have a negative impact on the place of origin of migration since it increases the dependency ratio and draws off more productive members of the population. To the extent that education is generally available, migrants tend to be the more educated, thus increasing the drain of human resources from rural areas. On the other hand, out-migration can be an advantage to the place of origin. It may ease population pressures in rural areas, which benefit from remittances sent back by out-migrants and from the flow of progressive urban ideas back to rural areas via out-migrants who retain some contacts with and make visits back to their place of origin. The net of negative and positive impacts on the place of origin of migrants cannot be stated in general terms as it will be heavily determined by specific local conditions.

The impact of migrants on points of destination is also mixed. On the one hand, the influx of young adults increases the productive human resources in the area. It is generally observed that new migrants are less likely to be unemployed than the comparable nonmigrant urban populations, possibly because they accept jobs that natives will not, or are not forced to take. This may mean only that migrants are more underemployed than nonmigrants, although in any event their work does constitute a productive benefit to the city.

Currently there is greater recognition of the problems and obstacles to development generated by high rates of urban in-migration. Heavy pressure on housing is seen in the pervasiveness of massive urban slum areas with substandard housing. Pressure on land is seen in the speed with which squatter settlements spring up in vacant land. Pressure on urban public services is reflected in the shortages of piped water, drainage, controlled sewage, electricity, and transportation that constitute some of the overwhelming problems of most Third World cities. Heavy pressures on educational and health services are also part of a landscape that implies poverty for the masses and headaches for the planners.

Although both advantages and disadvantages to the sending and receiving areas are observed, there appears today to be a growing consensus that the disadvantages outweigh the advantages in both areas. While the social and economic trade-offs are not yet well understood, the older free market view (in which internal migration was thought to be useful in drawing labor from rural surplus areas to urban employment, fueling the growing urban industrial system) is no longer adequate or acceptable. It is now being supplanted by a view that recognizes the detrimental impacts that can result from internal migration and suggests increasing attempts to manage the flow of migrants.

A 1974 United Nations study showed that half of the total number of UN member states permit migration from rural areas but seek to divert the movement from metropolitan areas to smaller urban areas. The management of migration is thus becoming a common element in national population policies. These policies generally develop by studying a perspective of differential benefits as the major determinant of migration and then attempting through various forms of taxation and subsidy to alter the distribution of benefits. European countries show substantial successes in this process with activities that focus on infrastructure development, incentive subsidies for, or controls on, industrial location, and direct government activity in locating public services and offices. Weiner has examined policies of a number of developing countries and finds that they are based on one or more of three different primary concerns: ethnic compositions of populations, regional imbalances, and the rate of urban growth. He notes that policies concerned with ethnic distributions tend to be formulated precisely, to be pursued with vigor, and to achieve their objectives with greater effectiveness than most migration management policies.

The recognition that differential distribution of services has a large impact on migration streams has led to the suggestion that urban public services should receive less emphasis in order to discourage in-migration and that greater support be given to rural services to reduce out-migration pressures. But the potential impact of this type of differential public investment may not be great. Urban public services are already highly inadequate, yet this does not appear to discourage in-migration. On the other hand, rural infrastructure and service development may increase out-migration as it facilitates access to other areas; for example, through improvements in communication and transportation flows.

Differential income policies are also suggested by the Harris and Todaro models, which propose that urban in-migration is primarily a function of higher employment and income opportunities in the urban areas. Governments may directly affect income in urban and rural areas or indirectly affect them through incentives to industries that locate in rural or smaller urban areas. Some governments decentralize their own administrative services in the hope that this will produce a multiplier effect on smaller urban areas. Finally, direct controls over migration are used in some countries; for example, in the Union of South Africa and the Peoples' Republic of China. (We show later that such direct controls are difficult to operate and place heavy administrative demands on governments.)

One problem with all attempts to manage or control migration lies in the inadequacy of data required for effective policy implementation. Most metropolitan areas fail to perceive changes as they occur and therefore fail to react to them in a timely fashion. Thus any migration management policy will require sensitive indicators, quickly collected, to permit planners to manage effectively the migration streams that are generated by powerful market forces.

One of the lowest cost policy instruments has often been found to have considerable impact on migration streams. European countries provide extensive information to potential migrants to affect the rate and direction of flows. Many researchers suggest that simply providing information to potential migrants about opportunities in planned growth centers can appreciably increase the rate of movement to those areas.

For effective management of migration, much more research needs to be done on the determinants of migration flows. To affect migration, planners need to know more about the determinants and consequences of in- and out-migration, the impact of various public policies on migration, the character of existing urban-rural linkages, the effects of migration on fertility, and more about the individual decision-making processes that are involved in migration. In all of these areas more and better data should be collected systematically and relatively quickly. Finally, more effective theoretical developments on migration are required, both to guide data collection and to integrate those data into effective public policy decision-making processes.

RURAL POPULATION REDISTRIBUTION

If urbanization in the developing countries constitutes the most visible and dramatic migration pattern in the world today, rural-to-rural migration *is even greater in magnitude,* possibly more profound in its implications, and certainly far more neglected, far less studied, and less understood. The largest component of world population movement today consists of individuals and groups moving from one rural location to another. Recent estimates indicate that the current rate of new rural land settlement is four to five million hectares annually, with about 75 percent of this due to spontaneous new settlement. Unchecked population redistribution in rural areas may ultimately pose greater problems than those of overurbanization. Overpopulation in rural areas can result in poverty that makes urban slums seem almost paradise by comparison. When rural populations expand into forest reserves, river watersheds, or dry land margins, the impact may be ecological disasters that dwarf the worst inconveniences of overurbanization. Further, while most of the ills of overurbanization permit reversals and solutions through public policy, the consequences of rural ecological disasters may be irreversible and insoluble. Yet spontaneous rural migration is the least studied aspect of modern population movements: most governments have virtually no data on rural migrations, and few studies exist to parallel the attention given rural-to-urban migration. Given the magnitude and seriousness of spontaneous rural-to-rural migration and the lack of detailed knowledge about it, there is great need for both research and planning activities to be directed toward this type of movement.

Managing Spontaneous Rural-to-Rural Population Redistribution

In spontaneous rural migration, people are usually moving specifically to better their lives or their opportunities. Increases or decreases in security in an area often produce rapid and dramatic movements. Government programs that affect the accessibility, productivity, or health of a region similarly can be counted on to give rise to rural-to-rural migration. Even sponsored population movements, such as land resettlement programs, typically also bring with them an important component of spontaneous movement as others follow the opportunities generated by the sponsored movement. Thus the management of spontaneous rural migration must first begin with a recognition that it does occur and that it typically follows from many other forms of development programming.

This has led to one suggestion that all development programs should contain *migration impact studies* similar to the environmental impact studies required by some governments before any significant publicly controlled development is permitted.

To avoid the worst ecological consequences of spontaneous rural migration, a policy of *exclusion* is often used. This strategy tends to be successful in developed countries where forest reserves and other types of public land are closed to settlement or managed for ecologically safe habitation and production levels. In developing countries, however, exclusion tends to be unsuccessful. It is often politically unpopular and tends to demand greater administrative efficiency than is typically available. Further, radical differences in traditional land rights often work against effective exclusion policies. In many developing countries, traditional land systems provide usufructuary rights and rest on the assumption that all undeveloped land is available for occupation; the act of clearing land provides title claim. These populations do not accept exclusion from government lands, which are consequently riddled with squatter occupants. Moreover, exclusion from public land is usually acceptable only if alternative opportunities are available to squatters; so long as public land is the best hope of the rural poor, nothing can keep them from using it.

Sponsored Rural Population Redistribution

In sponsored rural-to-rural migration some central authority plans and executes population redistribution, giving attention both to the source and selection of migrants and to the development of the destination area. Two general types of programs can be identified. *Land settlement* will refer to those land development programs in which rural peoples have some options to move or to remain where they are. *Resettlement* will be used to refer to forced movement, in which rural populations are forcibly moved either for security or development purposes. There is a great deal of experience with both types of movement in the developing areas, but there has as yet been no systematic attempt to analyze this experience to identify the determinants of successful redistribution. Here we make a preliminary effort at this type of analysis.

Land settlement schemes have been a common element of government economic development programs in the developing countries over the past three decades. Many of these continue policies originated by colonial governments, but independence has usually involved a rapid expansion of such activities as new governments showed greater commitment to development goals than did their colonial predecessors. In 1954

W. Arthur Lewis reflected on his observation of land settlement programs and identified seven major factors that would determine success or failure of schemes. The mere enumeration of these elements immediately indicates that high levels of administrative effectiveness are required in the development authority. This is an important point to which we shall return. The seven determining factors are: (1) site selection—the land must be productive; (2) settler selection—productive young adult families are preferable; (3) site preparation—it should be prepared for production and habitation; (4) settlers' capital—provision of subsistence allowance is necessary; (5) organization of group activities—some organization preferable; (6) acreage per settler—usually 10–30 is optimum; and (7) condition of tenure—specified freeholding lease with some restrictions on fragmentation is optimum.

We have attempted to specify the range of conditions under each of these factors and to assign weights to each of the conditions. The resulting point system is shown in Table 12.1. We then assigned appropriate points to seven major development schemes for which descriptions are sufficiently complete to permit both judgments on each of the factors and a summary judgment of the degree of success achieved by each scheme. This is admittedly a preliminary effort, but we believe it points to the type of systematic assessment of land settlement schemes that can be useful in future planning. The results of this analysis appear in Table 12.2.

The data in Table 12.2 provide a number of insights or propositions concerning the determinants of success in land schemes. First, the individual scores in the seven factors appear to scale. That is, there is a tendency to show high scores in all the factors or in none. This may be taken to indicate that a generally effective administration of settlement schemes will attend to all of the conditions necessary for success. This perception is reinforced by an examination of the cost per family. Land settlement appears to require heavy investment, and it appears that the greater the investment, the greater are the chances of success. Thus the major underlying determinant may be said to be a combination of administrative effectiveness and the political commitment necessary to achieve high levels of resource allocation to the program. Effective land settlement is expensive, both in financial and organizational terms.

Land settlement typically involves many dilemmas for the planners, but one in particular should be especially noted. Most settlement schemes are production-oriented, but some also include aims of relieving population pressures, such as the Indonesian *transmigrasi* programs which since the Dutch colonial period have moved only about one million people. When production-oriented settlement schemes are successful, however, the immediate impact may be to increase population growth rates and thus

TABLE 12.1
Factors for Evaluating Performance of Land Settlement

	Points
Factor I: Site Selection	
1. Marginal land, inaccessible	0
2. Marginal land, accessible	1
3. Productive land, inaccessible	15
4. Productive land, accessible	20
Factor II: Settler Selection	
1. Poor and/or landless	1
2. Limited capital and/or land	2
3. Limited capital and/or land and adult agricultural experience	3
4. Limited capital and/or land, agricultural experience, mature married male with children	4
5. All of the above, together with prime age and good health	5
Factor III: Site Preparation	
1. No preparation at all	0
2. Temporary shelter provided	1
3. Village area cleared	2
4. Permanent houses built	3
5. Part of farm area cleared	4
6. Whole of farm area cleared	5
7. Main crops planted	6
Factor IV: Settlers' Capital	
1. Settlers with no capital/no credit provided	0
2. Settlers with capital	1
3. Settlers with capital and some form of credit provided	2
4. Supervised credit program	3
5. Rigidly administered subsistence allowance	4
Factor V: Organization of Group Activities	
1. No organization	0
2. Independent family farms	1
3. Settlers cooperatives	2
4. Centralized control of farm operations, extension, supervision, processing, marketing, etc.	3
5. Some form of compulsion applied to follow centrally organized activities	4
Factor VI: Acreage per Settler (Southeast Asian allocations)	
1. Less than 5 acres and more than 30 acres	1
2. 20–30 acres	2
3. 5–9 acres	3
4. 10–19 acres	4
Factor VII: Conditions of Tenure	
1. Unspecified and/or uncontrolled	0
2. Non-ownership/*de jure* or *de facto* tenancy	1
3. Leasehold/freehold without restrictions	2
4. Leasehold/freehold with restrictions	3

TABLE 12.2
Scheme/Program Characteristics. Scheme Performance Level

Scheme	Site selection	Settler selection	Site preparation	Settlers' capital	Organization of group activities	Acreage/settler	Conditions of tenure	Total points
Alto Beni I Bolivia	1	3	2	2	1	1	2	12
Alto Beni II	1	3	1	1	1	1	2	10
Farm Settlement Western Nigeria	1	1	5	2	1	3	0	13
FELDA Malaysia	20	5	6	4	4	4	3	46
Igbariam Eastern Nigeria	20	4	3	3	4	4	3	41
PLS Region 5 Sara Buri Thailand	20	4	6	2	4	4	2	42
Wauna-Yarakita Guyana	1	1	1	0	0	2	0	5

SOURCES: Tunku Shamsul Bahrin and P. D. A. Pereira, *FELDA: Twenty-One Years of Land Development* (Kuala Lumpur: FELDA, 1977). C. Boonman, S. Tongpang, and C. Konjing, *Socio-Economic Conditions and Agricultural Planning of Phra Buddhabat Land Settlement, Saraburi* (Bangkok: Kasetsart University, 1969). B. S. Floyd and M. Adine, "Farm Settlement in Eastern Nigeria:

to reduce the medium or longterm population absorptive capacity of the receiving area. This is a problem currently facing the successful Malaysian FELDA schemes. Those schemes also point to the critical nature of settler organization activities, however, for it is through the group organization that the new government family planning program is being channelled.

Resettlement schemes involve the highest level of government intervention. They are typically carried out either for *security* or *development* reasons. Security resettlement has been carried out for political purposes—usually to deny insurgents access to the support base provided by scattered and unprotected rural populations. It is implemented under wartime conditions, in haste, usually without adequate planning, and often by the military. Development resettlement is carried out for public economic benefit—to make way for dams, highways, or other national infrastucture projects. The removal is carried out under more peaceful conditions, usually by a special agency designed to facilitate the movement and resettle-

Table 12.2, continued
Scheme/Program Characteristics. Scheme Performance Level

Performance Level Rated by source	% Planned number of settlers	Cost/ family	Net income/ family/ year
Medium	50	U.S. $ 6621	U.S. $ 350
Medium		U.S. $ 2154	U.S. $ 250
Less Successful	38	U.S. $ 5600	U.S. $ 220
Impressive	100	U.S. $11,000	U.S. $1750
Successful	100	U.S. $ 5000	U.S. $1200
Successful	N/A	N/A	U.S. $ 540
Failure	N/A	N/A	N/A

A Geographical Appraisal," *Economic Geography* 43 (3). Michael Nelson, *The Development of Tropical Lands* (Baltimore: Johns Hopkins University Press, 1973). Werner Roider, *Farm Settlements for Socio-Economic Development: The Western Nigerian Case* (New York: Humanities Press, 1971). James W. Vining, "Site Development and Settlement Scheme Failure in Guyana," *Journal of Tropical Geography* 42.

ment. Despite the time available for advance planning, however, most development resettlement resembles security resettlement in the absence of adequate planning.

The most common form of *development resettlement* involves relocating people flooded out of dam reservoirs. Table 12.3 provides a list of some displaced persons over the past 25 years. Even this incomplete listing, especially incomplete in failing to include large projects in the USSR and China, shows approximately three-quarters of a million people displaced. A more complete count would undoubtedly push the figure to at least 2 million.

Like land settlement schemes, resettlement is costly in both organizational and financial terms. The two are also similar in that the degree of success is largely a function of the level of public investment included. In resettlement, however, problems are compounded and opportunities for

TABLE 12.3
Numbers of People Evacuated in Association with Some Large Dams in Less Developed Countries

Country	Dam	Year dam closed	Number of evacuees (nearest thousand)
India	Damodar Valley (4 projects)	1953–59	93,000
Zambia/Rhodesia	Kariba	1958	29,000–11,000
Egypt/The Sudan	Aswan	1964	70,000–48,000
Ghana	Volta	1964	82,000
Pakistan	Mangla	1967	90,000
Nigeria	Kainji	1968	44,000
Ivory Coast	Kossou	1971	75,000
Philippines	Upper Pampanga	1973	14,000
Pakistan	Tarbela	1974	86,000
Thailand	(11 projects)	1963–77	130,000
		Total	713,000

SOURCE: L. A. P. Gosling *et al.*, *Pa Mong Resettlement* (Ann Arbor: University of Michigan, Department of Geography, 1978).

corruption are increased by the necessity of paying compensation to individuals for loss of property. Compensation itself is quite complex, since it raises issues of the range of losses for which compensation is paid, the range of persons to whom it is paid, and the level of payment. A desirable goal is to compensate for the loss of all productive and valuable property; to include all damaged persons—for example, nearby townspeople who suffer a loss of demand for their services even though they may not be directly flooded out; and to provide sufficient compensation to restore income at least to prior levels. Resettlement should also aim to provide migrants with some choices in their future location. It should allow for adequate preparation, the best form of which is often to pay settlers to go in search of alternative locations themselves before they are flooded out. It should aim to maintain levels of public services to settlers, to protect them from various forms of corruption, and to assist in their full resettlement. It will come as no surprise to observe that most resettlement projects fail considerably against these standards, and that a major cause of the failure lies in lack of adequate compensation.

Table 12.4 shows the estimated per capita direct resettlement costs for a number of dam projects. The Thai estimates are based on extensive fieldwork to determine adequate direct costs, which approach $1,600 per capita. This cost level is similar to that projected by the World Bank for Transmigration Projects in Indonesia. These are admittedly incomplete

TABLE 12.4
Estimated Per Capita Direct* Resettlement Costs

Volta	$ 350+
Kainji	$ 500
Tarbela	$ 766
Nam Pong, Thailand	$ 540
Upper Pampanga, Philippines	$ 640
Kossou	$ 865
Kwai Yai, Thailand†	$1,250
Pa Mong†	$1,578

* Does not include indirect support, such as World Food Program supplies.
† Pre-project calculation; project not completed to date.
SOURCE: L. A. P. Gosling *et al.*, *Pa Mong Resettlement* (Ann Arbor: University of Michigan, Department of Geography, 1978).

cost estimates, but they give some rough idea of the magnitude of the problem of providing adequately for this form of development resettlement.

Security resettlement has most often involved colonial governments moving scattered rural populations into concentrated villages so that contact with indigenous insurgent forces can be denied. Well-documented programs are found in Malaysia, Vietnam, Algeria, Mozambique, and Angola. Of all the security resettlement programs, only the Malaysian one can be said to have achieved part of its security goals. It did restrict support to the insurgents, and Malaysia achieved independence without their inclusion in government. In every other case, the colonial power that initiated the strategic resettlement was defeated, and the insurgents that the resettlement was designed to isolate now rule the nation. In all cases, Malaysia included, it is apparent that whatever security gains there were from cutting insurgents off from supplies were probably offset—sometimes decisively so—by increased political support for the insurgents from the relocated population. The forced movement of peoples is not the best way to "win hearts and minds." To the extent that security resettlement was successful, it was based on economic conditions and opportunities provided in the new areas. If resettlement communities provided more amenities, higher income levels, and a good administration, there was less direct anti-government reaction. In most cases, however, resettlement was a degrading experience, resulting in an impoverished population located in what amounted to detention camps under brutal leadership, and the reaction was increased solidarity with the insurgents.

In general, then, security resettlement can be seen as a control measure which is seldom successful in its security aims and is economically successful only if it includes an adequate development framework. Development resettlement is usually seen as an opportunity to benefit the resettled population by improving their lives in the process of relocating them. The goal is worthy, but implementation is difficult and requires comprehensive planning, together with high levels of intervention and investment. At an estimated minimum $U.S. 1500 per capita, which must be accepted as a level necessary for successful resettlement, most alternatives are cheaper and more acceptable.

Implications for Planned Rural Population Redistribution

The largest component of rural population movement is spontaneous. It is little understood and little studied but apparently is strongly affected by economic pressures. This suggests that a range of low-level intervention strategies is available to governments, from the simple provision of information on migration opportunities to the differential location of economic opportunities through various development policies and projects. Greater impact on spontaneous movement might be gained by increasing intervention to the level of providing subsidies for desired patterns of migration. In ecologically fragile areas, some form of exclusion of population is often deemed necessary to prevent long-term disasters, but the experience of developing areas does not hold much hope for successful exclusion policies. Land settlement or resettlement schemes require very high levels of intervention. Both monetary and organizational requirements for success are very high indeed, and the failure of governments to meet these requirements in the past has led to great increases in human misery. If such sponsored movements are to be more common in the future, which is quite likely, it is imperative that the high costs be understood and accepted. Resettlement for security reasons has not proved successful in the past, and it is difficult to see any change in this in the future.

Most of this analysis applies primarily to market-oriented economies. Centrally planned economies, at least in theory, control the pattern of rural population movement through a series of mechanisms similar to the high-level intervention policies discussed above. Little is known about actual rural movements in these situations, but it is apparent that they require levels of investment and organizational skills similar to those required in the market-oriented economies.

URBAN POPULATION REDISTRIBUTION

Urban centers in the developing countries are growing at a rate much more rapid than that of cities in the developed world at the equivalent period of their industrial development. Problems of urban unemployment and poverty, overcrowding and squalor are highly visible and dramatic in developing countries, but there is little hope that the rapid rate of urbanization will decline. Nor do governments in these countries have the resources—information, financial resources, and administrative capacity—to halt or slow this process of overurbanization and the cumulation of human problems it brings with it.

Differences between developed and developing countries' urbanization processes are sufficient to preclude using policies of the former as a guide for the latter. There is, however, one set of policies that appears to be effective in the industrialized countries and in some of the less developed countries. If urbanization cannot be halted, it can be redirected. Many countries are now attempting to decentralize the process of urbanization to prevent the great build-up of one or a few major primate cities and to redirect populations toward a larger number of smaller towns, which are planned to act as growth poles for their own hinterlands. *Newtowns* are common, and relatively well documented in both developed and developing countries. Experience indicates that if adequate infrastructural investments are made, these can attract new industry to provide regional growth poles and also provide adequate housing and services for the population.

Urban development, in the form of slum clearance and urban renewal, has been notoriously unsuccessful in American cities with failures deriving from inadequate planning and investment. Two cases in the developing countries, however, are noteworthy for their greater success and have been suggested as models for the rest of the Third World. Singapore provides probably the most successful case of urban renewal, with a combination of effective public housing and industrial development. An efficient Housing and Development Board has produced what is certainly the most impressive housing program anywhere in the world. Its large high-rise estates currently house about 60 percent of Singapore's 2.3 million people. Hong Kong's public housing program is less impressive than Singapore's, in that housing is generally of a more modest quality, but the program can nonetheless be called a considerable success. Low-cost public housing now provides for close to 50 percent of the city's 4.5 million persons. Hong Kong's program did not aim at population redistribution as much as the simple provision of adequate housing where the population was already located. Singapore's program has been more ambitious and has succeeded in moving large numbers of people out of the city center into satellite towns around the island which include industrial and service facilities as well as self-contained residential estates.

Squatter settlements have been a typical aspect of all urban experiences in the developing world. Early public policies toward squatters were primarily negative and punitive. Squatting was considered a major problem usually dealt with through forced relocation and demolition of dwellings. Recently policy has become more tolerant, and it is recognized that squatters may provide more of a solution than a cause of urban problems. In some cases, observation over time indicates that squatter areas gradually improve in quality and show great stability in providing low-cost housing for the population. Policies based on these observations attempt to assist squatter settlements with the public provision of some utilities and amenities and restrictions to prevent the more serious problems of overcrowding and unsafe construction.

URBAN-TO-RURAL POPULATION REDISTRIBUTION

Spontaneous population movements from urban to rural areas are small in magnitude relative to the dominant migration stream toward cities but are often related to it as shown by various studies on counterstream, return, and circular migration. Some new urban migrants maintain ties to their rural places of origin through periodic visits or seasonal movements. In other cases, urban living is continuous but temporary, ending in a permanent move back to the place of origin. Return migration is a component of both international and internal migration flows throughout the world. Much of it involves moves from large urban areas back to smaller towns in or near the migrant's place of origin, rather than to the original rural village. Economic forces seem to determine counterstream population movements as they do the mainstream movements, with people leaving urban areas for a variety of urban push factors (such as employment layoffs) and rural pull factors.

Managed movements from urban to rural areas involve government intervention to strengthen these push and pull factors through controls and direct policies. More and more developing countries, especially in Asia, are resorting to coercive and restrictive measures in desperate attempts to halt the uncontrolled growth of primate cities. A variety of "closed city" policies have been enacted, including periodic squatter evictions and demolition of squatter communities, compulsory registration of "legal" urban migrants (those who have jobs in the city), mass round-ups of "illegal" migrants and their return to rural areas, the outlawing of many self-employed activities in the cities such as hawking and operating pedicabs, which are the main sources of employment for recent urban migrants. South Africa employs a draconian "pass-law" system to restrict the entry of blacks to cities, confining the families of urban workers to remote rural "homelands," while China has a system of direct controls including registration and the manipulation of ration cards to keep new migrants out of its cities. All these policies require considerable coercion, are administratively costly, and are generally ineffective in reversing the flow of rural-urban migrants. Policies to supplement pull factors in rural areas include the provision of information and assistance to return migrants and specific rural development projects but have so far been limited and not very effective. For example, some rural development projects may stimulate urban migration through improved access to the cities.

Sponsored urban-to-rural population redistribution has not been attempted on any significant scale or with any significant degree of success except by some Asian socialist countries which have attempted to move populations from urban to rural areas as an integral part of overall national development plans. The most dramatic recent example was the apparently forced mass evacuation of the city of Phnom Penh in Cambodia in 1975 which few other governments are ever likely to attempt. Vietnam is currently planning a large-scale movement of urban populations in both the north and the south of the country to New Economic Zones in rural areas as a means both of relieving high levels of urban unemployment, especially in Ho Chi Minh City, and of increasing agricultural production. Various incentives are offered including free transportation, food rations, provision of initial agricultural inputs, and general infrastructural development in the New Economic Zones. However, so far there has only been a limited response to these incentives because of the reluctance of both established and relatively recent urban dwellers (many of them refugees) to take up rural life and work, and the government may eventually resort to more forcible measures of relocation.

The People's Republic of China has had the longest and most successful experience with government-sponsored urban-to-rural population redistribution, mostly through its rustication program for urban youth. Between 1968 and 1975, 12 million urban youths were sent to the countryside, thereby removing about 10 percent of the urban population from the urban sector. The program was aimed at eliminating urban unemployment by permanently removing potential surplus labor from urban areas, at accelerating rural development through the transfer to rural areas of educated youth who would presumably contribute to agricultural production, and at effecting ideological transformation. It has been very successful in preventing large-scale unemployment of educated urban youth, in permitting the growth of productivity and output through capital-intensive industrial development without generating high unemployment, in reducing birth rates and natural population increase in the cities, and in reducing the pressures on urban services, the costs of which are borne by the state. At the same time, the productive integration of the rusticated youth into the rural areas and agricultural production has been less successful, and there is some return to the cities of disaffected youth.

China's rustication program has been an integral part of its overall development program and has been conducted in the context of other policies and programs which enhance its chances of success. It is likely to be of limited relevance for other developing countries because of the unique organizational and ideological capacities which the Chinese have been able to use to make the program work, and which are not present in other countries. The Chinese program has also not been without its own problems and failures.

In general, both low-intervention and high-intervention government policies to redistribute population from urban to rural areas have proved to be both costly and ineffective in developing countries with the partial exception of the Chinese rustication program. The city continues to exert a strong attraction over the countryside as a place to live and, hopefully, to find work. Policies to redistribute population away from cities go against powerful popular preferences and the working of market forces and can only succeed if both these factors are supplanted.

REFUGEES AS A SPECIAL CASE OF POPULATION REDISTRIBUTION

Throughout human history, political upheavals, wars, and natural disasters have produced large waves of redistribution of refugee populations. Over the past quarter of a century, a conservative estimate puts the figure of refugees at approximately 14 million. Refugee movements are found in all continents and occur both within and across national, and indeed continental, boundaries. A rough estimate shows that approximately one-fifth of the world's refugees have settled in urban areas, about a third in rural areas, while another third remain in refugee camps, and about a tenth have been repatriated. Table 12.5 shows our estimate of the recent world experience with refugees.

Refugee experiences run the full gamut of those of other migrants. Refugees may be both innovative and stagnant; at times they become highly productive communities, and at times they continue to be a heavy and permanent drain on public resources. Governments are typically under heavy obligation to assist refugees, in part because they constitute visible and compact groups who arrive together in large numbers and cannot easily be ignored. Assistance programs vary considerably, but it is possible

TABLE 12.5
Refugee Settlement Responses by Continent

Continent	Resettlement Alternatives								Total	
	Repatriation		Refugee Camp		Rural Resettlement		Urban Resettlement			
Africa	1,187,000	33%	716,000	19%	1,748,500	47%	21,800	1%	3,673,300	100%
Asia										
Southeast	125,000	4%	100,400	3%	2,741,700	93%	200		2,967,300	100%
East	—		200		—		148,000	99%	148,200	100%
South	—		619,900	81%	136,400	18%	8,800	1%	765,100	100%
Middle East	—		2,748,000	60%	936,800	21%	878,000	19%	4,562,800	100%
Oceania	—		—		—		32,500	100%	32,500	100%
Europe	—		201,500	16%	11,000	1%	1,087,500	84%	1,300,000	100%
Latin America	—		6,000	44%	100	1%	7,600	55%	13,700	100%
North America	—		—		—		818,100	100%	818,100	100%
TOTAL	1,312,000	9%	4,392,000	31%	5,574,500	39%	3,002,500	21%	14,281,000	100%

SOURCE: Maxine Olson, "Flight Settlement and Adjustment: Refugees in Laos and Other Developing Countries." Ph.D. dissertation, University of Michigan, 1978.

to propose some generalizations about the conditions of assistance that have proved most successful. If infrastructure facilities for refugees are made relatively permanent, if plans are made to assist refugees to become productive—especially in ways that complement rather than compete with native populations—and if refugees are permitted to participate in planning for their own care, they can often be turned into useful and productive members of the new community.

POPULATION REDISTRIBUTION AND HUMAN RIGHTS

Freedom of movement and residence within national boundaries has been proclaimed as a basic human right in the 1948 U.N. Universal Declaration of Human Rights. This right has been frequently reaffirmed; for example, at the 1972 Stockholm Environment Conference, the 1974 Bucharest Population Conference, and the 1976 Vancouver Habitat Conference. It is imbedded in the written constitutions of some states and accepted as part of traditional rights in many others.

The exercise of the right to free movement and residence is never without constraint, however. The rights of private property constitute one major constraint. Another is the widely recognized right of governments to appropriate private property for public purposes. The United Nations International Covenant on Civil and Political Rights also recognizes that rights of both movement and residence may be derogated in times of public emergency. Environmental protection and national economic development are commonly accepted as goals whose achievement may require derogation of movement and residence rights. Limitations on these rights in practice is apparently as universal as proclamations of their existence.

If the rights to free movement are more strongly proclaimed than practiced, the actual limitation of free movement is extremely difficult to effect. A wide range of legal, coercive, and economic tactics are used to restrict movement. But since population movements typically represent reactions to perceived variance in the spatial distribution of economic rewards, most restrictive procedures do not appear very effective. Even coercion is often of limited effectiveness, and its costs are usually very high, both in terms of organizational demands on the government and in terms of popular alienation. This suggests that greater efficiency and greater consistency with the human rights declarations will be achieved through programs that aim to reduce or eliminate spatial differences in economic opportunities. For further discussion of the human rights aspects of population redistribution and broader context, see Chapter 14.

POPULATION REDISTRIBUTION AND ECONOMIC DEVELOPMENT

Migration management does not stem the flow of people to cities. Land settlements do not solve the problems of crowded rural slums, nor do they keep people from ecologically hazardous pioneering in watershed forests. Squatter resettlement does not solve the problems of overurbanization and urban unemployment; it is difficult to keep migrants out of the city or rustics down on the farm. In general, the measures currently used to control or direct population redistribution are not consistently successful in achieving even the piecemeal goals set for these various programs. In developed nations, where there are long-standing, elaborate, and expensive population redistribution programs, involving new towns, regional growth poles, investment incentives and disincentives, and direct migrant subsidies, the results are ambivalent, and many cannot be clearly traced to program components. In developing nations, whatever measures are attempted have even less effect, with the exceptions of some examples in the centrally planned economy of China.

There are several reasons for this somewhat dismal record. First, there is little formal population redistribution planning. Population redistribution simply results from measures undertaken for other purposes, such as industrialization or increasing agricultural production. Second, redistribution measures which are attempted often conflict with, and cancel out, each other. The separate analysis in the foregoing sections of rural-to-urban, rural-to-rural, urban-to-urban, and urban-to-rural movement obscures the connections among them. For example, any successful migration management plan to keep people from entering towns leaves them in the rural areas to add to redistribution problems there. Restrictions on farming forest reserves forces would-be rural migrants into towns, while programs for de-urbanization return them to the rural areas again. Third, not only are there conflicting goals among different population redistribution efforts, but there are also conflicts between these goals and national planning priorities in other areas. Thus it is unlikely that national development plans which focus on urban-based industrialization can be linked with population redistribution programs which attempt to inhibit migration to urban areas. This suggests that before there can be any effective population redistribution programs, there must be *integrated* population redistribution planning as a part of comprehensive national development planning.

Population Redistribution in Market Economies

Spontaneous population redistribution, or voluntary migration, is most strongly influenced by economic motives: people move in search of better economic opportunity for themselves and, as individuals, usually find it. Population redistribution policy in market economy countries tries to control, influence, or redirect spontaneous population movements by changing the structure of market incentives which generates aggregate maldistribution of population and resources. A set of what might be called "tax-and-subsidy" policies are enacted to tax or penalize people who locate in areas considered to be overcrowded and to subsidize or reward people who leave such areas and move toward or remain in more "suitable"—less socially costly—locations. These tax-and-subsidy policies, aimed at achieving a better allocation of resources and population than the market will create, can take many forms, all of them geared toward manipulating the economic incentives and disincentives to which the individual migrant responds in his or her locational decision-making.

Such microeconomic policies, like all attempts to interfere with market forces, tend to be very costly. That is, a high level of government expenditure, especially on subsidies, is required before the structure of economic incentives can be sufficiently changed to induce movements counter to those indicated by the market. Not only must the migrant be made better off in the planned than in the market situation, but the differential in favor of the planned receiving areas has to be maintained over time to prevent remigration. For example, attempts to reverse the flow of rural-to-urban migrants must make staying in or returning to the rural areas more attractive in economic terms than moving to or staying in the cities.

In many if not most developing countries, governments already try, not always with success, to influence market forces through national macroeconomic development planning, especially via public investment or public policies to influence private investment decisions. This has an effect on the structure of economic incentives facing the migrant and, hence, on population redistribution. For example, a campaign of agricultural modernization aimed at increasing agricultural productivity, such as the Green Revolution, may introduce capital-intensive technology into the rural sector, thus generating rural out-migration as labor is displaced in the countryside. Policies to encourage industrialization, such as foreign investment in manufacturing, may generate an urban bias in the structure of incentives to the extent that factory jobs are created in or near urban areas. Clearly, population redistribution policies at the microeconomic level must take cognizance of these larger economic developments, in order that they not contradict each other and prove even more costly and less effective.

It should be noted, however, that economic growth and development goals probably take precedence and priority over population redistribution goals in the objectives of national governments, and these goals may well conflict. For example, modern industrialization almost invariably involves urbanization, and the most developed urban locations offer businesses the greatest economies of scale and agglomeration, the best infrastructure, and so on. The economic logic of location of industry would tend, other things being equal, to reinforce the growth of the primate city. Government incentives to encourage the regional dispersion of industry are likely to be very costly if they are to be effective in offsetting the market advantages of major urban areas. For example, there would be heavy costs in creating duplicate fixed infrastructural facilities for industry in various regions, such as highways, developed industrial sites, and airports. In developing countries, labor is often a more mobile resource than fixed capital, so the tendency is to let labor adjust to the locational decisions of private investment; that is, migration to where economic opportunities are located, usually in the major cities.

In the relationship between economic growth and development and population redistribution, the former is clearly determinant. To be successful, then, redistribution policies must be integrated into comprehensive national development plans. Where socially optimal population redistribution patterns conflict with individual maximization of economic benefit—an increasingly likely situation given growing overall population pressure in many countries—higher levels of government intervention will be required to achieve the desired population redistribution. As private and social costs and benefits continue to diverge, the free market increasingly maldistributes population and undermines redistribution policies and programs which go against the grain of the market. Increasingly, governments for whom population redistribution is an important national goal will have to move away from reliance on market mechanisms and partial equilibrium measures to affect these mechanisms. Instead, the underlying structure of market incentives to which migrants respond will have to be brought under the control of a general planning mechanism which can effectively allocate resources among different sectors of the economy and direct population movements in consonance with such allocations. Otherwise, population redistribution policies run the risk of being frustrated—first, by predominant market forces, and second, by macroeconomic development policies which have an effect on population redistribution.

Thus the tendency in market economies is to move toward greater government intervention and joint central planning of the economy and of population, in order to solve population distribution problems. While the economy limits the success of population redistribution policies carried out in isolation from planned or market economic changes, it also provides the possibility for successful population redistribution through joint planning. This may, of course, entail some sacrifice of net economic growth, at least in the short run, for a more balanced population distribution in the long run.

Population Redistribution in Centrally Planned Economies

In the Soviet Union and other Eastern European countries, planning under socialism deliberately attempts to change existing patterns of population distribution and settlement in order to achieve greater regional equalization of population and economic activity. Spatial population policy is closely integrated with national sectoral and regional development planning. Both incentive and control measures are used to secure a redistribution of population in line with national development goals.

Most of the incentive measures are economic in nature. The primary incentive measures involve the location or diversion of new industrial development funds in such a way as to influence migration to, and settlement in, desired regions or centers. This is possible in states where the government is responsible for all industrial capital investment and can divert it to small and medium-sized centers if it so wishes, free of private profit maximization concerns which might dictate investing in large cities instead. The next most important incentive measure is the location or diversion of investment in housing and other social overhead capital projects, since housing availability is an important migration inducement. Government can also create regional wage differentials (since it is the only national employer) and provide wage supplements and relocation allowances. It can provide information and propaganda through national organized labor recruitment systems and mass exhortation, education, and persuasion campaigns. Control measures have imposed spatially selective bans on new or expanded industrial growth and have even moved existing enterprises to control growth. Other control measures include police registration, administrative-legal controls, job transfers, and work assignments for new graduates.

Despite this impressive array of incentive and control measures, spatial population policy has been quite ineffective in controlling and directing internal migration, especially in the USSR. There has not been a close and explicit match between national economic development strategies and population redistribution. The Soviet model of development (heavy industry, backward agriculture) *reinforced* rather than countered market forces leading to regional and sectoral imbalances in population distribution. State industrial and social investments in general induced movement in opposite directions from what was socially desired by generating agglomerations in major cities and neglecting rural areas, while people were left relatively free to choose their occupations and geographical locations. Administrative controls, where enacted, were more effective than incentive measures, but it was incentive measures (which have not been successful in market-economy countries either) which were emphasized in redistribution policy. Where there is free population movement, even in a centrally planned economy, market forces still dominate in the redistribution of population.

The lessons of the Eastern European experience with population redistribution policy for developing countries are limited by the differences between them in economic structure. The centrally planned economies of Eastern Europe are much more highly developed and urbanized than developing countries today; they have already controlled fertility, and have full employment in the cities. Their population redistribution problems arise from sectoral imbalances which any growing economy is bound to suffer from, and the concern of redistribution policy is with adjustments to spot shortages and surpluses of labor. While planned economic development has a marked urban bias—and economically the cities can indeed absorb more population (as shown by the widespread practice of commuting to city employment, with city residence limited by the housing shortage)—this is resisted for social and ideological reasons.

In developing countries, on the other hand, the maldistribution of population is more serious and fundamental, the costs of free movement of population are greater, and population continues to grow. Urbanization is proceeding at a rate greater than the rate of industrial job creation in the cities, and there exists a general labor surplus in both urban and rural areas. Whereas some of the centrally planned developed countries are moving toward more free market redistribution of population, developing countries should learn from the planning mistakes of these countries. A more complete, consistent, and integrated joint planning of economic growth (especially employment creation) and population redistribution is needed in the developing countries than has been practiced in Eastern Europe.

Since current population redistribution concerns and policies center on preventing the flow of population to cities, the "solution" most commonly suggested is a rural one. Further urbanization is to be inhibited by attempts to retain potential migrants in rural areas, to resettle potential urban migrants in land settlements, to prevent rural people from entering cities, or to force those already in the cities back into the countryside. While alternative urban solutions have also been proposed, such as the creation of dispersed urban centers to which population can be directed, the main emphasis of redistribution programs is still on rural solutions to the problem of overurbanization. However, increasing numbers of people are seeking, with their feet, an ultimately urban solution to their personally perceived "redistribution problem." Driven by rural poverty, they are redistributing themselves in locations where their economic opportunities are perceived to be better, usually in the city. In the following sections, we discuss the relative potential of the urban and rural redistribution solutions.

While population growth is obviously a very important factor affecting any redistribution solution, for the purposes of this discussion we assume that this growth will be controlled, as it has to be to avoid overwhelming all resources. Thus we will examine the proposed urban and rural solutions in the most favorable context for redistribution, i.e., limited population growth, since most of the population to be redistributed in the immediate planning future has already been born.

The Urban Redistribution Solution

The city is the most spatially and economically efficient location for the production and distribution of an extremely wide range of goods and services. Externalities and economies of scale and agglomeration lead to the concentration of infrastructure and industry and the centralization of administrative, distributive, and service functions in relatively small physical areas capable of supporting large population densities. The historical evolution of cities accelerated with the growth and spread of the market economy, and today, continued urban growth and concentration is largely the result of market forces, attracting ever larger numbers of people to move to and settle in the city. This creates problems in present-day developing countries where the growth of urban populations through natural increase and migration has exceeded the capacity of urban functions to generate employment and income opportunities, on the one hand, and to provide an adequate level of urban services, particularly infrastructural services, on the other. The observed natural forces in favor of cities and the revealed preference of many people for city life suggests that an urban-based solution to the maldistribution of population may be the most efficient. This must involve a restructuring of the city economy to make it more absorptive of population. There are at least two possibilities.

RESTRUCTURING THE NATURE OF INDUSTRIAL EMPLOYMENT

Since the colonial era, many of the functions of cities in developing countries have been preempted by the developed countries. The international division of labor concentrates certain urban functions in the developed world, beginning with colonial government functions and extending to most of the manufacturing industry and highly-skilled services which are produced in the world today. Labor-absorptive economic functions, such as manufacturing, and various technical and commercial services (research, marketing, finance) are concentrated in developed countries, from which developing countries import the manufactured goods (both capital and consumer goods), technology, and services that they need. If more of these functions were performed in the developing countries, more jobs would be created in urban areas, both directly and indirectly.

Recently, new changes seem to be occurring in the international division of labor, suggesting that as the developed countries move into the "post-industrial" phase of economic development, more of their manufacturing functions—especially those which are more labor intensive—may be dispersed to developing countries through the multinational corporation. However, there are limitations to this process, and though new urban-industrial employment may be created in some developing countries in the short run, the long-run benefit of export-oriented industrialization is ambiguous.

National government actions can help effect a restructuring of the economy in directions which will generate increased urban employment in developing countries, e.g., through the "import substitution" of capital goods, technology, and services as well as of manufactured consumer goods. This is a long-range prospect.

Industrial growth in present-day developing countries has so far been limited by market forces, especially the structure of national as well as international demand for manufactured products made in developing countries. The unequal distribution of incomes and the predominantly private-enterprise, profit-motivated character of most manufacturing industry in developing countries means that there is only a small and stagnant market for most manufactured goods, which tend to be luxury consumer goods (e.g., automobiles, color televisions) produced for a high-income domestic elite or for export, using capital-intensive technologies which do not generate many jobs. Because of the low incomes of the mass of the population in these countries, it is not profitable to produce cheap mass consumer goods (e.g., shoes, clothes) for domestic consumption, though this would use labor-intensive technologies and create more urban jobs. Equalizing domestic incomes to create mass purchasing power and/or substituting public investment in labor-intensive mass consumer goods industries for private investment in capital-intensive luxury goods industries are two possible, albeit perhaps extreme, strategies to increase urban-industrial employment. Government intervention in the economy to reduce its orientation toward production for foreign markets (which lends a capital-intensive bias to domestic production) may also be necessary. It should be noted that some sacrifice of aggregate economic growth for better distribution of employment and income opportunities is probably inevitable.

If, however, technological constraints (such as the greater productivity of capital-intensive techniques in many industries) and/or market and resource constraints limit the number of jobs which can be created even using labor-intensive techniques, more radical solutions, such as reducing the number of hours worked per person (work- and income-sharing) to spread the available jobs around larger numbers of people, may be required. Such "planned underemployment" need not be seen as a pernicious thing if every worker makes a living wage for the work he does do and has more leisure to enjoy besides.

RESTRUCTURING THE FORM OF THE CITY

The currently highly centralized and rigidly zoned primate city, where most of the problems of overurbanization are discerned, may be modified physically in a number of ways to accommodate more population. The development of "satellite towns" outside the main city can help to decentralize urban employment and population by spreading it over a wider spatial area without losing the benefits of urbanization. Regional dispersal of industry, and of government functions, to smaller new or existing urban centers in different parts of the country will also diffuse overcrowding in the primate city as well as provide a wider choice of alternative urban locations for migrants and city residents. The location of new industrial zones in rural areas is expensive, but they can form "growth poles" for regional urbanization, perhaps taking the form of "urban villages" capable of agricultural as well as industrial production.

Radical changes in city layout, transportation networks, immediate food support zones, and sources of energy may all be included in planning for new cities. High cost services, such as the provision of public housing, may be replaced by management of squatter construction of their own homes, with the government providing sites and basic infrastructure. These are some of the variety of measures by which cities can be modified in form and operation to make them more efficient in providing for large populations without substantially reducing services or the quality of urban life.

The Rural Redistribution Solution

The rural solution encompasses rural development measures to retain population in the rural areas and divert excess urban population to these areas. This necessitates the provision of more economic opportunities capable of generating substantially higher incomes in rural areas than currently exist. Not all of these opportunities can be provided in agriculture, since labor-intensive agriculture is generally unattractive because of the hard physical labor and low incomes involved. Indeed, increasing agricultural productivity—a necessity if increasing populations are to be adequately fed—is often accompanied by the increasing capital-intensity of production, eventually culminating in the highly productive, very highly mechanized agriculture found in the developed countries today. Diversified productive activities will have to be provided in the rural areas in order to absorb the labor which might be displaced by increased agricultural productivity, as well as net population increase.

Since incomes in industry are higher than incomes in agriculture, some dispersal of industry to rural areas is necessary in order to raise rural incomes and narrow rural-urban wage differentials. Industry may be located around existing villages, in land settlement schemes, or in new locations in rural areas. Services such as education and health, which are more costly and less efficiently produced in small amounts, will still have to be somewhat centralized, but may be established in multiple urban or semi-urban locations, rather than just in the primate city. Spatial dispersal of services and industry can help to eliminate the rigid identification of productive sectors (agriculture/industry/services) with spatial location (rural/urban) and spread development more evenly throughout the country. There will be a great need for efficient transportation and communications services in order for this dispersal not to be counterproductive.

The decentralization and dispersal of industry and urban services to rural areas are part of both the urban and rural solutions; indeed, in this the two solutions merge into each other. The choice between solutions is really one between centralization or decentralization, rather than between urban and rural. In the first strategy (centralization) one can maintain and improve one or a few major cities, providing adequate employment opportunities and services to accommodate their large and increasing populations (e.g., through the modified urban employment and structure discussed above), while simultaneously developing agriculture in the countryside so that the few who remain there enjoy adequately high incomes and delivery of services. This is the situation found in most developed countries today. In the second strategy (decentralization), one can de-emphasize the major city and disperse its functions through the countryside, contributing to a blurring of the distinction between rural and urban areas and of the corresponding spatially distinct locations of agriculture and industry, i.e., "urbanization of rural areas." In each case the distribution of population will be different, but one cannot be said to be "better" than the other if there is no imbalance between population and resources in either situation. Where sectoral and regional incomes have been equalized and full employment is assured, the spatial distribution of population ceases to be a matter of concern; i.e., the population redistribution "problem" is largely solved. This again shows the primacy of economic development over population redistribution. Employment and income creation is ultimately the main tool of population redistribution policy. When the first problem is solved, the other mostly disappears. Cities, however large they are, which can adequately house and efficiently service and employ all their residents pose no population distribution problem, nor do well-developed, diversified rural areas with adequate jobs and services.

BIBLIOGRAPHY

Bahrin, Tunku Shamsul, and Pereira, P. D. A. *FELDA: Twenty-One Years of Land Development*. Kuala Lumpur: FELDA, 1977.

Bernstein, Thomas P. *Up to the Mountains and Down to the Villages: The Transfer of Youth from Urban to Rural China*. New Haven: Yale University Press, 1977.

Berry, B. J. L. *The Human Consequences of Urbanization*. New York: St. Martin's Press, 1973.

Breeze, G. W. *Urbanization in Newly Developing Countries*. Englewood Cliffs, N.J.: Prentice-Hall, 1966.

Brokensha, David, and Schudder, Thayer. "Resettlement." In *Dams in Africa,* edited by W. M. Warren and N. Rubin. New York: Augustus Kelley, 1968.

Byerlee, Derek. "Rural-Urban Migration in Africa: Theory, Policy and Research Implications." *International Migration Review* 8(1974):543–66.

Connell, John, Biplab Dasgupta, Roy Laishley, and Michael Lipton. *Migration from Rural Areas: The Evidence from Village Studies*. Delhi: Oxford University Press, 1976.

Davis, Kingsley. "The Migrations of Human Populations." *Scientific American* (September 1974):53–65.

du Guerny, J. "Migration and Rural Development." UNFAO Social and Economic Development Paper No. 3. Rome: FAO, 1978.

Fallenbuch, Zbigniew M. "Internal Migration and Economic Development under Socialism: The Case of Poland." In *Internal Migration: A Comparative Perspective,* edited by Alan Brown and E. Neuberger. New York: Academic Press, 1977, pp. 305–27.

Fisher, Joseph L. "The Relationship of Material Resources and Population to Economic and Social Development." *Papers of the World Population Conference* (Bucharest) 1(1974).

Fuchs, Roland J., and Demko, George J. "Spatial Population Policies in the Socialist Countries of Eastern Europe." *Social Science Quarterly* 5(June 1977):66–67.

Fuller, Theodore P. "Cityward Migration and Social Stratification in Northeast Thailand." Ph.D. dissertation, University of Michigan, 1977.

Galeotti, Guido. "Les Migrations Rurales et Urbaines en Italie." *IUSSP Proceeding* (Liege, 1971).

Goldstein, Sidney. "Facets of Redistribution: Research Challenges and Opportunities." *Demography* 13(1976):423–34.

Golger, O. J. *Squatters and Resettlement: Symptoms of An Urban Crisis; Environmental Conditions of Low-Standard Housing in Hong Kong.* Wiesbaden: O. Herrassowitz, 1972.

Gosling, L. A. P. *et al. Pa Mong Resettlement.* Ann Arbor: University of Michigan, Department of Geography, 1978.

Harjono, J. N. *Transmigration in Indonesia.* Kuala Lumpur: Oxford University Press, 1977.

Harris, J. R., and Todaro, M. P., "Migration, Unemployment and Development: A Two-Sector Analysis." *American Economic Review* 60 (1) (1970): 126–42.

Hauser, P. M. and Senore, L. F., eds. *The Study of Urbanization.* New York: Wiley, 1965.

Holborn, Louise. *Refugees: A Problem of Our Time.* Metuchen: Scarecrow Press, 1975.

Humphrey, J. "Population Resettlement in Malaya." Ph.D. dissertation, Northwestern University, 1971.

Ivory, Paul E., and Lavely, William R. "Rustication, Demographic Change, and Development in Shanghai." *Asian Survey* 17(May 1977):440–55.

Kim, Son Ung, and Donaldson, Peter J., "Redistribution of Seoul's Population: Government Plans and Their Implementation." Paper presented at the 30th Annual Meeting of the Association for Asian Studies, Chicago, April 2, 1978.

Lee, Everett S. "A Theory of Migration." *Demography* 3 (1) (1966).

Lewis, W. Arthur, "Thoughts of Land Settlement." *Journal of Agricultural Economics* 2 (1) (1954).

Lightfoot, R. Paul. "Planning Problems in the Resettlement of Reservoir Evacuees in Less-Developed Countries." Ph.D. dissertation, University of Michigan, 1976.

Mabogunje, Akin L. "A Typology of Population Pressure on Resources in West Africa." In *Geography and a Crowding World,* edited by Wilbur Zelinsky *et al.* New York: Oxford University Press, 1970.

Mabogunje, Akin L. *Regional Mobility and Resource Development in West Africa.* Montreal: McGill-Queen's University Press, 1972.

Mabogunje, Akin L., "Systems Approach to a Theory of Rural-Urban Migration." *Geographical Analysis* 2(1970):1–18.

MacAndrews, C. *Mobility and Modernization: The Work of the Federal Land Development Authority.* Yogyakarta, Indonesia: University of Gadjah Mada Press, 1977.

Mazie, Sara Milla, ed. *Population, Distribution, and Policy.* U.S. Commission on Population Growth and the American Future, Vol. 5 of Commission Research Reports. Washington, D.C.: USGPO, 1972.

McGee, T. G. *The Southeast Asian City: A Social Geography of the Primate Cities of Southeast Asia*. London: Bell and Sons, 1976.

Morrison, Peter A. *Migration and Rights of Access: New Public Concern for the 1970s*. Santa Monica, Calif.: Rand Corp., 1977.

Morrison, Peter A., and Wheeler, Judith P. *Local Growth Control Versus the Freedom to Migrate*. Santa Monica, Calif.: Rand Corp., 1974. ,

Olson, Maxine. "Flight, Settlement and Adjustment: Refugees in Laos and Other Developing Countries." Ph.D. dissertation, University of Michigan, 1978.

Palmer, Gary. "The Ecology of Resettlement Schemes." *Human Organization* 33(3:1974).

Pryor, Robin J. "Methods of Analyzing Population Redistribution Policies." Population Redistribution Policies, IGU Commission on Population Geography, Edmonton, Alberta, 1978.

Rothenberg, Jerome. "On the Microeconomics of Internal Migration." in *Internal Migration: A Comparative Perspective,* edited by Alan Brown and E. Neuberger, 1977, New York: Academic Press, pp. 183–205.

Rothenberg, Jerome. "Urban Renewal Programs." In *Measuring Benefits of Government Investments,* edited by R. Dorfman. Washington, D.C.: Brookings, 1965.

Scudder, Thayer. "Man-Made Lakes and Population Resettlement in Africa." In *Man Made Lakes,* edited by R. H. McConnell. New York: Academic Press, 1966.

Scudder, Thayer. "The Human Ecology of Big Projects: River Basin Development and Resettlement." *Annual Review of Anthropology* 2(1973): 44–45.

Simmons, Alan B. *Slowing Metropolitan City Growth in Asia: A Review of Policies, Programs and Results*. Ottawa: International Research Centre, 1978.

Sundquist, James. *Dispersing Population: What America Can Learn From Europe*. Washington, D.C.: Brookings, 1975.

Todaro, Michael P. *Internal Migration in Developing Countries: a Review of Theory, Evidence, Methodology, and Research Priorities*. Geneva: International Labour Office, 1976.

United Nations Department of Economic and Social Affairs. "Population Distribution, Internal Migration and Urbanization." *The Determinants and Consequences of Population Trends* 1 (Population Studies No. 50, 1973).

United Nations. *United Nations Standards Concerning the Relationship Between Human Rights and Various Population Questions*. Conference Background Paper, E/CONF.60/CBP/6, 1974.

United Nations. *Spatial Re-Distribution of Population in Africa*. Economic Commission for Africa, E/CN.14/POP/45, 1971.

U.S. Bureau of the Census. *Planning for Internal Migration: A Review of Issues and Policies in Developing Countries*. Washington, D.C.: USGPO, ISP-RD-4, 1977.

Wander, Hilde. "Policies and Implementation Methods in the Internal Redistribution of Population." *International Population Conference Proceeding* 3 (London, 1969).

Weiner, Myron. "Internal Migration Policies: Purposes, Interests, Instruments, Effects." Working Paper MDG/75-1 of the Center for International Studies.

Wolpert, Julian. "Behavioral Aspects of the Decision to Migrate." *Proceedings of the Regional Science Association* 15 (1965).

13

Women, Population, and Development

CHRISTINE OPPONG AND ELINA HAAVIO-MANNILA

THE 1970s: THE INTERNATIONAL FOCUS ON WOMEN, POPULATION, AND DEVELOPMENT

Bucharest

SINCE THE 1974 World Population Conference in Bucharest, there has been increasing realization of the intricacy of the relationships existing between population variables and economic development, politics, ideology, religion, and last but perhaps centrally critical, changing sex roles and family structure. The interrelationship of population and development and the equalization of the status of men and women were among the basic principles enunciated at the World Population Conference. It was stated that the free participation of women on an equal basis with men should be encouraged in all aspects of socioeconomic development, including population and family planning. It was also asserted that improved status of women can contribute to smaller family size and that planned births will have a reciprocally positive effect on women's status.

The determination of social and demographic processes within the family life cycle and the study of family structure, function, and dynamics were among the research priorities selected by the Conference. Recommendations for action included strengthening the family, marriage, and the rights of spouses and children, and promotion of equal status between men and women. Significantly, it was only at the Conference itself that the crucial paragraphs highlighting the importance of women's roles and the family were incorporated; they had not been included in the draft plan.[1]

1. Bernard Berelson, "The World Population Plan of Action: Where Now?" *Population and Development Review* 1 (September 1975): 1. According to Berelson a content analysis of imperative sentences in the Plan indicated that no less than 22 percent were concerned with reproduction, family, and women. As for the comparison of the draft and the Plan and changes made at the Conference, he found the

International Women's Year (IWY)

The following year, 1975, was selected as International Women's Year. In 1975, delegates from one hundred countries gathered in Mexico and decided to adopt a World Plan of Action to be carried out in the decade 1975–85. This plan contained guidelines for each state to achieve complete equality between men and women. It covered a wide range of issues which affect women and, by extension, family size: education and literacy, employment and wage opportunities, home responsibilities, and family planning. With respect to family planning, the plan noted the importance of the right of women to decide on the number and spacing of their children—and their need to have adequate information upon which to base such decisions. In addition to these major substantive problems, other lesser problems which affect women—prostitution, illicit traffic in women, and female criminality on the social side, statistical underrepresentation of women in the labor force and the non-recognition of the value of women's work in the home, on the administrative side—were also covered.

The seventies have been a period of critical re-evaluation of policies, programs, and research concerning women, as well as of a massive increase in the amount of material resources and technical assistance allocated to population activities.[2] There is increased recognition of the need to develop new research methods and to frame new theories on the role of women in society. These new methods and theories will then lead to new, hopefully more effective strategies in dealing with the role of women in the contemporary world. The emphasis on economic factors in much of the research on fertility in less developed countries and the relative absence of women as researchers in fertility studies and as policy decision makers has perhaps skewed some of the results of the past 20 years, and future work must try to overcome these biases if it is to be useful in leading to more effective policy directions.[3]

---

following additions: 14g on the family; 14h on women's rights to integration and participation; 15e promotion of the status of women; 41–43 the participation of women; 40b the legal responsibilities of parenthood; 78o–q research on the family and women's status.

2. Halvor Gille, "Recent Trends in International Population Assistance," in *Inventory of Population Projects in Developing Countries Around the World 1976–1977* (New York: UNFPA, 1977), notes an increase in the amount of international assistance for population activities from $2 million in 1960 to $314 million in 1976.

3. Geoffrey Hawthorn, "Introduction," *Journal of Development Studies* 14 (July 1978), special issue on the economic bias; Judith Bruce, "Setting the System

The Response of the United Nations Fund for Population Activities

The UNFPA, wishing to respond quickly to the recommendations in the Action Plan of the IWY Conference of 1975, appointed a special internal task force to study the involvement of women in the formulation and implementation of population projects supported by the Fund, to recommend necessary changes in attitude and approach, and to devise guidelines. The latter have been accepted and published in *Population Profiles* 7 as "Women, Population and Development." In this document, several manifest and latent biases against women in demographic studies and population programs were identified: the sexist bias inherent in census definitions such as "work," "head of household," and "homemaker"; the bias of fertility surveys directed only at female respondents; the bias of the science and technology which have produced contraceptives mainly for women; the adverse impact of many development activities on women.[4] The significance was stressed of women's rights and functions in decision making—notably family planning, in employment and wage opportunities, in education, and in almost all aspects of human economic and social development.

The guidelines of the task force included an emphasis upon basic research in fields not previously dealt with by population researchers: the processes of gender-role conditioning in different cultures; the dimensions of traditional parental roles; traditions and taboos about human sexuality and fertility; and the relationship between equal participation of women, fertility change, and development. As in the IWY Plan, the UNFPA guidelines stressed both a more adequate recording of women's contributions to the economy and the necessity for recruiting qualified women as workers in the programs. These recommendations imply that the concepts, theories, methods, and sets of empirical findings of psychology, of history, and of social anthropology or comparative sociology are needed as a counterbalance to the domination of population studies currently held by economics, sociology, demography, and statistics.

---

to Work for Women," *Populi* 4 (1) (1977); Perdita Huston, "To be Born a Woman is a Sin," *Populi* 4 (3) (1977); Sandra Tangri, "A Feminist Perspective on Some Ethical Issues in Population Programs," *Signs* 1 (4) (1976): 895–904; Paula Hollenbach Hass, "Contraceptive Choices for Latin American Women," *Populi* 3 (4) (1976); and Michelle Z. Rosaldo and Louise Lamphere, *Woman, Culture and Society* (Stanford: Stanford University Press, 1974), on the bias against women.

4. *Population Profiles 7*, "Women, Population and Development" (New York: UNFPA, n.d.)

In order to move from these recognitions to policy and guideline formulation and from these to action, development agencies must not only analyze women's roles but also design special modes of action, enabling women to take part in and ultimately rethink development.[5] Programs which may actually reinforce and contribute to women's low status must be re-examined. UNFPA has already taken the first step, if not leap, and has begun to take the second.

Some of the issues and problems relevant to this move will now briefly be examined: (1) equality; (2) basic indicators of the position of women, such as political participation, education, work, and fertility; (3) a global comparison of the social and economic position of women, particularly their productive role in society and the effects of cultural determinants on women's position in society; and (4) the central importance of family systems, both for the role of women in reproduction and production and for development as a whole.

EQUALITY OF WOMEN AND MEN

Implications for Development and Fertility

As Reid has noted, there are obvious similarities between the demands by women and by developing countries for equality of treatment, but while the debate on the New International Economic Order continues in forum after forum, that on the position of women seems to have ended with International Women's Year. Moreover, what is particularly ironical is that: "Those demanding a new economic order want to end the humiliation and degradation of their past and present oppression. Yet their understanding of their own oppression has given them no insight into their own roles as oppressors, no understanding of the agony and extent of women's subjugation."[6]

Equality of women and men has been viewed as an integral component of development, especially in the matter of control over fertility.[7] In her recent study sponsored by UNFPA, Huston stressed the significance of women's lack of power to control their own reproductive processes and lives and claimed that this was the most salient finding of her 200 inter-

5. Bruce, "Setting the System."

6. Elizabeth Reid, "The Forgotten Fifty Per Cent," *Populi* 4 (1) (1977).

7. Speaking at the United Nations International Women's Year in 1975, Rafael M. Salas, Executive Director of UNFPA, stated: "For many women the power of decision over this one basic function would represent a major step toward equality."

views with rural women in six nations. Thus based on her impressionistic multinational study of rural women, Huston felt that *personal autonomy* of women emerged everywhere as *the key issue* and was of the opinion that *male dominance of women's lives is the greatest single barrier to population efforts.* "Over and over in Africa, in Asia and in the New World [rural women] spoke of the absence of choice in their lives, of the lack of the personal autonomy. They would like to have more control over their destinies, to be able to choose their mates and the size of their families, to participate in society and to contribute to it."[8]

She enumerated the many barriers to those goals. In some places, new laws and regulations are required. In others, women's legal rights exist but are not understood as well as they might be nor enforced as they should be. And everywhere literacy, skill-training, self-confidence, and personal autonomy are needed to surmount "the myths, taboos, traditions and male supremacy that stifle women's wish to participate." "Most disabling of all, and influencing everything else, is the fear of male dominance; wife beating, polygamy, restricted mobility and lack of legal protection continue to hold [many] women in resigned apathy." The ability to leave the domestic context and to interact with people is obviously an important resource of women, and yet women in many cultures do not even have this basic human right. Even a short journey to a nearby training center can be an important advance in a male-dominated system, particularly one where purdah is practiced.[9] The disadvantageous consequences for the family and community, as well as for the individual, of the social and economic dependence of women resulting from such seclusion are clear.[10]

Significantly, Huston's findings have been paralleled by those of Reining *et al.,* who carried out studies of rural women in Kenya, Mexico, and the Philippines with the aim of finding out how changes brought about by modernization might influence family size.[11] Their important finding

8. Perdita Huston, *Message from the Village* (New York: Epoch B. Foundation, 1978), p. 136. See also her "To be Born a Woman," and the works of S. B. Kar, "Individual Aspirations as Related to Early and Late Acceptance of Contraception," *The Journal of Social Psychology* 83(1971):235–45, who notes that those who feel powerless are less likely to use contraceptives; or Alan B. Keller *et al.,* "Psychological Sources of 'Resistance' to Family Planning," *Merrill Palmer Quarterly* 16 (1970):286–302.

9. Sandra A. Zeidenstein, "A Short Step for Woman," *Populi* 4 (4) (1977).

10. Ruth B. Dixon, "The Roles of Rural Women: Female Seclusion, Economic Production and Reproductive Choice," in *Population and Development: The Search for the Selective Interventions,* edited by Ronald G. Ridker (Baltimore: Johns Hopkins University Press, 1976), p. 305.

11. Priscilla Reining *et al., Village Women, Their Changing Lives and Fertility: Studies in Kenya, Mexico and the Philippines* (A.A.A.S., 1977).

was that in the three contrasting cultural settings the women who were demographic innovators were those who were *hopeful* and *confident* in their own ability to *direct* their own lives and to help improve those of their children.

Sexual Asymmetry: A Cultural Product

Male domination, female subordination, and sexual asymmetry have been accepted by many to be universal facts of human social life. A number of recent studies, as well as some earlier ones, have found, however, that sexual asymmetry is not a necessary condition of human societies but a cultural product which varies from society to society and is subject to change. The social roles and powers of women, their public status, and their cultural definitions vary from one society to the next far more than has often been assumed.[12]

There has been increasing documentation of the extent of female power and of women's role in social processes and of the social, cultural, and economic correlates of their variation. Women use resources available to them in support of interests often opposed to those of men, and women's power strategies have been seen to be directly related to the power and authority structure of the domestic group.[13] Women's role in production and their control over the products they produce have been selected by some feminist anthropologists as critical indicators of women's power and status in different peasant and hunting societies.[14]

12. Rosaldo and Lamphere eds., *Woman, Culture and Society;* Margaret Mead, *Male and Female: A Study of the Sexes in a Changing World* (New York: Monow, 1949); and Phyllis M. Kaberry, *Aboriginal Women Sacred and Profane* (London, 1939), and *Women of the Grassfields* (London, 1952).

13. Carol B. Stack, *All Our Kin: Strategies for Survival in a Black Community* (New York: Harper and Row, 1974); Christine Oppong, *Marriage Among a Matrilineal Elite: A Family Study of Ghanaian Civil Servants* (Cambridge: Cambridge University Press, 1974); and several of the studies in *Woman, Culture and Society,* edited by Rosaldo and Lamphere, that examine the forms and quality of women's strategies and powers and are seen as being consistent with earlier theoretical developments in anthropology, which attempted a more dynamic interpretation of political processes—e.g., Frederik Barth, *Political Leadership among the Swat Pathans* (London: University of London, Athlone Press, London School of Economics, Monograph 19, 1959).

14. See several of the studies in *Woman, Culture and Society,* edited by Rosaldo and Lamphere, and J. K. Brown, "Iroquois Women: An Ethnohistoric Note," in *Towards an Anthropology of Women,* edited by Rayna Reiter (New York: Monthly Review Press, 1974).

Two different ideological frameworks have recently been proposed to answer the question as to where and why women have occupied a subordinate position in society, and how the variations in the form and intensity of their subordination can be explained. On the one hand feminists have addressed themselves to "patriarchal ideology," which defines the system of male domination and female subjugation as based upon biological differences between the sexes; on the other hand Marxist analyses have located the origins of female subordination in the phenomenon of private property, so that different forms of male domination would reflect different modes of production. Feminists argue that the sexual caste system preceded private property and survives its abolition, that it shows no more sign of breaking down in socialist countries than in capitalist. Thus the feminist analysis has been able to account for the differences in life chances between men and women, but has fallen short of a credible explanation of the differences among women. On the other hand the Marxist analysis has been persuasive in explaining the class differences, but copes less well in explaining status differences between men and women.[15] Some, such as Saffioti, have combined these two approaches and examined, among other questions, sex as a barrier keeping many women outside the occupational structure (or at least the most desirable parts of it).[16]

Leacock has argued that contemporary assertions of male dominance as biologically based and/or universal serve several functions, besides that of directly rationalizing the *status quo*.[17] One is that they perpetuate an idea of social organization as necessarily involving structures of dominance and submission. Thus matriarchy is set up as a historical alternative to patriarchy. At the same time, the existence of primitive communist societies, in which relationships between the sexes were or are egalitarian, is obscured. Such images of masculine dominance reinforce contemporary images of men as basically aggressive and competitive. But perhaps what is even more pernicious in its effects is that the notion of sexual equality—the liberation of women—is presented as Western and foreign to the tradition of Third World peoples, whereas Leacock and others would argue that egalitarian reciprocity between the sexes characterized precolonial life among some of them.

Recent anthropological investigations using data on traits from many diverse cultures have in fact indicated that many aspects of the position of

15. Roberta Hamilton, *The Liberation of Women: A Study of Patriarchy and Capitalism* (New York: Allen and Unwin, 1978), pp. 11–13.

16. Heleieth Saffioti, *Women in Class Society* (New York: Monthly Review Press, 1978).

17. Eleanor Leacock, "Introduction," in *ibid.*

women relative to men are not closely correlated, making it difficult or impossible to assume the existence of a unitary phenomenon—*the status of women.* However, Whyte did discover small groups of variables which were correlated with one another. Nine separate clusters of three to five variables each were found, including *the relative property rights of women, their domestic authority, the separate solidarity of men and women,* and *the relative controls on women's sexual and marital lives.* This probably indicates the value of dividing these several issues and dealing with each one separately in future studies.[18]

There is also a gap between appearance and reality with regard to women's status and the ambiguous character of some status indicators such as sexual taboos and deferential public behavior.[19] In the subsequent analysis, examination of indicators of the status of women will perforce be confined to those which have already been collected in national censuses—typical demographic variables such as fertility, work force participation, and schooling. Yet the inadequacies of such limited data are clear, and a closer consideration of the problem of women's status must include the collection of broader sets of data if it is to be placed in the context of related social, economic, legal, and political problems.

INDICATORS OF THE POSITION OF WOMEN

Political Participation

Citizenship in the sense of full membership with equal rights in society is taken for granted in some nations. But for women the position is often different since certain social attitudes and customs have continued to hinder women's realization of full citizenship rights, and for many their legal status as dependents continues. But neither did the right to vote automatically ensure other political and economic rights, and the recognition of women as social equals continues to be a long and tedious process.[20] Recent surveys indicate that women in positions of economic and political decision making at the national and international level continue to be few.

18. Martin K. Whyte, "Cross Cultural Codes Dealing with the Relative Status of Women," *Ethnology* 18 (April 1978):214–15.

19. S. C. Rogers, "Female Forms of Power and the Myth of Male Dominance: A Model of Female/Male Interaction in Peasant Society," *American Ethnologist* 2 (4) (1975).

20. Josephine Milburn, "Women as Citizens: A Comparative Review," *Contemporary Political Sociology Series,* Vol. 2, a Sage professional paper (New York: Sage Publications, 1976).

For example, only 6 percent of the delegates of the UN General Assemblies from 1946 to 1974 were women—a percentage that was true for the postindustrial, industrial, and developing countries alike. Nor does the economic development of a country correlate with the proportion of women in its parliaments, at least in Western Europe.[21]

Education

In the modern world, educational level is a crucial determinant of both societal development and individual status. The Universal Declaration of Human Rights proclaimed that every individual has a right to an education. The Declaration on the Elimination of Discrimination against Women stated that girls and women, whether or not they are married, have equal rights with boys and men in education at all levels and of all types.[22]

Yet sex differentials in literacy are widespread. In the 94 countries of the world for which data were available in 1968, women were less than 50 percent of the illiterates in only eight, while they composed more than 60 percent of the illiterate population in 37 countries.[23] At the higher levels of education there are also marked differences between the sexes. Even though there are some countries where more than half of the students at the educational institutions are female, in some 20 to 30 percent of the countries for which information was available in 1975 fewer than 40 percent of the students enrolled in schools or universities were female. When individual countries, irrespective of their size, are used as units of analysis, the world averages for the proportion of women among students are 45 percent at the first level, 42 percent at the second, and 34 percent at the third level of education.[24]

Tables 13.1, 13.2, and 13.3 show that female education is related to high proportions of both industrial and service populations in the total economically active population and that both the level of female education and the proportion of women among students is highest in postindustrial societies.

21. Elina Haavio-Mannila, "How Women Become Political Actors," *Department of Sociology, University of Helsinki, Working Paper 6,* and "Changes in Sex Roles in Politics as an Indicator of Structural Change in Society," *International Journal of Sociology* 8 (3) (1978):56–85.

22. United Nations, *Human Rights: A Compilation of International Instruments of the United Nations* (New York: UN, 1973), article 26, p. 3; article 9, p. 40.

23. Elise Boulding *et al., Handbook of International Data on Women* (New York: Wiley, 1976), pp. 134–35.

24. UN, *Statistical Yearbook, 1976* (New York: UN, 1976), table 207.

Work

Married and unmarried women are supposed to have equal rights with men with regard to work, free choice of employment, fair and favorable working conditions, protection against unemployment, fair pay, and equal pay for equal work. Measures ought also to be taken to prevent their dismissal in the event of marriage or maternity, to provide paid

TABLE 13.1
Crude Birth Rate and Educational and Political Positions of Women According to Proportion of Persons Working in Industry of All Economically Active Population. Averages Based on Country Averages

Birth rate and position of women	(N)*	Percentage of industrial population: –15 (25)	16–25 (21)	26– (35)	Total (150)	Statistical sign F†
Around year 1968						
Crude birthrate (births per 1,000 inhabitants)		43	39	21	35	60.71+++
Educational position of women						
Mean years of school attendance among women aged						
15–24		2.0	2.7	5.5	3.6	15.43+++
25–64		1.1	1.6	4.2	2.6	15.80+++
Student enrollment ratio for girls (percent of age category) at the first and second level of education		45	62	77	54	14.24+++
Proportion of women at the third level of education %		30	30	34	28	1.50
Around year 1975						
Proportion of women at the first level of education, %		41	47	48	45	9.50+++
second level of education		36	44	48	42	10.79+++
third level of education		32	31	40	34	5.30+
Political position of women						
Year when universal suffrage was attained for women		1949	1951	1931	1945	14.14+++
Proportion of women of delegates to United Nations General Assemblies 1946–74, %		8	7	5	6	1.34

* In many cases the number of countries is smaller. Total includes also countries for which data on the independent variable is lacking.

† Level of statistical significance: +++ = .001, ++ = .01, and + = .05.

SOURCES: E. Boulding *et al.*, *Handbook of International Data on Women* (New York: Wiley, 1976), pp. 250–57. UN Centre for Social and Humanitarian Affairs, *Les Femmes aux Nations Unies* (New York: UN, 1977).

maternity leave and the guarantee of returning to former employment, and to provide child-care facilities as well as other social services.[25] Obviously, the major adverse effects of poor working conditions, including unemployment, underemployment, and low wages, are felt by women and men. But women are often particularly vulnerable to poor working conditions and find it especially hard to enter the same kinds of jobs and to earn the same levels of pay as men.

Women are less likely than men to be in what is classified as eco-

TABLE 13.2
Crude Birth Rate and Educational and Political Position of Women According to Proportion of Persons Working in Services of all Economically Active Population. Averages Based on Country Averages

Birth rate and position of women		Percentage of service population				
	(N)	−15 (22)	16–25 (49)	26– (24)	Total (150)	Statistical sign F*
Around year 1968						
Crude birthrate (births per 1,000 inhabitants)		39	33	24	35	8.82+++
Educational position of women						
Mean years of school attendance among women aged						
15–24		3.0	3.4	6.6	3.6	9.36+++
25–64		2.0	2.2	5.5	2.6	11.89+++
Student enrollment ratio for girls (percent of age category) at first and second level of education		49	64	80	54	9.91+++
Proportion of women at the third level of education, %		27	31	36	28	3.55+
Around year 1975						
Proportion of women at the first level of education, %		44	46	49	45	2.63
second level of education		41	44	48	42	2.92
third level of education		37	35	41	34	1.77
Political position of women						
Year when universal suffrage was attained for women		1945	1944	1933	1945	3.30+
Proportion of women of delegates to United Nations General Assemblies 1946–74, %		8	6	6	6	0.92

* Level of statistical significance: +++ = .001, ++ = .01, and + = .05.

SOURCES: E. Boulding *et al.*, *Handbook of International Data on Women* (New York: Wiley, 1976). UN Centre for Social and Humanitarian Affairs, *Les Femmes aux Nations Unies* (New York: UN, 1977).

25. *Human Rights,* article 43, p. 2; article 10, p. 40.

nomic activity. However, they may be working very hard in domestic and, in some countries at least, farm tasks even though they do not appear in the statistics. Indeed, a major stumbling block to accurate analysis of women's labor force participation has been the sexist bias of census statistics which have been accused of rendering women almost invisible.[26] They

TABLE 13.3
Crude Birth Rate and Educational and Political Position of Women According to Type of Society. Averages Based on Country Averages

Birth rate and position of women	(N)	Type of society* Agri-cultural (31)	Indus-trial (83)	Post-indus-trial (19)	Total (134)	Statistical sign F†
Around year 1968						
Crude birth rate (births per 1,000 inhabitants)		42	36	23	35	17.79+++
Educational position of women						
Mean years of school attendance among women aged						
15–24		2.3	3.6	6.9	3.6	13.79+++
25–64		1.3	2.5	5.8	2.6	19.34+++
Students enrollment ratio for girls (percent of age category) at first and second level of education		46	50	81	54	11.46+++
Proportion of women at third level of education, %		26	26	37	28	5.66+++
Around year 1975						
Proportion of women at						
first level of education		43	45	49	45	2.85
second level of education		39	42	48	42	3.52+
third level of education		32	33	41	34	3.00
Political position of women						
Year when universal suffrage was attained for women		1949	1947	1932	1945	8.66+++
Percentage of women among delegates to the UN General Assemblies 1946–74		6	5	6	6	0.97

* Agricultural = more than 50% of economically active population work in agriculture. Industrial = at most 55% of economically active population work in agriculture and industry, but the agricultural population does not exceed 50%. This category also includes countries for which no data are available for their economic structure. Postindustrial = more than 45% of the economically active population work in services.

† Level of statistical significance: +++ = .001, ++ = .01, and + = .05.

SOURCES: E. Boulding *et al., Handbook of International Data on Women* (New York: Wiley, 1976). UN Centre for Social and Humanitarian Affairs, *Les Femmes aux Nations Unies* (New York: UN, 1977).

26. Guy Standing, *Labour Force Participation and Development* (Geneva: ILO, 1978), p. 3.

frequently list women as dependent persons even when that is not the case. Additionally, more and more women around the world in both industrialized and industrializing nations are even the sole providers for their own dependents, mainly their children, a phenomenon which is increasingly documented for a number of different cultures.[27] Thus a major basic problem in the analysis of much data on women's work is the ambiguity of such concepts as "unpaid family worker" and "homemaker." A decrease in the proportion of women classified as "homemaker" from one point in time to another may mean that more women are engaged in productive activity outside the home, or it may simply mean that the concept has been differently construed. Thus recent studies of women's labor force participation in some countries have found that earlier estimates need considerable revision. It is remarkable that changes in census categorization have not always become less sexist. Sometimes change has been on the opposite direction. For example, the idea of a male wage earner supporting a family, or of the wives of farmers and small businessmen being outside the working population is foreign to early British censuses, whereas these assumptions are made in twentieth-century ones.[28]

In cross-cultural and comparative studies, of course, a basic consideration is the extent to which home and work or the spheres of reproduction, consumption, and production are in fact functionally and spatially separate. In peasant economies, the three may be very much integrated or overlapping, hence the conceptual problem involved—a problem to which subsequent consideration will be given.

Another factor complicating the documentation of the female work force is its volatility. The rapid population growth of the past three decades has been associated with correspondingly rapid rates of labor force growth and urbanization. Rising unemployment and radical changes in the levels and incidence of labor force participation have accompanied these phenomena as well as changes in the pattern of income-earning opportunities. These changes have had great effects upon women as well as men. Indeed, in most countries women form the component of the labor force whose participation is most sensitive to economic and social pressures.[29]

The number of married women in the work force in Western Europe

27. For the European context see: Alice H. Cook, *The Working Mother: A Survey of Problems and Programs in Nine Countries* (New York: New York State School of Industrial and Labor Relations, Cornell University, 1978), p. 5.

28. H. Land, "The Myth of the Male Bread Winner," *New Society* 9 (October 1975).

29. Guy Standing, "Labour Force Participation in Historical Perspective: Proletarianisation in Jamaica," *Population and Employment Working Paper No. 50* (Geneva: ILO, 1977), p. 2.

has been increasing rapidly, but this phenomenon has not always been adequately documented in census figures.[30] In Eastern Europe, the number of women employed in social production is changing, and the proportion of women in the total number of workers and civil servants is growing during the process of industrialization.[31] However, there is evidence of marked decline in female labor force participation in other areas. For example, women's employment in industry in developing countries over time has declined in many areas.[32]

There is a wide variation in the crude labor force participation rates for women in 1975. In Eastern Europe and the USSR, and in a few Central and Southern African countries, more than 40 percent of the women of all ages work, whereas in Northern Africa and the Middle East less than 10 percent are included in the registered labor force. The crude labor force participation rate for women is curvilinearly related to the proportion of both the industrial and the service population of the total economically active population. It is higher in the least and the most industrialized and service-centered societies (Tables 13.4 and 13.5). However, when the countries of the world are divided into three groups—agricultural, industrial, and postindustrial—no statistically significant differences can be seen (Table 13.6).

It is also clear that women are discriminated against in terms of economic activities classified by status, industry, and occupation. On the basis of the information given in the *International Handbook of Data on Women,* the world average for sex discrimination by status is 20 percent, by industry 35 percent, and by occupation 37 percent. The indices of sex discrimination by status, industry, or occupation are "interpreted as the proportions of economically active females (or males) who would have to change their status, industrial, or occupational classification for there to be an equal distribution of women in the various status, industrial, or occupational sectors of the economy."[33]

30. Cook, *The Working Mother.*

31. V. Bodrova, "Fertility and Female Employment in Social Production: Current and Coming Problems (on the Example of European Socialist Countries)," Helsinki Conference on Economic and Demographic Changes: Issues for the 1980s (Helsinki: IUSSP, 1978).

32. See, among others, June Nash and Helen Safa (eds.), *Sex and Class in Latin America* (New York: Praeger, 1976).

33. Boulding, *Handbook,* p. 323. They base their indices of segregation of economic activity by states, industry, and occupation on the indices of segregation outlined by Otis Duncan and Beverly Duncan, "A Methodological Analysis of Segregation Indices," *American Sociological Review* 20(April):210–17; and E. Gross, "Plus ça change . . . ? The Sexual Structure of Occupation Over Time," *Social Problems* 16:188–208. These indices are used here. Actual calculations are based

Sex discrimination by status is thus less frequent than that by industry and occupation (as Tables 13.4 to 13.6 show). In 1968 women composed on the average 19 percent of the self-employed, 24 percent of the employees, and 45 percent of the family workers in the countries of the world (when countries were used as the research units). The range was smaller than in the femaleness of different industries; there the proportion of women fluctuated from 4 percent in construction to 39 percent in services. The gap between different occupations was also wide: women were 11 percent of the workers in administrative and managerial jobs but 50 percent of those in service jobs.

There is little evidence for change in the degree of discrimination against women within the labor market over the past quarter century. Furthermore, the fact that the idea of equal pay for equal work is widely subscribed to and supported by law does not automatically guarantee women opportunities and remuneration. And even in circumstances where the law is upheld, women still have lower levels of pay because they remain in jobs needing lower skills and educational qualifications. As Cook points out, once women are in a separate labor market there is little application for such laws about equal pay. In addition, many women also work part-time, which lowers their incomes considerably.[34]

Women in Agriculture

Women play an important role in agriculture throughout the world. In the developing countries, women are most commonly included in the agricultural labor force in Central and Southern Africa and in Southeastern Asia. In South America, North Africa, and the Middle East, the proportion of women workers in agriculture is lower. Women's work in agriculture is also curvilinearly related to the proportion of industrial popu-

---

on a comparison of the proportion of females in each status/industry/occupation category of all females economically active by status/industry/occupation, defined as the distribution index for females and the proportion of males in each category economically active by status/industry/occupation, which could be defined as a distribution index for males. The index of segregation is the sum of the absolute values of the differences between these proportions or distribution indices for female and male economic activity in each category, divided by two. Countries for which one-half the data for women and men by status were not available were excluded from the indices presented. Indices of segregation, "are read as percentages and may be interpreted as the percentage of females (or males) who would have to change . . . in order that the distribution of sexes. . . . should be the same" (Gross, p. 202).

34. Cook, *The Working Mother.*

TABLE 13.4
Position of Women in Economic Activity According to Proportion of Persons Working in Industry and Construction of all Economically Active Population. Averages Based on Country Averages

Position of women in economic activity	(N)	Percentage of industrial population −15 (24)	16–25 (22)	26– (35)	Total (123)	Statistical sign F*
Around year 1968						
Crude labor force participation rate for women		23	14	24	24	4.77+
Proportion of women of all economically active population		28	21	30	28	4.01+
Proportion of women in different status groups:						
self-employed		18	17	19	19	0.36
employees		21	18	29	24	9.13+++
family workers		46	27	52	45	6.15++
Proportion of women in different industries:						
agriculture		25	15	23	23	2.45
mining and quarrying		12	6	6	8	2.13
manufacturing		23	27	27	25	0.81
electrical, gas		5	7	9	8	1.70
construction		3	3	4	4	1.59
commerce		29	27	36	30	1.84
transport		5	5	11	7	12.99+++
services		34	40	47	39	4.63+
Proportion of women in different occupational groups:						
professional and technical work		32	38	41	38	4.58+
administrative and managerial work		14	7	12	11	1.97
clerical work		26	25	46	35	11.14+++
sales work		29	29	39	33	1.83
service work		40	47	60	50	6.98++
agricultural and related work		28	14	23	22	3.21+
production and related work		15	16	17	16	0.38
Around year 1975						
Crude labor force participation rate for women		21	14	26	24	6.82++
Sex ratio (female/male) in labor force participation rates		42	31	46	45	3.98+

* Level of statistical significance: +++ = .001, ++ = .01, and + = .05.

Sources: ILO *Year Book of Labor Statistics, 1976.* E. Boulding *et al.*, *Handbook of International Data on Women* (New York: Wiley, 1976). UN Centre for Social and Humanitarian Affairs, *Les Femmes aux Nations Unies* (New York: UN, 1977).

TABLE 13.5
Position of Women in Economic Activity According to Proportion of Persons Working in Services of All Economically Active Population. Averages Based on Country Averages

Position of women in economic activity	(N)	Percentage of service population -20 (22)	21–45 (49)	46– (23)	Total (123)	Statistical sign F*
Around year 1968		Percent				
Crude labor force participation rate for women		29	17	33	24	7.93+++
Proportion of women of all economically active population		34	23	32	28	9.33+++
Proportion of women in different status groups:						
self-employed		25	17	18	19	3.07
employees		22	22	29	24	3.96
family workers		52	36	59	45	7.04
Proportion of women in different industries:						
agriculture		34	19	20	23	6.76++
mining and quarrying		13	6	6	8	2.59
manufacturing		26	26	27	25	0.06
electrical, gas		7	8	8	8	0.24
construction		4	3	4	4	0.68
commerce		34	28	37	30	2.01
transport		6	6	12	7	8.02+++
services		38	40	48	39	2.45
Proportion of women in different occupational groups:						
professional and technical work		32	38	42	38	4.09+
administrative and managerial work		18	9	12	11	3.44+
clerical work		28	30	50	35	9.26+++
sales work		36	30	38	33	1.49
service work		44	49	61	50	3.73+
agricultural and related work		36	19	18	22	8.36+++
production and related work		17	15	16	16	0.14
Around year 1975						
Crude labor force participation rate for women		28	18	26	24	5.75++
Sex ratio (female/male) in labor force participation rates		53	36	47	45	4.79++

* Level of statistical significance: +++ = .001, ++ = .01, and + = .05.

SOURCES: ILO *Year Book of Labor Statistics, 1976.* E. Boulding *et al.*, *Handbook of International Data on Women* (New York: Wiley, 1976). UN Centre for Social and Humanitarian Affairs, *Les Femmes aux Nations Unies* (New York: UN, 1977).

TABLE 13.6
Position of Women in Economic Activity According to Type of Society. Average Based on Country Averages

Position of women in economic activity	(N)	Type of society* Agricultural (34)	Industrial (67)	Post-industrial (22)	Total (123)	Statistical sign F†
Around year 1968				Percent		
Crude labor force participation rate of women		22	25	24	24	0.55
Proportion of women of all economically active population		26	26	32	28	1.87
Proportion of women in different status groups:						
self-employed		20	18	18	19	0.19
employees		19	25	29	24	7.71+++
family workers		41	40	61	45	4.82+++
Proportion of women in different industries:						
agriculture		26	22	20	23	0.76
mining and quarrying		9	7	7	8	0.17
manufacturing		24	26	26	25	0.13
electrical, gas		6	10	8	8	2.30
construction		3	5	4	4	1.07
commerce		28	29	37	30	1.77
transport		4	7	12	7	13.17++
services		36	38	48	39	2.87
Proportion of women in different occupational groups:						
professional and technical work		33	40	42	38	4.14+
administrative and managerial work		7	13	12	11	1.91
clerical work		20	36	51	35	18.70++
sales work		28	35	38	33	1.67
service work		41	53	61	50	5.81++
agricultural and related work		26	22	20	23	0.77
production and related work		15	16	15	16	0.19
Around year 1975						
Crude labor force participation rate of women		21	25	26	24	1.28
Sex ratio (female/male) in labor force participation rates		41	47	48	45	0.79

* Agricultural = more than 50% of economically active population work in agriculture. Industrial = at most 55% of economically active population work in agriculture and industry, but the agricultural population does not exceed 50%. This category also includes countries for which no data are available for their economic structure. Post-industrial = more than 45% of the economically active population work in services.

† Level of statistical significance: +++ = .001, ++ = .01, and + = .05.

SOURCES: ILO *Year Book of Labor Statistics, 1976*. E. Boulding *et al., Handbook of International Data on Women* (New York: Wiley, 1976). UN Centre for Social and Humanitarian Affairs, *Les Femmes aux Nations Unies* (New York: UN, 1977).

lation in a country: in the least and the most industrialized countries there are more women in agriculture than in those where industry employs only a few people (Table 13.4). A high proportion of service population is, however, clearly associated with a low proportion of women in agriculture (Table 13.5). Commercial agriculture has had effects similar to those of industrialization in rural developing areas: the green revolution has vastly increased yields, but at the expense of the displacement of small farmers, of the creation of regional inequalities and of the accentuation of income differences.[35] In many cases, women in particular have suffered from this modernization of agriculture.

Ahmed has recently attempted a preliminary assessment of the nature and impact of technological change on the condition of rural women, especially the changes in rural women's employment and income-earning opportunities. The impact of drudgery and the burden of work following technological change, and the extent of rural women's access to technology, extension services, and other resources are also reviewed. As Ahmed stresses, the nature of relations between men and women in the *household* must be examined in order to understand the locus of the sexual division of labor and the effects of technological change. Ahmed's study concludes that it is quite clear, from the survey evidence brought together, that the neglect of women's key roles in the rural economy, especially their contribution to agriculture and food production, including processing, distribution, and animal husbandry, and of the importance of technology in their activities could seriously hinder rural development.[36]

The heavy burden rural women in developing countries bear in their dual roles as producers and reproducers (housewives and mothers) has been increasingly stressed and documented and the cultural variations in the sexual division of labor explored. Thus, for instance, the Basic Needs Strategy adopted by the ILO World Employment Conference recommended under the special Programme of Action at the national level that "special emphasis should be placed in developing countries on promoting the status, education, development and employment of women."[37]

35. June Nash, *The Integration of Women in the Development Process as Equal Partners with Men* (Mexico City: International Women's Year, 1975).

36. I. Ahmed, "Technological Change and the Condition of Rural Women: A Preliminary Assessment," World Employment Program, *Technology and Employment Working Paper* (Geneva: ILO, 1978).

37. ILO, *Meeting Basic Needs: Strategies for Eradicating Mass Poverty and Unemployment,* Conclusions of the World Employment Conference (Geneva, 1976), p. 28; Idem, *A Basic Needs Strategy for Africa: Report of the Director General,* Report I, Part I, Fifth ILO African Regional Conference (Abidjan, September–October, 1977).

Women in Industry and Services

The proportion of women in manufacturing is about as high as that in agriculture. The world averages were 25 and 23 percent respectively around 1968. (The averages were counted on the basis of information from 98 and 107 countries, using country averages as the unit of analysis.) Women in other secondary industries—electrical, gas, water and sanitary services, and in construction—are fewer (4–8 percent). However, many women working in factories are engaged in clerical or service work; the world average for production work is only 16 percent. Women working in factories are relatively common in America, Europe, Asia, and Australia, but not in Africa and the Middle East.

The proportion of women in manufacturing and other secondary industries seems to be totally unrelated to the structure of the economically active population and varies little in agricultural, industrial, and post-industrial societies (Tables 13.4, 13.5, and 13.6). There are, however, variations in two indicators of the position of women in the tertiary service sector of the economy: proportions of women in services (government, community, business, recreation, and personal services) and in clerical work. The proportion of women in services is, on the average, 39 percent (108 countries), and in clerical work it is 35 percent (87 countries). In addition, there are regional variations: there are many women in services in most of the world except Africa (excluding South Africa) and the Middle East, while women in clerical work are rare in those areas and in Central and South America and Asia (excluding Japan and the Philippines).

In Latin America, women have a long tradition of working as domestic servants, which explains their high proportion in service in that area. But these women have not been able to enter into the more modern female occupations such as clerical work. This is a clear indication of the way in which those with greater resources in certain societies are able to benefit from the use of cheap domestic labor extracted from those less fortunate, especially poor women. It is an advantage which the elites are loathe to give up when other opportunities for higher status and more lucrative employment open up for their household help, and the pool of potential maids diminishes. At a meeting organized by the Ghana National Council on Women in Development, Dzidzienyo noted that in a culture in which women, not men, do "housework," housemaids are vital in keeping the educated and trained sector of the female labor force free to work outside the home. This is, however, at the price of severely restricting the life chances of a whole segment of the children of the poor. She phrased the dilemma as follows: "If we keep children in school and restrict child employment, we raise the cost of household help to the point where it is prohibitive and drives many women out of work. If we do not, we guarantee illiteracy and underdevelopment for another segment of our Ghanaian womenhood."

Women work somewhat more often in services and markedly more in clerical work in industrial and postindustrial societies than in agricultural societies. There is also a clear increase of female participation in transport and communications, as well as in professional and technical work when one moves from agricultural toward industrial and postindustrial societies (Tables 13.4, 13.5, and 13.6).

The ILO has adopted a number of conventions, which member nations have been expected to ratify as part of their national labor codes, including prohibitions against night-work, lifting heavy weights, and underground work. Recently there has been opposition to such prohibitions against women, partly because they upheld segregation of the sexes in the labor market. Rights and legal provisions for childbirth and the succeeding months vary a great deal among the industrialized nations, from provision of lengthy paid child-care leave (for example, in Australia, Finland, Hungary, and Sweden) to lack of any provision of even a national health insurance plan covering medical expenses including those of childbirth. The social policies governing retirement health plans and other welfare programs for women in many industrialized countries are confused and contradictory, often treating women as spouses or widows rather than as workers or citizens in their own right.

The proportion of working women who are members of unions is usually lower than in the case of men. There are, however, also exceptions: in Finland, women are organized in trade unions as often as men, and the increase in the number of Finnish union members in the 1970s is totally due to the growing number of women joining the unions. In many countries and industries union scales and rates are lower for women and they receive fewer fringe benefits.[38] Indeed many high-paying occupations exclude women completely. This union opposition to women entering some occupations also helps account for the sex-segregated labor market. Even in the cases where women form the majority in a union, such as in the textile and garment trades, women are seldom if ever the leaders of the unions. Women's trade union caucuses, however, have emerged in the seventies in some countries.

38. Cook, *The Working Mother,* chapters 12 and 13. She also notes, p. x, the high "cost of equality" for women and men considering the special problems involved. Nonetheless, some countries, such as Sweden, have decided to accept these costs through a commitment to equality and a conviction that ultimately such an investment will pay off for the nation as a whole.

Fertility

The individual's right to plan births, their number and timing is one which has long been proclaimed as a basic human right by the United Nations, one which has been accounted essential to physical and mental health. It is a right which, when translated through power to decision and action, has a dramatic impact on the status of women.[39]

There are marked variations in crude birth rates in different parts of the world, varying from less than 13 to more than 52 per thousand around 1968. The latest figures from 1975 range from 10 to 52 per thousand.[40] The high birth rate areas include Central America, Western South America, most of Africa, and parts of Asia. Analysis of global data shows that with industrialization (Table 13.1) and with increasing employment of people in service occupations (Table 13.2) there is a significant decrease in the crude birth rate. Table 13.3 also shows that there is a significant drop in the crude birth rate from agricultural to industrial and from industrial to postindustrial societies. There is also a vast literature indicating the presence of an inverse relationship between urbanization and fertility across a wide range of less developed countries. Individual studies, however, do not always show the same kind of correlation between urban/rural residence or city size or agricultural occupation and fertility.[41] Reproductive behavior is also correlated with individuals' circumstances and economic behavior as well as with sociological variables, such as class,

39. In 1966 the United Nations proclaimed that "the size of the family should be a free choice of each individual family" [General Assembly Resolution 2211 (XXI)]. In 1968 the International Conference on Human Rights announced that couples have a basic human right to decide freely and responsibly on the number and spacing of their children and a right to adequate education and information about birth planning (resolution XVIII). In 1969 the right to means to space and limit births was declared (General Assembly Resolution 2542 (XXIV), Article 22). On the health aspects of these problems see: United Nations World Health Organization, "Health Aspects of Family Planning," Technical Reports Series No. 442 (Geneva: WHO, 1970) and International Planned Parenthood Federation, "The Relationship between Family Size and Maternal and Child Health," Working Paper No. 5 (London: IPPF, July 1970). The impact of the right to plan births has been documented by Frederick L. Campbell, "Family Growth and Variation in Family Role Structure," *Journal of Marriage and the Family* 32(1970):45–53.

40. UN, *Demographic Yearbook, 1976* (New York: UN, 1976).

41. This literature is covered in W. P. McGreevey et al., "The Policy Relevance of Recent Social Research on Fertility," Occasional Monographs Series, No. 2 (Washington: Smithsonian Institution, 1974). Among the authors who treat this problem are: W. Robinson, "Urban Rural Differences in Indian Fertility," *Population Studies* 14(March 1961):218–34; and Janit Abu-Lughod, "Urban Rural Differences as a Function of the Demographic Transition," *American Journal of Sociology* 69(March 1964):476–90.

caste, and community.[42] Recently, as was noted above, the idea has become increasingly prevalent that the status of women and their role in decision making and reproduction have an important bearing on the success of family-planning programs and the long-term reduction in fertility of a country.[43] A basic assumption is that in societies in which women are mainly concerned with the domestic domain of life and child-rearing, fertility will be higher. Thus associations have been observed between the desire for a large family and what has been termed "the traditionalism" of women's roles.[44] Certainly many studies have underlined the fact that children provide important avenues to social recognition, economic security, and happiness for women. There is evidence from many different cultures that among the nuclear family relationships, the relationship between mother and child is the most loving and least ambivalent (except perhaps in those cultures in which almost the total responsibility of parenthood is born by the mother and from which there is growing evidence of violent behavior on the part of parents towards their children). For most women of the world, motherhood is defined as their major role in life, and it may even be a prerequisite to their recognition as mature members of a community. Even the concept of being an adult woman without children may be difficult to comprehend, and the lot of the barren women can be a hard one fraught with suspicion. The role of wife may also be crucial for social respectability.[45]

It has been noticed that improvements in health increase the potential capacity for having larger numbers of children, since there is evidence that improvements in the diet may lead to earlier menarche and later menopause and shorter periods of postpartum amenorrhea in nursing mothers. Historical as well as contemporary data support the contention that varia-

42. Richard Anker, "The Effect of Group Level Variables on Fertility in a Rural Indian Sample," *Journal of Development Studies* 14(October 1977).

43. Rafiqul H. Chaudhury, "Female Status and Fertility Behaviour in a Metropolitan Urban Area of Bangladesh," *Population Studies* 32 (2) (1978); Joseph Banks and Olive Banks, *Feminism and Family Planning in Victorian England* (New York: Schocken, 1972), have pointed out that much of the interest in relations between the status of women and demographic changes, especially family planning, may have arisen as a result of the fact that the rise of feminism and the fall of the birth rate coincided in Victorian England and were thus thought to be causally connected.

44. Janet Z. Giele, *Women's Roles and Status in Eight Countries* (New York: Wiley, 1977).

45. For an example of the position of barren women among an African people, see Christine Oppong, *Growing Up in Dagbon* (Accra: Ghana Publishing Corp., 1973). Among the Hausa, all unmarried women are verbally categorized with prostitutes.

tions in marital fertility rates across different social and economic groups may be a result of varying health and nutrition conditions and differing habits of breast-feeding and need not necessarily be explained by conscious family planning. Thus, for instance, studies in rural Bangladesh have indicated that maternal malnutrition and lack of high-quality supplementary feeding for infants are associated with longer periods of lactational amenorrhea which consequently postpone the possibility of further pregnancies.[46] Again it is important to note that indicators of modernity in some social contexts are not seen to be associated with a desire for fewer children but rather the reverse.[47]

One of the aspects of reproduction critical for women's educational and employment status, as well as for their ultimate fertility levels, is the age at which their reproductive career begins. Since becoming educated is a prerequisite for occupational advancement for women as well as men, the interruption or termination of education as a result of pregnancy is likely to have ill effects on a woman's eventual status in nondomestic roles.[48]

Child marriage and the betrothal of young girls before puberty are supposed to be prohibited, and women should have the same right as men to free choice of spouses and indeed of marriage itself.[49] The minimum age of marriage is supposed to be 15, and all marriages are supposed to be officially registered. In spite of these United Nations declarations, in actual fact the recognized legal minimum ages for the first marriage of girls varies from 12 to 20 years. In most cases there is legal inequality in that the minimum age for males is higher than that of women. In many regions, in particular Africa and India, there are strong social pressures to marry girls off early. In countries where girls marry young there is often a 10 to 15 year gap between the ages of wife and husband.

Each year 12–18 million babies are born to girls younger than 20. The percentage of live births to mothers under 20 varies in different countries and cultures, from 25 percent in several Central American and Caribbean countries, and nearly 20 percent in the United States, to as low as one percent in Japan. In the United States, where three-quarters of these

46. S. L. Huffman et al., "Nutrition and Post Partum Amenorrhea in Rural Bangladesh," *Population Studies* 32 (July 1978); Jeroen van Ginneken, "Prolonged Breast-feeding as a Birth Spacing Method," *Studies in Family Planning* (June 1974): 201–206.

47. R. W. Thompson, "Fertility Aspirations and Modernisation in Urban Uganda: A Case of Resilient Cultural Values," *Urban Anthropology* 7 (2) (1978).

48. See for example: M. B. Presser, "Age at Menarche: Socio-sexual Behavior and Fertility," *Social Biology* 25 (2) (1978).

49. United Nations, *Human Rights,* article 16, p. 2; article 6, pp. 39–40; pp. 43–44.

teenage mothers are unmarried, the percentage of such births is about three times the level of 1940. Where in 1960, 14 percent of births were to teenagers, by 1972 this figure reached 19 percent. As Kantner and Zelnick point out, the high and probably increasing level of sexual activity among teenagers, combined with the continuing high levels of unwanted pregnancy and births to unmarried women, constitute one of the serious remaining population problems in the United States. These teenage mothers are often poor, unmarried, and from economically underprivileged minority groups. Their education is often curtailed as a consequence, and their chances for upwardly mobile careers reduced. In addition, the health risks for their babies are higher than those of other mothers.

The basic causes of early motherhood have been seen as cultural. Thus, for instance, in traditional Islamic cultures early marriage is characteristic and attempts to raise the legal marriage age for girls may meet with widespread and powerful opposition. In the majority of West Asian countries 40–50 percent of girls are married before age 20. A study of Iran ten years ago showed that one-third of rural women and a quarter of women in Teheran were married before the age of 15. In Islamic countries the proportion of married teenage girls varies from 31 percent in the United Arab Republic to 73 percent in Pakistan.[50] In early Islam, marriage took place at the time the girl reached puberty, and this is still the case in many rural areas. The effects on fertility of an early commencement are of course significant. Raising the age of marriage and delaying childbirth may be an important element in a state's attempt to reduce population growth.

A somewhat related phenomenon, in terms of its connection with fertility and assumption of control over juvenile female genitalia, is the various forms of genital mutilation practiced in a range of societies. Female circumcision or clitoridectomy in its various forms is traditionally practiced on young girls in some 26 countries of Africa and Asia. The resulting severe health hazards are better known and documented than the potential psychological and sexual effects.[51] Infibulation is also practiced to control female sexual expression and incidentally reduce fertility. This is apparently still a sociocultural feature of several different peoples throughout East Africa. At least in the Sudan it is reported to be not an archaic survival but a vital and integrated part of the contemporary sociocultural system, even though it has officially been illegal for almost 30 years.[52]

50. See the articles in *Mothers Too Soon,* Draper World Population Fund Report, No. 1 (Autumn 1975).

51. *Women's International Network News* 4 (2) (1978):43–44.

52. R. O. Hayes, "Female Genital Mutilation, Fertility Control and Women's Role and the Patrilineage in Modern Sudan: A Functional Analysis," *American Ethnologist* 2 (4) (1975).

Reproduction and Production

Three phenomena are noted to have characterized the more developed societies in the twentieth century—a decline in marital fertility rates, a rise in the labor force participation of married women, and an emphasis on the importance of the mother in child-rearing which is unparalleled in other cultural areas.[53] An increase in women's access to education and employment is therefore a frequently discussed mode of reducing fertility through radically affecting the availability of their time, energy, and maternal resources, as well as by changing their aspirations and social contacts. Certain changes in women's status brought about in this way may contribute to fertility reduction, but they are neither a necessary nor a sufficient condition for such a change in birth rates. Indeed, the findings of a range of recent studies are conflicting.[54]

The hypothesis that an increase in women's access to employment opportunities and control of productive resources such as income and education would lead to a decline in fertility levels is based on two different premises. The first is the assumed incompatibility of women's productive and reproductive activities. This hypothesis assumes that in modern industrialized societies mother and worker roles are incompatible so that women who try to combine the roles will have fewer children. This incompatibility of work and maternal roles is considered to arise out of a bureaucratized occupational system, which does not allow the kind of flexibility needed for the simultaneous taking on of parental responsibilities, and out of the nuclear family role structure—*closed/segregated*—which in the absence of parental role substitutes—either husbands, kin, or others—leaves women to take on the total task of child-rearing.[55]

The second premise is based on the assumption that increasing women's resources will increase their say in domestic decision making. This would lead to greater control of their own reproductive capacities and lower fertility, on the assumption that many of the children women are having are surplus children they did not decide to have. Thus it is presumed that female autonomy or power will be associated with both demographic and contraceptive innovation.

53. S. Kupinsky, ed., *The Fertility of Working Women—A Synthesis of International Research* (New York: Praeger, 1977).

54. See for example J. L. McCabe and M. R. Rosenzweig, "Female Employment Creation and Family Size," in *Population and Development*, edited by Ridker.

55. J. Mayone Stycos and Robert Weller, "Female Working Roles and Fertility," *Demography* 4 (1) (1967), is one such study. For an explanation of the terms "closed" and "segregated," as used here in relation to nuclear family functioning, see Chapter 1 of Oppong, *Marriage*.

This hypothesis has been stated and tested in the most rigorous way by the New Household Economists who have examined women's market wage rates and viewed them as having two kinds of effects: (1) increasing household income and making it possible to afford more children; and (2) increasing the opportunity cost of the wife's time used up in nonmarket activities, encouraging her to reallocate her time toward profitable market conditions. In fact no generally consistent relationships have been found between women's employment status and family size. Studies in industrialized countries have shown a negative relationship between women's employment and fertility and have led to an assumption that the price effect on women's time tends to be more important in affecting fertility than the effect of increasing income. Studies in countries at different stages of economic development, however, have not always shown this kind of relationship.

Examined cross culturally, the relationship between female employment and fertility is not nearly so systematic as the New Home Economics would imply. Areas with similar levels of labor force participation are found to have different fertility levels and vice versa. What is discovered to be crucial is the type of work leading to a separation of the domestic, reproductive, and productive spheres. When this does not occur, fertility is not necessarily altered; indeed it may be positively affected.[56]

It is only employment in the modern urban sector which appears to depress fertility, but women employed in this sector are a very small proportion of all working women. Most women of the world are working in agriculture, family crafts, and trading. In these situations there is little incompatibility between productive work and socialization.

Among social cultural groupings where "extended family ties" make child-care arrangements relatively easy, there is no role incompatibility for working women.[57] Hence the negative relationship between female labor force participation and fertility level does not hold in such areas. Thus a number of studies have pointed out that where employment and maternal roles are not incompatible, as when surrogate mothers are readily available, employment can be an addition rather than an alternative to reproduction and the employment-fertility relationship may be nil or even positive. Neither fertility, the presence of children under five, nor the presence of another adult female appear to make a significant difference in the possibility of female participation in either rural or urban areas of Africa. It

56. Nancy Birdsall, "Women and Population Studies: Review Essay," *Signs* 1 (3) (1976).

57. J. W. Salaff and A. K. Wong, "Chinese Women at Work," in *The Fertility of Working Women,* edited by Kupinsky. P. S. Weisner and R. Gallimore, "My Brother's Keeper: Child and Sibling Caretaking," *Current Anthropology* 18 (2) (1977).

seems that the child-care burden does not significantly affect female labor force participation in Kenya, and a recent analysis of Nigerian evidence also gives no suggestion that childbearing has severely restricted female labor force participation rates there.[58]

Based on an analysis of the international data on women collected by Boulding and associates, the global variance of fertility, measured by *crude birth rate,* is explained very well (74.6 percent of the variance) by using a regression analysis which has as independent variables indicators of women's position and general economic and cultural characteristics of the countries.

These findings can be related to Kasarda's comparative study of 49 nations. It showed that in each country the level of education was related to the proportion of females employed for wages and salaries, which in turn was negatively associated with fertility. Holsinger and Kasarda have claimed that as educational levels of women rise we may expect a larger proportion to be employed outside the home, and the fertility rates to be lower.[59] A factor analysis by the authors shows that low birth rate is related mainly to women's education and participation in clerical, service, professional and technical work, not to their manual work. Further analysis shows that the birth rate is more closely associated with women's education than with their proportion of the economically active population, even though this relationship is also statistically significant.

Negative relationships between fertility and nonagricultural economic activity have also been recorded in other areas.[60] In Greece, Safilios Rothschild found that higher degrees of work commitment were associated with more rational contraceptive behavior and lower levels of fertility. This points to the need for the study of the work commitment of the employed

58. Richard Anker and J. C. Knowles, "A Micro-Analysis of Female Labour Force Participation in Africa," in *Labour Force,* edited by Standing and Sheehan; and Guy Standing and Glen Sheehan, "Economic Activity of Women in Nigeria," in *ibid.*

59. J. D. Kasarda, "Economic Structure and Fertility: A Comparative Analysis," *Demography* 8(August 1971):307–17. D. B. Holsinger and J. Kasarda, "Education and Human Fertility: Sociological Perspectives," in *Population and Development,* edited by Ridker.

60. In an examination of European data, Elina Haavio-Mannila, "Fertility and Economic Activity of Women in Historical and Cross-National Perspective," Conference on Economic and Demographic Change: Issues for the 1980s (Helsinki: IUSSP, 1978), found that 16 countries had fertility decline with the onset of increased nonagricultural activity for women, while seven did not. See also the articles in Standing and Sheehan, *Labour Force.* On the suggestion that fertility will be higher in those societies where women are mainly concerned with domestic affairs, see Chaudhury, "Female Status."

and the need to separate full-time workers from part-time or intermittent ones.[61] Similarly, the degree of satisfaction with nonworking status must be examined, as there is a widespread assumption that employment outside the home provides women with alternative satisfactions that can compete with child-raising.

The linkage between education and fertility has been termed paradoxical for both researchers and policy makers.[62] While it has probably the strongest negative association with fertility of all the commonly measured variables, some studies have shown, however, that the relationship is positive for women with only a few years of primary education. The correlations which do exist—both negative and positive—have until now remained unexplained. Changing family relationships may be an important intervening explanatory variable however, so the causal mechanism must be adequately specified and submitted to empirical testing.[63]

It may be that the number of years of schooling is simply the most apparent and measurable element in a whole cluster of interdependent forces affecting fertility: that it is not higher education *per se* but other factors with which it is associated such as "openness to new ideas, higher standards of living, exposure to urban environments and a greater range of options and interest outside the home that is responsible for the apparent influence of education on fertility."[64] Higher education for women may influence fertility levels in a number of ways, however, such as delaying the age of marriage, increasing the likelihood of not marrying because of increased aspirations for higher levels of living, increasing interest and involvement in employment and other activities outside the home, and improving the potential capacity to plan and control births.

Education can also trigger off substantial social and spatial mobility, especially for the newly educated. This mobility is likely to have a far-reaching impact upon kinship ties and family relations (as discussed below), which may themselves be the critical links in a chain of change

61. Constantina Safilios-Rothschild, "The Relationship between Women's Work and Fertility: Some Methodological and Theoretical Issues," in *The Fertility of Working Women,* edited by Kupinsky, and idem, "The Relationship between Work Commitment and Fertility," *International Journal of Sociology* 2 (March 1972). On the alternative satisfaction of work outside the home see Judith Blake, "Demographic Science and the Redirection of Population Policy," in *Public Health and Population Change,* edited by Sheps and J. C. Ridley (Pittsburgh: University of Pittsburgh Press, 1965):41–69.

62. See the articles in Ridker, *Population and Development.*

63. Christine Oppong, "A Note on Chains of Change in Family Systems and Family Size," *Journal of Marriage and the Family* (August 1977):615–21.

64. Dixon, "Roles of Rural Women."

in reproductive aspirations and behavior. They may also engender the kind of individualism which could ultimately be critical in fertility control.[65]

Certainly the position that rising levels of education result in lower fertility rates is widely held by population scholars, and many studies have supported this view. Thus, for example, data from Bangladesh have shown education to be inversely related to fertility and positively associated with the practice of contraception, with female education having relatively more effect than male. It is also associated with longer spacing and with earlier use of contraception. However, some multivariate analyses have shown literacy to be only one among a set of variables, such as child survival and access to and availability of land, explaining fertility differentials.[66]

The negative relationship between birth rate and a high proportion of hired labor, as opposed to self-employed and family workers in the active population, indicates that when societies move into a direction where most people are engaged in paid work, mainly outside the home, fertility is likely to drop.

WOMEN'S POSITION IN DIFFERENT TYPES OF SOCIETIES AND LEVELS OF ECONOMIC DEVELOPMENT

Varying attempts have been made to relate modernization or economic development (using such indices as urbanization, societal complexity, industrialization) to the changing comparative equality of sex roles in terms of relative power, the division of labor, influence and authority in the domestic and public domains (insofar as these are separate), and to levels of female reproductive and productive activity. Their outcomes have been conflicting in terms of the directions of change. Feminist anthropologists have recently argued that sexual egalitarianism and female autonomy have been a feature of at least some hunting and gathering societies.[67] This situation has been documented to change drastically with the beginnings of sedentary agriculture.[68] Giele proposed a curvilinear relationship between

65. John C. Caldwell, "The Demographic Implications of the Extension of Education in a Developing Country: Ghana," *Population Studies* (2) (Legon) (1968):90–100.

66. T. Merrick, "Fertility and Land Availability in Rural Brazil," *Demography* 15 (3) (1978).

67. Eleanor Leacock, "Women's Status in Egalitarian Society: Implications for Social Evolution," *Anthropology* 19 (2) (1978).

68. P. Draper, "Kung Women Contrasts in Sexual Egalitarianism in Foraging and Sedentary Contexts," in *Toward an Anthropology of Women*, edited by Reiter.

societal complexity and sex equality—with the intermediate level of societal complexity being the most deleterious to the status of women, a view contradicted by Safilios-Rothschild.[69]

Boserup was one of the first to study on a global scale what happens to women as socially and economically productive members of their communities when a society starts to modernize its agriculture and urban living. Her analysis demonstrated that "development often causes a diminunition of the productivity and the status of women." In the earlier stages of technological development in which families produce and consume their own goods, labor is divided on sex lines which differ from culture to culture. In her study she defined two basic kinds of agriculture, based on the respective roles of women of countries in Asia, Africa, and Latin America. In many parts of Africa (and a few in Asia and Latin America), women do much of the work involved in farming and have as a consequence considerable economic responsibility and independence and freedom of movement.[70]

Boserup characterized male-dominated agricultural areas as those using the plough, draft animals, and hired labor, which may include women. The farmers' wives are often secluded and dependent upon their husbands. In the first type of situation, she argued, development plans and programs favored men, who have in many cases monopolized new agricultural methods and resources. Another tendency has been for jobs in the modern sector to go to men. One problem noted is that of the employment of urban women whose economic productivity may be lost by migrating from the village. Boserup argued that, to prevent further decline in the status and productivity of women with modernization, there is a need for proper education and training. Whereas formerly men and women were economically productive and both sexes were illiterate, now more men than women are learning new skills. Boserup's work and the subsequent studies it stimulated have greatly supported the argument that there must be provision and encouragement of education and job training for women in order to prevent women from becoming or remaining a backward class.

Nash recently reiterated that the position of women has deteriorated in spite of development activities in many parts of the world.[71] The scope of many development programs, she argues, has been narrowed by the

69. Giele, "Women's Roles," and Constantina Safilios-Rothschild, "A Cross-Cultural Examination of Women's Marital, Educational and Occupational Options," *Acta Sociologica* 14 (1–2) (1971).

70. Ester Boserup, *Women's Role in Economic Development* (New York: St. Martin's, 1970).

71. June Nash, *The Integration of Women* (Mexico City: International Women's Year, 1975).

concept of production for profit rather than for the welfare of the population. Stating the situation in microeconomic terms, she writes that "marginal productivity becomes the rationalization for increasing technological substitutes for human labour." As a result of this public and private development agencies fail to invest enough in the subsistence-based rural production mainly sustained by women in Africa, Asia, and some parts of Latin America. In industry, this substitution of capital for labor has meant increases in numbers of unemployed. Even in those countries with equality of access to employment, women often bear the double burden of home care and work.

The industrial revolution involves profound economic and social changes which have triggered off changes in the roles and status of women as well as changes in the three population variables—mortality, fertility, and migration. Although changes were first observed in Europe and North America, as industrialization has moved to other parts of the world, other societies are experiencing them in a variety of ways.

Many scholars agree that at least in Western societies there existed greater equality between men and women before industrialization and urbanization occurred.[72] Indeed, it has been argued that with the transition from a peasant to a rural proletarian community the position of women has deteriorated, both in the absolute sense and in relation to men.[73] A major factor for equality between men and women in peasant societies was the lack of differentiation in economic and familial roles.

In some sectors of the early industrial population women retained, at least among the working class, their dual economic and familial functions. Among other sectors, however, they relinquished it, and it was later demographic changes which made it possible for them to resume an economic role in society, resulting in increasing rates of female labor force participation in industrialized nations in the last few decades.[74]

While attempts have been made to compare women's participation in the labor force in more developed and less developed areas, Nash argues that while overall employment rates reflect the difference between more developed and less developed areas, women's activity rates do not. Women in the working force in the more developed areas are experiencing the same insecurities—the first to be laid off (along with other minorities) and the last to be hired—that women in less developed countries have

72. J. C. Ridley, "The Effect of Population Change on the Roles and Status of Women: Perspectives and Speculation," in *Towards a Sociology of Women,* edited by Constantina Safilios-Rothschild (1972).

73. A. Rubbo, "The Spread of Capitalism in Rural Columbia: Effects on Poor Women," in *Toward an Anthropology of Women,* edited by Reiter.

74. Ridley, "The Effect of Population Change."

experienced for some time. The major differences between more developed centers and less developed periphery are in the extremity of unemployment and the narrow margin of welfare benefits in less developed compared with more developed countries. Another difference is that while women are treated as a reserve labor force in the developed world, in the developing areas a large segment are excluded from any but the most marginal activities. Nash also argues that the variation throughout the world in the participation of women in the labor force depends not so much on the question of developed versus developing countries, but the commitment to a full employment policy versus the treatment of labor as a commodity equivalent to other factors of production and subject to the same fluctuations in demand.[75]

A basic question to be answered in a society is whether there should be social and community support for the welfare and education of the nation's young or whether parents, especially mothers, should solve the problems of reproduction and production on an individual basis. A number of nations, including the USSR and China, have succeeded in mobilizing woman as well as manpower for national development, through establishing training, childcare, health, educational, and recreational institutions at the cost of the community or state. But in most countries women are left to solve their dilemmas of conflicting responsibilities alone or with their husbands and kin; it remains to be seen whether or not countries with economic and political structures different from those of the USSR and China could do the same.[76]

According to comparisons of countries at different stages of development of industrialization (Tables 13.1 to 13.6 above) and at different levels of economic prosperity (measured, for example, by GNP per capita) the labor force participation of women is much less associated with economic development than is women's education and fertility. Only in the tertiary sector of the economy, particularly in clerical and service work, is the proportion of women higher the more economically developed a country is.

The position of women cannot be explained only by the levels of economic development of a country, however, cultural and historical traditions are also important. The influence of the political system can be seen in the high economic activity of women in the socialist countries of Eastern Europe, where the women are more frequently engaged in economic activity than their sisters in Western Europe.[77] The position of women would also seem to be related to some extent to religion. In gen-

75. Nash, *Integration*, p. 166.

76. Cook, *The Working Mother*, p. 65.

77. Haavio-Mannila, "Fertility and Economic Activity"; Boulding, *Handbook*.

eral, the areas of Islamic culture have a tendency to be characterized by low education and low economic activity for women, the African and Asian cultures (excluding Islamic areas) by low education and high economic activity for women, the European cultural area by both high education and high economic activity, and the Latin areas by high education but low economic activity.[78]

THE FAMILY: THE CONTEXT OF PRODUCTION, REPRODUCTION, AND WOMAN'S ROLE

The new emphasis upon the domestic domain of social life in the statements following the World Population Conference, as well as the references to the importance of the domestic context for women's status in the IWY Conference in Mexico have already been mentioned above.[79] At both meetings domestic organization was highlighted as a critical area for investigation and consideration in the design of future programs and research. This emphasis was again apparent in the deliberations of the UNFPA task force.[80]

Family systems of varying types are the primary settings of reproduction and in peasant societies they are also the places of production. Thus family systems have been viewed as social devices for coping with problems of replacement and resource exploitation and as dynamic generators of material and human resources—as depicted in a number of anthropological studies.[81] At the same time, family structure has been seen as the mechanism through which general social values are transferred into action at the interpersonal level.[82] And as has been noted above, it is in

78. For details of this analysis, see Elina Haavio-Mannila and Matti Korteinen, "Demographic, Economic, and Cultural Backgrounds of Women's Work and Education," paper presented at 9th World Congress of Sociology, Uppsala, August 1978.

79. Nash, *Integration.*

80. Cf. also, for example, the statements and discussions of the Ghana National Council on Women and Development in which there are frequent references to the effects of kinship obligations, "extended family" ties, and conjugal duties upon women's roles.

81. Norman B. Ryder, "Fertility and the Family," in *The Study of Population,* edited by Philip Hauser and Otis Duncan (Chicago: University of Chicago Press, 1959); Jack Goody, ed., *The Developmental Cycle in Domestic Groups* (Cambridge: Cambridge University Press, Cambridge Papers in Social Anthropology, no. 1, 1958).

82. Kurt W. Back and Paula Hollerbach Hass, "Family Structure and Fertility Control," in *Psychological Perspectives on Population,* edited by James T. Fawcett (New York: Basic Books, 1973).

their familial roles as daughters, mothers, and wives that women experience the most compelling constraints, preventing them or urging them to take part in productive activities and granting them or withholding from them equal rights and responsibilities with brothers and husbands.

Historical Developments: The Household

Population scholars, in particular economists and demographers, use some common pairs of concepts, based on certain processes of historical development, when analyzing the domestic domain. These pairs of concepts include: *production* and *consumption, work* and *home, work* and *housework, public* and *private,* all of which arose with the coming of capitalism and the separation of people from the means of providing for their own livelihood.[83] When preindustrial, precapitalistic economies are the subject of study these dichotomies no longer apply. In peasant or precapitalist economies *production* and *consumption* are both embedded in the economy of the *domestic group* though not necessarily completely congruent.[84] There is considerable historical data to show the process of change of the separation of the *domestic, private domain* of consumption, reproduction, and women from the *public domain* of men, work, and *breadwinning* and the corresponding development of the role of *housewife:* a role which is virtually unknown in preindustrial, hunting or agricultural economies.[85] These historical data show that in sixteenth-century Europe, just as in much of the developing world today, family life and work were not separate, but part of the same series of activities in the same vicinity. With the movement to capitalism and the removal of economic production from the household, women became increasingly dependent upon their husbands, who did not necessarily have any adequate means to support them.[86] Parallel data may be drawn from the developing world today.[87]

Using historical data from Britain, Hamilton argues that the fundamental changes occurred in the family as a result of *capitalism* not indus-

83. Hamilton, "Liberation."

84. Jack Goody, *Domestic Groups* (Reading, Mass.: Addison-Wesley Modules in Anthropology 28, 1972).

85. Ann Oakley, *Women's Work: The Housewife Past and Present* (New York: Vintage, 1976).

86. Philippe Ariès, *Centuries of Childhood: A Social History of Family Life* (New York: Vintage, 1962).

87. Hamilton, "Liberation."

trialization, just as fundamental changes have been noted to be taking place in areas of the developing world in which there is not necessarily any significant level of industrialization.[88] Leacock has stressed the importance to the development and persistence of capitalistic economic systems of kinship structures based upon economically independent nuclear family units.[89] In these units the male wage earner is supposed to support his dependent wife and children, and within them women are at once a reserve labor force, subject to manipulation by the needs of firms and at the same time an unpaid labor force, providing domestic services to men and socializing and reproducing the next generation of workers.

Significantly, conventional economic theory, developed in the capitalist context of industrial Europe, has assumed two decision-making entities, which are presumed to operate rationally—maximizing their satisfactions or profits. One is the *household,* a unitary concept within which there is assumed to be a conjugal family, with a male head/breadwinner and which is the locus of both consumption and reproduction. The other is the *firm,* the place of production. It is this concept of household which the New Household Economists have been attempting to use in their explanations of differential fertility. The inadequacy of this concept for work in most of the world's cultures has already been discussed at length elsewhere.[90]

Leibenstein has criticized this traditional economists' concept of the household and has chosen to use instead individuals as basic decision-making units.[91] An aspect of the concept of the *household* as used by the New Household Economists which is not supported by historical or contemporary cross-cultural data is the idea that the biological mother is entirely responsible for the socialization and care of her children from birth. Historical and contemporary evidence, however, indicates that full-time motherhood and domesticity were not archaic, premodern, or universal practices. Rather they are the product of a specialization of functions and roles: a modern phenomenon peculiar to a restricted cultural area. The very individualized mother role in Europe and North America (where even maternal relationships established by second marriages are distinguished by special verbal forms) has been contrasted with the diffuseness of the mother-child bonds in households which contain several wife/mother figures, and where there may be a category of women classi-

88. Christine Oppong *et al.*, eds. *Marriage, Parenthood and Fertility in West Africa* (Canberra: Australian National University Press, 1978).

89. Leacock, Introduction, in Saffioti, *Women in Class Society.*

90. See Oppong, "Ghanaian Household Models."

91. Harvey Leibenstein, "Beyond Economic Man: Economics, Politics and the Population Problem," *Population and Development Review* 3 (3) (1977).

fied as "mothers," as, for instance, in African societies.[92] There is an ethnocentric focus upon the single (biological) mother figure in much child development literature written in Europe and North America as well as a corresponding neglect of the roles of nonmaternal child caretakers. Indeed, family settings in which mothers alone care for their young unaided are in fact very unusual, when viewed within a cross-cultural perspective.[93]

Anthropology: Kinship and Domestic Groups

Fortes has pointed out that the preoccupation with the age of first marriage and the tendency to seek economic explanations for demographic facts have obscured what is most important from the anthropological point of view regarding the type of family system taken for granted in the Hajnal model of demographic theory: namely that it is the monogamous, independently co-residential, conjugal, or nuclear family that has been the legal, modal, and social norm in Western Europe since at least the sixteenth century. This is the family type in which the marital relationship is the basic tie, whether or not augmented by collateral relatives, servants, apprentices, and foster children. Some have claimed that it is based on the religious ideology and the sexual morality and procreative ideals of Christianity. Others, including Fortes, would give this type a more ancient historical origin. Certainly the family type of a number of hunting and gathering societies has been classed as nuclear.[94]

The important point made by Fortes is that when demographers and economists and most sociologists write of *the family* this is the model they have in mind. And often there is an associated idea that it is also the ideal, the inevitable, and the most appropriate family form for every modern society. This, however, as Fortes emphasizes, is not how anthropologists see it. Their broader view is based on ethnographic data from a range of global systems, which vary in modes of reckoning descent, residential patterns, kinship terminologies, marriage forms, as well as in domestic organization and patterns of socialization.

92. Harriet Barry, Josephson Lauer, and Catherine Marshall, "Agents and Techniques for Child Training: Cross Cultural Codes 6," *Ethnology* 16 (2) (1977).

93. Jack Goody, *Production and Reproduction: A Comparative Study of the Domestic Domain* (Cambridge: Cambridge University Press, Cambridge Studies in Social Anthropology, no. 17, 1976). Weisner and Gallimore, "My Brother's Keeper." T. Hareven, "Modernization and Family History: Perspectives on Social Change," *Signs* 2 (1) (1976).

94. Meyer Fortes, "Family, Marriage and Fertility in West Africa," in *Marriage, Parenthood and Fertility*, edited by Oppong.

Kinship and Fertility

As MacFarlane has distinguished, there have been two separate strands of arguments attempting to link kinship organization with fertility.[95] On the one hand, there has been a correlation with the so-called "household structure," that is the residential patterns or modes of cohabitation. On the other hand, the latter has been taken as merely one aspect of the total kinship system, including the kinship terminology and method of reckoning descent. Lorimer argued as far back as 1954 that *unilineal descent groups* would be associated with high fertility.[96] Meanwhile, cultures with bilateral kinship systems and lacking the unilineal descent group systems were categorized as being likely to have low fertility, an argument which, as MacFarlane points out, was plausible given the existing facts. Indeed unilineal descent group systems are often characterized by complex residential groupings, so-called *extended families.*[97]

Davis spelled out the reasons why such groups would encourage high fertility, including the fact that the economic cost of child-rearing was spread to a larger set of people than the parents alone—both the costs of material goods and of time and energy.[98] Again in such contexts, since newly married couples are not independent, they may be young at marriage. As MacFarlane admits and others have shown, this was an attractive argument and many have tried, inconclusively, to prove it.[99] Thus Nag, in his analysis of anthropological data attempting to integrate available literature from three disciplines (anthropology, sociology, and demography) regarding the relationships between fertility and several aspects of marriage and kinship, especially in nonindustrialized societies, found that statistical tests did not support the hypothesis that the *extended family* is associated with higher fertility.[100] Nor did the data support the hypothesis that societies emphasizing unilineal corporate descent groups have higher fertility.

95. A. MacFarlane, "Modes of Production," *Journal of Development Studies* 14 (July 1978).

96. Frank Lorimer, *Culture and Human Fertility: A Study of the Relation of Cultural Conditions to Fertility in Non-industrial and Traditional Societies* (Paris: UNESCO, 1954).

97. MacFarlane, "Modes of Production."

98. K. Davis, "International Patterns Favouring High Fertility in Underdeveloped Areas," *Eugenics Quarterly* 2(March 1955):33–39.

99. MacFarlane, "Modes of Production"; Back and Hass, "Family Structure."

100. Moni Nag, "Marriage and Kinship in Relation to Human Fertility," in *Population and Social Organisation,* edited by Moni Nag (The Hague: Mouton, 1975), pp. 11–54.

Shifting to a combination of factors including domestic functions and resources, MacFarlane puts forward a changed hypothesis, which would appear to be much more logically relevant to potential connections between production, reproduction, and family structure. He proposes that, "where the basic unit of production/consumption is the domestic group [that is unit of reproduction and socialization], whether coresidential or operationally united in work and consumption, there fertility will be highly valued." This "peasant" pattern of reproduction and production and consumption is contrasted with the pattern of *individualism* in which the lowest unit engaged in these functions is the individual, not the domestic group, and the kinship system is correspondingly ego centered.[101] Certainly, data collected and analyzed in Ghana over the past decade and testing similar hypotheses combining changes in kin ties, increasing individual responsibilities, and restricted resources have been supportive of such a hypothesis, although in those studies there has been a more specific separation of different types of resources and the additional dynamic of domestic power.[102] Certainly this hypothesis calls our attention to a critically important issue, the congruence of the units of production, reproduction, and consumption and their size and composition in any society under study and points to the necessity for a historical perspective and a time dimension.

Conjugal Relationships

Conjugal affection, marital power, the "strength" of the conjugal bond, conjugal division of labor, sex-role definitions and mores have all been hypothesized in different contexts as influencing family planning and family size aspirations, ideals, and behavior. Stycos pointed to the importance of easy communication between husband and wife, a point which has been taken up in subsequent studies and also related to education.[103]

Again the degree of *segregation* of husband and wife's roles or the strictness of the division of labor between them has been explored in terms of its relationship to fertility norms and behavior. Hypotheses regarding the association between marital power and modes of decision making in relation to demographic and contraceptive innovation have been explored. It has been maintained that more "egalitarian" family sys-

101. MacFarlane, "Modes of Production."

102. Oppong, "Family Type and Size: Some Recent Evidence from Ghana," in R. Ruzicka.

103. J. Mayone Stycos, *Human Fertility in Latin America: Sociological Perspectives* (Ithaca, N.Y.: Cornell University Press, 1968).

tems are a function of "modernism" and have an effect (on fertility) independent or additional to the effects of independent variables such as education.[104] However, "modernization" does not necessarily increase the proportion of "egalitarian" families. They may be rare forms even in industrial societies. Indeed contemporary trends may tend to reduce female power and autonomy leading to a decline in the possibility for such conjugal family forms.[105] Moreover, analysis of varying sets of data from single geographical areas indicates the emergence of multiple family forms associated with the increasingly diverse modes in which individuals are earning a living.

The theory that male-dominant family systems are causally related to high fertility has been proposed several times. Elements of the patriarchal structure thought to be associated with high fertility are husband dominance, the importance of demonstrating male virility in terms of producing male offspring, the separation of males from the costs and burdens of child-rearing, and the limited opportunity for women to experience nondomestic roles.

Dixon has recently reviewed some of the studies indicating that the distribution of decision-making power between husbands and wives shows that the greater the influence the wife has in decision making the more likely it is that husbands and wives communicate with one another about sex, family size desires, and family planning, and the more likely they are to practice effective birth control.[106] For example, Mitchell found that in Hong Kong women are more likely to practice family planning if they have high levels of influence over family decision making, but that if husbands and wives differ in their attitudes towards family limitation, the husband's preferences are most likely to predominate.[107] A UN survey in 1972 of couples in urban India, Iran, the Philippines, and Singapore, found that males dominated family decision making in all four places, especially in the first three.[108] In all four samples the husband-dominated

104. D. Goldberg, "Modernism: The Extensiveness of Women's Roles and Attitudes," *World Fertility Survey Occasional Paper No. 14,* 1974.

105. J. Scanzoni, *Sexual Bargaining Power Politics in American Marriage* (Englewood Cliffs, N.J.: Prentice Hall, 1972).

106. Dixon, "Roles of Rural Women."

107. R. E. Mitchell, "Husband-Wife Relations and Family Planning Practices in Urban Hong Kong," *Journal of Marriage and the Family* 34(February 1972): 139–40.

108. United Nations, *Economic Commission for Asia and the Far East, The Status of Women and Family Planning,* paper prepared for the United Nations Seminar on the Status of Women and Family Planning, Jogjakarta, Indonesia (June 20–30, 1975).

couples were less likely to practice birth control and less likely to talk to one another about sex and family planning than were couples who share decisions. Again Mukherjee, based on a survey of married women in urban and rural areas of three Indian states, showed that women were most likely to know about and practice contraception if they took part in syncratic decisions with their husbands and reported their status in the household to be high.[109] Goldberg has also shown with data from Mexico and Turkey that husband-dominated couples have more live births, expect more children and are less likely to have used contraception than couples among whom both decide or among whom the wife usually or always makes the decisions.[110] Thus Mukherjee and others have suggested that the dominance of men over women and lack of conjugal communication are obstacles to the diffusion of family planning and reduction of fertility.[111]

Given the demonstrated associations between syncratic decision making and the adoption of demographic and contraceptive innovation, attempts have been made to specify the conditions under which syncratic decision making is most likely to occur. Data from some areas have indicated that it is wives whose resources are more nearly equal to those of their husbands, in terms of experience, education, income, and assumption of financial responsibilities, who are most often in *joint* conjugal role relationships and who also have the most egalitarian syncratic relationships.[112] Control over economic resources and education may not be the only necessary conditions, however, as a further relevant resource can be freedom of movement outside the home.[113]

The precise nature of the decision-making unit as well as the decision-making process remain part of the matters pertaining to fertility which require explanation, just as the influence of social norms and pressures and biological factors cannot be discounted from future analysis of the problem.[114]

109. Ramkrishna Mukherjee, "Condensed Report of the Survey of Women and Family Planning India," part II (New Delhi Council for Social Development, 1973, unpublished).

110. Goldberg, "Modernism."

111. Ramkrishna Mukherjee, "Status of Women as Related to Family Planning," *Journal of Population Research* 2(1975):5–33.

112. Goldberg, "Modernism"; Oppong, *Marriage;* Mitchell, "Husband-Wife Relations."

113. Dixon, "Roles of Rural Women."

114. P. McNicoll, "Population and Development: Outlines for a Structuralist Approach," *Journal of Development Studies* 14(July 1978).

The Division of Labor

There is widespread insistence by feminists that equality for men and women demands that men should share equally with women the responsibilities and tasks associated with reproduction and socialization and that women should share in the production and control of economically valuable resources. Rosaldo and Lamphere have argued that societies that do not elaborate the opposition of male and female and that place positive value on the conjugal relationship and the involvement of both men and women in the home seem to be the most egalitarian in terms of sex roles.[115] For, as they point out, when a man is involved in domestic labor, in childcare and cooking he cannot establish an aura of authority and distance. They go on to suggest that men will recognize women as true equals only when they themselves help to raise new generations by taking on the responsibilities of the home.

There is considerable data showing the extent to which women rather than men bear the major part of domestic tasks in both industrialized and rural communities. This inequitable distribution of tasks and responsibilities is one which has been debated hotly in conferences and seminars.[116] The World Conference of International Women's Year recommended that measures should be taken at the national level—including legislation to ensure that in marriage both partners not only perform an active role in the home but also share jointly in domestic decision making.

A recent attempt to clarify types of conjugal family systems with regard to the amount of role support received by wives from their husbands, kin, or other agencies in the performance of household tasks and childcare responsibilities showed that liberation movements have occurred where women are most bereft of supports from all sides and, at the same time, have levels comparative to men of material and intellectual resources.[117] There is also evidence which shows that stress is inevitable among mobile, educated women who try to follow traditional ways of productive and reproductive behavior despite changing socioeconomic

115. Rosaldo and Lamphere, *Woman, Culture and Society*, pp. 14, 39.

116. See UN, Inter-regional seminar on "The Family in a Changing Society."

117. Christine Oppong, "Women's Roles and Conjugal Family Systems," in *The Changing Role of Women in Family and Society: A Cross Cultural Comparison*, edited by J. Lupri (Leiden: Brill, 1979).

contexts in which the traditional supports of high fertility appear to be crumbling.[118]

Sexuality and Emotion

The discussion of fertility rates and of changes in fertility under different conditions has generally omitted the human aspect, particularly the relationship of sexual behavior and human reproduction to attitudes and emotions. The detachment of most studies on fertility may be partly seen as an effect of the predominance of economics and demography in this field of study, and the fact that those two disciplines were developed in societies in which the separation of work and home has already taken place. The role of the family was by then somewhat obscure and family life, intimacy, sexuality, and love came to be seen as totally separated from the economic system. Thus fertility became disassociated with the human factors—love, tenderness, a sense of responsibility to others—that influence it. The considerable variety of precapitalist and preindustrial societies in their ideas about men and women and the proper relationships between them, including love and sexuality, have for several decades been an area for systematic inquiry within the scope of social anthropology.[119] However, little attempt has yet been made to study the relationship between sexual practices, emotional experiences, and human fertility.[120] Even those anthropological studies which have provided the most explicit accounts of sexual behavior have not been found very relevant to the study of fertility.[121]

A recent survey of data from Africa concluded that there was relatively little detailed information on the subject of love and sexuality in contrast to the copious literature on marriage and kinship.[122] A review of data for West African societies noted that there is a singular lack of information on the management of sexual relations. Thus it is, for instance,

118. Christine Oppong, "The Crumbling of High Fertility Supports," in *The Persistence of High Fertility: Population Prospects in the Third World* (Canberra: Australian National University Press, 1977).

119. P. H. Hass, "Family Structure and Fertility Control," in *Psychological Perspectives on Population,* edited by J. T. Fawcett (New York: Basic Books, 1973). Pierre Pradervand, "Why is There No Love in Population?" *Populi* 4 (2) (1977).

120. Moni Nag, "Sex, Culture and Human Fertility: India and the United States," *Current Anthropology* 13 (April 1972).

121. Bronslaw Malinowski, *The Sexual Life of Savages* (London: George Routledge, 1929).

122. W. Bleek, *Sexual Relationships and Birth Control in Ghana: A Case Study of a Rural Town* (Amsterdam: Universiteit van Amsterdam, 1976).

impossible to answer such questions as whether there is any connection between coital frequency in marriage and residential arrangements.[123] Studies of traditional societies in West Africa show that a woman's legal and economic status depends on where the rights of disposal over her reproductive and sexual capacities are lodged. This leads to the question as to the degrees of freedom over their own sexuality exercised by women in different cultural or kinship systems and whether this freedom is correlated with greater freedom with respect to other issues.[124]

There are indications from some cultures that sexual mores which stress feminine modesty, matrimonial fidelity, and jealousy regarding the husband's sexual monopoly affect fertility control. The associated influence of formality, modesty, and avoidance of intimacy—a characteristic which may be required for domestic planning—also seems to be related to fertility.[125] Greek data show the relevance of marital and sexual satisfaction for the practice of birth control and that conjugal love has an extremely significant effect upon the balance of conjugal power.[126]

Motherhood has tended to be viewed as an end to sexuality in some cultures and *mother* and *good woman* may be synonymous.[127] In such social contexts pregnancy and motherhood are likely to help women to feel virtuous and worthy. Children can also provide the affiliation and love which women and men crave. This affiliation and love are often more secure than those arising from marriage, as the latter can be traumatically ended by divorce or widowhood.[128]

CONCLUDING REMARKS

This brief review of a small segment of the relevant literature and the analyses of available quantitative data has underlined several of the emphases initially present in the declarations of the World Population Con-

123. Fortes, "Family, Marriage and Fertility," p. 47.

124. Goody, "Production and Reproduction."

125. Rainwater, *The Poor Get Children;* Stycos, "Human Fertility."

126. Constantina Safilios-Rothschild, "Socio-Psychological Factors Affecting Fertility in Urban Greece: A Preliminary Report," *Journal of Marriage and the Family* 31(August, 1969):595–606; and idem, "A Macro-Micro Examination of Family Power and Love: An Exchange Model," *Journal of Marriage and the Family* (1976).

127. L. W. Hoffman and M. L. Hoffman, "The Value of Children to Parents," in *Psychological Perspectives on Population,* edited by J. T. Fawcett (New York: Basic Books, 1973).

128. Rainwater, *The Poor Get Children.*

ference and of International Women's Year. These include the necessity for a more systematic research focus on demographic processes within the family cycle and the cross-cultural study of family structures, functions, and dynamics in relation to sexuality, reproduction, marriage, and parenthood. They also include the need for more sophisticated and accurate modes of collecting, measuring, and comparing data on aspects of women's positions in different cultures, particularly with respect to their productive contributions.

At each stage of the analysis and discussion, the importance of cultural variation and the necessity for concepts and models that are not culture bound have been stressed. This focus upon the significance of cultural considerations supports the contention that the role of anthropology in population studies is likely to increase in the coming decade, as is the importance of interdisciplinary endeavors. One point seems clear: the changes in concepts and attitudes needed to free research on the domestic domain from cultural bonds will be just as radical as those needed to eradicate sexism from the study of women's roles.

It has been argued that the equality of women and men cannot be achieved through reforms in educational, occupational, or family policies but only through fundamental transformations. Similarly, it has been suggested that only major social changes that would entail the restructuring of incentives and the erosion of familistic values and existing domestic and social structures are adequate to change the fertility of a population. A third argument states that the demographic revolution, just like the sexual revolution, is dependent upon profound changes in personal relationships, especially within the domestic domain.

The most pressing issues of development that have been singled out are the sensitive ones of distribution of wealth, services, and political power—issues often not touched upon in research and programs focusing on development. It is evident that profound social changes affecting relationships between men and women and between family members and community members cannot be undertaken without disruption and social conflict. These kinds of structural modifications would bring about changes in reproductive behavior and women's role in production and opportunity to participate more effectively in development.

Programs have already begun to attempt to meet these various kinds of challenges regarding policy formulation, research, and action on population issues. Thus, for instance, seminars and workshops have been sponsored in which women are participants and not mere targets. Projects are being funded to collect and analyze new and existing basic data on women in order to determine better what women are doing and to promote improved systems as important contributions to development efforts. Interdisciplinary research is also being funded to establish more clearly the intricate interaction between aspects of women's status and demographic issues. The basic precept is being accepted that the social, cultural, and economic profile of a community must be analyzed before an approach to implementing assistance programs can be developed, and it is recognized that a wide range of cultural, social, and economic factors affect demographic issues. With increasing understanding of these factors, policies and programs should be made more responsive to what people need.

14

Human Rights Aspects of Population Programs

DANIEL G. PARTAN

INTRODUCTION

GOVERNMENT POPULATION POLICIES and programs frequently affect the conduct of people in intimate aspects of their lives and therefore inevitably raise questions of their effect upon the "inherent dignity of the human person," from which international human rights concepts are derived.[1] This chapter explores the relationship of human rights standards to population policies and programs in the context of the work of United Nations agencies. It attempts to articulate the extent to which human rights standards bear upon the work of the UN agencies and the ways in which their action might serve to further the "universal respect for, and observance of, human rights and fundamental freedoms" referred to in the Charter of the United Nations.[2]

The chapter begins a survey of the range of standards relevant to the work of UN agencies in the population field. Past discussions of human rights in the context of population policies have tended to emphasize the human rights aspects of family planning. This is perhaps to be expected considering the emphasis placed on family planning in many national popu-

1. The United Nations covenants on human rights, the International Covenant on Civil and Political Rights, and the International Covenant on Economic, Social, and Cultural Rights, state that the rights framed in the covenants "derive from the inherent dignity of the human person." See UN, *Human Rights: A Compilation of International Instruments of the United Nations* (UN Pub. Sales No. E.73.XIV.2, 1973), hereinafter cited as *UN Human Rights Compilation*. The Universal Declaration of Human Rights, adopted by General Assembly Resolution 217 A(III) (1948), states that "recognition of the inherent dignity and of the equal and inalienable rights of all members of the human family is the foundation of freedom, justice and peace in the world."

2. UN Charter, Article 55 (c).

lation programs, and the direct relevance to family planning of human rights standards, but it is nonetheless clear that human rights considerations are relevant to all aspects of population activities. A review of the 1974 World Population Plan of Action[3] shows plainly the pervasiveness of human rights considerations in this field.

The chapter also examines three broad issues that underlie much of the discussion in this field: (1) the legal status of human rights; (2) concepts of "individual rights" as contrasted with "collective rights"; and (3) the relationship between the free will of the individual and coercion by government action. This discussion is followed by a review of specific human rights in the context of population policies and programs and an human rights in the context of national population policies and programs and an exploration of the role of UN agencies in relation to such programs.

HUMAN RIGHTS IN THE WORLD POPULATION PLAN OF ACTION

The World Population Plan of Action recognizes the sovereign right of each nation to formulate and implement its own population policies, acknowledging at the same time that action pursuant to the plan should be consistent with the purposes and principles of the United Nations Charter and with the provisions of the Universal Declaration of Human Rights.[4] In stating the principles upon which it is based, the Plan of Action refers both in general and in specific terms to a wide range of human rights considerations. These are briefly summarized here to show the breadth of the considerations raised, and to indicate the degree to which the consensus supporting the Plan of Action may have embraced specific formulations of relevant human rights.

In the broadest terms, the Plan of Action characterizes the principal aim of socioeconomic development policies, of which population policies are a part, as improving levels of living and the quality of life of the people.[5] While development policies serve socioeconomic objectives, the Plan of Action states that such policies "should be consistent with internationally and nationally recognized human rights of individual freedom, justice, and the survival of national, regional, and minority groups."[6] All

3. See UN, *Report of the United Nations World Population Conference,* 1974 (UN Doc. E/CONF.60/19, Sales No. E.75.XIII.3, 1975), hereinafter cited as *1974 World Population Conference Report.*

4. World Population Plan of Action, para. 14, *ibid.,* pp. 6–7.

5. *Ibid.,* para. 14(a), p. 7.

6. *Ibid.,* para. 14(d), p. 7.

development policies, including population policies, must respect "the dignity of the individual" and seek the "elimination of discrimination in all its forms."[7] Population activities in their entirety, being elements of socio-economic development activities, are thus subject to the full range of relevant human rights considerations.

Some human rights are also mentioned in specific terms. The Plan of Action states that "respect for human life is basic to all human societies."[8] It also states that: "The family is the basic unit of society and should be protected by appropriate legislation and policy."[9] The status of women is given special attention: "Women have the right to complete integration in the development process particularly by means of an equal access to education and equal participation in social, economic, cultural, and political life."[10] The plan calls for action to "promote the status of women" and their "full participation in the formulation and implementation of socio-economic policy including population policies."[11]

Family planning is treated in the most specific terms. The Plan of Action states that: "All couples and individuals have the basic right to decide freely and responsibly the number and spacing of their children and to have the information, education, and means to do so; the responsibility of couples and individuals in the exercise of this right takes into account the needs of their living and future children, and their responsibilities towards the community."[12]

The specific human rights mentioned in the World Population Plan of Action do not exhaust the human rights considerations relevant to population activities. Other rights are embraced by the broad references in the plan to the dignity of the individual, to the human rights of individual freedom and justice, and to human rights expressed in the United Nations Charter and in the Universal Declaration of Human Rights.[13] Human rights relevant to population programs are explored in later sections, in which each such right is discussed in terms of its application to the population field and in terms of the issues on which attention might be expected to be focused in the future.

7. *Ibid.*, para. 14(b), p. 7.
8. *Ibid.*, para. 14(e), p. 7.
9. *Ibid.*, para. 14(g), p. 7.
10. *Ibid.*, para. 14(h), p. 7.
11. *Ibid.*, para. 15(e), p. 9.
12. *Ibid.*, para. 14(f), p. 7.
13. See generally paras. 14 and 15, pp. 6–9.

GENERAL ISSUES

Human Rights as Legal Rights

Discussion of human rights in the population field frequently raises the issue of the legal status of internationally defined human rights. This issue is often framed as a choice between the classification of human rights as legal rights in the sense that governments are obliged under international law to respect such rights, and the classification of human rights as ethical principles to which governments should pay heed, but to which they have no formal legal obligation.[14] Having framed the issue in this way, some commentators are led to inquire into the differences between the various forms in which United Nations definitions of human rights have appeared: multilateral treaties, such as the international covenants on economic, social, and cultural rights, and on civil and political rights; General Assembly declarations, such as the Universal Declaration of Human Rights; and resolutions and decisions adopted by the General Assembly or by other international bodies. In each case the relevant inquiry would be whether and to what extent the rights defined in a particular instrument may be regarded as having become part of general international law. Inquiry should also consider to what extent the rights in question should be regarded as legally binding with respect to particular states or classes of states, such as those that supported or became parties to the instrument, those that abstained or did not participate in the drafting and adoption of the instrument, and those that opposed or voted against the particular right under consideration.

For example, in the population field the basic human right of couples and individuals to determine freely and responsibly the number and spacing of their children has been affirmed several times: in the World Population Plan of Action, in resolutions adopted by the General Assembly and the Economic and Social Council, and in declarations and resolutions adopted by other international bodies.[15] To determine the extent to which such a

14. The legal status of human rights has been the subject of considerable scholarly commentary and debate. For a discussion of human rights in the population field, see Partan, *Population in the United Nations System,* ch. 2, "Human Rights Aspects of Family Planning," and ch. 3, "The Legal Status of the Family Planning Rights," pp. 16–39 (1973).

15. See text note 12 *supra,* and see General Assembly Resolution 2211 (XXI), preamble (1966), and Resolution 2542 (XXIV), "Declaration on Social Progress and Development," Article 4 (1969). See also Resolution XVIII adopted at the UN International Conference on Human Rights at Teheran in 1968. The

right has passed into general international law and has therefore become legally binding on all states, it would be necessary to assess the attitudes of governments toward that right, both in the discussions leading up to the adoption of the instruments articulating the right and in their actual acceptance of obligations to respect that right in the period following its articulation in the international instruments. Generally speaking, since the right in question has been framed in declarations and recommendations rather than in international agreements, its status in international law would depend upon its actual acceptance as a right in the practice of states.[16]

Thus in the population field, as in other fields in which human rights bear upon government action, the legal status of particular rights will require careful investigation and will present controversies that are not easily laid to rest. In this context, what is the proper role for UN agencies?

Two points are clear. First, UN agencies will not be in a position to determine whether with regard to particular states particular individual human rights have become legally binding in the sense of imposing obligations on such states under international law. In the present status of international relations, authoritative determinations of this nature are only rarely made and depend for their validity on the consent of the states involved. Second, however, UN agencies need not resolve the legal status issue to obtain policy guidance from international human rights standards. The role of UN agencies is to determine what they will support as elements of national population programs, not to assess the conformity of national policy and action with international law. In carrying out this task, UN agencies may properly seek guidance in international human rights standards expressed in United Nations instruments, whether or not such standards have acquired the status of legally binding rights in international law.

To return to the example of the human right to determine the number and spacing of children, since such a right has been endorsed by the General Assembly and has been enunciated as one of the principles underlying the World Population Plan of Action, the right should be respected by UN agencies whether or not that right is properly termed a legal right binding upon states. Such respect for the family-planning right would flow from the policy guidance given by the General Assembly and the World Population Plan of Action. It would not necessarily imply that the

---

three resolutions cited are reprinted in UNFPA, *The United Nations and Population: Major Resolutions and Instruments,* pp. 81–82, 53, and 50–51, respectively (1974).

16. See Partan, *Population in the United Nations System,* ch. 3, pp. 30–39 (1973).

right is a legal right that must be honored by states in formulating and implementing their own population programs.

Three tasks fall to UN agencies in utilizing international human rights standards for policy guidance. First, as will be shown by the discussion of specific rights, many human rights standards are not entirely clear in their fore, undertake to stimulate discussion of such standards, leading to their clarification and elaboration in the context of UN agency programs. Second, UN agency programs should seek to support the realization of relevant human rights standards through the medium of national population programs. This can be done by favoring in the allocation of UN agency funds the support of activities that will bring about progressive realization of human rights as defined in the relevant United Nations instruments. Third, although as shown above, the UN agencies will not be able to characterize as contrary to international obligation particular national practices that run counter to internationally defined human rights, they will be justified in regarding such practices as inconsistent with UN policies founded on human rights. Therefore, UN agencies may view programs founded upon such policies as ineligible for their assistance. In this way UN agencies will both support actions that further human rights and withhold their support from actions that impair respect for human rights. In both cases the human rights standards that thereby become part of UN agency programs will be drawn from United Nations instruments defining the rights in question as human rights. In neither case will it be necessary to show that such rights have become legal rights binding on states under international law.

Individual Rights and Collective Rights

The balancing of individual rights to freedom of action against the rights of society or the state to restrain individual action in the interests of the people as a whole is a characteristic of human rights in general as well as of human rights in the population field. This balancing is sometimes referred to in terms of responsibility: it is said that the individual has the responsibility of considering the needs of society as a whole in making the choices that are embraced by the individual's rights. Responsibility in this sense does not rest solely with the individual; society, acting through the government, may constrain individual choices in ways required to protect its collective rights.

The idea of individual responsibility is expressed in the preamble in both United Nations human rights covenants in the following terms: "the individual, having duties to other individuals and to the community to which he belongs, is under a responsibility to strive for the promotion and observance of the rights recognized in the present Covenant."[17]

In one sense the idea of collective rights merely indicates that the individual right is not absolute: all rights exist within society and must reflect the needs of the society as a whole as well as the needs of the individual. In this sense the collective right is the limit on the individual right, flowing from the needs of the society. There are many examples of limits of this nature in which governments are regarded as justified in taking action to limit the exercise of individual rights in order to safeguard the rights of others or the interests of society as a whole.[18]

In another sense, the concept of collective rights takes on more vitality as an affirmative right of society to condition the exercise of individual rights. Under such a concept the government would appear to have a greater directive role, shaping the exercise of individual rights to serve the collective ends of society as a whole, rather than merely restraining individual choice when needed to prevent damage to the interests of society. Collective rights in this wider sense may not be inconsistent with human rights contained in international instruments (see the discussion in later section on population distribution and internal migration). The individual rights framed in such documents, however, generally appear to put the interests of the individual ahead of those of the state, leaving to the latter the capacity to protect the collective rights of society only when individual freedom of choice threatens damage to those rights.

In either case, however, a major difficulty for the external observer, such as a UN agency, interested in promoting respect for specific human rights, is that judgments as to the needs of society must be made in each society by the government of that society. In the absence of special agreement, no international institution is competent to weigh the needs of the individual against the collective needs of society as determined by the government of that society.

One example is the individual's right "freely and responsibly" to determine the number and spacing of children. It has been observed that the word responsibly may imply the collective right of society to achieve a balance between population size and resources.[19] If so, the question is:

17. See note 1 *supra*.

18. The International Covenant on Civil and Political Rights provides explicitly in Article 4, para. 1, that: "In time of public emergency which threatens the life of the nation . . . , the States Parties to the present Covenant may take measures derogating from their obligations under the present Covenant," subject to certain limitations.

19. See, e.g., UN Doc. E/CONF.60/SYM.IV/3, "United Nations Standards concerning the Relationship between Human Rights and Various Population Questions," paras. 9–34 (1974).

may the government impose measures to limit family size in order to assure that the free exercise of the individual's rights will not threaten society, that is, that the individual's rights will be exercised "responsibly" as well as "freely"? Whether measures of this nature are seen, essentially, as measures of last resort, imposed to ward off impending damage to society, or as measures designed to guide and set a framework for the exercise of individual rights, it is the government that must make the judgment and take the necessary action. In the present state of international relations, that decision will not be subjected to international review.

What, in this context, is the proper role for UN agencies? Three types of action might be possible in connection with their assistance to national population programs.

First, the UN agencies might seek to stimulate discussion of the relationship between the rights of the individual and the needs of society to clarify in particular contexts the role of the government in its exercise of collective rights. This task is similar to the task of seeking greater clarity in human rights standards as they bear upon population programs generally.

Second, while working with governments on the formulation of their national population programs, the UN agencies might focus attention on the human rights aspects, to assure that action restricting individual rights is not taken without first exploring all available alternatives.

Third, in extreme cases where the UN agencies might disagree as to the need for particular restrictive measures, they might decline to support such measures as part of the national population program, citing human rights as the basis for its action.

Individual Free Will Subjected to Government Coercion

In addressing the need for government programs to provide family-planning guidance, information, and services, Resolution XVI of the World Population Conference, entitled "Population Policies," offers three guidelines for such programs: "(1) that they [family-planning programs] are carried out with absolute respect for the fundamental rights of the human being; (2) that they preserve the dignity of the family; and (3) that no coercive measures are used."[20] The three guidelines were stated by the conference in the context of family-planning programs but can be applied as well to other aspects of population policies. All such policies should give "absolute respect" to fundamental human rights and to the "dignity of the family" as protected under international human rights standards. Whether "coercive measures" may be used, however, appears to be gov-

20. *1974 World Population Conference Report,* pp. 43–44.

erned by the meaning given to the concept of coercion, and by the impact expected from the particular coercive measures on the fundamental human rights to which "absolute respect" must be given.

It has been pointed out that all rights, including human rights, exist within society, and that even basic human rights are conditioned in their exercise on respect for the needs of others, expressed as respect for the needs of society.[21] Examples relevant to the population field include compulsory sterilization for eugenic reasons, epitomized in the United States by Mr. Justice Holmes's statement that "three generations of imbeciles are enough." Other examples include restrictions on marriage, such as minimum age and health and education requirements, and restrictions on freedom of movement or residence made necessary by public decisions concerning land use or population redistribution. In each case, "absolute respect" for the human rights involved does not mean that the rights are in themselves absolute. The scope and meaning of each right are structured by the human values held by the people, which are in themselves influenced by the needs of society. To assess free will as opposed to coercion it is therefore necessary to examine both the traditions of individual liberty and the concepts of individual responsibility as part of a dynamic process that will effectively protect individual rights while serving the needs of society.

Returning to free will and coercion in the family-planning context, it is clear that in this field traditions of individual liberty are quite strong and will not easily give way through government coercion to accomplish government-determined goals reflecting a society's need to reduce rates of population growth. Indeed, the objective of recent efforts has been to enlarge individual freedom through removing restrictions on access to fertility control information and means. While it is true that the effect of such changes has sometimes been a reduction in fertility, and that to some extent change of this nature has been motivated by society's need to reduce fertility, it remains true that free access to the knowledge and means needed for family planning is most often considered as a measure designed to promote freedom of choice. Undoubtedly, it is considerations of this kind that led the World Population Conference to couple its call for respect for human rights with the stricture that no coercive measures be used in family planning programs.

What of the future? If, in some societies, population growth should threaten the well-being of the society, impairing the quality of life for all,

21. See note 19 *supra,* and *Human Rights and Population: Proceedings of the Second Annual Meeting of the International Advisory Committee on Population and Law,* Tokyo, 1972. See also *Report of the Symposium on Population and Human Rights,* UN Doc. E/CONF.60/CPB/4 (1974).

would it be consistent with human rights standards to impose fertility restrictions such as a limit to the number of children for each couple or each individual?

Leaving aside the practical problems posed by restrictions of this nature, the question seems to be whether, when persuasion fails, the individual's right to free choice in determining the number and spacing of children must give way to the presumed need of society to limit population growth. In other words, having done everything possible to induce voluntary restraint in population growth, may the government, as legitimate determiner of the interests of society as a whole, use coercion to accomplish the goal of lowered population growth, or, indeed, of a stationary population size, or even of a reduced population size?

Several important issues are raised by this question. They are explored here to show the way in which free will and coercion may be balanced in population programs.

First, the question implies that the government's articulated population size goals can be attained only through the imposition on the individual of absolute limits on the number of children that the individual may have. While it is true that each additional child adds to total population size, it may not be true that the only, or the best, way to attain overall goals as to population size is to prevent those who may desire larger families from having more children. So many factors affect fertility, and fertility determinants are so poorly understood, that it may not today be possible to assert with any assurance that individual family size limits are required if population size goals are to be attained.[22] If, before restricting the individual's freedom to determine the number and spacing of children, a government must exhaust other means of controlling population growth, coercive measures may not be justified in the present state of knowledge, and it is not clear at what point such measures would be justifiable in the near future.

Second, assuming that a government has tried all available methods of persuasion and has done what it can to influence the values bearing on choice of family size, and that, nonetheless, population growth and size continue to exceed the norm sought by the government, two conflicting attitudes are possible. The first attitude is that the government would then be justified in restricting through coercive measures the right to free choice in family size. Second, in contrast, it might be said that the unwillingness of the people to change their values and actions to meet government population size goals casts doubt on the validity of those goals. If, having full

22. See, e.g., *Report of the Symposium on Population and the Family,* UN Doc. E/CONF.60/CPB/2 (1973).

knowledge of the consequences of their actions, and enjoying free access to the means required for fertility control, sufficient numbers of people reject the suggested limit on family size so as to jeopardize overall population growth and size goals, perhaps the goals themselves must be reevaluated rather than coercion used to impose those goals on an unwilling people.

Third, the issue just stated raises the question of participation by the people in setting population policy, which is related to the question of whether all avenues have been exhausted in the effort to influence fertility. Is it reasonable to assume that if the people, in fact, effectively participate in setting population goals the goals will be met without resort to coercion?

The difficulty in relying upon the informed individual's freedom of action to meet society's population size goals is that accomplishing such goals will require only that the average number of births per family fall to the point at which total population can conform to the desired numbers, not that every family remain below a specified family size. Allowing larger families for some individuals and not others as a result of free choice may lead to a failure to achieve the overall goal even though that goal has the support of the majority. Thus in some cases the failure of a minority to conform to the needs of society will threaten the accomplishment of the overall goal, and discretion must be exercised in balancing the collective needs of society against the needs of the individual as reflected in unwillingness to accept norms required by societal population goals.

Fourth, it seems clear that free access to all necessary family planning knowledge and means should be assured before resorting to coercive measures that may impair human rights. Presumably, this would mean that in addition to the usual contraceptive measures, people should have access to postconception fertility control measures, and perhaps to abortion where that is required for effective exercise of freedom of choice in limiting family size. It would appear arbitrary and unfair to impose coercive fertility control measures in a context in which limits have been placed on access to voluntary measures. As noted above, this factor is also important in comparing restraints on individual freedom with actions of society as a whole. Why should individuals lose their freedom to choose a larger family if the societal problem of overcrowding results in part from restrictions on fertility control measures actually made available to all people in the society?

Finally, it has been assumed up to this point for purposes of discussion that the coercive nature of the measures to limit fertility has been clearly established. The most discussed example is compulsory sterilization. The question in this case is: when is a sterilization program compulsory or coercive in the sense condemned by the World Population Conference

Resolution quoted above, and when should such a program be regarded as persuasive but not coercive? As will be shown in the discussion of incentives and disincentives later in the chapter, the line between persuasion and coercion is not always clear. Depending in particular upon the economic situation of the individual and the alternatives available, government benefits offered as incentives may sometimes be coercive, and the withdrawal or withholding of government benefits may be even more clearly coercive. Each case calls for its own close analysis, with all factors taken into account.

The issues raised in relation to free will and coercion in the family-planning context can be applied in other areas of population programs. Population redistribution is an example. As will be shown later in the section on population distribution and internal migration, pertinent questions are: Can the government's goals be accomplished by measures short of the use of coercion to relocate individuals against their will? Have the people participated in formulating the population redistribution scheme? Do they have all the information necessary for an informed choice? Should the government measures involved be regarded as coercive rather than merely as persuasive? Where incentives and disincentives are used, has a proper balance been achieved between the needs of the individual and the needs of society? Where, notwithstanding careful attention to such issues, urgent population redistribution goals are not met, the government may in some circumstances consider itself justified in resorting to coercive measures to accomplish such goals even though the measures chosen may impair the individual's right to freedom of movement.

HUMAN RIGHTS STANDARDS IN THE POPULATION FIELD

For the purposes of this discussion, international human rights standards can be divided into two classes: those that seek to guarantee or to protect individual freedoms, and those that contemplate the provision of government benefits or services to enable individuals more fully to enjoy their human rights. The two types of rights appear to raise different issues in the context of population programs and are therefore discussed separately in the sections that follow. In each case, the emphasis is on the relationship between human rights and government action in population programs, and on the extent to which the rights in question may affect the work of UN agencies.

In the case of rights involving the provision of government benefits or services, UN agency assistance would generally be designed to help the government attain the realization of the right in question. Three issues might be raised in the context of such assistance. First, considering the demands made upon agencies' funds, what priority should be assigned to assistance designed to secure realization of a particular human right? Second, to what extent, if any, does the government program for which agencies' assistance is sought incorporate limits on the services or benefits involved that would in effect secure less than the full realization of the right in question? Third, would the program for which agencies' assistance is sought discriminate among recipients of government services or benefits in such a way as to conflict with international standards of nondiscrimination? These issues are addressed in the section that follows.

In the case of individual freedoms as contrasted with rights to government services or benefits, the issues go beyond priorities, balance, and nondiscrimination. In such cases the program for which UN agency assistance is sought may involve restrictions on the rights involved, raising questions as to whether such assistance would help in the realization of such rights or would in fact contribute to a diminution of respect for human rights. Cases of this latter type can be expected to present the most difficult problems for UN agencies in their efforts to promote awareness of, and respect for, international human rights standards.

RIGHTS TO GOVERNMENT BENEFITS AND SERVICES

Population policies affect, and are affected by, a broad range of economic and social rights which are thereby made relevant to the work of UN agencies. In the broadest sense, all or almost all economic and social standards have some bearing on population. Population policies, including policies as to population size, growth rates, and distribution, bear indirectly but importantly upon the quality of life enjoyed by people in the society. Each such policy is directly related to development and to the scale of the resources that can be devoted to achieving economic and social standards that form the basis for enjoyment by the individual of improvements in the quality of life.[23]

Furthermore, a review of the specific rights articulated in the International Covenant on Economic, Social and Cultural Rights shows in many cases a direct relationship to population policies. For example, rights to protection and assistance for the family, and to an adequate standard of living, including adequate food, clothing, and housing, require expenditure of government resources that may be clearly related to the core population

23. See, e.g., *Report of the Symposium on Population and Development,* UN Doc. E/CONF.60/CPB/1 (1974).

policy areas of fertility, mortality, and migration. The same is true of rights to education, to employment and technical and vocational training, to social security, to adequate nutrition, and to the highest attainable standard of physical and mental health.[24] In each case the resources that can be devoted to fulfillment of such rights are affected by the overall development policies of the government, of which population policies are a part. Furthermore, each of the economic and social rights mentioned above itself affects population policies, since its relative degree of realization affects and is affected by the individual's choice of family size. Thus there is in each society a complex interdependence between economic and social policies and population policies, in which population policies affect the achievement of economic and social rights, and in which levels of achievement of such rights affect the achievement of population policy goals.

In view of the interrelationship between population policies and economic and social rights, UN agency assistance may be designed to help to achieve economic and social goals, thereby contributing to the success of the country's population program. Agency assistance of this nature can be expected to raise three kinds of issues: (1) issues of priorities in the allocation of agency resources in economic and social programs; (2) issues of completeness and of balance in the realization of the rights in question; and (3) issues of nondiscrimination in access to the government services and benefits involved in such programs.

Priorities in Allocating UN Agency Resources

The issue of priorities in assistance programs is always complex and may involve many variables, but it does not require special treatment from the human rights point of view. Rights to government services and benefits are interrelated, but such rights are not framed in a hierarchical structure in which particular sets of such rights are regarded as entitled to precedence in relation to other such rights.

In a recent publication entitled *Priorities in Future Allocation of UNFPA Resources,*[25] it is acknowledged that the term "population activities" may broadly encompass everything related to the determinants and consequences of population change, but that UNFPA resources should be devoted primarily to supporting "the population aspects of development, defined as the causes, conditions and consequences of changes in fertility,

24. International Covenant on Economic, Social, and Cultural Rights, Articles 8, 11, 12, and 13.

25. UNFPA, *Reports and Documents* (1) (1978).

mortality, and mobility as they affect developmental propects and the human welfare resulting therefrom."[26] In this light, the primary role of the UNFPA would be to support activities aimed at "bringing about a fuller understanding of the population aspects of development and at influencing population factors through the formulation and implementation of policies concerning the size, growth, and structure and distribution of population, to improve levels of living and quality of life."[27]

In response to the need to focus use of its scarce resources within the broad field of population activities, the UNFPA has articulated a "core program of assistance" that embraces the following areas: "basic population data collection and analysis, population policy formulation and implementation including family planning and population redistribution, population education and training, and applied research."[28] The main emphasis in the core program is given to population policy formulation and implementation. This will not be an inflexible boundary, but support outside the core program is expected to be limited to related activities such as the following: "expansion and strengthening of maternal and child health delivery systems; adaptation of regional, rural, and community development programs to include population elements; and measures to deal with spatial distribution of population, including urbanization."[29]

As has been noted, the UNFPA core program framework flows from the Fund's assessment of the most pressing population needs, not from any ranking of the human rights considerations involved. Indeed, no such ranking can be derived from the United Nations instruments or from discussions underlying the various rights to government benefits and services under discussion here. Such rights are certainly interrelated. For example, rights to employment and to social security are frequently tied in practice to rights to medical care, in that medical care services may be provided in conjunction with employment or social security benefits. In addition, in a broader sense, rights to benefits or services of this kind are competitors for shares in a finite public purse. Nonetheless, no effort has been made or could be made to determine on a universal scale which of these rights is to be preferred to the others. Choices of this nature are left to the government exercising the sovereign rights of the state in the light of its economic and social system and of its judgment as to the needs to its people.[30]

26. *Ibid.*, p. 12. The quoted language is drawn from the Final Report of the UNFPA/UN Interregional Consultative Group of Experts on the World Population Plan of Action, UN Doc. UNFPA/WPPA/20/Rev.1.

27. *Ibid.*, pp. 12–13.

28. *Ibid.*, p. 13.

29. *Ibid.*, pp. 13–14.

30. The World Population Plan of Action is founded upon the premise that: "The formulation and implementation of population policies is the sovereign right of

As can be seen in the UNFPA core program framework, human rights considerations are essentially neutral in the choice of priorities, leaving it to the governments and the UN agency concerned to determine whether in a particular context to prefer support for one set of government services and benefits to another. Thus there remain for consideration the issues of completeness or balance in the services or benefits provided, and of nondiscrimination in access to such services or benefits.

Limitations on Government Services or Benefits

Two types of limitations on government services or benefits appear to be relevant to programs in the population field. First, in the family-planning area in which couples and individuals have the right to the "education and means" necessary to practice family planning[31] some governments may be willing to provide some types of education or means, but not others. Thus programs designed by such governments might support the partial but not the complete realization of the right to government services and benefits in the field of family planning. Second, in the area of the provision of government services or benefits generally, some governments may wish to condition access to some benefits, such as education or housing, on the willingness of the recipient to conform to government-prescribed family planning norms. In both cases the question for UN agencies is: should agency assistance be made available to support such programs notwithstanding the fact that their result will be less than full realization of the rights in question?

Where, as in the family-planning "education and means" example, governments might support some measures but not others, two factors likely to be present in most such cases appear to indicate that UN agency support need not be withheld from such programs.

First, the major reason leading a government to be willing to support some education and means measures but not others is likely to be disagreement as to whether the disapproved measures fall within the education and means right. For example, some have said that abortion should be considered a legitimate means of family planning that should be supported by government assistance programs, while others consider that in most circumstances abortion should not be supported by the government. Where the means in question is subject to such differences of opinion, the UN

---

each nation . . . to be exercised in accordance with national objectives and needs and without external interference." *1974 World Population Conference Report*, para. 14, p. 6.

31. See *ibid.*, para. 14(f), p. 7, quoted in the text note 12 *supra*.

agencies would not be in a position to resolve the issue or to require that governments accept a particular view of the legitimacy of abortion as a means of family planning.

Second, even where such differences of opinion do not exist, it must be remembered that resources are limited, and that neither governments nor UN agencies will be able to assure in all cases that fully adequate family-planning means are in fact made available to all persons. Choices must be made, and it is the role of the government to make such choices. In such cases, governments exercise national sovereignty but may be assisted by UN agencies within the limits of resources and of their core program priorities.

In general, subject to careful review in each case, UN agencies may take the view that partial achievement of particular human rights standards would be beneficial and thus worthy of their support, notwithstanding the unwillingness of the government to provide the services required for full realization of such rights.

Incentives and Disincentives

More difficult issues are presented when governments seek to condition receipt of government services or benefits on acceptance of official policies. Prominent examples occur in the areas of family planning and of population redistribution. In both areas some governments have sought to accomplish policy goals by offering special advantages to persons who act in accordance with a desired policy (incentives) or by limiting or reducing government services or benefits to those who fail to conform to such a policy (disincentives). Considering that the government services or benefits involved (such as education, housing, employment, or medical care) are aspects of human rights in economic and social fields, what should be the attitude of UN agencies towards support of such programs?

Examples of incentives in the family-planning field include cash payments or increased medical or social security benefits made available to persons who accept sterilization or who show records of no births over a specified time period. Examples of disincentives include reductions in the usual social security benefits or exclusions from public employment or from public housing for persons whose families exceed a certain number of children, or who, having attained a specified family size, refuse to undergo sterilization. Disincentive programs might also include the exclusion from public education benefits of, for example, the fourth child and later children, or a progressively increasing scale of accouchement fees depending upon the number of children already born to the mother.

Examples of incentives in the population redistribution field include cash payments or the provision of public employment, or access to farm land or to public housing made available to persons willing to relocate in new towns or in underpopulated areas. Examples of disincentives include the removal from public welfare assistance rolls, or the exclusion from public employment or from public housing, of persons who decline transfer to such areas.

One answer to the problem of proper UN agency role in such programs might attempt to distinguish incentives from disincentives. The argument might be that although the withdrawal or the withholding of government services or benefits from persons who fail to conform to the desired policy would raise issues of unfair discrimination and of improper coercion, the government should have unhampered discretion to allocate new or additional resources to incentives designed to influence individual choice in the service of society as a whole. The line thus drawn would mean the continuation of existing services and benefits for most people in a substantially static condition, with opportunities for change or improvement being used to accomplish the government's population policy goals through incentives provided to those who are willing to act in accordance with that policy.

Although in some circumstances the distinction suggested may be sound and will avoid issues of the human rights impact of disincentive programs, under other circumstances there may be too fine a line between incentives and disincentives to indicate which is sound and which is unsound policy. For example, the provision of jobs, housing, and other benefits in a new town for those willing to make the move would certainly appear to be proper as a government choice in the allocation of resources designed to accomplish the redistribution of population. In contrast, the removal from government assistance rolls of persons who decline such transfer would raise issues of improper coercion impairing the free exercise of the human right to freedom of movement and of residence, as discussed in a later section on changing concepts of human rights.

Taking an example from the family-planning field, there is a question as to whether it should make a difference whether persons with too large a family by the official standard are excluded from public housing or from public employment, as contrasted with the incentive concept in which public housing or public employment is made available to those who keep their family size within the officially sanctioned bounds. In either case the effect is the same: the public housing or employment benefit is reserved to those who serve the presumed public interest in moderating the rate of population growth. It should make no difference in evaluating such a policy whether it is termed one of incentives or one of disincentives chosen to attain the desired end.

The suggested distinction between incentives and disincentives leads to difficulties in another respect. Since the distinction would result in the channeling of new resources to the incentive programs, rather than to programs benefitting all persons equally, the result will be to favor certain groups over others, and in some cases to advance the enjoyment of economic and social rights by the favored groups while leaving others with few or no benefits in the areas involved. Where resources are limited, and where levels of government services and benefits are not high, the incentives provided to the favored groups may be indistinguishable in effect from the discrimination and coercion that use disincentives to attain the same ends. In other words, in conditions of extreme deprivation, incentives may appear to be just as discriminatory and as coercive as disincentives. In such circumstances both types of programs should be judged by the same standard.

Discrimination in Incentive and Disincentive Programs

The discriminatory and coercive elements of disincentive programs, which as shown above may also affect incentive programs, raise two kinds of questions: Does the discrimination inherent in such programs conflict with the international human rights standard calling for the "elimination of discrimination in all its forms"?[32] Second, considered in the context of conditions in the society for which it is proposed, would the discrimination and coercion inherent in the program so impair respect for human rights as to make it unwise or improper for UN agencies to support the program?

The statement of both issues implies a balancing of the needs of society as reflected in the government's formulation of the disincentive—or incentive—program, against the need to achieve full realization of the human rights affected by the program. It should be remembered that the rights under discussion here are rights to government benefits and services in the economic and social fields, not the individual liberties or personal freedoms discussed in the next section. Whatever might be said about the latter rights, it seems clear that a balancing of the individual's position against the needs of society must always occur in setting priorities for government support of programs in the economic and social field. It is also clear that it is the government that must undertake the required balancing: although UN agency aid will be available in policy formulation and other

32. UN Charter Article 55(c) mandates United Nations promotion of "human rights and fundamental freedoms for all without distinction as to race, sex, language, or religion."

activities as needed, the program is defined and carried out by the government. As was stated in the World Population Plan of Action, the "main responsibility for national population policies and programmes lies with the national authorities."[33]

Thus it can be seen that the evaluation of disincentive proposals, and of some types of incentive proposals, calls for a sensitive inquiry into the need for such measures in relation to national policy goals and to the expected impact of such measures on the realization of human rights to economic and social benefits and services. The inquiry relates more to the wisdom and appropriateness of incentive and disincentive measures in relation to the goals of the society than it does to the propriety of such measures in the legal sense. Having the task of choosing priorities and of allocating resources, the government must have discretion to shift its resources in such a way as to serve the policy interests it has defined. In making such choices, however, the government should consider the human rights impact, and should be sensitive to the need to advance respect for international human rights standards as they affect all of its people.

There is little more that can be said at the level of general principle. The protection of human rights in economic and social fields results from a series of decisions on resource allocation made in each society in accordance with its needs and its resources. Support for favored groups will always result in "discrimination" in their favor; support for those willing to carry out government policies will always "coerce" others into acceptance of those policies. Whether a government's choices in this regard are sound is a question of judgment that must first be answered by the government itself in the light of relevant international policies, including human rights policies. The role of UN agencies should be to assure by their review and consultation with the government that human rights policies are, in fact, fully considered, so that the government's choices will be responsive to the human rights needs of all of its people.

Within this general framework, a few specific observations can be made. First, in considering programs in societies in which there has been little progress in some areas, such as in education or in health care, linking major government benefits to family-planning norms might be strongly coercive and discriminatory, raising questions of proper balance between family planning and other goals. This is not to say that such incentives and disincentives may not be strong; it is to say that attention must be given to meeting minimum needs of all people together with the use of incentives and disincentives designed to accomplish family-planning goals.

Second, in planning disincentive programs, the choice of measures

33. *1974 World Population Conference Report,* para. 14, p. 6.

affecting children's rights raises difficult issues. For example, considering the needs of society and of the individuals involved, it may not be sensible to exclude the "fourth child" from educational opportunities made available to children generally. Even if such measures could be shown to foster effective family planning, which may be doubted, the burden would ultimately fall upon the child. Although the child had been given no opportunity for choice in the matter of its conception, the child would suffer the burden of exclusion from access to government benefits.

Third, with regard to government planning of disincentive programs, it may be necessary to protect community expectations that particular services or benefits provided in the past will be continued in the future. In the case of government employment, for example, although there may be no right to continue in the job, it would seem harsh and highly punitive to discharge employees on the birth of the fourth child, in contrast to offering preference in employment or in advancement to persons who have maintained a smaller family size.

Finally, community perceptions of justice and of propriety in particular incentive and disincentive programs will be affected by the degree to which such measures are seen to be rationally related to the goals sought by the government. Jobs, housing, and medical care in new towns, for example, clearly relate directly to the goal of developing the new settlement. Enhanced social security benefits for persons having small families also clearly relate to the goal of controlling population growth. Exclusion of the "fourth child" from educational benefits, or denial of nutrition services to children of large families, would be less clearly related to population growth rates, and for that reason may be both less effective and less likely to be accepted as an appropriate government choice in the allocation of resources.

INDIVIDUAL FREEDOMS

This section discusses international human rights standards of individual freedoms in the core population areas of fertility, mortality, and mobility. Unlike the preceding section, which discussed the considerations affecting government choice in the allocation of funds in economic and social areas, this section focuses on individual rights to freedom of action, asking in each case the extent to which the right has been clearly articulated in international instruments and the extent to which its free exercise may be restricted by the government for the purpose of accomplishing national population policy goals.

The order in which individual freedoms are discussed is not intended to imply an order of importance; as with human rights in the economic and social fields, international instruments do not rank individual freedoms in order of importance.

The Right to Life

Article 3 of the Universal Declaration of Human Rights and Article 6, paragraph 1, of the International Covenant on Civil and Political Rights define in general terms the "right to life." The Universal Declaration states that "everyone" has the right to life; the International Covenant states that "every human being" has the "inherent" right to life. No distinction appears to have been intended by the different formulations used in the two instruments.

In the case of each instrument, efforts were made at the drafting stage to add language to the effect that the right to life applies "from the moment of conception."[34] In both cases the proposed amendments were rejected, but their rejection was not regarded as expressing a view on the controversial problem of abortion. In light of this, it seems clear that the concept of a right to life cannot be taken as a solution to the abortion issue in United Nations practice.

Two regional instruments are relevant in considering the meaning of the right to life in relation to abortions. The European Convention for the Protection of Human Rights and Fundamental Freedoms provides in Article 2, paragraph 1, that: "Everyone's right to life shall be protected by law."[35] There is no reference in the convention to the point at which a person's life begins. The American Convention on Human Rights provides in Article 4, paragraph 1, that the right to life "shall be protected by law and, in general, from the moment of conception."[36] The words "in general" appear to reduce the scope of the moment of conception language, but there is otherwise no indication of the intended relationship between abortion and the right to life.

In addition, Article 6, paragraph 5, of the Covenant on Civil and Political Rights provides that the death sentence "shall not be carried out

34. See *United Nations Standards concerning the Relationship between Human Rights and Various Population Questions,* UN Doc. E/CONF.60/ SYM.IV/3, paras. 38–41 (1974).

35. Convention for the Protection of Human Rights and Fundamental Freedoms, signed in Rome, November 4, 1950, 213 U.N.T.S. 221.

36. American Convention on Human Rights, signed at San José, Costa Rica, November 22, 1969, OAS Treaty Series, No. 36.

on pregnant women." While some have inferred from this provision that the right to life must extend from the moment of conception, at least in the context of the death penalty imposed on the mother, the provision does not by itself settle the issue of the woman's right to voluntary abortion. Whereas in the former case society is taking the life of the woman in consequence of some infraction committed by her, an act that would coincidentally terminate the pregnancy, in the latter case the pregnancy is the direct object of the act, and its termination is the result of the will of the woman. Considerations that bear upon the postponement of the death penalty until after the birth of the pregnant woman's child have no bearing upon an evaluation of the pregnant woman's decision to end her own pregnancy.

Therefore, whatever may be the proper meaning and application of the right to life provisions in other contexts, it cannot be concluded in the present state of the law that this right impairs whatever freedom a woman may have to choose to terminate her own pregnancy.

Abortion, Menstrual Regulation, and the Right to Life

As indicated above, existing international instruments do not settle the issue of the relationship between abortion and the right to life. This issue has two major facets: the scope of the right to life, which is dealt with here, and the relationship between that right and the woman's right to determine the number and spacing of her children, which is considered later in the sections on the family-planning right, persons entitled to exercise the right, and access to the means for family planning.

Taking the moment of conception as the beginning point of the right to life leads to practical difficulties that may under some circumstances deprive the concept of practical effect.

The moment of conception will not always be known; indeed, there will normally be no way for the woman to know that she is in fact pregnant until some time after the moment of conception. In these circumstances, how are postcoital family-planning measures to be evaluated? The use of such measures, e.g., the "morning-after" pill, will sometimes amount to abortion and sometimes not, but in neither case will the user actually know whether or not she had become pregnant. The same is true of menstrual regulation techniques: the woman using such a technique will normally not know whether she had in fact been pregnant. There is thus no meaningful way to apply the moment of conception concept as the beginning point to the right to life. It could only be said that since such family-planning techniques would deny the right to life should conception actually have occurred, such techniques may not be used even though at the time of use it is not known whether or not conception had occurred.

Similarly, the intrauterine device which functions to prevent implantation in the uterus of the fertilized ovum after conception, rather than to prevent conception, would have to be considered to conflict with the right to life, should that right be considered to begin at the moment of conception. Notwithstanding its acknowledged postconception effect, however, the IUD appears generally to be considered a contraceptive device, rather than an abortion technique.[37]

In the light of the controversy over the meaning of the right to life, it is perhaps significant that some countries that have maintained strict antiabortion legislation appear to permit both IUDs and menstrual regulation, considering both methods to be contraceptive measures.[38] With national opinion moving in this direction, it might be concluded that the moment of conception cannot be taken as the beginning point of the right to life.

If the moment of conception is not to be considered the beginning point of the right to life, at what point should that right be considered to begin? Choosing any point prior to birth results in two kinds of difficulties. First, on what basis is such a beginning point to be determined? Second, under what circumstances and through what procedures should the assumed fetal right to life be sacrificed to other rights, such as those of the mother or of society?

In considering the analogous question in the United States of a state's power under the federal constitution to regulate abortion, the United States Supreme Court has held that while the fetus is not a "person" entitled to constitutional protections, the state has certain compelling interests that entitle it to regulate abortion, but only after the first trimester, that is, after the first twelve weeks of pregnancy.[39] The Court held that for the first trimester the abortion decision must be left to the woman and her doctor. Beyond that point, the state would be permitted to regulate abortion for the purpose of protecting the health of the mother, that is, such regulation must be reasonably related to maternal health. On the point at which the fetus becomes viable, that is, capable of surviving if born, however, the Court held that the state may prohibit abortion except where abortion is necessary to preserve the life or the health of the mother.

37. See, e.g., Stepan & Kellogg, *The World's Laws on Contraceptives,* pp. 20–21 (1974).

38. See, e.g., Potts, "The Regulation of Fertility," in UNESCO, *Readings on Population for Law Students,* ch. 5, pp. 91–103 (1977).

39. Roe v. Wade, 410 U.S. 113 (1973).

Applying the United States decision to the right to life concept, the first trimester line would appear to have no relationship to that concept, but a case could be made for the viability standard as the beginning point of the right to life. One problem with such a standard, however, is that, in general, the woman would not know at the time of the abortion decision whether the fetus is viable in the sense of being capable of surviving if born. As with menstrual regulation, the woman undergoing the abortion would not know whether she was, in fact, aborting a fetus protected by the right to life, since in the normal case at such a stage the woman would be attended by a physician. However, from the woman's point of view this difficulty could be solved by leaving it to the physician, or to the hospital authorities, to determine whether the fetus should be considered viable.

Whatever the point chosen as the start of a fetal right to life, there remains the problem of balancing that right against other rights, principally the rights of the pregnant woman.

Some abortion laws permit abortion only under certain specified circumstances that might be taken as a rough guide to some of the considerations that would be involved in balancing the rights of the woman, or of society, against the right to life of the fetus.[40] The physical or mental health, or the life, of the pregnant woman is probably the most common such reason. Another is the degree of risk that the child would be born with a grave physical or mental defect. A third is the case in which the pregnancy resulted from rape or incest. The common use of these three exceptions to prohibitions of abortion implies that the woman has a right to life, or even to good physical and mental health, that is superior to the fetal right to life. It also implies that society, or perhaps the woman together with society, should enjoy a right to avoid the birth of children having serious physical or mental defects, and of children conceived through serious infractions of legal and moral standards. In both cases the right implied would be superior to the fetal right to life.

One difficulty with the approach just described is that it appears to permit the taking of a life, that is, of the fetal life, assumed here to be protected by the right to life standard. The taking of the fetal life would occur through procedures much less formal, and much less subject to control, than the procedures contemplated by the right to life articles in the Universal Declaration of Human Rights and in the Covenant on Civil and Political Rights. In contrast to the judicial procedures required under the covenant,[41] the typical abortion statute leaves the abortion decision to

40. See, e.g., Dourlen-Rollier, "Legal Problems related to Abortion and Menstrual Regulation," *Columbia Human Rights Law Review* 7(1975):120.

41. Article 6 of the International Covenant on Civil and Political Rights provides due process protections to be applied in cases in which the death penalty is imposed.

the attending physician or to a health agency, acting under the general standard stated in the statute. If the fetus has a protected right to life, that right is administered and protected in a far less formal and effective way than is required in other cases by the international instruments that define the right to life.

A second difficulty is that the articulation through abortion statutes of circumstances under which the fetal right to life must yield to other rights and interests is by no means exhausted by the three examples listed above. Additional grounds frequently also appear as sufficient to permit abortion. Examples include family hardship, the number of living children, and the fact that the pregnancy resulted from a failure of a contraceptive method or device. Giving such wide latitude to abortion reduces the fetal right to life to the vanishing point.

Finally, the woman's right to determine the number and spacing of her children, considered in a later section, is also recognized in some countries as adequate grounds for abortion. Respect for such a right implies that the fetus has no right to life.

Marriage and the Family

Article 16, paragraph 1, of the Universal Declaration of Human Rights provides that men and women have the "right to marry and to found a family." Paragraph 3 of the same article provides that: "The family is the natural and fundamental group unit of society and is entitled to protection by society and the State." These provisions are reflected in nearly identical language in Article 23, paragraphs 1 and 2, of the International Covenant on Civil and Political Rights, and in Article 10, paragraph 1, of the International Covenant on Economic, Social, and Cultural Rights.

The right to marry is normally made subject both to medical conditions and to age requirements laid down by national legislation. A minimum age for marriage is also called for in international instruments. The 1962 Convention on Consent to Marriage, Minimum Age for Marriage, and Registration of Marriages states in Article 2 that parties to the convention "shall take legislative action to specify a minimum age for marriage."[42] In 1965, a General Assembly recommendation on the same subject called upon states to take "legislative action to specify a minimum age for marriage, which in any case shall not be less than fifteen years of age."[43] In fact, most states appear today to set a higher minimum, and the exercise

42. *UN Human Rights Compilation,* p. 92.

43. General Assembly Resolution 2018 (XX) (1965), *ibid.,* p. 93.

by governments of legislative power to set such minimums does not appear to have been challenged at either the national or the international level.

The right to "found a family" is stated in the Universal Declaration in conjunction with the right to marry, but there is no other indication that the right to found a family is to be enjoyed only by those who marry. Neither instrument contains a definition of the term family; they merely state that the family is the "natural and fundamental group unit of society." The same is true of the World Population Plan of Action, which provides only that: "The family is the basic unit of society and should be protected by appropriate legislation and policy."[44]

Since there has been no international definition of the concept of a family, there would appear to be no need to confine that concept to marriage. Thus the implication may be that any person may found a family, which might be taken to mean a group of persons bound together in a legal relationship by legally recognized family ties, such as marriage, parentage, or guardianship. The family need not necessarily have or produce children; its members might acquire that status through the operation of law rather than through birth. Thus the fact that men and women, presumably either separately or as a couple, have the right to found a family does not for this reason alone mean that they have the right to produce children in that family: a family membership can be constituted in other ways.

The Family-Planning Right

Neither the Universal Declaration of Human Rights nor the international human rights covenants mention the right of individuals and couples to determine "freely and responsibly the number and spacing of their children." That right, termed here the family-planning right, was first articulated by the General Assembly in 1966,[45] and has since appeared in several international documents, including most recently the World Population Plan of Action.[46] Although the right thus has no formal status in United Nations human rights treaties, its incorporation into resolutions and declarations of the General Assembly and other United Nations bodies gives it the status required for acceptance as a determinant of UN agency policy in the population field.

44. *1974 World Population Conference Report,* para. 14(g), p. 7.

45. General Assembly Resolution 2211 (XXI), "Population Growth and Economic Development" (1966).

46. *1974 World Population Conference Report,* para. 14(f), p. 7.

The family-planning right, coupled with the right to found a family, implies that individuals and couples have a right to bear children at least in the context of a family. The right is stated, however, to be subject to a requirement of responsibility most recently termed the "responsibility of couples and individuals . . . [to take into account] the needs of their living and future children, and their responsibilities towards the community."

The formulation of the family-planning right just quoted, adopted by consensus at the 1974 World Population Conference, has a number of elements that ought to be considered separately.

The right is said to belong to all couples and individuals. It is characterized as a basic right to decide freely and responsibly the number and spacing of children, and to have the information, education, and means to do so. The concept of responsibility, mentioned above, refers both to the parents' other children and to responsibilities towards the community.

The right to have the information, education, and means necessary for family planning has been discussed earlier in relation to individual rights to the provision of government benefits or services in the economic and social fields. The persons entitled to the family planning right, the scope of family planning "means" covered by the right, and the concepts of freedom and responsibility in the exercise of that right are discussed in the sections that follow.

Persons Entitled to Exercise the Family-Planning Right

In the more than a dozen years that have elapsed since the General Assembly first formulated the family-planning right in 1966 as "the principle that the size of the family should be the free choice of each individual family," the right has been declared to belong to the following: all parents, all couples, and all persons.

The word *parents* was used in some instruments in preference to the word *family* to make clear that, in determining the size of the family, the wishes of the parents should prevail over the wishes of other members of the family who might seek to influence the parents' choice of family size. The word *couples* was introduced in other instruments to show, at least by implication, that the couple has the right to choose to have no children; therefore the couple would not properly be termed parents. Finally, the word *persons* was used in one instrument in preference to *couples* to make clear that unmarried mothers shared the right to free choice in determining the number and spacing of their children. This latter instrument, the 1970 "Program of Concerted International Action for the Advancement of

Women," called for making available to "all persons who so desire the necessary information and advice to enable them to decide freely and responsibly on the number and spacing of their children."[47]

The formulation used in the World Population Plan of Action, "all couples and individuals," undoubtedly combines the breadth of the previous terms, showing that the right belongs to all couples, married and unmarried, and to all individuals, men and women, including, of course, the individual woman. What is left unclear, however, is the position of the couple when the partners differ in their desire as to number and spacing of children.

National laws and practices differ widely on the rights of parties within the family when one spouse wishes to have children and the other does not. It thus has not been possible to resolve the issue at the international level in terms of which spouse should have the dominant voice in making the choice as to number and spacing of children.

Considering that it is the woman who bears the child, however, it is sometimes said that the woman should have the final decision. Recent trends permitting abortion in some countries early in pregnancy reinforce this view to the extent that the decision to abort is considered to rest with the woman and her physician. The same would be true with regard to sterilization in the sense that the woman who chooses sterilization would have exercised the final choice in limiting family size, as would her husband had he chosen sterilization. In such cases, however, the choice may not be "free"; abortion and sterilization affects the marriage and under national law may give rise to rights of the partner to terminate the marriage. Where this is true, the woman may have the capacity under the applicable law to exercise the final choice, but may not in fact be able to do so because of the expected impact on the marriage.

Access to the Means for Family Planning

The basic right to determine freely and responsibly the number and spacing of children clearly requires free access to the means to do so. The question of the provision of such means through government benefit programs has already been discussed. This section deals with the range of family-planning means to which free access must be assured to carry out the individual's family planning choices.

47. See *United Nations Standards concerning the Relationship between Human Rights and Various Population Questions,* UN Doc. E/CONF.60/ SYM.IV/3, paras. 9–34 (1974).

The concept of the means which are necessary for family planning is not defined in the United Nations instruments on the subject. Discussion has included all presently available means actually used for fertility regulation, including contraception, voluntary sterilization, abortion, and menstrual regulation. Since under some circumstances each of these means has been found actually necessary for successful control of the number and spacing of children, in principle each such means should be embraced by the family-planning right and made available to those who need it for regulating the size of their families.

The view just stated has not been uniformly endorsed by governments participating in family-planning debates at the United Nations. Indeed, some governments continue to maintain national laws and practices that in effect restrict access to contraceptives generally, while others limit or forbid free access to such practices as voluntary sterilization or abortion as methods of family planning.

Contraception and Menstrual Regulation

The right of free access to contraceptive methods and devices affects a wide range of laws and practices that have historically had the effect of reducing or preventing access to such measures. For example, laws requiring a doctor's prescription for contraceptive devices or supplies will in effect make them unavailable in large parts of the world where doctors are scarce and where many medical services must be provided by medical personnel. Similarly, laws restricting the import, shipment, advertisement for sale, or sale of contraceptive devices will in practice make them unavailable to much of the population. While change is occurring rapidly in this field, such restrictive practices continue to prevail in many countries.

Two current issues require special comment. First, the distinction between contraceptive and other measures of fertility regulation is no longer clear due to the development of the IUD and of postcoital contraceptive measures and menstrual regulation techniques.[48] The distinction may be important in countries in which abortion is prohibited or is restricted by law. In such countries, the classification of the IUD, the "morning-after" pill, and menstrual regulation as contraceptive rather than abortive techniques will open the way for use of these methods of fertility control without the necessity of changing the abortion laws. It may be concluded that since the measures in question do not fall within the pur-

48. See, e.g., Lee & Paxman, "Legal Aspects of Menstrual Regulation," *Lawasia* 5(1974):128–57.

poses of national antiabortion laws, such measures should be viewed as measures of contraception rather than abortion.

Second, the role of the medical profession in relation to contraception needs re-examination in many countries.[49] It is certainly true that modern contraceptive methods involve risks for the user, and that medical assistance should be available to monitor such risks and to safeguard the health of the user. In some cases, however, existing laws may be too stringent in requiring prescriptions for contraceptive devices or in requiring the services of a physician for the use of such devices. For example, laws requiring a doctor's prescription for contraceptive pills, or limiting to physicians the insertion of IUD's in effect deny the use of these devices to people in many areas. In view of the successful use of paramedical personnel for such tasks in some countries, inquiry should be made as to whether it might not be possible to change such restrictive laws and practices in other countries.

The considerations just reviewed are of special importance in developing countries. In some such countries existing laws both directly restrict access to contraceptive methods and indirectly restrict such access through requirements that physicians perform tasks that could be performed by paramedical personnel. Review and revision of such laws would open the way for more effective realization of the right to determine the number and spacing of children.

Voluntary Sterilization

In recent years, fears and taboos surrounding sterilization have lessened in some countries, leading to the widespread acceptance of voluntary sterilization as a contraceptive technique.[50] This development has been hampered by a lack of clarity in some countries as to the legal position of contraception. While under the older laws still in force in some countries, performance of sterilization operations has been regarded as a crime, in others there are no clear legal provisions bearing on voluntary sterilization. In both cases the legal framework should be reviewed and the necessary action taken to clear the way for voluntary sterilization for contraceptive purposes.

From the human rights standpoint, two issues are presented by voluntary sterilization. First, as noted above, since it is actually used as a con-

49. See, e.g., Paxman, Lee & Hopkins, *Expanded Roles for Non-Physicians in Fertility Regulation: Legal Perspectives* (1976).

50. See, e.g., Stepan & Kellogg, *The World's Laws on Voluntary Sterilization for Family Planning Purposes* (1976).

traceptive technique, and since it is vitally needed in many areas for contraceptive purposes, voluntary sterilization should be regarded as one of the means to which persons are entitled to have free access in making family-planning choices.

Second, voluntary sterilization must be assured to be voluntary. Compulsory sterilization should normally be regarded as a serious invasion of the person, and, unless warranted by extraordinary medical circumstances, as a serious infringement of the right to found a family and to have freedom of choice in determining family size. It is therefore important to assure that national legal frameworks permitting voluntary sterilization for contraceptive purposes effectively guarantee freedom of choice in individual decisions to accept sterilization.

In this regard, attention should be given to the legal guidelines recommended in 1976 by the "Workshop on Legal Aspects of Sterilization" of the Third International Conference on Voluntary Sterilization. The workshop recommended that the term sterilization be replaced by the term surgical contraception to remove the stigma attached to the concept and to emphasize its contraceptive purposes. The legal guidelines adopted by the workshop would guarantee free and informed consent and thus ensure that sterilization is in fact voluntary. The workshop guidelines provide as follows:

> 1. Every individual male, and female, who has the legal capacity to give informed consent, has the right to obtain surgical contraception, and the State has an obligation to make available appropriate services subject to the following:
>
> 1.1 When performed by qualified personnel in accordance with accepted medical standards, voluntary surgical contraceptive is lawful. The decision must be voluntary, meaning that it is based upon informed consent on the part of the patient, who has been advised of the alternative means of family planning as well as of the immediate, the probable, and the possible long-term consequences of surgical contraception.
>
> 1.2 There shall be no civil or criminal liability for voluntary surgical contraception performed without negligence.
>
> 2. Nothing in these provisions of law shall compel any individual to participate in a voluntary surgical contraceptive procedure, but any individual declining to participate shall have the obligation to inform the requesting individual of other persons or facilities which offer such procedures. State-supported facilities with appropriate medical resources shall be obliged, however, to make surgical contraception services available.
>
> 3. The State shall adopt procedures to protect those incapable of making an informed consent to surgical contraception and shall make surgical

contraception available to such persons with appropriate safeguards to protect their rights as individuals.[51]

Considering that voluntary sterilization, unlike abortion, has never been opposed on human rights grounds so long as the voluntary nature of the act is assured, there would appear to be no reason in principle why every country should not provide through its lawful freedom of access to voluntary sterilization for contraceptive purposes in accordance with the above quoted legal guidelines.

Abortion

Human rights issues concerning the relation between abortion and menstrual regulation and the right to life have been discussed earlier. If, as indicated by the trend in national laws, freedom of abortion at least in the earlier stages of pregnancy does not conflict with the right to life, there would be no reason in principle to prevent free access to abortion as a means of fertility regulation. In fact, abortion is used for this purpose in many parts of the world; indeed abortion is sometimes the only effective measure available to some segments of the population. As such, abortion should be regarded as one of the means necessary to give full effect to the right to determine the number and spacing of children.

Where abortion is regarded as restricted by the right to life of the fetus, as, for example, where the fetus has reached the stage of being capable of survival if born, there may be a need to balance the rights of the woman and of society against the assumed fetal right to life. Considerations of this nature have already been reviewed. The major point here is that the fetal right to life, where it is said to exist, does not require an absolute ban on abortion. It requires, instead, a sensitive balancing of that right against the impact both upon the woman and upon society of requiring that the woman carry the fetus for a full term and give birth to a child.

In this context, in addition to the woman's right to freedom of choice in family planning, consideration should be given to the woman's right to health and to the impact upon her physical and mental health of being forced to carry through with an unwanted pregnancy. India's abortion law of 1971 brings the two rights together in an especially helpful fashion. That law authorizes abortion if continued pregnancy would involve a risk of grave injury to the physical or mental health of the woman. In an explanation of the basis for the protection given to the mental health of the woman, the following is stated in that law: "Where any pregnancy occurs as a result

51. *Summary Report of Workshop M-9 Third International Conference on Voluntary Sterilization,* Tunis, 1976.

of failure of any device or method used by any married woman or her husband for the purpose of limiting the number of children, the anguish caused by such unwanted pregnancy may be presumed to constitute a grave injury to the mental health of the pregnant woman."[52]

Consideration of the legal position of abortion should also focus on the practical consequences of limiting access to abortion. A foremost consideration is that laws proscribing abortion have not worked. Abortion is known to be widespread even in countries in which it is forbidden by law. In effect, this means that women denied opportunities for lawful abortion will turn to self-help, and will seek assistance outside regular medical channels, which enormously increases the risk of harm to the woman. Thus as a result of prohibitions on abortion, women in fact suffer much greater damage through abortion than they would if abortions were available as part of regular health care.

Second, and equally important to policy making, prohibitions on abortion discriminate against the poor. Wealthy women desiring abortions are generally able to travel to places where they are lawful and are performed safely in medically sound procedures. Poor women, who make up the bulk of the population requiring abortions, cannot normally go beyond the local medical services and will thus have no medical assistance in countries in which abortions are unlawful. Such a law thus discriminates against those least able to care for themselves, while as a whole it will fail to accomplish its stated purpose.

Finally, inability to obtain a desired abortion often results in the birth of an unwanted child. This fact can severely affect the quality of life for the mother, for the child, and for the family as a whole. Once the birth has occurred, there can be no fully satisfactory solution to the new situation since the child has become part of the family. Considering the role of the government in prohibiting an abortion that would have avoided the situation, however, it should perhaps be said that society bears a special responsibility to take measures that would alleviate the burden on the mother, on the child, and on the family.

Freedom and Responsibility in Exercising the Right to Determine Family Size

Freedom has been linked to responsibility throughout the development of the family-planning right, but there has been little clarification of the meaning to be given to the concept of responsibility.

52. India, Medical Termination of Pregnancy Act of 1971, Explanation II to Section 3, Paragraph 2, quoted from *Population Report,* Series F, No. 1, George Washington Medical Center, 1973.

One approach to the concept of responsibility is contained in Article 29 of the Universal Declaration of Human Rights, which provides in part that persons exercising rights and freedoms are subject to limitations determined by law "for the purpose of securing due recognition and respect for the rights and freedoms of others and of meeting the just requirements of morality, public order, and the general welfare in a democratic society." In the context of the right to determine the number and spacing of children, the chief impact of this concept would be to require that persons exercising the family-planning right take into account the impact on society of their having children, especially as that may contribute to undesirable levels of population growth.

Another approach is to stress that responsibility means responsible parenthood in the sense of having only that number of children for whom adequate food, health, education, housing, and personal love and attention can be given. Persons choosing to have more children than they can fully care for in this all-embracing sense can be regarded as having failed in their duty to act responsibly since, through their actions, they have contributed to a failure in the protection of the human rights of all of their children.

While there is thus some measure of agreement that the concept of responsibility means responsibility both to society and to the family, no solution is apparent where parents fail to act responsibly. Perhaps all that can be said is that individuals must pay heed to their duties of responsible parenthood, and that the state might require some formal measures, such as family-planning instruction, in this regard. Measures going beyond instruction, education, and persuasion to enforce a particular government-defined concept of responsibility would amount to coercion, possibly conflicting with the standard of individual freedom made part of the family planning right.

As defined in the international instruments quoted earlier, the right to freedom of choice in determining family size is said to give to individuals and couples the right to act freely and responsibly to choose the number and spacing of their children. If, following persuasive efforts by the government, including incentives and disincentives discussed earlier, individuals persist in choosing a larger number of children than that desired by the state, coercion to follow state policy would negate this right of free choice. Freedom may coexist with responsibility, but freedom may also include freedom to make wrong choices and freedom to reject official policy.

POPULATION DISTRIBUTION AND INTERNAL MIGRATION

The World Population Plan of Action succinctly identified both the reasons underlying the need to consider population distribution and redistribution as part of national social and economic planning, and the human rights framework within which such measures should be taken. The plan's section headed "Population Distribution and Internal Migration" begins with the statement that: "Urbanization in most countries is characterized by a number of adverse factors: drain from rural areas through migration of individuals who cannot be absorbed by productive employment in urban areas, serious disequilibrium in the growth of urban centers, contamination of the environment, inadequate housing and services and social psychological stress."[53] The Plan of Action then recommends that government policies aimed at influencing population flows into urban areas should consider certain guidelines, the first of which relates to international human rights standards. The Plan of Action states that, in formulating and implementing internal migration policies: "Measures should be avoided which infringe the right of freedom of movement and residence within the borders of each State as enunciated in the Universal Declaration of Human Rights and other international instruments."[54]

This chapter briefly reviews relevant international human rights standards and explores the relationship between such standards and national population redistribution programs. The operating premises are, first, that population redistribution will sometimes have an important role in national population policies and programs; second, that UN agencies will be called upon to participate in national population redistribution programs; and, third, that such agency participation should be consistent with and should further respect for international human rights standards.

The Right to Freedom of Movement

The Universal Declaration of Human Rights states in Article 13, paragraph 1, that "everyone has the right to freedom of movement and residence within the borders of each State." The Universal Declaration also makes clear, however, that rights of the individual, such as the right to freedom of movement, are exercised within the framework of the community with concomitant duties to the community. Article 29, paragraph 2, articulates those duties in the following fashion: "In the exercise of his rights and freedoms, everyone shall be subject only to such limitations as are determined by law solely for the purpose of securing due recognition and respect for the rights and freedoms of others and of meeting the just requirements of morality, public order, and the general welfare in a democratic society."

53. *1974 World Population Conference Report,* para. 44, p. 14.

54. *Ibid.,* para 46 (a), p. 15.

The same pattern of rights and duties appears in the International Covenant on Civil and Political Rights. Article 12, paragraph 1, of that covenant formulates the right to freedom of movement in the following terms: "Everyone lawfully within the territory of a State shall, within that territory, have the right to liberty of movement and freedom to choose his residence." Paragraph 3 of the same article clearly indicates, however, that the individual's right to liberty of movement and freedom to choose the place of residence is exercised within the framework of community needs. That paragraph provides as follows: "The above-mentioned rights shall not be subject to any restrictions except those which are provided by law, are necessary to protect national security, public order (*ordre public*), public health or morals, or the rights and freedoms of others, and are consistent with the other rights in the present Covenant."

It should be observed that the restrictions on the right to freedom of movement contemplated in Article 12 of the Covenant on Civil and Political Rights are seen in the covenant as reflecting the ordinary powers of government in the service of the needs of the community. Such restrictions, reflecting, for example, public health or public order requirements, do not depend for their validity upon the existence of a public emergency. Article 4, paragraph 1, provides generally that in the extraordinary circumstances of a "public emergency which threatens the life of the nation," states parties to the covenant may take "measures derogating from their obligations" under the covenant to the extent required by the emergency situation and subject to certain restrictions not relevant here. In contrast, Article 12 places the exercise of rights to freedom of movement and to free choice of place of residence explicitly within the context of the usual process for the determination of community needs. The limits on restrictions in the rights framed in Article 12 flow first, from the other rights recognized in the Covenant on Civil and Political Rights, and second, from the concepts of national security, public order, and public health or morals referred to in paragraph 3 of Article 12.

Restrictions on Freedom of Movement

Government actions and programs restraining freedom of movement, or directing the redistribution of populations, may be designed to serve several differing goals. For example, security in border areas might be enhanced by new settlements, or by resettlement of existing populations. Social goals might be sought through programs aimed at achieving racial integration, or a more balanced mix of religious or ethnic groups. Economic development goals might underlie policies of urban redevelopment, policies restricting migration to urban areas, or policies fostering the growth of new settlements in underpopulated areas. In many cases a population distribution or redistribution policy may be designed to serve several goals. Since the focus here is on the role of UN agencies in relation to national population programs, the following discussion is confined to government policies that might be expected to underlie population redistribution measures undertaken as part of national population programs.

The goals of population redistribution in national population programs focus upon economic and social development and upon the enhancement of the quality of life. Rapid and excessive urbanization has been a major impetus for such programs. Goals may include more balanced distribution of population and more equitable regional development, together with enhanced employment opportunities and more adequate social services for the people involved. Other goals may include slum clearance and urban redevelopment, increased agricultural production in new town areas, and industrial development through large projects such as highway or dam construction. In each case the goals form part of the country's population program, integrated with its social and economic development planning. The question here is the extent to which international human rights standards impose restrictions on the accomplishment of such goals through population redistribution programs.

As has been observed, the individual's right to freedom of movement exists within a framework of duties to the community and is subordinated to community needs characterized in terms of national security, public order, and public health or morals. Taken together, these categories of community needs are broad enough to embrace population redistribution goals formulated as part of national economic and social development plans. The central concept is public order, drawn from the civil law concept of *ordre public;* the two terms are used together in Article 12, paragraph 3, of Covenant on Civil and Political Rights. Consistent with their appreciation of the needs of the *ordre public,* for example, governments would be regarded as competent to direct the removal of persons from areas designated for slum clearance, or from areas to be flooded through new dam construction. The control of urbanization, the resettlement of rural areas, and other measures to achieve balanced population distribution and enhanced social and economic development, can also be seen as reflections of the needs of the *ordre public.* Choices of this nature made by a government in achieving its economic and social policy goals may result in restrictions on the individual's right to freedom of movement. In themselves, however, such restrictions merely may reflect legitimate community needs and do not improperly abridge internationally protected human rights standards.

Although the goals of population redistribution in national economic and social development plans fall within the range of restrictions on freedom of movement permitted under Article 12 of the Covenant on Civil and Political Rights, questions may arise concerning the procedures or methods used to give effect to such goals. Such questions fall into two categories: first, conformity of the program as a whole with the general human rights norm of nondiscrimination; and, second, an evaluation of particular aspects of such programs in the light of international human rights standards. The general question of nondiscrimination is discussed here; human rights issues related to particular components of population redistribution programs are explored in the next section.

Nondiscrimination has become a central feature of international human rights standards. Article 2, paragraph 1, of the International Covenant on Civil and Political Rights contains the most comprehensive statement of the nondiscrimination norm: "Each State Party to the present Covenant undertakes to respect and to ensure to all individuals within its territory and subject to its jurisdiction the rights recognized in the present Covenant, without distinction of any kind, such as race, color, sex, language, religion, political or other opinion, national or social origin, property, birth, or other status." Article 26 reinforces the nondiscrmination norm by imposing obligations upon governments to act to prevent discrimination. That article provides: "All persons are equal before the law and are entitled without any discrimination to the equal protection of the law. In this respect, the law shall prohibit any discrimination on any ground such as race, color, sex, language, religion, political or other opinion, national or social origin, property, birth, or other status."

These provisions apply to population redistribution programs as well as to other forms of government action. There is thus no doubt that under international human rights standards population redistribution programs must apply equally to all without discrimination on grounds of "race, color, sex, language, religion, political or other opinion, national origin, property, birth, or other status." The population redistribution goals included in economic and social development planning are compatible with the nondiscrimination norm. Particular programs and measures adopted to give effect to such goals must also be subject to the nondiscrimination norm. Such measures and programs are considered in the next section.

Population Redistribution Programs

For the purposes of the present discussion, population redistribution programs might be divided into three categories: (1) programs that provide for the exclusion of persons from certain areas; (2) programs that provide for the removal of persons from certain areas; and (3) programs that provide for the transfer of persons to certain areas. Although particular programs may combine two or even all three of these elements, each presents distinct human rights issues that are most conveniently discussed separately.

RESTRICTIONS ON SETTLEMENT

In line with their economic and social development needs, governments may consider that certain areas should not be settled, or that new or additional settlement should be excluded from certain areas. The latter is most prominently the case where an urban area is considered overcrowded and incapable of sustaining additional population growth. In such cases the government may exclude all persons seeking to move into the area, or it may establish a preference or priority scheme under which some persons, but not others, would be granted permission to settle in the city or in the area in question.

As indicated by the discussion in the previous section, although the government's action would restrict freedom of movement, and especially freedom to choose a place of residence, the restriction would be legitimate as an exercise of the government's authority to make choices as part of its economic and social development planning. In making such choices, however, the government would be constrained to observe the general nondiscrimination norm developed through United Nations human rights practice.

There is thus a point of potential conflict. As articulated in the Covenant on Civil and Political Rights, quoted in the last section, the nondiscrimination norm proscribes discrimination on the basis of property as well as on the basis of race, color, and sex, etc. If, for example, a government were to permit propertied persons freedom of movement to urban areas while excluding those who have no property, would such a distinction amount to discrimination on the basis of property?

The question just stated has no clear or settled answer, but the issue is not likely to arise in so simple a form. In most cases the basis for the government's distinction is likely to be employment or housing, rather than property. An overcrowded urban area may be characterized by a lack of adequate housing and employment opportunities; in such circumstances a government choosing to restrict migration into the area on the basis of the possession by the individual of adequate housing and employment would not be guilty of discrimination on the basis of property as that term is used in the Covenant on Civil and Political Rights.

The problem here is analogous to conditions placed upon access to government benefits: migration into the area under the assumed circumstances would be a privilege or benefit dispensed by the government in furthering its social and economic policy goals. As such, the conditions for access to the benefit are subject to the government's overriding nondiscrimination duty, and the particular content and application of that duty should be drawn from normal government practice in its allocation of benefits equally to all without discrimination as that concept is defined in international human rights law.

REMOVAL OF POPULATIONS

Government policies requiring the removal of populations from specified areas are likely to arise in two distinct classes of cases: evacuations for purposes of development or renewal, and removals for purposes of lowering population density and reducing overcrowding.

The first case is the simplest. Where, for example, a dam is to be built, or a slum cleared, all the people must be removed, and there is consequently no scope for practices that might be characterized as discriminatory. In the second case, that of removals to lower density and to eliminate overcrowding, the nondiscrimination norm is relevant in the same manner as has been discussed above. The government should be regarded as competent to make the social and economic policy choices that require removal of a portion of the population, but in carrying out that policy, it must select the persons to be removed without discrimination on the basis of "race, color, sex, language, religion, political or other opinion, national or social origin, property, birth, or other status."

Removals of a portion of the population thus may be judged as related to the manner in which the choice is made as to which individuals are to be removed and which are to be permitted to remain. Nondiscrimination is one dimension of the problem. Freedom of choice versus coercion is the other. In some circumstances the government's goals might be satisfied by recruitment of volunteers for removal. In such cases the recruitment might be done through incentives to removal, such as cash payments or housing or employment at the new location. Where the incentive is large and the need great, the choice, though theoretically voluntary, may in fact be coerced. The unemployed offered no job benefits in the city may be coerced to accept employment and other benefits through removal to other areas. In other cases the element of coercion may be more direct. For example, the government might determine that a portion of the existing population selected upon some nondiscriminatory basis should be removed to other areas to alleviate an overcrowded urban condition. To the extent that there is no provision for the exercise of individual choice, even of the kind conditioned by powerful incentive measures, the impact on freedom of movement and free choice of place of residence becomes more severe.

Acknowledging that the government may have authority to impose coercive measures when required to accomplish economic and social development goals, nevertheless the degree of impact upon individual freedom of choice should dictate careful exploration of alternatives before coercive measures are used. Although a government may consider that an urban area has become so overcrowded as to impair the quality of life for all its people, and to render impossible the accomplishment of economic and social goals, it should exhaust the potential of persuasion and incentives before it resorts to a policy of forced removals even when that policy is carried out on a nondiscriminatory basis.

TRANSFER OF POPULATIONS

The final element in population redistribution programs envisages the transfer of populations to an area selected for development. Here again, the main human rights issue is freedom of choice versus coercion. The focus, however, is on transfer to the new area, rather than on selection for removal from the former area of residence.

In the context of transfer to new areas, incentives are likely to be a major element in the government's program and a central issue for UN agencies. As noted above, incentives are in principle inducements to voluntary action, but in practice may amount to indirect coercion. If a government has determined that new towns, or new development areas, are required to accomplish its social and economic goals, the reality may be that some measure of coercion will be needed to induce relevant populations to transfer to those areas. The problem is made more intense where the government determines both that the new area should be settled and that the population should come from existing overcrowded areas. In such cases, alternatives preserving free choice may be quickly exhausted and coercion required, perhaps extending to mandatory removals from the overcrowded city and mandatory resettlement in the new towns.

In such circumstances, the conflict between the need to accomplish economic and social development goals and the right of individual choice of place of residence is plain and perhaps cannot be wholly satisfactorily resolved. One measure is possible, however; the population that is to be transferred to the new towns might be given both a role in making the decision and as much freedom of choice as that decision would allow.

These ideas are reflected in the Vancouver Declaration on Human Settlements, adopted in 1976 by the United Nations Conference on Human Settlements. The Vancouver Declaration affirmed the general principle of the right of free movement, stating that: "The right of free movement and the right of each individual to choose the place of settlement within the domain of his own country should be recognized and safeguarded."[55] At the same time, the Vancouver Declaration refers repeatedly to the role of governments in determining land use policy for the state. In particular, the Vancouver Action Plan proposes that governments adopt measures to reduce the disparity between conditions in the different regions within their countries, including the use of incentives and disincentives to encourage more equitable population distribution. Perhaps as a means of reconciling the latter statements with the expressed rights of free movement the following principle is stated in the Vancouver Declaration: "Basic human dignity is the right of people, individually and collectively, to participate directly in the policies and programs affecting their lives. The process of choosing and carrying out a given course of action for human settlement improvement should be designed expressly to fulfill that right. Effective human settlement policies require a continuous co-operative relationship between a Government and its people at all levels."[56] This seems to imply that effective participation of the people in the decisions that affect their lives will enable a government to undertake policies restricting, or even directing population redistribution. While such policies would restrict freedom of movement, and the individual's free choice of a place of residence, they would in a larger sense conform to human rights standards by giving to the persons affected an opportunity to participate in making basic choices.

As was observed in the case of removals from overcrowded areas, in cases of transfers to new towns or to areas of lower population density, the line between free will and coercion may be difficult to draw. In both cases, persuasion and inducement by such incentives as cash payments and the provision of housing and employment will sometimes accomplish the government's goal. When this is true, it will sometimes be because modest incentive levels will make the move sufficiently attractive to sufficient numbers; at other times, however, the motivation to accept the move will be conditioned more by dire need than by free choice between acceptable alternatives. In the latter cases, the incentives used may be in a real sense coercive: the individuals may feel that they had no real choice and that

55. Vancouver Declaration on Human Settlements, Part II, para. 6, *Habitat: United Nations Conference on Human Settlements, Report* (1976).

56. *Ibid.*, Part III, para. 10.

survival required acceptance of the move in order to gain the benefits offered as incentives. In this context, all that can be asked of the government is that it make every effort through persuasion and through maintenance of normal social welfare programs to accomplish its population redistribution goals without moving further than necessary towards coercion in its use of incentive measures.

Persuasion and incentives will not always be successful, however, especially in cases of transfers from overcrowded urban areas to new towns. In many such cases the people who have chosen to settle in the city, notwithstanding its inadequate housing, the lack of employment, and minimal public welfare services, will prefer to remain in the city rather than accept the unknown burdens of a move to a newly developed town or rural area. The problem is made more difficult where the government lacks sufficient resources to make the new area truly attractive. Where this is true, neither persuasion nor the levels of incentives that the government is capable of providing will suffice to induce large enough numbers to make the move. In such a context, the government must balance the need for population redistribution against the individual's right to freedom of movement and to choose a place of residence. It cannot be said that the government lacks authority to decide that in some circumstances the individual's rights must be subordinated to the needs of the community; indeed, Article 12 of the Covenant on Civil and Political Rights expressly contemplates subordination of the rights of free movement to the requirement of the *ordre public*. Where such decisions are made, however, sensitivity to the government's duty to further observance of human rights dictates that the government should first exhaust every possibility of inducing voluntary action through persuasion and incentives; second, afford to the individuals involved an opportunity to participate in the decision leading to their mandatory resettlement; and third, allow the affected individuals as much freedom of choice as possible, consistent with the accomplishment of the urgent need for population redistribution. Finally, as is true throughout the range of government population redistribution measures, such measures must conform to the nondiscrimination norm developed in international human rights law.

UN Agency Participation in Population Redistribution Programs

As observed at the outset, population redistribution will sometimes form an important part of national population programs, and UN agencies will be called upon to participate in such programs. Considering that population redistribution is affected by international human rights standards, such participation should both be consistent with these standards and be designed to promote respect for the human rights involved.

To accomplish these goals, UN agencies should seek to ensure that the guidelines suggested above are satisfied in population redistribution programs for which their assistance is sought. First, they should ensure that there is no discrimination on grounds of race, color, sex, language, religion, political or other opinion, national or social origin, property, birth, or other status.[57] Respect for this nondiscrimination norm will require that classifications and distinctions made in the national population redistribution program be designed directly and narrowly to meet the govenment's social and economic development goals. Second, UN agencies should give priority to measures designed to induce voluntary compliance with population redistribution goals, rather than measures that will have the direct or indirect effect of coercing unwilling compliance with government directives. Third, where coercion is nonetheless found necessary, UN agencies should seek to ensure that maximum freedom of choice is preserved for the individuals involved. Finally, UN agencies should support measures designed to secure participation of the affected people in decisions leading to their removal and resettlement.

Within the framework suggested, UN agency assistance might focus on the design of population resettlement schemes at the planning stage to ensure adequate attention to the human rights aspects identified in this chapter. At the operational or implementation stage, such assistance might concentrate on elements that would tend to maximize freedom of choice. Such elements might include, for example, information programs designed to provide full information on the quality of life to be expected in the new areas and on the reasons for making the move. It might also include support for incentive programs and for the services and benefits to be made available in the new areas, which would provide positive reasons for making the move and hence minimize the need for coercion. In the short range, emphasis by UN agencies on full information and on enhancement of the quality of life through the redistribution of population can be expected to maximize willingness to enter voluntarily into the redistribution program, and thereby minimize the need for coercion and foster the feeling among the people involved that they have a role in decisions that affect their lives. In the longer range, perceptions that the move had been a voluntary choice will tend to increase the satisfaction of the people involved and reduce the likelihood that they will wish to move again and perhaps to return to the place from which they had come in the redistribution program. In this sense, freedom of choice, and UN agencies participation in bringing about the conditions in which such

57. International Covenant on Civil and Political Rights, Article 2, para. 1.

freedom can be exercised, may prove to be the most valuable element in a national population redistribution program.

CHANGING CONCEPTS OF HUMAN RIGHTS

As much of the preceding discussion has shown, human rights is not a static concept. Changes in the conditions of society and changes in human values bring about changes in concepts of human rights. Through their programs, and through their assistance to national population programs, UN agencies will be active participants in this process of change. This means that UN agencies must be sensitive to the currents of change, and that they should attempt to stimulate active consideration of the need for change by the governments involved. In this way UN agencies will assure that changing concepts of human rights are taken into account in developing UN population assistance programs.

The preceding sections have dealt with existing human rights concepts and with their relationship to population programs. While change is difficult to predict, several potential developments should be mentioned that may lead to change in concepts of human rights relevant to UN population assistance programs.

Considerable attention has been given in recent years to the issue of when life begins. As dicussed in the section on individual freedoms, this issue is relevant to the question of the relationship between the right to life and the right to determine the number and spacing of children. There is at present little agreement on such aspects of this issue as the right to abortion, but continued attention must be given to such questions in their relationship to UN agency programs.

Attention should also be given to the issue of when life ends, and to the human rights implications of artificial means of prolonging life, as well as to the position of the individual who may wish to end his own life. Issues of this kind are now discussed in some societies and are likely to become of greater importance in the next decade. Such issues have a direct bearing upon population programs and might usefully be given systematic, if preliminary, attention in UN agencies planning for the future.

Similarly, attitudes towards marriage and the family are undergoing change that might affect both human rights standards and UN agency programs. One example of such change is the development of the right to determine the number and spacing of children. That right, which began as the right of the family or of the couple, now includes the right of the individual, a change that may have implications for the concept of the family. Another example is the practice in some societies of groups of unrelated individuals coming together as a new form of extended family, which may seek recognition and protection equivalent to that given the nuclear family. Change in this sphere may have implications for population policies and for UN agency programs.

Another potential area of change is in attitudes towards homosexuality which may affect both the concept of the family and population policies. Increasingly, in some societies, homosexuality is claimed as an aspect of the human right to free choice in matters of sexuality; UN agencies may have to consider their relationships either to government policies protecting the rights of homosexuals or to government policies suppressing homosexuality.

Moving further in the direction of change, developments in human fertility and reproduction may raise human rights issues relevant to UN agency programs. Contraception is such a field. The development of a universal oral contraceptive capable of administration through water supplies, or otherwise to the general population, would present human rights and population policy issues not yet examined. So, also, the capacity to predetermine the sex of children, or to endow children with predetermined genetic traits, may require examination from the perspective of human rights and population policies. Developments in technology in such areas will lead to changing concepts of human rights and to implications for population programs that will require close attention by UN agencies.

CONCLUSIONS AND RECOMMENDATIONS

The foregoing review of human rights standards in the context of population programs, and of the central policy issues relevant to the work of UN agencies, leads to certain conclusions about the role of UN agencies that may usefully be restated here. The restatement of conclusions is followed by suggestions for action to ensure that human rights considerations are given proper emphasis in the work population of the UN agencies.

Human Rights Standards as Policy Guidelines

International human rights standards are in a developmental stage in which their legal status, content, and application in the population field is also not always clear. In this context it is concluded that UN agencies should, to the extent possible, use United Nations human rights standards as policy guidelines in the development of their programs. To this end, they should take the following action:

1. Stimulate the clarification of international human rights standards as they apply to national and international population programs.

2. Support national action to give effect to international human rights standards in population programs.

3. Decline to lend their support to national action inconsistent with human rights standards as defined in United Nations practice.

Taking into account the ongoing process of change in international concepts of human rights, UN agencies must keep these developments continuously under review and adjust their programs accordingly.

Rights, Responsibilities, and Coercion

International standards defining human rights frequently incorporate concepts of responsibility, lending emphasis to the idea that all rights, including human rights, exist within society, and that individuals in exercising such rights must respect the interests of society as a whole. The juxtaposition of rights with responsibilities leads to the question of the extent to which the government, acting for society, may impose constraints on the exercise of individual rights to assure respect for the collective rights of society.

In this regard, UN agencies act within a policy framework set by United Nations decisions, including human rights standards, General Assembly resolutions, and the World Population Plan of Action, that, in the family-planning field, emphasizes the free will of the individual and seeks to avoid both discrimination and the use of coercion. Incentives and disincentives used in family-planning programs always raise issues of discrimination and of coercion since they reserve public benefits to the segment of society that is willing to accept government-defined family-planning goals. Incentive and disincentive programs thus call for a balancing of the needs of society against the economic and social needs of the individual. UN agencies should assure, through consultation with each government, that human rights policies are fully considered in incentive and disincentive programs, and in particular that:

1. resources used as incentives in family-planning programs do not exclude the provision of basic human services to all segments of the population;

2. exclusions of families from public benefits (as disincentives) do not deprive children of their basic human rights;

3. the removal or witholding of government services or benefits (as disincentives) does not defeat justifiable expectations in the continuation of such services or benefits; and

4. incentives and disincentives are rationally related to the goals sought by the government.

With regard to coercive measures in general, where such measures are regarded as permissible, and where a government has concluded that the individual's right to freedom of choice must yield to the overall needs of society, UN agencies should assure through consultation with the government that human rights policies have been fully considered, and, in particular, that:

1. adequate study has shown the urgency of the situation and the need for coercive measures;

2. all available measures short of coercion have been exhausted;

3. the people have been consulted and have participated in the decision to use coercion; and

4. the coercive measures to be used are reasonably related to the goal sought and are carefully designed to minimize impact on human rights.

Human Rights and Family Planning

The discussion of human rights aspects of fertility regulation, including contraception, voluntary sterilization, abortion, and menstrual regulation, shows that there is still considerable lack of clarity as to the meaning and application of human rights standards in this field. It is thus important for UN agencies to stimulate discussion of these issues at both the national and the international levels. The following are some of the major issues and, based on United Nations instruments and current practice, the attitudes that UN agencies might adopt as to those issues as they bear upon their programs. In each case the attitudes expressed represent the dominant trend in national and international thought on the issue; they do not exclude the maintenance by some governments and authorities of other attitudes.

1. The right to life is not established as a right extending to the fetus, whether measured from the moment of conception or otherwise.

2. The right to life, therefore, does not exclude resort to abortion when required as a means of family planning.

3. Abortion need not always be the free choice of the woman and her physician; in particular, the state may act to restrict abortion in the later stages of pregnancy.

4. The right to marry and to found a family need not necessarily include a right to conceive and to give birth to children.

5. The right to determine the number and spacing of children (here called the family-planning right) is to be exercised responsibly, by in

this respect freedom of choice may not be restrained by coercive measures.

6. The family-planning right belongs to all couples and to all individuals; in the event of differences of opinion in the case of a couple, the dominant voice should be that of the woman, who would bear the child. The information, education, and means required for the family-planning right extend to all means required for family planning, that is, to contraception, voluntary sterilization, abortion, and menstrual regulation, where those methods are important means of family planning.

7. Where some means of family planning, abortion or voluntary sterilization for example, are restricted or excluded by national law or practice, UN agencies may, nonetheless, extend their support to national programs designed to make other such means available to the people.

8. Menstrual regulation and other postcoital methods of fertility regulation should be distinguished from abortion; considering the short time span within which such methods are used, and the frequent inability to know whether the woman is in fact pregnant, national laws restricting abortion should not be applied to postcoital contraceptive measures, including the "morning-after" pill, the IUD, and menstrual regulation.

9. Voluntary sterilization should be made freely available as a contraceptive technique, subject only to proper guidelines to ensure that the sterilization is performed with informed consent and is in fact voluntary.

Population Redistribution Programs

The discussion of population distribution and internal migration has shown that the individual's right to freedom of movement and to free choice of place of residence exists within a framework of duties to the community and is subordinated to community needs expressed in terms of public order and public health or morals. While this framework gives full support to population redistribution goals formulated as part of national economic and social development programs, UN agency participation in such programs should be designed to promote respect for the human rights standards involved.

1. UN agencies should ensure that population redistribution programs do not discriminate on grounds of race, color, sex, language, religion, political or other opinion, national or social origin, property, birth, or other status.

2. Priority should be given to measures designed to induce voluntary compliance with population redistribution goals, rather than to coercive measures.

3. Where coercion is required, the maximum area of freedom of choice should be preserved to the individuals involved.

4. To maximize freedom of choice, UN agencies should support measures designed to ensure participation by the affected population in decisions leading to their removal and resettlement.

5. To maximize voluntary participation, UN agencies should support measures designed to enhance the quality of life of the affected population in the areas in which they are to be resettled.

A SYSTEMATIC REVIEW OF HUMAN RIGHTS AND POPULATION PROGRAMS

Human rights considerations affect UN population programs in a great many respects, and many aspects of the human rights involved are inadequately understood and only sporadically applied. Thus there is need for explicit attention to human rights in the population work of UN agencies which might be accomplished in the following two ways.

First, human rights considerations should be raised by UN agencies in their discussions with governments on the formulation and implementation of national population programs. The issues identified in this chapter are issues that should be raised as they apply in particular national programs. Full consideration should be sought for such issues at the earliest possible stage, and whenever UN agency participation or assistance is sought for such programs. UN agencies would apply international human rights standards defined in United Nations practice in determining whether their assistance should be extended to particular national population programs.

Second, UN agencies should seek to stimulate national review and consideration of human rights standards as they apply to all aspects of population programs. This might be done through a series of regional or subregional meetings at which the appropriate national officials exchange information and views on the laws and practices of their countries relevant to their national population programs. The goal of such meetings would be to promote study of the legal and ethical dimensions of population programs from the point of view of human rights, and to bring about the systematic review in each country of the action taken in that country to protect human rights in the context of its population program.

The first suggestion, that is, that UN agencies raise human rights considerations in their discussions with governments about the formulation and implementation of national population programs, could be carried out by action within given agencies. The guidelines within which such discussions are conducted should include a comprehensive review of human rights aspects relevant to the country's population program, and the application of a human rights framework within which UN agency assistance would be made available to national population programs.

The second suggestion, that of a series of regional or subregional meetings on population and human rights, would call for detailed advance planning and possibly the availability of funds to give effect to suggestions for national action advanced at the meeting. Each meeting might, for example, be held on the basis of country reports prepared for each participant according to a common framework that would show the position in each country of specified human rights standards relevant to population programs. The meeting might then bring together the ministers of health, education, and labor from each country, who would discuss their country's positions on the relevant human rights standards and endeavor to propose a series of "next steps" that might be taken within the countries to advance respect for and the protection of human rights. These next steps could form the basis for UN agency assistance to that country to translate the willingness to take the "next step" into the reality of advancement of human rights in the population field.

15

Beyond Integration, Toward Guidability

AMITAI ETZIONI

INTRODUCTION

INTEGRATION OF POPULATION and development policies is a sound idea, but it provides insufficient basis for devising relevant public policies. Missing, first and foremost, is a systematic concern with the structures and

The author greatly benefited from several discussions with Dr. Rafael Salas, Executive Director of UNFPA, and Dr. A. Thavarajah, Chief, Office of Policy Analysis and Statistics, UNFPA, and their staffs. Dr. Hirofumi Ando was especially helpful. Dr. George Brown of the Population Council, Dr. Lee Jay Cho of the East-West Population Institute, Dr. Paul Demeny of the Population Council, Dr. James Fawcett of the East-West Population Institute, Dr. Oscar Harkavy of The Ford Foundation, Dr. Allan Rosenfield of Columbia University, Ms. Anne Sheffield of the International Planned Parenthood Federation, Western Hemisphere Region, Dr. Michael P. Todaro and Mr. George Zeidenstein both of the Population Council gave freely of their time in educating the author and directing him to new sources.

The hundred or more persons in developing nations who helped this project cannot all be listed here. Particular thanks are due to the following persons in developing nations who extensively exchanged ideas, information, and insights with the author. In the Philippines: Dr. Mercedes Concepcion, Director, Population Institute, University of the Philippines; Mr. Dominador P. Labit, Provincial Population Office, Santa Cruz, Laguna; Mr. Felicisimo T. San Luis, Governor, Santa Cruz, Laguna; Dr. Ozzie Simmons, Program Officer, The Ford Foundation; and Mr. Felix Zorrilla, Jr., Regional Director, Population Commission, Region IV-A. In Singapore: Dr. Kernial Sandhu, Director, Institute of Southeast Asian Studies. In Indonesia: Maja Cubarrobia, National Family Planning Coordinating Board, Jakarta; Dr. Sofjan Effency and Dr. Terence H. Hull, Population Institute, Gadjah Mada University, Yogyakarta; Dr. Thomas H. Reese III, Chief, Office of Population, AID; and Dr. Haryono Suyono, Deputy Chairman for Research and Development, National Family Planning Coordinating Board, Jakarta. Linda Belotti served as Research Assistant on this project from its inception through its conclusion and rendered valuable research assistance in all its phases. Jill Dugan helped edit the original draft.

processes necessary to achieve the desired outcome: a higher quality of life both for the people of the world today and for future generations.

The following analysis indicates that integration is well supported by all we know about the nature of societal systems, but that we need to concern ourselves (1) with the *transmitting processes* which link population programs, including family planning with developmental activities; (2) with distinct, separate *institutionalization* (or embodiment) of population program activities within the development context; and (3) with the quantity and quality of *knowledge* produced, which serves policymakers in this area. Furthermore, population policies must be linked with development policies in a comprehensive way, including those concerning mortality and morbidity, the ecological distribution of population, the composition of populations, the quality of the population, and the future of the family. Without such a linkage the expected quality-of-life benefits may elude the world's populace.

To state this differently: study of the relevant literature, interviews with key officials, visits in the field, and prior sociological training, knowledge, and experience all suggest that the time is ripe to move beyond the 1974 Bucharest consensus—not to replace it, but to build upon it. For reasons delineated below, the concept of integration provides a valid but limited guideline for action; and it is necessary to enrich it with additional guiding principles, both to reduce its philosophical vagueness and to secure a wider, deeper basis for relevant public policies.

INTEGRATION: SOUND SYSTEM THEORY

Integration: The Concept

The evolution of the often-cited concept of integration is well known to those active in the population field. It is briefly and schematically reviewed here for those not working in this field, and as a backdrop for the following analysis. Attention is first focused on family planning because, apart from fact-gathering activities in census and sample survey operations, family planning has been, up to this point, the major area of population policy and program.

Out of a background of inattention to family planning, there arose in the late fifties and early sixties a concern with the "population explosion." While some indications of the early interest came from developing nations, most of the drive, funds, and action were initiated by private groups and governments of the West. Third World countries and socialist republics tended to focus on the need for economic development and often rejected the notion of family planning. Crudely summarized, family planners sought to improve the quality of life by having fewer people put demands on scarce resources, while the developers' route to the same result was to increase the available resources. In economic terms, one group was concerned with demand, the other with supply. The "great debate" between these positions, which has many subtle aspects and asides, has been admirably reviewed by Bernard Berelson[1] and need not be repeated here.

The idea of integration, supported by a worldwide conference of governments in Bucharest in 1974, had two main levels: on a value level, it recognized the need to move on both fronts—family planning and economic development—although it tended to stress more the developmental context with which population policies were to be integrated. It signified a greater Western commitment to economic development and a greater willingness of Third World and socialist countries to recognize the need for family planning—although the limited consensus reflected in the conference document refers to "population policies" rather than "family planning" (let alone "birth control"), and stresses the primacy of socioeconomic development: "The explicit aim of the World Population Plan of Action is to help coordinate population trends and the trends of economic and social development. The basis for an effective solution of population problems is, above all, socioeconomic transformation."[2]

A similar debate—and partial consensus ("reduction of dissensus" might be more accurate)—seems to have taken place within the social science community.[3] Before Bucharest, some social scientists openly argued for family planning exclusively. Indeed, they suggested that better distribution of modern contraceptives would go a long way toward resolving the population problem and toward the related quality-of-life issue, and programs were evolved on that assumption. However, slow progress in implementing family planning, along with the "great debate," has led a growing number of social scientists to question the role of other societal changes in effecting family planning. The family-planning approach was called inadequate, for example, in an often-cited 1967 article by Kingsley Davis, because it "does not undertake to influence most of the determinants of human reproduction."[4] Family-planning programs as they have been

1. Bernard Berelson, *The Great Debate On Population Policy* (New York: Population Council, 1975).

2. Report of the *United Nations World Population Conference, United Nations Conference 60/19, 1974* (New York: UN, 1975), p. 3.

3. On the Bucharest role as one which "reconciles" the two viewpoints, see Rafael M. Salas, *People: An International Choice* (Oxford: Penguin, 1976), p. 131.

4. Kingsley Davis, "Population Policy: Will Current Programs Succeed?" *Science* 158 (November 10, 1967):731.

constituted, according to Davis, can only reduce births to the extent that unwanted births exceed wanted births because they neglect those factors which affect the motivation to have smaller families. Since factors affecting the birth rate (such as a woman's age at marriage) are chiefly influenced by social and economic conditions, Davis argued that family-planning programs "must be supplemented with equal or greater investments in research and experimentation to determine the required socioeconomic measures."[5] This position has gained in influence since Bucharest, to the extent that even those who previously dealt with family planning almost exclusively now pay at least some homage to it. It should be noted, however, that despite the reduced dissensus, there continued significant differences of emphasis on development versus family planning, both intellectually and in program orientation. There are still those who stress socioeconomic development as the most important avenue to improved quality of life *and* the best way to curb population (if such a goal is desired) and those who view family planning (coordinated with socioeconomic development) as an activity worthy of nurturing in its own right and a most effective contribution to socioeconomic development. Members of both camps, and those who define themselves as in between, point to the wide latitude the concept of integration contains (i.e., its limited specificity and hence weak guiding capacity), both philosophically and as to which lines policymakers are to follow.[6]

Integration and Sociological Theory

From the viewpoint of sociological theory and research, the limited consensus implied in the concept of integration is well founded. Sociological system theory (not to be equated with general system theory) has evolved a view of society as a semiorganic, or systemic, being. This contrasts sharply with the psychological stimuli-response and the anthropological diffusion theories.

According to sociological system theory, the effects of a new input—whether they be due to a change in the available resources, a new technology, or a new birth control technique—are determined, only in part, by the nature (or attributes) of the input. They are, however, significantly, if not largely, shaped by the internal structure and processes of the social system into which the input is introduced. For instance, the effects of the level and nature of foreign aid given to a society are largely determined

5. *Ibid.*, p. 739.

6. For the views up to Bucharest, see Michael S. Teitelbaum, "Population and Development: Is a Consensus Possible?" *Foreign Affairs* 52 (4) (July 1974):742–60.

by the structural condition of the recipient society rather than by the donor society.

System theory contrasts sharply with the stimulus-response theory,[7] which derives its core image from the Pavlovian experiments: the bell rings; the dog's saliva flows. Or, take away the toys of a group of children and they all become aggressive with each other. According to this theory, specific stimuli elicit specific responses. System theory, in contrast, expects the same stimulus to produce different responses. In the last example, for instance (here the system being the children's personalities or the small group), the same stimulus—removal of the toys—would produce rather different behavior (aggress or regress, attack or cry, act individually or in unison—or even ignore the stimulus), depending on the children's personalities and relationships.

Similarly, diffusion theory is greatly interested in the intersocietal flow of technologies, techniques, ideas.[8] Where did tobacco, the plow, or whatever come from? Is it imported or native? The image behind this is often that of the white missionary or trader bringing a new culture to the "primitives," although it also deals with diffusion among preliterate societies. System theory, in contrast, suggests that the item's origin (e.g., foreign) is less significant than whether it is adopted or rejected by the system and, if accepted, how it is internalized. (Most Latin American republics, for example, theoretically copied the constitution of the United States, but its pragmatic meaning in those countries reflects their own politics, so it is quite different from that of the U.S.)[9]

Applying this notion to the field of socioeconomic development and population policies, whether large shipments of rice from overseas are used to conserve a nation's resources, to evolve its infrastructure, to further enrich the elite, or to feed the poor, is largely determined by the sociopolitical-economic structure of the recipient country—not by the amount or quality of rice, or by the attributes of its senders. This is not to suggest that the rice shipments and the conditions under which they are provided have no effect, but that the effect is, to a considerable extent, determined

---

For a later report, see *A Report on UNFPA-EWPI Technical Working Group Meeting of Family Planning With Rural Development* (Honolulu: East-West Center, Feb. 15–18, 1978), p. 3.

7. Ernest R. Hilgard and Gordon H. Bower, *Theories of Learning,* 3rd ed. (Englewood Cliffs, N.J.: Prentice-Hall, 1966), pp. 8–11.

8. A. L. Kroeber, "Diffusionism," in *The Encyclopedia of the Social Sciences,* edited by Edwin R. A. Seligman and Alvin Johnson (New York: Macmillan, 3rd ed., 1937), III:139–42.

9. Jacques Lambert, *Latin America* (Berkeley: University of California Press, 1967), pp. 267–71.

internally. The underlying reason for this view of societies, of great consequence for this study, is contained in the notion that societies are "integrated"—that they typically have mechanisms which keep their parts related to each other, and which seek to maintain the internal format of these relationships, i.e., the structure of the system.

System theory has been criticized for assuming excessive integration and, indeed, it must be recognized that some societies are only poorly integrated.[10] System theory has also been criticized for focusing on the wrong system unit—tribes, regions, ethnic groups, or classes—rather than on the national society which is said to be the integrated unit[11] (e.g., on "French Canada" and "English Canada," rather than on "Canada").[12]

The concept of societal integration on the national level is useful, especially when treated as an hypothesis. In other words, it is not necessary to assume *a priori* that societal integration is high and that the relevant unit of analysis is the nation. For each social system, one must determine the extent of its integration empirically and know what the relevant units of integration are. At the same time, past studies suggest that for many contemporary social systems, the level of integration of nation-societies is sufficiently high to expect that changes in one sector will interact with changes in other sectors and that the net or ultimate change which results will be significantly affected by this internal interaction. Thus the basic underlying notion of integration is fully supported by sociological analyses and studies, and one cannot prudently proceed with family planning or other population programs without taking into account the linkages which the impacted sector has with other societal sectors. The conditions in, and processes of, other sectors—from health services to income to educational structure, from public administration to local/metropolitan relations—will affect population program efforts. Those conditions and processes may hinder, support, or sidetrack the population program efforts, but they are never irrelevant.

An integrated policy, which seeks to take these intersector linkages into account and, when necessary, to move other sectors simultaneously with (or even prior to) making advances in family planning or other population programs, should be more effective in the long run than non-integrated, isolated population policies which ignore these linkages, the bases of societal integration. Or, to put it differently, the reality of societal

10. Arthur S. Banks, *Political Handbook of the World, 1977* (Washington, D.C.: USGPO, July 1977), pp. 66–68.

11. Ralf Dahrendorf, *Class and Class Conflict in Industrial Society* (Stanford, Calif.: Stanford University Press, 1965).

12. Everett C. Hughes, *French Canada in Transition* (Chicago: University of Chicago Press, 1963).

integration favors the concept of policy integration for those who seek to change one or more societal facets.

It also follows that, since the linkages are basically internal, external inputs (such as importation of birth control techniques and technologies or subsidies of family-planning programs) particularly need to be designed with the internal structure in mind. This is especially so because initiators of such inputs are not typically subject to the impacted society's interacting processes and are hence more likely to try to ignore them.

Main Qualifications

While the integration of population and development policies is basically supported by the system view of society, sociological analysis also points to three main caveats, ignored in at least some of the formulations of the integration position.

1. Societal integration, while commonly found, varies significantly in its level and intensity. The support or the "drag" (constraints) provided by factors and sectors of a society other than the one impacted will be high only in highly integrated societies, lower in poorly integrated ones. It is erroneous to assume *a priori* that integration is high in all societies. The level is to be determined empirically, and the implications of whatever level is found must be taken into account. For example, one would generally expect a higher level of integration in many traditional villages and clans than in urban slums. (Although here, too, significant differences are to be expected among levels of integration for a given type of social unit. Edward Banfield, for instance, reported on a poorly integrated village.[13]) In introducing contraceptives to a well-integrated village, one would expect to make good progress if the village system and structure are favorable (as they are reported to be in contemporary Bali[14]), and to do rather poorly if such programs are incompatible, as they are, say, in some traditional Catholic countries.[15] In contrast, a typical poorly integrated slum

13. Edward C. Banfield, *The Moral Basis of a Backward Society* (Glencoe, Ill.: Free Press, 1958).

14. Haryono Suyono *et al., Village Family Planning—The Indonesian Model: Institutionalizing Contraceptive Practice* (Jakarta, Indonesia: National Family Planning Coordinating Board), Technical Report Series, Monograph No. 13, July 1976. Terence H. Hull, Valerie J. Hull, and Masri Singarimbun, "Indonesia's Family Planning Story: Success and Challenge," *Population Bulletin* 32 (6) (Washington, D.C.: Population Reference Bureau, 1977).

15. Benjamin Viel, *The Demographic Explosion* (New York: Irvington, 1976), pp. 178–79. J. Mayone Stycos, *Ideology, Faith and Family Planning in Latin America* (New York: McGraw-Hill, 1971). p. 84.

will offer both much less support and much less resistance because it is socially more neutral. Thus while it is sociologically supported that integration is relevant, it should not be assumed that it is unfavorable to population programs including family planning. Integration is a powerful mechanism which can propel or retard, depending on its reaction to the substance of the policy.[16]

Greep *et al.* made this point in respect of family planning (without referring to its analytical basis) in urging that a wide variety of contraceptive technologies and techniques be developed and promoted to suit the specific sociocultural needs of various people.[17] Several of the individuals interviewed favored "customized," rather than global or regional, population policies, adapted to a particular nation's character, conditions, and level of integration. In some nations, for example, working only with the national central government may be sufficient, while in others, which are highly fragmented and less politically intensive, working with nongovernment organizations, multisectors, and geographical areas may be essential for success.

2. System theory, which stresses intersectoral linkages, would lead one to expect that the effects will be interactional rather than monodirectional. In the literature on integration, however, many more references are made to the effects of socioeconomic development on population policies and programs than to the contributions of population policies and programs to socioeconomic development.

While slower population growth is often expected to increase the quality of life, it is less often recognized as directly affecting development (which is defined here as an increasing productive capacity of whatever adjective—economic, social, or political—goes with development). This may reflect the fact that scores of factors are subsumed under the concept of development, but only a few under population programs including family planning. Consequently, it may be natural to expect that more effect will flow from development to population management than vice versa. Nevertheless, it should be stressed that effects flow both ways—that not only does development enhance population programs including family planning, but population programs also enhance development. For example, family planning—to the extent that it frees women to work (where

16. For additional discussion and documentation, see Amitai Etzioni, *A Comparative Analysis of Complex Organizations*, rev. ed. (New York: Free Press, 1975), Chapter 11.

17. Roy O. Greep, Marjorie A. Koblinsky, Frederick S. Jaffe, *Reproduction and Human Welfare: A Challenge to Research* (Cambridge, Mass.: MIT Press, 1976), p. 25.

there is no labor surplus) and to the extent that it reduces the consumption of resources—frees resources for development quite directly.[18]

3. While integration may be high or low and while its actual level, in a specific society in a specific historical period, must be determined empirically, scores of studies of interfactor linkages strongly suggest that, at each point in time, there tends to be considerable intersector "play" and lag. That is, granted the integration (or interaction) assumption, under many conditions, it is to be expected that varying degrees of progress can be made by changing one facet without working on the others. This will either be due to the fact that societal sectors are often loosely, rather than tightly linked, i.e., that there is a measure of "play" among connected facets; or that some have moved previously and hence the factor one is working on is lagging, and can be made to catch up without working on the others. The significance of these two concepts for the present discussion will be considered next.

Intervariable play exists, for instance, in goodwill. If one introduces a high level of austerity (e.g., price and wage control) into a society where there is a good labor-management relationship based on many years of working together and economic growth, the new policy often may initially produce very few strikes, discernible side effects on productivity, or other indications of disturbed industrial relations. If, on the other hand, the same austerity policy is introduced into a situation of growing labor disaffection and unrest, it may raise the level of labor-management conflict quickly and severely. Even where goodwill is high, a prolonged wage freeze accompanied by rising prices (due to imports, for example) will sooner or later exhaust it, and the expected consequences will follow. Goodwill here defines the extent of intervariable play.

Economists use a similar concept in the term "slack,"[19] which refers to unemployed resources or unused capacity. It suggests that as long as there are idle resources, higher output can be generated without new inputs or system changes. If there is no slack, or once it is exhausted, this is no longer the case.

The same phenomenon of play is recognized in studies of population programs such as family planning, although it is occasionally ignored in the more rigid and abstract discussions of integration. There are reports of significant progress in family planning, which is not accompanied, or even

18. On the producing role of women in developing nations, see Adrienne Germain, "Poor Rural Women: A Policy Perspective," *Journal of International Affairs* 30 (2) (Fall/Winter 1976–77):161–72.

19. Alpha Chiang, *Fundamental Methods of Mathematical Economics* (New York: McGraw Hill, 1967), pp. 598–99.

preceded, by economic development.[20] In some instances, this even occurs following economic retreat or underdevelopment (e.g., Sri Lanka, in recent years).[21] This is sometimes attributed to simultaneous, or antecedent, development in some sector other than the economic one (e.g., increase in literacy). But as long as such other development is not shown to be the responsible factor, its attribution is more an indication of willingness to give population programs such as family planning any room for independent action than it is evidence of social linkages. To acknowledge play is not to assume policy stance built upon it. Play only suggests that some progress can be made in one area without working on the other societal facets. Providing people with the means to avoid unwanted pregnancies is a case in point. Meeting unmet demands is another expression of the same idea. Whether the scope of such play is trivial or considerable is a point which will be further considered in a moment—but first, let us consider a related idea, that of intervariable lag.

Lag is said to exist when one factor, or set of factors, is advanced, while one or more others stay behind.[22] These lagging factors can then catch up, without further advancing the others. Lag will occur when, for example, work opportunities for women, family income, and literacy (factors believed to correlate with acceptance of birth control) have gradually increased, but little or no increase in acceptance of birth control has yet occurred. When a birth control program is now launched, it is expected to make relatively rapid progress without working on these factors and still benefit from the progress they have already made.

Both concepts—play and lag—suggest a measure of flexibility within the interaction-integration view of society and lead to the same basic policy implications: (1) under some circumstances, progress can be made while working only on population programs, such as family planning, and (2) once the play or lag is exhausted, the other factors will have to be advanced before additional progress can be made. Both suggest that progress in population programs without simultaneous development in other areas does not disprove the integration thesis but that such progress does agitate against the rigid assumption that nothing will be gained unless prior or simultaneous development is achieved.

The scope of play and lag becomes a rather crucial issue here. If it

20. R. T. Ravenholt and John Chao, "Availability of Family Planning Services: The Key to Rapid Fertility Reduction," *Family Planning Perspectives* 6 (4) (Fall 1974).

21. Private communication.

22. On the concept of lag, see William F. Ogburn, *Social Change* (New York: Viking, 1922), pp. 200–212.

is small, the issue is largely one of mere theoretical interest; but if it is considerable (and under certain circumstances, such as low societal integration, it may be quite large), the policy implications for population programs including family planning are very significant. This is because population programs tend to be less demanding in terms of resources, funds, work force, managerial attention, and time than many programs of socioeconomic development. (Reference here is not being made to, for instance, one plant versus one family-planning clinic, but to the industrialization of a country versus the modernization of family planning or implementation of other population programs such as those relating to population distribution.) Consequently, if the scope of progress which can be made in population programs is considerable, at least under certain circumstances, then it is cost-effective to do so.

Before addressing the question of whether play and lag are ever substantial and to what extent, it may be useful to explore a general underlying posture. The significance of play and lag is not determined solely by the size of the unmet demand (which in some societies may encompass 20 to 30 percent, or even more, of what is needed to bring population growth, or distribution, to the desired level). Their significance is equally affected by how voluntaristic one is in viewing societal change. If one is highly voluntaristic and, as such, socioeconomic development can be attained rather readily, at least under favorable conditions (e.g., high level of Western contribution to new international trade arrangements), then the size of unmet demand is relatively unimportant. If one assumes, as does the voluntarist, that the other factors (e.g., economic and educational) can be moved—and that they can be moved rather quickly—and if those factors are recognized as both valuable in their own right and necessary for full implementation of family planning or other population programs, at least in the long run, then why concern oneself with the difference between, for instance, 3 percent and 30 percent of unmet demand? Indeed, as one leading family-planning policy researcher put it: "People want to have sex and children; unless their views of these are changed, no improvement in contraceptive techniques, technology, or delivery system will solve the problem of developing nations."[23]

The key phrase here is "will solve the problem of developing nations," which is, of course, highly voluntaristic. A less voluntaristic observer would assume that no policy available during the foreseeable future "will solve the problem of development," and hence that any significant progress, wherever it is achieved, and whether it be on one or more fronts, is of great interest. People who desire light bulbs which

23. Private communication.

utilize electricity only to produce light, but to waste no energy on heat, will find of very little interest the difference between bulbs which are 4.5 percent effective and those which are 5.5 percent effective. In contrast, people who see the total variance available for the foreseeable future as ranging between 4.5 and 5.5 percent will be greatly interested in the 5.5 percent bulbs. Berelson made a similar point when he wrote: "Would an anti-TB campaign be regarded as a failure if 'only' one-third of the decline in TB could be attributed to the campaign efforts? I would judge it a smashing success."[24]

The author sides with those who are less voluntaristic.[25] Socioeconomic development is perceived as a highly desirable purpose—but not one that is readily achieved for most nations under most circumstances. Out of commitment to the quality of life goal, one must have great interest in any front on which significant progress can be made, expending resources for that area as cost effectively as possible. This might mean using up some play here, exhausting some lag there—rather than first focusing on the conditions which require simultaneous (and coordinated) attack on numerous fronts.

What is the size of the unmet (or ready-made) demand for family planning? No universal answer to this question can be given because unmet demand differs from society to society and over time. There are indications, however, that, under some circumstances at least, it seems to be sizable. For example, about 20 percent of all births to married couples in the United States between 1960 and 1965 were unwanted, according to an estimate by Bumpass and Westoff.[26] (It seems safe to assume that if unmarried women were also included, the proportion would be higher, especially in view of the high pregnancy rates among teenagers.) Using world fertility survey data, Westoff also examined unmet demand in Korea, Malaysia, Nepal, Pakistan, and Thailand. Defining unmet demand as the proportion of women who were currently married and exposed to the risk of conception and who said they did not want more children but were not practicing contraception, Westoff estimated the range of unmet demand to be between 21 and 32 percent across the five countries.[27] To the less voluntaristic observer, this suggests that family planning should be

24. Bernard Berelson, *The Great Debate on Population Policy*, p. 12. For elaboration and reasons, see Amitai Etzioni, *The Active Society* (New York: Free Press, 1968), chs. 4–5.

25. For additional discussion, see Etzioni, *The Active Society*, Ch. 4.

26. Larry Bumpass and Charles F. Westoff, "The 'Perfect Contraceptive' Population," *Science* 169 (September 18, 1970):1180.

27. Charles F. Westoff, "The Unmet Need for Birth Control in Five Asian Countries," *Family Planning Perspectives* 10 (3) (May/June 1968):181.

stressed in these situations and greater emphasis made on an integrated approach where the unmet demand is much smaller—rather than integration policy being mechanically applied in the same manner under all circumstances. Similar considerations could be involved if population policy and programs were generated in relation to population distribution or to improvement of population quality as considered in Chapters 9 and 10.

THE ROLE OF SPECIALIZED TRANSMISSION MECHANISMS

Up to this point, an effort has been made to show that: (1) integration as a policy stance is basically a sound idea since society acts as an integrated entity; but that (2) the level of integration varies from society to society and varies over time, hence—because of play and lag—may allow for substantial progress on any one front without simultaneous progress on the others. It may now be suggested that public policy must concern itself with the transmitting mechanisms—even when the societal level of integration is high and there is little play and no lag. The transmitting mechanisms are those specialized processes which either transmit progress in one area to progress in another or put pressure on that other area to catch up. Such transmittal, as a general rule, is never fully automatic, and the more public policy can contribute to the improvement of these mechanisms, the more progress will be achieved in related areas and the more benefits will be derived out of integration. Thus, for example, while a general rise in level of education will enhance a nation's industrialization, the industrialization efforts will benefit substantially more if the procedures for hiring employees are also changed—drawing more on those with better education and training while reducing nepotism, tribalism, and corruption. This would not, of course, automatically result from increasing the level of education. (The specialized transmitting mechanisms here—operating between the educated people and the industrial labor force—are the hiring procedures.)

This concept may usefully be applied to development and population programs. There is a widely held assumption—often more implicit that explicit—that progress in socioeconomic development by itself will lead to the desired population results. Ozzie G. Simmons and Lyle Saunders summarize this viewpoint well in respect of fertility: "One approach to the problem of excessive fertility that has enjoyed substantial popularity is the notion that employment of policy measures to promote economic and social development and modernization will surely bring in their wake fertility decline. In short, it is argued, development policy *is* fertility policy."[28] They

28. Ozzie Simmons and Lyle Saunders, "The Present and Prospective State of Policy Approaches to Fertility," Papers of the East-West Population Institute, no. 33 (June 1975):11.

go on to cite Paul Demeny: "One version of this position advocates exclusive concentration on development policy as narrowly defined, that is without any direct attention to fertility effects as such."[29]

In contrast, the author agrees with those who expect only some of such benefits to follow automatically, and who maintain that the rest must be helped along—that those benefits which would take place without specialized transmitting mechanisms would do so more rapidly if encouraged. Hence one of the main recommendations made in this chapter is that the conceptual and experimental development of transmitting mechanisms, from socioeconomic development to population action programs, be one of the major tasks of agencies concerned with such programs, so that these concepts become available to public policymakers.[30]

An example based on family planning might serve to illustrate this idea. Many people allegedly desire a greater number of children than population programs wish they would, both as insurance against loss of children due to death and to secure economic and social support prior to and throughout old age.[31] Assume that a new health program reduced the infant mortality rate in a given country. Without explicit and effective efforts to point out the implication of the lower death rate achieved by the new health programs for contraceptive behavior, it might take a decade or more for a community to become aware of the changing death rate (which is, after all, very gradual and most noticeable only in statistical aggregates), much less to draw the "proper" conclusion from it.[32] It will take still more time, education, and resources for the changed preference regarding desired number of children to be reflected in learning about the use of birth control techniques and technologies and to gain access to such technologies, i.e., implementation of, or change in, the delivery system.

In discussing with population experts the need to formulate and test ways in which the family planning payoff of new socioeconomic development could be increased, two major viewpoints were encountered: enthusiastic endorsement by some and the assertion of two important counter-

29. Paper by Paul Demeny cited in "Population Policy: The Role of National Governments," 1974, p. 11.

30. This position has been taken by George Zeidenstein in lecturing before the Select Committee on Population, House of Representatives, April 20, 1978. George Zeidenstein, "Population and Development: Overview, Trends, Consequences, Perspectives and Issues," 95th Congress, Second Session, vol. 1 (April 1978):5.

31. Fred Arnold *et al., The Value of Children: A Cross-National Study,* vol. 1 (Honolulu: East-West Population Institute, 1975).

32. For a review of the relevant literature and insights into the problems of the "learning curve" following improvements in child health, see Peter Kunstadter, "Interactions of Child Mortality with Maternal Parity," unpublished paper, June 1978.

points by others. One of these counterpoints concerns the relationship between motivation and action; the other, the value of information, education, and communication.

Proponents of the first point claim that, once people no longer want more children, "they know what to do"—that they proved, long before massive programs of modern contraceptives were available, that they know how to have fewer babies.[33]

There are three steps to this argument. The first concerns the link between socioeconomic development and preference for children—and, consequently, motivation to employ family planning; the second, willingness to use modern contraceptive methods; and the third, availability of relevant technologies.

The issue regarding the first step is an empirical one, subject to the verdict of data rather than argument. The author subscribes to the hypothesis that socioeconomic development, if not aided by education explicitly aimed at promoting a changed norm in the desired number of children, will be significantly more gradual in leading to a reduction in that norm than when explicit educational efforts accompany or follow the socioeconomic development. The reason for expecting that education would be valuable here is that there is no necessary link between higher level of income, education, or health and having fewer children. The link, therefore, must be forged via changed views concerning the value of additional offspring. How much education could do here to contribute to this process is an empirical question.

The importance of the second and third steps can be shown on the basis of logic and requires little new research. Consider first the role of modern contraception. The argument that "if people want it badly enough they know what to do" exemplifies a common misunderstanding about the interaction between motivation and action. (Similar arguments are made about the alcoholic's will to stop drinking, or the addict's to stop using drugs, overeating and so on.)[34] Implicitly, it is assumed that, if motivation is present, the proper action will follow; but if not, action cannot be expected until motivation is generated. It is further pointed out that, even if people are somehow convinced to use contraceptives, if there is no real motivation they soon stop using them—hence the high dropout rates.[35]

33. Paul Demeny, "Early Fertility Decline in Austria-Hungary," *Daedalus* 97 (1968):520–21. Michael S. Teitelbaum, "Relevance of Demographic Transition Theory for Developing Countries," *Science* 188 (4187) (May 2, 1975):423.

34. See chapter on alcoholism in Amitai Etzioni and Richard Remp, *Technological Shortcuts to Social Change* (New York: Russell Sage Foundation, 1973), pp. 53–102.

35. High dropout rates were reported in sample studies of oral contraceptives

While the basic argument here is quite valid, it proceeds on a level of thinking which treats motivation as a dichotomous variable: either present or absent. Motivation (and most other variables) is better treated as a continuous variable (which, of course, researchers—but not many conceptualizers—tend to do). It follows that there is, for any given population (or subpopulation) at any given point in time, a certain level of motivation to regulate future births, ranging from aversion to disinterest to highest possible interest. Large segments of the world's people seem to be somewhere between the extreme poles. It is for them that the specific motivation requirement of each technology is expected to make a significant difference. Thus, for instance, given a low level of interest, a technology which is easily available and not demanding would be more widely used by people with a "middling" level of motivation than a technology which is costly, difficult to obtain, demanding, and full of side effects.

Thus, all other things being equal, variations in technologies and in their availability make a difference in the frequency and continuity of family planning. Indeed, it seems impossible to speak about the size of the unmet demand without making reference to a specific mix of technologies, costs, and delivery systems. The basic reason for this is that no two technologies are equal in their human, economic, and administrative costs. For example, if, given the same population in terms of age, education, income, health, and motivation, a shift is made from a technology which is costly, difficult to obtain, and socially taboo (e.g., birth control pills in an orthodox Catholic country, available only by prescription) to the opposite situation (free birth control pills in an approving culture, dispensed without prescription although with a medical history and checklist), a greater utilization—or unmet demand—can be expected. To state this differently, the population motivation profile varies from smaller to larger, depending on the nature of the technology and access to it. Some of the relevant variables which influence motivation are cost, distance to supply points, legitimacy, need for repeated decisions, fear of side effects, and actual side effects.

(The connection between the nature and availability of a technology and motivation was made vivid during a visit to a Philippine village in which women line up for a contraceptive injection which they prefer over the Pill or IUD because they fear its side effects less, consider injections to

---

in a number of countries. Within one year after initiating use of the contraceptive, the percentage of dropouts was 88 in Bangladesh, 60.7 percent in a survey of urban centers in India, 53 percent in Colombia, and 41.8 percent in Hong Kong. Philip Kreager, *Family Planning Drop-Outs Reconsidered* (London: International Planned Parenthood Federation, 1977), p. 90.

be akin to health treatments, and believe the injections to be more potent than ingested or inserted matter.)

Out of the attributes which affect motivation, one can derive the profile of an appropriate technology which maximizes unmet demand without making other changes. This would result from a method which would be available at little or no cost, without the need to travel for resupplies (i.e., it would be available at points visited regularly, such as the well or village store), to which no stigma is attached, and which is culturally welcomed. It would also be a method which could be applied for a long period of time—preferably until conception is desired—but which could be easily reversed. Finally, it would have no undesirable side effects on either health or sexual relations.

Hence the author sides with those who favor additional research and development effects on contraceptives and is against those who see such efforts as no longer needed, and with the Ford Foundation panel, headed by Roy O. Greep, which concluded that: "A variety of safe and effective methods of fertility regulation beyond those now available is urgently needed. . . . Two decades of experience with oral contraceptives and intra-uterine devices have made it evident that these methods have significant limitations. New methods that have fewer health hazards than existing methods, that are more acceptable and convenient for individual couples, and that are simpler to distribute are needed."[36]

(A similar position was taken by the president of the Population Council, George Zeidenstein, in a May 16, 1978, address to the Symposium on Contraceptive Technology, sponsored by the National Academy of Sciences. The head of the Population Office at the Ford Foundation, Oscar Harkavy, also advanced this position in testimony before the Select Committee on Population in April 1978, as did a hereto unpublished report by the National Research Council's Panel on Population, Health, and Nutrition.)

This position is supported not because dramatic breakthroughs can be confidently expected but because in any significant progress there will be a potential for increased demand—a demand which can be satisfied relatively cost effectively. (In other words, the costs of the improved technologies can be expected to be lower per user than, for instance, educating potential users—although education, of course, is of value in its own right, whereas technological progress has no such secondary value.)

It is further argued that, while differences in technology and access (or delivery) may increase unmet demand, they will not "make or break" the population problem, and hence are basically insignificant.

36. Greep, *Reproduction and Human Welfare,* p. 25.

Here one position regarding voluntarism is pivotal. If one seeks to "solve the population problem," and develops scores of nations, (some of which have few prerequisites in terms of resources, infrastructure, or cybernetic capacities) both to raise the quality of life and to gain the bonus of fertility reduction, and does so on relatively short order, then the achievements of technological improvements in contraceptives and other family-planning activities may indeed seem small by comparison. If, on the other hand, one recognizes that problems of such magnitude are rarely "solved"—that most development plans achieve fewer gains in development than birth control plans achieve in fertility reduction; and that progress, when achieved, although high in some countries, averages out over the years for most countries—then one realizes that the impact of technological and delivery system improvements, while small in absolute terms, may be quite considerable when compared to those of other programs and efforts. Indeed, the less optimistic one is about guidability (without, however, despairing), and the more conscious one is of scarcity, the more is one concerned with where practical results can be obtained, especially at relatively low costs and relatively quickly.

Finally, resources for other efforts (such as development) are freed by attending first to whatever unmet demand already exists—or is generated by improved technology and delivery—because, with this approach, fewer resources are used up for maternity and child care or by outright consumption. In Indonesia, for instance, it has been suggested that the cost of the rice which would be consumed if the births averted by family planning were not averted, would by itself exceed the costs of the family-planning program[37]—and perhaps even exceed the cost of the rice imported by Indonesia.[38]

Turning now to the second point, IEC (information, education, communication), again the criticism seems to be well taken—but not its implication. That slogans, placards, and commercials often do little to enhance family planning and that they are not cost effective—especially when they seek to change attitudes rather than to inform (e.g., about the

37. For "savings" for development from family planning, see an early but still significant work by A. J. Coale and E. M. Hooper, *Population Growth and Economic Development in Low-Income Countries* (Princeton: Princeton University Press, 1951). See also O. Simmons, "The Indian Investment in Family Planning," Population Council Occasional paper, p. 28.

38. Private communication. Soedarmadi and Thomas H. Reese, *The Indonesian National Family Planning Program: A Cost-Effectiveness Analysis 1971/1972–1973/1974* (Jakarta, Indonesia: National Family Planning Coordinating Board), Technical Report Series, Monograph No. 10, April 1975.

relative merits of various contraceptives)—is well supported by sociological work in other areas.[39]

The data strongly suggest that formal communication, as a rule, is a weak agent of social change. This does not hold for *other* means of education, however, which basically seek to mobilize the emotive and normative power of small groups. Some family planners may base their model on the tightly knit, single purpose groups. For example, the birth control program in Java is said to form groups specifically around contraceptive use.[40] Others mobilize existing social groups for family planning, as is said to work in Bali.[41] Groups may also be composed for other purposes, such as teaching or sewing, with birth control promoted as only one of its activities, which reportedly has been done in Bangladesh.[42]

In all these situations the main force is not the literature on contraception, the official outside input, or other formal communication provided by birth control agencies and outreach workers. These are, it is true, the mobilizing agents which link the local natural or newly composed groups to the desired program; but the education bite comes from the power of these groups, through which individuals are deeply bonded. They thus provide an example of an effective transmitting mechanism. They might not work, in the long run, if other forces are not supportive, but they can accelerate, magnify, and provide greater family-planning outcomes for development inputs than would be obtained without such transmitting mechanisms. Hence the recommendation follows that those concerned with integration study and help evolve these transmitting mechanisms, so that policymakers as well as mobilized citizens can increase the interaction effects (or payoffs) of family planning and other population programs for development.

SECTOR RANKING

The concept of intersector linkages and of transmitting mechanisms raises an additional question: Are all intersector bridges equally achievable and

39. Haryono Suyono and Thomas H. Reese, "Integrating Village and Family Planning and Primary Health Services—The Indonesian Perspective," unpublished paper, January 1978.

40. Terence H. Hull, Valerie J. Hull, and Masri Singarimbun, "Indonesia's Family Planning Story: Success and Challenge," *Population Bulletin* 32 (6) (Washington, D.C.: Population Reference Bureau, 1977), pp. 24–25; Terence H. Hull, "Where Credit Is Due: Policy Implications of the Recent Rapid Fertility Decline in Bali," Population Institute, Gadjah Mada University, Yogyakarta, Indonesia, unpublished paper, 1978, p. 6.

41. Private communication.

42. Private communication with Mrs. Rodriguez.

equally productive? If not, which are more productive for the purposes at hand—or can be made to be so? This issue may be of little interest to the hypervoluntarist. After all, if one assumes that a society can readily be guided toward higher levels of activity and achievement on all or most facets encompassed by development, one need not be concerned with the relative power of various linkages or the effectiveness of various transmitting mechanisms. On the other hand, the more one sees the difficulties involved in guidability and is concerned with making it more effective, the more relevant these questions become.

Concretely, the questions of where and how to integrate are raised on numerous levels: local services, regional and national administrations, planning and public policy, and even international agencies. In Indonesia, for example, the question is raised of whether family planning outreach workers should also provide health and nutritional advice in order to "give the villages something *they* want."[43] In the Philippines, an attempt is made to package family planning as part of a four-item program, "Project Compassion," in which health, nutrition, new modes of gardening, and environmental protection are contained together with birth control.

The author is not aware of any definitive data, either from population studies or other investigations, which would allow one to rank the various sectoral combinations. We cannot decide *a priori* that the integration of family planning with health services, let us say, is a more effective pairing for all or most societies than, for instance, family planning with new employment opportunities or increased educational or other efforts. Obviously, numerous factors could affect the relative success of various combinations. Nor are these combinations limited to two sectors at a time—which further increases the possible permutations and the complexity of the issue. Influencing factors include the relative lag versus the advanced state of the various sectors, the relative legitimation of intervention in these respective sectors (e.g., in the United States, federal intervention in securing jobs is somewhat more acceptable than in sex education), power relations among the agencies involved (e.g., health versus welfare, where they are separate institutions), and numerous others.

Few general observations based on sociological analysis can, however, be made on this subject. All other things being equal:

1. The wider the sectoral reach of the integration policy and the more encompassing the scope of planning and coordination in terms of the sectors involved, the more unlikely is progress—but, if progress is accomplished, the more effective it will be. The reason for this suggestion is that coordination is a highly taxing task; but the system, at the same time,

43. Private communication with Dr. Terence H. Hull, Population Institute, Gadjah Mada University, Yogyakarta, Indonesia.

is anchored at numerous points, and hence all those points must *eventually* be moved if it is to change in a significant way. This can be accomplished either: (a) by planning ahead and working on all fronts at once; or (b) by advancing some sectors, in the process exerting pressure on the others to progress, even if their progress is not planned *a priori* or secured simultaneously.

2. Activities which have relatively clear and measurable outcomes may lose out when integrated with those whose outcomes are less obvious. The basic reason for this is that evaluation and supervision, difficult under the best of circumstances, becomes even more difficult when outcomes are vague—and efficient program management is rare, of course, without effective evaluation and supervision. Hence, integrating family planning (which has relatively clear measures of "process," e.g., number and proportion of "acceptors," or continuity of use and of outcome, e.g., reduction in births) with, for instance, general education (whose measures of outcome are comparatively less clear and whose tasks, while more ambitious, are also more amorphous)[44] contrasts with integrating family planning with, let us say, specific health services (such as vaccination) or with providing jobs to the unemployed.

These questions, and many others, arise when attempts are made to integrate family planning into a general development program concretely on either the service, management, or planning level.[45] One issue, that of the independent institutionalization of family planning and, more generally, of population policies, programs, and activities, seems to be so pivotal that it deserves special attention.

INSTITUTIONAL EMBODIMENT OF POPULATION

The issue is under what structural conditions will an integrated program of development and population programs make the highest degree of combined progress? By combined progress is meant advancement both of the goals of development and of the population program objectives either

44. In suggesting that family planning is more measurable than many services we are not unmindful of the many measurement difficulties involved. See, for instance, Hull *et al.*, "Indonesia's Family Planning Story: Success and Challenge," *Population Bulletin* 32 (6) (Washington, D.C.: Population Reference Bureau, 1977); and *Pakistan Fertility Survey* (Pakistan: Population Planning Council of Pakistan, Oct. 1976), pp. 2–3. *The Survey of Fertility in Thailand: Country Report,* vol. 1 (Bangkok: Institute of Population Studies, Chulalongkorn University and Population Survey Division, National Statistical Office, 1977), p. 1.

45. For excellent discussions of some of the programs see William Paul McGreevey and Associates, "Population and Development," assistance to USAID, un-

because this is assumed to be a necessary part of a development program or in itself a direct way to advance quality of life. In this sense, not only development, but also the population program becomes an instrument or ultimate goal of integration.

Logically, using the family-planning example, the alternatives are:

1. Complete fusion of family planning into some developmental activities, such as health services. (It has already been indicated why it is held that specific family-planning activities are necessary and that sheer reliance on fallout effects of other programs would retard both family planning and development.)

2. Complete institutional embodiment in a segregated administrative hierarchy, reaching all the way into the village and subvillage, drawing on a separate family-planning agency involving outreach workers and volunteers. Here family planning has its own authority and communication lines, budget, labor force, and ministry. Coordination and integration occur, as with other separate agencies (e.g., education and health), in local interagency committees, planning boards and informal contacts, regional and national planning, coordination committees and informal contacts, and the leadership of village heads, mayors, governors, and national authorities (such as the president or prime minister).

3. Various mixes in which family planning has some, but not all, of the above characteristics. For example, it may have its own commission and access routes to the national government, governors, and mayors, but as "staff" rather than "line" authority, providing advisory and promotional authority but not decision-making power.

Thus under most circumstances, independent, "line," institutionalization seems more productive for population programs—and for integration—than the other arrangements. The reason for supporting this position and a review of some of the counterarguments and exceptions to the rule follow.

On the basis of general organizational analysis and experience,[46] one must note that independent institutionalization, to one degree or another, is extremely common. Few activities are combined into a general or specialized category of action without at least some segregated institutional-

---

published report, June 1977; Gayl D. Ness, "On Integration in Family Planning Programs: A Background Paper," prepared for a technical working group meeting at East-West Center, Feb. 1978; Anne Sheffield, "The Integrated Approach to Family Planning, Population and Development," unpublished IPPF paper, Sept. 29, 1976.

46. William H. Newman, *Administrative Action* (Englewood Cliffs, N.J.: Prentice-Hall, 1950), p. 128; J. G. March and H. Simon, *Organizations* (New York: Wiley, 1958), pp. 369–89; H. A. Simon, D. W. Smithburg, and V. A. Thompson, *Public Administration* (New York: Knopf, 1959). See also Amitai Etzioni, *Modern Organizations* (Englewood Cliffs, N.J.: Prentice-Hall, 1964), pp. 24–25.

ization. Thus manufacturing corporations have separate departments for production, marketing, and labor relations—each with its own hierarchy, labor force, and budget—because each set of activities is considered to benefit from such separate institutionalization. Hospitals, universities, armies, and practically all other organizations are internally differentiated in the same manner.

Moreover, historically, whenever it was desired to secure budget, attention, and impact to a new line of activities or programs, those activities and programs received distinct institutional embodiment. Thus English received its own department at Harvard when the significance of modern language next to Latin and ancient Greek was recognized. Social sciences were set apart from humanities once their importance in academia was established. On the national level, for instance, as economic policy was considered of greater value in the United States, the president was given a Council of Economic Advisors rather than continue to rely on his general staff for assistance in this matter.[47] The same was true for science and technology with the 1962 formation of the Office of Science and Technology in the White House.[48] The United States Air Force, once a branch of the army, was given departmental status in 1947;[49] space activities were given an agency of their own (NASA) after Sputnik; and the National Science Foundation (NSF) was established once it was felt that basic research was being neglected.

In reviewing those activities which receive no separate institutionalization, one quickly realizes that these are few and far between. From accounting to physical education to acquiring supplies, all are secured by separate institutionalization on both corporate and national levels, although some activities receive higher levels of institutionalization than others (e.g., in the U.S. national government, "education" is presently an agency within a department, whereas "labor" has departmental status).

Activities left completely uninstitutionalized, or on a low level of institutionalization, tend to be weak in the sense of being poorly legitimated, vulnerable, and low in budget, labor force, and managerial attention, with their low level of institutionalization either reflecting or exacerbating their weakness. Thus in U.S. public schools, attention to ethics and character development is supposed to be "everyone's" business, meshed in with other teaching or course-related activities, but in reality is rather neglected. (In

47. Corrine Silverman, *The President's Economic Advisers,* (University, Ala.: University of Alabama Press, 1959), pp. 1–3.

48. Milton Lomask, *A Minor Miracle—An Informal History of the National Science Foundation* (Washington, D.C.: National Science Foundation, 1976), p. 266.

49. *Questions and Answers,* United States Air Force Pamphlet 190–1 (Washington, D.C.: Department of the Air Force, February, 1977), p. 1.

some societies, homeroom teachers or clergy faculty are given primary responsibility for this area. In the United States, assigning character development to the coach, whose principal duty is another activity, often results in preoccupation with physical education—from development of the body to the desire to win—and in neglect of character development in any other respect—from playing by the rules to being sensitive to others.) On the national level, social sciences in the United States, once destined for a separate agency and presidential council, were kept as a division within the National Science Foundation, with no White House representative, which reflected and augmented their weakness.[50]

If one compares most of the countries in which family planning has no distinct embodiment to those in which it has, family planning is observed to be less legitimate, active, endowed, and effective in those countries in which it is submerged than in those where it is distinctly embodied.[51]

Here, too, where family planning is particularly weak (e.g., in coun-

50. *The National Foundation for the Social Sciences Act of 1966,* proposed by Sen. Fred Harris (D-Okla.), supported creation of a National Foundation for the Social Sciences, to be similar to but separate from the National Science Foundation. The purpose of the bill was to encourage and support research in the social and behavioral sciences.

The following year, Sen. Walter F. Mondale (D-Minn.) introduced legislation to establish a Council of Social Advisers, comparable to the Council of Economic Advisers, which would report directly to the president.

Some of the major criticisms concerning both bills focused on lack of intellectual strength of the social sciences and an inadequate supply of top-level researchers. Testifying at Senate hearings on the proposed Council of Social Advisers, Lewis Butler, then Assistant Secretary for Planning and Evaluation at HEW, questioned the utility of such a council because of "limitations in our theoretical knowledge and understanding of the social system, limitations which are greater and which extend to more subject areas than faced the Council of Economic Advisers." Lewis Butler, Hearings before the Special Subcommittee on Evaluation and Planning of Social Programs of the Committee on Labor and Public Welfare, U.S. Senate, 91st Congress, on S.5 (Washington, D.C.: USGPO, 1970), p. 151.

Hearings on the National Social Science Foundation produced criticism from Robert A. Levine, then Assistant Director for Research Plans, Programs and Evaluations, Office of Economic Opportunity. Levine argued that institutionalizing disciplines with "limited availability of first class social research manpower" would not increment the quantity or quality of productive research, but would create a "resource bottleneck—the funds being applied to obtain a product the supply of which is limited by the absence of a key input." Robert A. Levine, Hearings before the Subcommittee on Government Research of the Committee on Government Operations, U.S. Senate, 90th Congress, on S.836 (Washington, D.C.: USGPO, 1970), pp. 25–26.

51. For a list of countries which include family planning in their national plans and which do not, see B. Maxwell Stamper, *Population and Planning in Developing Nations* (New York: Population Council, 1977), pp. 72–73.

tries whose religion agitates against it), keeping family planning low in embodiment—for instance, by presenting it as a health service—may actually serve to protect it. Nevertheless, the necessity of maintaining such a low profile obviously reflects weakness. Also, when distinctly embodied, the relative clout, status, budget, and line versus staff authority, all other things being equal, are expected to correlate with impact. (As there seems to be no systematic study of this point, it should, of course, be viewed as a hypothesis rather than an established fact until it can be empirically validated. Note, also, that one must take into account that other differences between any two countries could obliviate the differences at hand. For example, if country A has a separate and well-endowed family-planning agency but a poorer civil service and greater villager opposition to national guidance than country B, country A may well have a less effective family planning program.) Hence, comparisons are easier for program changes within the same country than from one country to another. (Here, too, other factors may impinge on progress, e.g., the country's development may slow down as the family planning is separately institutionalized, which would affect the overall results. But such changes seem easier to take into account than numerous cross-country differences. The same point holds true for analyzing changes within the same part of a country versus comparison of parts.)

All other things being equal, the author supports the hypothesis that, aside from situations in which family planning must "hide," separate institutionalization will generally enhance progress by providing family planning with its own volunteers, outreach workers, and local services (although some legitimate secondary activities may aid this progress when they are treated as instrumental rather than competitive). This hypothesis applies to all levels: national, regional, state, and local for planning, administrative organization, and delivery of services. The same point was already made with reference to international agencies.[52]

The main exception to this hypothesis is a situation in which the whole national program, a major agency, or a program other than family planning, makes family planning its first priority, or at least one of its core projects. Singapore is said to have approximated this model nationally in recent years.[53] There, it is reported, the "whole government" made family

52. On the troubles WHO had in dealing with family planning, see Jason L. Finkle and Barbara B. Crane, "The World Health Organization and the Population Issue: Organizational Values in the United Nations," *Population and Development Review* 2 (3–4) (Sept. and Dec. 1976):pp. 367–93, especially pp. 369 ff.

53. "Singapore," *Population Profiles*, no. 1 (New York: UNFPA 1978); Wan Fook Lee, Margaret Loh, "Singapore," *Family Planning in the Developing World*, Walter B. Watson, ed. (New York: Population Council, 1975), p. 21.

planning its high priority, with the national leadership highlighting the virtue of small families by offering tax incentives, other economic rewards, and education privileges to those who planned their families.[54] (For example, choice school attendance was granted to those women who had had tubal ligations after two children.) In Thailand, the public health program is reported to have granted such a priority to family planning that Thailand's annual population growth fell from a rate of 2.3 percent in 1966, to 1.3 percent in 1976—without the aid of specialized family-planning agencies.

While the author has not studied these two countries, their family planning achievements are very impressive and seem to have been made in defiance of the thesis of the impact of separate institutionalized embodiment for family planning. Nevertheless, these situations may be exceptions which prove the rule. The reason is as elementary as it is compelling: no country or program whose prime purpose is not family planning can in the long run maintain family planning as its first priority. This is possible only for a limited period. Otherwise, its other goals would be neglected or it would turn into a family-planning agency! And once the priorities shift, it may be hypothesized that family planning will require its own institution to maintain momentum or it will become relatively weak.

Questions have been raised regarding the implications of the institutionalization thesis for the labor force. It is said that, while such a thesis may hold for the United States and other modern countries with large managerial labor pools, how can nations with little such talent and capability "afford" such specialized agencies? Where the managerial labor force is scarce, specialized institutions may not be possible, but this is not to suggest that development effort, such as family planning will not suffer as a result. It might be necessary to defer or avoid specialization, but that as a rule is likely to result in less family planning. It is difficult to imagine family planning being as well attended to as part of a long list of duties, as when it is a prime duty and responsibility locally, regionally, nationally, and internationally.

54. On the success of the Thai program using existing health personnel and clinics, see Yawarat Porpakkhan, Peter J. Donaldson, and Thavisak Svetszen, "Thailand's Field-Worker Evaluation Project," *Studies in Family Planning* 6 (7) (July 1975):201–204; Ronald Freedman and Bernard Berelson, "The Record of Family Planning Programs," *Studies in Family Planning* (New York: The Population Council, Jan. 1976) 7 (1):24–25; "Thailand," *Population Profiles,* no. 8, (New York: UNFPA), pp. 14–15, 33–34; and *The Survey of Fertility in Thailand: Country Report,* vol. 1 (Bangkok, Thailand: Institute of Population Studies, Chulalongkorn University and Population Survey Division, National Statistical Office, 1977), pp. 1–3.

THE SOURCES OF RELEVANT KNOWLEDGE, POLICY, RESEARCH, AND PLANNING

The production of knowledge relevant to population programs, especially for policy research, is mentioned briefly here because of its relevance and significance, but its scope requires separate study. At issue here is integration, not on the level of local services or national administrations, but in policy formation and planning—a task which is part "intellectual" or knowledge making and part cybernetic, providing relevant inputs to policymakers. Briefly, to the extent that integration proceeds on service and administrative levels, effective policy research would be based on the best knowledge available rather than on trial and error, uneducated "hunches," misinformation, and ideologies. To the extent that integration is not forthcoming, policy research can substitute for it in part, at least, by securing the coordination of programs which are separate in the field on the conceptual and perhaps planning levels.

In the literature on both population and development, the value of policy research is often underscored, but there is little concern with the specific prerequisites needed to make policy research effective. There seems to be a considerable degree of optimism about the ability to provide it (indeed, in some countries it was promised as "forthcoming" not only on the national level but in each district as well) but less than full realization of how taxing this mission is and how scarce the necessary workers or the required access to policymakers are.[55]

CONCLUSION

Integration of population policies and programs and development policies is judged to be a solid concept because it builds on linkages found in society. In its present state, however, it provides insufficient guidance for the relevant public policies concerning the articulation of family planning and other population programs and development. To provide such guidance it is necessary to know not only that a society is integrated but at what level it is integrated. (Where integration is weak, the opportunity for building on societal linkages may be rather limited.) It is also necessary to take into account the degree of intersectoral play and lag—which may allow for significant progress in family planning or other population pro-

55. For additional discussion, see Amitai Etzioni, "Policy Research," *The American Sociologist* 6, Supplementary Issue (June 1971):8–12.

grams without simultaneously working on development. Above all, we must maximize the population program interaction effects of development by better understanding and developing those socioeconomic activities which have the greatest interaction benefits for population programs and vice versa. Here the importance of properly institutionalizing population programs stands out (not to violate the concept of integration, but to secure the place of the program within the integrated context). By pursuing these recommendations, population policy researchers and population policymakers might be more assured that their work is indeed in the service of quality of life for the world's present and future generations.

16

Management of National Population Programs

SAGAR C. JAIN, FEDERICO JOUBERT, AND
JAY K. SATIA

INTRODUCTION

THIS CHAPTER SEEKS to clarify the definition and scope of the term "management." There seems to be a pervasive confusion in this regard in the population field, causing serious communication barriers, professional rivalries, and other dysfunctional behavior. We hope to identify the primary managerial issues in the population field, to discuss the various efforts under way to improve the quality of population program management, and to make a series of recommendations regarding the nature and direction of activities which are needed in order to facilitate further improvement in the management of population programs.

MANAGEMENT: CONCEPTUAL ISSUES

Background

There are several hundred studies on managerial roles; each of these has attempted an authoritative statement on the nature and scope of managerial responsibilities and activities. Some of these studies are largely conceptual and tend to present deductive models of the management function. A good many of these studies, based on empirical data collected through a variety of methodologies, are attempts to present inductive models—functions and activities actually performed. Since scholars tend to view the world

Two colleagues to whom we owe a special debt are Dr. Khalil Asayesh, a Visiting Fellow at the University of North Carolina, Dr. Laurel Files, a member of the faculty of the University of North Carolina. This project would not have reached its final shape without Mary Johnson's able and cheerful management of many details.

from their special perches, using their favorite instruments, their observations suffer from distortions caused by the peculiarities of their vantage points and instruments. Some get a nearsighted view and others are farsighted. Some want a microscopic view, while others are interested in a megascopic view. Some have a panoramic view, while others have only a partial view. Some views are focused while others seem out of focus. The net result is a multiplicity of images, each different from the others, each reflecting the bias and the limitations of its originator.

By and large, disagreement among scholars is both a fact of life and functional for the achievement of a larger social good. However, from time to time scholarly debate may degenerate into a brawl. In such cases, objectivity, analysis, and the pursuit of truth may become subservient to the egotistic needs of these scholars. In the population field, discussions of the role and function of managers are showing symptoms of an incipient brawl.

The population field is dominated by demographers, social scientists, and health professionals. Largely unfamiliar with the management literature, each professional in the population field has tended to take a highly personalized view of management, based or his/her own experience with issues of unique concern. This has added a new dimension to the ongoing debate on the managerial role. Several key actors in this debate in the population field control vast amounts of resources, which are invested in those activities considered to be highly salient. Any marked distortion in the perception of the managerial role can result in an unnecessarily skewed investment in management development activities.

In the population field, the debate on the concept of management has three main focuses: (1) is the primary need of the population field for leaders and entrepreneneurs, or for managers? (2) is formal training in management an essential prerequisite for effective managerial performance? (3) are modern management techniques relevant for development-oriented public-sector programs or for Third World countries?

No useful purpose is likely to be served by joining this debate and becoming partisan. Further, an adjudicative posture may be rightly viewed as pretentious, arrogant, and arbitrary. At the same time, this study would fail in its responsibilities if these issues were ignored and left unaddressed. Therefore, it is important to make an explicit statement of our conceptualization of management, with special reference to the three points of contention noted above.

Managers and Administrators

First of all, it should be stated that the management function in an organization is lodged with, and carried out by, many persons; it is not limited to a chief executive officer, or even the four or five persons on the top. Therefore, it is not correct to equate the roles and activities of the chief and top executives with the totality of the management function. We shall thus use the term management in its generic sense and not in relation to the role of top-level executives. Concomitantly, in using the term manager, we shall refer to the composite of all those charged with the management function, and not to any single individual.

Secondly, we shall use the terms manager and administrator interchangeably. Some equate managers with top-level management functions, and administrators with middle- and low middle-level managerial activities; another group takes an absolutely contrary view. This controversy is essentially culture-bound; those oriented to the world of business and industry tend to subscribe to the former point of view, while those associated with the tradition of public administration tend to advocate the latter view. This controversy is unnecessary and can be avoided by the use of appropriate adjectives, such as top, middle, and beginning, to specify the level of managerial/administrative responsibilities.

Management: A Systems View

Turning to the central issue of the definition and scope of *management,* we believe that the management function is best visualized by the use of the systems approach. This approach has the advantage of being able to accommodate the findings of all other authors as vital pieces in a jigsaw puzzle. Stated simply, a system has five main properties: (1) a defined environment; (2) a measurable set of resources; (3) an identifiable but pervasive information network; (4) an output that seems to achieve a set of goals or objectives; and (5) a capacity for manipulating and converting resources, environment, and the information network to specific ends. A more concrete way of describing a system is to say that its anatomy consists of five basic components: environment, input (resources), information network, output (intended as well as incidental products), and process (conversion capability); while its physiology is characterized by the interdependence of these components—any change in one component vibrates through all other components. The greater the degree of interdependence among components, the more cohesive is the system.

Environment is all those variables over which the system has no direct control but which bear significantly on the working of the system. In the population field, environmental variables will include the following: (1) size, distribution, characteristics, and vital rates of the population; (2) socioeconomic and political structure of the society, with special references to power elites and the significance attached by them to the size, distribution, composition, and characteristics of the population; (3) overall strategy of the society for its socioeconomic development, and recognition given to the population variables in this connection; (4) structure of the government with special reference to decision-making, resource allocation, and management processes; (5) laws and policies pertaining to population growth, distribution, composition and characteristics, and the nature and degree of commitment to these laws and policies; (6) knowledge, attitude and practice (KAP) regarding fertility, mortality, migration and family composition characteristics; (7) history of population programs in the country as well as the world; (8) status of technology bearing on fertility, mortality, distribution, composition, and characteristics of population; (9) availability of labor, mobilization, and development systems; (10) communication and transport systems; (11) social services system; and (12) production and distribution systems for industrial goods with specific reference to supplies needed by the population programs.

Inputs are the resources flowing into the system which provide basic energy for the working of the system. Input variables, as distinct from environmental variables, are subject to the direct control of the process component. The processor, subject to environmental constraints, is free to decide on the what, when, where, and how of any resource. Inputs to a population program will include various population and behavioral science theories, manpower, technology, supplies and equipment, physical plant, clients, funds, time and goodwill.

The *information network* in a system has the same kind of function as the sensory, nervous and impulse system in a body, namely, transmission of information regarding the state of being of various components of the body to all other components. This permits the body to adjust, to cope with, and to benefit from all new developments. A comprehensive, accurate, and sensitive information network is vital not only for the efficient functioning of the system, but also for its very survival. It should constantly and accurately monitor all developments in all components of the system and transmit all relevant information to all concerned parties. In all organized societal programs, including population programs, the information network consists of three main channels: (1) an official channel under the direct control of those responsible for managing the system producing official reports, studies, statements, news releases, public relations activities, and management information systems (MIS) data; (2) an organized unofficial channel, not subject to the direct control of the program managers, which is shared by the scientific and professional community and the mass media. This channel produces scientific, professional and popular publications, research reports and pronouncements, and mass media reports; and (3) an unorganized, unofficial channel which is a free-for-all arrangement. Its main products are rumors, gossip, whisper campaigns, and personal pronouncements. The relative importance of these channels varies greatly from program to program, culture to culture, and time to time.

Output refers to two distinct but interdependent types of products generated by the system. The first type may be called *intended outputs,* consisting of all those products for which the system was conceived, in other words, these outputs relate directly and positively to the objectives and goals of the system. However, in the process of obtaining the intended output, often a series of by-products also get produced; these by-products comprise the *incidental output* of a system. In the population field, program goals and objectives tend to vary among countries. Several countries have mounted their population programs primarily to reduce the fertility rate; some are mainly concerned with the distribution of their populations; others are interested only in child spacing and parity to enhance the health and social status of their populations, and so on. In the process of achieving any of these intended outputs, the system is also likely to generate several incidental outputs, e.g., goodwill or illwill toward the program, changes in technology, changes in the strategy of development, changes in the infrastructure of government and service systems, changes in family and social structure, changes in social norms. A good manager anticipates all major *incidental outputs* so that they may be used creatively to enhance the *intended outputs.*

Process in an organizational or program context refers to both the production and managerial functions. The latter functions are aimed at helping the system to achieve its intended output efficiently. Operationally, the managerial process involves five functions: (1) making the environment of a system increasingly hospitable to its growth and development; (2) attracting desired inputs into the system; (3) mobilizing the inputs toward an optimal state of production; (4) ensuring that data from the information network are promptly received, efficiently processed, and creatively utilized; and (5) helping the system refine and, if necessary, revise its goals and objectives in the light of new information.

Dynamics of Managerial Role

Each management function entails very different sets of tasks, needing very different kinds of qualifications. Furthermore, all management functions do not receive equal weight at all times in the life of an organization. In some ways, organizations may not be too different from organisms: they are born, they go through the early developmental years of infancy and childhood, they proceed through adolescence and maturity, and they also grow old and die. The dominant needs of an organization change from one stage of life to another, and these new needs require new approaches, methods, and skills for fulfillment. A schematic presentation of this analogy is given in Table 16.1.

We should hasten to point out that the biological model of organizational growth (as in Table 16.1) is at best an analogy, and must not be taken literally. Further, in listing the managerial tasks and qualifications necessary for each stage of organizational growth, our approach has been deductive. Despite these limitations, Table 16.1 presents a useful way of thinking, which in turn suggests an analytical framework for examining the three main bones of contention (noted earlier) regarding management in the population field viz., the need for leaders, entrepreneurs, or managers; the role of formal training; and the relevance of modern management techniques.

Entrepreneurs, Leaders, and Managers

> In 1966, when a major U.S. university was in the process of designing a population center, the leader of the planning group made a flat statement that "management hocus pocus" is irrelevant to the needs of the field; what is needed is effective leadership.
>
> In 1972, in an international meeting of population experts, it was observed that the "population field may need 95% entrepreneurship, and only 5% management."
>
> In 1978, in another international meeting, yet another population expert opined that he would rather have a poorly managed program going North (when it needed to go North) than a well-managed program heading South. He concluded that the field needed leaders and entrepreneurs rather than managers.

These are only three of many such statements that continue to be made in the population field by men and women of good will and stature. There are an equal number of pro-management statements made by others of comparable good will and stature. This controversy seems to be rooted in the differences of perception regarding the managerial role and in a failure of communication. The entrepreneurial school appears to equate the managerial role with the use of sophisticated electronic mathematical social science methodologies for the manipulation of intraorganizational processes. This stereotype of the managerial role may have been generated by the tables of contents of textbooks in business administration. The pro-management school tends to present two types of counterarguments—a

TABLE 16.1
Biological Model of Organizational Growth

Stage of growth	Main concerns	Primary managerial task	Essential managerial qualities
Birth and infancy	Healthy birth, survival	Developing and maintaining rapport with powerful constituencies	Charisma, creativity, commitment, connections, communication skills, resourcefulness, risk-taking ability, and high degree of optimism
Childhood	Proper growth and development	Obtaining increased amount of resources and proper mobilization of these resources	All of the above. In addition, go-getting abilities, sound understanding of relevant scientific, technical, and organizational issues, and sound PR skills
Adolescence	Adjustment to rapid growth	Obtaining vast amount of additional resources, dealing with emerging complexity and impersonality	Know-how for managing complex systems, skills in conflict resolution and direction, foresight, fairness, firmness, and good will
Maturity	Ensuring continued good health and productivity	Maintaining and improving all operations of the system	Broad vision, ability to delegate, skill in forecasting, planning, directing, coordinating, and controlling
Old age	Redefinition of raison d'être	Redefining organizational goals and purposes, and directing the organization towards these goals by making necessary adjustments in resources as well as in operations	Incisive organizational diagnostic skills, will and ability to take needed actions, sound social skills, and good will

manager *is* a leader, and entrepreneurship is not only *not* inimical to the managerial role but is inherent in it; and modern management techniques are badly needed in the population field to deal with emerging complexities in policy and program planning, with obtaining funding logistics, supply, information, control, allocation, scheduling, and other operational problems. The issue is not 5 percent versus 95 percent, but rather the difference between success and failure.

Unfortunately, these two groups are not dialoging but are talking past each other. To facilitate communication, let us first note the definition of the key terms. The *Oxford Universal Dictionary on Historical Principles* notes that the term *entrepreneur* was originally used for directors of public musical institutions; it was later used to describe contractors acting as intermediaries between capital and labor. In recent years, the term has been used to describe those who are inclined toward daring and creative behavior in removing obstacles in the way of their enterprise. A *leader* is defined as one who leads a group of followers. Leadership status may be acquired by birth, force, election, appointment, purchase of ownership, charisma, or unique achievements. A *manager* is a system processor responsible for so manipulating and utilizing the environment, inputs, and information network components of the system as to generate the intended outputs. In carrying out this role, the manager must give varying degrees of attention to different components at different points in the life of the system. Also, to achieve the system goals at their optimum level, the manager must ensure that all actors in the system are making a unified effort toward achievement of these goals.

A close and careful examination of the definition of these three terms would indicate that the term entrepreneur, as used in modern times, is characterized by a mode of behavior, not by a reference to status or role; the term leader essentially describes status; and the term manager implies, above everything, a specific role. A closer look will show that a manager tends to be an appointed leader in the organization, and that, to successfully fulfill this role, entrepreneurial qualities are critical in the early stages of organizational growth; know-how, to help the organization deal with increasing complexity in the middle stages of organizational life; and diagnostic, surgical and more importantly preventive skills, necessary to save the organization from the ills of old age.

Management Training

The population field is dominated by physicians, demographers, and social scientists. Many of them have done a truly outstanding job of making the societal environment hospitable to population programs and in designing, as well as in running, these programs. In a few cases, these programs started to show signs of strain as they grew beyond the take-off stage and gained complexity. Many program watchers attributed these strains to the fact that the managers of these programs did not have formal training in management and were not using modern management techniques. This initiated the controversy about the need for formal training in management. Is it essential? What should it contain?

The need and the nature of formal training can be determined only in the context of the nature of tasks to be performed, the role of knowledge, attitudes, and skills needed for performing these tasks, and the efficiency of available pedagogies for developing such knowledge, attitudes and skills. In this context, drawing on our earlier discussion of managerial functions, tasks, and qualifications the following assertions may be made:

1. Successful performance of the managerial role requires five different elements: (A) a secure and creative personality; (B) well-developed social skills; (C) a sound understanding of the enterprise and its environment; (D) a good grasp of the theories and methods of manipulative dynamics of organizations; and (E) an appropriate mind-set: role perception, role commitment, and personal values. However, not all managers need all these elements in equal measures at all times.

2. Obviously, successful performance of a managerial role requires considerably more than theoretical and methodological know-how for manipulation of organizational dynamics. In fact, this element of managerial makeup starts to acquire significance only when the organization gains complexity.

3. Irrespective of the stage of organizational growth, the primary function of top management tends to be policy determination, resource development, and constituency cultivation. For successful performance of these functions, top-level managers are likely to draw more on elements A, B, and E than on elements C or D, which basically involve information that can be obtained from other sources. This does not mean that top-level managers need not have any strength in elements C and D; in fact, sound policy decisions cannot be made without a proper understanding of operational complexities, together with the knowledge and know-how to surmount these complexities. What is implied here is that while information related to element D (and element C) can be obtained by top management from those in charge of implementation, and from other experts, the top managers will be paralyzed in decision-making tasks without the proper personality characteristics, mind-set, and social skills. It should quickly be added that personal competence in elements C and D, in addition to A, B, and E will noticeably improve the efficiency of the top management.

4. Competence in element D is critical for middle and beginning-level managers, especially those occupying staff positions. The managerial ranks start to become hierarchical when the organization reaches a certain size and gains a certain level of complexity, which is usually between childhood and adolescence of organizational growth. At that time, the top management assumes primary responsibility for dealing with environmental and output components of the system and delegates all planning and implementation functions to lower level of management. These functions cannot be performed effectively in a complex organization without a sound command of element D.

The managerial role requires more than knowledge of facts, theories, and methods; it also entails a variety of skills, a certain mind-set, and certain personality characteristics. Further, for success in certain situations the cognitive elements of the managerial role may not be as important as other elements. Therefore, the nature of preparation for successful performance of the managerial role need not be uniform, but should be determined by the demands of the situation.

Now, turning to the potential of available pedagogy for the preparation of managers, it should be stated that because of preoccupation of the educational and training system with cognitive learning, there have been important advances in the pedagogy for teaching "what" and "why." Moreover, in technical and vocational fields, there is increasing sophistication in the teaching of "how." However, proven methods for teaching social skills, personality development, and manipulation of mind-set are either nonexistent or are in early and crude stages of development. Faced with these pedagogical limitations, formal training in management can accomplish a great deal in relation to elements C and D, and may succeed partially with element E, but it is unlikely to make much headway with element B, and still less with element A. It is not surprising that most of the formal training programs in management tend to concentrate on those aspects of teaching for which reliable pedagogy is available, viz., the transmission of a variety of methods and techniques, as well as relevant historical and current information. In recent years, pedagogical breakthroughs have been made which permit students to gain insight into their mind-set and personality structures, and which help them to learn about the efficacy of their social skills, but which offer very limited assistance in achieving improvements and change. All the same, such new frontiers in management education have moved it several notches closer to comprehensiveness.

In conclusion, our stand on the question "Is formal training essential for all managers?" may be summarized as follows: while formal training in management may not be essential for all managers, it would be helpful; but, given the limitations of the available pedagogy which can impart only certain kinds of learning, formal training, although helpful, is no guarantee for the successful performance of all management functions.

Modern Management Techniques and the Third World

There are serious questions in many minds about the relevance and utility of so-called modern management techniques to the developmental concerns of the Third World. A resurgence of nationalism has infused a new spirit into this discussion. The proponents of these techniques argue that modern management is nothing but a set of specialized analytical and operational techniques designed to deal with overall complexity in policy, planning, operation, and evaluation decisions. Given a certain degree of complexity, no organization can function efficiently without the use of some of these techniques. The opponents' arguments express a variety of concerns and reservations. Their main arguments, and the proponents' rejoinders are presented in Table 16.2.

A review of these debates clearly indicates that the question of relevance is not wholly scientific and technical; it is largely a matter of mind-set. People on different sides of the argument seem to have different values, different perceptions of managerial roles, and different stylistic inclinations. There is also a hint that some opponents may be having a rather uneasy time adjusting to the fact that in the lives of all organizations a time comes when some of the old ways must be traded for new ones. At the same time, it should be also said that the advocates of modern management may often be too zealous to admit the limitations of their methods in relation to the developmental concerns of the Third World countries. The modern management techniques hold high potentials for the population field, but these techniques may require several adjustments and refinements before they are fully capable of meeting the needs of program managers in this field. However, as this would be true of any application of the techniques, the issue is one of degree, not of kind.

MANAGEMENT OF POPULATION PROGRAMS: CURRENT STATUS AND CONCERNS

Growth of Population Programs

From time immemorial, societies have been concerned with the size, composition, and distribution of their population and have utilized a variety of informal and formal means to achieve their goals in this regard. However, formal and organized programs for fertility manipulation are relatively recent.

TABLE 16.2
Modern Management Techniques and the Third World: Reservations and Rejoinders

Reservation	Rejoinder
1. Several modern management techniques are quantitative and require high-quality data. Most Third World countries lack such data. The development of data-generation capability requires a great deal of time and resources, neither of which these countries may be able to afford.	1a. Nonavailability of data poses a handicap, but this can be overcome. Fundamentally, mathematical techniques of management are a systematic way of thinking—organizing and sorting issues in a given fashion. This is a way of approaching complex tasks which goes beyond "playing" with numbers. Some of these techniques are being usefully adpated to the "poor data" situation. For example, see Wolfgang E. Stolper, *Planning Without Facts: Lessons in Resource Allocation from Nigeria's Development* (Cambridge, Mass.: Harvard University Press, 1966).
	1b. A comprehensive and sensitive information network is critical to the efficient functioning of a system. The Third World countries are engaged in massive organized efforts for their socioeconomic development. These efforts will result in a morass of uncoordinated confusion if they are not properly monitored. The development of a sound information system is essential for planned development.
2. A good deal of data which goes into decision making is qualitative, and must be artificially reduced to numbers to suit the convenience of quantitative techniques. This could inject a serious flaw in the decision-making process, which might outweigh the advantages of using modern management techniques.	2. This is a pervasive issue and is not limited to Third World countries. The manipulation of qualitative data to facilitate the use of quantitative techniques means assigning precise numeric values: not an easy task in any culture. If there is a lack of consensus on the numeric value of qualitative data, then a range of values may be used. If such quantitative techniques are not used, decisions will have to be made on the basis of intuition or some extraneous factor. Where

TABLE 16.2 *(continued)*

Reservation	Rejoinder
	is the guarantee that the latter decisions will be sounder than those based on careful analysis?
3. Social science–based theories and techniques of organizational behavior, development, and change are likely to be culturally biased insofar as they are based on data from industrialized Western cultures.	3. This argument has a very high prima facie validity. Systematic comparative research is needed to determine the nature and significance of cultural variables.
4. The modern management scientist tends to be obsessed with matters of concern to business and industry, but to have paid little attention to nonprofitmaking human service enterprises.	4. In a broad historical sense, the observation may be correct. Large and complex organizations surfaced a lot earlier in the business and industrial world, while human service organizations have only recently moved into this category. However, the growth in size and complexity of human service organizations will not, in itself, result in the development of appropriate management methodologies; significant new investments are needed for the development of methods and techniques which will effectively address the special concerns of the human service field.
5. Modern management techniques tend to be maintenance and control oriented. Development programs are change and accountability oriented. Obviously, the available management techniques are not suitable for developmental programs.	5. This argument may suffer from exaggeration, but it is not without merit. The need for development-oriented management techniques can be met only by significant and sustained investments in their development.
6. In public sector enterprise management, political considerations play a paramount role. This calls for an ability to adapt and change rapidly. Management techniques, with their cumbersome tasks of data collection, analysis, and evaluation, reduce such flexibility.	6a. Valid information can be a powerful political weapon. 6b. Data storage, retrieval, and processing tasks need not be time-consuming. EDP systems are rapidly decreasing in price, and are increasingly portable. 6c. A manager who must constantly bend to each new political breeze may survive (with a backache), but is not likely to be an organizational leader.

Although small-scale family planning activities under the auspices of a variety of voluntary welfare agencies may be traced to the early 1930s, governmental involvement in this field did not come about until the 1950s (see Table 16.3). In the fifties however, the available technology for fertility manipulation did not provide an adequate base for large-scale programs. It was only in the sixties, when the intrauterine device (IUD)

TABLE 16.3
Evolution of Population Programs in 19 Countries

	Activities in the population field		
Country	Early nongovernmental activities	Early governmental activities	First official statement on population
Bangladesh	1953 Voluntary organization established by group of dedicated social workers	1957 A grant made to the private family planning organization	1960 (as part of Pakistan) 1971 (As an inde-pendent country)
Colombia	1960 Isolated individual concern 1964 Services and research organized by ASCOFAME. Service delivery by private organ-ization called PROFAMILIA	1969 Limited family planning services made available as part of maternal & child health services	1970
Egypt	1930 Importance of population variables in the develop-ment of the country noted by various authors 1953 Egyptian Family Plan-ning Assn. established	1939 Newly established Min-istry of Health charged with a systematic study of issues related to family & population size 1953 Nat'l. population comm. appointed by government	1965
Ghana	1967 Planned Parenthood Association of Ghana	1965 Interdepartmental com-mittee appointed to develop appropriate popu-lation policy	1969

TABLE 16.3 (*continued*)

Country	Activities in the population field: Early nongovernmental activities	Early governmental activities	First official statement on population
India	1930s Planners and economists recognized importance of population variables; 1952 Family Planning Assn. of India established	1948–1950 Documents related to the development plans recognize the importance of population variable 1951 Census report called for birth control	1952
Indonesia	1953 Small group of concerned individuals began activities leading to the formation of Indonesian Family Planning Assn. in 1957	1965 Government participated in a national conference on family planning	1967
Iran	1957 Family Guidance Assn. of Iran (IPPF) established	1966 Invited an expert mission from the population council to help develop a suitable policy on population	1967
Jamaica	1939 Jamaican Family Planning League 1956 Jamaican Family Planning Assn. (IPPF)	1956 Supported a family planning study	1966
Kenya	In 1950s Pathfinder Fund initiated small-scale family planning activities 1957 Family Planning Assn. established at Kenya	1965 First request to population council by government for assistance	1966
Malaysia	1953 Malaysian Federation Family Planning established	1962 All 11 states offered family planning services	1965
Mexico	1959 Assn. for the welfare of the family founded by small group 1965 FEPCA was established and affiliated with IPPF	1972 Family planning services made available thru Govt's. Maternal & Child Health Service	1974

TABLE 16.3 (*continued*)

Country	Activities in the population field		
	Early nongovernmental activities	Early governmental activities	First official statement on population
Nigeria	1949 Variety of small-scale voluntary efforts to provide family planning education 1964 Family Planning Council of Nigeria established	1958 Govt. health clinics offered to provide family planning services on behalf of the voluntary organizations	1970
Pakistan	1953 Family Planning Association of Pakistan established	1955 The first development plan recognized the importance of population variables 1958 First national Family Planning Conference	1960
Philippines	1957 First educational service offered by Family Relations Center, a church affiliate 1965 Planned Parenthood of Philippines established	1969 Limited family planning services offered through MCH centers	1970
Rep. of Korea	1957–58 Mothers' clubs activities in family planning education 1961 Planned Parenthood of Korea established	1961 National development policy recognized importance of population variables	1961
Singapore	1949 Singapore Family Planning Assn. established	1958 Official concern with high birth rate publicly expressed	1965
Thailand	1958 Family Planning Assn. of Thailand established	1963 A committee on family planning formed within prime minister's office	1970
Tunisia	1968 Tunisian Family Planning Assn. established	1962 Govt. invited a Ford Foundation/Pop. Council expert team to help develop a suitable population policy	1964

TABLE 16.3 (*continued*)

Country	Activities in the population field		
	Early nongovernmental activities	Early governmental activities	First official statement on population
Turkey	1963 Planned Parenthood Assn. of Turkey (TAPP) established	1958 Formal expression of concern about population growth rate 1963 Govt. request to Pop. Council for an expert team	1965

SOURCES: Country program reports and Dorothy Nortman *et al.*, *Population and Family Planning Programs: A Fact Book* (New York: Population Council, 1978), Table 6, pp. 19–36.

became available, that governmental activities in this field came to life. New breakthroughs in fertility-related technology, combined with an increased appreciation of the relationship between socioeconomic development and population dynamics, led to seemingly exponential growth in population programs oriented toward fertility manipulation. By the early seventies, a vast majority of developing countries had active population policies designed to reduce the population growth rate, to improve health, and to ensure the human right to control one's own fertility (see Table 16.3).

At the same time, there was a tremendous expansion in the size of the population programs of individual countries (see Table 16.4). However, the pace of expansion has not been the same in all parts of the world. As noted in Table 16.4, by 1974 sixty-three developing countries had adopted a population policy and were committed to achieving its goals. By 1977, two additional countries (one in Africa and one in Latin America) had joined these ranks. However, only in less than half of these countries (including twenty-six programs shown in Table 16.5), have population programs gained noticeable momentum. Countries having high density, high commitment to a planned approach to socioeconomic development, and an established infrastructure of human services have tended to move more rapidly in the development of their population programs. These countries also tend to give special emphasis to a reduction of their population growth rate in their program objectives.

In addition to differences in their policy objectives and the pace of program growth, the countries differ in at least four other major areas: (1) programmatic strategy; (2) location and structure of programs; (3)

TABLE 16.4
Population Policy Status of 74 Developing Countries in 1974

Region	Number of countries having a formal policy: To reduce population growth*	To promote MCH/human rights	Neutral/ opposed to fertility control	Total
Africa	7	11	5	23
Asia and Oceania	19	5	5	29
Latin America	7	14	1	22
Total	33	30	11	74

* Most of these programs also aim to achieve improved maternal and child health (MCH) as well as to ensure the human right to control fertility.

SOURCE: Dorothy Nortman *et al., Population and Family Planning Programs: A Fact Book,* Number Two (New York: Population Council, December 1974), pp. 25–35.

number of methods made available for birth control; and (4) source of their funds. Since these variables have important managerial implications, as do policy objectives and program size, it is useful to describe each of these differences briefly.

Strategies of Population Programs

The sixty-five developing countries which have declared themselves in favor of organized population programs fall into two basic categories. The thirty-five Type A countries are primarily concerned with reducing the growth rate of their population, and the remaining thirty Type B countries are interested in child spacing and birth control programs to enhance the health status of their population, as well as to enhance the status of their women.

The program strategy of the Type B group of countries (of which fifteen are located in Africa, twelve in Latin America, two in West Asia, and one in East Asia) is essentially limited to the provision of family-planning education and services. In most of these countries, these activities are carried out inconspicuously as part and parcel of maternal and child health (MCH) services, with voluntary organizations playing an important role. Only in rare cases have significant new resources been mobilized to support their family-planning activities.

Type A programs started in Asia and now cover most of that continent (19 countries). Latin America (8) and Africa (8) also have their

TABLE 16.5
Growth of Population Programs in 26 Countries

Region/Country	Annual/per capita budget/expenditure (in U.S. cents)		Total number of employees (including part-time)		Total number of acceptors (in thousands)	
	from	to	from	to	from	to
AFRICA						
Egypt	5.70	4.50	8,500	13,524	148.0	187.0
	(1968)	(1975)	(1969)	(1976)	(1969)	(1976)
Ghana	14.00	21.00	110	503	2.6	32.0
	(1970)	(1976)	(1971)	(1976)	(1969)	(1976)
Kenya	3.30	54.00	300	NA	9.5	48.4
	(1967)	(1976)	(1969)		(1968)	(1975)
Morocco	1.10	5.50	865	7,945	6.0	78.0
	(1968)	(1973)	(1969)	(1972)	(1966)	(1976)
Tunisia	22.20	22.60	218	676	1.4	73.5
	(1968)	(1973)	(1969)	(1975)	(1964)	(1976)
ASIA						
Bangladesh	5.00	18.00	3,823	32,038	142.5	1,103.1
	(1972)	(1976)	(1973)	(1976)	(1972)	(1976)
India	0.05	28.00	138,000	58,857	318.0	12,456.0
	(1956)	(1976)	(1969)	(1976)	(1965)	(1976)
Indonesia	0.60	16.00	691	16,159	21.2	2,213.0
	(1968)	(1976)	(1969)	(1976)	(1968)	(1976)
Iran	2.10	88.00	2,780	5,610	10.4	572.0
	(1968)	(1976)	(1969)	(1975)	(1967)	(1976)
Malaysia	3.30	40.00	230	577	20.7	75.2
	(1976)	(1977)	(1969)	(1976)	(1967)	(1976)
Nepal	0.50	11.00	107	985	0.6	138.8
	(1968)	(1975)	(1969)	(1976)	(1966)	(1976)
Pakistan	5.00	34.00	8,526	10,051	147.8	2,086.0
	(1965)	(1976)	(1969)	(1974)	(1965)	(1975)
Philippines	2.70	58.00	16,139	10,605	70.0	643.0
	(1969)	(1976)	(1971)	(1976)	(1969)	(1976)

Region/Country	Annual/per capita budget/expenditure (in U.S. cents)		Total number of employees (including part-time)		Total number of acceptors (in thousands)	
	from	to	from	to	from	to
Singapore	16.00	41.00	96	164	10.3	39.2
	(1969)	(1976)	(1969)	(1976)	(1965)	(1976)
Sri Lanka	NA	(1977)	2,774	12,873	15.0	95.3
		11.40	(1969)	(1975)	(1966)	(1973)
Rep. of Korea	4.40	22.00	6,191	5,741	233.0	3.340.0
	(1965)	(1976)	(1969)	(1976)	(1965)	(1975)
Thailand	2.30	8.00	1,311	23,556	3.0	527.0
	(1968)	(1975)	(1969)	(1976)	(1964)	(1976)
Taiwan	1.00	17.00	1,776	2,516	99.0	325.0
	(1964)	(1977)	(1969)	(1976)	(1965)	(1976)
Turkey	3.30	5.00	6,403	7,038	5.0	NA
	(1976)	(1975)	(1969)	(1974)	(1965)	
LATIN AMERICA						
Colombia	NA	23.00	2,044	5,537	0.5	263.8
		(1974)	(1969)	(1974)	(1965)	(1976)
Costa Rica	34.00	86.00	391	509	6.1	28.8
	(1973)	(1976)	(1972)	(1975)	(1968)	(1976)
Dominican Republic	4.10	43.60	69	370	3.6	61.5
	(1968)	(1976)	(1970)	(1975)	(1968)	(1976)
Ecuador	NA	NA	114	1,356	3.1	32.3
			(1971)	(1974)	(1968)	(1976)
Guatemala	13.00	12.00	220	46	7.6	NA
	(1972)	(1974)	(1971)	(1976)	(1968)	
Jamaica	3.40	96.00	202	661	19.3	27.0
	(1976)	(1976)	(1970)	(1973)	(1970)	(1975)
Mexico	8.00	46.00	701	NA	19.7	608.0
	(1972)	(1973)	(1973)		(1969)	(1975)

SOURCE: Computed from 1969 through 1978 editions of Dorothy Nortman *et al.*, *Population and Family Planning Programs: A Fact Book* (New York: Population Council).

share of such programs. Since these programs are mainly devoted to the reduction of population growth rate, and thus tend to concentrate on reduction of the birth rate, their program strategies have been very largely influenced by a variety of theories regarding fertility. In this respect, there are at least four schools of thought:

1. Significant improvement in the socioeconomic status of the population is essential for achieving and sustaining a declining birth rate. Therefore, population programs should be aimed at impacting those critical development variables which are most closely associated with fertility. This strategy calls for the systematic assessment of all developmental investments in terms of their impact on fertility so as to maximize achievement of the goal of lower fertility.

2. Birth control is not a very high priority concern of the people. Often health and social welfare matters are of greater importance, and if these more important issues are not addressed, the family-planning programs are likely to generate suspicion and even hostility. Therefore, family-planning programs should go hand in hand with health and social welfare programs.

3. It is essential to bring down the rate of infant mortality before people will agree to reduce births. This calls for significant improvements in maternal and child health programs, together with investments in family-planning activities.

4. KAP studies indicate a pervasive desire for smaller families and improved child spacing. Therefore, provision of family-planning services is both an effective and an expedient strategy. It is argued that through organized family-planning education activities, supplemented by culturally appropriate incentives, this strategy is likely to produce a relatively rapid decline in fertility.

Most programs concerned with population growth rates originated in a realization that a rapidly growing population was a major obstacle to socioeconomic development. Historically, the early programs started with a frontal attack on the birth rate based on family-planning services (strategy four); but recently, especially after the 1974 World Population Conference at Bucharest, more and more programs have moved toward strategies two and three.

Program Location and Structure

Initial concepts of population program design, guided by a family planning-oriented strategy, tended to be simplistic, having only one main concern: the development of contraceptive services. Since provision of these services required the use of medical labor, most of the early population programs were located in ministries of health. In Type B countries (having a population policy aimed at the improvement of health status), these programs tended to be merged with existing maternal and child health services; but in Type A countries (having a population policy aimed at reduction of population growth rate), population programs were given a separate identity within the structure of appropriate ministries.

In most of the Type B countries, the original arrangement has continued, but in Type A countries, the location and organization of population programs have been the subjects of considerable experimentation and innovation. The latter countries soon realized that the creation of a service supply system was not adequate; equal, if not more attention needed to be given to generating demand as well as creating logistic arrangements to bring supply and demand together. They also realized the limitation of the clinic-oriented service delivery system. These types of considerations resulted in the development of (1) information education communication (IEC) activities; (2) a complex service delivery system (e.g., fixed clinics, mobile clinics, camps, storage facilities, and commercial and community distribution systems); and (3) a reward/punishment incentive system (impacting matters such as legal age of marriage, adoption laws, and abortion laws, as well as distributive policies on employment, housing, education, food subsidies, medical services, and social security).

With the development of these new dimensions of the population programs, active involvement and participation of many other ministries of government (and in many cases, also private sector organizations) became imperative. This in turn, made it necessary to rethink the initial decisions regarding location and organization of the program. This resulted in three types of models:

Model 1. Creation of a high-level (usually at the highest level) interministerial council which makes broad policy decisions and specifies roles and responsibilities of each ministry in the implementation of these decisions. The ministry of health, through a division of the population/family-planning program, continues to have the lead role in the development of policy proposals, as well as in planning, coordination, research and evaluation, and a variety of supporting and facilitating activities. India typifies this model.

Model 2. An interministerial council (as in Model 1, above) is created, but the lead role regarding policy, program development, and planning is given to a new ministry of population/family planning. Bangladesh experimented with a separate ministry of population control for a short while, but then reverted to the model in which Health and Population functions are combined into a single ministry.

Model 3. A high-level interministerial council sets broad policies, defines overall strategy, specifies responsibilities of each ministry in the implementation of these decisions, and monitors and coordinates the activities of all ministries, as well as carrying out all activities assigned to the ministry of health/population/family planning in Models 1 and 2 above. To carry out these functions, the council creates its own executive body with a full-time staff. Egypt and Mexico are probably the most prominent examples of this model.

Countries which have become active in the population field more recently have benefitted from the experience of their predecessors. Many of them have adopted one or the other of the three advanced organization models immediately but have made local adjustments. For example, Ghana has adopted Model 1, but the lead ministry is planning, rather than health. Both the Indonesian and Malaysian programs follow Model 3; however, the executive wings of these interministerial boards carry much greater responsibility for program development than in Egypt. Further, the Malaysian Council includes a very large representation of public interest, including industry, commerce, trade unions, and the professions. The policy-making structure in the Philippines is not too different from the one in Malaysia, but in the Philippines the voluntary agencies play a considerably more active role in program implementation.

In the post-Bucharest era, the countries committed to the Type A population policy have shown an increasing interest in achieving an effective interface between population and development programs. This concern is ideally expressed under the rubric of integration. This new posture has not yet resulted in any significant revisions in the location and structure of population programs at the national level. However, there may be some behavioral changes, such as increased attention to fertility-inhibiting developmental activities; improved communication and coordination with selected ministries, particularly those concerned with planning, labor, and human services; and a general broadening of the scope of the population concern to include distribution, characteristic, and quality considerations.

At the implementation level, several interesting organizational innovations have been developed for improved integration. These include (1) the use of multipurpose community development workers (who provide generalized counseling and service in such diverse fields as health, family planning, nutrition, sanitation, housing, education, recreation, and agriculture extension); (2) use of a single outlet for providing a variety of human services (e.g., family welfare centers in India, Mothers' Clubs in the Republic of Korea); (3) the delegation of all developmental and population-related responsibility to community-level governments (e.g., use of *banjars* in Bali and communes in mainland China); and (4) creation of specialized development groups at the local level with responsibility for all developmental programs including family planning (e.g., the Republic of Korea's *Saemaul Undong* program). Since each of these arrangements has capitalized on some unique institution or development in the country, it is unlikely that they will gain significant currency in other countries. However, it is very likely that other countries will make their own innovations, which will make each program structure increasingly individual.

Birth Control Methods Made Available

The number of birth control methods made available and the nature of these methods have important implications not only for the effectiveness of the programs, but also for their complexity and costs. Table 16.6 provides data on birth control methods offered and most frequently used in twenty-four countries with active family-planning services. These data indicate that there are some very notable differences.

1. Tunisia is the only country which uses all methods (with the exception of male sterilization) more or less equally.
2. The IUD's popularity has dropped a great deal; only nine countries use this as one of the important methods, and only South Korea uses it as its primary method.
3. Oral contraception is the single most popular method. All countries offer it; twenty-one countries report it to be one of the most popular methods; and in Kenya, Morocco, Indonesia, Iran, Malaysia, Costa Rica, the Dominican Republic, and Jamaica, it is the most popular method.
4. Sterilization is gaining in popularity, but more countries offer it to females than to males. Only Tunisia (female only), India, Singapore (females), Sri Lanka, and Thailand (female) have placed significant reliance on this method.
5. Only four countries offer abortion, and only Tunisia and Singapore use it as one of their primary methods.
6. While all countries offer the use of condoms, foams, jelly, and similar methods, only nine countries reported high use of these methods.

These twenty-four-country data sets may not represent the experience of all other countries accurately, but they do indicate that an increasing number of countries are building the family-planning programs around methods in which medical labor is not critical; e.g., in most of these countries, oral contraceptives are supplied without a medical examination.

TABLE 16.6
Birth Control Methods Offered by 24 Countries in 1977

Region/ Country	IUD	Oral	Sterilization		Abortion	Others
			Male	Female		
AFRICA						
Egypt	2	2	0	0	0	1
Ghana	1	2	0	0	0	2
Kenya	1	2	0	0	0	1
Morocco	1	2	0	0	0	1
Tunisia	2	2	0	2	2	2
ASIA						
Bangladesh	1	2	1	1	0	2
India	1	1	2	2	1	2
Indonesia	1	2	1	1	0	1
Iran	1	2	1	1	0	1
Malaysia	1	2	1	1	0	1
Nepal	1	2	1	1	0	2
Pakistan	1	2	1	1	0	2
Philippines	1	2	1	1	0	2
Rep. of Korea	2	1	1	1	0	2
Singapore	1	2	1	2	2	1
Sri Lanka	2	1	2	2	0	1
Thailand	2	2	1	2	0	1
Taiwan	2	2	1	1	0	2
LATIN AMERICA						
Colombia	2	2	1	1	1	1
Costa Rica	1	2	0	0	0	1
Dominican Republic	1	2	0	0	0	1
Ecuador	2	2	0	0	0	1
Jamaica	1	2	0	1	0	1
Mexico	2	2	1	1	0	1

Key = 1 Method available
2 Method very frequently used
0 Method not available

SOURCE: Dorothy Nortman *et al., Population and Family Planning Programs: A Fact Book*, 9th ed. (New York: Population Council, 1978), Table 16, pp. 53–56.

Increasing reliance on nonclinical methods implies a need for permanent and reliable supply lines to service consumers, and for installation of appropriate information and motivation systems. However, the use of these methods does permit the utilization of established commercial distribution channels as well as of nonprofessional personnel, and this, in turn, should permit many creative organizational innovations.

Sterilization-based programs are likely to be less concerned with permanent supply lines and follow-up services, but their high reliance on medical labor may keep them tied to the clinical model of service delivery. Nevertheless, the use of sterilization is gaining in popularity, especially in Asia.

However, there will always be countries, such as Tunisia, Singapore, and Thailand, which will strike a balance between the clinical and nonclinical methods. The delivery system of these programs is likely to be the most complex.

Sources of Program Funds

In the last ten years, investments in the population program have experienced nearly a fivefold increase. From Table 16.5 we can calculate that the average per capita expenditures in the twenty-six countries went up from 6.46 cents to 32.46 cents. Table 16.7, which includes information on total funds invested in the programs of nineteen countries for the years 1970 and 1976, also indicates a very rapid growth of investments in the population field. Where are these funds coming from? The answer to this question should provide clues to important managerial concerns regarding governmental commitment, program image, growth potential, degree of autonomy, and even future direction of these programs.

A review of Tables 16.7 and 16.8 provides the following information on the sources of funds in the population field:

1. In their initial stages, the population programs relied heavily on funds from overseas: e.g., developed countries in the West, international agencies, foundations, and private organizations such as the Population Council and the International Planned Parenthood Federation (IPPF). In 1970, these outside sources were responsible for more than half of the total investments in the programs of the *nineteen countries* included in Table 16.7. However, these countries are rapidly becoming self-reliant. By 1976, their share of the investments rose to nearly 60%, and this change took place despite the fact that the total investment grew four to five times.

2. Despite the increasing financial independence of the countries with established programs, the total overseas investments in the population field have continued to rise. These investments nearly quadrupled between 1970 and 1976.

3. The progress of the population programs toward financial self-reliance is not uniform. In 1976, of the countries included in these tables, only Iran and Taiwan were wholly on their own, with Singapore almost fully self-reliant. It is important to note that in achieving this self-suffi-

TABLE 16.7
Total Funds for Population Programs by Major Sources for 19 Countries, 1970 and 1976

	Amounts of Funds (in thousands of U.S. Dollars) by Sources					
	Government		Foreign Govts. Int'l. Agencies & Other Overseas Sources		Total	
Country	1970	1976	1970	1976	1970	1976
Ghana	325	1,782	985	170	1,310	1,952
Indonesia	1,250	16,007	3,716	5,000	4,966	21,007
Iran	4,186*	29,600	2,907*	0	7,093*	29,600
Jamaica	482†	NA	177†	NA	659†	NA
Kenya	28†	10,000	910‡	26,600	938‡	36,600
Malaysia	533†	4,508	674†	NA	1,207†	NA
Nepal	85	1,138§	305	302§	390	1,440§
Philippines	0	16,524	1,350	8,734	1,350	25,258
Rep. of Korea	2,670	6,105	2,130	1,514	4,800	7,619
Taiwan	650	2,785	358	0	1,008	2,785
Thailand	862	935	1,617	2,751§	2,479	3,686§
Tunisia	280	888	502	1,700	782	2,588
Turkey	1,925	2,000	465	NA	2,390	NA
Costa Rica	NA	643§	NA	1,052§	NA	1,695§
Dominican Republic	80	1,009	216	1,203	296	2,212
Egypt	NA	197§	NA	1,489§	NA	1,686§
Pakistan	NA	8,000	NA	16,000	NA	24,000
Singapore	NA	926	NA	5	NA	931
Sri Lanka	NA	0	NA	6,247	NA	6,247
Total	13,356	103,047	16,312	72,767	29,668	169,306
%	45	60	55	40	100	100

* For 1971
† For 1968
‡ For 1969
§ For 1975

SOURCE: Dorothy Nortman *et al., Population and Family Planning Programs: A Fact Book,* 4th and 9th ed. (New York: Population Council), Tables 17 and 10, respectively.

ciency, these countries do not seem to have arrested the growth of their programs. On the other hand, in Ghana the reduction in foreign assistance may explain the setback in the program growth. Other countries which have become largely self-sufficient are Indonesia, Nepal, the Philippines, and the Republic of Korea.

Several countries are still wholly or largely dependent on outside

TABLE 16.8
Funds in Percentage for Population Programs by Major Sources for 16 Countries, 1976

Region/ Country	Percentage of Funds by Source			
	Government	Foreign government and intelligence agencies	Private organization	Total
AFRICA				
Egypt*	12 (NA)†	86	2	100
Ghana	91 (25)	9	0	100
Tunisia	34 (36)	66	0	100
ASIA				
Bangladesh	32 (NA)	64.5	3.5	100
Indonesia	76 (25)	24	0	100
Iran	100 (59)	0	0	100
Nepal	79 (21)	21	0	100
Pakistan	33 (NA)	67	0	100
Philippines	65 (0)	30	5	100
Rep. of Korea	80 (56)	18	2	100
Singapore	99 (NA)	1	0	100
Sri Lanka	0 (NA)	100	0	100
Taiwan	100 (64)	0	0	100
Thailand	25 (35)	74	1	100
LATIN AMERICA				
Costa Rica	38 (NA)	39	23	100
Dominican Republic	46 (NA)	23	31	100

* Data are for 1975
† Figures in parentheses are for 1970
SOURCE: Computed from Dorothy Nortman *et al.*, *Population and Family Planning Programs: A Fact Book*, 9th ed, (New York: Population Council, 1978), Table 10, pp. 38–40.

funds. These include Sri Lanka, Egypt, Tunisia, Bangladesh, Pakistan, and Thailand. Only in Thailand and Tunisia did the proportion of foreign investments rise between 1970 and 1976.

Major Managerial Concerns

The preceeding discussion, although based on less than comprehensive data, makes a reasonable case that population programs are in different stages of growth and, therefore, have different concerns. There are several obvious regional patterns worth noting:

EAST ASIA

Many developing countries in this region (notably Taiwan, the Republic of Korea, Singapore, Indonesia, Hong Kong, Malaysia, Thailand, and the Philippines) with a high population density and a standard of living barely above the poverty level, recognized relatively early the importance of population variables in their developmental schemes and, as a result, assigned high priority to control of their population growth rate. These countries have thus developed fairly significant and clearly identifiable population programs, employing a sizable number of people, and consuming large amounts of resources. On the basis of their relatively long history, stability, and complexity, most of the programs in this region should be considered to be in the very early to middle adolescent stage of growth. The dominant managerial concerns seem to be with gaining an increased degree of self-reliance and self-confidence by developing an assured local support system through the commitment of local resources and the increasing use and development of local expertise. There is a growing awareness of the managerial problems caused by increased program complexities, and several programs are attempting to deal with these problems in innovative ways, but the gap between the need for managerial know-how and achievements based on local innovations is not narrowing.

SOUTH ASIA

Population programs in this region (consisting of five countries: India, Bangladesh, Pakistan, Sri Lanka, and Nepal) are in very different stages because of significant differences in their age and the pace of growth. India and Pakistan/Bangladesh were among the first countries in the world to adopt the Type A population policy and to establish official population programs. Although these countries have shown an impending crisis orientation in controlling the growth rate of their populations, political realities have allowed only a checkered growth of their population programs. Sri Lanka and Nepal are relative newcomers in the population field and are highly dependent on foreign assistance for supporting their population programs. In terms of stage of growth, the programs in this region range from early childhood to adolescence. Correspondingly, the managerial concerns of the programs span the whole gamut from sheer survival to coping with emergent complexity and transitional needs.

MIDDLE EAST

Only three countries in the region (Iran, Egypt, and Turkey) are noted for organized and official population programs. However, the history, orientation, and organization of the population programs in these countries are very different from each other. Egypt is considered a pioneer of the Type A population policy in the region and was among the first countries in the world to establish an official population program. After an initial surge of activities and growth, the Egyptian program seems to have experienced a fairly long period of the doldrums, but is on the move again. Turkey, leaning toward the Type B population policy, was also an early leader in the region, but has been unable to sustain its initial momentum. With the sudden discovery of its oil wealth, Iran's initial commitment to its Type A population policy seems to have diffused with a corresponding impact on its population program. In terms of stages of growth, these programs are probably best described in terms of "arrested childhood." Per capita investment in Egyptian programs declined between 1968 and 1975 from 5.7¢ to 4.5¢, and the total number of acceptors moved from 148,000 to 187,000 between 1967 and 1976. In Turkey, the per capita expenditure in 1966 was 3.3¢ but in the next ten years it reached a mere 5¢ level (if this figure were adjusted for inflation, the per capita expenditure in constant dollars would actually show a decline). The number of acceptors in Turkey rose rapidly from 5,000 in 1965 to 77,000 in 1969. But by 1973 (the last year for which data are available) this number fell to 54,000. Fragmented data from Iran presents a similar picture. If the "arrested growth" description of these programs is more or less accurate, then the managerial concerns would be of the type noted for old age, viz., refocusing the program to its original, or new, goals and energizing it to achieve these goals.

AFRICA

With the exception of Ghana, Tunisia, and Kenya, most of the African countries which have a population policy are not concerned with population control, but rather perceive family-planning services as an important but not critical element in their maternal and child health programs. Highly fragmented data available on the programs of these countries indicate that only in a few cases have noticeable investments been made, and, in most of these cases, a good deal of these investments have come from outside. In most of these countries most of the action seems to be limited to public rhetoric. Given the brief history, small size, relative lack of complexity, and stability of these programs, they may be described as newborn, although some are clearly in only a gestation stage. The dominant concerns in relation to these programs would naturally be of the type best described as prevention of stillbirths, infant mortality, and arrested growth. In other words, the primary managerial tasks are largely developmental: working with the leadership in each of these countries to ensure that an identifiable program is established, appropriate activities are developed, adequate resources are found, and backlash is prevented.

The programs in Ghana, Tunisia, and Kenya do not fit the mold for the rest of the continent. The case of Ghana shows many parallels with Egypt and Turkey. Ghana was the first African country to subscribe to the Type A population policy and to establish an official population program. The number of acceptors climbed from 2,600 in 1969 to 32,000 in 1972. But since 1972, the program has shown no growth. The program in Tunisia presents a clear contrast to Ghana. It came into its own a bit late but has grown steadily and rapidly. The number of acceptors grew from 1,400 in 1964 to 73,500 in 1976; the number of employees rose from 218 in 1969 to 676 in 1975. However, the Tunisian program continues to be very largely dependent on foreign assistance for its resources. Kenya is an in-between case: the number of acceptors increased from 9,500 to 48,400 between 1968 and 1975; but the per capita expenditure rose sharply from 3.3¢ to 54¢ between 1967 and 1976. Although its dependence on foreign assistance is declining, the last available figures (from 1976) indicate that Kenya received nearly 75% of its population program funds from overseas. In terms of stages of growth, while Ghana seems in the stage of arrested childhood, Tunisia seems to have grown out of childhood, and Kenya is still cutting its teeth.

LATIN AMERICA

The growth of population programs in Latin American countries is more advanced than in Africa, but it is far short of the levels reached in Asia. Of the twenty-one countries with an identifiable population policy, only seven have adopted the Type A policy. Given their relative low density and middling standard of living, even these seven countries have shown no real sense of urgency in dealing with their population problem. By and large, the population programs in all twenty-one countries are organized as part and parcel of health services, with voluntary organizations playing a very significant role both in generating demand and supplying services. The programs are showing steady growth, but they are still not very large. The notable programs are in Mexico, Colombia, the Dominican Republic, Costa Rica, Jamaica, Chile, Ecuador, and Guatemala, and in terms of their stage of growth they could be described as growing children. Most of them are not fully faced with issues of complexity and transition, but if they maintain their rate of growth, it should not be long before these issues become their main concerns.

Before this discussion is concluded, it is most essential to point out that the placement of countries in any system of categories is at best a hazardous exercise. Undoubtedly, we must have made mistakes in our effort to categorize. But for the purpose of this discussion, which country is placed in what category is not important. It is more important to know that population programs of different countries are in different stages of growth, and therefore have different types of managerial concerns. It would be a grave mistake to take a homogenized view of this matter.

ORGANIZATIONAL AND MANAGEMENT DEVELOPMENT ACTIVITIES IN THE POPULATION FIELD

Definition of Terms

The term "organizational development" is broader than "management development." The former covers all activities aimed at improving the performance of an organization as a whole; the purpose of management development activities is to improve the performance of an individual or a group of managers. Management development is often an important element in strategies for organizational development.

In the management literature, often the term O.D. (for organizational development) is used to signify a particular approach of organizational development. It is important to point out that the achievement of organizational development is not dependent upon any single approach. There are many approaches to organizational development, and the selection of the appropriate approach should be a function of the nature of the organizational problem.

Systematic organization/management development (O/MD) has three broad phases: (1) diagnosis: to determine the nature of the problem as well as its possible cause or causes; (2) treatment: the subject is put through appropriate processes indicated by the diagnosis, with a view to correcting the problem; and (3) follow-up: the outcome of the treatment is evaluated, new treatment is initiated if indicated, and a plan of action is developed and operationalized to prevent future occurrences of the problem.

All these activities may be carried out by a single person or group, or different expertise may be used for different phases. However, it is important that a sound diagnosis is established before investments are made in treatment. Unfortunately, this obvious fact is more often than not ignored, because diagnosis is often expensive and time consuming and may result in a very different definition of the problem than its original construct.

Available data on organizational/management development in the population field are highly sketchy and fragmented. They consist essentially of the reports of various expert program review committees, proceeedings of international, regional, and national conferences, workshops, seminars, and meetings; and an occasional research study. Most programs do not maintain and report data which would permit easy distillation of basic information, such as the size of a program's management group, their training and background, turnover data, proportion of program budget devoted to managerial activities, and the size of their investment in organizational/management development activities. In the light of this lack of data, we are able to address only two of our original questions, viz., (1) perceptions regarding critical organizational and managerial issues faced by the population programs, and (2) who is doing what regarding organizational/management development in the population field.

Perceptions of Important Issues: Fads and Foibles

The population field has some unique characteristics: it is a relatively young field; it has expanded very rapidly; it relies heavily on foreign assistance which comes from a very small number of sources; and the information network among its leaders is pervasive ("Join the population 'club' and see the world"). Yet another important feature of this field is that while most countries' programs have had a high turnover in their leadership, the leadership of the foreign funding sources has enjoyed a remarkable stability.

All of these circumstances provide fertile ground for the propagation of fads and foibles, and no area of the population field is more rife with these than organization/management development. The personal opinions of some individuals—especially those connected with important sources of funds—regarding what might be wrong with a program tend to gain instant currency as pervasive management issues of critical importance. These "important issues" then become the subject of seemingly endless international and national meetings, in which energy is devoted to the resolution of these issues on the *a priori* assumption that they really exist and are faced by many programs. The following list of "important issues" has been gleaned from recent expert reports, proceedings of international meetings, and writings of population program management experts:

1. Population programs need to be integrated with other social welfare and developmental programs. How should this be achieved?

2. The programs need to have an active involvement of communities. How should this participation be achieved?

3. The programs are too centralized, making little provision for participation of lower-level program personnel in decision making. Program structures providing for decentralization and significant delegation need to be developed and operationalized. How should these goals be achieved?

4. The program managers tend to be too authoritarian. The "participatory management" approach needs to be adopted. How should this be achieved?

5. The programs need improved management information systems. How should this be achieved?

6. The programs need to make a greater use of "modern management" techniques to improve their planning, control, and coordination activities. How should this be achieved?

7. The program managers need to have comprehensive formal management training. How should this be achieved?

8. The commitment of political leadership to population programs is still not very strong. How should this commitment be improved?

9. The programs are suffering because of their location in the health ministries, which have low prestige and power in the political decision-making system of government. How should this problem be corrected?

10. The programs need charismatic, creative, committed, and competent leaders. How should this be achieved?

11. The outside donors have an unholy influence on the programs. How should the programs protect themselves from undue pressure from the donors?

12. What is the proper role of voluntary agencies in the population field? How can this role be ensured?

13. The commercial/industrial sectors should have an active role in the population field. How can they be involved?

14. The programs need to get away from the clinical model of service delivery. How should this goal be achieved?

15. The programs need to make increasing use of paramedical personnel. How should this be achieved?

The list goes on and on, with topics falling out of favor only to be resurrected later. Indeed, some of these issues are important to some of the programs, but all of these issues are unlikely to be important to all of the programs. A universal approach to organizational/management development issues, when programs are in vastly different stages of growth, is not only dysfunctional but may actually be dangerous. At the risk of repetition, it should be re-emphasized that organizational/management development is serious business, and it must not be treated glibly. This area of activity does not lend itself to an "epidemic-control" approach; instead, each case should be diagnosed and treated individually.

Who is Doing What?

The responsibility for organization/management development (O/MD) rests with each program, which must find the necessary ways and means to carry it out, but many others may be able to assist. To sharpen the focus, this discussion has been divided into two parts: O/MD activities of the population programs and support activities of other organizations.

ACTIVITIES OF THE POPULATION PROGRAMS

The leaders of the national population programs seemed to have realized the need and importance of O/MD almost as soon as the programs started to come into being. As early as 1963, they expressed their concern on the subject and requested help. (UN, ECAFE, *The Asia Population Conference, 1963,* E/CN.11/670, New York, 1964—Sales No. 65 II.F.II—pp. 32 and 51.) In the following year, the programs developed a variety of activities which may be grouped under (1) training, (2) research, and (3) technical assistance. Table 16.9 provides information on the size of investments made by twelve countries in recent years for which data were available. (No expenditure data could be found on technical assistance activities.) Based on these and related data on training and research activities in the annual reports of the programs, the following observations are made:

1. On the average, the countries are spending approximately 5 percent of their program budgets on training, and probably a little more on research. Although only a small proportion of these expenditures may be going toward management training and research, these are sizable investments in organizational development. However, there is little evidence, except in a few countries, that the programs have developed any systematic mechanism to channel these investments toward well-defined goals. Indeed, training and planning/evaluation divisions are found in most of the pro-

TABLE 16.9
Expenditures on Training and Research by Population Programs in 12 Countries

Country and year	Total budget of the population program (in 1,000 U.S. $)	Percent expended on	
		Training	Research and evaluation
Bangladesh 1976	14,420	0	1
Brazil 1975	3,784	5	3
Costa Rica 1975	1,695	13	2
Dominican Republic 1976	2,212	3	7
Ghana 1976	1,952	8	10
Hong Kong 1976	787	0	4
India 1975	91,920	3	11*
Iran 1976	29,600	8	7
Malaysia 1977	4,508	5	5
Puerto Rico 1975	6,493	1	3
Singapore	849	10	7
Rep. of Korea	7,619	4	4

* Includes expenditure (10%) for the India Population Project

SOURCE: Dorothy Nortman *et al., Population and Family Planning Programs: A Fact Book,* 9th ed. (New York: Population Council, 1978), Table 11, p. 42.

grams, but only in rase cases have plans for organizational and labor development and agenda for research been developed. The posture of the programs in these matters seems to have been largely reactive.

2. Organized management development activities are recent, few and far between, and consist largely of management training through short courses. No program seems to have developed a well-organized system of management audit, managerial appraisal, on-the-job management training, a junior executive program, training-within-industry (TWI) for supervisory personnel, or an executive counseling service. Even for management courses, most programs rely on the resources of educational institutions (often located in other countries) and international agencies. Management

research seems to have received even less attention. All this is not surprising, given the fact that a large majority of the programs are still fairly young and are not yet faced with the organizational complexities which tend to force attention on management development. Also, management development as an area of organized activity is relatively new to most developing countries; therefore, while it is a subject of increasing curiosity, there is a general lack of experience in conceptualizing and organizing this activity in most sectors of public as well as private activity.

3. A review of the contents, organization, pedagogy, and the faculty of management courses for population program managers (offered by U.S. universities and other training organizations, and by British universities, as well as by institutes of management, universities, and other organizations in developing countries) indicates that there has been an all-around improvement in their sophistication, but there is still a long way to go.

For meaningful progress in this regard, several steps would be necessary. These include:

A. an organized system of communication between program managers and management educators, to inform the educators about the managers' needs and to help the managers appreciate the strengths and limitations of the training system;

B. increased attention to management research to facilitate development of capabilities for sound organizational diagnosis and treatment;

C. an organized effort toward development of teaching materials relevant to a given country's program, to permit the quick focus so essential in short training courses; and

D. sustained investment in faculty and institutional development to ensure the building of a critical mass of needed talent large enough to withstand the vagaries of turnover and to be able to regenerate itself.

Before concluding this observation, it should be noted that training is a powerful weapon. When properly aimed and used, it can do a great deal of good; when misused, it can also do a great deal of harm. To ensure positive results, the training should be preceded by appropriate organizational diagnoses and followed by post-training technical assistance.

4. Given the large size of foreign investment in the population programs, it is safe to assume that they have been recipients of a fair amount of external technical assistance. A good proportion of this assistance may have been focused on organization and management matters.

In recent years, for a variety of good and bad reasons, there is an increasing degree of resistance to foreign "experts." As a result, there has been a sharp reduction in the number of such experts. In many cases, such experts are truly not needed, but many a program will benefit from the perspectives of trained and seasoned outsiders. These outsiders do not have to be foreigners, if in-country expertise can be mobilized.

There is another aspect of technical assistance which deals with issues faced at the middle and lower levels of the programs. Once the national level decisions have been taken, the action moves to these levels, and unless their needs are properly met, the programs are unlikely to achieve very much. However, few programs have developed any O/MD technical assistance capability which could help not only in diagnosing and treating managerial problems as soon as they arise, but also in preventing these problems. Development of such a capability should be important for those programs which are already fairly large and complex.

ACTIVITIES OF OTHER ORGANIZATIONS

A variety of organizations, institutions, and groups have made important contributions to O/MD activities of the population programs. This history of assistance is almost as old as the history of the programs themselves. A comprehensive treatment of this subject should make an interesting and useful treatise, but a detailed study is beyond the scope of the report in hand. Limiting ourselves to only those organizations which have played a fairly significant role in relation to O/MD activities in the population field, we have grouped these organizations into four broad categories (multilateral agencies, bilateral agencies, nongovernmental organizations, and universities and other similar institutions) and compressed the available information into Table 16.10.

A review of Table 16.10 leads us to the following observations:

1. Until about 1975 the number of organizations supporting O/MD activities was steadily increasing. But since then, sources of direct assistance have been declining as a result of a shift in the priorities of U.S. foundations and because more and more countries are channeling their assistance through multilateral agencies. As a result, the population field is left with only three dominant assistance agencies: the United Nations Fund for Population Activities (UNFPA), World Bank, and United States Agency for International Development (USAID). The priorities of these three agencies are likely to gain a new importance in the population field.

2. In past years, most of the assistance in relation to O/MD was concentrated on organizational development, and relatively little on management development. Given the fact that in these years the population programs were new, this was the proper thing to do. But now a number of programs are already quite large, while many others are growing fairly

TABLE 16.10
Selected Organizations and their Activities in O/MD in the Population Field

Name	Nature of O/MD Activities	Early History of O/MD Initiatives	Current Status
A. Multilateral Agencies			
1. United Nations Fund for Population Activities (UNFPA)	A UN body established in 1969 specifically to provide support to population programs, UNFPA makes grants to governments, private sector programs, and various UN system agencies for their population activities. It recognized the importance of management variables in the success of population programs very early in its life. Its primary management development activities include provision of funds on a project basis for training conferences and technical assistance, as well as for research. Only rarely has it taken a direct initiative to organize these activities under its own name.	In the 1971 Population Conference held in Bellagio, Italy, UNFPA presented a review of the state of organization and administration of population programs, proposing a five-year program of comparative management research to understand the determinants of program effectiveness and efficiency. In 1972, it held an international meeting of program managers on "Issues in Population Program Administration," and supported a piggyback workshop at the University of North Carolina on "Systems Approach to Population Program Management." It has become an important benefactor of the International Committee on Management of Population Programmes (ICOMP).	The UNFPA supports a large number of activities at international, regional, and country levels, but maintains a responsive posture for its investments in management development.
2. The World Bank	Established to provide assistance to national governments for developmental projects, the Bank entered the population field nearly ten years ago and has developed a full-fledged organizational unit for this purpose. Historically, the bank has given a great deal of attention to organizational and managerial capabilities in the appraisal of the suitability of any project for which a loan is sought. This approach continues in the population field. The Bank's Economic Development Institute organizes 2 or 3 month-long courses for senior government officials. Some of these courses have focused on managerial issues.	In 1970 the World Bank initiated its first project in the population field. In appraising the merits of this project, a great deal of attention was given to organizational and management aspects, resulting in significant reorganization of a country's population program.	The size of its investment in the population field has markedly increased. Special attention is being given to the development of an interface between population and other developmental projects (especially education, health, rural development, housing, and agriculture), and to this end a series of workshops for senior bank officials has been organized.
3. World Health Organization (WHO)	After resisting any direct participation in the population field, nearly ten years ago, WHO entered this field. Primary concern is with family-planning services, which are perceived as a subsystem of health services. In this connection, it has been very active in helping countries prepare comprehensive	In 1970, WHO attempted to introduce modern management methods in the planning of health services (Project Systems Analysis). In 1971 WHO made an aborted effort to produce a document	The World Health Assembly has given WHO a specific mandate for helping countries improve the management capability of their health system, but WHO has yet to develop a comprehensive strategy and plan of action.

	health plans, but has paid very limited attention to management issues beyond planning. Management development activities include fellowships, technical assistance, expert meetings, technical reports, and short courses.	identifying critical managerial tasks at the national, state, and local levels in the organization and delivery of family-planning services.	Under another directive of the Assembly, the primary locus of activity is shifting to regional offices. In the management development area, limited initiatives have been taken by some of the regional offices, but this activity continues to be directed more to health services in general than population programs *per se*.
4. United Nations Educational, Scientific and Cultural Organization (UNESCO)	Established to help develop educational, scientific, and cultural activities, UNESCO's primary activities in the population field are focused on information-education-communication (IEC) matters. In this connection, it has given special attention to the integration of population IEC activities with similar activities of other developmental programs. Since IEC activities in the population field tend to be fairly large, UNESCO has given some attention to development of IEC planning, management, and education methodologies.	In 1971, UNESCO initiated studies on the relationship between population, development and the environment. In 1973, it initiated a program for developing Manuals on the Management and Evaluation of Family Planning Communication. In 1974, it initiated the International Study of the Conceptualization and Methodology of Population Education (ISCOMPE).	UNESCO continues to be active in its traditional role, but is largely dependent on UNFPA grants for its activities in the population field. Historically, management education has not been a forte of UNESCO, and there are no indications that this situation will change in the near future.
5. Food and Agriculture Organization (FAO)	FAO's involvement in the population field is marginal and limited to random explorations of the interface between nutrition and population, agriculture extension and family-planning education, and population dynamics and agricultural planning.	In 1973, FAO initiated a plan of Agro-Demographic surveys to promote collection of data for the study of the relationship between food consumption, nutrition, and agricultural change with demographic factors.	Largely dependent on UNFPA grants for its population activities, FAO seems to have no plan to expand the scope or size of its work in this field.
6. International Labour Organization (ILO)	Involvement of the ILO in the population field is both recent, limited, and largely dependent on financial support from UNFPA. O/MD activities are limited to technical assistance to organized industrial sector, and occasional sponsorship of meetings.	In 1973, ILO cosponsored with Government of Bangladesh, "Management Seminar in Population Planning" held in Dacca. In 1974, organized Asian Regional Seminar on "Management of Family Planning Program" held in Singapore.	Largely dependent on UNFPA grants for its population activities, ILO currently seems to be in a holding pattern of little activity in this field.
7. U.N. Regional Organizations: a) Economic and Social Commission for Asia and the Pacific (ESCAP) b) Economic Commission for Africa (ECA) c) Economic Commission for Latin America (ECLA) d) Economic Commission for West Asia (ECWA)	Of all the regional organizations, ESCAP is the only one which has developed O/MD activities in the population field. However, these activities are very limited and consist of the occasional convening of expert groups, and infrequent sponsorship of management training and research activities.	ESCAP was the first organization to devote special attention to the managerial aspects of population programs; In 1966, it convened a working group on the subject which led to the first publication on population program management viz., *Administrative Aspects of Family Planning Programmes* (New York: United Nations, 1966). Sale No. 66.II.F.10. Document No. E/CN. 11(742).	ESCAP, as well as other regional organizations are largely dependent on UNFPA for financial support of its activities in the population field. These organizations are not seen as a major source of assistance in O/MD activities by the population programs because these organizations lack a critical mass of needed talents.

TABLE 16.10 *(continued)*

Name	Nature of O/MD Activities	Early History of O/MD Initiatives	Current Status
B. Bilateral Agencies			
1. U.S. Agency for International Development (USAID)	In 1965, the U.S. Government started to give direct assistance to countries for their population programs. USAID is now the largest single source of bilateral assistance in the population field. It is also a major source of revenue for a number of multilateral agencies, nongovernmental organizations, universities, and other similar organizations active in the population field. It provides assistance for practically all aspects of population programs. Its investments in organizational development-related activities, especially in the areas of policy, planning, evaluation, and manpower development, are very significant.	In 1965, USAID made institutional development grants to a number of educational institutions both in the U.S. and overseas for development of training and research programs in the population field to prepare urgently needed program leadership.	USAID continues to be mainly interested in organizational development as against management development.
2. Swedish International Development Authority (SIDA)	Sweden was the first country to develop a formal program of bilateral assistance for population activities. However, given the small size of its assistance funds, it has opted to concentrate on a small number of countries in Africa and Southeast Asia. Without advertising a grand strategy of its own for dealing with the population issue, it plays an active role in support of each country's plans and programs in a variety of ways. In recent years, it has channeled more and more of its resources through multilateral agencies. Its involvement with O/MD activities is not direct and visible, with the exception of its support to ICOMP (see under nongovernmental agencies).	In 1958, SIDA established a pilot project in Ceylon to determine the acceptability and feasibility of family-planning services in a rural area, and to develop an integrated model of MCH-family planning services.	SIDA continues to be an important source of assistance in the population field. It maintains a very low profile and prefers to work through others. There is no evidence that SIDA leadership does not recognize the importance of investment in O/MD, but it does not seem to be willing to initiate any action in this area on its own.
3. Danish International Development Agency (DANIDA)	DANIDA has been providing small-scale support to selected projects in the population field for a little more than ten years. A good proportion of its funds are channeled through and in support of multilateral agencies. It is taking a special interest in developing management capability of governments and public sector enterprises in selected African countries.	In 1966, DANIDA made a grant to IPPF to support its Eighth International Conference held in Chile, in which a great deal of attention was given to a variety of managerial issues, with special reference to voluntary organizations.	DANIDA continues to have a special interest in O/MD-related activities, but its resources are relatively small. Therefore, its investments in this field are highly selective and "supplementary" in nature.
4. British Ministry for Overseas Development (MOD)	British bilateral aid in the population field started in 1964. In 1968, MOD established a Population Bureau to coordinate its activities in this field. Many of the activities have been concentrated on provision of	Information not available.	MOD assigns a very high priority to the development of manpower needed by the population programs. In this connection, special attention is given to management

	technical assistance services to countries and support of training programs, which are increasingly focused on management issues, organized by Sussex University and British Family Planning Association. It is also an important source of funds to IPPF.		development activities. However, investments are small scale and largely limited to support of training activities held in England.
5. Other Bilateral Agencies: a) Canadian International Development Agency (CIDA) b) Norwegian Agency for International Development (NORAID) c) Japan International Cooperation Agency (JICA)	In recent years, increasing numbers of countries have started to contribute to population programs of developing countries through bilateral and multilateral channels. Their preferences for these investments, which tend to be small, are not yet clearly established. As a result they tend to provide supplementary support to a variety of activities including training, research and conferences.	Varies from country to country.	These countries are not set in their focus yet, and therefore tend to be reactive and not proactive. Several countries have a historical appreciation for the critical importance of management in the success of any enterprise, but any concerted activity in this field is yet to be developed. NORAID is an important supporter of ICOMP; JICA provides support for O/MD activities in selected East Asian countries, through the Japanese Organization for International Cooperation in Family Planning.
C. Nongovernmental Organizations: 1. The Ford Foundation	A leader in both development of management education and population programs in developing countries, the Ford Foundation has also been a leader in recognizing the importance of management development in the population field. Its activities include assistance in the establishment of a number of elite management institutes in Asia, Africa, and Latin America; support to a number of universities in the U.S. and other countries (as well as to many nongovernmental organizations) for population management training and research activities; O/MD-related technical assistance to population programs; sponsorship of meetings and conferences on O/MD in population; and support to ICOMP.	In the early fifties, the Ford Foundation supported the visit of Dr. Abraham Stone to India to popularize the rhythm method. In 1963, it established a population office under the leadership of a management expert; in 1965 it cosponsored the International Conference on Family Planning Programs held in Geneva, which devoted a whole section to O/MD issues. It made a series of grants to U.S. universities for development of training and research capabilities in population program development and management. The Foundation is largely responsible for the establishment of ICOMP.	While its overall budgets have been sharply reduced from levels of the early 1970s, the Foundation continues to give high priority to support of work in population. It continues its emphasis on population program management with special attention to its implications for social development management more broadly conceived.
2. The Rockefeller Foundation	Enjoying a long and distinguished history of interest and activities in the health field, it became increasingly involved in the population field through its historical association with the Population Council. In addition to supporting the Technical Assistance Division of the Council, it has concentrated on development of family-planning units in medical schools for	In 1965, the Rockefeller Foundation supported the International Conference on Family Planning Programs held in Geneva, and provided institutional development grants to a number of U.S. universities for development of research and training activities in the population field.	Its support activities in the population field have declined significantly; further, the Foundation does not avow any interest in O/MD activities in this field.

TABLE 16.10 *(continued)*

Name	Nature of O/MD Activities	Early History of O/MD Initiatives	Current Status
	teaching and research in this field. On occasion, it has also supported development of demonstration programs for the organization and delivery of family-planning services through medical schools. However, its interest in management development has been indirect, resulting in sporadic limited-support activities.		
3. The Population Council	Established in 1952, the Council is concerned with advancement of knowledge in the broad field of population by fostering research, training, and technical consultation and assistance in social and biomedical sciences. With its involvement with technical assistance, the Council became increasingly interested in programmatic and organizational issues. It sponsored The International Committee on Applied Research in Population (ICARP) to promote the systematic study of service design and delivery issues. Also, it has been a source of fellowships for advanced training for program managers.	In 1965, the Council cosponsored the International Conference on Family Planning Programs held in Geneva. Also, in 1966 it cosponsored with ECAFE the regional meeting on "Administrative Aspects of Family Planning Programmes." Its *Reports on Population/Family Planning*, and other series and publications, are the main source of organized information in the population field.	Recent changes in the funding, structure, as well as in the leadership of the Council have generated an impression of lack of clarity regarding its direction. Meanwhile, most of its previous activities are continuing on a somewhat reduced scale.
4. International Planned Parenthood Federation (IPPF)	Established in 1952, the IPPF has a mandate and responsibility to stimulate the formation and development of family-planning associations. With this as its primary concern, IPPF has been devoting a great deal of its energy to O/MD activities in relation to its affiliates. For this purpose, it arranges training and technical assistance. It has also published a number of reports dealing with various aspects of O/MD for family-planning associations.	The establishment of IPPF itself was a major milestone in O/MD activities in the population field.	With the rapid expansion of governmental involvement in the population field, the family-planning associations are increasingly faced with the issue of "proper roles." This is bringing about new pressures for ensuring that the current activities of these associations are as efficient as possible. These pressures are not likely to be reduced in the near future.
5. International Committee on the Management of Population Programmes (ICOMP)	Established nearly five years ago, ICOMP's membership is open to chief executives of national population programs and selected management institutes from developing countries. Its primary goal is to help improve the management of member countries' population programs. With the assistance of a full-time executive director, its primary activity consists of an annual meeting of members at which selected management issues are addressed through specially prepared papers and cases. Other activities include institutional development grants to	Its organizational meeting took place in 1974 in London.	ICOMP is still in the process of development. Its annual meetings serve as advanced management seminars for population program managers. It continues to be dependent on financial sources other than its members but must essentially become self-supporting if its long-term viability is to be assured.

	selected management institutes, technical assistance activities, and management training-related activities.		
D. Universities and Other Institutions 1. In the United States	Several universities in the U.S. have been active in the field of demography and public health for many years. But starting in 1965, with assistance from USAID and foundations, several of these universities developed interdisciplinary population programs. As a result, some of these universities (e.g., University of Michigan, Johns Hopkins University, Columbia University, University of North Carolina, and Tulane University) became actively involved with O/MD in the population field through training, program research, and consultation. The University of North Carolina, assisted by an eight-year grant from the Ford Foundation, for the International Project for Teaching Cases in Family Planning Administration (PopCase) and The International Project in Population Program Administration (IPPA) has enjoyed special visibility with regard to management development activities.	Around 1965, a number of universities formally established multidisciplinary population centers to promote training and research in the population field. In 1972, a one-week workshop was organized by the University of North Carolina to examine the role of modern techniques of management in the population field. This workshop, attended by top-level program managers from eighteen countries, generated the idea which led to the formation of ICOMP.	With the termination/reduction of USAID and foundation support, these programs are in a state of confusion. The critical mass of faculty talent mobilized for training and research activities in the population field is rapidly being directed to other fields.
2. In Other Developed Countries	With the exception of a few universities in England (notably Sussex and Cardiff), there does not seem to be any significant involvement of universities and other educational institutions in the population field. These few British universities seem quite interested and active in management development activities.	Information not available.	Information not available.
3. In Developing Countries	Involvement of universities and other training and research institutions in the population field in developing countries is fairly pervasive, but this involvement, in most cases, tends to be limited, episodic, and highly transient. There are notable exceptions, e.g., National Institute of Health and Family Planning in India has been created to ensure long-term sustained and focused attention to the population field. A number of universities in several countries have established interdisciplinary population centers on the U.S. models. A number of schools of public health have created specialized programs in family planning and population. Several management institutes	In 1965, at the request of the Indian Government, the Indian Institute of Management-Calcutta conducted a feasibility study to determine the role of the organized commerical sector in condom distribution.	Continued availability of a significant amount of resources on a sustained long-term basis continues to be a critical variable in maintaining and enhancing the interest and activities of these institutions in the population field. In the long run, the support has to come from the countries themselves, but in the meanwhile, the gain made in development of institutional and faculty involvement in the population field (largely through foreign assistance which is rapidly decreasing) seems in jeopardy.

TABLE 16.10 *(continued)*

Name	Nature of O/MD Activities	Early History of O/MD Initiatives	Current Status
	(notably Asian Institute of Management, Indian Institute of Management-Ahmedabad, Administrative Staff College of India, Indian Institute of Management, Bangalore, Instituto Centroamericano de Administracion de Empresas, Instituto de Estudios Superiores de Administracion, Ghana Institute of Management & Public Administration, National Institute of Development Administration-Thailand, and Asian Centre for Development Administration) have developed more than a casual interest in the population field and have become a valuable source of training, research, and technical assistance.		

rapidly and becoming increasingly complex. These developments necessitate greater attention to management development.

3. Earlier, it was noted that only a few programs were moving to build in-house capability for management development, and that the vast majority of the programs relied on the resources of the universities and management institutes. Faced with a rapid decline in financial support for their population activities, most of the universities in the U.S. are redirecting their resources to other programs; and the situation in other countries does not look any better.

These observations paint a rather disconcerting picture. As the population programs are growing, they are facing internal complexity on one hand, and new organizational issues (e.g., need for improved integration with other developmental programs) on the other hand. As a result, their need for O/MD is surfacing in a variety of ways, and in the next few years this need is likely to gain greater momentum. Unfortunately, the currently available sources of O/MD assistance seem to be in the process of closing their shops. Most of the population programs have not even started a planning process to develop their own O/MD capability. As a result, when O/MD assistance is most needed by the population programs, there may be nobody to effectively provide it.

FACING THE FUTURE

Concluding Observations

This survey of management needs in the population field leads to three main conclusions.

1. The population programs, although in different stages of growth, are gaining in complexity as they grow. Recent renewed recognition of the interaction between socioeconomic development and population dynamics is adding a new dimension to this complexity. Further, the programs and their environments being in a continual dynamic state of tension, the complexity issue is not a one-time issue; the nature and the degree of complexity will continue to change with shifts in the equation of this tension. This indicates that the population field needs a long-term strategy for O/MD for dealing with issues of today as well as those of tomorrow. The success or the failure of this strategy may have an important influence on the future course of the population programs.

2. Most population programs have given little systematic attention to issues pertaining to O/MD. However, a few small and scattered pockets

of population field-oriented O/MD capability have grown in the universities and other educational institutions of developing, as well as developed, countries. This has happened largely as a result of a systematic and sustained effort by a handful of assistance-giving agencies. Some of these agencies, for a variety of reasons, seem unwilling to continue making their investments. As a result, the little O/MD capability that now exists in the population field is in danger of being refocused on other fields. If this happens, the population field will end up having the least O/MD capability when its need is at its greatest.

3. After a rapid proliferation of aid-giving agencies in the population field, there is a new significant trend toward consolidation. If the trend continues, then the population field is likely to be left with only three primary aid agencies: the World Bank as a loan/assistance agency, UNFPA as the primary source of multilateral assistance, and USAID as the major source of bilateral assistance. While this process of consolidation has many positive aspects, it will also add new weight to the preferences and priorities of these agencies. This, in turn, should place a new responsibility on these agencies for guarding against personal whims and fancies.

Given these three sets of data, what should be done to ensure that population programs do not suffer as a result of inadequate management? To put it positively, what should be done to ensure that the population programs have the full benefit of O/MD? The answer lies in the development of two mutually supportive steps. The first step would be the development of a set of management development activities within the program, such as a junior executive program, junior boards, training within industry, management counseling service, management audit, executive appraisal, or any other arrangement feasible under the unique conditions of each program. A small investment in this aspect of O/MD could have a high payoff in improving the quality of individual managers.

The second step would be the development of an adequate O/MD capability available to help a program deal with those difficult management problems which it cannot overcome solely by using its own resources. The term adequate is critical in this discussion and should be defined clearly. The concept of adequacy in the context of O/MD refers to the size, nature, and function of the talent pool. Briefly, the size should be large enough to meet the needs of not only the top management but all levels of management. The nature of the O/MD talent pool is to be determined by the complexity of the program. Complexity is largely a function of variety, and the variety in issues requires a variety in talents for dealing with these issues. It was noted earlier that effective O/MD consists of three phases—diagnosis, treatment, and follow-up. Organizational diagnosis implies research (both epidemiologic and case study). Treatment may be in the form of changes in structure, process, and/or behavior, and these changes may be affected with or without training. Follow-up implies evaluation of the results of the change, adjustment in the treatment plans and/or diagnosis when so indicated by the evaluation data (this process of evaluation and adjustment is to be continued until desired results are achieved), and developing and executing a plan for the prevention of similar problems in the future. Another way of describing this aspect of O/MD is to call it action-research.

From the above definition, it is clear that development of O/MD capability means considerably more than having a couple of management trainers in an organization. It implies a pool of multidisciplinary talent capable of dealing with a variety of managerial issues of varying degrees of complexity and sophistication.

Where should this capability be located; inside or outside the programs? The answer to this question depends on answers to two related questions: first, who can best attract and sustain this kind of talent? Experience indicates that the government-managed programs, even the large ones, have not proven very attractive to high-quality educators and researchers, unless the latter were hired by an operationally autonomous educational institute affiliated with the program. On the other hand, universities and specialized institutes have a remarkable ability to attract and retain such talent, but the autonomy of these organizations, combined with the academic freedom of their faculty, often makes them less than fully responsive to the needs of the operating programs. This problem may be surmounted through long-term service contracts between an educational institute and a population program; but even under such an arrangement, the faculty of these institutions are unlikely to assign high priority to those mundane operational concerns of the program manager which are perceived as academically unchallenging. An optimum solution lies in a two-tier arrangement: developing an in-house O/MD capability for routine and low-level issues, and developing a backyard capacity (outside the program structure, but within easy reach) for complex issues.

The second question which should be considered regards the relative importance of personal loyalty and objectivity in dealing with sensitive organizational and managerial issues. It is not uncommon for O/MD consultants from outside to take out their butcher knives to force imposition of their personal values on a system. It is also not uncommon for program managers to hamstring their own O/MD staffs by limiting their diagnostic and treatment work to symptoms and not allowing them to address the root causes of such symptoms. Also, managers at lower levels of the organizations tend to be uneasy in dealing with the O/MD in-house staffs from the headquarters, who are often perceived as inspectors instead of facilitators.

There are no simple answers to these problems, but we tend to believe that, on the whole, the programs are likely to be served better by outsiders, in situations where a high quality analysis of the issues is important and when the treatment plan may call for significant changes. However, in the selection of these consultants, as much attention should be given to their personality characteristics as to their know-how.

A Proposal for Action

The following plan of action is proposed to resolve the various issues relating to the important emerging problem of O/MD capability.

1. The population programs and aid-giving agencies should join hands in developing a mutually reinforcing norm for investment in O/MD activities. Available data indicate that currently, programs may be spending on an average as much as 10% of their budgets on training and research activities, and the proportion of budgets of the funding agencies devoted to such activities may be in the neighborhood of 25%. In the light of this, it may be useful to consider that the programs devote at least 1% of their budget to O/MD, and the assistance agencies allocate 5% of their funds to help develop needed O/MD capability, both inside and outside the population programs.

2. Each population program should consider the possibility of preparing a formal five-year plan for development of its O/MD capability in relation to its O/MD needs and activities. These plans should help in facilitating the development of systematic investments in O/MD. They should also help identify the critical resource needs bottlenecking the O/MD activities, so that these needs may be addressed on a priority basis. The International Committee on Management of Population Programs (ICOMP) may be invited to devote special energy in the next few years to helping the countries develop such plans.

3. The aid-giving agencies should join hands with the population programs and other relevant organizations in ensuring that the highly scarce O/MD capability which is now currently available in a number of universities and other similar institutions is safeguarded, is further developed if necessary, and is mobilized as a critical developmental resource.

4. Each of the three major aid-giving agencies (UNFPA, the World Bank, and USAID) in the population field should consider the possibility of developing a small, specialized unit concerned primarily with O/MD to help each agency plan and implement its activities in this field.

17

Organizational Issues in International Population Assistance

GAYL D. NESS

ORGANIZATIONAL ISSUES

LARGE-SCALE, bureaucratic forms of organization are a dominant fact of life in the modern world. In production, consumption, trade, governance, welfare, and intellectual pursuits, the large scale organization has become the single most powerful instrument for arranging and controlling human activity. Most current human problems are in large part created by this modern form of organization, and if solutions are found they will require some form of large-scale organizational activity for their implementation.

A preliminary version of this chapter served as a background paper for a conference on organizational issues in international population assistance organized in Tunis, Tunisia, October 1978, by the University of Michigan Center for Population Planning with the cooperation of the University of Tunis Centre d'Etudes et des Recherches Economiques et Sociales. The participants provided excellent criticisms, many of which will be reflected here. They should certainly not be held responsible for any of the materials presented, however. The participants were as follows. Dr. Ataollah Amini (Iran), Dr. Mongi Behir (Tunisia), Professor Robert Cox (Canada), Dr. Laila S. El Hamamsy (Egypt), Professor Dr. Louis Emmerij (the Netherlands), Professor Jason Finkle (USA), Professor Philip Hauser (USA), Professor Toshio Kuroda (Japan), Dr. Muheddine Mabrukh (Tunisia), Dr. Milos Macura (Yugoslavia), Dr. Dordana Masmoudi (Tunisia), Dr. Nor Laily Aziz (Malaysia), Dr. Visoo A. Pai Panandiaker (India), Dr. Moncer Rouissi (Tunisia). Dr. Marco Cittone (Tunisia), Dr. A. Thavarajah (Sri Lanka), Dr. Hirofumi Ando (Japan), and Dr. S.N.L. Rao (India), all of UNFPA, also attended the meeting as observers.

The fine research assistance of Jeffrey Rodanar, Mark Lundgren, Ellen Murphey, and Kathryn Tilly is gratefully acknowledged. Jason L. Finkle has provided much direction and valued criticism in my studies of population affairs over the past decade; I am pleased to note his special contributions. Finally, I have benefitted from many personal interviews with UN officials, US AID officials, various government family-planning officials, and the staffs of private foundations.

Thus any assessment of current human problems, and any proposed solution, must consider the organizational issues implied both by the problem and by its solutions.

This is nowhere more evident than in the area of population policies. The successful work of large-scale organizations was mainly responsible for the continuing reduction in world mortality, which in turn is the immediate cause of rapid population growth. That rapid population growth constitutes a serious problem, and that the problem is complex and multidimensional, was given official world recognition at New York in 1966 and at Bucharest in 1974. The larger social causes and consequences of rapid population growth are acknowledged to lie in political, economic, social, cultural, and health conditions. Solutions to the problem are thus seen to require changes of all of these conditions. Further, and most important, these desired changes have become the mandates of various forms of national and international organization. A problem created in part by large-scale organizations is to be solved in part by large-scale organizations.

Will these organizations be able to help in solving the problem? Will they be able to carry out their mandates? And if they are successful, will this produce the desired changes? These questions remain open. The outcome will have profound implications for the future of human welfare. The answers to these questions lie in part in the very conditions that are to be changed and in the institutional structures that underlie those conditions.

Can human poverty, sickness, and illiteracy be attacked with the same success that human mortality has been attacked? Are the institutional structures that underlie those conditions amenable to adjustment and change by large-scale organizations? The answer to this question lies not only in the character of human institutions, but also in the character of the large-scale organizations that are designed to deal with the problems. It is to the organizational issues, especially those seen in the United Nations system, that this chapter is directed.

Organizational issues involve much more than questions of structure and functions, leadership and resources, and scope of authority, which have been the common fare of much administrative analysis. Modern theory and research suggest that in addition the environment of action and the nature of the technology used play a large role in determining what kind of organizational design is most appropriate to a given set of problems. From this theory and research we can identify the following four questions that will be especially useful in dealing with the organizational issues in international population assistance.

1. What is the character of the environments within which the organizations must operate?

2. What is the nature of the problem they face and the technology available to confront that problem?
3. What are the organizational requirements that follow from the character of the environment and the problem?
4. What is the nature of the United Nations system and to what extent is this system capable of meeting the organizational requirements presented by the environment and the problem?

At the risk of considerable oversimplification, we can briefly summarize our answers to these questions here. Each of these answers will comprise the content of the four major sections of this chapter. A final section will deal with general principles that should inform organizational design for work in international population assistance. The analysis will focus largely on the United Nations and its Fund for Population Activities (UNFPA), since UNFPA has become the largest single multilateral agency in international population assistance.

First, the critical environments for international population assistance are found in the world political condition, in the condition of national population policies, and in the sociodemographic conditions of nations that permit external assistance in population questions. These environments are complex, heterogeneous, and changing.

Secondly, the current population problem involves deep moral and ethical issues. It does not involve conflict with major organized economic interest. It is a problem whose strategies of solution involve volatile conditions and precarious values. Although there is an extensive and effective contraceptive technology available, the broader technology for changing reproductive behavior is highly complex and not by any means well understood. In addition, the character of the population problem is changing. The problem of growth is losing its dominant and almost exclusive position, and is giving way to a broader concern with the more complex and elusive problem of "the quality of life."

Third, these environmental and problem conditions require organizations that are highly flexible, adaptive, innovative, and service oriented. This in turn requires flat, decentralized structures, extensive specialization with flexible integrative mechanisms, and considerable freedom given to the application of human discretion. The precarious nature of problem-solving strategies requires strong legitimizing support for whatever organizations are charged with addressing the problem.

Fourth, the United Nations provides both the broad legitimacy, and a wide range of the technical competence needed for international population assistance. But to be effective, the UN must provide support for the different types of organizational activity needed. The system has produced a differentiated set of technical units, but in each unit bureaucratic forces tend to produce a centralized, hierarchic structure engaging in routine and standardized activities. This also implies little integration of the differentiated units. All of this contrasts with the flat, decentralized structures capable of flexible and innovative actions that population assistance requires.

The final section of the chapter will deal with some technical principles of organizational design suggested by our analysis. Organizational design always involves both political and technical considerations. Technical considerations can suggest some of the organizational characteristics that should be protected in order to achieve a given end. Political considerations will determine how such things as formal mandates, authority, and resources are to be arranged in order to produce the needed organizational characteristics. The political considerations are the responsibility and authority of the General Assembly and the committees, governing councils, and agencies that constitute the political decision-making units of the UN system. They will have to decide on the specific features of organizational design used to promote international population assistance. These are not properly the concern of this chapter. It is our task, however, to provide some of the needed technical considerations. By necessity these will be stated in the form of general principles rather than recommendations for specific changes.

THE COMPLEX, CHANGING ENVIRONMENTS OF INTERNATIONAL POPULATION ASSISTANCE ORGANIZATION

International organizations in population assistance are constrained in three important ways. First their goals, mandates, and resource mobilization procedures are established by the General Assembly and their Governing Councils, whose members are sovereign states. Second, they enter into member-state territories for population work only if allowed by national governments and for the specific purposes decided upon by each government's policies. Third, the specific work they must do is determined in large part by the sociodemographic condition of the population with which they work. Thus the UN population assistance organizations are affected by political, policy, and sociodemographic environments. The basic observation of these environments is that all are highly heterogeneous, complex, and changing.

The World Political Environment

The high complexity and rapid change of the world political environment is widely recognized and commented upon in the popular press, in political circles, and among scholars. It does not require extensive documentation here, but it is useful to recount the major elements of this phenomenon to remind ourselves of the impact it has on population assistance organizations.

The simplest view of the change is gained from noting the increase in numbers of the United Nations members. Although the actual strength and independence of these members varies greatly, they all constitute units with voting rights and thus will have some capacity to play initiating and activating roles in the world forum. Table 17.1 shows the increase in the sheer number of members by year and by region. It shows rapid growth and increasing heterogeneity.

The early years of the United Nations saw dominant influence held by the developed countries. Asian numerical growth occurred in the first decade. The second and third decade saw a rapid increase of new members from the developing countries. The increase in numbers itself would be expected to add greater heterogeneity to the membership, and the great increase in representation from the developing countries, only reinforces the perception of increasing heterogeneity.

Writing more than a decade ago, Inis L. Claude reflected on the increase in number and diversity of United Nations membership and made a series of important observations. This numeric growth reflected a trend toward both universality in the United Nations, and the de-Europeanization of international affairs, making world politics truly the politics of the whole world. With this the United Nations roster has become not only "unprecedentedly comprehensive," but "unprecedentedly heterogeneous" as well.[1]

TABLE 17.1
UN Members by Region and Year of Admission, 1945–78

Year	Africa	Asia	Europe and N. America*	Latin America	South and East Mediterranean	Total	(Cumulative)
1945	3	5	18	20	5	51	
1946–49	—	4	2	—	2	8	(59)
1950–54	—	1	—	—	—	1	(60)
1955–59	3	6	10	—	4	23	(83)
1960–64	24	1	—	2	5	32	(115)
1965–69	6	2	—	2	1	11	(126)
1970–79	7	8	3	3	4	25	(151)
	43	27	33	27	21	151	

* Includes the North Atlantic extensions of Australia and New Zealand.

1. Inis L. Claude, *The Changing United Nations* (New York: Random House, 1967), pp. 62–3.

The developing countries have become increasingly sophisticated in the General Assembly and especially in their demands for a new international economic order. They have been joined as well by influential voices from among the developed countries, but the struggle is by no means one sided. Developed countries still control the major financial arms of the United Nations and still provide a major share of its economic resources. Further, in the budgetary policies of the United Nations, we see a complex struggle over resource mobilization that has a profound impact on the character of international assistance in population as well as in the broader field of development or economic change.

United Nations activities are supported by two different types of funds—those assessed member nations by the General Assembly, and those provided through the voluntary funds. The former represent a form of international assessment, and the major UN donors have shown considerable interest in arresting the growth of the assessed budget for both economic and political reasons.[2] The voluntary funds are not assessments and thus give nations more direct control over their contributions, both in absolute amounts and in the specific activities for which the funds are to be used. This has led to a considerable increase in the use of voluntary funds, especially to finance world development activities. Voluntary funds have grown from about 45 percent of total UN expenditures (excluding the World Bank Group[3]) in the first decade to well over 50 percent of total expenditures in the 1970s. The United Nations Development Programme (UNDP), the World Food Program, United Nations International Children's Emergency Fund (UNICEF), the United Nations High Commissioner of Refugees (UNHCR), and the United Nations Fund for Population Activities (UNFPA) account for the major share of these voluntary funds.

The voluntary nature of its Fund places a severe strain on international population activities. Contributions are made annually, and thus are potentially subject to wide fluctuations. This makes it extremely difficult for UNFPA to make long-term commitments to its recipients. It also raises the possibility of very rapid reductions in total resources if any of the major donor nations should withhold support. Table 17.2 shows the distribution of UNFPA funding sources over the past decade. It indicates that the concentration is diminishing slightly, introducing more heterogeneity into the financial base, but it also shows how far the diversification has yet to go to reduce the reliance on a very narrow base.

2. Mahdi Elmandjra, *The United Nations System: An Analysis* (Hamden, Ct.: Archon, 1973).

3. The World Bank is excluded from this analysis since it is a net income earner.

TABLE 17.2
Total and Percentage Distribution of Pledges to UNFPA by Major Donors, 1967–78

	1967–71	1972	1973	1974	1975	1976	1977	1978
Total Pledged								
($ million)	48.8	30.6	42.4	54.1	63.2	79.1	91.7	107.3
(Cumulative)	(48.8)	(79.4)	(121.8)	(175.9)	(239.1)	(318.2)	(409.9)	(517.2)
Major Donors (%)								
Canada	6	7	5	5	5	6	7	6
Denmark	1	2	4	3	3	4	4	4
Federal Republic of Germany	6	8	10	11	12	9	8	11
Japan	6	—	6	9	11	11	12	13
The Netherlands	2	9	9	11	11	10	10	11
Norway	4	7	6	6	6	7	8	10
Sweden	10	10	8	8	9	8	8	8
U.K.	5	7	5	4	6	5	6	7
U.S.	53	46	42	37	32	25	32	25
Total	93	96	95	94	95	85	95	95

SOURCE: *UNFPA Annual Reports* from 1969 through 1977.

Even this high concentration of donors, however, overstates the homogeneity of the funding source. In the past, some major donors emphasized fertility control and contraceptive distribution as an almost exclusive means of achieving fertility control. More recently, donors have shown greater interest in supporting a wider range of population activities and of broader-based development programs as ways of addressing the population problem.

In the Stockholm Environment Conference of 1972 and the Bucharest Population Conference in 1974 we can also see examples of another change in the character of the world political environment. The initiative for both the conferences came largely from the Western developed nations. These nations had two dominant approaches in these conferences—curtailing industrial pollution at the first, and promoting fertility decline through family planning programs at the second. In the preparations for Stockholm and at Bucharest itself, these approaches were redefined by Third World participants.[4] In Stockholm, the developing countries noted the dangers of

4. On Stockholm see T. E. J. Campbell, "The Political Meaning of Stockholm: Third World Participation in the Environment Conference Process," *Stanford Journal of International Affairs* (Spring 1973):138–53. On Bucharest see Jason L.

using environmental protection to justify curtailing development, and poverty was redefined as one of the most pressing forms of pollution. In Bucharest, family planning was defined as a limited palliative, and a greater emphasis was placed on using economic development and increasing equality in the distribution of wealth as a more profound tactic for the reduction of fertility.

Claude noted a decade ago that the outcome of these and other conferences is far from certain. While it is hopeful to note the positive voices raised in these conferences, it is also necessary to ask the amount of actual change they produce. It is common to note that the action plans of the conferences often lack implementation.

Despite those questions, the conflicting voices are present and persistent, and they are most assuredly an integral part of the complexity, the heterogeneity, and the rapid change that constitutes the world political environment of the international organizations.

The Population Policy Environment

A first view of the changes in population policies in developing countries is gained by using the Population Council's three-part classification. Countries either (1) adopted fertility limitation policies *and* programs; (2) have no policy but support family-planning programs; or (3) have neither policy nor programs. By 1960 only three countries—India, Pakistan, and China—had adopted official fertility limitation policies. By the time of the UN's new population resolution, December 1966, twenty countries had adopted official fertility limitation policies, and another six provided public support for such programs. In 1977 sixty countries (thirty-one with official policies, twenty-nine with program support only) provided public support for family-planning programs. This expansion of policy decisions opened the respective countries to actions by international organizations in population assistance, making them a part of the environment of those organizations.

Along with the expansion of policies, their rationale and motivation have increased in complexity. The earliest countries to adopt official fertility limitation policies were motivated primarily by aims and considerations of national economic development. Rapid population growth was defined as an obstacle to economic development, and fertility reduction

---

Finkle and Barbara B. Crane, "The Politics of Bucharest: Population, Development and the New International Order," *Population and Development Review* 1 (1) (September 1975): 87–114.

programs were adopted as part of the package of economic development programs. By 1977 sufficient information had become available on the consequences of high fertility to lead even nations with pronatalist aims to adopt public family-planning programs. In these cases, family-planning programming is justified on grounds of maternal and child health rather than on grounds of obstructing economic development.

Using the description of national population positions provided in the UNFPA's extensive inventory of activities, we can classify national policy positions on Table 17.3 with a six-part classification.[5]

TABLE 17.3
119 Developing Countries Classified by Population Policies

Policy	Number of Countries
Official antinatalist policy and public family-planning program	36
No official antinatalist policy*; public family-planning programs in existence and justified largely on grounds of economic development and welfare	19
No official antinatalist policy* but public family-planning program justified largely on grounds of maternal and child health	32
No official antinatalist policy* or public program, but private family-planning programs permitted to operate	20
Official pronatalist policy, public and private family-planning activity not permitted to operate	5
No official antinatalist policy* but public fertility reduction program are in existence and based on various revolutionary aims and ideologies	7
Total	119

* This often but not always implies some degree of policy orientation for population growth.

SOURCE: UNFPA, *Inventory of Population Projects in Developing Countries Around the World, 1976–77* (New York: UNFPA, 1976).

5. We must acknowledge our debt to the UNFPA and especially to Jack Voelpel for his painstaking work in drawing up the UNFPA Inventory. This work provides a mine of systematic and relatively comparable information which we have drawn upon for the quantitative analysis provided in this section. Like the Population Council's Factbook, the Inventory provides extensive information on population policies, programs, projects, expenditures, and demographic data. Its advantage over the Factbook is that it contains information on a larger number of countries, and especially on many of the new small countries, which are omitted from the Factbook. This, of course, reflects the distinctive "universal" character of the United Nations.

Today even countries that do not espouse fertility limitation policies, and may even prefer population growth, have become part of the environment of the international organization concerned with population planning. Only 5 out of the 119 high fertility countries remained officially outside of this definition of the environment in 1977. Even this is an understatement of the scope of the environment, however. We can see this by examining the location of UNFPA country programs in two points in time.

In 1970 UNFPA was engaged in 64 country products in 34 high fertility countries. By 1977 UNFPA had actual or budgeted expenditures covering more than 200 projects in 104 of the 119 developing countries. We cannot reconstruct the more extended classification of population policies for 1970, but we can return to the simpler Population Council Classification for a direct comparison of policies and UNFPA country project expenditures in the two periods. The data for this comparison are shown in Table 17.4.

A number of important observations can be made from Table 17.4. First, the number of countries with UNFPA country projects has increased greatly. From only 34 countries in 1970, UNFPA country activity today includes virtually all (104) of the high fertility countries. Second, the relatively high concentration on Asian programs (35 percent) in the early period has considerably decreased. Third, in the early stage there was a great concentration (44 percent) of activity in countries with official antinatalist policies. By 1977 the distribution of activity across different policy categories was much more equal.

In summary, the early years found UNFPA working in a small number of countries, which primarily wanted to reduce their rates of population growth, and more than a third of these were in Asia. Today the UNFPA works in a larger number of countries, spread across more different policy positions, and across a wider geographic distribution. That is, its national population policy environment has become larger, more heterogeneous, more complex, and more differentiated.

The overall pattern of UNFPA expenditures reflects this change as well, showing an increasing allocation to the highly diverse world of individual countries. There are two ways to express this change. In its first three years of operation the UNFPA allocated 42 percent of its funds to country projects and 59 percent to regional and global projects.[6] In 1977 country projects received 67 percent of total allocations. Another aspect of this change is seen in the changing organizational units through which allocations are made. UNFPA has pioneered in making direct transfers to national governments for their own programs. In its first three years of

6. The data are from UNFPA annual reports.

TABLE 17.4
Number of Countries with UNFPA Country Project Expenditures by Region and Country Population Policy Classification,* 1970 and 1977

	Africa (sub-Saharan)	Asia and Pacific	Latin America and Caribbean	Mediterranean and Middle East	Total
Total countries	36	28	38	17	119
1970 Countries with UNFPA projects	7	12	7	8	34
Country Population Policy Class					
A. Official antinatalist policy and public family-planning program	1	9	3	2	15
B. No antinatalist policy but public support for a family-planning program	2	—	4	—	6
C. No antinatalist policy, no program support	1	1	—	3	5
D. No information in classification system or from Population Council consideration	3	2	—	3	8
1977 Countries with UNFPA projects	34	25	28	17	104
Country Population Policy Class*					
A. Official antinatalist policy and public family-planning program	4	15	7	4	30
B. No antinatalist policy but public support for a family-planning program	6	2	11	3	22
C. No antinatalist policy, no program support	5	2	—	3	10
D. No information in classification system, omitted from Population Council consideration	19	6	10	7	42

* Population Council Policy Classification.

operation UNFPA allocated 53 percent of its funds through the specialized agencies and another 34 percent through the UN, primarily its regional commissions. By 1977 the specialized agencies received only 38 percent of the total, and the UNFPA itself used 32 percent of its funds primarily for direct transfers to country programs. The greatest share of this amout went directly to national governments. Thus the UNFPA began by dealing primarily with the homogeneous environment of large-scale UN organizations. While it continues to deal with these units, it now channels a growing proportion of its funds through the heterogeneous group of national governments.

The Sociodemographic Environment

The actual work demanded by the UNFPA or other international population assistance organizations will depend in large measure on the sociodemographic environment in which it works. For example, if such organizations were permitted to work only in more developed countries, they would face conditions of low fertility and a large range of conditions closely associated with low fertility. In this sense, the socioeconomic environment would be relatively homogeneous and would demand very much the same kind of work in most settings.

It is well recognized, of course, that the UNFPA and other international population assistance organizations work largely in developing countries. But the questions still remain of the extent to which the sociodemographic conditions of these nations are similar. There is a general impression that developing nations share conditions of high fertility, rapid population growth, and a wide range of other social and demographic conditions indicating a highly homogeneous environment for the UNFPA. Closer and more systematic inspection of the environment, however, reveals considerable heterogeneity. To demonstrate this, we can use a simple correlational analysis of the relation between a wide number of sociodemographic indicators and the level of UNFPA country activity. High correlation coefficients would indicate relatively homogeneous environment; low coefficients would indicate a more heterogeneous environment.

For sociodemographic conditions, we have collected 53 indicators of national level demographic, economic, and social conditions for the 119 countries. The measure would fit any standard list of national indicators taken from the tables of the UN statistical, demographic, and World Bank yearbooks. Demographic measures include population size, vital rates, rates of growth, life expectancy, urbanization, and density. The economic measures include gross and per capita output levels, their rates of change over various periods, per capita energy consumption, and rates of change in agricultural and industrial production indices. The social indicators include literacy, per capita and change rates for school attendance, mail flows, telephones, and medical and hospital facilities.

For the level of UNFPA activity eight different items were coded from the 1976–77 inventory. Five of these are standard financial measures—cumulated actual expenditures through 1976, post-1976 budgeted figures, the total of the two, and the first and last calculated in per capita terms. The number of different *projects* was counted for each country, which included both UNFPA and other project sources; all of the different *agencies* mentioned for each country's population program; and finally the number of *pages* used to describe each country's program.

The rationale for assessing financial inputs is quite clear. The more money UNFPA is putting into a country, the larger its level of activity there. But it is also possible that a large amount of funds could be directed to a single program, indicating a high degree of homogeneity in the activity, since only one set of negotiations and assessments would be required. Counting the number of *projects* a country has in the population field provides a partial correction. A larger number of projects indicates greater differentiation of activity. The number of *agencies* involved also indicates the degree of organizational differentiation required in the host country environment. If only one agency provides all the external support, the host country's own organizational orientation toward such external support can be highly homogeneous. The more different agencies are involved, the more the host country must differentiate its own activity in dealing with foreign donors. Finally, the number of pages used to describe a country's program is used as an unobtrusive measure of its size and heterogeneity.

Of the fifty-five socioeconomic indicators, only two show high and significant levels of correlation with the absolute, *but not per capita,* level of UNFPA financial activity: total population (r = .47 to .78) and total school enrollment (r = .59 to .81). These two measures are themselves highly intercorrelated (r = .59), of course. The different measures of UNFPA activity tell an interesting story, however. Country size is most highly correlated with actual expenditures (r = .62), future budgets (r = .80), and the total of these two (r = .78). The correlations with number of agencies and number of projects is lower, however (r = .74 and .51 respectively). That is, understandably more money is actually spent and budgeted in larger countries, but even the medium and smaller countries have a large number of different projects and different external agencies working in them.

Four other measures show statistical significance, but much smaller correlation coefficients. These are adjusted primary school enrollment in 1960 and 1970 (r = .33 and .38 respectively), the change in adjusted secondary school enrollment figures from 1960 to 1970 (r = −.25) and telephones per capita in 1970 (r = −.21). It is difficult to make anything of these correlations, and their low values argue against pushing too hard for an interpretation. In effect, except for total national population, we find virtually no social, economic, or demographic measure that is strongly associated with the level of UNFPA activity in a country. The basic socioeconomic conditions in the environment, which in part determine the type of work to be done, are highly varied. Again, heterogeneity rather than homogeneity characterizes the environment. It should be expected that the type of work done by UNFPA would be both varied and changing.

Although country socioeconomic conditions are not closely related to UNFPA activity, they do show another configuration that is significant for organized population assistance. If we examine each of these social indicators by region, we find that there are significant differences between regions for most of the indicators. (Forty-three are different at levels of significance greater than 5 percent; three are different at about 10 percent significant levels; and twelve are not significantly different.) For all classs of indicators—economic, demographic, social—there is more difference between the regions than within them. In effect, there is some ground for considering the regions relatively homogeneous in their socioeconomic conditions. Tables 17.5 and 17.6 provide two examples of indicators that differ significantly by this regional breakdown.

TABLE 17.5
Levels of Female Life Expectancy at Birth by Region

Region	Number of countries	Mean	Standard deviation
Africa (sub-Saharan)	34	46.8 yrs.	5.13
Asia and Pacific	28	56.7	9.70
Latin America and Caribbean	37	66.1	6.28
Mediterranean and Middle East	17	54.5	6.90
Total	116	54.5	10.34

SOURCE: UNFPA, *Inventory of Population Projects in Developing Countries Around the World, 1976–77* (New York: UNFPA, 1976).

In Table 17.5 we show female life expectancy, which may be taken as a general indicator of a society's level of well-being. The difference in mean levels is quite large between the regions, and note that Latin America has the highest level, Africa the lowest, and Asia and Mediterranean lie in between. Table 17.6 shows the change in literacy rates between 1960 and 1970. Here the rank order of regions is the reverse of that in

TABLE 17.6
Percent Change in Literacy Rates by Region

Region	Number of countries	Mean	Standard deviation
Africa	4	120.5	103.09
Asia	8	53.7	26.00
Latin America	16	15.3	24.52
Mediterranean	7	52.4	37.13
Total	35	43.5	51.94

SOURCE: UNFPA, *Inventory of Population Projects in Developing Countries Around the World, 1976–77* (New York: UNFPA, 1976).

Table 17.5. Africa shows the largest rate of change, Latin America the lowest, and Asia and the Mediterranean are in between, and again quite similar.

These tables illustrate a broad classification that can be applied to the four regions. Latin America ranks highest in most of the measures of social and economic development. Life expectancy, literacy, school enrollment, doctors per capita, mail flows, and phones per capita are all higher than in the other regions. Conversely, death rates and infant mortality rates are lowest, as are the rates of change in the social indicators. Africa lies at the other end of the ranking. Social indicators are lowest, but often the rates of change in the indicators are highest, as might be expected since low initial rates would produce high growth rates. Further, in most of the rates, Asia ranks between Africa and Latin America. The Mediterranean region shows wider variation in rates of change. For some the rates are similar to those found in Asia. For others, for example changes in energy consumption, it shows the highest rate of change.

Thus although there has been a large increase in the numbers of different countries entering directly into the population activity environment, and although those countries show wide differences in many of their socioeconomic conditions, there is some homogeneity among regions and difference between regions. In effect, UNFPA faces an environment that is heterogeneous, complex, and changing at the country level, but more homogeneous at the level of the four different regions.

There has indeed been considerable change over the past decade in the type of population activity carried out by international organizations. This is most readily seen, if somewhat oversimplified, in the proportion of UNFPA country support for its two major types of activity: basic population data collection, and assistance to family-planning programs. Table 17.7 shows the relevant statistics for cumulated expenditures through 1976.

TABLE 17.7
Percent UNFPA Cumulated Total Country Expenditures for Basic Data Collection and Family-Planning Programs by Region, through 1976

Region*	Number of Countries	Basic Data Collection Mean (%)	Basic Data Collection Standard Deviation (%)	Family-Planning Program Mean (%)	Family-Planning Program Standard Deviation (%)
Africa	35	55	46	17	33
Asia	28	21	34	53	40
Latin America	38	21	34	24	37
Mediterranean	17	45	46	30	39
Grand Mean	118	34	42	30	39

* Regional differences are significant at .01 level for both types of expenditures.

Most UNFPA expenditure in Asia has been concentrated in family-planning program support. Africa and the Mediterranean have shown a higher concentration in basic data collection. The differences are large and striking, but this static view understates the difference, because it does not show the changes that have occurred over time. These are shown in Figure 17.1. Asia shows stability in the high concentration on family-planning program even with rapid increases in UNFPA expenditures. This reflects the earlier movement to official antinatalist policies in Asia. Many countries in the region had made these policy decisions before UNFPA began extensive work in population, thus it simply moved in to provide support for programs previously designed by the countries of the region. Latin America has experienced rapid change from high early proportions of expenditures in basic population data to high proportions in family-planning

FIGURE 17.1
Amount of UNFPA Support to Country Programs by Region and Its Proportion to Basic Population Data Collection and to Family Planning

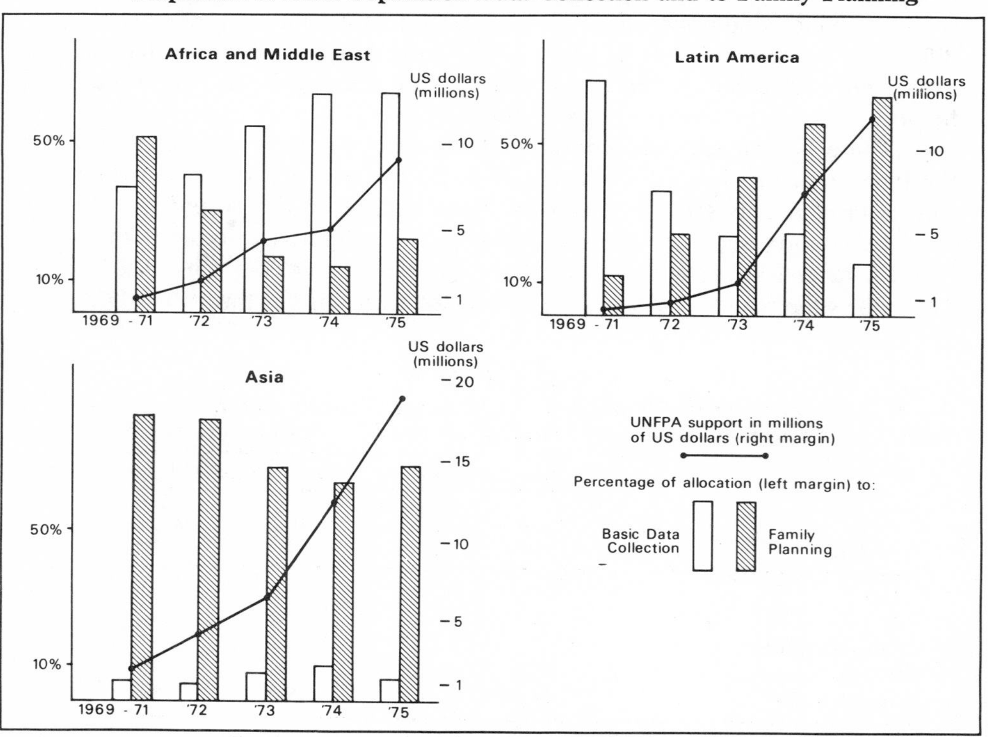

programs as total expenditures grew. Africa moved in the opposite direction, however, from high concentrations in family planning to high concentrations in basic data collection, as the total amount of UNFPA expenditures grew rapidly.

The data in Figure 17.1 permit the interpretation of a distinct process in international organizational activity in population. If countries have made the antinatalist decision for themselves, as they did in Asia, international organizations may move in to supply assistance in implementing those decisions through supporting family-planning programs. Where these decisions have not been made, the international organizations may enter to provide assistance in collecting basic data on population. Where local infrastructures were well developed, as in Latin America, this data collection leads quickly to national decisions for some form of antinatalist activity, which the international organizations then assist in implementing through supporting family-planning programs. Where the basic data collection infrastructure is underdeveloped, as it is in much of Africa and the Mediterranean, increased activity by the international organization will involve more concentrated efforts in early phase activity of data collection.

In summary, all three elements of the environment of UNFPA are marked by great heterogeneity, complexity, and instability. The United Nations as a system of nation states has become larger, more universal in its membership, and has given rise to articulated conflicts of interest. Policies of member governments have become increasingly specific concerning population issues. This brings an increase in the numbers of political units in which UNFPA must operate, and in the diversity of their population policies. Although UNFPA works primarily in the developing nations, these show a high degree of diversity in the socioeconomic conditions that define in part what kind of work has to be done. Within major geographic regions, however, there are important elements of similarity, just as there are major differences between regions.

THE NATURE OF THE POPULATION PROBLEM AND THE TECHNOLOGY FOR ITS SOLUTION

In one sense the population problem is simple and simply stated. Rates of population growth are considered to be too high. They cannot be sustained for very long, and in many poor countries, high growth rates are considered an obstacle to economic development. This condition arises from the rapid decline in mortality and the continuation of high fertility control. This is basically the perception that the developed countries carried when they went to Bucharest for the World Population Conference in 1974.[7]

This statement of the problem in its simplest terms—growth and reproduction control—immediately raises two major types of complexity: demographic and political. On the demographic side, issues of mortality and distribution intervene. On the political side, the issue is the extent to which the demographic conditions can be separated from other political-economic conditions. Let us consider each of these dimensions of complexity briefly.

If problems of rapid growth arise from low mortality, we immediately observe that mortality is not universally low. Some of the world's poorer countries still have relatively high levels of mortality. Thus the prospect of success in further mortality reductions raises the spectre of even more rapid rates of growth in the near future. Further, low mortality and fertility are not themselves guarantees that growth rates will not increase, as baby booms in the industrial nations have shown.

Second, issues of population distribution intervene to produce even greater complexities. High growth rates appear especially costly where population density is high. Rapid urbanization with attendant slum living represents only part of the costs. Perhaps most important are the costs that arise from environmental degradation. For example, population growth in the Himalayan foothills leads to excessive deforestation, with attendant destructive flooding farther down the watershed. On the other hand, where population densities are low it is the very shortage of human resources that results in the underutilization of the natural resources. This condition leads governments to adopt pronatalist policies. Thus the variance in the basic demographic conditions of population growth produces a "problem" that exhibits great complexity.

On the political side the population debate is intense and is closely related to the broader debate over the conditions of human betterment. One side of this debate holds that population growth is a relatively separable problem that can be addressed through direct and specialized activities promoting fertility control. The other side holds that population growth is a problem derived from a basic inequality in the distribution of wealth. From this position the problem is addressed through major efforts to restructure the worldwide political-economic system.

From both demographic and political debates there is strong pressure to broaden the definition of the population problem. The demographers

7. This is also the view that *continues* to mark the orientation of the World Bank. See, for example, Robert S. McNamara, "Address to the Massachusetts Institute of Technology," April 28, 1977.

who less than half a century ago urged that growth would soon present a major problem are today urging that problems of distribution, urbanization, and labor utilization will soon be the major problems the world must confront. The political debate has already shifted much attention from the isolated problem of growth to the complex of human institutions whose deficiency and oppresiveness present problems that must be confronted. Despite these pressures from broadening the perception of the population problem, growth and reproduction control remain critical problems. Further, it can be argued that there is a growing consensus on the urgency of the problem and the need to attack it through direct concerns with reproduction and fertility limitation. Even where demographic conditions indicate that population growth is not a serious problem, fertility limitation programs are seen as a part of the range of services that must be provided to raise the general health and welfare of the population. And even the most extreme proponents of the need for radical restructuring of the world's economic system engage in concerted efforts at reproduction control as part of their own attempts to reshape their national societies.

Regardless of demographic or political conditions, the problem of population growth and fertility limitation is distinctive and especially difficult for three reasons: those concerning its economic and cultural implications, the precarious character of relevant public policy, and the technology available to address the problem.

Economic and Cultural Implications

Population affairs are affected by cultural, ethnic, and legal factors. They are usually not affected by organized economic factors. Other international development programs sometimes experience opposition on economic grounds. This is one type of opposition that population planners do not usually experience.

Population issues are, however, ladened with deep cultural, ethnic and legal considerations, especially where fertility limitation is an important part of public policy. Deep cultural and religious traditions support the continuation of life. Profound and delicate changes are required to adjust this deep human value to the norms in favor of fertility limitation. Human life is often identified with a distinct ethos, or a way of life. It is a near universal observation that wherever a society contains different ethnic groups, fertility limitation programs will be perceived by some groups as a threat to their very existence. Population planning especially concerning fertility regulation usually requires some change of legislation. It is never easy to change legal codes, especially where legislative changes are public and provide opportunities for moral entrepreneurs to mobilize mass sentiments.

It is important to recognize the relative importance of economic and cultural factors for population offices, since they will require different organizational strategies. Economic interests must be confronted with wealth and power. Cultural interests are confronted and managed with other values. Since population issues do not usually involve economic conflicts but do involve at least potential cultural conflicts, population organizations need to be sensitive, adaptive and diplomatic rather than rigidly powerful.

The Precarious Quality of Population Programs

Second, and in part following from the first, is the observation that population programs are precarious. Political leaders typically avoid raising population problems for public debate. There is little gain for political leaders in promoting family planning or contraceptive distribution, and there is often great liability, either perceived in potential or experienced in reality. Political and bureaucratic public leaders have in the past lost office and influence through support of public fertility limitation programs.[8]

Further, specialized agencies of the United Nations have shown considerable reluctance to move into population affairs, even with the encouragement and financial support offered by UNFPA. A review of annual reports of the Directors General of FAO, WHO, UNICEF, UNESCO, and ILO shows very little space and attention devoted to the discussion of population problems and projects. These agencies have developed their own specialized capacities, constituencies and interest. They have also built substantial budgets. Against these, the resources provided by UNFPA are only very small fractions of the total. As much as one may argue rationally that population problems are deeply involved in problems of health, education, employment or food production, the attempt to promote population activities in the respective specialized agencies is often seen as a diversion of activities from higher to lower priorities.[9]

8. The Malaysia leader Khir Johari perceives some considerable loss of influence due to his support for family planning. Richard Symmonds and Michael Carder, *The United Nations and the Population Question* (New York: McGraw Hill, 1973), pp. 127–32, argue that Dr. B. R. Sen's promotion of the population discussion in FAO was in part responsible for his failure to gain re-election as director general in 1968.

9. This point is well exposed in Jason S. Finkle and Barbara Crane, "The World Health Organization and the Population Issue: Organizational Values in the United Nations," *Population and Development Review* 2 (3–4) (September/December 1976): 367–94.

In the question of precariousness, population issues are in part similar to, but in part different from general development issues. In the need for integration of efforts, the two are similarly weak. It is easy to argue that development requires a multifaceted effort, including the work of many different specializations. Yet both UNDP and the many new national development agencies often face difficult problems in gaining the attention and cooperation of existing specialized agencies either at international or national levels. In the general area of precariousness, however, it may be argued that population control programs are in a more difficult position. Development is, after all, a widely accepted value and there are few national or international conditions that oppose or reduce its power. Not so with population issues. We have often seen current exigencies—recessions, ethnic disputes, religious opposition—intrude to reduce national efforts in population planning. Thus the value of population-planning strategies must be counted far more volatile and therefore more precarious than the value of national economic development.

The Technology of Population Planning

Third, the technology available for population planning shows certain distinctive properties. In the first place there is a wide range of *material* technology available for population planning. This is most obvious in census taking, and fertility control. In both cases, the available technology is richly diverse, highly portable, relatively inexpensive, fairly effective, and constantly expanding. But as obvious as this is, it is equally obvious that this technology is not applied everywhere with the same effectiveness. National population censuses produce statistics of wide ranging validity and reliability. And the full range of fertility-limiting technologies is nowhere fully and effectively applied.

Underlying this material technology is an organizational or *human* technology that is both a critical determinant of the effectiveness of the material technology, and much more difficult to understand, to know, and to apply. For example, we know that there is a wide range of social and economic conditions associated with high level and rapid decline in fertility. No one is clear, however, on what specific mix of conditions operates under all conditions. Low levels of mortality, high levels of education or communication, generally effective administrative structures, contraceptive availability, economic pressures and incentives, and even political will, have all been advanced as important determinants of rapid fertility decline. Plausible cases can be made for each. But no one can be very clear on how any of these conditions is achieved, or on what its specific impact will be on fertility decline.

Thus it is clear that there are identifiable technologies available for fertility reduction, but it is not by any means clear now those technologies work, how they can be brought to bear on the problem, or what impact they will have under different conditions of application.

ORGANIZATIONAL REQUIREMENTS

We have taken this time and space to characterize the environment and the technology of international organizations in population assistance because these conditions have decisive importance for organizational design. Organizational analysis in the social sciences has grown over the past century and has grown enormously in the past generation. One of the strongest sets of findings from this analysis is that there is no one best way to organize anything. The "best" way to organize things depends primarily upon the goals of action, the environment within which that action is to take place, and the technology available to achieve the goals of action.

Two sets of generalizations can summarize the decisive elements in these findings. First, the goals of action will determine what compliance mechanisms are to be used.[10] As Etzioni argues, to achieve goals of order, organizations typically use coercion. To achieve goals of production of goods and services, organizations usually provide material rewards and incentives. On the other hand if goals involve creating a new normative or social system, organizations need to use symbolic rewards. Population planning involves a combination of goals—producing goods and especially services for human welfare, and creating a normative structure appropriate for policy aims. Achievement of these goals therefore requires money and supplies, and legitimacy, or valued programmatic means and ends. Further, since population activities involve deep moral sentiments and the programs often carry precarious and volatile values, the need for legitimacy may be greater than the need for material resources.

There is sufficient experience with disastrous results of forced family-planning programs to support the proposition that coercive compliance structures are inappropriate, and may be counterproductive, for the goals of population planning. On the positive side, there is sufficient linkage between effective socioeconomic development programs and fertility decline to support the proposition that both material and symbolic reward manipulation are of critical importance in achieving fertility de-

10. For a good review of this perspective and its empirical defense, see Amitai Etzioni, *A Comparative Analysis of Complex Organizations* (New York: The Free Press, 1975).

cline. Finally, the successes of the Chinese and more recently the Indonesian planned birth programs indicate that new forms of normative support, involving both national level political legitimacy and small group level actions, are probably of greater importance than material rewards alone in promoting fertility decline.

The second set of generalizations links organizational structure process to environmental and technological conditions.[11] When the environment is stable and homogeneous and when the technology is well known and capable of being separated into distinct integral units of action, the type of organization that works best is one that is hierarchic, highly centralized for unified decision making, relatively closed to its environment, and involving a large number of highly routinized procedures. Within this type of organization there are clear lines of authority and responsibility arranged hierarchically, with rather strict subordination of lower to upper units along the chain. These characteristics are often associated with the term "bureaucracy" in common parlance, or with the more technical term "mechanical" forms of organization.

When the environment is heterogeneous and constantly changing, and when the technology for action is not well known and cannot be broken down readily into separate and repeatable acts, a totally different type of organization works best. This is one that is flat, highly decentralized, with many specialized activities loosely integrated through numerous flexible linking mechanisms, and a free flow of information. In such organizations there is little routine activity, much interaction with the environment and a constant emphasis upon problem solving and innovation. This set of conditions usually characterizes more professional groups, and it is referred to in technical language as the "organic" type of organization.

It should be clear from the previous analysis that international population assistance under current environmental and technological conditions requires the flat, decentralized, professionalized, and open type of organization which uses reason and persuasion rather than coercion to achieve its goals. It is also important to recognize that the terms "organic" and "mechanical" applied to the two different forms refer not only to the formal elements of the structure, those boxes and lines that are typically shown in organizational charts. The terms refer more to the character of the organization, its style of action, the processes that give it its distinctive identity. While the formal structure is an important determinant of organ-

11. For two excellent reviews of this portion of the literature see Charles Perrow, *Complex Organizations, A Critical Essay* (Glenview, Ill.: Scott, Foresman, 1972), and Bengt Abrahamson, *Bureaucracy or Participation* (Beverly Hills, Calif.: Sage, 1977).

izational character, it is only one of the determinants. Other determinants are less visible and less easy to identify with standard operational concepts. They include administrative styles, recruitment and internal control mechanisms, and the resources and demands on the organization generated by the external sources.

There is also a set of questions for which past organizational analyses in the social sciences provide no ready answers. What kind of organization is needed when the environment is made up of sovereign states among which power and resources are unequally divided? One observation appears readily supportable. Organizations external to a state are severely limited in the changes they can effect within that state.[12] External assistance may provide critical resources and leverage, but it will only be effective to the extent that indigenous human, political, and administrative resources are equal to the task. Systematic inspection may well reveal this to be the single most powerful generalization to be derived from three decades of international assistance in national economic development. Development may be assisted or obstructed in critical ways from the outside; it cannot be achieved from the outside.[13]

A final observation must be made of a set of enduring characteristics of modern large-scale organizations. It is widely held that all large-scale organizations are subject to inevitable and powerful pressures toward serving themselves and their members rather than serving their creators or clients. They become excessively concerned with their own survival, and they lose the capacity for innovation and flexible action.

However, organizations can be made efficient and effective. It is possible to make organizational survival and growth contingent upon serving wider societal aims, and it is possible to reward individuals for performance and service to clients. Much experience and some research suggests that the critical requirements for linking rewards to performance lie in openness, free flows of information, public scrutiny, public accountability, and in the development and utilization of human talents. These general principles can be useful if they can be translated into specific organizational structures and processes, a task that is the special responsibility of leaders and governing bodies. A crucial question now is the extent to which the United Nations System is capable of producing the type of organizations needed for international population system. To answer this question we must consider the nature of the UN system.

12. I have dealt with this problem in an analysis of land reform in a number of countries in the period 1945–60. "Foreign Policy and Social Change," in *Foreign Policy and Development,* edited by Richard Butwell.

13. For one summary statement of this view see Brandon Robinson, "Foreign Assistance and National Decisions," *International Development Review* 15 (1) (1973):13–16.

THE NATURE OF THE UNITED NATIONS SYSTEM

The United Nations is a *representative system* in which the members are *sovereign states*. That the system is representative, and almost universally representative at that, implies that it has some moral authority. Along with this advantage, however, there are certain disadvantages for the UN organizations. That the members are sovereign states implies that the system has no independent political power over its executive agencies, that its financial resources are at best uncertain, and that its technical competence has been organized in the form of decentralized specialization. All of these conditions have profound implications for the organization of international population assistance.

Representativeness: Advantages and Disadvantages

The moral authority of the United Nations is easily overlooked, but it is perhaps the most important type of influence the system has.[14] In the area of population affairs this influence has been growing in important ways over the past decade. When the United Nations decided in 1966 that population affairs constitute a legitimate area of concern *and* technical assistance, this provided powerful support for population activities throughout the world.

Universal representativeness provides useful legitimacy for UN population organizations, but it provides certain liabilities as well. One liability derives from the demand that UN population organizations work everywhere, gain support from all member states, and provide assistance and service to all states. Private foundations gain some advantage in their freedom from this demand. Part of the advantage enjoyed by the private foundations derives from their abilities to decide where they will work. They can decide to stay out of areas in which they are not welcome or in which the problems are judged overwhelming. This will naturally tend to maximize success and minimize failures, though the latter are by no means unknown to the foundations. The UN population organizations on the other hand, *must* gain acceptance, and they *must* operate in all countries, especially in the most difficult circumstances.

A second liability of representativeness lies in the political pressure it produces in staffing. Where these pressures have been effectively resisted, as they have in some UN agencies, it appears that both small size and high

14. This point is perceptively and eloquently presented in Connor Cruise O'Brien, *The UN Sacred Drama* (New York: Simon and Schuster, 1968).

professional orientations have been important in helping them to protect their integrity and thus to remain efficient and effective.

Member Sovereignty

One of the most serious organizational implications of the sovereignty of the United Nations' 151 members lies in the resultant lack of supra-bureaucratic power.[15] Having many heads, often demanding different things of the organization, is often much the same as having no head at all. The General Assembly and the governing councils of the specialized agencies and regional commissions often lack the will and capacity to establish clear priorities for their agencies and to hold them accountable for goal achievement. In part this occurs precisely because the United Nations system is representative and its members are sovereign states, often with different orientations and interests in different issues. On the one hand this lack of a single coherent political head is the condition that permits large-scale organizations to drift toward serving themselves and their officials rather than their clients or creators. It is also the condition that creates weakness by pulling the organizations in different directions in the attempt to serve many interests that are often conflicting. Much of the popular criticism of the UN bureaucracy is focused on this self-serving rather than client-serving quality.

Under these conditions the question is not why the UN is inefficient, but why it remains as efficient and effective as it is. The answer lies in part in the professional specialization of individual units. This allows units to establish clear-cut professional standards for performance and to protect these standards. Such professionalism usually works more effectively in small than in large units. This is what apparently lies behind the generally accepted observation that some of the UN units are more effective than others.

A second organizational weakness derived from member sovereignty lies in the instability of UN financial resources. We have seen that member states resist the implied international taxation that rests in the regular assessed budget process. Members are also able to withhold their regular assessments, and they have done so in some circumstances of international political conflict. The result was almost the total destruction of the UN system.[16] It is also member sovereignty that is in large part responsible for

15. Edward M. Martin, "The United Nations System and Review and Appraisal of the Second Development Decade Strategy," *International Development Review* 14 (4):9–12; and "Interview with Myer Cohen," *ibid.* 15 (2) (1973):2.

16. This occurred in the mid-1960s and has been the topic of many popular treatments of the UN.

the growth of voluntary funds, by which major donors have regained some of the budgetary control they lost in the General Assembly. We have also seen that the voluntary nature of many special funds, for example, UNFPA, pose serious problems for the long-term planning and commitment that are necessary for rational international assistance. On the other hand, the voluntary funds do provide for a measure of accountability, at least to the major donors with different population interests, which UN agencies lack by virtue of the size and diversity of the General Assembly as a decision-making body.

Finally, member sovereignty produces a serious organizational problem in the area of differentiation and integration. It is widely recognized that the UN system was originally and deliberately designed to be a decentralized system,[17] with many technically specialized units to carry the tasks of promoting world peace, welfare and development. Each of the specialized units was given its own governing body, which theoretically had the expertise to guide the unit. Thus the task of organizational governance was defined as a technical rather than a political task. This may have been useful in accommodating to the dictates of member sovereignty, and it may also provide some measure of protection for professional standards of individual performance, but it also produces a serious organizational problem.

One of the most enduring organizational complaints of the UN Secretaries General has been of the continuing and excessive fragmentation of the UN system. Specialized agencies proliferate and grow, and special funds, centers, commissions, and committees constantly spring up and appear indestructable.[18] The resulting alleged duplication of effort, overlapping functions, and lack of coordination constitute the most persistent subject of criticism of the system from within, and have given rise to periodic internal drives for reorganization. These typically take the form of the creation of special committees, or offices for administrative coordination, for the consideration of budget questions, for civil service issues, and special units for oversight and inspection. Internal reorganizational efforts constitute the continued struggle of the administrative center to check the process of feudal decentralization. This clearly reflects the lack of a powerful political center above the administration, which can establish clear goals and hold the administrative structure accountable for goal achievement. Some knowledgeable observers have also held that the constant

17. Elmandjra, *UN System*, p. 29–30.

18. See, for example, "Introduction to the Report of the Secretary-General on the Work of the Organization, August, 1976," in *Annual Review of United Nations Affairs, 1976*, edited by W. A. Landekran (New York: Oceana Publications, 1977), pp. 18–20.

struggle for internal reorganization represents an attempt to undermine the UN itself. Gunnar Myrdal wrote in 1973: "An entirely disproportionate part of the energy of delegates and secretaries is concerned with 'coordination.' In view of the low effectiveness to reach substantive results, this stands out as an escape and a substitute for action. That the governments of the great powers have been using the demand for 'coordination' in order to curtail the organizations' effectiveness in substantive issues is my personal experience."[19]

There are also many new restructuring proposals that come from sources outside of the administrative structure itself.[20] Some of the proposals come from the General Assembly, reflecting the increasing voice of the developing nations. If there is not a strong political center, there is at least an increasingly vocal center demanding a more effective administrative structure. These voices from the General Assembly demand an administration that will be more accountable and more open to scrutiny, especially in the administration of worldwide development activities. Thus the demand for a new international economic order is giving rise to rational attempts to construct the type of world administrative structure required to build the new order. This dynamic process in the United Nations is clearly hopeful, although it is as yet too early to predict its outcome.

There is a clear need for the integration of specialized skills for development. This is recognized in restructuring efforts that come from internal UN administrative interests, from external political interests of the developing nations, and from the technical requirements of development. Together these represent a series of organizational strategies that confront member sovereignty and its consequence: the lack of the political power to establish goals and to demand goal achievement of high performance in the administrative structure. It is not likely that either member sovereignty, its consequence for organizational leadership, or the resulting strategies for reorganization and adaptation will change radically in the near future. Thus international population assistance will most likely face the same problems for the next decade that it has faced for the past decade.

19. Elmandjra, *UN System,* p. 13.

20. See, for example, the following illustrative items: "What Now," *The 1975 Dag Hammersjold Report on Development and International Cooperation,* a special issue of *Development Dialogue,* Numbers 1 and 2, 1975; Martin Hill, *Towards Greater Order, Coherence and Co-operation in the United Nations System* (New York: UN Institute for Training and Research, 1974); UN, *A New United Nations Structure for Global Economic Cooperation* (New York: UN, 1975), E/AC.62/9; and Amon J. Nsekela, "The World Bank and the New International Economic Order," *Development Dialogue* 1 (1977): 75–84.

TOWARD EFFECTIVENESS IN ORGANIZED POPULATION ASSISTANCE

Before considering some of the specific implications of the foregoing analysis for UNFPA, it is necessary to review briefly some of the more positive characteristics of the Fund's actions to date. First, the Fund has grown enormously since its inception. From a small trust fund of one or two million dollars, it has grown to a fund of more than $120 million in 1979, with a cumulative total over the last ten years of more than $600 million. This makes UNFPA the largest multinational agency in population assistance. Further, as a UN agency it occupies a special place in the world community in that it carries the legitimacy of an organization representing the consensus of that community. Its rapid growth represents a remarkable degree of mobilization of support and acceptance from virtually all members of the world community. This is not a small achievement and certainly does credit to the governing bodies and the officials that have helped to chart the growth. Second, the Fund has been relatively successful in increasing cooperation of the UN, the specialized agencies and the regional commissions by supporting population activities and infrastructures within these other units. Third, the Fund has shown considerable organizational flexibility and innovativeness. It has, for example, innovated in direct transfers to national governments for their population programs. It has remained small and professional, showing very low levels (approximately 7 percent) of administrative overhead costs. It has led in the development of modern management information systems, in the use of modern participative management styles and in its beginnings at systematic project evaluation. Finally, it has been characterized by its openness, making links to such external groups as nongovernmental organizations, universities, development planners, and parliamentarians. Overall in its organizational activities, the record has been good and the dynamic processes appear to move basically toward greater effectiveness.

Yet the future effectiveness of any large-scale organization and certainly of any UN agency must constantly be validated. The external and internal conditions UNFPA will face over the coming decade will pose serious problems and must be managed to maintain and strengthen its innovativeness and effectiveness. This management will require constant attention and an accurate identification of those conditions that both obstruct and enhance organizational performance. The aim of this analysis has been to assist in this identification process. The focus on organizational environments and technologies for addressing major problems can lead us to propose certain guidelines for action that will promote effectiveness.

One set of limitations for these guidelines must be noted, however. While it is not fully satisfactory to distinguish between technical and political determinants of organizational behavior, there is a sense in which the distinction is useful. The above analysis of environments and technologies has been more technical in that it proceeds to abstract generalizations from observations of many concrete cases. Thus it leads to general guidelines, or principles of organizational action, that are likely to promote certain types of behavior. It cannot identify the specific mechanisms by which the principles are to be worked out in any given situation. These involve what we can call more political issues. For example, it is possible for us to suggest that the value of population activities will require considerable support and expansion. We cannot specify, however, the organizational mechanisms by which this will be achieved. The mandate of a specific organizational unit concerned with population, its position in the larger system of authority and responsibility, and the resources it commands will be decided upon under specific constitutional rules, and must take account of the internal political conditions of the system within which it operates. Specifying these organizational mechanisms for UN population assistance—mandates, resources and authority—is the legitimate province of the General Assembly. In addition, decisions on these questions must be informed by a sensitive understanding of the internal politics of the UN system. This has not been the subject of our analysis. In what follows, then, these political issues will be left aside, and we shall focus attention on the technical issues, which provide us with general guidelines for organizational design.

In the above analysis we described the environment of UNFPA as complex and unstable. It is marked by both great variety and considerable change in the numbers of sovereign member states, in their definitions of the "population problem," in the public policies with which they confront problems, and in their basic sociodemographic conditions. It is also a highly volatile environment in that population issues touch upon points of potential deep conflict within most societies. These environmental conditions require that any population organization must enjoy considerable support for its separate identity, and that it must be highly flexible and adaptable. The first is necessary for its basic survival, and thus for continued rational attention to population problems, the second to enable it to fit effectively into the great variety of situations in which it must act.

We also noted that the technology required to address population problems remains obscure, unknown, or at best one that cannot readily be standardized and routinized. Whatever is needed to address population problems will require a great deal of human intelligence, discretion, and technical skill. These technological conditions imply that an effective organization in international population assistance will require considerable technical competence in its staff, and a capacity to integrate the distinct mix of specialized skills needed by any given problem. Thus the general principles for organizational considerations that can be advanced here lie in four interrelated areas: *value enhancement and identity, flexibility and adaptability, technical competence and innovation,* and *integration* of special skills.[21] Each of these can be considered in turn.

Value Enhancement

One can confidently predict two things for the coming decade. First, member states will continue to guard their sovereignty with great vigor. They will continue to define their population problems as they wish, and it is unlikely that anything approaching a single, uniform worldwide population policy can be developed. Second, the ethnic, religious, national sources of identity will persist in most states and will show considerable volatility as groups are mobilized at various times around various public issues. Both conditions imply that the value of population programming will always have to be reappraised periodically. Population programming will require the attention of governments to keep its activities distinct and identifiable.

Development provides only one source of value protection for population assistance; another important source lies in the value of human rights. Resolutions of the General Assembly (1966), the Teheran Human Rights Conference (1968), and the Bucharest World Population Conference (1974) all proclaimed that the right of families to decide on the number and spacing of children is a basic human right. This provides a microsociological complement to the aggregate rights proclaimed in the values of economic development. If development implies a right of the society to plan for the aggregate population, human rights implies that individuals should have access to population-planning capacities for themselves.

The need of the international population assistance organization is to continue and to strengthen the connection with human rights in its activities. The interests of population planning can be well served by greater attention to its human rights aspects. The studies of law and population constitute a beginning,[22] but only a beginning in the analysis that can indicate how

21. These are interrelated in that value protection and adaptability, required by environmental conditions, provide the material and symbolic resources needed for producing the needed nonroutine technology. Similarly, the technical competence and integration required by the condition of the technology will also promote the survival and adaptability of the organization in its varied and potentially hostile environment.

22. See, for example, Luke Lee, *Population and Law* (Durham, N.C.: Rule of Law Press, 1971), and "Legal Implications of the World Population Plan of Action," *Journal of International Law and Economics* 9 (3) (1974).

public policies can more effectively link population and human rights considerations. A second and potentially powerful linkage is currently being forged by UNFPA in association with policy-makers, planners, and legislators through a series of conferences. It is most likely that the continued development of these linkages will lead toward more rational population policies.

Finally, enhancing the value by association with other units and activities must be balanced by protecting the separate identity of population activities. Although many forms of cooperative linkages will be required with other activities, population will require a separate and distinctive identity to assure that it gains the attention it needs in the agenda of world problems. The importance of its distinctive identity is clearly reflected in the rapid growth in the size of the Fund. Greater value enhancement for population activities is likely to be gained by regularizing the constitutional and budgetary position of UNFPA in the UN system.

Flexibility and Adaptability

The flexibility and adaptability demanded by the elimination of the population problem requires a substantial degree of organizational autonomy. Autonomy promotes flexibility in part by maintaining small size, and in part by permitting greater discretion in programming. Each deserves special consideration.

It is unlikely that the economies of scale operate very far or very effectively when organizations are faced with heterogeneous and dynamic environments. Small size is advantageous in such situations because it implies less specialization, less routinization of actions, and greater use of human discretion in organizational action. This is especially clear in financial and accounting procedures, but it applies also to simple routine matters such as mail flows. It is a common practice for large-scale organizations to duplicate layer after layer of financial scrutiny, especially when organizations grow in size and complexity. It is equally common practice in organization and methods reviews to eliminate successive layers of accounting.[23] It is quite possible for superordinate units to maintain effective control over subordinate units through broad budgetary reviews, and to leave to the subordinate units responsibility for routine accounting procedures. Such separation of routine procedures permits organizational units

23. For a good example of this in the modern Malaysian setting, see Milton J. Esman, *Administration and Development in Malaysia* (Ithaca, N.Y.: Cornell University Press, 1972), especially chapters 3 and 7.

to remain relatively small and unspecialized and thus to retain greater capacities for the flexible and adaptable behavior that is a basic character of acts requiring much human discretion.

If the external conditions requiring population planning were stable and relatively homogeneous, it would be possible, and preferable, to routinize many decisions on program strategy. With a situation that is constantly changing human discretion is continually required. Countries have changed population policies, often very rapidly, and in different directions. External assistance organizations must be capable of responding to such changes with appropriate forms of assistance.

At this time it is not possible for UNFPA to make long term commitments, and this is often a source of problems for recipient countries. In large part, the grounds for this inability lie outside of the control of UNFPA, since it is a voluntary fund with year to year commitments from donors.

Supporting organizational conditions for greater flexibility and adaptability should go a long way toward meeting some of the most common criticisms recipient country officials have of international organizations in general. These typically focus on time required for simple correspondence and for support negotiations, and the complex and cumbersome procedures governing assistance. Small size and discretion in programming strategies should promote greater organizational flexibility and thus meet some of these common criticisms.

Competence and Innovation

Organizational competence and innovativeness can be promoted through both structural and personnel strategies. The two are, of course, closely interlinked. Organizations are more innovative when their internal processes are open, loose and informal, and systematically self-evaluating. Frequent staff meetings break down the isolation of specialized units, keeping them aware of what others are doing and multiplying integrative actions between them. The use of small task forces of different technical specialists helps to focus staff activities on problem identification and solving rather than jurisdictional protection. And a constant pressure to examine and assess organizational processes and outputs helps to keep energy focused on performance rather than security. These are precisely the strategies UNFPA appears to have used to achieve relatively high levels of innovativeness, and one can only propose that the strategies be strengthened and that constant pressure be applied to the thrust for innovation. It is likely that the Fund's small size helps greatly to sustain this dynamic structure, and this of course, strengthens the case for autonomy and continued small size.

Integration

Population planning, as any task in development or human welfare policy, requires the use of highly developed technical skills. This typically implies a high degree of specialization. At the same time, effective programming requires that different skills be brought together at the appropriate time and in the appropriate mix for any specific setting. That is, both specialization and integration are required.

In population activities the term "integration" has unfortunately become almost exclusively associated with very specific proposals to place family-planning programs under the organizational jurisdiction of maternal and child health programs, making them simply subordinate units of this portion of public health administration. Although this specific form of organizational linkage might be indicated under certain conditions, it does not begin to answer the broad need for integration or the effective coordination of specialized skills in overall population activities.

UNFPA has devoted some attention to the question of integration, asking what forms it takes, how it is to be assessed, and what impact it has on organizational performance.[24] Some ESCAP countries are currently engaged in a field study of linkages between family planning and other agencies in an attempt to assess levels of integration and to determine whether it has any impact on program effectiveness or efficiency. All of this work is careful to point out that integration involves both structural and behavioral meanings. Structurally, integration can imply that one unit has jurisdiction over a number of other specialized units or skill groups. Behaviorally, integration implies that these different units or skill groups actually are in contact and work with one another. It is important to note that the structural linkages are neither necessary nor sufficient to achieve actual linkages in work and behavior, and that it is the behavior rather than the structure that is necessary for effective development programming.

It is easy to observe that the extent of integrated activity within the UN system is not great. Field projects, research activities, even conferences and meetings tend to be the special preserve of one or another of the

24. See, for example, ESCAP, Population Division, *Report on an Expert Group Meeting on Organizational Aspect of Integrating Family Planning with Development Programmes* (Bangkok: November 29–December 4, 1976); and UNFPA. *Report on the UNFPA/EWPI Technical Working Group Meeting on Integration of Family Planning with Rural Development* (Honolulu: February 15–18, 1978).

specialized agencies rather than to involve a number of them. It is easy to propose that the techniques of modern project management be more extensively used to achieve the needed integration. These techniques involve extensive use of task forces that pull together specialists from many different units for a specific task. When the task is completed the specialists disperse and other groups are brought together for other tasks. In each case the mix of specialists is fitted to the requirements of the task. These observations and recommendations are relatively easy to make. It is more difficult to identify the underlying obstacles to this type of effective coordination and to design organizational procedures to overcome these obstacles. The solution appears to have eluded legions of UN reviewers and their recommendations.

The UNFPA procedures of supporting population offices and activities in many of the specialized agencies have been designed to achieve more effective coordination. Still, the level of effective interaction could be raised. It appears clear that the stronger the national development capacity and effort of a given country, the greater should be its capacity to coordinate external specialists. UNFPA assistance to country planners should help to increase the effective interaction of specialists at the national level. It is possible that work on country level planning capacities will be most effective in achieving the necessary integration, since this is where the required political power lies. At the same time, however, past efforts to negotiate formal agreements and to arrange informal contacts with other specialized agencies and units should certainly be continued.

It is also possible to observe that coordination of population activities can be effected through regional as well as national level activities. It was shown above that although country characteristics relevant to population policies vary considerably, there is significant homogeneity at the regional level. Activity at the regional level, which UNFPA has recently initiated, provides the opportunity to increase international consensus and cooperation, as member nations with relatively similar problems can develop common approaches and assist one another in solving their problems.

In the final analysis it is useful to recall the success UNFPA has achieved in promoting the development of rational and human population activities. This is reflected especially in the wide acceptance and rapid financial growth of the Fund. It is also important to recall that this growth has been associated with a maintenance of small size, professional orientation, flexibility, and a rather high degree of innovativeness. It will require mature and thorough study by the relevant political bodies to preserve and improve this model of existing population assistance.

Epilogue

PHILIP M. HAUSER

THE SEVENTEEN CHAPTERS preceding these closing remarks examine what constitutes major national and international problems, now and for decades to come well into the next century. Most of humankind still possess high fertility and high rates of population growth; and they still live, by the standards of the more developed nations, in abject poverty, with widespread illiteracy, relatively low life expectancy, and a gloomy outlook for the future. Furthermore, the gap in levels of living between the "haves," and "have nots" has been increasing since the end of World War II, despite some rise in absolute living levels in less developed countries and despite multilateral and bilateral programs of the more developed nations to help the poorer nations to achieve their national aspirations for development.

As has been indicated, many aspects of population and social and economic development are closely related. The long-standing debate on whether decreased fertility and population growth are prerequisite to development or whether development must be achieved so that fertility and growth decline can follow is increasingly recognized as being based on a false issue, a misconstruing of the relationship between population factors and development. Decreased birth rates and population growth rates do not necessarily result in increased economic development; and economic growth is not necessarily quickly followed by fertility and population growth declines. There is growing evidence that the birth rates can be lowered before economic development is achieved, as in the case of Sri Lanka; and that continued high fertility and population growth can accompany economic growth as in Mexico, but there is also increasing evidence that declines in fertility and population growth rates can contribute to development and that development can contribute to lower tempos of fertility and population growth.

Some of the developing nations have achieved lower fertility with the help of strong family programs and success in varying degree in attaining higher levels of living. A major challenge confronts the other LDCs: can they manage to reduce their birth rates with little or modest gains in their economies? Can pathways laid down by such nations as Egypt, Thailand, and Indonesia—which have achieved significantly reduced birth rates with minimal gains in development—be followed by other LDCs? Success in meeting this challenge may not only affect the future of successful nations, but also prospects for diminishing tensions between the "have not" and "have" nations, for the attainment of lower fertility can be a significant step toward raising the level of living.

Major challenges also face the LDCs on the economic front. Can they increase their productivity in both the agricultural and the industrial sectors? Can their economies develop adequately to provide jobs for the some 900 million workers that would be added to their labor force by the end of the century? Can not only income per capita be increased but simultaneously can income distribution be improved in order to increase the share of their poorest people—say the lower one-fifth of their households?

There are obviously no easy, ready answers to these problems, nor is there any easy road to achieving these goals. If a population control challenge is satisfactorily met, however, the struggle for economic development would at least be eased.

These challenges confronting the LDCs have significant implication for the MDCs. The economies of the advanced nations are also faced with a major and, as yet, unmet challenge arising from the inequitable distribution of national levels of living. Can the MDCs increase their contribution to multilateral and bilateral assistance programs to help diminish the gap in levels of living between the "have" and "have not" nations? The UN proposal for the developed nations to contribute at least 1 percent of GNP toward assistance programs remains an unreached goal; and the LDC demand for a New International Economic Order has met with further resistance on the part of MDCs. Furthermore, the OPEC nations have thus far increased rather than decreased the economic burdens of the non–oil-producing LDCs. In this shrinking world necessarily shared by all nations, failure to diminish the income gap between the LDCs and the MDCs could, obviously, have bitter consequences, not excluding violent confrontation.

While the LDCs lack adequate capital for investment to increase productivity—investment both in capital goods and in human capital—the world is at present expending over $400 billion per annum for military goods and services. It is relevant to point out that the LDC share of world expenditures for military purposes has been rising.

The major challenges also face population and development agencies and programs, national and international, public and private. Can population programs be coordinated with health, education, welfare, and general economic development programs? Integration of these programs requires astute management, professional competence, intense dedication, and minimal bureaucratic rivalries and conflicts, while the individual agencies retain their own identity and autonomy. Can the approach to development and an improvement in the quality of life in the LDCs and throughout the world be a comprehensive, holistic approach with elements which are effective and cumulative?

The resolution of the difficult and dangerous problems that confront the whole world in the coming decades depends on a sound foundation of knowledge and its effective application. At the present time the physical, biological, and social sciences do not yet possess enough knowledge easily to meet the challenges which have been outlined above.

Despite great gains made in the understanding of human reproduction and the resultant improved means of fertility control, there is no means of conception control acceptable enough, effective enough, and cheap enough to effect fertility reduction as efficiently and quickly as desirable. Moreover, the present inability of the biological and related sciences to make possible more effective means of fertility control is matched by social and behavioral sciences in not possessing enough knowledge to permit family planning agencies more readily to increase acceptance of such control methods. Similarly, the physical sciences yet have much to learn to solve the worsening energy crunch, to improve the production of food, and to diminish environmental pollution and degradation. Can the sciences step up the tempo of research so as to meet the challenge of sorely needed knowledge? Furthermore, if the knowledge is gained, can the management and action personnel—physical, biological, and social engineers—rise to the challenge of effectively applying the knowledge? Virtually all of the sciences face the challenge of increasing and improving their research output to provide a better base of knowledge than now exists to help meet the major challenges which have been noted. It has been made clear that many facets of population, other than high fertility and growth rates, affect development and the quality of life. The world as a whole has become aware of the problems generated by high fertility and population growth. The control of human reproduction, which not long ago was a taboo subject in many places and agencies, has become accepted as legitimate not only for discussion but also for public and private agency policy and programming. National and international programs have proliferated in recent years to help reduce fertility, and funding for such programs, though by no means completely adequate, has greatly increased.

However, there is comparable awareness of the problems generated by the population implosion, urbanization, and its attendant migration streams; and there are no comparable policies and programs to deal with the problems stemming from rapid urbanization, migration, and the maldistribution of population. Although there is a growing awareness of these problems in some quarters, individual nations and international agencies have yet to meet the challenge of formulating policies and programs to ameliorate the problems. Can the LDCs meet the challenge posed by the tripling of their urban populations by the century's end? Can the MDCs meet the challenge of providing the necessary assistance to help? There can be little doubt that in the short run there will be more human misery arising from rapid urbanization, mass migration, and population maldistribution.

Another major challenge to humankind is manifest in diversity. Yet under the impact of the revolution of rising expectations, minority groups throughout the world are insisting on equality of opportunity, and they have expressed their insistence not only with rhetoric but also with physical violence. Can majority populations meet the challenge of providing minorities with equality of opportunity? Can adamant minorities in some countries meet the challenge by enabling suppressed majorities to share equitably in the good life? Can evenly balanced but diverse populations find ways to reduce tensions arising from inequalities in income distribution or social studies or political power?

What are the prospects of success for meeting the challenges set forth? In contemplating the future, there is reason for both pessimism and optimism as the authors of the individual chapters of this book have shown. Undoubtedly one critical element affecting the answer to this problem lies in the capacity of this planet to provide enough resources to make possible continued increases in the levels of living of the MDCs even while the levels of living increase more rapidly in the LDCs to narrow the gap. If this should be the case, the prospect is relatively bright, but only with the passage of time. On the other hand, if all resources should prove to be too limited to enable LDC living levels to rise, without decreasing MDC levels, then the prospect is certainly much more gloomy. The zero-sum game in the relation of levels of living of LDCs and MDCs, as has been indicated, would only mean increased tension, alienation, hostility, and potentially great violence.

This volume might well have been entitled "World Survival Imperatives—Management of Population and Development." The first part of such a title would not have been hyperbole. Although there is a basis both for pessimism and optimism in the short run, there can be no disagreement with the fact that present rates of world population growth cannot persist for very long into the future, nor can present, let alone increasing disparities persist between the MDCs and the LDCs in levels of living, without culminating in Doomsday. Yet Dawnsday is within the reach of humankind if rational policies and programs are adopted both with respect to population and to development.

The second part of the unused title of this volume, "Management of Population and Development," holds forth not only the prospect of survival but also of fulfillment—significant improvement in the quality of life. Modernization has brought in its wake great increases in years of life, in the less developed as well as the more developed nations. But inadequate management of population and development could well undo this accomplishment and threaten, also, to decrease rather than to enhance the quality of life of all human beings.

At this juncture of history, the all-embracing challenge to humankind is how to preserve and increase added years of life while adding life to years—especially for the predominant proportion of the world's population resident in the less developed countries. Failure to meet this challenge may well guarantee the advent of Doomsday rather than Dawnsday.

INDEX

WORLD POPULATION AND DEVELOPMENT

was composed in 10-point Linotype Times Roman and leaded two points,
with display type in handset Goudy Open and Times Roman,
printed offset on acid-free 50-pound Perkins & Squier Offset by Joe Mann Associates, Inc.;
Smyth-sewn and bound over 88-point binder's boards in Columbia Bayside Linen,
and also adhesive bound with Corvon 220-13 paper covers,
by Riverside Book Bindery, Inc.;
and published by

SYRACUSE UNIVERSITY PRESS
SYRACUSE, NEW YORK 13210